THE LAW OF CHRIST

THE LAW

Volume Two:

SPECIAL MORAL THEOLOGY:

*Life in Fellowship with
God and Fellow Man*

Moral Theology
for Priests and Laity

OF CHRIST

by Bernard Häring, C.SS.R.

Translated by EDWIN G. KAISER, C.PP.S.

THE NEWMAN PRESS · 1966 · WESTMINSTER, MARYLAND

Fifth Printing 1966

This translation was made from the sixth edition of
Das Gesetz Christi, published by Erich Wewel Verlag,
Freiburg im Breisgau, Germany, in 1960.

Imprimi potest: VERY REV. JOHN E. BYRNE, C.PP.S.
      Provincial
      March 12, 1962

Nihil Obstat: FREDERICK J. HUNNEFELD, C.PP.S.,
      S.T.D.
      Censor Librorum

Imprimatur: JOHN J. CARBERRY, D.D.
      Bishop of Lafayette, Indiana
      March 7, 1962

TRANSLATOR'S PREFACE

THE translation of Volume Two of *The Law of Christ* is taken from the sixth German edition. This volume deals with man's communion or fellowship with God (in the first book) and with his fellow man (in the second book). Under this fellowship with God we consider the theological virtues and the virtue of religion; under the fellowship of man we present love of neighbor. The third volume is to treat of man's loving acceptance of the all-embracing sovereignty of God in all areas of earthly life.

With practically no exception our English translation of Volume One was welcomed with the same enthusiasm that greeted the work of the noted Redemptorist theologian throughout the rest of the world. As in the first volume, so too, in this one, we are deeply indebted to the members of the Precious Blood Society who cooperated in our enterprise. Most of all we are grateful for the painstaking precision of Father Fred Hunnefeld of Saint Charles Seminary faculty, Carthagena, Ohio, without which our work could lay little claim to theological accuracy. For constant encouragement in the entire task, from text to finished volume, we are indebted to Father Joseph Smolar of Saint Joseph's College, East Chicago, Indiana, to Father Raymond Cera, and Father Joseph Lazur of Saint Joseph's College, Rensselaer, Indiana. The bibliography is largely the work of Father Lazur.

EDWIN G. KAISER, C.PP.S.

St. Joseph's College
Rensselaer, Indiana
Feast of St. John Chrysostom,
January 27, 1962

CONTENTS

BOOK ONE

Life in Fellowship with God

PART ONE:

THE THEOLOGICAL VIRTUES

BOOK TWO

Love in Human Fellowship

AUTHOR'S PREFACE

In the providential fulness of time Jesus proclaimed the coming of the kingdom of God. Salvation was at hand, offered to men with the urgent and ecstatic invitation: "The time is fulfilled, and the kingdom of God is at hand. Repent and believe in the gospel" (Mk 1:15). With similar words on the first Pentecost Peter announced to the people the good tidings: "Him, when delivered up by the settled purpose and foreknowledge of God, you have crucified and slain by the hands of wicked men. But God has raised him up, having loosed the sorrows of hell, because it was not possible that he should be held fast by it. . . . Therefore, let all the house of Israel know most assuredly that God has made both Lord and Christ, this Jesus whom you crucified" (Acts 2:23, 36). The people responded with the question, "'Brethren, what shall we do?' But Peter said to them, 'Repent and be baptized every one of you in the name of Jesus Christ for the forgiveness of your sins; and you will receive the gift of the Holy Spirit'" (Acts 2:37f.).

The basic query of Christian moral will always be the same: How can we respond to the incomprehensible love which the Father has spoken to us in His Incarnate Son, the Word, Jesus Christ? How can we respond to this Word ceaselessly spoken to us in God's love? The Lord did not answer this question with an enumeration of individual duties or virtues. Nor did St. Peter. What is most fundamental in the Christian order of existence is openness to the good tidings of salvation. First of all, we must accept it with open hearts and submit in faith to Jesus Christ: He is the Word of the Father addressed to us. In Him and through Him the Father bestows the Holy Spirit upon us, as His supreme Gift and the most generous pledge of His personal love.

In the light of this insight, which is totally personal, our *general* moral (treated in Volume One) presented the picture of the Christian life as inner conversion of heart. In the Christian life all depends on this interior conversion and from this all transformation in the world about us proceeds. According to our exposition, Christian conversion is far more than a moral sense of duty or even a virtuous spirit or disposition. It is rather a personal encounter with Christ whom we are assured to meet in the sacraments, an encounter in which our life task is presented and accepted in a new spirit: "How shall I make a return to the Lord for all the good he has done for me?" (Ps 115:3).

The fruits of conversion, of the acceptance of Christ, as found in the first Christian assembly, the primitive community of Christians, are described vividly in the Acts of the Apostles: "And they continued steadfastly in the teaching of the apostles and in the communion of the breaking of the bread and in the prayers. And fear came upon every soul; many wonders also and signs were done by means of the apostles in Jerusalem, and great fear came upon all. And all who believed were together and held all things in common, and would sell their possessions and goods and distribute them among all according as any one had need. And continuing daily with one accord in the temple, and breaking bread in their houses, they took their food with gladness and simplicity of heart, praising God and being in favor with all the people" (Acts 2:42ff.).

Special moral theology should be a development and enlargement of this impressive picture of Christian life. The study clearly follows two grand lines of development:

I. Life in Fellowship with God.

II. Life in Fellowship with Fellow Man.

It would be utterly false to assume that community with God (in the three divine virtues, faith, hope, love, and in the worship of God through the virtue of religion) removes man from human fellowship and places him exclusively in solitary personal encounter with God. Quite the contrary! When man is torn from the faceless existence of the masses, he experiences in this very fellowship in the divine life the good fortune of the fellowship of human salvation. Life in the community of the brethren is rooted in the fellowship of faith, in the good tidings of salvation, in the solidarity of the one hope, in the love of the one Father and the one Lord Jesus Christ, in the unity of the Holy Spirit, in the community of praise offered to the Triune God. All this is quite evident from the text of Acts, cited above. The very first objective above all others in our scientific moral theology is to present this fundamental structure of the Christian life. In other words: the Great Commandment of love is the foundation for Christian personalism and as well the deep source of the Christian spirit of fellowship and family. The divine summons to us, which is something utterly personal, and its acceptance on our part, which must likewise be altogether personal, is the foundation of fellowship with God and at the same time of brotherly community with men. All authentic responsibility of man for his fellows and all responsibility for the social order in the world flows from our response to the redemptive Word of God. From this response it draws its life and inspiration; to this response it constantly returns.

PRELUDE: THE BIBLICAL SOURCE

Prophecy and parable of the personal mission of the Word of the Father through the incarnation are the characteristic utterances which run through the entire Old Testament: Thus spoke the Lord, the word of God, God spoke, etc. Most jubilant in the glad tidings of the New Testament is the great fact that the Word of Truth appeared to us in human form, that the Father spoke to us the definitive essential Word of His love in Jesus, His well-beloved Son. Conversely, the Father received the response, infinite in value and good pleasure, from the heart of mankind in the sacrifice of Christ. Through His resurrection from the dead and ascension to the throne at the right of the Father, He is forever accredited as true priest and ambassador to mankind. His eternal glory is witness that He has fulfilled His task as the Father's Word of love to us and loving, adoring response of obedience to the Father in our name (cf. Jn 15:10).

To its very roots Christian moral is religious. It is essentially dialog-response,[1] which means that it springs from the response of man to the redemptive word of God committed to him. In consequence moral theology in all its considerations must flow from the word of God. How do we stand in relation to the word of God? What kind of response does the word of God demand of us? In these few pages we can do no more than attempt to present the grand outlines which the Holy Scriptures press upon us, only the major directives which guide us in the presentation of individual problems! It surely will prove helpful in this study to gain an insight into the Old Testament in order to come to a clear understanding of the New Testament fulfillment of the ancient dialog of love and worship.

I. GOD'S WORD AND MAN'S RESPONSE IN THE OLD TESTAMENT

The revelation of God's word to Israel presents two facets which are equally essential and mutually related. The one is the revelation of the divine plan of salvation for the people, its creative, prophetic history whose content centers in the sacred alliance or covenant. The other is the self-revelation of God or, according to Semitic idiom, the revelation of His name.[2] God speaks to man to reveal to him the mystery of salvation and at the same time the mystery of His own divine life. Or perhaps we should rather say He reveals the twofold mystery with an ever increasing clarity and unity. Israel must respond with a grateful heart and embrace this dual mystery.

1. *The Self-Revelation of God*

God revealed the mystery of His awesome transcendence (the *mysterium tremendum*) progressively. This Old Testament revelation forms three groups centering in as many Semitic concepts in the Holy Scripture. These key concepts are: the name (*shem*), the holiness (*qadósh*), and glory (*ḳabód*) of God. Above all others Israel was to experience uniquely how incomprehensible and exalted was the Lord, how absolute the obligation on man's part to dedicate himself to the divine worship.

We treat the theme at greater length under the virtue of religion. Here we are concerned only with the basic biblical trends in so far as they are definitive for the whole of moral theology.

God's name is ineffably great and wonderful. Man cannot claim a right to learn and experience it. When Jacob asked God, "What is your name?" the Lord answered, "Why do you ask my name?" (Gn 32:30; cf. Jgs 13:17f.) In a tremendous historical moment when God chose to communicate the marvel of His mystery to His people, He disclosed His name to Moses: He is Yahweh, fulness of being. "I am who am" (Ex 3:14). Undoubtedly, this unique name is a solemn corroboration of God's supreme dignity and transcendence. Only unique being, One Who is, transcending all existing, can exercise sovereignty over all things. In a supreme act of freedom He can intervene to show mercy to His people: "I . . . show favors to whom I will, I . . . grant mercy to whom I will" (Ex 33:19). Awesome and terrifying is the divine name in its sovereign grandeur: "You shall not take the name of the Lord, your God, in vain. For the Lord will not leave unpunished him who takes his name in vain" (Ex 20:7).

God is holy, without shadow or limitation. He is totally other (*qadósh*, "separated," "set apart"). His presence is dynamic. It affects men with awe and terror (*mysterium tremendum*). Sinful man cannot bear to face God, the All-Holy. "Who shall be able to stand before the Lord this holy God?" (1 Sm 6:20). For sinful man to face God is to die, unless God stay the hand of death by a miracle of mercy. "Jacob named the place Phanuel, saying, 'I have seen a heavenly being face to face, yet my life has been spared'" (Gn 32:31). "But my face you cannot see, for no man sees me and still lives (Ex 33:20; cf. Jgs 13:22; Is 6:3ff.). We can take up the divine utterance from the all-holy God and communicate it to men only if God Himself purges our lips (our thoughts, our hearts, our very lives) with the glowing coal from the altar of His sanctity (cf. Is 6:6).

Mere man cannot see the inaccessibly holy God face to face. Only a visible reflection of the hidden glory is revealed to him. God manifests His glory (His *ḳabód*) in the dark cloud, which is also a glowing pillar of fire (Ex 13:21). Sign of mercy to the Chosen People, this cloud is a portent of destruction for their enemies (Ex 14:19ff.). "And the sight of the glory of the Lord was like a burning fire upon the top of the mount, in the eyes of the children of Israel" (Ex 24:17). And after Moses had seen the glory of God as from the "back" and "passing" before him (Ex 33:23; 34:5f.), the reflection of the divine glory he had been permitted to see remained impressed on his countenance. So awesome was it that, when Aaron and the other Israelites saw Moses and "noticed how radiant the skin of his face had become, they were afraid to come near him" (Ex 34:30). When Solomon dedicated the temple to the Lord, "the glory of the Lord had filled the house of the Lord. Then Solomon said: 'The Lord said that he would dwell in a cloud'" (3 Kgs 8:11f.). In the vision of Ezechiel the "glory of the Lord left the threshold of the temple and rested upon the cherubim." "And the glory of the Lord rose from the city and took a stand on the mountain which is to the east of the city." God reveals His glory for the exiled captives so that they give Him due honor. He will manifest His glory anew in the temple at Jerusalem and wherever it suits His mysterious design, in His own good time (cf. Ez 10:18; 11:23; also Ez 39–43).

God's disclosure of Himself is more than bare instruction on the divine greatness. It is the dynamic manifestation of the hidden mystery which fills the people with holy awe and reverence, forcing them to their knees in adoration. Thus God lays down His commandment: "The Lord, your God, shall you fear; him shall you serve. . . . You shall not follow other gods, such as those of the surrounding nations . . . for the Lord, your

God, who is in your midst, is a jealous God" (Dt 6:13ff.; cf. Mt 4:10). The first table of the Law of Sinai and all cultal directives of the Old Testament must be studied in the light of this revelation, which forms the background for all study of Old Testament worship of God. For us, too, the divine self-disclosure is the basis of all worship. The entire foundation of our life as manifested in the light of the divine self-revelation is religion. Through religion we honor and worship God. We adore the Lord: "You shall be to me a kingdom of priests, a holy nation" (Ex 19:6). In the light of God's manifestation of Himself, religion is the *first pillar* of our life.

2. Revelation of the Mystery of Salvation

a. Word and Act of God

In God's revelation of Himself the divine mystery of salvation unfolds. As God makes Himself known, He manifests to His people the merciful designs of His love. Israel's salvation lies in her thankful and heartfelt acceptance of the plan of salvation offered by Yahweh.

The world, since man's doleful fall, is filled with tragedy, pain, and odium. In His plan to save fallen man, God chose a people of His own as model and forerunner of the Church which was to bring salvation to all mankind. With patience and condescension a providential pedagogy shaped and formed the plan of salvation to suit the unique character of the Jewish people, who were still steeped in earthly thinking. Yahweh in His revelation repeatedly manifests Himself as the Savior of Israel from earthly evil: He leads the people out of Egypt with its cruel bonds. He guides them through the Reed Sea to a land flowing with milk and honey. All of which is the type of a far more glorious redemption with a grander promise.

But the worst of all evils is sin. Yahweh will free His people from the enslavement of sin. God inaugurates this work of salvation from sin by giving His Law to the people, the Law, which according to Paul is fulfilled in love: "Love does no evil to a neighbor. Love therefore is the fulfillment of the Law" (Rom 13:10). The second table of the Mosaic Law regulates all human relations in the spirit of love. Though their express formulation is surely negative, in content and total presupposition the commandments of Sinai are entirely positive. They are concerned with the mutual relations in human conduct. They deal with men in contact with other men, all of them conscious of the bond of divine love which unites them. In the Law and also in the Prophets, love is the power by which God wills to break the bonds of sin. With ever increasing clarity this concept of love in opposition to sin comes to the fore in the sacred pages of the Old Testament. Thus the commandments decisively presuppose the positive, love.

Soon the eschatological outlines with their promise of greater things take shape, though they are constantly obscured and placed in jeopardy by a narrow-minded nationalistic thinking. There looms the great promise of the Messianic Kingdom with universal and everlasting peace. Death shall reign no more. "For God formed man to be imperishable; the image of his own nature he made him" (Wis 2:23). God will carry out His original plan. Wonderful shall be the fulfillment: His true servant will suffer and be exalted. "If he gives his life as an offering for sin, he shall see his descendants in a long life, and the will of the Lord shall be accomplished through him. Because of his affliction he shall see the light in fullness of days; Through his suffering, my servant shall justify many, and their guilt he shall bear" (Is 53:10f.).

b. Israel Responds

Israel's noblest children accepted this revelation of the mystery of salvation through faith (Heb 11:1). Faith is at once acceptance and response, trustful submission of self to the loving designs of God. Faith is the force which enabled the children of Israel to place themselves trustfully in the hands of Providence directing the history of salvation to its appointed end. Faith taught them to refrain from proudly taking their destiny in their own hands, vaunting their own strength and glory. "By faith (they) conquered kingdoms, wrought justice, obtained promises, stopped the mouths of lions, quenched the violence of fire, escaped the edge of the sword, recovered strength from weakness, became valiant in battle, put to flight armies of aliens" (Heb 11:33f.). In brief: faith was characterized by redemption from physical evil.

By faith they "wrought justice" (Heb 11:33). Thus they were like David, "who kept my [God's] commandments, and followed me with all his heart, doing that which was well pleasing in my sight" (3 Kgs 14:8). Faith was the beginning of the triumph over sin. Faith induced them to "seek after a better, that is, a heavenly, country" (Heb 11:16). Many "were tortured, refusing to accept release, that they might find a better resurrection" (Heb 11:35).

Through faith, in response to the revelation of the divine plan of salvation, the just of the Old Testament conformed their will to God's will. They placed their trust in His promises. They said *yes* to the moral ideal set before them by God's revelation. They sought to live in accordance with this revealed ideal of man in all his human contacts.

In the light of divine revelation we clearly discern the *second foundation stone* of our life here on earth. It is the moral life considered in the strict sense as assent to the creative designs of God. It is faith-full obedience to God who discloses His covenant-plan of salvation and His promises of eternal life. The beginnings may be imperfect indeed! But despite all their imperfection the day will come when the Messianic peace shall bear the fruit of perfect fulfillment: "Justice shall walk before him, and salvation, along the way of his steps" (Ps 84:14).

3. *Mutual Mystery: Divine Self-Revelation and Plan of Man's Salvation*

The religious and moral life in the Old Testament are not merely contiguous or parallel. As we just noted, in Israel the moral directives and demands flow from the religious life. This unity of religion and morality must now be studied more thoroughly and in greater detail. God Himself directed His self-revelation, the disclosure of His name, His holiness, and His glory to our own salvation.

In the revelation of His name God lays stress on His supreme and transcendent dignity. But the context of the divine communication reveals something else much more clearly: in His name God reveals Himself to us as the Lord of the whole history of salvation. That Israel can invoke Him, must invoke His name, is sign of His salvific will. "And God spoke further to Moses, 'Thus shall you say to the Israelites: The Lord, the God of your fathers, the God of Abraham, the God of Isaac, the God of Jacob, has sent me to you. This is my name forever; this is my title for all generations'" (Ex 3:15).

The name of Yahweh does not convey to the people of Israel a conceptual or abstract notion of self-existent Being, though indeed He is truly all that, but rather the image of the God who is mighty in deeds, who chooses to be close to His people with His protection. He is the Lord God who says, "I, the Lord, am your God, who brought you out of the land of Egypt, that place of slavery" (Ex 20:2). There are similar texts: two of many are Lv 11:45 and Dt 5:6. Thus the name of God which denotes His dignity and transcendence becomes through divine condescension the *leitmotif* of our salvation. For no reason but His love did God manifest His name to Israel. "Israel is my son, my first-born" (Ex 4:22). "When Israel was a child I loved him, out of Egypt I called my son" (Os 11:1).

The book of Isaias in all its parts bears the profound impress of the threefold *Holy,* which the Cherubim utter before the throne in adoration. God is simply the Holy One of Israel. But this expression of the *mysterium tremendum* also connotes the *mysterium fascinosum* of our salvation. "I will help you, says the Lord; your redeemer is the Holy One of Israel" (Is 41:14). "For he who has become your husband is your Maker; his name is the Lord of hosts; Your redeemer is the Holy One of Israel, called God of all the earth" (Is 54:5). God, the all-holy, manifests His holiness and thus sanctifies a people as His very own, who shall worship Him. "For I, the Lord, am your God; and you shall make and keep yourselves holy, because I am holy" (Lv 11.44). With the bounty of an unmerited love God sanctifies this wretched people: "For you are a people sacred to the Lord, your God; he has chosen you from all the nations on the face of the earth to be a people peculiarly his own. It was not because you are the largest of all nations that the Lord set his heart on you and chose you, for you are really the smallest of all nations. It was because the Lord loved you . . ." (Dt 7:6ff.).

The revelation of the glory of God is both awesome and beatifying. God lives in the midst of His people through His glory: he shelters it and lends ear to its petitions, so that finally it may be permitted to behold His glory in all its fulness (Is 66:11ff.). It might even appear, in the light of what is said repeatedly in the Old Testament, as though God subordinates His own glory to the salvation mystery. God glorifies Himself precisely in bringing salvation to men. But precisely because of this, man must seek his salvation entirely and utterly in the adoration and glorification of God. Only in the measure in which we know and love the name of God can we hope for the fulness of the salvation proffered to us by God's loving mercy. Only in the measure in which we adore the all-holy God and thus respond to the revelation of the glory of God by dedicating our entire existence to His glory!

All self-revelation of God in the Old Testament has as its goal the

beatifying realization that "God is love." In this lies the great mystery of
the New Testament that divine transcendence stoops to lowly man in
infinite love. God manifests His supreme glory as loving majesty. He
glorifies Himself by drawing us to His tender embrace with the ineffable
power of His love.

In the light of the marvellous unity of God's self-disclosure and the
communication of His salvific plan there can be only one response on
man's part. Only a love that obeys and adores can be man's true response,
a love which penetrates and animates the whole religious and moral life
of man. Only such love can respond to God's self-revealing offer of grace
and mercy. The love of God directed to man demands first of all adoration, loving adoration of God. And this love of God is authenticated by
loving submission to God, an obedience which submits to all the divine
commands and directives in every realm of moral life.

"The bond of love (*agápe*) with the virtue of religion or of piety is
obvious. Love for God ardently longing to manifest itself in prayer of
praise and in good works adores and serves Him, submits to Him, and
makes His will the loftiest motive of daily conduct and of all virtues. . . .
The love (i.e. the loving, *agapân*) of the Israelites is love of adoration, of
worship. It is truly a cultal love, the worship of praise for the sovereign,
transcendent God and dedication of life to His service." Thus writes the
noted Dominican exegete, C. Spicq, who cites the text, "Hear, O Israel!
The Lord is our God, the Lord alone! Therefore, you shall love the Lord,
your God, with all your heart, and with all your soul, and with all your
strength. Take to heart these words which I enjoin on you today. Drill
them into your children. Speak of them at home and abroad, whether you
are busy or at rest. Bind them at your wrist as a sign and let them be as a
pendant on your forehead. Write them on the doorposts of your houses
and on your gates" (Dt 6:4ff.). "Thus it is evident," says Spicq, "that the
love of God is the one thing important. One is to think of nothing else.
Nor is there anything else of which to speak. This is man's unique, life-
long occupation, his *agápe* that embraces faith, worship of God, and the
whole moral life."[3]

God's love for His people is the condescending love of the All-Holy, the
manifestation of His glory to them. Consequently man's response to God
must be with all his heart. It must be totally worshipful love. Love expressed in divine cult! And the love and adoration must be authenticated
through obedience to the commandments of God, which demand moral

effort and dedication. "And now, Israel, what does the Lord, your God, ask of you but to fear the Lord, your God, and follow his ways exactly, to love and serve the Lord, your God, with all your heart and all your soul, to keep the commandments and statutes of the Lord, which I enjoin on you today for your own good? . . . Love the Lord, your God, therefore, and always heed his charge: his statutes, decrees, and commandments" (Dt 10:12f.; 11:1). From this magnificent text it is evident that the fear of God is response in love to the mystery of the divine sanctity. Also evident is it that love cannot be satisfied with anything less than total consecration to the God of love.

Israel was not always open to the love of God, did not always return His love with full faith and unconditional submission. In consequence Israel as a whole did not attain to that justice which should lead to Christ. Israel did not possess full justice in supernatural faith. "What then shall we say? . . . Israel, by pursuing a law of justice, has not attained to the law of justice. And why? Because they sought it not from faith, but, as it were, from works" (Rom 9:30ff.). It had need of the New Law which is engraved on the hearts of men, of a renewed spirit and a new heart. "I will place my law within them, and write it upon their hearts; I will be their God, and they shall be my people" (Jer 31:33). "I will give you a new heart and place a new spirit within you" (Ez 36:26). We may not doubt that the order of salvation in the Old Testament was just and holy according to God's design and will: "the law indeed is holy and the commandment holy and just and good" (Rom 7:12). It was an order of bountiful and unmerited love on God's part, which was to call forth love in return. And yet the Old Testament was no more than the period of promise. It was not the perfect fulfillment, but rather only its anticipation. The full revelation for which this time of promise prepared man was in Christ. In Him the Word was fully revealed, for the Word became man and lived among us (Jn 1:14).

II. GOD'S WORD AND MAN'S RESPONSE IN CHRIST

According to the letter to Hebrews, God who spoke in times past through the prophets "last of all in these days has spoken to us by his Son" (Heb 1:2). The mystery of man's salvation and the mystery of God's self-revelation has been unveiled for us in the one mystery of Christ Jesus. In and through Jesus, the Father turns His countenance toward us with all His glory and love. In Him and through Him mankind can in turn truly honor and please God in a manner worthy of His supreme dignity. In Christ we are saved. "This life [i.e., the eternal life] is in his Son. He who has the Son has the life. He who has not the Son has not the life" (1 Jn 5:12). Jesus Christ is the ultimate and definitive Word of God's love to us, and also the sole worthy response of man to God's love. In Him alone have we a response of infinite and ultimate value to Infinite Love.

The only-begotten Son of God "came down from heaven for our sake and for our salvation" (*Credo* of the Mass), took our sins upon Himself, offering Himself to the Father for us. Though veiled in our humanity the loving majesty of God was revealed in Him, the "glory as of the only-begotten of the Father—full of grace and of truth" (Jn 1:14). God's holiness and glory are unfolded in the mystery of the redemption. Thus in ultimate clarity is revealed the supreme mystery of love: God is Infinite Love. His glory is totally and utterly loving majesty. As in Christ, love for the Father in heaven and love for men unfolded in the harmony of perfect unity, so too must our love of adoration embrace Christ's whole company of the redeemed. If we would sincerely love our fellows, we must open our hearts wide to this love of God which is brought to us in Christ.

1. *The Mystery of God's Self-Revelation in Christ*

The grand themes, the name, the holiness, and glory of God are revealed in the Old Testament only incipiently. What God begins to reveal to Israel is spoken again by Jesus with new richness and fulness of divine truth. And even more important: the One who speaks is the Divine Person. We see and hear the God-man. In Him the grand themes are the revelation of the Holy Trinity. We learn from this Teacher that God is Love for us, because He is in Himself a Trinity of Love: "Everyone who loves is born of God, and knows God . . . for God is love. In this has the love of God been shown in our case, that God has sent his only-begotten Son into the world that we may live through him. In this is the love, not that we have loved God, but that he has first loved us . . . God is love, and he who abides in love abides in God, and God in him" (1 Jn 4:7ff.; 4:16).

Our religious life, our response to this revelation in the divine virtues, in the divine worship, and in the practice of religion is henceforth manifested as fellowship with the Triune God in and through Jesus. In Him, with Him, and through Him, we profess our faith, our hope, our love. And faith, hope, and love become a worthy prayer of praise of the name, the holiness, and the glory of God.

Jesus reveals the name of Father to us. The Father of the beloved only-begotten Son is now also "Our Father," since the "Father has sent his Son to be the Savior of the world. Whoever confesses that Jesus is the Son of God, God abides in him and he in God" (1 Jn 4:14ff.). "He who has not spared even his own Son but has delivered him for us all, how can he fail to grant us also all things with him?" (Rom 8:32). All things, even the name and right of child of God! "Behold what manner of love the Father has bestowed upon us, that we should be called the children of God; and such we are" (1 Jn 3:1). "Behold now we are the children of God, and it has not yet appeared what we shall be. We know that, when he appears, we shall be like to him, for we shall see him just as he is. And everyone who has this hope in him makes himself holy, just as he also is holy" (1 Jn 3:2f.). Jesus rejoices that He has revealed the Father's name to those who knew that He received all from the Father: "I have manifested thy name to the men whom thou hast given me out of the world. They were thine, and thou hast given them to me, and they have kept thy word. Now they have learnt that whatever thou hast given me is from thee; because the words that thou hast given me I have given to them" (Jn 17:6ff.; cf. also Mt 11:25f.).

The Father has bestowed upon His Incarnate Son "the name that is above every name" (Phil 2:9). In this inexpressible name, the Apostles rejoice to suffer (Acts 5:41). In Jesus, our Lord and Brother, the love of the Father abides with us and in us, so that we are able to do all things in the name of the Lord. We do all in His name, since we pray to God the Father through Him: "Whatever you do in word or in work, do all in the name of the Lord Jesus, giving thanks to God the Father through him" (Col 3:17).

We are able to do this through the Spirit of Love. "You have been washed, you have been sanctified, you have been justified in the name of our Lord Jesus Christ, and in the spirit of our God" (1 Cor 6:11). The Spirit, whom the Lord has sent us from the Father, cries out in our hearts: "Abba! Father!" (Rom 8:15). In consequence our life, even though in an obscure manner, is taken into the mystery of the Triune God. Our incomprehensibly exalted vocation is to live—such is the meaning of the baptismal invocation of the Trinity—in the name of the Father, the Son, and the Holy Spirit.

"Holy Father" (Jn 17:11), Jesus prays in the high priestly prayer. He sanctifies Himself for His own, so that they "may be sanctified in truth" (Jn 17:19). He sanctifies Himself as an offering of love. The Father manifests in His tender providence and in the work of redemption His holiness, His perfection, His loving kindness (cf. Mt 5:48). The All-Holy is the All-Loving!

Jesus Himself is "the Holy One of God" (many MSS have this reading in Jn 6:70). St. Peter, stricken with holy awe at the miracles of Jesus, calls to mind the prophet Isaias before the throne of the thrice-holy God. But the Apostle who exclaimed in dread, "Depart from me, for I am a sinful man" (Lk 5:8), was also wonderfully drawn to the *mysterium fascinosum* of the love of Jesus: "Lord, to whom shall we go? Thou hast words of everlasting life" (Jn 6:69).

Again we must note: The revelation of the mystery of holiness leads to the mystery of the Holy Trinity, and therewith to the mystery of love, which summons us to participation. The Holy Spirit, the Spirit of Holiness, in whom Christ sanctifies and offers Himself for us, is bestowed upon us so that in this way, in truth, we also are consecrated to a life of love and sacrifice (Jn 17:19). We are baptized "with the Holy Spirit" (Mt 3:11; Acts 1:5). The Holy Spirit operates in all the sacraments (they are sanctifying, effective signs of salvation) in order to form and fashion Christ in us. From this grace-giving font of the Spirit of Holiness there issues the grace-bearing imperative: "Do not grieve the Holy Spirit of God, in whom you were sealed for the day of redemption. . . . Walk in love, as Christ also loved us and delivered himself up for us as an offering and a sacrifice to God to ascend in fragrant odor" (Eph 4:30; 5:2).

The theme of majesty or glory (*dóxa, gloria*) in the New Testament is constantly traced back to the ultimate of all mysteries, the Most Holy Trinity. For the Father is the Father of glory, who eternally communicates His own loving glory to His only-begotten Son, the "brightness of his glory and the image of his substance" (Heb 1:3; cf. Jn 1:14).

The Word Incarnate is the new temple in which the majesty of God is now enthroned. He is now the dwelling, the presence of the Most High among us, the *shekinah* (cf. Jn 1:14). In the resurrected Christ this glory embraces the entire blessed humanity, including the body. He is the *Kyrios*, the "Lord of glory" (1 Cor 2:8).

The Eternal Word humbled Himself for our sake. For us the Incarnate

Word merited exaltation through the most abject humiliation so that by sending the Holy Spirit, the Spirit of glory, He might take us up into the work of glorification and lead us to eternal life. "The glory that thou hast given me, I have given to them" (Jn 17:22; cf. also Jn 7:39). If we are "partakers of the sufferings of Christ," then we shall "rejoice with exultation in the revelation of his glory . . . the honor, the glory and the power of God and his Spirit" will rest upon us (1 Pt 4:13f.). All that we do, whether we eat or drink, or do anything else, we should do "for the glory of God" (1 Cor 10:31). By His obedience unto the death of the cross the Incarnate Word gave glory to His Father and was in turn raised up from the dead by the Father, being glorified also in His Body. Through Him who from His throne in splendor sends the Spirit of glory, our life receives its final appeal to loyalty: "to him be glory in the Church and in Christ Jesus down through all the ages of time without end. Amen. . . . for from him and through him and unto him are all things. To him be the glory forever. Amen" (Eph 3:21; Rom 11:36).

The sublime mystery of the Holy Trinity which these biblical themes proclaim is brought to us in the most marvelous condescension: in the mystery of the Incarnation-Redemption in Jesus Christ. In the Old Testament the mighty name of Yahweh was explained by the biblical utterance: Your God, who saved you from Egypt. Now the name of the Lord is simply Jesus, which means Redeemer, Savior. Responding gratefully with love to the prevenient love of God, we can consecrate our whole existence to this name. In the reflected splendor of His holiness we dedicate our lives to His honor and glory.

The mystery of love, which we may honor thus, is the mystery of Eternal Love: the Trinity and Love-Fellowship of the three divine Persons. The mystical unity or identity (*identificatio*) established by love between Jesus and ourselves brings forth new children to God, children by adoption. In an incomprehensibly glorious way we are taken up into the life and the love of the Triune God. The Spirit of God Himself in person, the Spirit of Love, cries out in us: "Abba! Father!" "The Spirit Himself gives testimony to our spirit that we are sons of God" (Rom 8:16). Our religious life, therefore, is an articulation of divine life, of divine power (the theological virtues). An inexpressible inner dialog of love goes on between the three divine Persons and ourselves. In this I-Thou of love the frame of human personality, fashioned in the image of God, receives its final fulfillment.

It is entirely obvious that such an unmerited dialog of love cannot dispense us from the obligation of adoration. Quite the contrary! Now our lives are much more urgently dedicated to that adoration of God which blesses and consecrates. In fact our whole existence is adoration, but always loving adoration, adoring love. The Spirit who moves us to pray, "Abba, Father!" also inspires us with the realization that the "Father in heaven," the All-Holy, wishes to be our Father. In childlike adoration we share in the glory which the Son possessed with Him before the creation of the world and which is revealed to us in the paschal mystery of Christ's death and resurrection. The New Testament commandment: "Thou shalt love the Lord thy God" is the commandment of loving childlike adoration of God. Childlike piety which is all love, all adoration! Expressed in theological terms this means the "unity of the virtues of love and religion."[4]

The first part of our special moral theology—life in fellowship with God—fully corresponds with this biblical basis: the theological virtues, their summit in love, are articulate in the virtue of religion (paying honor to God). The very center and focus of religion is the mystery of salvation, of the incarnation, death, resurrection, and ascension of Christ, which we celebrate in the Eucharistic Sacrifice and in the sacraments. We cannot fail to note how central is the position of the sacraments in this order; for in the sacraments there is unveiled for us, in the most intimate personal contact, the mystery of God disclosing Himself to man. In the community of the Church, with all the urgency of actuality, the revealing God glorifies His name in the mystery of redemption, holding us fast with its presence and power.

The duties prescribed in the first tablet of the Law of Sinai and in the first part of the Great Commandment are to be treated in our special moral theology, part one. This treatment of the first tablet of the Law of Sinai is very far from a mere exposition of obligations. These duties are to be viewed rather as essential expression of the New and Eternal Alliance. They are the task committed to the baptized, the confirmed, the ordained and consecrated, the priest and layman, virgin and spouse, unmarried and married, by the very fact of sacramental consecration which they share. This sacramental consecration it is which commits man to the glorification of the Triune God through Christ, with Him and in Him! Soul and center is the sacrifice of Christ and the Church.

Obviously there is the closest bond between the two parts of our special moral. Life in the fellowship of brotherhood is intimately bound up with the life in fellowship with God. Love of neighbor and its realization in the various realms of life finds its highest motive in the love and worship of God, in the virtues of charity and religion. Charity and religion furnish far more than motive, however. They are the very foundation, the fount and source of the love of brotherhood. One cannot live "in Christ Jesus," one cannot truly glorify the name of our common Father in heaven, one cannot love God in His Holy Spirit without loving one's neighbor in Christ and with Christ and in His Holy Spirit. Did not Christ offer Himself for our neighbor, vicariously and in the bond of human solidarity, in order to present to the Father in heaven infinite glory? As Head of the entire race He obtained salvation for all mankind in giving supreme honor to His Father. In consequence the life in human fellowship cannot be severed from the life in fellowship with God. Thus the *moral* life of the Christian in its strict and proper sense forms a peerless unity with the *religious*.

Our arrangement is exegetically sound and correct, according to C. Spicq in his exposition of Pauline theology: "What should we say man must answer to God's love so freely given to him with its demands? The Apostle states the case in the form of cultal gratitude: one must sacrifice self, one's body, as a living, holy oblation, well-pleasing to God. Such is the service which the renewal of heart demands we give to God. . . . 'I exhort you . . . to present your bodies as a sacrifice, living, holy, pleasing to God —your spiritual service' (Rom 12:1). All the moral virtues which are mentioned subsequently spring from gratitude and praise as sacrificial oblations. . . . For Paul this spiritual service and sacrifice is the moral life in its profoundest sense."[5]

2. The Mystery of Man Redeemed

An angel could have brought us the message of the mystery of a triune God who in His love deigned to rescue us through the redemptive power of His grace: However, the word of the angel would have been merely external, remote from the heart of the mystery. It was not so with Christ, who is both true God and true man. He is the Incarnate Word of the Father sent to us, the Word in whom the Father communicates all His love and His glory. But He is also the perfect response of loving adoration addressed to the Father by the renewed mankind whose Head He is. He is the first fruit of the "new earth and the new heavens." In the paschal mystery of His death and His resurrection the visible public participation of mankind in the divine life begins: participation in the love of the Father given in the Incarnate Son, who gives Himself with equal love to the Father and bears the stamp of the Father's approval in His resurrection from the dead.

The paschal mystery reveals how mankind becomes one, insofar as the redeemed live entirely on the love flowing from the heavenly Father and can return the gift by loving oblation of themselves. In the Eucharist Jesus not only embraces us in His oblation and His adoration of the Father, He also shares with us His own love for the community of the brethren. His adoring love is likewise a sacrificial love for them: "Greater love than this no one has, that one lay down his life for his friends" (Jn 15:13). Because Christ, the risen Savior, embraces us in His love, we the redeemed can offer the heavenly Father the greatest glorification by loving one another with the love Christ Himself has shown us: "As the Father has loved me, I also have loved you. Abide in my love. . . . This is my commandment: that you love one another as I have loved you" (Jn 15:9, 12).

In wondrous wise the promise to Israel has been fulfilled: participation in the paschal mystery of the death and resurrection of Christ is our pledge of the perfect fulfillment in the final consummation of all things at the end of time.

A question arises regarding the participation in the mystery of Christ's death: are we freed through Him from physical pain and suffering? The answer is yes and no. We are liberated from meaningless, fruitless suffering if we assent to our assimilation to the crucified Christ, if we assent also to His sacrificial love for our neighbor! Jesus healed the sick and fed the hungry. He bestowed all the warmth of a special affection on the poor. As the Good Samaritan who heals the wounds of our bodies, He teaches us that our salvation and the divine judgment depends on our attitude toward our suffering and persecuted fellow man. Were all men profoundly motivated by the love of Christ, the pain and sorrow in the world would be greatly lessened. The sharpest sting of physical evil would be removed.

The Lord did not promise an earthly paradise to His followers. He demands that we accept our daily cross. For those who embrace it, this cross is no longer a curse but becomes the bearer of salvation. It is the mark of superabundant redemption and the noblest badge of honor for the Christian to complete his days with a life wracked with earthly pain. Those who suffer with Christ and for Christ may well bear in mind the word and example of St. Paul: "I rejoice now in the sufferings I bear for your sake; and what is lacking of the sufferings of Christ I fill up in my flesh for his body, which is the Church" (1 Col: 24).

Christ freed us from the great evil of earthly enmity, on the pattern of the liberation of the Hebrews from their harsh enslavement in Egypt. In Christ we are all one body. We are members of one another (Eph 4:25). The walls of separation created by egoism, scorn, and hatred of individuals and groups break down in principle as soon as we willingly accept the great commandment: Love one another as I have loved you. The love of Christ can prevail in us even over hatred of enemies. Hatred will lose its power to contaminate and corrode our minds and hearts, if we learn through a spirit of solidarity and concern for our neighbor's salvation to overcome evil with good. "If thy enemy is hungry, give him food; if he is thirsty, give him drink. For by so doing thou wilt heap coals of fire upon his head" (Rom 12:20).

Christ freed us from the bondage of Satan and sin: "To this end the Son of God appeared, that he might destroy the works of the devil" (1 Jn 3:8). "Because children have blood and flesh in common, so he in like manner has shared in these; that through death he might destroy him who had the empire of death, that is, the devil; and might deliver them, who throughout their life were kept in servitude by the fear of death" (Heb 2:14f.). "He has rescued us from the power of darkness and transferred us into the kingdom of his beloved Son, in whom we have our redemption, the remission of our sins" (Col 1:13f.).

We are not only cleansed of the guilt of past sins, "but the law of the Spirit of the life in Christ Jesus has delivered" us "from the law of sin and of death" (Rom 8:2). If the law of sin implies a melancholy solidarity in the loss of grace, then surely we should submit to the law of divine grace and dedicate ourselves entirely to the service of the solidarity of salvation. Then even a vile and poisoned atmosphere cannot corrupt and enslave us. The law of the spirit, which has written the great command-ment of love in our hearts, has also freed us from death. In the measure in which we assent to this law we need no longer dread the death of judg-ment and punishment. We are freed from an evil death by being in-corporated in the salvific death of Christ; we participate in His death in the great hope of the resurrection.

Christ has prepared the way for our resurrection. He has opened the portals through His loving, humble obedience to the Father in a solidarity of salvation with the brethren, suffering for us even to the death of the cross. In imitation of Him through our obedience to His law, to the law of love written in the very core of our being by the Spirit, we attain to the freedom of the children of God, awaiting in joyful confidence the consummation of revelation: the full possession of the glory of God and the freedom of His children. But this freedom and this hope—coming to us through the power and instrumentality of the Christ in glory—is ours only at the price of love. We must be ready to pay this price day by day in self-oblation and mystico-real death with Christ; we must accept all the sacrifices which fraternal peace and harmony demand, all the sacrifices required by the solidarity of interest in the salvation of our neighbor.

Such is the picture of man renewed in Christ. He is assured of that life in glory which our faith sees in the risen Christ, its Author and Model. We have Him constantly in mind when in this second part of our special moral theology we treat of the life in the love of brotherly fellowship. Faith in Him, hope in Him, make possible the realization of love amid the harsh realities of this world in which the old constantly clashes with the new, so that ceaseless sacrifice and conformity with the Crucified is always demanded.

SUMMARY

Our life must be response both to the self-revelation of the all-holy God and to the revelation of the mystery of man redeemed. In this twofold mystery the two grand divisions of our special moral theology are clearly indicated: life in the fellowship with God, life in the community of brotherly love. These two grand perspectives in turn permit of a similar twofold division: our fellowship with God includes the three theological virtues which are splendidly articulated in the virtue of religion (divine worship); love of neighbor must turn to all the moral virtues, using them in all the realms of human life. Love of others must be the form and fashion of one's entire life. When charity-structured, our whole life is submission to the loving dominion of God: man's assent to God's sovereignty in love.

ABBREVIATIONS

AAS	*Acta Apostolicae Sedis*
AmCl	*Ami du clergé*
AER	*American Ecclesiastical Review*
Ang	*Angelicum*
Blf	*Blackfriars*
CC	*Civiltà Cattolica*
CiTh	*Ciencia Tomista*
ClerRev	*Clergy Review*
CM	*Catholic Mind*
CrCr	*Cross and Crown*
DivThom (F)	*Divus Thomas (Freiburg)*
DivThom (P)	*Divus Thomas (Piacenza)*
DR	*Downside Review*
DSp	*Dictionnaire de Spiritualité*
DTC	*Dictionnaire de la Théologie Catholique*
DubR	*Dublin Review*
EphThLov	*Ephemerides theologicae Lovanienses*
FrancStud	*Franciscan Studies*
FranzStud	*Franziscanische Studien*
Fur	*Furrow*
GeistLeben	*Geist und Leben*
Greg	*Gregorianum*
HerderKorr	*Herder-Korrespondenz*
Ho	*Hochland*
HPR	*Homiletic and Pastoral Review*
IER	*Irish Ecclesiastical Record*
IMo	*Irish Monthly*
ITQ	*Irish Theological Quarterly*
JRI	*Journal of Religious Instruction*
Jur	*Jurist*
LebS	*Lebendige Seelsorge*

LiSp	*Life of the Spirit*
Lit	*Liturgy*
LitLeb	*Liturgie und Leben*
LThK	*Lexikon fuer Theologie und Leben*
LumVie	*Lumiere et Vie*
LumVit	*Lumen Vitae*
MélScRel	*Mélanges de science religieuse*
Mo	*Month*
MThZ	*Muenchener Theologische Zeitschrift*
NO	*Neue Ordnung*
NRTh	*Nouvelle Revue Théologique*
NZMW	*Neue Zeitschrift fuer Missionswissenschaft*
OF	*Orate Fratres*
PhJb	*Philosophisches Jahrbuch*
PRM	*Periodica de re morali*
RACh	*Reallexikon fuer Antike und Christentum*
RAM	*Revue d'ascétique et de mystique*
Rb	*Revue biblique*
RevApol	*Revue Apologétique*
RevSpir	*Revista de Espiritualidad*
RevThom	*Revue Thomiste*
RR	*Review for Religious*
RThP	*Revue de théologie et philosophie*
SC	*Scuola Cattolica*
ScEccle	*Sciences Ecclésiastiques*
Schol	*Scholastik*
StimmenZeit	*Stimmen der Zeit*
TD	*Theology Digest*
TH	*Thought*
TheolS	*Theological Studies*
ThG	*Theologie und Glaube*
Thm	*Thomist*
ThPrQschr	*Theologisch-praktische Quartalschrift*
ThQschr	*Theologische Quartalschrift*
ThW	*Theologisches Woerterbuch zum Neuen Testament*
ThZschr	*Theologische Zeitschrift*
TrThZ	*Trierer theologische Zeitschrift*
VerbDom	*Verbum Domini*

VieIntell	*La Vie intellectuelle*
VieSpir	*Vie Spirituelle*
VieSpirSupp	*Supplément de la Vie Spirituelle*
WissWeish	*Wissenschaft und Weisheit*
Wor	*Worship*
WW	*Wort und Wahrheit*
ZAM	*Zeitschrift fuer Aszese und Mystik* (now *Geist und Leben*)
ZKathTh	*Zeitschrift fuer katholische Theologie*

Book One

Life in Fellowship With God

Part One:

THE THEOLOGICAL VIRTUES

CHAPTER ONE

THE THEOLOGICAL VIRTUES IN GENERAL

1. *The Theological Virtues as the Foundation of Supernatural Moral Life*

Not only must the Christian be really and objectively ennobled by grace, his faculties or powers must be elevated through grace so that his actions can be supernatural in form and worth. In fact Christian morality is nothing less than the life flowing from sanctifying grace. It is the life flowing from the dynamism of the divine Sonship and vested with its dignity.

Sanctifying grace is not dead capital but the foundation of a life formed in God. It is participation in the divine life (2 Pt 1:4), a sharing in the knowledge and love which Father and Son have for each other in the Holy Spirit. This is evident from the splendor of the noble retinue of the life of grace, the divine virtues, through which grace makes the powers of the soul capable of the vital activities of the child of God. Thus in the virtue of divine faith, reason is elevated as a faculty made capable of participation in the divine fulness of truth. In hope the will, reaching out toward happiness, is directed toward the divine inheritance of the child of God, the heavenly bliss. In love man's power to love, the power which says *yes* to value, is made capable of a joyous response to the absolute love-value which is God Himself. It is given a true capacity for the repose-in-joy in God which is fruitful in works and in loving communion with God.

Sanctifying grace and the theological virtues are not simply parallel or companionate, standing alongside one another. They form an intimate and vital unity. Without these three divine virtues, sanctifying grace, which surely means life, would be incapable of its own vital activity. And the virtues themselves without sanctifying grace would be capacity for supernatural vital manifestations without an innermost vital principle. It is true there is a kind of separability, for at least faith and hope can abide in the soul and be active, although imperfectly, without sanctifying grace and the virtue of love; but then they are only the capacity for acts which seek after the supernatural life, which cry out for the supernatural life-forms, of which they are bereft. They are only the cry after the missing forms of virtue (*virtutes informes*). If faith does not spring from its true

3

vital principle, it is in the proper sense of the word a dead faith (*fides mortua*). This is equally true of supernatural hope if it is no longer struggling after the attainment of beatitude (that is, after love). Totally inseparable from habitual grace is the act of love which is the act most essential and proper for the child of God.

In the child of God love enlightens and animates everything. The contrast between the faith and hope in him and faith and hope in one deprived of the life of grace and love can hardly be exaggerated. It is no easy task for the theologian to present so detached an explanation of the divine virtues of faith and hope that his statements are equally true of dead faith and hope as of faith and hope animated by love. In the one instance the reference is to faith and hope which merely tend toward or seek love; in the other they bask in the warm rays of God's love. It is true that in our theology we treat each virtue distinctly with all its own individuality or formality, but ultimately it is love that believes, love that hopes. Only through love are faith and hope in the full sense of the word true virtues.[1] And yet we may not deny the value even of dead faith and hope: we must always see in them the way and call to conversion.

The three theological virtues are virtues in an eminent sense of the word, because they are basic endowment, equipment, orientation, capacity. They are qualifications for actions which would be utterly impossible without them. However, we should not overlook the fact that qualification for individual transient supernatural acts is certainly possible through the operation of actual graces. This point is clearly established by the fact that the acts which prepare the sinner for justification are by their nature and character supernatural acts belonging to these virtues. Even the sinner who has never been in possession of the gift of faith, who is converted from infidelity to faith and to the state of grace, elicits acts of faith and hope before he comes to a possession of these virtues.

Faith, hope, and love are called theological or divine virtues, because (1) only God can give them to us and man is incapable of contributing anything positive toward effecting them beyond the mere readiness to receive them; (2) these virtues communicate to us a participation in that which properly belongs to God alone: in His fulness of truth which transcends all created power to acquire or grasp; in His own eternal bliss and in the community of His intimate divine love; (3) God is their end and motive (material and formal object). He is the end (material object): faith has God in His infinite self-knowledge, God all-truthful as its end and object, insofar as He opens up to man the infinite resources of His own divine mind. Hope reaches out toward God, infinite bliss, bestowing the bounty of His own beatitude. Love rests in the absolute loving value which is the infinite goodness of God Himself. God Himself is likewise the motive (formal object) of the divine virtues: the motive of faith is God all-truthful, the divine Truth. The foundation or motive of hope is the all-good, omnipotent, and faithful God (which is to say, the promised treasure of the love of God). The foundation of love is the absolute lovableness of God, God all-amiable, God all-good.

This "trinity" of divine virtues in the "unity" of sanctifying grace is an image of the Most Holy Trinity, one in nature, three in person. The three theological virtues may be said to correspond to the spiritual powers of man, intellect or the power of knowing, the will or the power of striving, and its power to love. St. Paul expressly refers to the threefold number: "So there abide faith, hope and charity, these three" (1 Cor 13:13). These three virtues are "the permanent essential conditions of our Christian existence."[2] All manifestations of the Christian life must conform entirely to these three virtues and be founded in them. Moreover, the three are comprehensively grouped in many passages in Scripture: Heb 10:22-24; Rom 5:1-5; Gal 5:5f.; Col 1:4f.; 1 Thes 1:3; 5, 8 (in the latter text reference is made to the equipment of the Christian fighter for the cause of God). Augustine looks upon the three theological virtues as an epitome of the whole Christian morality (*Enchiridion sive de fide, spe et caritate*).

Reference to the three virtues as three and only three does not settle the question regarding the position of the virtue of religion: must it be reckoned among the theological or moral virtues? This much is certain: the theologians of the school of Salamanca and many other writers very strongly opposed the opinion that the virtue of religion should be subordinated to the moral virtue of justice. It can very correctly be considered a component part of the divine virtues and as their primary manifestation.

2. The Theological Virtues as Foundation and Epitome of the Mysterious Dialog between God and Man

The primary purpose of the theological virtues is not to equip man for a mission or vocation in the world—though of course they do promote and exalt this assignment tremendously—but to open the sacred dialog between God and man, which is to be completed and perfected in eternal bliss. Nor are these divine virtues to be considered in the first instance as human achievements. They are rather the special endowment of man equipping him through divine grace for basic activities of Christian existence. These fundamental activities are not world betterment, not striving for self-perfection, but orientation to God, participation in the fulness of divine life.

Before man says *yes* to God in faith, God says *yes* to man. He offers man (this individual man) a supernatural participation in the truth which attests the riches of His love and bliss (through His revelation and the infusion of the grace of faith, or more specifically through the virtue of faith). Before man reaches out his hand in hope toward the supernatural beatitude in God, God Himself extends His fatherly hand to man (through His promises and through the infusion of divine hope). Before man comes to rest in the love-value which is God, God embraces him as His child, clasps Him to His bosom in communication of His divine love and His own intimate divine life. The dialog always begins with God, who reaches out to man with His transforming grace, endowing him with the capacity to respond.

In the order and process of conversion of the adult this takes place first through the transient acts of faith and hope under the influence of actual grace. In the instance of infant baptism the three virtues are infused with sanctifying grace at the very beginning of the whole Christian life, with the acts of the virtues to follow only later when the child attains to reason and is instructed in the faith. Thus there is an actual expression given to the divinely infused power of response to God's word and love.

Most marvelous is this mutual interrelation and interpenetration of the dialog proceeding from God and grasped by man in the first act (and in the virtue) of divine love in man's conversion to God. The act of love does not come into existence without man's response through faith and hope to the loving call of the revelation and promise of God. In His own unique immanent love, God communicates Himself to man in order to make him capable of the act and life of sonship, for this gift is never bestowed without the Giver Himself. And no sooner is the act of love expressed than the lover receives the divine response, insofar as God unites Himself with him in permanent purpose and infuses into him, together with the objective reality of the first God-like act of love (and to an extent as divine response to it), the very virtue of love, and with it sanctifying grace itself. And all the good one so favored does or wills henceforth, he does through the dynamism of this divine capacity, hence as immediate response to God's loving address and invitation which inwardly renews him.

The theological virtues do not directly and immediately abide in the realm of the external act. Rather they belong to the inner spirit and the Word because they are directly and totally turned to God. More specifically they reflect the loving glance of God immediately directed to man and man's response to it, the movement of life and love between God and man.

But since these virtues are infused in this earthly life and lay hold of man on his pilgrim's sojourn in this world, they must bear a relation to his activity here below. They place man, the pilgrim, with all his external activity, with all his tasks in the world (that is, in his total moral bearing and orientation) before God His final end, in his response and his responsibility. This implies that all the vital manifestations of the moral virtues of man in the state of grace are laid hold of by the divine virtues and transformed and placed into the dialog with God. And surely wherever man faces the world and sets his hand to the tasks in the world, wherever man deals with the temporal order, there are moral tasks and virtues (and with some restriction, also in the worship of God when man undertakes to form and penetrate space, time, and community through cult). But such is the vital dynamic of these three virtues that they render the entire earth their sphere of activity, transparent with the countenance of the Christian always shining through earthly realities and turned to God. In consequence, once man lives from the dynamism of the theological virtues, there no longer exists a mere moral life for him, but henceforth only a religious-moral life. This is the *yes* of world-responsibility spoken to God, arising from the gift of divine love within us.

3. The Theological Virtues as Inner Dynamism of the Imitation

Through the theological virtues we are placed in dialog with God, but only in and through Christ. Through faith Christ, the eternal Word of the Father and the Word of God to mankind, is our Truth, our Teacher. Because God unlocks for us the treasury of the truth of the Godhead, the inner ear of faith is attuned utterly and totally to Christ as our Teacher. Through hope Christ is our path to heavenly bliss. He revealed and proposed Himself to us in the redemption as our way and through His resurrection He manifested the power of His redemptive love. Only because of this are we able to hope. Wherefore the inner force of the virtue of hope rests entirely on Christ, our way, our hope. Through infused love Christ is our life (cf. Jn 14:6). In Christ the love of the Father was manifested toward us. Christ sends to us the Spirit of love, who infuses love into our souls (Rom 5:5). Through incorporation into Christ, and only through this incorporation, do we share in the love of Christ for the Father and in the love of the Father for Christ.

The theological virtues give to us an interior relationship to Christ, our Teacher, Redeemer, and Friend. They are the inner capacity, the divine invitation and obligation to imitate Christ, because Christ is for us the sole cause of this God-like life. Life flowing from these virtues is nothing other than actual imitation of Christ, harkening to Christ, hoping in Christ, obediently loving Christ.

4. Sacramental Formation of the Divine Virtues

The dialog with God, in faith, hope, and love, is in no wise banished into the purely interior confines of contemplation without word or gesture. There is a reflection of God's invisible nature in the visible creation, which He created in His own Word, Who is the Image of His substance. In the splendor of His visible creation God reveals Himself, if only we harken to its inner voice and respond to the divine message. But mightier by far is the supernatural message: The Word of the Father willed to become visible and audible to us in a Person. "And the Word was made flesh, and dwelt among us" (Jn 1:14). "And we have seen, and do testify, that the Father has sent his Son to be Savior of the World" (1 Jn 4:14). "I write of what was from the beginning, what we have heard, what we have seen with our eyes, what we have looked upon and our hands have handled: of the Word of Life" (1 Jn 1:1f.).

Christ is truly the basic, primordial sacrament. He is the sign in which and through which we experience the promise and the love of the Father. And in turn through and in Him we are able to speak effectively and worthily to God in response to His love.

Himself visible witness to the love of the Father, Jesus willed that even after His ascension His truth, His salvific will, His love should remain visible and perceptible on earth in the mystery of His Church. The Church is a visible sign of the continuing love of Christ in the world.

Precisely as visible and perceptible does the Church, linked with Christ in the covenant of love, live from His redemptive words. She is His full response to the Father, the basic, primal sacrament of Christ, the redemptive sign of Christ's love which saves all and embraces all in loving response. She is the sacrament of Christ as He, the Incarnate Son of the Father in His visible Sacrifice and in the visible sign of His resurrected humanity, is the basic, primordial sacrament, the redemptive sign of the love of the Father.

God glorifies His name not merely through a love for men in secret; the salvific work of God is much rather a revelation and manifestation of His loving majesty. There must be visible and perceptible in the sacramental celebration (administration and reception), and in the life flowing from sacramental grace and in conformity with sacramental summons to duty, that love of God and that loving response of the redeemed: the love of God manifested in Christ and the Church, the loving response offered by the redeemed filled with faith and trust.

The decisive mystery of our salvation is that the Father sent us His only-begotten Son as Redeemer in the visible guise of flesh: faith of man in this decisive mystery is essentially linked with the covenant of love between Christ and the Church manifested in the celebration of the sacraments. In all the sacraments, but most especially in the Eucharist, the covenant of love manifests itself; and in a life befitting the sacramental graces it bears witness to Christ the Savior. Through the sacraments faith establishes its bond with the mystery of salvation.

The community of faith and cult and the loving salvific fellowship of the redeemed flowing from it must depend on the visible and perceptible. It is God's will that we see with our eyes in the sacramental sign and hear with our ears and experience how great a love He has shown us and what richness of salvation He has prepared for us. We are dealing with a concrete order of salvation. It belongs to this order that we cannot experience, without the visible signs of the sacraments, how tremendous is the revelation of the beatifying truth which the Father makes known to us when He calls us His much-beloved children.

Precisely this visible character of the experience of faith and the dialog of love in the sacramental celebration directs our life to the full and complete manifestation of our salvation. Surely by comparison with the great day of the Lord, in which the "new heaven and the new earth" shall be manifest to all creatures, we can only say of the sacramental visible sign and the externally perceived community of love in "this last hour of salvation": "It has not yet appeared what we shall be. We know that, when he appears, we shall be like to him, for we shall see him just as he is" (1 Jn 3:2). In the last analysis our hope in the final splendor and glory of the loving majesty of God is sustained by the visible manifestation of the kingdom of God. We look forward to the final unfolding of that which begins here on earth. It is already manifested in the incarnation of the Son of God, in the paschal mystery of the Lord, in the Church and her sacraments.

The final goal of the whole history of salvation, the goal as well of the divine virtues is the *parousia* of the Lord. In this Second Coming of the Lord the loving majesty of God and His Anointed and our participation in Him will be revealed in all its splendor. Made as we are, essentially of body and soul, we do not await an exclusively interior beatitude. Beatitude in the Christian sense of the word consists of the complete unfolding of the loving glory of God before us in a perfect dialog of love. In this the reflection of the divine majesty in our bodies and in the visible bodily fellowship is not something accidental. The life of grace here below is the germ of eternal glory. It is bestowed upon us in the sacraments, and unfolds in the dialog of faith, hope, and love. Accordingly grace, and with grace the basic divine powers of faith, hope, and love tend to make visible the truth and love received. Manifested in this world they blossom forth finally in the blessed fellowship of God's love in eternity.

The sacramental order takes a very earnest view of the realism of the visible sign and the audible word in which truth, promise, and love of God flow to us and qualify us for the response in the fellowship of the Church. For this reason the formation of the divine virtues belongs essentially to the Church and to the *eschata:* in the sacraments we have the beginnings which we see and experience. From these we strive toward the full revelation of that truth and love of the Father which lays hold of our whole existence and summons us to response. From these sacramental beginnings we strive upward toward this truth and love of the Father in the glory of the Son and His Bride, the holy Church. "And every one who has this hope in him makes himself holy, just as he also is holy" (1 Jn 3:3).

The sharp accentuation of the divine truth and love as visible and tangible in the community of faith and love, which is the Church, and in her sacraments belongs essentially to the discernment of spirits: "Beloved, do not believe every spirit, but test the spirits to see whether they are of God; . . . By this is the spirit of God known: every spirit that confesses that Jesus Christ has come in the flesh, is of God" (1 Jn 4:1ff.).

It is not theologically sound to classify the activity of the theological virtues specifically with contemplation—without word or gesture—and accordingly rank contemplation and meditation in solitude and quiet above the celebration of the divine mysteries.[3]

Sacrament and faith—we have in mind in the first instance faith animated with hope and love—are indissolubly linked in this concrete order of salvation. St. Thomas states this truth in his classic dictum: "We receive salvation through faith in Christ, who was born and suffered for us. And the sacraments are chosen signs which announce and profess the faith by which man is justified."[4]

Scientific exegesis in the last decades has taken extraordinary pains to demonstrate the marvelous inner unity of two series of New Testament texts: the one stresses the redemption through faith, the other the reception of salvation in the sacraments. The two are not merely loosely parallel, much less contrasting opposites; they form a wonderful unity. In the sacrament of faith God assures us of His actual salvific will, which becomes a present salvific event. We are to live in faith and, in the believing celebration of the sacraments of faith, live a life flowing from sacramental grace and in harmony with the challenge and summons of grace. Thus sustained by grace we accede to the grace offered us in the word of salvation.[5]

The two principal themes of the Johannine theology are the divine gift of grace (the will of divine bounty) and its grateful human acceptance. God bestows His gifts freely, and man trustfully submits himself to the will of the bounteous Giver. The divine bounty is evident in all the devices of the divine providence, which is climaxed by the communication of the gift of the Holy Spirit, above all in the mystery of the Incarnation-Redemption showering its riches upon us in the celebration of the sacraments. As regards the gift, it is the first and fundamental task of man to open his heart and mind to the gracious God in faith, to believe His word and respond to it trustfully.

In a pre-eminent sense tradition looks upon baptism and the Eucharist as "sacraments of faith." In all the sacraments, but particularly in these two, the Church, our Mother, celebrates and proclaims her belief in the mysteries of salvation and enkindles in us the light of faith. In the

sacraments the Church, the Bride of Christ, believingly accepts the
covenant of love and submits in grateful faith to her divine Bridegroom.
The faith of the individual is essentially nourished on the testimony of
the Church's belief in a community which exults in the possession of
vigorous and vital faith.

In the administration of baptism Mother Church asks the catechumen
what he desires of her. He answers, "Faith." The Church imparts to him
not only the unfathomably rich treasure of the divine truths, but also
communicates to him in the salvific event which is baptism the saving
word of faith. The faith of salvation which brings assurance to the individual so that he is sanctified and made a child of God is constantly experienced anew in the sacrament of faith by the assembly which shares
in the celebration. Hence it is inevitable that the joy and warmth of the
individual's belief depends in a very considerable measure on the vigor
of the Christian community's faith at the celebration of the sacraments.
The belief of the Christian is nourished more essentially by the celebration of the sacraments of faith than through individual meditation or
contemplation. Reception of the sacraments and participation in the
celebration of the sacraments, especially in the offering of the holy
Eucharistic Sacrifice, implies openness to both the word of faith and likewise, in union with the people of God, to the *redonatio fidei* (renewal of
faith),[6] the grateful response of faith.

"Faith then depends on hearing, and hearing on the word of Christ"
(Rom 10:17). The announcement of the faith of salvation to the people
(the *kerygma fidei*) centers in the mysteries of salvation which the Church
celebrates and proclaims in the sacraments. Therefore the liturgy is essentially an expression of faith. Through it man listens and responds, submits
himself completely in grateful acceptance of the word of salvation. From
this standpoint it is quite obvious that there are certain indispensable requirements for the manner and mode of the sacramental celebration.
Formalism and ritualism are utterly contrary to the "sacrament of the
faith" and to the sacramental celebration by the people of God, a believing
celebration which constantly stimulates and sustains the faith.

The word of faith is also one of promise. In the sacrament we receive
the promise and pledge of the Savior: "I am the salvation of the people,
I am thy salvation." Here in our earthly life we are as pilgrims in a sacred
bond with Christ constantly looking forward to the heavenly goal: it
follows that we must be eschatologically formed, alerted, and renewed

with all the vigor of Christian hope through the sacramental celebration, through the sacred and solemn signs which stimulate and strengthen hope.

The liturgy, properly and decorously celebrated, awakens in the faithful the realization that their salvation depends on the revelation of the loving majesty of God and the corresponding willingness of the individual himself to give glory to God. It would be altogether unChristian and inhuman to set up a "pure cult" with the pretence and presumption that it has nothing to do with the soul's salvation or the divine virtue of hope. No less mistaken would it be to relegate the virtue of hope and its exercise primarily to the invisible realms of pure contemplation and to loosen it from firm sacramental moorings.

The most central expression of the divine virtue of love also flows from the sacramental celebration and the Eucharistic sacrifice. By participation in the celebration of the sacraments in faith and trust we constantly share inwardly in the covenant between Christ and the Church. The sacraments signify and effect above all the love which brings back and unites to God those who have fallen from Him. The love of the Lord restores the unity of all that has been severed. It demands of us a loving response to Him, peace and harmony with our fellows, for we are all given a share in the love of the Lord which makes all things one. At the Last Supper the Lord gave us His new commandment when He instituted the Eucharist: "A new commandment I give you, that you love one another: that as I have loved you, you also love one another" (Jn 13:34; cf. also 15:12).

The sacramental structure of the theological virtues, as we have just presented it, stresses its character as dialog, as basis and source of fellowship, as tending to the visible and manifest. As such it is indeed a far cry from "sacramentalism" or so-called "liturgicism." Quite the contrary to being a loose parallel to the life of virtue, it means the grace and call to a corresponding life-formation which is a truly virtuous. As are the sacramental grace and the sacramental dedication, so also are the divine virtues dynamically directed to the totality of life.

BIBLIOGRAPHY

The Theological Virtues in General

BERNARD, R., O.P. "La vertu théologale," *VieSpir*, 41 (1934), 146–167.
DELHAYE, PH. *Rencontre de Dieu et de l'homme*. Vol. 1: *Vertus théologales en général*. Tournai, 1957.
KRAUTWIG, N. "Jetzt bleiben Glaube, Hoffnung, Liebe," *WissWeish*, 11 (1944), 1–10.
LECLERCQ, JEAN, *"Alone with God,"* New York: Farrar, Straus, 1961.

MERSCH, E. "La grâce et les vertus théologales," *NRTh*, 64 (1937), 802–817.

PEINADOR, A. *De virtutibus theologicis et de prudentia*. Madrid, 1951.

PFLIEGLER, M. "Glaube, Hoffnung und Liebe als Lebens- und Geschichtsmaechte," *Seelsorger*, 22 (1951), 476–489.

SOIRON, TH. *Glaube, Hoffnung und Leibe*. Regensburg, 1934.

VOGTLAND, F. *Die theologischen Tugenden nach dem heiligen Paulus*. Mainz, 1917.

WALTER, E. *Glaube, Hoffnung und Liebe im Neuen Testament*. Freiburg i. Br., 1940.

Additional Works in English

AUGUSTINE, SAINT. *Faith, Hope and Charity* (Ancient Christian Writers, 3). Westminster, Md.: Newman, 1947.

BARS, HENRY. *Faith, Hope and Charity* (Twentieth Century Encyclopedia of Catholicism, 27). New York: Hawthorn, 1961.

FARRELL, WALTER, O.P. *Swift Victory: Essays on the Gifts of the Holy Ghost*. New York: Sheed and Ward, 1955.

JOHN OF ST. THOMAS, O.P. *The Gifts of the Holy Ghost*. New York: Sheed and Ward, 1951.

KELLY, BERNARD J., C.S.Sp. *The Seven Gifts of the Holy Ghost*. New York: Sheed and Ward, 1942.

LANSLOTS, ILDEFONS. *Three Divine Virtues*. New York: Pustet, 1925.

The Virtues and States of Life (Theology Library, v. 4), ed. A. M. Henry, O.P. Chicago: Fides, 1957. "Faith" (A. Liégé), pp. 1–59. "Hope" (B. Olivier), pp. 61–126. "Charity" (B. Olivier), pp. 127–208. "The Virtue of Religion" (A. Mennessier), pp. 393–444. "The Social Virtues" (M. Gerland), pp. 445–485 (on obedience, piety, liberality).

Periodical Literature in English

DEMAN, T. "Towards an Objective Spiritual Life," *LiSp*, 11 (Oct.–Nov., 1956), 148–57, 200–208.

JOHN XXIII. "The Practice of the Theological Virtues," an address given at the close of the Roman Synod, *AAS* 52: 285–296. English Translation: *Australasian Catholic Record*: 37 (April, 1960), 89–99.

KELLY, G. "Notes on Moral Theology," *TheolS*, 10 (March, 1949), 70–77.

"Life of Faith," *RR*, 2 (Jan. 15, 1943), 41–51.

McCARTHY, J. "The Supernatural Order," *IER*, 50 (Sept., 1937), 247–270.

VAGNOZZI, E. "States of Perfection and the Theological Virtues," *AER*, (Nov., 1961), 289–300.

VERBILLION, J. "Faith, Hope, and Charity, These Three," *CrCr*, 13 (March, 1961), 81–104.

CHAPTER TWO

THE VIRTUE OF FAITH

T HE CHRISTIAN is a believer. Through the revelation of the deep mysteries of His heart, God enters into communion with man who opens his own heart to God in faith. Faith is the foundation of the community of life and love with God. On the foundation of the community of faith in the Church there is built up the community of cult and the solidarity of salvation of the faithful. Faith tears the mask from the ancient forces of evil and manifests the new world to which the community of the redeemed is to devote its efforts. The entire Christian life must be viewed from the standpoint of faith as well as under the aspect of love.

We must, in the very first place, attempt to explain the essence of faith as right response to the divine revelation (I). From this the duties which immediately flow from faith will be apparent (II). Finally we must discuss the sins which directly destroy faith itself (III).

I. THE ESSENCE OF FAITH

We believe what God has revealed to us in Christ and teaches us to believe through the Holy Catholic Church. But the mystery of faith is not to be explained in the first instance as the simple assent to a specific set of dogmas. Moral theology which has the totality of life and the whole man as its object views faith above all as a personal adherence to the Father of Light, who through His Son communicates to us a participation in the richness of His beatifying truth. Thus St. Thomas says: "Since faith is the assent to the word of another, it seems that in the act of faith what is fundamental and, as it were, the end is the person to whose word assent is given, and secondarily that which one wills to accept by assenting to him."[7]

The mystery of faith therefore can be rightly expressed in the terms of biblical personalism: 1) Faith is the personal encounter with God in Christ. 2) The psychology of faith cannot proceed from man. It must come from God, who, in Christ and in the Holy Spirit, is Light for the intellect which opens itself to Him. 3) Through the word of faith and light and motion of grace the conscience of man is stirred and summoned to response. 4) How profoundly true is the concept of faith as encounter with God, communion with God, becomes entirely evident to us only when we study it as salvific. 5) Faith means a giving as well as a receiving, and in this disposition the sacraments of faith (*sacramenta fidei*) are to be celebrated. Yet faith at the same time draws its life from them. 6) Faith is perfected through the gifts of the Holy Spirit.

1. *Personal Encounter with God in Christ and the Church*

Faith rests on the revelation of God through His grace, on the free self-manifestation of God to man. It is not intuition, not evidence, not the result of a logical deduction which leads us to belief. Persons can meet and know each other only through personal encounter and mutual self-manifestation. Since faith is more than mere knowledge about God, is an actual encounter with God, it can arise only through God's manifestation of Himself to man through revelation. God manifests Himself already in creation, which is nothing less than a word of God uttered externally. It becomes a word of God to man through the act by which God gives to man the capacity and His help to understand the word rightly (this may be by means of logical deductions).

Supernatural faith, of which we are speaking here, rests on a divine self-manifestation or revelation quite different from that of mere creation and reason: The triune God unlocks the deep mysteries of His heart; He opens the portals to His most secret and intimate truths which are in no way contained in the word of creation and which never can be learned from creation. In revelation God manifests Himself in direct conversation with man; and through the grace of faith, specifically through the infused virtue of faith, He opens the intellect and heart of man so that he can rightly accept His revelation.

Man himself, however, must do his part and actively cooperate in the divine action and actively accept the divine word. Man must permit God to unlock his intellect and thus be truly open to the word of God. Faith is dialog with God. God speaks His revealed word to the heart and spirit of man and at the same time gives to man the ear to hear, and man does hear and responds in faith.

God's self-manifestation is through Christ. By means of His almighty and eternal Word (the second Person of the Trinity) God manifested

Himself to man as Lord and Giver of life in creation. Through the incarnation of the Word, through the divine-human theandric words of the eternal Word, God tells us in accents of fatherly love about His mysteries. The grace of faith and the virtue of faith is a power from Christ. It is a gift of the resurrected Christ and the Holy Spirit sent to us by Him.

Our response and obedience in faith are response in Christ. As we accept the authentic word through and in Him, so in turn through His Spirit may we join with Him in His perfect response to the Father. Far beyond our fondest dreams our personality unfolds in a loving faith which gives us a share in the dialog of love between Father and Son in the Holy Spirit. Faith is the beginning and the presupposition of the imitation of Christ.

Since Christ speaks to us in His Mystical Body, the Church, and in her offers our word of faith to the Father in heaven, our faith is essentially bound up with the Church. In gratitude we must accept her mediation. The Church does not form a wall of separation between us and Christ. She is not a stumbling block on our way to Him. On the contrary she leads us to personal encounter with God. Through the Holy Spirit she forms the fruitful "milieu," the mother earth from which we draw nourishment. In her fruitful bosom Jesus gives us the life of faith and grace, particularly through the sacraments, above all through baptism. All saving faith includes at least implicitly the acceptance of the Church and her work of mediation. From this it is evident what faith implies: personal fellowship with God indicates community of faith with men, a new, more exalted encounter of men among themselves in the Holy Spirit, an emancipating fellowship of conscience.

Life does not always follow the procedure of logic in its unfolding and development: through the Church to Jesus, through Jesus to the triune God. "In one instance faith is enkindled by turning to the Father, even though the individual is scarcely aware that he possesses the Father only through Christ. For him faith is simply bowing to the Father who shelters and protects him. With this beginning faith develops further and gradually gains new insights. Another comes first to Christ, to His figure in history, to His word in the Bible. Through Christ he is led to the Father and the Spirit. There may be another who first grasps the work of the Spirit, the forms and aspects of holiness, the voice of the Church. . . . Only then does he learn of the Son and the Father."[8]

2. Faith Is Light of the Intellect

"It was the true light that enlightens every man who comes into the world" (Jn 1:9). Faith is not the result of our effort and achievement, as though we enkindled the light of our understanding, but it is the enlightening, expanding, and deepening of our knowledge through participation in the divine knowing by means of revelation. The intellect of man in adoring gratitude bows in faith, bows before the authority of the revealing God. It follows that faith rests in authority. Nor is human intelligence limited to its own powers equal to the truth of the mystery of salvation, even after it has been brought to us. "Flesh and blood" (Mt 16:17), insight and wisdom of petty man are totally disproportionate to the supernatural revelation (cf. Mt 11:25; 1 Cor 2:5). Our faith and our progress in faith is clear proof of the divine power. Supernatural faith rests in authority, because God Himself is the Author of the faith in our hearts. In order that we are able to believe as we must to attain salvation, God Himself must enlighten us: "God, who commanded light to shine out of darkness, has shone in our hearts, to give enlightenment concerning the knowledge of the glory of God, shining on the face of Christ Jesus" (2 Cor 4:6; cf. the variant reading; cf. also Eph 1:17f.). "It is written in the Prophets, 'And they all shall be taught of God.' Every one who has listened to the Father, and has learned, comes to me," Jesus Himself says of the grace of faith (Jn 6:45). He who believes in the Son does not owe his faith to the light of his own mind. No matter how essential it is that the human mind and heart be open to faith and cooperate in the reception of faith, it is still true that "He who believes in the Son of God has the testimony of God in himself" (1 Jn 5:10). "It is the Spirit that bears witness that Christ is the truth" (1 Jn 5:6). "No one can say 'Jesus is Lord,' except in the Holy Spirit" (1 Cor 12:3).

The human intelligence endowed with faith also submits to the judgment of the magisterium of the Church established by God. Therefore we speak of "Catholic faith." The reason lies in the enlightenment and movement of the one Holy Spirit: the one divine Spirit animates the Church and directs her to teach the truth vitally and without error: the one divine Spirit enlightens the heart and the spirit of each and every believer.

The faith which is light and gift from above is, nevertheless, also reasonable. It presupposes the judgment of credibility and credendity.

Before one makes the act, "I believe," he is convinced by sound arguments that his faith is basically reasonable, that it is vouched for by divine signs.[9] For the Church the faith is in no wise a "blind thrust into the dark."[10] "The one who believes does not deny his reason as though faith were opposed to reason. Much rather does he rise above mere reason (*eam transcendit*), insofar as he submits himself to the light of the First Truth, for the things of faith do indeed transcend (*supra*) reason, but they are not contrary to reason (*non contra*)."[11] The act of faith is not a surrender of reason, but an unmerited enlightenment and fulfillment, wonderful beyond all human conception.[12]

The basic attitudes toward the word of God suggested by a reasonable faith are humility, gratitude, sincere and active openness. Within the limits of our capacity we should make every effort to penetrate the mysteries of faith and learn all we can of the richness of this great treasure. The supernatural mysteries, we well know, are far beyond all human comprehension: we adore the incomprehensible majesty of God, sincerely confessing that He is infinitely greater than our intellect and spirit. The more we realize how far removed these mysteries are from our power to master them with our frail intellects, the more open we must be to the light from above. St. Peter demands that we be able to give an account of that which we hope for: "Be ready always with an answer to everyone who asks a reason for the hope that is in you" (1 Pt 3:15). And the first Vatican Council declared that reason enlightened by faith can acquire a very fruitful knowledge of the mysteries of faith, even though the knowledge be limited. This knowledge is acquired above all by a study of their analogy with natural things and of the relation of the truths of faith to one another and to the ultimate end of man.[13]

In the light of the mysteries of salvation all things acquire a new splendor for they are seen under a new aspect. The believer comes to a new insight, a far deeper insight into his own life and into all human history: he sees how God manifests his love and brings about the salvation of men. In the light of the deep mysteries of God's own Heart man no longer looks upon himself in pain and perplexity as an insoluble riddle. Pondering the mysteries of faith in the spirit of adoration we are able to catch a glimpse of eternity, the aurora of dawn presaging the clear bright sun of midday. Thus the blessed vision of God emits a faint ray of its overwhelming splendor. There are times of grace when we are immersed in the mystery of the Most Holy Trinity and in the unfathomable revelation of love in Jesus. We dare not venture to plumb the depths of the divine mysteries; in fact we may seem blinded by the divine majesty itself: but this is not due to lack of light. It is rather that we are overwhelmed by its heavenly brilliance.

3. Faith and Conscience

By faith we hold as true what God has revealed. Thus revelation is directed to the intellect seeking the truth. But faith is not the result of persuasion effected through rational arguments. (Of course the motives of credibility are more than adequate to convince the mind that faith is reasonable.) Faith is the result of illuminating grace enlightening the intellect and likewise of the movement of grace affecting the will. The Apostle says: He "has called us by his own glory and power" (2 Pt 1:3). God calls us to faith by the attraction of the external evidence or testimony, but equally through the inner force and glory of His grace, which lays hold of intellect and will, though it does not coerce the will but rather elevates it and evokes and perfects the freedom of its act. Were faith based on clear and necessary insight into evidence for the truths of faith, then the negative freedom to refuse to believe would be excluded. But such is not the case. The truths of faith are a light to the mind, but a light reflected, shrouded in a veil of obscurity in this life.

The will is free in the act of faith. We can, in the first place, freely ignore the motives of credibility no matter how clear they may be. (We can, to cite an example, concentrate all our attention on business or work or other activities having nothing to do with faith.) Or if one takes up the study of the truths of faith, he may with a kind of intellectual dishonesty focus all attention on the arguments opposed to the faith. With nagging persistence he may concern himself with the difficulties and obscurities inherent in the mysteries, while ignoring the grandeur of the divine evidence for the fact of revelation and the transcendent sublimity of the revealed truths themselves. Man can always refuse to believe.

The truths of faith are not mere abstractions but tremendous realities which lay claim to man's whole being and existence. Therefore the consent of faith implies a true recognition and acceptance of this claim of faith, a claim which penetrates to the very marrow of our being. For this reason the words of St. Augustine are pertinent: "Only one who wills to believe can believe,"[14] as are the words of St. Thomas: "Faith is only in the intellect to the extent that it is commanded by the will."[15] The Council of the Vatican condemns those who deny that faith is free: "If any one says that the assent to the Christian faith is not free, but is necessarily produced by arguments of human reason, let him be anathema!"[16]

Faith imposes itself upon the human conscience. Conscience makes the demand for earnest inquiry and research, commands one to make further inquiry as soon as one is confronted by the possibility of a divine revelation. But conscience also forbids one to accept as certain and give firm adherence to any alleged revelation as long as there is reasonable doubt regarding an essential fact or truth in the mind of the sincere inquirer. Preceding the act of faith there must be the judgment of conscience that we may and must believe.[17]

The "shipwreck of faith" follows on the violation of conscience (1 Tm 1:19). The pure conscience is the guardian of "the mystery of faith" (1 Tm 3:9). Conscience is the tireless monitor urging man to seek after faith, to persevere in the faith.

From all that we have said thus far, it should be apparent how faith encompasses the whole man. In the act of assent to truth intellect and free will participate; the receptive spirit and the responsible power of decision, the understanding and the conscience join. Faith turns not merely to the understanding and the naked will but also to the heart (the entire inner man with his conscience). Beautiful is the thought of the inspired writer: "*Cor creditur ad justitiam.*" "For with the heart a man believes unto justice, and with the mouth profession of faith is made unto salvation" (Rom 10:10). In faith the religious encounter of God all-truthful and man enlightened by God takes place. And yet faith is also a free moral act flowing from the force of love. Moral prerequisites and dispositions are, therefore, necessary for faith: the act is in itself a moral-religious act; though primarily a religious decision, it is also a moral one.

a. Moral Prerequisites for Faith

Faith is not the achievement of the moral excellence of man. There is no bridge between man himself with all his moral excellence and the inaccessible treasures of God's truth. Faith comes only from the revelation of God and the divine endowment of man through grace by which he is made capable of turning receptively to the revealed word and responding to it. If the personal encounter between man and man is possible only through self-manifestation, then surely the encounter with God is primarily the result of God's own manifestation of Himself through revelation and grace. It follows that man must also open his heart to God (permit God to open his heart) with such utter completeness that his own moral freedom is challenged to the very depth of his being. In all its depth and breadth man's freedom is summoned to respond to the divine invitation.

Faith is not simply an acceptance of speculative or abstract truths and principles with no further demand on the mind and heart of man. It is rather the revelation of truth with all the inexorable insistence of the good. The truth revealed is the good which must be loved, for the truth is the Truth which is God Himself. For this reason the decision of man regarding revelation will depend essentially on the inner attitude which lies in the profoundest depths of his being. Individual faults, occasional moral offenses, though they may be disturbingly grievous and are never to be excused or defended, do not create hindrances or obstacles to faith as nearly insurmountable as an habitual bad attitude of mind and heart. Such a persistently negative spirit clearly indicates a stubborn and unrepentant will. The greatest obstacle to faith is *pride* (cf. Mt 11:25f.); for to open one's heart to God directly implies that one submits to Him, subjects one's self to Him. Moreover carnal bondage, enslavement to the flesh, once it has taken hold of the whole man, is also one of the chief obstacles to faith, for devotion of the mind to the divine truth is irreconcilable with total enslavement of the senses.

b. Faith Demands the Beginning of Love

Above all, faith demands a good disposition with a loving readiness to harken to revelation which flows from God's love and is directed to elicit love in return. It is itself entirely and utterly a movement from love toward love. Revelation takes place in the Word of God. And the Word is the Son of God. "The Son however is the Word, not just any word or other, but the Word breathing love."[18] Faith is not yet love, in fact it can exist really distinct from love, even though its existence be stunted and coupled with fearful hazard of complete destruction. In its whole essence faith is directed toward love. Therefore it is inwardly impossible to accept faith without some movement of love toward love. Not that one must necessarily possess the supreme love of utter submission if one has faith but at least an incipient love, at least a loving acceptance of the Word of God who approaches us in person. In fact faith essentially requires grace for the will, which can only be a movement by the breath of the divine Love! This movement of love proceeding from the will must set the intellect aglow. Only in such wise can it truly become seeing. "Only loving eyes have insight into the essence."[19] "Love alone is the attitude which opens the eyes to what the other really is."[20] "The attitude of love opens the eyes of faith, but every reinvigoration of this vision gives love further room and greater clarity. One may say as well that faith springs from love, as love from faith, for the two in their profoundest depths are one."[21]

Keeping in mind the words of St. John that "God is love," we can readily accept the assumption of Scheler: "Love lays the foundation for knowing and willing as the spiritually deeper act."[22] But we must not fail to distinguish between the love-breath of grace with the loving disposition accepting it, preceding the individual will-act and knowledge-act, and the conscious love-response and love-act following in consequence of clear and conscious knowledge. Knowing and loving mysteriously intermingle in a way which faintly resembles the eternal love movement of the Trinity; for the Word proceeds from the loving Father, united in the breath of love which is the breath of the Holy Spirit (*perichoresis*). "According to St. Thomas the essence of faith consists in the intermingling of knowing and loving directed Godward. Wrought by the Holy Spirit and imparted as His gift of grace, faith is light to the mind, movement to the will. It is both the anchoring of self in God and the pressing on toward Him."[23]

c. The Act of Faith, a Moral Act

The act of faith, as religious response to God, is a moral act for the simple reason that it is a free decision for God. However, it also supposes and involves a moral decision in a narrower sense: it is a fundamental recognition of our duty of obedience in all our activity in the world and in time. This is apparent from the fact that revelation does not embrace merely the blessed truth that God is our Father but also the assignment of duty from God our sovereign Lord, who lays claim upon our whole life. It is true that the act of faith is not in itself absolutely bound up with the firm resolution to do all that is demanded by faith, but it is essentially a recognition of the just claim of the assignment which faith imposes upon us. For this reason faith implies an acknowledgement of our obligation to obey God without reserve.

Even the believing sinner elicits this moral act or implies it when he makes an act of divine faith: he acknowledges the claim of faith and the verdict of guilt insofar as the act of faith itself confronts him with the accusation of his sinful conduct. So long as he has not totally averted his eyes from the truth of faith, and insofar as he still looks to the faith and clings to it even in his sinfulness, he still makes the decision against himself, a sinner, and for the rights of God's dominion.

There is a contradiction of course deep down in the heart of the believing sinner, because he fails to act in conformity with his belief. The decision in his act of faith and in his attitude to the faith does not enter into his moral conduct as decisive or final. In fact his sin may be more heinous or malicious than the offense of one who has not received the light of faith. The man who sins despite his faith sins in the very sight of God by acting against a clear conscience enlightened by faith. But even his sin is far less malicious than the offense of the apostate who in his spite has extinguished the light of faith. One who has renounced the faith presumes consciously and in principle to repudiate the sovereign rights of God. Moreover in his every sinful act he hurls the weight of that total renunciation of the rights of God onto the scale. But the believing sinner, despite his sin, still has an awareness of sin which is an incipient sorrow or approach to sorrow and conversion whose value is to be measured by the vitality of the faith he still possesses. He still possesses the basis and principle of conversion.

This is true because in faith itself he implicitly professes his guilt and recognizes at least in principle his duties of obedience. In his faith he clings to the sovereign rights of God and manifests an incipient good will. "If in man himself there is nothing by way of inner response to the claim and demand for decision, if there is no inner disposition toward the object of decision,"[24] then the consent of faith is permanently impossible, unless it should be no more than an utterly fatuous and sterile faith, completely empty, mechanical, isolated, habitual.

Genuine faith, above all a profoundly penetrating faith, is possible only when it is coupled with the works of faith. The Lord Himself says: "My teaching is not my own, but his who sent me. If anyone desires to do his will, he will know of the teaching whether it is from God" (Jn 7:16f.).

The man who in the spirit of self-glorification follows only his own will and craves only his own honor closes his mind and heart to the very witness by whom God Himself authenticates His word: "You search the Scriptures, because in them you think that you have life everlasting. And it is they that bear witness to me, yet you are not willing to come to me that you may have life" (Jn 5:39f.). Only the man who is fully attentive to the inner value and its challenge to duty found in the signs and objects by which God prepares the way to faith, is capable of understanding their words. Only in doing the known good does man become entirely one with God. Even without being fully conscious of it, he becomes one with the saving will of God, the good itself in person.

Thus he is best prepared rightly to hear and to understand the call of God to faith and to fulfillment of the demand of faith. Only the man whose heart is morally open grasps the faith in its life value, which surely belongs to faith altogether essentially. Just as the Word of God is eternally fruitful in the intimate divine life, so the word of revelation uttered in time must be essentially fruitful. It is the manifestation of the transcendent paternal love of God toward us. Only in the measure in which we are prepared to fulfill with love God's loving will, does faith impart to us the vital experience of His love.

4. *Faith as Salutary Faith*

Faith as a divine virtue is in its whole essence bound up with our salvation. According to the Council of Trent, "Faith is the beginning of man's salvation, the foundation and root of all justification."[25] In a celebrated passage St. Paul says that "He who is just lives by faith" (Gal 3:11; Heb 10:38; Hb 2:4). Again in a phrase which enunciates the theme of the epistle to the Romans the Apostle says: "For I am not ashamed of the gospel, for it is the power of God unto salvation to everyone who believes . . . For in it the justice of God is revealed, from faith unto faith, as it is written, 'He who is just lives by faith'" (Rom 1:16f.). Paul does not speak merely of a justice which is according to faith or in conformity with the faith, but of a justice which is born of the faith. The just man lives in conformity with the faith, but he also derives his life (*Zoé, sotería*) from it.

In order to understand this fundamental declaration of Pauline theology one must bear in mind that faith in biblical thought is infinitely more than a mere intellectual "holding as true." Basically and in principle, faith is so open to the life-giving word of God that through it we submit our whole existence to Him who reveals Himself to us as the all-truthful and all-good God. Faith is submission to Christ, our salvation. Faith is transformation of our mode of life and existence through the Spirit of Christ, who wills to preserve us unsullied and constantly renewed against the day of resurrection, and who even now restores in us moral integrity through the good works which He brings forth in us through faith.

Salvation of man means simply preservation from evil as such, from physical and moral destruction. It is the work of the Holy Spirit that enables the man of faith to escape this evil and overcome the spirit and forces of contradiction and death which harass him in this earthly existence. Let us note, however, that God bestowed the Holy Spirit upon man not because of just works but because of faith. St. Paul speaks of the blessing coming to the Gentiles through Christ, "that through faith we might receive the promise of the Spirit" (Gal 3:14). In this sense we must confess that "man is justified by faith independently of the works of the Law" (Rom 3:28). It follows that any presumptuous vaunting of our own achievement must be summarily dismissed: "Salvation does not derive from ourselves, but is God's gift."[26]

But precisely because we are saved by grace, because we are a new creature in Christ Jesus, we may and must do good works. Says the Apostle: "For by grace you have been saved through faith; and that not from yourselves, for it is the gift of God; not as the outcome of works, lest anyone may boast. For his workmanship, we are created in Christ Jesus in good works, which God has made ready beforehand that we may walk in them" (Eph 2:8ff.). It follows that only then does man finally and effectively have salvation from faith, when this faith manifests itself through love as submission to Christ in our life (Gal 5:6; Mt 7:21; Jas 2:14-26).

In its very core faith is salvific. God does not reveal Himself to us in order that we may have some information about Him, but that through participation in His glorious truth we may attain to salvation. In His revelation of the truths of faith God's plan embraces not merely Himself and His glory, but also us and our eternal bliss. He reveals His glory so that we shall seek our happiness in it. "When I profess my faith and say, 'I believe in the living triune God, etc.,' I include in the totality of my belief myself and the whole mystery of my Christian existence. The Christian belongs to the *Credo* as the one called to faith and responding in faith. Responding in such wise that he knows that he himself is meant as a vital part of what he professes! Through that which he confesses as Christian truth in the profession of faith he himself is included."[27]

Faith is "consciousness of holy reality, but in such a way that my own existence is drawn from it and is directed toward it."[28] When we pray, "I believe in God," we wish not merely and first of all to say that we believe in a certain number of truths which God has revealed to us, but primarily and most of all we wish to say we believe that we with our whole existence are bound to God, the Revealer of the saving truth. In faith we experience most of all that God means us ourselves and we in the act of faith mean God Himself who is our salvation. Also in each detail of truth which we accept in faith because God has revealed it, we experience some reference to our eternal salvation, to God, who is our salvation. God's truth is always a summons and an appeal. It is always life-giving and points out the way to eternity with the promise of eventual beatitude.

"The faith as salutary faith" implies not merely that the faith brings salvation to the believer if he lives by it, but likewise that it will be a "judgment" for anyone who fails to live by it. Dreadful is the threat to any one who consciously rejects the claim of the divine revelation to the faith of man. Dreadful the claim of the faith to a life in accordance with the faith. "What will it profit, my brethren, if a man says he has faith, but does not have works? Can the faith save him? . . . So faith too, unless it has works, is dead in itself. . . . Thou believest that there is one God. Thou dost well. The devils also believe, and tremble" (Jas 2:14, 17, 19).

If the faith has lost every dynamic of action, every life-force to grasp salvation, then it is dead. But then too it ceases to be a virtue in the full sense of the word. "In Thomas such faith has no grace. . . . The 'dead faith' (fides informis) which does not send living roots into the whole man, is no virtue, and therefore is excluded from the structural elements, and all the more from the life-giving elements of the Christian life."[29]

The virtue of faith is not destroyed by every mortal sin, for the very conversion of the sinner who still believes is a clear and striking proof that his faith—though not at the actual time when the sin is committed, but afterwards—manifests itself as a vital force, which permits him to grasp salvation anew. There is therefore an "unformed faith" which is salutary in the sense that it can at least clear the way for a return to salvation. But there is also an "unformed faith" that is altogether dead, a purely "empty faith" which is mere formalism and routine, something

entirely conceptual and therefore no longer a true virtue. Salvific faith
and virtue in the full sense, however, must be faith animated with love,
operative in love (Gal 5:6; cf. 1 Cor 13).

Salutary faith implies an inner essential relation to Christ. As He is the
source of our faith, as He completes and perfects it, so He is our Salvation. Therefore salvific faith implies a living hold on Christ. Through
faith Christ lives in our hearts (Eph 3:17). "He who believes in the Son
has everlasting life" (Jn 3:36). "He who believes in me enters into me.
Who enters into me, possesses me. To possess me means to have eternal
life."[30]

It is apparent that salutary faith is not merely a conceptual or doc-
trinaire "holding as true." It is rather a vital adherence to Christ, the
Truth and Salvation. In St. Paul, and in revelation generally, the word
is regularly used to express the "faith of the heart," which means faith
with understanding and heart. *"Corde creditur ad iustitiam"* (Rom 10:10).
Only faith in the heart, living union with Christ, the truth and the life,
is in the full sense of the term salutary faith.

Believing, we are baptized in the passion and the resurrection of Christ.
In nothing does faith manifest its salvific character and effect so singularly
and triumphantly as in suffering for the sake of salvation. "And this is the
victory that overcomes the world, our faith" (1 Jn 5:4f.). Living salutary
faith robs the seductive world of its glamor and lure. Above all it imparts
a new and deeper meaning to suffering. And suffering becomes a dynamic
force for salvation through faith and trust in the suffering of Christ.

Faith essentially introduces us to the virtue of Christian hope (cf. Heb
11:1). And it is really through hope that we contemplate and lay hold of
salvation in Christ. Hope is not something extrinsically superadded to
faith. Rather of its own inner essence faith seeks to be salutary and calls
forth hope from its own inner depth. It is normal that one who believes
should hope, for faith creates confidence. And faith and hope postulate
charity. Because the salvation of those who believe rests in the love of God
made manifest in Christ, salutary faith in the full and adequate sense of
the term demands faith that is effective in love.[31]

5. *Faith and the Sacrament of Faith*

Adherence to Christ through faith and the vital incorporation in Him
through baptism, which is *par excellence* the sacrament of faith,[32] forms

one inner bond of unity. "He who believes and is baptized shall be saved" (Mk 16:16). In the sacrament of baptism Christ grafts us into His Mystical Body. As children of the Church, our Mother, we partake of the treasure of revealed truths He has given her. In the sacrament Christ also communicates to us, with the life of grace and the divine virtue of love, the spirit and sense of children, without which we could never penetrate into the profoundest depths of the faith.

The adult who is about to be baptized must first make an act of faith. Only in faith can one receive the full fruits of the sacrament of faith. This means that the mind, the will, and the heart must be open to the truths of salvation. For the infant and for any one who has never attained the use of reason the faith of the Church is present, awaiting the awakening of reason. Both the Church and the parents or guardians have the right and duty to provide for the child's education. Jointly they assume the responsibility that the words of salvation addressed to the child in the administration of the sacrament will be properly explained in due time, progressively and adequately. All the education to faith in the baptized must be based on the exhilarating reality that the Lord Himself has laid the supernatural foundations. With the grace of divine Sonship He has placed in the heart of the child a childlike spirit and sense of the faith. Not only should the Christian family and the parish ordinarily share in the celebration of the baptism; they also assume the responsibility that the child's spirit and knowledge of the faith be given the opportunity to develop in an atmosphere of faith. Baptism places us in the sacred orbit of truth where we are able to accept from the Church, our Mother, the word of the Father imparted to us in Christ. In baptism we become inwardly and with all the objective reality of grace, disciples of Christ, docile hearers of the word of God in the Catholic Church.

At baptism we receive from the Church not only the confession of faith, but also the word of sanctification and salvation, a word which is directed to us individually and personally. It lies in the very nature of our faith that we are called by God to holiness. In the gracious bounty of God's good will at every participation in the celebration of baptism and above all through the reception of the other sacraments, our faith should ever be deepened and revitalized. The development of the spirit of faith in great part depends on the celebration of the sacrament of the faith in a vitally interested and believing manner which appeals to the heart. And an essential part of all this is the active participation of all the faithful.

Formalism and individualism in a mere "administration" of the sacraments, on the other hand, tends as does no other act or neglect, to affect the faith with a destructive force.

In case of necessity baptism of blood (i.e., martyrdom) or baptism of desire (perfect love of God, or perfect contrition) can supply for sacramental baptism (baptism by water). But there is no substitute for faith. Without faith there is no salvation for anyone who has attained the use of reason.[33] "He who does not believe is already judged" (Jn. 3:18). "Without faith it is impossible to please God" (Heb 11:5). However, the salutary faith which saves us always points to the "sacrament of faith." Without the saving mystery of our redemption, which we celebrate in the sacrament and which is extended to all men in the sacrament, there would be no salvific faith at all. This interior bond between the act of faith and the sacrament of faith is even effective in instances when there is salvific faith without any actual or explicit knowledge of the sacraments.

According to the more probable teaching, which today is the view more commonly held, only faith in the existence of God who is our salvation (this means faith in God who mercifully rewards, who justly punishes) is absolutely and indispensably necessary for salvation. This faith is necessary by an absolute necessity of means, which nothing can supplant, whereas faith in Christ the Incarnate Son of the eternal Father, who died for us, who arose from the dead and sent us the Holy Spirit, is necessary for the salvation of those only to whom Christ is actually made known. But nonetheless Christ alone is the salvation of all. And no matter how limited the objective content of the act of faith, by which one is saved, faith itself in all instances forges that inner bond with Christ by which we attain salvation. Saving faith is interior openness unto grace and the commitment to Christ, which under ordinary conditions is effectively and authoritatively imparted to us in the sacrament.

6. Faith Perfected through the Gifts of the Holy Spirit

The spirit of faith is sustained and kept alive in the soul not merely through supernatural grace, but also through the presence of the Holy Spirit who breathes the virtue of faith and the other virtues into us. The spirit of living faith demands the presence of the Holy Spirit with His heavenly gifts. The gift of wisdom (completion and perfection of divine love) unlocks the richest treasures and gives the profoundest insights into the beauty and sublimity of faith. Understanding and knowledge are special gifts of the Holy Spirit relating to the depth and breadth of the knowledge of faith. Understanding imparts such a luminous insight into the motive of faith that man is fired with enthusiasm for the certainty and clarity of his faith. The fruit of this gift is the blessed joy of basking in the bright light of the faith. In antithesis to this joy is spiritual blindness, dullness of perception, defect of sense for the joys of faith. Through the gift of knowledge the one who believes is rendered judicious in his appreciation of what belongs to faith and what to the discernment of reason. If wisdom enables one to look lovingly toward God Himself, the gift of knowledge imparts, above all, the believing perception of things created, a believing and trustful instinct for the providential plan and Christian solution in all the situations and trials of life. Opposed to the faith enlightened by the gift of knowledge is credulity, uncritical approval of ill-founded religious opinions, and hasty acceptance of private revelations and prophecies.

II. DUTIES FLOWING DIRECTLY FROM FAITH

By its very nature divine revelation demands acceptance by man. And faith demands most universally action in accordance with faith, life in the design and pattern of faith. The entire life of the Christian is depicted in the Sacred Scriptures as "practicing" the truth in our lives, "doing" the truths of faith in love (Jn 3:21; Eph 4:15; 1 Jn 1:6). Just as the entire moral and religious life of man is ordered to salvation, so also all salutary conduct ultimately flows from faith, for faith is the mainspring of all action leading to salvation.[34] However, this is not to say that all the manifold duties of the Christian life flow directly from the virtue of faith as such. Our present concern is with those commandments which do directly flow from this virtue.

1. The Duty of Knowing the Truths of Faith

Faith is communication of the treasure of divine truth to the human mind. It follows that man has a strict obligation to accept this heavenly treasure of truth as well as he can. And this implies that he has the duty of learning to know his faith as well as he can. The degree of obligation is determined by one's intellectual capacities and one's position in life, particularly in relation to the challenge of one's surroundings. Danger to faith incurred from the hostility to divine revelation clearly imposes the obligation to safeguard the treasure for one's self and those committed to one's care. What might have been sufficient knowledge, possibly barely sufficient, in former times when most men could not read and write is no longer adequate in our time when every conceivable error is broadcast to the masses through the most efficient media of mass communication.

It is not easy to determine exactly the extent of the obligation to memorize the fixed formulas in which the truths of faith or its duties are expressed (for example the Ten Commandments and the Creed). If there is no other means of appropriating the rich treasure of the divine truths, then learning the formulas by heart becomes an obligation. Thus in former times committing the creed and the Our Father to memory was required before an adult would be admitted to baptism. Yet far more important than learning by heart is a true penetration into the meaning of the Divine Word accepted by faith, for faith is the reflection of the light of God's truth. The Savior speaks of Himself as our light: "I am the light of the world. He who follows me does not walk in darkness, but will have the light of life" (Jn 8:12).

Faith can enlighten our earthly existence only insofar as it penetrates into our spirit. Therefore the constant deepening of the knowledge of his faith is among the first and most rigorous obligations of the Christian. This is effected more readily by meditation than by mere abstract study of the truths of revelation.

The Church introduces us to the faith. She carries the light of Christ on through the ages of time. Therefore faith demands adherence to the Church, full submission to her teaching magisterium. Profound insight into the world of faith is assured only through the life in and with the Church, a life in harmony with the mind and heart of the Church, as expressed in the phrase, *sentire cum ecclesia*. This union with the Church and possession of the *mind* of the Church places the Christian with heart and mind in the light of Christ.

The exultant faith of the Church comes to us principally in the sacraments of faith, above all in the sacraments of baptism and the Eucharist. For this reason the celebration of the sacraments must be a matter of great concern to priest and layman. It is one of the basic obligations of the priest and the faithful who celebrate with him to proceed with great decorum. The liturgy—the mysteries of faith—should be celebrated with such dignity and formality that the faith, joy in the faith, and understanding of the faith are constantly enriched and deepened.

To neglect the study of the truths of faith altogether or to make only superficial efforts to acquire a knowledge of the revealed doctrine is a grave violation of the obligation to be properly informed in matters of faith. Habitual neglect of the Sunday sermon by those who have no other means of instruction in such matters is surely a mortal sin, for they neglect the one source of alerting and deepening the knowledge of their faith. Even the educated man sins by such neglect if in matters of religion his knowledge is altogether disproportionate to his cultural standing in other spheres. Particularly grave is the neglect that constitutes a proximate danger of shipwreck to the faith itself. This danger arises most commonly in the circles of the educated who are insufficiently prepared to face the doubt and denial of their surroundings. Parents, teachers, educators, and especially priests entrusted with the care of souls are obliged to provide effectively for the religious instruction and guidance of those subject to them. This is impossible unless they themselves are properly trained in sacred doctrine.

It is the duty of the *priest* who administers the sacraments to the faithful to give serious attention to the recipient's fitness: the priest should see that he is equipped with the knowledge of the truths of faith at least as to essentials and possessed of the dispositions necessary for the fruitful reception of the sacrament. Children who through fault of their own neglect to attend catechetical or other instruction in religion and parents who fail to provide that those under them obtain such instruction are not to be absolved in the sacrament of penance unless they manifest sorrow for their neglect and promise amendment.

2. The Obligation to Elicit Acts of Faith

The obligation to elicit acts of faith is particularly binding when the divine revelation is first recognized as credible. For the adult to be baptized the act of faith is obligatory above all on the occasion of the reception of the sacrament;[35] for those baptized in infancy the obligation begins with their instruction in the truths of the faith. When the Church defines an article of faith through the exercise of her infallible teaching authority, every adult Catholic must accept the doctrine as divinely revealed. One who has not given assent of faith to the doctrine, whether it be because of denial or reservation of judgment or lack of knowledge about it, must give his assent to it after the definition by an explicit act of divine faith. When faith is seriously assailed by temptation against this divine virtue, the act of faith is necessary for resistance to temptation and the firm defence against this great danger.

Every right-living Christian makes numerous acts of faith implicitly every day: by active participation in the liturgy, by every prayer he utters, every sign of the cross he makes, every triumph he scores over temptation for God's sake. All these are activation of the faith; all implicitly, and often explicitly, contain the act of faith. Nevertheless the faithful should be urged to elicit explicit acts of faith frequently on other occasions. The result will be a readiness and promptness to combat temptations against faith whenever they arise, and all other temptations, with the motive and spirit of faith. No proof or evidence of faith is clearer or nobler than the exercise and practice of faith through prayer. Living faith draws its life nourishment from prayer just as prayer in turn is fed and nourished by living faith. Both center in the warm and vital celebration of the sacraments of faith.

3. The Obligation to Profess One's Faith

There is a strict and sacred obligation to profess one's faith in word and deed, whenever the divine honor and glory and the salvation of our neighbor may demand it. To deny one's faith is never allowed under any circumstances. There can never be any threat of evil so great as to justify the denial of the faith. The dread of suffering or death even with the most excruciating pains of martyrdom cannot justify even a fictitous or merely external denial of the faith by some articulate word or sign. The guilt of denial is incurred—and it is among the most heinous of sins—even though the denial is merely external and the mind and will interiorly still cling to the truths of revelation. Our Savior speaks expressly of the profession of faith when He says: "Every one who acknowledges me before men, I also will acknowledge him before my Father in heaven. But whoever disowns me before men, I in turn will disown him before my Father in heaven" (Mt. 10:32f.; cf. Mk 8:38; Lk 9:26; 2 Tm 2:12f.; Rom 10:10).

Active participation in heretical rites or in the rites of any false religion, particularly attempting marriage before an heretical minister, is tantamount to denial of one's faith. As a matter of fact, these rites are often the occasion of an explicit profession of a false religion, no matter what the individual's religion may be nor what he actually believes.

Joining with non-Catholics in common prayer on civic occasions or in prayer for Christian unity in faith may be a mutual sign of Christian love. It can prove a meritorious testimony to loving zeal on the part of Catholic and non-Catholic. All the activity of the *Una Sancta* movement is clearly motivated by the stern realization that any compromise of principle is out of question where matters of faith are at stake. The supreme concern is rather a deeper penetration into the truths of faith and a vitalization of the spirit of faith in the Church.

Though the denial of faith is always evil, the concealment of one's religion may be permitted for grave motives. Yet even then only temporary concealment can be justified, with the proviso that one is always ready to profess his faith openly when the obligation to do so arises. On such occasions one must be willing to risk life itself rather than refuse to profess the true religion. But no reason can ever be sufficient to justify the failure to profess one's faith or even to conceal it, if this is practically equivalent to a denial of faith. For this reason one must testify clearly regarding one's faith in response to a legitimate inquiry by lawful superiors, though surely an evasive or equivocal answer may be given to a private and unauthorized questioner, provided there is a good reason to do so.

Per se one who has been converted from unbelief or heresy must profess his faith also exteriorly as soon as possible after his conversion. But for weighty reasons (for example to avoid the wrecking of one's marriage or to prevent overt attacks against the Church by means of a prudent delay in publicizing the conversion) a temporary postponement of the public profession could be justified. But in no instance may acts be performed during this interim which are equivalent to approbation of heresy or unbelief. Thus a Protestant, to cite an example, who has come to the conviction of the truth of the Catholic Church may no longer participate in the "Lord's Supper" at a Protestant Church. Because of a sense of what is honorable in the profession of one's religion, Protestant groups likewise forbid participation in the Last Supper with certain other groups whose teaching is not in harmony with their own. From the standpoint of profession of faith, the judgment against participation by Catholics in the Eucharistic celebration of the dissident Eastern Churches is not so severe. The problem in such instances is not really a question of faith (at least not regarding the Eucharist) so much as of unity of the Church.

It may happen that a dying man is willing to profess the Catholic faith in the presence of a priest, even though he could not be prevailed upon to do so in the presence of his own relatives and friends. In such an instance the priest would be permitted to receive the sick man into the Church privately. But if it is at all possible, the profession of faith should surely be attested by the presence of witnesses who would later at the proper time testify publicly to the conversion. The testimony of the witnesses may be of great apologetic value for the Church, particularly if the convert was a man of considerable stature or notorious as an enemy of the Church who had wrought harm to the faith.

In time of persecution one is permitted to hide or flee from the center of persecution. But it is never lawful to conceal one's faith if the concealment imperils the faith of others or is prejudicial to the cause of the faith or religion. Therefore every effort must be made to avoid the slightest semblance of vacillation, or even more so, of denial of faith in the presence of Christians who are weak in their religion. The shepherds of souls placed over the flock of Christ (bishops and pastors) may not forsake the flock entrusted to their care through flight from persecution, to the neglect of souls, so long as there is some hope that the necessary spiritual ministrations can be exercised for the flock. "The good shepherd lays down his life for his sheep. But the hireling . . . leaves the sheep and flees" (Jn 10:11f.). However, if the flight of the pastors at least in the long view be for the good of souls, then the words of the Lord apply: "When they persecute you in one town, flee to another" (Mt 10:23).

When certain "rites" prescribed by civil authorities are in themselves ambiguous and capable of a double meaning, so that they can be considered an expression of a false cult or of a morally unobjectionable civil homage or honor, then the Catholic may participate in the exercise of such rites. But he must have a serious reason for doing so and manifest very clearly through his entire behavior or even by means of an express declaration that he is taking part not in a religious rite but only in a purely civil ceremony. In accordance with this principle the Church has recently manifested a very generous-minded attitude in the matter of the veneration of the statues of Confucius, the tablets of ancestors and the sacred shrines in China, Japan, Siam, and other countries. The Church took this position largely because of the assurances given by competent authorities that these rites were not so much professions of religious faith and exercise of rites of religion as purely civil ceremonies and acts of civil and national patriotism.[36]

4. *The Duty of Spreading the Faith*

The Holy Catholic Church has the divine mission and therefore also the *divine right* to preach the faith all over the world. The very term *Catholic* indicates this mission and right (Mt 28:19; Mk 16:15). Any one who appreciates the great blessing of the true faith must be filled with zeal and a passionate desire to communicate it to others. Any one who is animated with zeal for the honor of God and His Church will always be pained at the thought that there are still so many men who do not honor God, who do not know Christ, or are separated from the true Church.

It is not at all compatible with the right attitude toward the "kingdom of God and grace" to be so concerned "with religious harmony" as to renounce every effort to lead unbelievers or heretics and men of different faiths to the truth of the one faith. Only culpable indifference or a total misconception of truth can characterize as *proselytism* the burning missionary zeal which leaves nothing undone in the endeavor to lead all men to the true faith.

There is, of course, a proselytism in the pejorative sense. It would be present in any effort to win others to the faith merely externally without regard for inner conviction and conscience. True zeal for the faith stands aloof from all motives of finance and power politics and all dishonorable methods in the work of conversion.

Zeal for the spread of the faith may not be based on the false—and for many, the offensive—assumption that all those who do not explicitly profess the Catholic faith and acknowledge the Church's authority will be lost. The faith must be spread, above all, by true zeal for the manifestation of the kingdom of divine love, for the revelation of the abundance of salvation in the kingdom of saving truth and love. This kingdom of God's redemptive truth and love with its fulness of salvation welcomes all men. Even those still outside the Church may be on the way to salvation before they arrive at the explicit profession of the faith in all its fulness. Yet they do not have free access to the abundant treasures of grace and truth found in the Church. True zeal seeks to open to all men this infinite treasure.

In such zeal for the cause of Christ, every true Christian must indeed be grieved by the bloody wounds in the Lord's dear body, grieved by the alienation of so many millions from the unity of the true Church and in part from her sacraments. To win back to the one true Church founded by Christ all those who bear the Christian name must be the great concern of our prayer and our apostolate. Only deep understanding and sympathetic love motivated by prudent zeal will find a way to the hearts of the separated brethren.

The entire ecumenical activity and particularly the *Una Sancta* movement and all sincere efforts to promote Christian unity deserve our hearty support. The Instruction of the Holy Office clearly indicates the Church's attitude of approval.[37] The establishment of a special Secretariate for the Promotion of Christian Unity places the whole movement for one-ness in an entirely new stage. Many Catholics are convinced that the Holy Spirit is at work in the ecumenical movement among the Christians who are separated from Rome. Unmistakably clear are the repeated admonitions which the Holy Father, John XXIII, addressed to all Catholic Christendom. The Pope urges us to be so deeply and profoundly renewed in love, in solidarity of unity and in the spirit of faith, that all the separated brethren will learn to look upon the Father's house, the Church, as a true home which invites them to enter and remain. Compromise in matters of faith is vile and utterly excluded. But acrid discussion and a quarrelsome spirit must likewise be cast aside as failing in true love. Instead we must first of all attempt to understand the real concern and interest of those who do not share our faith and bond with the Church. We must learn to grasp the true meaning of the religious diversity in words and their use (our terms may have a totally different meaning in the mind and use of Protestants), and above all in the cultural backgrounds. Meanwhile, if once we are able to breach the walls of misunderstanding, and reveal to all the separated brethren the tender pastoral love of the Church with its all-embracing solicitude, much will have been accomplished indeed.

The duty of propagating the faith binds first of all the ecclesiastical hierarchy which has the obligation to direct and to supervise the whole preaching of the faith.[38] The religious communities and congregations are obliged to place themselves at the disposal of the Church authorities for this task as far as they are able to do so. Canon 1350 impresses upon the bishops and pastors the importance of the obligation of looking upon themselves not only as shepherds of their flock, the faithful, but also as responsible for all who live in their territory. They must realize that they have a serious responsibility for the unbelievers and those of other faiths living within their dioceses and parishes.

Those who have the care of souls contribute toward the spread of the faith through encouragement of the various organizations established for the *support* of the missions, and above all through awakening and fostering vocations for the work of the mission. The faithful must contribute by edifying example, fervent prayer for the spread of the kingdom of God, and according to their means, also by financial support to the cause of the missions. Any one who totally neglects the missions and of set purpose fails to contribute from his superfluity to the cause can scarcely be excused from mortal sin. Every believer must work in his own way and with the means at his disposal to spread the faith through word and example.

It is a moot point whether there is ever an obligation for the individual to enter the mission field and work as a missionary. *Per se* the duty to care for the great spiritual need of the heathens concerns the Church as a whole, not the individual as such. However, the Church can carry out her task only through individual, self-sacrificing Christians. One point is certain and may not be overlooked: God endows and inwardly calls a sufficient number of individuals for this task! The rejection of the divine call on the part of many actually means a serious handicap in this great undertaking. In my opinion, any one who seriously discerns a call to the missions is for that reason, but above all because of the law of grace, obliged to follow the call of grace. In any instance religious men and women who have bound themselves by vow or promise to a life of Christian perfection must follow the command of their ecclesiastical superiors to enter mission work without any hesitation. The plea that the vow does not bind any one to such tasks is valid at best for those who are not adequately equipped for the task.

If any one prompted by unworthy motives should seek to dissuade another who feels the call to the mission field from responding to the divine summons of grace, he can scarcely be excused from the guilt of mortal sin. Ecclesiastical authorities must realize that egoism of the group is just as contrary to the solidarity of the community of faith as individual or private egoism. The bishops of the Church must themselves actively cooperate in the encouragement of vocations to the missions in their dioceses. As to the opposition to mission vocations, even the passionate devotion of parents can in no wise justify a stubborn opposition or interference in the matter of their children's vocation to mission work. However, the blindness of human affection may diminish their subjective guilt.

5. *The Obligation to Safeguard the Faith*

We bear this gift which is absolutely essential for our salvation in a fragile vessel. Therefore we must pray unceasingly to God that He help us keep the faith, but we must also do our part to safeguard it against unnecessary risks and to protect it when it is imperiled. Today the multiplicity of contacts with the masses of unbelievers and men of different faiths creates many dangers to faith which cannot be entirely averted. Nevertheless, through zeal for the faith, solidarity in good, ardent prayer, vigilance, and deepening of the knowledge of the divine truths, immanent dangers can and must be made remote. Wherever serious dangers to faith can be avoided one must actually shun them, no matter how great the sacrifice.

We have already stressed the great danger inherent in an evil life which is an utter contradiction to the revealed principles of morals and the ideals of faith. The danger is greatest in the life of continued and unrepented sin, in the evil life which is based on principles utterly opposed to the truths of faith. The evil life may finally be made a rule of faith, so that one begins to believe what he practices.

A similar hazard to the faith arises from lack of the living warmth of love which should set our faith aglow in works of charity. Of its inmost nature faith seeks this glow of love, seeks to be animated by love. Equally dangerous is the state of mental vagueness and confusion in the grasp of the truths of faith arising from lack of training and stern mental discipline and from false intellectual attitudes toward the revealed mysteries and the supernatural life. Defective understanding of the truths of faith leaves one defenceless against the many objections arising from a hostile environment and the inner temptations arising from the obscurities of the sacred mysteries themselves. For the proud man and the worldly-minded these obscurities and the very supernatural character of the faith constitute the greatest hazard to faith.

Throughout the world today in varying degrees the stage, motion pictures, radio and television broadcasts, the press, magazines, books of every kind, not to mention countless forms of pornography, constitute a grave danger to both faith and morals. Surely such an atmosphere is responsible for a great weakening of the spirit of faith and Christian morality among our Catholic people, and for actual loss of faith. The extent of the evil influence can scarcely be reckoned, and therefore the most strenuous efforts must be exerted to deprive these potent influences of their dreadful power to poison the minds and hearts of our people. We must make every constructive effort to fill these same areas and centers of influence with a positive Christian spirit.

It is surely a mortal sin to attend any and every movie indiscriminately without any previous inquiry regarding its religious or moral nature. Certainly one may not ignore the warnings of religious leaders and the legion of decency lists. Similarly one may not subscribe to newspapers and magazines which are hostile to the faith except for a very serious reason, which may be economic or apologetic. However, no matter what the reason, only one who is strong in the faith and properly trained to detect the errors and hazards to faith and morals may read such literature. One must avoid the proximate occasion to sin. Moreover, the law of the Church[39] requires that proper permission be sought and granted before one is allowed to read literature of this kind.

To turn the dials of radio and television without any regard for the nature of the programs offered must be condemned outright. Under certain conditions it might be gravely sinful to expose families with children to the regular broadcast or telecast of stations which frequently have programs hostile to faith or morals. Often parents do not have the slightest notion of the spiritual harm they permit their children to suffer in these matters. Surely there is need for constant parental supervision and guidance so that the radio and television recreation and entertainment be made to serve the true needs of the children. Even educational programs must be orientated toward their true education and their spiritual good. This is particularly necessary if in the wide range of programs some are excellent, others indifferent, and some evil and dangerous. It must also be borne in mind that not every program which is unobjectionable for adults is free from all danger for children. Hence constant vigilance is necessary to keep the use of radio and television within sound moral limits. Such vigilance is surely not exercised by parents who permit the free use of the dials to all in the family until the hostility to faith and morals is forced upon them. They should be aware at all times of what is offered over the airways and forestall the danger of unwholesome recreation.

The instruction and exhortation of Christian families, particularly parents, regarding films, press, literature, radio, and television is an important part of the pastoral care. It is an urgent task imposed on the shepherds of souls to instruct and warn the flock of Christ against the dangers in these media of communication. Positively this duty includes the encouragement of good reading and wholesome entertainment. We might even suggest the establishment of good newsstands and bookstores. Nor should the shepherds of souls overlook the duty of instructing the faithful on the law of the Church which requires that certain kinds of literature be approved by her authority before publication and also on the law which forbids the reading of certain kinds of literature. The pastor should call attention likewise to the severe punishments of the Church for certain violations of her law in this matter. He will stress that far more is at stake than mere positive ecclesiastical law: the earnest Christian should be made to realize that the divine law itself forbids reading insidious literature which endangers his soul's salvation. This is a far cry from the current notion in Liberal circles that the Church's law on censorship and forbidden books is a reactionary imposition on men's minds and an arbitrary and indefensible restriction of human liberty.

There can be no doubt that up to the present the laws of the Church dealing with objectionable literature have been very severe by comparison with the ecclesiastical directives regarding films, radio, and television. We might suggest that the broad and generous attitude of these latter directives indicates the general tendency of the Church in effect: she displays almost extreme mildness in all her legal procedure today in order to place the moral obligations in the foreground. Stress is on the moral obligation arising from the well-informed conscience of the mature and well-instructed Christian.

Prominent in the struggle with present-day dangers to the faith, in nearly every country, is an anxious concern for the Christian school. The educational monopoly of the state today, especially of the unchristian state, is a grave affront to God, to the Church, the parents, and the children. Every Catholic child has a divine right to an education that is totally and integrally Catholic-Christian. In accordance with this right, which belongs to the child and its parents, we must demand of the state that it refrain from two courses of action: 1) it must not interfere with the establishment of Catholic schools (often called denominational or confessional schools); 2) it should not tax Catholic parents for support of non-religious or mixed schools and at the same time allow the Catholic people to bear the entire burden of support for the Catholic schools.

The state must support every legitimate type of school demanded by the parents or none at all. It may not discriminate against the Catholic group in a matter so essentially bound up with the basic rights of parents and children. Nor may the state so much as permit the establishment of schools which are hostile to faith and morals. This is a duty of the state even should there be no outcry against the evil on the part of the people. Such is the right of parents in the matter of education of their children that the state has no authority to require attendance at schools to which parents justly object. Even to force Catholics to support such schools by taxation is a grave violation of their natural rights.

Great as are the rights of parents in matters of education, their duties are equally serious. Wherever it is possible for them to send their children to a Catholic school, they are obliged to do so even at great sacrifice to themselves and their children. However, there may be reasons which would permit them to send the children to non-Catholic schools. Thus if the sole educational center in a particular area is non-Catholic, we should not have the right to demand that Catholic parents should under all conditions send their children to a Catholic school which is rather distant and perhaps even educationally backward or inadequate for the needs of the children. Nevertheless, even under these conditions it would be necessary for the parents to make sure in the light of all the circumstances involved that adequate religious instruction and also religious and moral guidance is provided for their children. If they should be constrained by law or circumstance to send their children to neutral schools (such as the public schools in the United States today), parents and pastors of souls have the absolute obligation to provide educational countermeasures removing the menace of unbelief or indifferentism or at least making the danger to faith or morals a remote danger.

We must distinguish between schools negatively dangerous and schools which are positively dangerous. Negatively dangerous are those which refrain from attacking the faith even though it is not the foundation of their system of education nor their guide in instruction. Positively dangerous are those schools in which the texts, the plan of instruction, the background and attitude of instructors, the whole atmosphere of the school life, conspire against the faith or Christian morals. In some instances only certain elements of the system, for example, certain courses or texts, are positively dangerous. In any instance, if there is no possible educational countermeasure which renders the danger a remote danger, then the parents have no valid excuse for sending their children to these schools. Should the state laws require attendance despite the evils, then all Christian parents must meet the unjust demand with massive passive resistance.

Confessors have no recourse in this matter except to refuse absolution to parents who go so far as to expose their own children to the proximate danger of loss of the faith, unless of course they show signs of repentance and promise to mend their ways. The same holds good for the children themselves if they share the guilt of the parents. Confessors and pastors should not fail to note that frequently parents send their children to non-Catholic schools for motives of social or educational prestige or even because of a mistaken patriotism, as though the Catholic or parochial school is not truly loyal to the principles of the nation, or exercises a divisive influence. Paradoxically such snobbery is both undemocratic and hazardous to the faith, at least in many instances.

In some countries political parties set up programs or platforms designed to deprive parents of their centers of Catholic education, the Catholic schools. To join such a party is undoubtedly a mortal sin, unless all the other parties are equally or even more hostile to the good cause. Catholics should be alerted not only to the danger inherent in such political parties and their programs, but also to the underlying principles which motivate them. The vehement attack of these parties against the Christian school may arise from hatred of all religion or it may be based on the dread heresy that "religion is a totally private matter." To make of religion a merely private matter is to attempt to form public life and especially public education without religion. It means a declaration that God is deposed in these important areas.[40] In some countries where religion is respected in a general way, the relegating of religion to the domain of private life or of individual preference makes for indifferentism. The so-called Christian "mixed" schools also are calculated to create a spirit of indifferentism, which is tantamount to saying that all religions are equally good or that it does not matter what one believes or to what church one belongs as long as one lives uprightly.

We must note that such equal treatment of all religions (or no religion) ignores the essential differences between the true faith and others: this prevents the objective approach to all reality in the light of the faith. There arises the danger of divorcing religion and life, more or less consciously and as a matter of principle. And this is one of the greatest temptations to the Christian of our time. In the face of such danger we must come to an ever clearer realization of the pressing obligation to Christianize all areas of human life. In no other way can we safeguard the faith of the weaker Christian so much in peril today.

We may add that many Catholics are totally unaware that many of their fellow men look upon all religion as a meaningless thing that is artificially structured into a *racket*. In the light of all these considerations Catholic training in the meaning of supernatural religion as found in the one true Church is of supreme importance.

Parents must be alerted to this great danger and to all other hazards to faith or morals arising from the positions their children hold as servants and teachers in non-Catholic families or institutions or regions. Especially when there is question of adolescents taking up employment in the service of those of other faiths or no faith, parents should provide, if possible by stipulation of contract, that the practice of the faith without hindrance, the fulfillment of Sunday obligations, and safeguards against insidious influences are guaranteed. To neglect these matters in a great concern for economic or social advancement of their children betrays a sinful lack of esteem for the faith.

The complexities of our modern life bring all religious denominations and groups together in many areas and in various cultural activities. Interdenominational organizations are formed along the most diverse lines (political parties, labor unions, civic groups, educational, philosophical, scientific, artistic associations, societies for relief of the needy, etc.). Such groups are permitted in our pluralistic society today particularly in those areas where there is a cultural or economic necessity for their formation, where great good is accomplished by concerted effort of Christians against unbelief, moral subversion of youth, etc. Common civic effort among all groups in a mixed society like that in the United States should be encouraged for the promotion of the public welfare in all areas. However, the caution must be observed: the interdenominational groups must maintain a strict neutrality regarding all disputed matters of faith. It must be clear in all instances that Catholics joining any of the above groups are not influenced by principles of indifferentism nor exposed to serious perils to their faith.

A very sensitive area is that of close personal friendship between Catholics and unbelievers and people of other religions, particularly among students or members of the armed forces, or between professor and student. Such close friendships may be permitted for mature Catholics who are firmly grounded in their faith, provided the non-Catholic friend has a sincere respect for the faith of the Catholic party. Friendship of this kind is truly good and absolutely devoid of danger only when the Catholic is animated by prudent apostolic zeal for the salvation of his friend's soul. Much good can be effected by such a noble form of friendship.

Catholics who form friendships with sectarian fanatics and visionaries are in constant danger either of growing weak in their religious convictions or of losing their faith altogether. Hence such friendships must be shunned, but not the love and zeal for the true faith which manifests itself in loving kindness to the erring brother! Children and adolescents who are not yet solidly grounded in knowledge and discipline of the faith must be altogether discouraged from forming very strong and affectionate attachments with people of other faiths. Parents must be on their guard lest the good and kind relationships of their children with their non-Catholic companions, which must always be maintained in a true spirit of Christian charity, do not develop into hazardous forms of friendship. The greatest prudence is required in this entire matter, particularly if it should be necessary to explain the dangers of certain friendships to children. The difficulty is greatest in areas where Catholics are few in number or where mixed marriages create a bond of close relationship between Catholic and non-Catholic.

Experience proves that there is scarcely a greater hazard to the faith than the mixed marriage. This is a primary reason why the Church in her love for her flock adjures the faithful so forthrightly to avoid marriage with those not of the faith.[41] A Catholic must be willing rather to renounce marriage altogether than to enter a union which places his own faith and that of his children in jeopardy. Only a zealous Catholic with apostolic zeal and ideals can prudently risk entering into marriage with an unbeliever or with one of a different religious faith. If the Catholic party has been somewhat lax in his religious practice hitherto, but now feels he has weighty reasons, such as are demanded by the Church, to enter a mixed marriage, he must do more than merely provide that the other party consents to the promises demanded by the ecclesiastical law (assurance of full and unhindered freedom for the Catholic party to practice his religion and assurance that all the children of the union will be given Catholic baptism and brought up as Catholics). He must work toward his own inner improvement by striving for a greater zeal in the faith and the corresponding apostolic spirit concerned with safeguarding the faith and communicating it to others.

Many attempts have been made by zealous priests to provide social contacts (for example, in parish centers) for Catholic young people with a view to bringing Catholic youth together and lessening the probabilities of mixed marriages. We must look upon Catholic social activities as part of this apostolate. Very much remains to be done in this important area of pastoral work.[42]

Active participation in non-Catholic rites or ceremonies which include a profession of a false religious doctrine is forbidden under all circumstances, because it is equivalent to a denial of the true faith. We have already referred to this point. Moreover, every participation in the cult or religious activities of other religions is sinful to the degree in which danger to faith is incurred or scandal is caused by such conduct. This holds also for radio and television participation in the non-Catholic religious service and sermon.

Passive participation in non-Catholic ceremonies (being present at baptisms, weddings, funerals, without joining in the recitation of prayers or acting in any official capacity such as best man, bridesmaid, etc.) in order to manifest respect based on relationship, friendship, citizenship, is *permitted* for a correspondingly serious reason. Of course one may never attend an attempt at marriage by a Catholic in a non-Catholic religious service. Participation for the sake of mere curiosity is not proper even when there is no scandal or danger to faith. Private (extra-liturgical) prayer with people of other faiths is permitted, if the prayers themselves are orthodox and there is no occasion of scandal because of special circumstance in a particular case.

Frequently the priest is asked by members of his parish or others whether it is lawful to assist as bridesmaid or best man at a Protestant or Jewish marriage or to be sponsor at a non-Catholic baptism. Beyond the general rule stated in our theology for any participation in the religious rites of non-Catholics already given, there are special directives laid down by many bishops for their dioceses. These clarifications of the principles involved and positive regulations must be strictly observed.

6. *Submission to the Magisterium*

There is a clear obligation to submit our minds to the teaching authority of the Church. The words of the Savior commanding the Apostles and their successors to teach necessarily include the obligation to harken to the word. "Go, therefore, and make disciples of all nations" (Mt 28:19). "He who hears you, hears me; and he who rejects you, rejects me; and he who rejects me, rejects him who sent me" (Lk 10:16). Faith subjects us to the teaching office of the Church, because Christ entrusted His truth to the Church and sent her the Spirit of Truth. In commanding us to submit to the Church Christ commanded us to submit to God Himself, but this submission is submission in the freedom of the children of God founded in faith and is far removed from any self-glorification and self-will. Salutary faith does not exclude good works but rather awakens them (Eph 2:9f.), and in like manner the freedom of the children of God in their faith means a joyous submission to God (cf. Rom 3:28, 31) and, in accordance with the will of God, to the teaching office of the Church. Faith in the freedom of the children of God becomes one with the joyous submission and obedience to God and the Church. Thus liberty does not destroy obedience nor obedience suppress freedom.

As the life of grace presses forward to good works, so too the "obedience in faith" (Rom 1:5) seeks union with our freedom. Perfect obedience to faith means perfect freedom. It is a dolorous and painful truth that in this earthly sojourn good works are always the fruit of a tenacious struggle, and likewise that the obedience of the believer always demands self-denial which must constantly be renewed. The reason is that our life of grace is still weak and our liberty imperfect as long as we are sojourning in this vale of tears. God wills to perfect our freedom through the community of faith in the Church and the obligatory subjection to it in order to prepare "in us the second coming of Christ, insofar as we die entirely to ourselves and arise to new life in the Holy Spirit."[43] But the obedience of faith which the Church demands of us is not the obedience or subjection of serfs. It ushers us into the inner beauty of the faith! It provides us with security and protection against the degenerate freedom which leads to arbitrary and vain-glorious decisions of error.

Submission to the decisions of the Church is not merely an obligation accessory to faith. It rests in the very nature of faith. Our faith is in its very content orientated toward the teaching of the Church. We believe what the Church teaches. "Faith depends on hearing." Surely in the virtue of faith it is directly God Himself who makes us capable of accepting His revelation. The Spirit of Pentecost Who is the soul of the Church teaches us in our hearts. In this sense we have no need that any one instruct us (cf. 1 Jn 2:27). The anointing which we have received from the Lord imparts to us the vision, so that we recognize that God has spoken in Christ and confided His message to the Church. But that which God has spoken we must grasp. The material content of revelation comes to us mediately. Taught in our hearts by the Spirit, who is the Spirit of the Church, we must receive the teaching externally. It is communicated to us by this same Church which has the assistance of the Spirit of truth (cf. 1 Jn 2:24; 2 Tm 1:13f.).

The Church is the community of faith which in unanimity of doctrine communicates to us and fixes for us the content of our faith. She determines by infallible doctrinal pronouncement what we must believe. The doctrinal magisterium of the pope and the bishops under him is the principal organ of this determinative function safeguarding us in the possession of divine truth. For all this we owe the Church the most profound and grateful obedience.

Enlightened obedience to the magisterium of the Church will recognize the importance of determining the limits of her charismatic infallibility. We must realize that it demands of us an absolute assent of divine faith only when it presents to us a truth as revealed. Beyond such absolute assent to the revealed truth, there is a reverential and filial adherence given in joyous freedom and confidence of truth to the decisions of the popes and bishops because of our believing attitude toward the Church, but this is not necessarily an assent of divine faith. The distinction is very important, as will appear in the discussion which follows. In all this we have various degrees of certainty to be measured by the nature and source of the pronouncement.

The solemn decisions of universal councils and the *ex cathedra* decisions of the Roman pontiffs defining doctrines as divinely revealed are to be accepted with an act of divine and Catholic faith. Likewise, all that the bishops of the entire world teach unanimously as truths of faith, divinely revealed, must be accepted on our part with the same absolute assent, for the ordinary universal magisterium of the Church is under the constant guidance of the Spirit of truth. Otherwise surely the Church would no longer be the "pillar and mainstay of truth" (1 Tm 3:15). There are also final decisions of universal councils and of the popes which do not have the truths of revelation for their object, though they are clearly bound up with them. These decisions are rightly considered infallible and irreversible and demand an absolute and perfect assent of the mind of every Catholic. And yet this is not specifically the assent of divine and Catholic faith.

The decisions of particular councils as such are not infallible, but they enjoy very great authority. The individual bishops, though teachers in their dioceses by divine right and law, are not infallible. But as teachers in their dioceses they must always be listened to with respect. What the individual bishop expressly teaches in matters of faith and morals must be accepted with faith, if it is taught as divinely revealed, unless there is a well-founded doubt regarding the agreement of the doctrine with the universal faith of the Church. The express teaching of the individual bishop on theological matters intimately related to the revealed truth must be accepted as of considerable authority though not as final. The opinions of individual bishops writing as theologians in matters which are not settled by the Church nor taught with unanimous agreement of theologians have the degree of authority which arises from the merit of the arguments presented in favor of the doctrine.

Decrees of the Roman congregations as such are not infallible pronouncements. Generally speaking, therefore, they do not demand that absolute and final assent which is given in the act of divine faith or in the assent to any other infallible decision. These decisions demand a real adherence of the mind but in accordance with their degree of certainty. There is some element of the hypothetical in the assent though this is usually not explicit in the mind. In giving assent one does so with the realization that a reversal of the decision is not altogether excluded. The same judgment is to be formed regarding the non-infallible doctrinal decisions of the pope, provided of course that the pontiff is not stating a teaching which is already defined through the Church's ordinary magisterium.

The doctrine is sufficiently important to demand a more detailed explanation. 1) It is certain that the decisions of the Church by comparison with the judgment of any individual scholar must be considered as weighted with greater soundness and certainty. Even though a decision may not be infallible, the authority of the Church gives it a presumption of correctness which no mere individual opinion can enjoy, for the official organs of the magisterium have a greater assurance of the guidance of the Holy Spirit than any scholar in his individual personal convictions. In the light of this guidance the individual who is affected by the Church's decision must humbly submit.

2) It is historically incontrovertible that certain individual decisions of papal congregations and commissions have been reversed by subsequent evidence. However, prudence is well-advised in this matter. In some instances decisions which at first blush seemed doctrinal may rather have been disciplinary. Thus, for example, the seeming condemnation of a doctrine with the statement that "it cannot be safely taught" (*tuto doceri non potest*) means specifically that there are cogent reasons militating against the actual present proposing of this view or opinion. It is not to be taught under the assumption that it is true, but at most as an hypothesis which is set forth as no more than an hypothesis. Should this same hypothesis in the light of subsequent study prove more adaptable to the whole system of the truths of faith after some clarification and purging of false connotations and phases; should it be presented in a less glaring light and no longer as a contradiction to a revealed truth or to other doctrine of the Church (at least to the doctrine which is universally admitted and certain), it may be that the presuppositions underlying the decisions of the papal congregation no longer are valid and consequently the decision would no longer apply as it once did.

The decision may be directed against an opinion which is actually true but couched in terms of a false philosophy with which it is so closely bound up as to make the proposition appear to contradict the teaching of the Church. In such instances the condemnation or prohibition is quite justified. In consequence the proposition must be withdrawn until it is purged of every false and rash assumption and then restated in an acceptable form. (The very terms *liberty, rights of man, progress,* on the lips of the nineteenth-century enemies of the Church were false and unacceptable.)

3) The decisions of the Holy See and more particularly those of the sacred congregations do not demand a firmness of assent out of proportion

to their own degree of certainty. Should there be question of a disciplinary decree, then disciplinary submission and interior respect for the authority making the decision and deferential acceptance of the reasons and motives for it is sufficient. It is a grave sin to rebel against a doctrinal decision by refusal to assent to it, even though the refusal is only in the mind. There is a valid presumption that the decree of the Church has been issued with the fullest understanding of all the arguments involved both favorable and unfavorable; unless by way of exception there are clear and compelling reasons to the contrary, the decision must be sincerely accepted and acknowledged as true and correct.

But what shall we say of an ecclesiastical writer, theologian, or scientist who thinks he has reasons to reject the judgment of the Church's authority, particularly if his own intellectual attitude or position has been affected? Should he be sincerely convinced that he has truly cogent reasons for opposition to a decision of a papal congregation or commission, he should first of all carefully study the form in which the case is being presented. Is the presentation such that it might prejudice the faith or sound theological teaching or disturb the minds of the weak and uninformed in matters of religion? Meanwhile all further public defence of his position must be studiously and respectfully avoided, unless he is absolutely convinced in conscience that defence of his condemned views is of great importance for the understanding or defence of the faith and for the promotion of Christian piety.

But if he may not remain silent, he has no right to be self-assertive and arrogant. The entire form and manner of presentation of his views must be such that his love of truth and complete submission to the doctrinal magisterium is unquestionable. Any desire to derogate from the authority of the Holy See must be far from his mind. Above all, as occasion arises for explanation of his position, the scholar must point out the merit of new information or new insights which the Holy See may not have taken into account. Even more important is the clear dissociation of false hypotheses or assumptions from his theories. These may well account for the Church's attitude of disfavor; for only dissociation from them justifies an attempt to study the whole problem anew. To be avoided in the entire presentation of the case is a sour and embittered attitude of criticism of the Church. The problem should be submitted with a spirit of modesty and objectivity.

III. SINS AGAINST FAITH

All offenses in violation of the duties springing from faith are (in a wider sense of the term) also sins against faith. Here, however, we plan to take up first of all those sins which by their direct opposition to faith destroy it. They break that inner bond by which we adhere to the faith and destroy its infused capacity or power. They destroy the habit of faith. These sins are: unbelief, heresy, apostasy, and wilful doubts against faith.

1. *Unbelief*

There is an inculpable unbelief, a culpable unbelief arising from neglect, and unbelief strictly as such. Hence we distinguish as follows: 1) There is the inculpable unbelief which is found in one who has never had the choice either for or against belief presented to his mind and will for a decision. This unbelief is inculpable, provided the individual has not incurred fault in the matter, has not been culpably responsible that the decision has never been presented to him. In consequence his unbelief or rather his "not-yet-believing" is not sin, though it may in some manner be the result of the fault of others, possibly many others. 2) There is also a kind of unbelief arising from personal and sinful neglect insofar as one has failed to fulfill his known duty of inquiring into the faith or at least has failed to give it serious and adequate attention. (The guilt in these instances must be assessed in accordance with the degree of neglect and the reasons which might account for it.) Even more culpable is actual resistance to the faith. No matter how great the culpable neglect in matters of faith may be, only conscious resistance to the known faith or to a known truth of faith constitutes the formal sin of unbelief or infidelity.[44]

Infidelity is one of the gravest sins, the most fatal of sins, because it destroys the very foundation on which all efforts for salvation rest. "He who does not believe shall be condemned" (Mk 16:16). "He who does not believe is already condemned" (Jn 3:18). The dreadful malice of this sin is shown in its true light only through revelation. In the light of the revelation in Christ, Incarnate Word of the Father, the malice of infidelity appears in all its enormity. It is the supreme sin that the world refuses to believe Him who is Truth itself (cf. Jn 16:19). The unbelief of the one who has known the mission of Jesus in the Holy Spirit and still rebels against it, even condemns and curses it (because faith disturbs the complacency of his world of self) is "blasphemy against the Spirit," "an everlasting sin" (Mt 12:31; Mk 3:29; cf. 1 Jn 5:16f.; Heb 6:4ff.; 10:26).

2. The Sin of Heresy

We must distinguish between the sin of heresy (formal heresy) and inculpable error[45] regarding a truth of faith (material heresy). The Christian who culpably refuses to accept one or other divinely revealed truth which the Church proposes for our belief is guilty of formal heresy. The Christian who repudiates the entire body of revealed truth is guilty of apostasy.[46] These two sins, heresy and even more so apostasy, are among the most heinous offenses against God.[47]

Heresy is a species of unbelief. The heretic presumes to question the absolute truthfulness of God which is of the very essence of faith. He directly questions God's own revealed word which is the basis of our faith. Because of a presumptuous and disordered confidence in his own limited rational insight he rejects an individual (or more than one) revealed truth, or makes his own choice of the truths of faith, accepting those which please him and discarding those which do not.

One incurs guilt by a neglect of inquiry into the full Christian truth which leads to the acceptance of doctrines and views opposed to faith. The guilt in such instances must be measured by the degree of neglect itself in this most important matter. However, the actual negligence as such does not constitute formal heresy, provided the will and disposition to believe all that God has revealed is not lost.

The ignorance of the truths of faith arising not only from neglect but from the deliberate will not to be informed (*ignorantia affectata*) must be classed as heresy in all instances in which the will is totally intransigent in its opposition to the truth in question. Nevertheless, this "will to be uninformed," in itself a sign of a very dire spiritual condition, may in many instances spring from a fixed determination to hold to one's own opinion and remain loyal to one's own religious sect. If this mistaken loyalty is such that it does not destroy the general good will to accept all of God's word and all the known revealed truths, then the guilt of heresy is not incurred. Heresy by its very nature destroys the virtue of faith and is incompatible with the general will to believe the whole of God's word, with the will to accept all that God has revealed. Nevertheless, though we do not condemn all affected ignorance as heresy, it is always a serious offence against God and may readily lead to the sin of actual heresy.

The stubborn and obstinate resistance to points of doctrine universally held in the Church or designated by all theologians as theologically *certain* is not heresy as long as there is a disposition to accept the doctrine should the Church formally define it. But obstinacy in such matters is usually due to sinful rashness and disrespect for authority in things closely bound up with the truths of faith. Actual guilt must be determined by the circumstances. Frequently the obstinacy is due to lack of instruction regarding the duties of Catholics in areas of doctrine which are not explicitly defined, though they may be theologically certain.

Though it is a very grievous sin to deny the faith or any article of the faith merely in words or by external acts, such denial is not the sin of heresy as long as the faith is not interiorly rejected. The sin is a gross violation of the obligation to profess the faith, and the Church rightly proceeds against the offender as against a heretic. Within him the faith still remains, but it is a dead faith, an accusing faith. Nevertheless it is the necessary basis for a return to living faith. It is the first step toward conversion.

Can a Catholic desert the Church and her faith without necessarily incurring the subjective guilt of heresy? The First Vatican Council discussed this matter: Catholic Christians who have received the faith under the magisterium of the Church, "never can possess a valid reason for changing this faith or calling it into doubt."[48] Such is the clear statement of the Council of the Vatican. In addition the Council very specifically defined that the status of the Catholic is not at all the same as that of the individual who has not yet arrived at the true faith. In consequence the Catholic who has already accepted the true faith under the guidance of the teaching magisterium of the Church can never have a sound reason to doubt his faith.[49]

It seems entirely certain that the Council is not referring merely to the possibility of having sound objective reasons for doubt against faith. Such a proposition is surely obvious, for even the confirmed unbeliever or heretic can have no true and objectively valid reason for his error. Obviously, it is clear from the context that the Council refers to subjective reasons and subjective guilt: not only does it stress the clear and convincing motives of credibility which the Church herself presents to all men who really are acquainted with her, but also, and this very emphatically, the grace of God which never forsakes those who have not first forsaken it.[50] It is quite clear that we may not equate the judgment of conscience of a non-Catholic who with the aid of divine grace has attained the insight that he must "change" his faith and become a Catholic, and the state of conscience of an apostate Catholic who has formed the judgment leading to his rejection of the faith. A Catholic under the guidance of a conscience entirely orientated toward God can never come to the conclusion that he must change his faith. No Catholic can with true conviction form the erroneous judgment that he must give up the faith which he has held in the Church and in which he has been adequately instructed, unless his conscience has been stained by mortal sin and obscured in its concept of truth and duty. Turning from faith is thus an aversion from God for which he must be held responsible in some way.

We do not say that in every instance the sin is a direct sin against faith. The opinion that apostasy or doubt against faith on the part of a Catholic who has been properly instructed is not necessarily a direct sin against faith can be reconciled with the teaching of the Vatican which we have just explained. Should the sin not be in direct opposition to the virtue of faith, but some other sin of which the apostasy or heresy is but the poisoned fruit, then it could be maintained that the virtue of faith might still be retained in some instances in which Catholics leave the Church. However, one should not readily assume that the sin is not an actual sin against faith and destructive of the virtue of faith.

The situation of the uninstructed Catholic seems to demand a different solution. The Council has left the matter open, whether or not a Catholic poorly instructed in the faith could doubt the Catholic truth without committing a grave sin. If we hold that this is possible, we might in the last analysis go so far as to say that he could even join an heretical sect without formal sin against the faith and even without any mortal sin at all.[51]

In any instance the plight of the Catholic who has left the Church despite adequate instruction in his religion is tragic. This surely must be held as a general rule, although we should refrain from forming a definitive judgment about any individual. We cannot be altogether certain that his education and training in the faith was sufficient for his particular situation and need, and if his failure was due to ignorance we do not know to what degree it was culpable ignorance. In fact the capacity for moral responsibility and the degree of responsibility in any individual is often shrouded in obscurity. But in all this one point is beyond discussion:

the doubt against faith or the abandonment of faith on the part of a Catholic can never possibly be based on a sincere and genuine mandate of a good and pure conscience in precisely the same way as the mandate of conscience in the instance of conversion to the Catholic faith on the part of one who has not been a Catholic. Men who look upon all religions as equally good and true may find it difficult to accept this Catholic position. In fact many Catholics imbued with liberalism and indifferentism have a totally false concept of the uniqueness of the Catholic truth and consequently of the dreadful evil of heresy and apostasy. Their attention should be called to the words of the Savior Himself warning against the sinister backgrounds of unbelief (Jn 3:19; 5:44; 8:37, 47).

Though we hold firmly to the conviction that a Catholic, fully responsible for his decisions and sufficiently instructed in Catholic truth, cannot lose the faith or fall away without serious antecedent fault on his part, we would not be allowed, at least not on the basis of the conciliar teaching (*Vatican*), to draw the conclusion that he is inevitably damned if he should die without openly having retraced his steps back to the Church. It is a conceivable and even a theologically defensible position that one who has abandoned the Church—and committed grave sin in so doing— can gradually acquire good faith (*bona fides*) in his heretical persuasion. He can acquire a good conscience in time and tread his way back to a spirit of love of God. This would implicitly at least include a readiness to correct his own initial error of desertion, if he should still be able to recognize it in its true light. However, such a position is not possible for one who has lost all supernatural faith, unless this too be restored by reacceptance of revealed truth. We speak of what is possible. What actually does take place in the souls of those who have left the Church is not known to us. Prayerfully and with deep gratitude for the gift of faith, we leave the matter to the mercy of God.

3. *Doubt against Faith*

The term *doubt against faith*[52] has a diversity of meanings in common usage: 1) There is the culpable doubt in matters of faith which is a presumptuous judgment questioning the certainty of the faith or of some article or articles of faith. It springs from a sinful conscience and is practically equivalent to the sin of unbelief, or more specifically the sin of heresy, as far as the disposition and spirit and the destructive effect on the virtue of faith are concerned. One who doubts deliberately prefers his own restricted insight to the testimony of God, like the heretic or un-believer who denies the truth outright. Deliberate doubt is wilful refusal to adhere firmly to the divine testimony. Ignoring this, the doubter usually centers attention on the revealed mystery itself and demands proof and clarity which is impossible, for the truths of faith are believed, not seen, in this life.

2) Essentially different from such culpable doubt is the attitude of interior indecision bound up with the sincere love of truth and the desire to find it and cling to it. This sincere inquiry which is not a repudiation of faith must be assessed as having a positive value. It is not the doubt of the instructed Catholic, for according to the doctrine of the First Vatican Council just referred to, the instructed Catholic cannot, without com-mitting a mortal sin, come to such a state of doubt regarding a truth which he knows the Church has infallibly proposed for our faith. But for one brought up in error or infidelity this "sincere doubt about faith" is the true path of conscience leading to faith. If conscience is followed sincerely and consistently, the end of the journey of inquiry will be the certainty and firmness of the virtue of faith, the gift of God's gracious bounty.

We do not hesitate to assert that a Christian in good faith, brought up in heresy, can pass through this stage of "doubt about faith" regarding the teaching of his own church or sect without losing his firm adherence or submission to the authority of God revealing, hence without losing, the virtue of faith. In fact his very search can be the fruit of a sincere and humble loyalty to faith, the evidence of its genuineness.

The unconditional assent to Catholic truth through faith is often preceded by an agonizing struggle, in all uprightness and sincerity, regarding the motives of credibility or regarding particular dogmas of the Church which are most difficult for certain individuals or groups to accept. Noted examples are John Henry Cardinal Newman and Frederick William Faber, whose lives are parables of love for the divine truth from their earliest years.

3) To doubt whether a specific doctrine or point of doctrine is actually an article of faith is not morally reprehensible, provided the uncertainty does not arise from indifference or culpable ignorance. Here one must clearly distinguish between the articles of faith which are generally known by all well-instructed Catholics and a refined understanding of the

theological notes. Quite often even the student of theology may hesitate if he is asked regarding a point of doctrine: is it *de fide* or only "theologically certain"?

4) Sincere Catholics of unimpeachable loyalty to the faith now and then accuse themselves of "doubts against faith." In reality they may have merely doubted, and with good reason, whether some point, sharply stressed in the Sunday sermon, was actually a truth which all must accept under pain of damnation. Thus, for example, a preacher may make extravagant claims based on private revelations or prophecies, which no good theologian would ever accept. Or in his eloquence he may state that all who do not sincerely love the rosary or harken to the warnings of Fatima will never be saved. The faithful who make some reservations about such statements should be prudently enlightened on the true nature of doubts against faith, and on the clear distinction between defined or certain teaching and opinions of some writers or preachers. The preacher is well-advised not to let his eloquence or ardent zeal betray him into utterances which sound theology could never justify.

5) Very important in pastoral care is the spiritual guidance of those who have difficulties in matters of faith. Their confession of doubts about revealed truth is frequently no more than the expression of a desire to resolve their perplexities about such points as the account of creation in Genesis, or of the tower of Babel and the confusion of tongues, the great age of the patriarchs, and similar incidents in the Old Testament. Often reasonable men who in every way wish to remain loyal to the Church cannot accept these accounts literally, but are unable to resolve their problems through a reasonable interpretation of the sacred text. They are harassed by a false dilemma: either to accept a literal interpretation according to the dictates of their faith—which seems impossible and absurd to them—or to reject the interpretation and be guilty of unbelief. The confessor should kindly probe into the source of the difficulty and suggest the proper instruction in these matters.

It is a general principle for his guidance that the method of combatting doubts against faith, or more specifically temptations against faith, is to be determined according to their nature and origin. Nervous reactions are to be overcome by simple and determined rejection of the doubt and wholesome relaxation and recreation and good general medical care. Cases of compulsive thoughts are best helped by an insight into the nature of the illness, coupled with the loving and insistent warning that in such attacks against faith one must place one's self entirely in the hands of God and not resort to vehement countermeasures, which would merely aggravate the evil.

Should there be question of biblical or scientific perplexity, the best remedy is a rational explanation of the problems as they arise. At times the director or confessor may have to concede that he himself cannot solve the problem, though he is convinced that experts in the field can give a very good account of the Church's position. Ordinarily the confessor should be able to know at least where the solution is to be found. Above all the director must avoid pretending to solve the problem or criticizing the inquirer for ever asking such questions. However, consideration for the feeling of the questioner should not be carried to the extreme of ignoring one of the commonest source of doubts. Frequently the priest will be forced to speak very frankly to one plagued by doubts against faith. In all seriousness he must warn him against exposing himself to dangers through reading of certain types of literature, through association with enemies of the faith, through neglect of strengthening his faith by the use of the means of grace. An evil life in constant contradiction to the faith may be responsible for the doubts and make the profession of faith most difficult for him. One cannot reconcile, at least not permanently, inner acceptance by the act of faith of that which is repudiated by immoral conduct with little or no evidence of interior sorrow and conversion. Finally, the difficulties arising from ignorance in matters of revealed truth suggest the only remedy: a more serious study of the truths of faith. The obligation to study one's religion is all the more serious, the higher the level of one's talent and culture in non-religious areas and the greater the hazard of exposure to doubt.

4. *Collective Apostasy and Doubt against Faith*

Faith is a treasure committed to the community. It is to be preserved in the fellowship of faith with strict accountability of the members. Each member shares in the spirit and joy of faith which the whole Church possesses. He also enjoys and directly experiences a participation in the community membership in which he lives. Here the words of St. Paul apply: "If one member suffers anything, all the members suffer with it, or if one member glories, all the members rejoice with it" (1 Cor 12:26). Let us presume that the entire Church in all her communities celebrates the sacraments of faith with living warmth and spirit, that all the preachers of the Gospel are men of deep faith, fervent witnesses to the divine truth, that the faith has taken hold of all the forms of the social order, that it is strong in every realm of life. The result could only be that the individual would readily triumph over all temptations against the faith. Let us assume, on the contrary, that in a certain parish, or even in an entire country, the liturgy is ordinarily celebrated listlessly, without comprehension of meaning and with mere rubrical formalism, that the faith of those whom God has placed as beacons in the Church is lukewarm, offering only lip service to truth; the result will be that the faith of the many, particularly of the weak and unstable, will be most gravely jeopardized.

It has been correctly observed that the faith of entire groups and social strata is in jeopardy in various countries in our time. In this collective phenomenon we are dealing, in one sense, with a sociological mechanism.[53] We speak of mechanism, but not at all in the sense of a deterministic denial of freedom and responsibility. Modern sociology, particularly empirical religious sociology, shows very clearly that the grand structures of social life (the colossal societies, the politics, the culture, the economy and industry, the recreational forms, public opinion, the impressive power of mass propaganda) were very largely developed of set intent and purpose according to an unchristian philosophy of life. In consequence they constitute a monstrous and terrifying peril to the faith of the masses. A peril, indeed, which develops appallingly, if on the part of Christians there are no vital and effective organizations to counteract the menace! And the hazard is compounded by the absence of understanding regarding the influence of the social structures.[54]

If the intellectual elite—those who have received five talents from the Creator and Savior—do not do their share to vitalize the spirit of faith and solidarity in the ecclesial and terrestrial order, they must bear a great blame for the gradual and imperceptible apostasy of the masses from Christian thinking. We should ponder the findings of sociology and social psychology in these areas. The result would be that we should in no wise lay the entire blame upon the weak and insecure for their doubts against faith and their indifferent attitude toward the Church. With sympathy for the fallen we should rather assess our own degree of responsibility. It is far better to examine our own conscience regarding our neglect and scandal than to condemn the weak. If it is hardly possible to come to a correct verdict about our own share of guilt, we should surely think of the words of Christ, when we are tempted to judge our fellow man: "Do not judge, that you may not be judged" (Mt 7:1). Fortunately the very renunciation of heartless and unqualified condemnation of others may be the beginning of a fruitful effort to progress spiritually ourselves. Thus we should strive for a better Christian social order.

BIBLIOGRAPHY

The Essence of Faith and the Duties Flowing from the Faith

ADAM, K. *Glaube und Glaubenswissenshaft im Katholizismus.* Rottenburg, 1923.

ANTWEILER, A. *Unser Glaube.* Muenchen, 1938.

ARNOLD, F. X. "Seelsorgliche Erziehung zum Glauben," *Anima,* 12 (1957), 125–136.

BACKES, I. "Der Glaube als Licht," *Pastor Bonus,* 47 (1937/38), 316–323.

BEUMER, J. "Ein Beitrag zur positiven Bewertung der fides informis," *Greg,* 22 (1941), 231–251.

BRUNNER, A. "Glaube und Gemeinschaft," *StimmenZeit,* 163 (1958/59), 439–451.

CHENU, M. D. "Vérité et liberté dans la foi du croyant," *Esprit,* 272 (1959), 598–619.

CIRNE-LIMA, *Der personale Glaube. Eine erkenntnismetaphysische Studie.* Innsbruck, 1959.

CONGAR, Y., O.P. "Konfessionelle Auseinandersetzung im Zeichen des Oekumenismus," *Catholica,* 12 (1959), 81–104.

DECOURTAY, A. "La conception johannique de la foi," *NRTh,* 81 (1959), 561–576.

Deutsche Thomasausgabe. Band 15: Glaube als Tugend (Commentary by F. Utz). Heidelberg-Graz, 1950.

GAILLARD, J., O.S.B. "Les sacrements de la foi," *RevThom,* 59 (1959), 5–31; 270–309.

GRUEN, ST. *Glaube als Last und Erloesung.* Muensterschwarzach, 1952.

GUARDINI, R. *The Life of Faith,* tr. by J. Chapin, Westminster, Md.: Newman Press, 1961.

HARTMANN, A. *Kirche und Freiheit. Kirchliches Lehramt und Freiheit des Denkens.* Kevelaer, 1956.

KLUG, H. "Die Lehre des heiligen Bonaventura ueber die Aufgabe der eingegossenen Tugend des Glaubens," *FranzStud,* 1937, 105–121.

LIPPERT, P., S.J. "Der glaeubige Mensch," *StimmenZeit,* 129 (1935), 145–155.

MORANT, P. "Der Glaube in der neutestamentlichen Theologie," *Anima,* 13 (1958), 5–14.

MOUROUX, J. *I Believe: the Personal Structure of Faith.* Translated by M. Turner. New York: Sheed and Ward.

RADEMACHER, A. *Der Glaube als einheitliche Lebensform.* Bonn, 1937.

RAHNER, K. Der Christ und seine unglaeubigen Verwandten," *GeistLeben,* 27 (1954), 171–184.

RANKE-HEINEMANN, U. "Vom Glauben," *GeistLeben,* 31 (1958), 404–411.

*ROESLE, M. UND CULLMAN, O. *Begegnung der Christen. Studien evangelischer und katholischer Theologen.* Stuttgart-Frankfurt, 1959.

SEITERICH, E. "Die Vernuenftigkeit des Glaubens nach dem NT," *TrThZ,* 59 (1950), 333–348.

SPAEMANN, H. *Das koenigliche Hochzeitmahl. Vom Wesen und Wachstum des Glaubens.* Muenster, 1939.

VILLETTE, L. *Foi et sacrament.* Paris, 1959.

Sins against the Faith

BARONI, G. *E possibilie perdere la fede cattolica senza peccato? Dottrina dei teologi dei secoli XVI–XVII*. Roma, 1937.

BOLKOVAC, P. *Glaube und Unglaube in der Krise*. Hamburg, 1948.

GAMBERONI, J. *Der Verkehr der Katholiken mit den Haeretikern*. Brixen, 1952.

GUZZETTI, G. B. *La perdita della fede nei cattolici*. Varese, 1940.

HAERING, B. "Unglaube und Umwelt," *Lebendige Seelsorge*, 9 (1958), 274–280. (Read the entire Volume 8, 1958: Psychologie des Unglaubens).

HANSSLER, B. *Das Gottesvolk der Kirche*. Duesseldorf, 1960.

JOURNET, C. "L'infidelité," *NZMW*, 4 (1948), 81–97.

LACROIX, J. *Le sens de l'athéisme modern*. Tournai-Paris, 1958.

LIENER, J. *Psychologie des Unglaubens*. Innsbruck, 1935.

LOMBARDI, R., S.J. *The Salvation of the Unbeliever*. Westminster, Md.: Newman, 1956.

PFUERTNER, ST. "Glaubensschwierigkeiten der heutigen Menschen," *Anima*, 13 (1958), 23–29 (Read the entire volume 1, 1958).

RUEMKE, H. C. *The Psychology of Unbelief*. London, 1952.

SCHAMONI, W. *Glaubensbewusstsein und Kirchenentfremdung*. Paderborn, 1958.

SCHMITT, P.-EGLIN. *Le mécanisme de la déchristianisation*. Paris, 1952.

SCHOELLGEN, W. "Der Unglaube der heutigen Welt," *Anima*, 13 (1958), 14–22.

Additional Works in English

ADAM, KARL. *Two Essays* (Second Essay: Love and Belief). New York and London: Sheed and Ward, 1930.

BAINVEL, JEAN V., S.J. *Faith and the Act of Faith*. St. Louis: B. Herder, 1926.

Bible Key Words. New York: Harper, 1961. Vol. 3: "Faith" (R. Bultmann and A. Weiser), pp. 1–110.

BORNE, ÉTIENNE. *Atheism* (Twentieth Century Encyclopedia of Catholicism, 91). New York: Hawthorn, 1961.

BRUNHES, GABRIEL. *Faith and Its Rational Justification*. St. Louis: B. Herder, 1931.

CALLAN, CHARLES J., O.P. *What Is Faith? and Other Essays*. New York: Devin-Adair, 1926.

COTTER, ANTHONY, C., S.J. *The Encyclical "Humani Generis."* Weston, Mass.: Weston College Press, 1951.

COVENTRY, JOHN, S.J. *Faith Seeks Understanding*. New York: Sheed and Ward, 1951.

CRISTIANI, LEON. *Why We Believe* (Twentieth Century Encyclopedia of Catholicism, 107). New York: Hawthorn, 1959.

———. *Heresies and Heretics* (Twentieth Century Encyclopedia of Catholicism, 136). New York: Hawthorn, 1959.

D'ARCY, MARTIN, C., S.J. *The Nature of Belief*. New York: Sheed and Ward, 1934. Revised Edition: St. Louis: B. Herder, 1958.

EMINYAN, MAURICE, S.J. *The Theology of Salvation*. Boston: St. Paul Editions, 1960.

Faith, Reason, and the Gospels. A Selection of Modern Thought on Faith and the Gospels, ed. John J. Heaney, S.J. Westminster, Md.: Newman, 1961.

FLANAGAN, PHILIP. *Newman, Faith and the Believer*. Westminster, Md.: Newman, 1946.

GROSSOUW, WILLEM, K. M. *Spirituality of the New Testament* (Cross and Crown Series of Spirituality, 19) St. Louis: B. Herder, 1961.

GUARDINI, ROMANO. *The Life of Faith*. Westminster, Md.: Newman, 1961.

JOLY, EUGÉNE. *What Is Faith?* (Twentieth Century Encyclopedia of Catholicism, 6). New York: Hawthorn, 1958.

JUERGENS, SYLVESTER, P., S.M., *Newman on the Psychology of Faith in the Individual.* New York: Macmillan, 1928.

McNABB, VINCENT, O.P. *Faith and Prayer.* Westminster, Md.: Newman, 1953.

MACKENZIE, ERIC F. *Delict of Heresy.* (Catholic University Studies in Canon Law, 77). Washington: Catholic Univ. Press, 1932.

NEWMAN, JOHN HENRY (Card.). *Essay in Aid of a Grammar of Assent.* New York: Longmans, 1892.

O'CONNOR, EDWARD D., C.S.C. *Faith in the Synoptic Gospels.* Notre Dame, Ind.: U. of Notre Dame Press, 1961.

PAUL-MARIE OF THE CROSS, O.C.D. *Spirituality of the Old Testament,* Vol. 1 (Cross and Crown Series of Spirituality, 18). St. Louis: B. Herder, 1961 (N.B. Revelation, Faith, Charity.)

QUIGLEY, JOSEPH. *Condemned Societies* (Catholic University Studies in Canon Law, 46). Washington: Catholic Univ. Press, 1927.

The God of Israel, the God of Christians: the Great Themes of Scripture, ed. Jean Giblet. New York: Desclée, 1961.

The Teaching of the Catholic Church (2 vols.), ed. George D. Smith. New York: Macmillan, 1949. "Faith and Revealed Truth" I, 1–37.

The Virtues and States of Life (Theology Library, v. 4), ed. A. M. Henry, O.P. Chicago: Fides, 1957. "Faith" (A. Liégé), pp. 1–59; "Hope" (B. Olivier), pp. 61–126; "Charity" (B. Olivier), pp. 127–208; "The Virtue of Religion" (A. Mennessier), pp. 393–444; "The Social Virtues" (M. Gerland), pp. 445–485 (on obedience, piety, liberality).

TRETHOWAN, ILLTYD, O.S.B. *The Basis of Belief* (Twentieth Century Encyclopedia of Catholicism, 13). New York: Hawthorn, 1961.

————. *Certainty: Philosophical and Theological.* London: Dacre Press, 1949.

VAN NOORT, GERARD, C. *Dogmatic Theology.* Vol. 3: The Sources of Revelation; Divine Faith. (See pp. 181–401.) Westminster, Md.: Newman, 1961.

Periodical Literature in English

BARROSSE, T. "Relationship of Love to Faith in St. John," *TheolS,* 18 (Dec., 1957), 538–59.

BECK, G. A. "Life of Faith," *BlJ,* 37 (April, 1956), 148–64.

BONNAR, A. "Religious Certainty," *ClerRev,* 20 (April, 1941), 307–25.

BRONNER, W. J. "Concept of Heresy," *CM,* 36 (Sept. 8, 1938), 339–46.

CARPENTER, H. J. "Reason and Faith," *BlJ,* 12 (March, 1931), 135–46.

CHRISTMANN, H. M. "Grandeur of Faith," *CrCr,* 4 (Sept., 1952), 344–55.

CONNELL, F. J. "Preserving the Faith Inviolate," *AER,* 114 (Jan., 1946), 34–47.

————. "Dangers to Faith within the Church," *AER,* 126 (June, 1952), 401–11.

CONWAY, P. "What the Modern Man Should Not Believe," *Thm,* 11 (July, 1948), 277–96.

COOKE, B. "Faith and the Human Personality," *CM,* 57 (Oct., 1959), 450–58.

DAVIS, C. "Faith and Dissident Christians," *ClerRev,* 44 (April, 1959), 201–20.

————. "Can Unbelievers Be Saved?" *ClerRev,* 47 (May, 1962), 257–63.

"Faith and Apologetics," *IER,* 82 (Nov., 1954), 310–21.

"Faith and Christianity," *ITQ,* 20 (Oct., 1953), 337–49.

"Faith, Man's Communion with God," *LumVit,* 9 (June, 1954), 182–92.

FARRELL, P. "Portals of Doubt," *Thm,* 8 (July, 1945), 293–368.

HAWKINS, D.J.B. "Plain Man's Motives of Credibility," *ClerRev,* 28 (Nov., 1947), 288–89.

HOARE, F. R. "Darkness of Faith," *DubR,* 191 (July, 1932), 105–16; 192 (Jan., 1933), 92–104.

HULL, R. "Authority and Belief," *IER,* 39 (Jan., 1932), 1–9.

Malik, C. "Crisis of Faith," *TH*, 25 (Dec., 1950), 581–90.

Murray, J. C. "Root of Faith; The Doctrine of M. J. Scheeben," *TheolS*, 9 (March, 1948), 20–46.

Philips, G. "Church and the Intellectual Believer," *LumVit*, 8 (July–Sept., 1953), 467–74.

Ring, G. C. "Motive and Freedom in the Act of Faith," *TheolS*, 6 (June, 1945), 147–62.

Simon, Y. R. "Rationality of the Christian Faith," *TH*, 31 (Winter, 1956), 495–508.

Smet, W. "Affective Tendencies and Belief in God," *LumVit*, 8 (March, 1953), 101–13.

Smith, G. D. "Must I Believe It?" *ClerRev*, 9 (April, 1935), 297–309.

White, V. "Faith," *BlJ*, 18 (Jan., 1937), 34–41.

CHAPTER THREE

THE VIRTUE OF HOPE

1. *Hope as Incentive to the Imitation*

THE entire foundation of our capacity to hope rests in the redemption through Jesus Christ. He is our only hope (1 Tm 1:1). Without Him we would be hopelessly immersed in sin. Since He alone has redeemed us from the serfdom of sin, from the hopelessness of our bondage in sin, the Christian may not place his hope in anything but Christ (cf. Acts 4:12). Even when he relies on the intercession of the Mother of God, he does no more than hope in Christ, who through His death calls us insistently to rely on this appeal of maternal mercy. Our invocation of the saints and our prayers for one another manifest our salvific solidarity in Christ.

When we say that "Christ is our hope," we mean that objectively we owe to Christ all that we trust to receive in supernatural values from God, and that all of us—the just as well as sinners—may, can, and must hope in Him, that He will save us all and lead us to eternal happiness (cf. 1 Tm 2:5f.). For the good Christian the phrase "Christ is our hope" means the joyous assurance and pledge that Christ is within us as our hope of glory (cf. Col 1:27).

"Christ is our hope" does not mean merely that Christ wills to save us, because He "wishes all men to be saved and to come to the knowledge of the truth" (1 Tm 2:4). It means also that there is a movement on our part toward Christ. It means that we reach out and grasp the hope extended to us in Christ, that for time and eternity we want nothing except what Christ offers to us in hope and promises. Christ our hope is far more than a simple universal hope in the loving-kindness of Christ as the Savior of all men. It is the particular and specific hope that Christ wills to be good to me personally and bring me to salvation. And it also means that I have resolved to tear myself away from every delusive hope in order to be able to place my trust in Christ, my true and only hope.

The promises of Christ are nothing other than the appeal of His love, the tender and urgent invitation, the most effective summons to man to follow Him to the Promised Land of eternal happiness. To one snared by sin and entangled in earthly interests the Lord cannot immediately open His Heart with the warm rays of His love. The sinner is not prepared to grasp the purest and most exalted language of love. But such is His loving generosity that the Savior can speak another language of love, a language so impressive that even the sinner, despite his evil state, can grasp it: it is the language of the promises and threats which really are essentially one, for the threats of Christ have the purpose of inviting man through the shock of fear and dread. They lead man all the way to holy hope and through this to love. When the sinner sees the Hand of the merciful Savior outstretched and offering him the rich treasure of His gifts, the Lord has already moved his heart and opened the eyes of his soul. To the first step of the Master's saving love there is the response of the first step of the disciple in imitation of the Master.

When the sinner, attracted by His promises, turns in hope to Christ, he first sees before him the proffered divine good as the most intimate treasure of the Heart of the Master Himself. But when in the following of Christ the Master continues ceaselessly to pour forth the rich treasures of His bounty, the disciple is led on through hope to love. The riches of the gifts of Christ continue to open up to him ever increasingly the loving heart of Christ. In this way hope constantly spurs us on to love, constantly unlocks the love of Christ which manifests itself and offers itself to the disciple in the glory of his hope. Hence the divine gift of hope in its profoundest depths must be looked upon as the first offer of divine love, as the spur moving man toward the imitation of Christ. Hope stimulates us to love and to loving obedience in the following of Christ.

For the earthly pilgrim, moreover, divine love as a constant incentive to love in return protects the initial frailty of love. The love of friendship which unites the disciple with the Master (*amor benevolentiae*) is not diminished by the love of hope (*amor concupiscentiae*). It is rather enkindled, protected, and invigorated. Love of hope is the love for salvation leading to the loving friendship with God. But it does not cease to exist once the friendship is established. Hope ever remains as the constant companion and the noblest fruit of love. The purer and loftier our love for Christ, the more will the loving-kindness, manifested in His promises and assured by His fidelity to them, enkindle love in us, the more will we treasure not only His riches but also, and most particularly, the good fortune of being His disciples.

Hope therefore is not only on its part a way to love, but love is likewise the way to ever stronger and more perfect hope. "O taste, and see that the Lord is sweet" (Ps 33:9). This holds true even more for the one who has

been tried and tested in his loving discipleship than for the newly converted. Only great love can in some measure grasp and in some degree
savor the greatness of the promises of the Lord, for in the last analysis all
Christian hope is totally ordered to the love of friendship. And here on
earth this love of friendship consists in giving honor and glory to Christ
by following in His footsteps, and in the other world it will be no less
than eternal community of love of God in and with Christ.

Hence the theological virtue of hope is not merely the first impulse
toward the imitation of Christ, but an impulse constantly renewed. Hope
enters essentially into the discipleship: to be a disciple in the school of
Christ means to be in the divine pilgrimage toward the Land of Promise;
it means to be placed under trial and test; it means to be really possessed
of hope.

Love is not diminished in its perfection by hope, but made more
perfect. The so-called "pure" or "disinterested" love without the essential
element of hope is not more perfect than the love of friendship seeking
salvation. It is in fact an utter caricature of the status of the divine
pilgrimage toward salvation, possible only through a complete misconception of our ceaseless dependence on Christ. Only in eternity will our hope
be transformed into joyous possession. Our love will be totally and
essentially a grateful receptive love no longer yearning for fulfillment,
whereas in this earthly sojourn it must be a correspondingly grateful love
looking forward hopefully in expectation of the glorious fulfillment.

"Christ our hope" means for the disciple of Christ the living conviction
that we can depend and rely on the love of Christ and His promises only
to the extent that we live with Christ, only to the extent that we fulfill the
commandments of Christ in love. If Christ Himself is our hope, then to
hope in Christ means to enter into Christ, to live in Christ. And this is
possible only if we are constantly loyal to the commandments of love
coming from Christ. Observing the commandments of God leads us ever
deeper into the love for Christ and consequently also ever deeper into
hope in Him. The more loyal our obedience to Christ, the more vital will
be our love for Him and the more firmly entrenched in love will be our
hope, for love thrives on obedience and nourishes and invigorates hope.
"Almighty God, grant that we may progress in faith, hope, and love! And
in order that we may merit to attain what you promise, grant that we may
love what you command" (Thirteenth Sunday after Pentecost).

Such therefore is the religious import of hope that it orientates us totally and utterly to Christ, that it summons us into the community of His love. Such is the religious-moral significance of hope that it spurs on all our moral forces toward the exalted goal in obedience to Christ, in patient suffering with Him, and in observance of His law. Since Christian hope places before us an infinitely exalted ideal, it is also able to arouse the most vigorous moral forces in man. It can unleash forces which far transcend his natural powers, because hope is a supernatural virtue, an exalted divine force, a basic endowment of the child of God bestowed upon him as one of the choicest of divine gifts. However, if the invisible goods which hope holds out to us in promise are really to spur us on vitally and effectively, we must be moved by the gifts of the Holy Spirit which come to us with hope and love. Only through these gifts are we entirely and utterly at home in the supernatural world of the sacred signs and motives.

2. Hope as a Supernatural Virtue

Hope is a theological virtue: a) God Himself is the object (the material object) of this virtue. "I am . . . thy reward exceeding great" (Gn 15:1; cf. Ap 22:12). The object we hope for from God is not the wages of a servant, but the recompense paid by God, our loving Father, to His child. It is admission into the intimate circle of God's own loving bliss. "You have received a spirit of adoption as sons, by virtue of which we cry, 'Abba! Father!' The Spirit himself gives testimony to our spirit that we are sons of God. But if we are sons, we are heirs also: heirs indeed of God and joint heirs with Christ" (Rom 8:15ff.).

The adequate object of hope embraces not only the end or God Himself, but also the means which are necessary to attain the end: above all, the great gift of final perseverance. However, since means derive value from end, the complete object of hope is God and the means by which we come to Him. One who serves God merely for temporal reward does not live from the virtue of hope. Nor does he possess true hope who looks to eternity for no more than the accidental rewards in heavenly bliss.

b) The motive (formal object) of hope is God-like: hope does not rely on human achievements (man's cooperation is only a condition of hope), but solely and entirely on the promises of God. In these promises we encounter the power, the love, the mercy, and the fidelity of God. Accordingly our hope in God is measured by our faith in the divine attributes and in the divine revelation which includes the promises (cf. Heb 11:1f.).

By hope man reaches out to God with the confident expectation that He will give Himself to us in eternal love. God Himself through His grace empowers us to trust in Him, obliges us to trust in Him. Supernatural hope therefore implies hoping for God from God through the promises of God who is all-good, almighty, and all-faithful (*sperare Deum a Deo per Deum*).

Another element essentially accompanies our hope as long as we are earthly pilgrims: the fear that we may miss our eternal reward (which in no wise weakens the divine motive in its absolute firmness). This fear included in the content of the divine virtue we understand as belonging to hope in a mere external sense, as taken up with it on the basis of our frailty, inconstancy, and sinfulness; we hope for all things from God, but from ourselves we fear everything. However, if we probe more profoundly, we see that even the motive of fear is included in the divine motive. Surely we fear to lose God, our last end, because we are wilful and frail, capable of deliberate refusal to serve Him. But ultimately we fear our exclusion from the divine love only because of the tremendous and all-holy earnestness of God's love, because of the infinite justice of God. Summarily, we may say that hope is unconditioned trust in the infinite power, goodness, and fidelity of God. We trust that He will grant us the fulfillment of the glorious promises of His love. But hope is also the firm conviction that God is just, and that in His justice He will infallibly carry out His threats against us if we do not persevere in our love for Him until death, thus dying in mortal sin.

Consequently there is in the virtue of hope that very element of tension (the "harmony of contrast") which Rudolph Otto maintains is the essential characteristic of religion as such: to be drawn by the beatifying love of God (the *mysterium fascinosum*) and at the same time quake before the terrifying majesty of the just love of God (the *mysterium tremendum*), to possess the child's jubilation over the good fortune of love and the child's dread and awe of the offense against the love of God. But these two elements are not strict contradictories; they do not cancel each other out or neutralize each other. Rather they merge into a higher synthesis: into awesome love, into chastened hope.[55]

Supernatural hope captures all the *dynamism* of natural hope. For the full effect of this dynamism we must repeatedly place before our eyes the grandeur and the beauty of supernatural hope in vivid life-like images.

From this point of view it is most desirable, if not altogether necessary, to present vividly in meditation, instruction, exhortation (for example in the sermons on heaven and hell) the objects of supernatural hope and fear. The result must be a natural reaction of stimulation or fright. But it would be totally incorrect to look upon this reaction or any realm of earthly images as the actual object of our hope. It must always be perfectly clear that the object of hope far transcends mundane fancy.

Supernatural hope must also embrace and transform the entire realm of earthly hope. All that we strive for in a natural manner with our natural powers of hoping, all that we seek for in natural goods, we must ultimately include in our supernatural hope. We must seek these things through the supernatural virtue of hope and order them to their supernatural end.

Health and riches, success and honor we may strive for and hope for— if we really wish to live entirely from the virtue of hope—only insofar as they are helpful for us in the attainment of eternal life, or at least do not hinder us in our efforts to attain our last end. Sickness and poverty, misfortune, suffering and disgrace we may fear only insofar as they, in view of our frailty, can prove obstacles to our love for Christ.

Supernatural hope deprives all that is purely earthly of its power—all, that is, which is detrimental to one's last end. But hope does not imply at all an alienation or estrangement from the genuine temporal tasks and duties in our lives. Only that which is alien to God in earthly sentiments and attitudes is dissolved in supernatural hope. The serious approach to the kingdom of God on earth with all its ramifications, diversities, and implications in the natural domain belongs to the sphere and motive of supernatural hope. Our tasks in time and space are the very arena of test and trial of hope. Hope produces trial as trial produces hope (cf. Rom 5:3f.).

3. Pledges of Hope

The promises of God in Christ are the pledges of our hope (note the eight beatitudes). Pledge and promise of our hope also includes all that God has already manifested to us through His love, for what God begins in love He also perfects and completes in His fidelity, as far as lies in Him. Supreme pledge of our hope is the suffering of our Savior. It manifests to us the infinite mercy of God and also His justice regarding sin. Most striking pledge of our hope is the resurrection of Christ, supreme testimony of the omnipotence of God and most convincing assurance of the fulfillment of God's promises to those who believe and hope. What God has begun and perfected in Christ He will also accomplish in us if we live in Christ and die in Christ.

All the sacraments are memorials of the passion of Christ, harbingers of eternal life (*signa prognostica vitae aeternae*). By means of the sacraments God has already rescued us "from the power of darkness and transferred us into the kingdom of his beloved Son, in whom we have our redemption, the remission of our sins" (Col 1:13f.). In the sacraments we receive the visible assurance that Christ is in us, our "hope of glory" (Col 1:27). Through the sacraments God "has brought us to life together with Christ . . . and raised us up together, and seated us together in heaven in Christ Jesus" (Eph 2:5f. cf. also Col 2:12; 3:1ff.). When we celebrate the Eucharistic Sacrifice, we realize that we are united to the "heavenly Jerusalem, and to the company of many thousands of angels, and to the Church of the firstborn who are enrolled in the heavens" (Heb 12:22f.). When in the sacraments, particularly in the Eucharist, we "proclaim the death of the Lord, until he comes" (1 Cor 11:26), then we experience in faith and hope that "our citizenship is in heaven from which also we eagerly await a Savior, our Lord Jesus Christ" (Phil 3:20). He indeed "will refashion the body of our lowliness, conforming it to the body of his glory" (Phil 3:21).

The Three Divine Persons are the surety of our hope. God the Father (with the Son and Holy Spirit) in a most admirable manner created us in the image and likeness of God and destined us for community of love with Him, and even more wonderfully restored our nature after its fall (cf. Offertory of the Mass). God the Son delivered us from the hopelessness of sin and invited us to share in the glory of His resurrection through membership in His kingdom into which we are already incorporated through His holy sacraments. The Holy Spirit, personal Gift of Father and Son in the life of the Trinity, is the supreme pledge of our hope. Even in this present life He grants us His love as earnest of the eternal embrace of love, inciting us through His celestial consolations to seek after divine things as He frees us from illusory earthly joys.

The sinner who has driven the Holy Spirit and divine love from his soul is not subjectively capable of the same ardor and fervor of hope as one who is endowed with the grace and love of the Holy Spirit. If he still possesses the virtue of supernatural hope at all, the element of fear must be more prominent, for he is a child of divine wrath rather than of love. In fact, only through the motive of fear is he able to come at all to conversion and to grace and thereby to the hope which rests on love rather than fear. From this it is evident that the sinner can hope. And he must hope. His sin does not destroy the virtue of hope unless it is directly opposed to hope or to faith itself. Should he have lost the virtue altogether, the virtue of faith remains the basis of a return through earnest prayer and contemplation of the mercy of God. God is always ready to save the sinner who turns to him sincerely and to grant him the grace of true sorrow.

The supernatural hope of the sinner, with its greater reliance on the motive of fear, differs from the filial hope of one in the state of grace most of all by an essentially weaker movement of the individual toward the object which is God. The sinner, who looks upon the transient good as here and now more important than the divine good of hope, requires an entirely new help of grace from God to direct himself to God with the same movement of hope as the child of God. The conversion by which the sinner turns again with his whole heart and soul to God's promises is a tremendous work of new creation. It is a new God-ward thrust in holy fear and hope. How important is the stress of the motive of hope sustained by fear in the instruction and exhortation on penance!

4. The Hope of Solidarity

Our hope has its foundation in Christ who proclaimed Himself one with us in true solidarity as our Head and who suffered and died for us. If we live in Christ, and Christ in us is our "hope of glory" (Col 1:27), we will give evidence of this union with Him above all through the solidarity of our hoping and striving. In Adam's fall we were trapped in a solidarity of perdition with its stifling effects arising from an existence according to the "old Adam," the flesh (sárx), and even more from a poisoned atmosphere created by "the world-rulers of this darkness, the spiritual forces of wickedness on high" (Eph 6:12). Such we were, but now through the "one baptism" we are called in "one body and one Spirit . . . in one hope" (Eph 4:4). In every way this common hope takes up and embraces in its entirety the individual hope of salvation. "For in one Spirit we were all baptized into one body" (1 Cor 12:13). Our salvation is founded in the love whose very core is the concern for the salvation of one another. It is a mutual harmonious concern in a hope of solidarity. "Bear one another's burdens, and so you will fulfill the law of Christ" (Gal 6:2). We cannot save ourselves from the solidarity of perdition except by working together in a conscious solidarity, in a spirit of readiness for sacrifice, placing our individual endowments of grace in the service of all (cf. 1 Cor 12) and showing ourselves ever willing to cooperate with all others in the Christianization of our realm of life.

Under this aspect the insights of modern social psychology and, to a greater degree, of pastoral sociology[56] assume a new importance and deserve special consideration. It is simply inevitable that the individualist concerned only with his own soul—we might call him a salvation egoist—is ever an easy prey to the evil and dangerous collectivism of his surrounding. His hope is gain. Our hope is well-founded and effective only when it is hope active in love, a hope in solidarity, whose effective signs are the holy sacraments. We hope for salvation as the people of God.

5. The Way of Hope

The way of hope begins with the fear of eternal punishment and exclusion from God's love, with high esteem for the supernatural goods promised by God. There must follow the breaking of the bonds which make us slaves of the allurements of transient joys and goods, and the gradual growth of trust in the goodness of God and His grace. Through all this one is placed on the way of divine hope, which is a way to joy and also a way of joy. But it is always and unavoidably a way of the cross through patience in suffering with Christ: "Did not the Christ have to suffer these things before entering into his glory?" (Lk 24:26; 1 Pt 4:1; 5:10; cf. Wis 3:4). Christ in His suffering stood the test of obedience (Heb 5:18). And for us also the patient acceptance of suffering sent by God is the supreme test of obedience and trust in Him. We are indeed sons of God. "But if we are sons, we are heirs also: heirs indeed of God and joint heirs with Christ, provided, however, we suffer with him that we may also be glorified with him" (Rom 8:17). The greater our progress in hope, the more precious its savor to us (since the Lord is its object), the more willing we are to follow Him on the way to the cross. With St. Paul we can say: "I reckon that the sufferings of the present time are not worthy to be compared with the glory to come that will be revealed in us" (Rom

8:18). The way of hope lies in the obedient fulfillment of God's law, epitomized in the one great commandment of love. "If thou wilt enter into life, keep the commandments" (Mt 19:17). If the Christian is steadfast in his fidelity to the commandments, he will receive the reward of the fulfillment of his hope.

In the fullest sense the way of hope is Christ. He is the new law of grace in us. It is His command that we abide in Him and walk hopefully in accordance with His Spirit. Indeed He Himself will be the reward of our hope (cf. Ap 22:12; Is 40:10), a reward which at its profoundest depths is the gift of His grace to be obtained above all by persevering prayer. Hence the way of hope is also a way of constant prayer. Prayer in union with Christ and in loving obedience to His law is the prayer of the perseverance which cannot be merited but which will be given to those who unceasingly beg for it.

The fear in our hope which constantly arouses us from our torpor and warns us against complacency in the divine service can also create a spirit of dejection and anxiety. Here too prayer is essential for our hope. If we are buoyed up by trustful, persevering prayer, our sinfulness and weakness no longer will terrify us, because prayer is the great assurance of the divine help. The divine promises are intimately connected with our humble prayer which is trustful submission to God. Prayer is the voice of hope, the vigor of hope, the guarantee of the goal of hope.

6. Hope Is Perfected through the Gifts of the Holy Spirit

Through the gifts of the Holy Spirit we are enabled almost instinctively to keep the commandments with a fulness of loving confidence in the divine promises. In the most tender response to the divine will we obey lovingly as we await with clear and unfailing hope the fulfillment of the promises in eternal glory. The gift of wisdom imparts a sweetness to the savor of love which is a true relish for the divine friendship and the supernatural goods we share in communion with God. Thus wisdom intensifies and heightens the yearning of hope, imparting a livelier trust in the goodness of God; for one who does not merely know but actually experiences God's love cannot readily doubt it.

According to St. Thomas the fear of the Lord is the special gift pointed to hope. It removes from hope all disturbing anxiety of spirit and deepens holy fear by transforming it into filial fear, which is concerned not so much with punishment for sin as with the malice and guilt of sin, which dreads the thought of offending God more than the thought of His punishment for the offense. However, we must caution that the "fear of the Lord" is truly fear and not merely reverence or awe.[57] And likewise that it does not halt at the beginning of wisdom, but accompanies all the stages of Christian life and perfection (Prv 1:7; 9:10; 15:33; Sir 1:14ff.; particularly 1:20: "To fear God is the fulness of wisdom").

The saint has the deepest insight into the malice of sin. He peers most deeply into its abysmal depths. He treasures the friendship of God supremely. Therefore his fear of offending and losing Him is supremely efficacious. The fear which is the gift of the Holy Spirit is of course not the abject fear which flees from the face of God in terror but the fear which flies from danger ever more and more into the arms of God. It is a holy fear taken up utterly and entirely in the unity and harmony of God's mercy and justice, which does not weaken our hope but actually invigorates it as well in the rhythm of its striving and yearning as in the firmness of its trust in God. Nothing so strengthens and secures our hope as prayer, and one of the principal fruits of the "fear of the Lord" is persevering prayer.

7. Sins against the Virtue of Hope

The obligations arising from Christian hope are positive and negative. The positive obligation requires that the Christian live in hope, that he increase the virtue within him day by day. The negative obligation forbids certain sins against the virtue. Since hope is kept alive by having the motives before one's mind, there is a positive obligation to elicit acts (motives) of hope and fear to the extent and degree which is necessary to avoid placing the religious-moral life in jeopardy.

Two kinds of destructive sin can be committed against the virtue of hope: despair and presumption.

a. Despair

There are two kinds of despair. They are distinct, but one more or less implies the other. 1) In the first species of despair there is no true desire for heavenly goods. The joy in heavenly things is wanting or weak because of a preference for the material and temporal rather than the spiritual. This weakness arises from defect of love for God and particularly from excessive attachment to earthly delights (especially the pleasures of the palate and the flesh). Essentially this type of despair, which is repugnance to spiritual things and lack of concern for the goods promised by the Savior, is nothing less than "spiritual sloth" (*acedia*). The repugnance is due either to a lack of appreciation for the spiritual by comparison with earthly goods in which one is immersed, or to the fear of the effort and sacrifice demanded by the sincere imitation of Christ. The dread of the effort and sacrifice is greater than the desire for the goal which is the blessed community of love. It is possible that this low and debased form of fear can be shaken by the shock of the true "fear of the Lord" which belongs to our hope. However, it will not be totally overcome except through the glory of Christian hope resplendent in divine love.

Spiritual sloth, and specifically the sin of despair of which we have been speaking, permits of a great diversity of degrees. Since it arises not so much from distrust of God's mercy as from earthly dispositions and attitudes of mind and heart, it may in some instances be no more than a venial sin. But it is always a grave sin to prefer the earthly to the divine simply and as such. No one can be guilty of outright preference of the material to the spiritual without grave sin.

2) The second kind of despair is a lack of confidence in the infinite goodness of God. In contradiction to the clear teaching of faith, one says that his sins are too heinous for the mercy of God. They are so monstrous that God cannot or will not pardon them or that one's sinful weakness is so great that God cannot or will not grant the grace for conversion, for a good life, and especially for a happy death. Here the sin against hope is compounded by a sin against faith itself.

The consummated sins against hope totally seal man's heart against effective action of the Holy Spirit. For this reason despair is reckoned among the sins against the Holy Spirit. It is a most fatal sin because in advance it renders sterile every attempt at salvation.

b. Presumption

Presumption is not directly and immediately opposed to the heavenward movement of our soul to God with trustful confidence in His promises, but to that essential element of wholesome fear which must be found in the theological virtue of hope. Whereas despair presupposes the condition of non-fulfillment, presumption rashly assumes the condition of the fulfillment of hope.[58] The presumptuous man either sins against the justice of God directly, thinking that God will grant him eternal happiness even though he does not turn to Him with all his heart and obey Him, or he sins against the supernatural character of hope by assuming that he is able to attain eternal happiness through mere natural powers or mere moral achievement.

Presumption is a sin against the dogma of the gratuitousness of the gift of perseverence, for the presumptuous man thinks he has already earned this gift or that he will be able in the future to merit it according to strict justice. Neglect of prayer for a happy death is hazardously close to the sin of presumption.

The root of presumption is pride. Often it is the pride of heresy, either that of Pelagianism, which exalted man's natural powers, or the doctrine of the Reformers that found the individual predestined and certain of his salvation. To postpone one's conversion and firmly trust all the while that God will not summon one by death before one actually is converted is not the consummate sin of presumption, but a grave sin against hope nonetheless. (In this sin there is lacking the genuine fear of the divine justice, an authentic and indispensable part of hope.) God has not promised to wait until the sinner finally makes up his mind to turn to Him again in sorrow, even though in the meanwhile he continues to reject the call of grace. In fact God has rather threatened him with damnation. Usually postponement of conversion is not the sin of presumption but a sinful hazarding of salvation arising from lack of appreciation of divine things. It is a sin which closely resembles despair. In any instance it seriously offends against hope and true love of self.

To multiply one's sins on the pretext that God forgives the more serious and numerous sins as readily as the less serious and single offense is a grave sin of presumption. The motive of hope is perverted into a motive for insolence in multiplying sin. Moreover, it is contrary to truth to say that God as readily forgives the more serious sins as the lesser offenses, or that He as readily pardons a host of violations as a few. Surely the longer one has continued in sin, the more numerous the sins, the deeper is the fall and the more difficult and improbable the conversion. No one can deny, of course, that God will pardon the most heinous sin. The hope that God will forgive even the greatest sinner, if he truly repents, just as mercifully as he will pardon the one less guilty is in perfect accord with the Catholic truth which teaches the infinite mercy of God. But the point at issue is whether postponement of conversion with the accumulation of sins will so readily be followed by a sincere repentance rather than by a hardening of the sinner's heart. God has not promised that at all times He will grant extraordinary graces of conversion even to those who have insolently rejected His call to repentance countless times.

Occasionally habitual mortal sin, though primarily the effect of violent passion and serious temptation, is due in part to an indifferent and easy-going attitude toward the gravity of the habit. The individual fancies that since he must confess the sins anyway, one or the other additional sin could not make any great difference. Though such an attitude does not make one guilty of the sin of presumption in the strict sense of the term, it does betray a gross defect of divine hope (an inadequate fear of the Lord) and a base ingratitude toward God's bounty and mercy in the sacrament of penance.

Particularly effective as a remedy against the temptation to give up hope through spiritual torpor or presumption is meditation on the four last things. One who is wrestling with the temptation to despair should be urged to turn his eyes hopefully to the Mother of mercy. A most beautiful prayer to recite on such occasions is the *Memorare*. Suggested likewise by good directors is the renewal of trust in the solidarity of salvation and cooperation in the community of the apostolate.

BIBLIOGRAPHY

The Virtue of Hope

Bo, C. *Scandalo della speranza*. Firenze, 1957.

BRUNNER, A., S.J. "Hoffnung," *StimmenZeit*, 146 (1950), 401–411.

CARRÉ, A. M. *Espérance et désespoir*. Paris, 1954.

DE LETTER, P. "Hope and Charity in St. Thomas," *Thm*, (1950), 204–248.

DELHAYE, PH.-BOULANGÉ, J. *Espérance et vie chrétienne*. Tournai, 1958.

DESBUQUOIS, G. *Die Hoffnung*. Uebertragen von Balmer-Basilius. Basil, 1950.

DE SOLAGES, B. *Le livre de l'espérance: Dieu, l'âme, la destinée*. Paris, 1955.

DE VILLARES, JUSTO. *La esperanza cristiana*. Bilboa, 1957.

GELIN, A. "L'esperance dans l'Ancien Testament," *LumVie*, (1959), 3–16, especially Vol. 1, 1959.

GRENTRUP, TH. *Hoffen und Vertrauen*. Wuerzburg, 1948.

GROSSOUW, W. "L'espérance dans le Nouveau Testament," *Rb*, 61 (1954), 508–532.

HAIBLE, E. "Gott wirft den Menschen ins Ziel. Bemerkungen zu einer Theologie der Hoffnung," *TrThZ*, 68 (1959), 271–284.

HENNIG, J. "Vom Wesen der Hoffnung," *GeistLeben*, 30 (1957), 257–262.

Hitz, P. "Krise der Hoffnung in der Seelsorge," *Anima*, 7 (1952), 102–107.

Hornstein, F. X. von "Die Hoffnung als Tugend in fragwuerdiger Zeit," *Anima*, 13 (1958), 103–111 (Note the entire Vol. 2, 1958).

Lain Entralgo, P. *La espera y la esperanza. Historia y teoria del esperar humano.* Madrid, 1956.

"L'Espérance chrétienne," *LumVit*, 9 (1954), No. III.

Loosen, J. "Menschliche Angst und christliche Hoffnung," *GeistLeben*, 30 (1957), 96–100.

Lucien de Marie-Joseph, P. *La communion dans l'attente.* Paris, 1952.

Marcel, G. *Homo Viator: Introduction to a Metaphysic of Hope.* Translated by Emma Craufurd. Chicago: Regnery, 1952.

Olivier, B. "Hoffnung als christliche Grundhaltung," *Theologischer Digest*, 1 (1958), 158–165.

———. *L'espérance chrétienne.* Paris, 1958.

Pieper, J. *Ueber die Hoffnung.* 4 ed., Muenchen, 1949.

Pott, A. *Das Hoffen im NT in seiner Beziehung zum Glauben.* Leipzig, 1915.

Schlier, H. "Ueber die Hoffnung. Eine neuetestamentliche besinnung." *GeistLeben*, 33 (1960), 16–26.

Spicq, C. *La révélation de l'espérance dans le Nouveau Testament.* Avignon, 1932.

Zimara, C. *Das Wesen der Hoffnung in Natur und Uebernatur.* Paderborn, 1933.

Additional Works in English

Carré, Ambroise M., O.P. *Hope or Despair.* New York: Kenedy, 1955.

Guillet, Jacques, S.J. *Themes of the Bible.* Chicago: Fides, 1961. "Hope" pp. 171–224.

Hasseveldt, Roger. *The Christian Meaning of Hope.* Westminster, Md.: Newman, 1958.

Kramer, Clayton, C.SS.R. *Fear and Hope According to St. Alphonsus Liguori* (Catholic University Studies in Sacred Theology, 2nd ser., 54). Washington: Catholic University Press, 1951.

Roguet, Aimon M., O.P. *The Season of Hope.* Collegeville, Minn.: Liturgical Press, 1961.

The Virtues and States of Life (Theology Library, v. 4). ed. A. M. Henry, O.P. Chicago: Fides, 1957. "Faith" (A. Liégé), pp. 1–59; "Hope" (B. Olivier), pp. 61–126; "Charity" (B. Olivier), pp. 127–208; "The Virtue of Religion" (A. Mennessier), pp. 393–444; "The Social Virtues" (M. Gerland), pp. 445–485 (on obedience, piety, liberality).

Periodical Literature in English

Conlon, W. M. "Certitude of Hope: a Survey among Theologians." *Thm*, 10 (Jan.–April, 1947), 75–119.

De Letter, P. "Hope and Charity in St. Thomas," *Thm*, 13 (April–July, 1950), 204–48, 325–53.

———. "Desire of God: Hope or Charity," *ITQ*, 23 (Oct., 1956), 393–404.

Kerns, V. "Virtue of Hope," *IER*, 79 (June, 1953), 409–21.

Lumbreras, P. "Hope, the Self-Seeker," *CrCr*, 3 (June, 1951), 174–89.

McCarthy, J. "Theological Hope," *IER*, 43 (June, 1934), 617–32.

McNarney, M. "Hope," *ClerRev*, 45 (April, 1960), 206–14.

McSorley, J. "Hope, the Forgotten Virtue," *CrCr*, 2 (Sept., 1950), 255–65.

Pieper, J. "Hiddenness of Hope and Despair," *CrCr*, 8 (March, 1956), 44–53.

CHAPTER FOUR

THE VIRTUE OF DIVINE LOVE

1. *The Love of God as Heart of the Imitation*

Through faith we are taught by Christ; through hope we turn to Christ our Mediator and Savior; in love we become His disciples, His friends. One who believes but is without love is not the friend and disciple of Christ; in fact he is not even a good pupil, for only one who sees with the eyes of love can perceive the deep and secret beauty of faith. Above all, it is the very person of Christ that unlocks that which is at faith's very depths; for His love bestows itself most generously only in mutual love. "The intimate center of the person of Christ is open only to one: His disciple."[59] Since the nature, the thoughts, and the actions of Christ are at their profoundest depths love, we can have with Him a community of life, of thought, of goods only through partnership in love which rests in the divine virtue of love. Just as love is the supreme motive of Christ in incarnation and redemption, so for man the sole response to God's supreme love is love in return.

Love without measure, self-giving, sacrificial, impelled the Son of God to become our Brother, Friend, and Master. We in turn can become His friends and disciples only through that love which truly makes Him our first concern. We are not to think of our salvation alone, nor even in the first place. "He who does not love believes in vain, even if the things he believes are true; he hopes in vain, even if the things he hopes for are taught to pertain to true happiness—unless he believes and hopes for this, that he may through prayer attain the gift of love. For, although hope is impossible without love, it may happen that a man fail to love something that is indispensable to the attainment of his hopes—for instance, if he hopes for eternal life . . . but does not love justice, which is indispensable to the attainment of eternal life."[60] Not love for goods promised by Christ but only love for Christ Himself makes us His disciples and imparts to our faith and hope the fulness of power unto salvation.

St. Thomas looks upon the theological virtue of love as a friendship between the soul and God.[61] The mystics, with Holy Writ, particularly the Song of Songs, in mind, refer to it with the warm and affectionate terms of betrothal and marriage. When we use the term *imitation* and the correlatives *Master* and *disciple,* we have similar thoughts in mind. The term *friendship,* employed by Jesus Himself, strikingly expresses unity of hearts with mutual love. The divine betrothal and marriage of mystical writers implies all the intimacy of affection between spouses and the indissolubility of their union (at least as to the ideal). *Imitation, following of Christ,* terms directly biblical, clearly indicate that the disciple imitates or follows the Master, and imply a bond of intimate love, yet at the same time an inequality, a loving relation of dependence and a corresponding guidance and leadership. In each of these tender concepts—friendship, espousal, imitation—love is at the very core. The very heart of the matter! It is the very heart of community with Christ. The theological virtue of love is love in and through Christ.

The relation of friend to friend, of spouse to spouse, of Master to disciple, presupposes intimate and spiritual relationship. Christ gives to the soul in and with His love a participation in His divine nature insofar as mere creatures can share in something so lofty; for whenever the Savior effectively bestows the gift of His love, He at the same time grants the life of grace to the soul. And with grace there is given the virtue of infused love so that we are truly made like to God, assimilated to Christ who recognizes us as His brothers, children of the same heavenly Father.

In friendship, in marriage, and even in the Master-disciple relationship, there must be a community of goods. The Master actually shares with His disciple the riches of His truth in love, for only in love can we come to a genuine intimate possession of the great revelations of the faith. The Lord Himself says: "I have called you friends, because all things that I have heard from my Father I have made known to you" (Jn 15:15).

The most profound communication between Father and Son is the eternal dialog of love in the Holy Spirit. This most intimate truth is grasped only by the loving disciple who is totally imbued with it. Faith and hope are presuppositions and at the same time part of the treasure of community goods in the friendship with God. But only through disciple-ship (only through divine love) do faith and hope become a living claim and incipient possession of permanent glory, so that we already share in germ the Savior's riches. Through this possession we have the power to know Him as He knows the Father and the Father knows Him; we have the right to the inheritance of the riches of His beatitude as He possesses it in the love of the Holy Spirit. Since He has communicated the full inheritance of His riches, He bestows on us the goods of His death and resurrection with the pledge of their eternal possession through participation of body and soul in His exaltation and glory.

In loving friendship for the Master the disciple also gives. As disciples we give ourselves, our entire being, and all our activity to the Lord. In giving we desire to retain nothing, to have nothing that does not belong utterly to Him. Disciple-love is self-giving from a bounty already received through God's grace. We give to God His own gift already bestowed upon us.

In friendship there is only one will between friend and friend. The same is true of loving spouses. The disciple has not only this sentiment of love for the master but also the will to be formed by him. The disciple of Christ has not only a loving friendship for his Master but likewise the firm will to permit the Master to form and mold him entirely in accordance with His will. He is resolved to consecrate himself entirely and without reserve to Christ and His kingdom. Hence, in loving imitation and consecration he will also keep the commandments: "You are my friends if you do the things I command you" (Jn 15:14). "This is my commandment, that you love one another as I have loved you" (Jn 15:12). Only in mutual love do we show that we are docile, obedient disciples of the Lord.

Friends seek each other's company. Spouses love to be together. The disciple loves the company of his master. All of this we have in our loving relation with Christ. The Son of God became man and lived among us. And the presence among men through the incarnation is continued by the Eucharistic presence and His whole activity in the Mystical Body. With Father and Holy Spirit the eternal Son is also present through the divine indwelling in the soul endowed with grace. The disciple on his part will seek to be at home with His Master by frequent visits to the Eucharistic hearth and above all will receive Him often in Holy Communion. In a constant spirit of prayer he walks in the presence of God, his mind pondering the words of the Master. "Faith believes; hope and charity pray. But without faith the other two cannot exist and, therefore, faith also prays."[62] Hope begs in the prayer of petition, love renders thanks and rejoices, praises, extols. In prayer love maintains authentic intimacy of friendship with God.

These grand prerogatives of the disciple are not won by one's own initiative and achievement but are the gift of an ineffable divine election. "You have not chosen me, but I have chosen you" (Jn 15:16). They are the fruit of the incomparable friendship of Christ: "Greater love than this no one has, that one lay down his life for his friends" (Jn 15:13). But if Christ has chosen the disciple, the disciple no less chooses Christ with all the dedication of loving friendship. Christ in dying for us invites us to the supreme friendship. In response the disciple must gratefully choose Him as the unique Friend for whom he is even ready to die and whom he loves for Himself and all else for His sake alone.

2. Participation in the Covenant of Love

The divine virtue of love in this concrete order of salvation means participation in the covenant of love between Christ and the Church. It is participation in that love which impelled the Son of God to become man and shed His Blood for us, so that in the water from His riven side, in the baptism of His passion and with the word—the sacrament—he might form and purify and sanctify His Bride, the Church (Eph 5:25ff.). As members of the People of God we are truly the "beloved of God" forming a mystical-real unity with the Church in whom and with whom we are able to love Christ with the same love which He has for her. Once we are admitted through baptism into the new and eternal covenant of love, we celebrate this covenant and with it our baptismal bond in the other sacraments, above all in the Eucharist which is the great and effective sign of the love-covenant.

The celebration of the sacraments bears this unmistakable message: we can remain in the divine love and progress in it only if we say *yes* to the bond of love between Christ and His Church, and *yes* to the covenant of love that binds all the members of the People of God. The mystery of the triune love of God was manifested openly here on earth through the paschal mystery of the death and resurrection of Christ and the sending of the Holy Spirit as fruit of that great mystery. As this mystery of God's love was present and active in the paschal events, so the divine virtue of love is imparted to us as a participation in the love of the triune God precisely through the participation in the covenant of love in the Church. Here the saving mystery of death, resurrection, ascension, and the descent of the Holy Spirit become for us a present salvific event. The paschal mystery is ever present in the Church's sacraments, particularly in the Eucharist.

3. *Participation in the Triune Love of God*

To be in Christ and in the covenant of His love with the Church means to be incorporated in the life of the triune God. Only in Christ do we have access to the mystery of the life and love of the Holy Trinity. Supernatural love is the divine virtue in a pre-eminent sense. For God Himself effects it. He is its source, its goal, its motive.

In the divine virtue of love we love God because He Himself gives us a share of the love with which He loves Himself.

God Himself, who in His Trinity is love, has so fashioned our innermost being that it is an image of Himself: we share in the fulfillment of the love with which the Father loves the Son and the Son loves the Father in the love of the Holy Spirit. God Himself shows us what love really is in the incarnation of His Only-begotten, in the love with which the Son glorifies the Father on the cross and with which the Father communicates all His glory to the Humanity of Jesus in the resurrection, in the sending of the Holy Spirit and in the Eucharist. He Himself grants us the divine power to love Him as His children by the fact that He, the God of love, dwells in our souls.

Every kind of love is an inclination toward some good based on consciousness of a value. The *love of desire* looks more to the profit or service as the value to be found in the good which is loved. However, where pride merely uses or exploits another without regard for his actual worth, there can be no love at all. Where desire is so caught up with self that one discerns in the other only advantage for one's self, there can be passion indeed but not love. Love, properly so-called, really begins with the sentiment of good pleasure arising in the soul on recognition of the value of another. One is drawn to that value in another or at least senses its presence and feels impelled toward it. The so-called love of desire (*amor concupiscentiae, love of concupiscence*) is genuine love, if in the object loved, in the *value-for-me*, one recognizes at least obscurely the *value-in-itself* and takes pleasure in it. Once man realizes that only God can make him happy, that he is ordered entirely and utterly to God, and accordingly begins to sacrifice everything which proves an obstacle to his effort to seek his happiness in God, then he already has true love even though at direct first blush it is no more than the movement of love of desire. Yet the perfect form of love is love of friendship (*amor benevo-*

lentiae). Possessed of this love, one rejoices over the value of another for his own sake, exults over him, has the desire to attest his love and esteem for him and in every way show him respect and honor.

On the supernatural plane love of desire corresponds to the divine virtue of hope, whereas the love of benevolence corresponds to the virtue of love. Supernatural hope is that undreamed-of fulfillment of the Greek (*Platonic*) eros on the highest level of the ideal, the loftiest flight of yearning and aspiring love, which knows no rest until it has ascended to the divine. And yet supernatural hope is essentially distinct from the Greek *eros*, for it does not spring from man himself but from the gracious and unmerited bounty and condescension of God who awakens and invites a hope transcending all created desire. It cannot be the flight of mere man no matter how lofty his aspirations. Even the hope of the Christian presupposes a concept and image of God totally different from that of the Greeks. For the Greeks God is the end and ideal which moves all things as the goal and object of love but does not itself love (*kineî dè hos erómenos*). But for us Christians God moves all things. He awakens God-like hope and love as the Sovereign Love. The love of the Son of God, love unto self-renunciation, love to the death of the cross was nothing less than a scandal, particularly for the Greeks whose "God" did not love but merely provoked human yearning and desire as a goal. The Christian concept of love as shown in Christ and the Christian response was something utterly new for mankind. Such love was an ineffable reality transcending all mere human power to conceive.

Supernatural hope, and even more so supernatural love, which we call charity, flows from love of God which stoops down from the divine heights and gives itself to us. It is the divine *agápe*. "In this is the love, not that we have loved God, but that he has first loved us" (1 Jn 4:10). "You have not chosen me, but I have chosen you" (Jn 15:16).

Without any merit on our part and without any demand or right of our nature, God freely gives us a love which can become our own love for Him through His gracious bounty. This love *from* Him, which becomes a love *for* Him, is an utterly undeserved participation in His own proper eternal love: "As the Father has loved me, I also have loved you" (Jn 15:9). We can and should abide lovingly in the love of the Savior as He abides in the love of the Father. The theological virtue of charity is a participation in the intimate life and love movement in the Trinity itself. As the Father in eternal knowing gives to the Son His entire being which is Love, as Father and Son mutually communicate themselves to each other in the breath of the Holy Spirit, thus through grace the Father gives us His Son, and Father and Son give us the Holy Spirit (insofar as this is possible in mere creatures). And now we too can give ourselves utterly to God in the love of the Holy Spirit who is infused into our hearts with that same gift of grace (Rom 5:5). As God's love is bounteous, overflowing, self-giving, so infused love given in sanctifying grace makes it possible for our love to be a grateful love overflowing into the hearts of all men: "This is my commandment, that you love one another as I have loved you" (Jn 15:12).

The virtue of love also has God for its object. We are privileged to love God Himself. Emil Brunner is surely guilty of a grave error, in fact of an assault on that which is most profoundly Christian, in his contention that God Himself accepts no love from us because He has no need of our love, that He permits Himself to be loved only "in our neighbor."[63] It is true that God has no need of our love, but He wills to be loved by us, first of all, because He Himself truly and earnestly loves us, and true love of friendship by its very nature demands the response of love. It is indeed an ineffable mystery that God, who is infinitely happy in Himself, should really show any concern for our love, and that we are privileged to turn to Him affectionately with the familiar *Thou* in our address. In a natural manner we would be able and indeed obliged to love God above all as the supreme value, but we would not be able to love Him with the utter intimacy of abiding personal friendship. But in the Christian order our love is immediately directed to God as our Father and Friend, because His love is directed immediately to us. It is meant entirely for us, utterly for us. It seeks us; it embraces us.

The motive of supernatural love for God is ultimately none other than God Himself: God's absolute love and lovableness, His own proper infinite worth, and His love of friendship embracing us. Love does not merely gaze on the absolute attributes of God. It must be inflamed by His goodness toward us, inflamed with gratitude for His marvelous benefactions toward us, for precisely through these do we most easily gain access to the inner sanctuary of His love. But the center, the heart, of the motive of love for God is not the thought that God's love is generous to us, beatifies us, but that it gives evidence of His own sovereign goodness.

If the love of gratitude primarily looks to our own well-being, it should rather be classified under the virtue of hope. If, on the other hand, it looks first to the goodness of God bestowing on men the blessings which we have experienced, it belongs to the virtue of love. It should always be the fruit of both, the manifestation and expression of both virtues.

Supernatural love is divine in its source, which is God, divine insofar as it gives us a participation in God's own life of love, divine because it has God for its object as well as its motive. Finally, it is divine because it leads us and our neighbor to God; for us the sole way to God is through the virtue of love of God. Supernatural love is necessary for salvation by a necessity of means. The final determinant of our destiny, it leads us to the eternal love-embrace of the Triune God and already in this life is a real and essential beginning of that union of love. Moreover, true love, or charity (*caritas*), leads all other things to God. Since the theological virtue is rooted in God as its very love-center, it is not merely love for God but also a partnership in loving and willing in union with God, a union which embraces all that God loves and wills. The love which is formed in God leads, as far as lies within us, all creatures to God. In consequence, the divine love enables us to transform all created things into a magnificent paean of praise and love to the glory of God.

Above all, our love of God bears our fellow man with us on our way to God, because this divine love empowers us to love him. We can and must love our neighbor as God loves him and because God loves him. In a certain sense we can and must love him with God's own love, and hence with a love that impels him in turn to love God. The evidence that our love for our neighbor is truly God-like, formed in God, lies in the fruits of the love. If it essentially tends to lead him closer to God and draw him into the sacred orbit of divine love, then we may say it is truly *God-formed*. It leads to God, for love formed in God "is not self-seeking" (1 Cor 13:5). It is not the will to lust or to power of domination over one's fellows. It is rather the will to render unselfish service to the highest values, to work for the loving glory of God and the salvation of others, all of which will redound to the greater glory of God and His love.

4. *Characteristics of Love*

a. Love Must Be Sovereign

We must love God above all things. Our love must be sovereign, for to love God no more than we love creatures or to love Him less than creatures is not really to love Him but to offer Him an unspeakable affront. It is the most abysmal misconception and disesteem of the highest good (cf. Mt 10:37; Lk 14:26). God is necessarily a "jealous God." His sanctity cannot admit of any equality with created values, much less of any inferiority to them.

"The measure of our love for God is to love Him without measure. Since the love which we bear for God has the immeasurable and infinite as its goal (for such is God), what limit could we set to our love or what measure? Particularly if we bear in mind that on our part it is not a gratuitous love but the debt of our duty toward God. That Love, which surpasses all knowing, loves us (Eph 3:19). God—whose greatness knows no limits (Ps 144:3), whose wisdom is immeasurable (Ps 146:5), whose peace surpasses all understanding (Phil 4:7)—loves us."[64] Shall we in response to this love set a measure or limit for our own? "God loves us with the whole fulness of His being (*ex se toto*); for the whole Trinity loves us."[65]

It is not at all required that our sovereign love surpass in emotional warmth and tenderness every other love, as for example the love of a mother for her infant. It is not necessary that it be emotionally the most lofty (*affective summus*); but such an ideal is well worth striving for. With the aid of the gifts of the Holy Spirit we can at least at times attain this lofty ideal, so that the spiritual experience of the affection or emotion in our love for God is more ardent and tender than the effect of any other love. Essential, however, in our love is its supreme esteem for God. It must be sovereign in appreciation (*appretiative summus*). We must esteem God above all other good and be firm in our resolution that no other love be placed above our love for Him. The strength and firmness of our love as truly sovereign often proves itself precisely in times of spiritual aridity when the heart seems cold with waning sentiment and enthusiasm. The principal act of love therefore is not exultation of fervor but submission to God based on the inmost esteem of true value. But the emotional or affective phases may never be disdained.

b. Interior and Effective

Love of God must be interior and efficacious. "Love is as strong as death, as hard as hell; the lamps thereof are fire and flames" (Ct 8:6). Love of God may not stop short at mere external sentiment and blissful feeling, even though, as we have already noted, the emotional life with the manifestation of our sentiment of love does play an important part. Insofar as it is not mere passing feeling and superficial sentimentality but a true reflection, a resonance, of the inner spiritual evaluation and submission, or an impulse toward a deepening of the interior orientation to God, the emotion in love possesses great value.

The inner dynamism and impulse of every feeling of love and, likewise, of every manifestation of love in acts must be the spirit of submission. In spiritual origin and development, the interior disposition of love, which is the basis for love's esteem and submission, the sensible affection and enthusiasm, and the manifestion of love in actions (which are the three essentials of love) have a distinct development of their own, though they interact vitally in the various stages of love. Should any of the three be altogether lacking (the external enthusiasm of love can of course wane considerably), love becomes arid and barren or altogether spurious. Particularly spurious is the inner sentiment of love which produces no acts of love. On the other hand, no matter how great the achievements for God and neighbor, without the inner spirit of love they are not acts of love at all. "My dear children, let us not love in word, neither with the tongue, but in deed and in truth" (1 Jn 3:18; cf. Mt 7:21ff.; 1 Cor 13:4ff.). "If the act of love, and always and only the act of love, enables us to discern the purity of spirit and disposition of love in the heart of man, it follows that the inner disposition of love in its true interiority and warmth must be the very soul of the act of love."[66]

c. Love Must Penetrate Nature

Even though it is altogether supernatural, the love of God must be solidly rooted in the nature of man. This means that man—as he really exists and acts—must be laid hold of in all his natural powers of love by the supernatural love of God. This means that the supernatural love may not be merely accessory to or parallel to the natural powers of enthusiasm and love. The supernatural is not merely placed upon the natural as one level upon the other. But the natural love with all that is noble and strong, in its tenderness and inflexible firmness, with its innermost tendency to inflame and embrace also the body-soul affections, must be imbued and impregnated and transformed by the supernatural love. Divine charity penetrates nature to its depths, subsumes and exalts it.

5. *The Effects of Love*

Charity brings to us the pardon for our sins and restoration of grace in the soul: "Her sins, many as they are, shall be forgiven her, because she has loved much" (Lk 7:47). "Charity covers a multitude of sins" (1 Pt 3:8). It brings the divine friendship and sonship: "He who loves me will be loved by my Father, and I will love him and manifest myself to him" (Jn 14:21). It brings merit in all our works which are performed in the love of God, eternal value of all our sufferings and joys accepted with love from the hand of God: 'Now we know that for those who love God all things work together unto good" (Rom 8:28).

Love imparts an insight into the beauty and profundity of the faith (cf. Eph 3:16ff.). If faith is the eye of love, then love is the light of the sun without which the eye cannot see clearly. The effects of charity are the fruits of love in the soul endowed with divine grace: joy, praise, bliss in the Holy Spirit, peace, zeal for God and the salvation of souls, mercy, patience in suffering, and love of the Cross (cf. Gal 5:22).

6. *Love and Obedience: Love and Law*

In every chapter of moral theology, if we conceive of it as the doctrine on the imitation of Christ, it is apparent that love and obedience taken together constitute the essential attitude of the disciple of Christ. We enjoy real friendship with Christ; and in Christ true friendship with the Father. We are united with Him in an ineffable bond of love. But humility, which attests to the truth and authenticity of this love, demands that we remain ever aware of the infinite chasm between our love and that of God, ever conscious of our essential dependence on the all-loving God. Our love for Christ is genuine only if it is reverential adoring love (according to the essence of Christianity as religion) and obedient love (according to the essence of Christian morality). Christ attested His love for the Father and for us through His divine condescension by obediently abasing Himself to the death of the cross. Through His obedient love He reestablished between man and God the communion of love which was disrupted by the sin of disobedience of our first parents. Our supernatural capacity for love derives from the act of obedience of the new Head of the human race. As with the race as a whole, so it is with the individual. Each individual Christian must prove and preserve his love through obedience. He must merit the eternal communion of love with God through loving obedience on earth. Our life has its supreme purpose and its profoundest meaning in love. Its highest mission is to prove our love in the test of obedience. On the most exalted level love and obedience are one.

In our friendship with Christ our love is always the love of the disciple of Christ. The disciple is always anxious to learn; he seeks to be a truly submissive disciple and never to fail to manifest his appreciation of the Master's authority through his obedience. Obviously the perfection of the disciple's obedience is found only in his love. The world must be made to recognize in our manifestation of obedience to Christ the evidence of our love as Christ attested His love for the Father through His obedience. "But he comes that the world may know that I love the Father, and that I do as the Father has commanded me" (Jn 14:31).

As love implies obedience, so it implies law, and love and law are essentially and mutually interchangeable. Obedience of love is surely more comprehensive than mere legal obedience for mere observance of law is the lowest degree of obedience. Mere legal obedience is not yet in the shadow of love. External laws are no more than universal regulations and therefore basically only minimum requirements. Universal rules cannot in fact even prescribe what is highest and best, since the best is not universal and cannot be demanded from men universally. On the contrary, love by its very nature strives for the highest and best and seeks the most perfect manifestation of its ideals in actions.

How can any one who does not fulfill the minimum requirements of the law progress toward that which is higher and better? Since the minimum requirements are basic for the fulfillment of the law of love, love may never violate or ignore the law. At the same time one who truly loves may not remain at the lowest level of obedience and be satisfied with the bare legal minimum.

In order to avoid confusion in this important matter we must clarify the term *law* as used here. If we understand by law the lowest limits of the least requirement (prescriptive laws), then indeed one must demand of love that in fulfilling the law (which it may never violate) it refuse to rest content with mere observance, but seek constantly to surpass the law. However, if by law (in its total meaning) we understand the directive toward ever loftier heights (laws directed to ends and ideals rather than merely to the prescription or prohibition of acts), then love and only love fulfills the law entirely. "Love . . . is the fulfillment of the law" (Rom 13:10). "For the whole law is fulfilled in one word: Thou shalt love thy neighbor as thyself" (Gal 5:14). "Now the purpose of this charge is charity" (1 Tm 1:5).

The new law which embraces everything is the love of Christ (Jn 13:34f.; Mt 22:36ff.). Each individual law or command, each individual precept is intended as an expression and a directive or application of the great commandment of love. Hence one can fulfill the individual laws according to their profoundest significance, only if one obeys them in the spirit of love, for only love divines and carries out the deepest purposes of every law.

As much as the virtue of love and the law are intimately correlated, so much do the spirit of love and the spirit of sheer legalism stand in irreconcilable opposition to each other. Love is entirely personal. It regards the person of the lawgiver, it has insight into his mind and purpose and the intention of the law. One possessed of this personal love feels called in person by the law giver, summoned to respond with all his powers and according to all the circumstances of the situation. One who is motivated by sheer legalism faces the impersonal law (even though it may not be the mere letter of the law) and asks only: what is the minimum requirement of the law, in order that I may avoid violation of law?

If love demands only this: what must be exactly done or avoided to shun loss of grace and the fall from love, it is very imperfect. But if the fulfillment of the law is still realized through such effort to avoid the total loss of love, the concern is not to be characterized as sheer legalism. Though such love is far from perfect, it is not without real value and genuinely fulfills the law.

Genuine charity, the great-hearted and magnanimous love of the disciple for the Master, is not satisfied with the minimum requirement of the law as ultimate norm, but looks to the loftiest ideals as its ultimate goal. But of course the disciple must be prudent! True charity will prompt him to ask humbly and modestly: In my own present situation, with the capacities now at my disposal (perhaps these are not very prepossessing), what is the better course for me, what is most pleasing to God for me?

The man whose love is truly penetrated with the spirit of humility will never be convinced that he can dispense with the norms laid down by universal law as long as he continues to come into contact with its sternest restrictions. The external law is essential for the discernment of spirits. One whose love is mingled with fear will not be altogether free from concern regarding his steadfastness and perseverance in doing good (although there can be no greater assurance of steadfastness in good than charity, according to the thought of St. Augustine: "Love and do what you will: *Ama et fac quod vis!*"). Humility will assure this steadfastness in good by creating in the loving disciple of the Master an unfailing instinct for the will of God; for humble love gives proof of its steadfastness in good and preserves the disciple in the good, precisely through the constant contacts with the law of God and above all through the living example of Christ. The clear path of love is learnt from the humble insight into God's law and the example of the Master, not for the purpose of discovering merely how to avoid sin but to find what must be done at any time to be able to progress to the higher levels of love.

The spirit of sheer legalism deadens, blinds, depersonalizes. On the contrary, love ceaselessly seeks the divine good pleasure and aims at the most perfect realization of the holy will of God. It sheds the clearest light on the individual commandment or precept of God and bids us harken to the call of the Master in each concrete situation. Love looks upon every command as an invitation of love and responds with love in obedience.

7. *Charity Is the Bond and Form of All Virtues*

St. Paul compares the equipment of virtue possessed by the Christian with a complete outfit of clothing in which love is the girdle, the "bond of perfection" (Col 3:14). Through charity or love the vesture of virtue is given its firmness and form, just as the girdle or cincture holds a garment together and imparts a certain unity to it. Hence St. Thomas is faithful to the biblical concept in following Peter Lombard in his characterization of supernatural love as the form of the virtues (*forma virtutum*).[67] But this is not to say that all the other virtues flow from charity in their very essence and special species, or that with charity they form one sole species of virtue. But the love of God confers on them a steadfast ordering toward the supernatural end, the eternal communion with God. Love is the inner dynamic principle which imparts to the whole life of virtue its firmness, inner warmth, and eternal value before God. In a manner of speaking, love is the principle or root of the supernatural qualification of all the good we do. In other words it is basically through charity that the other virtues are made capable of contributing toward the attainment of our eternal supernatural goal and thus rendering us ever more pleasing to God.

Love is not a virtue which merely parallels the others or reposes upon them. Rather it embraces all the others, animates them, directs, and guides them. We say it *informs* all the other virtues with its light and warmth. "Through love every virtue becomes a vital principle, which sets the life of man on the way to God and makes God her own possession."[68] This holds true also for love of neighbor. It becomes truly supernatural virtue, truly fraternal charity, love in God, only through the divine virtue of love which animates and forms it.

The entire Christian life is turned to God through the three theological virtues as a whole: "Faith points out this divine goal, hope releases the forces which strive for it, love unites us with it."[69] But since love alone is the perfect form of faith and hope which of themselves, apart from love, are only imperfect virtues, "unformed virtues" (*informes*), we may say simply that love is the form of all the virtues. Although a considerable number of the virtues may be present in the soul when supernatural charity is infused, they are imperfect virtues, supernaturally "unformed." On the contrary there are others which are typically Christian (for example, sacrificial abnegation, true humility, love of the cross). These spring up and develop only in the soil of faith warmed by the divine virtue of love. Our conclusion from all this is simply that love is the great commandment, the mother of all the virtues, their supernatural form and bond of unity.

Love discharges this lofty function as long as it is in some way vital and effective as the dynamic of form and motive. It is not necessary that a new and distinct act of love (the good intention) be explicitly elicited to accompany each and every act of virtue.

Love as the form of all the virtues joins religion and morality in a unique unsurpassable unity, for love animates all the moral activity of the child of God with the spirit of religion. Thus morality receives a religious form and is bound to God in the closest possible bond. Through love for God and in God we become partners with God in His own effective love for Himself and for all that He has created. We love God because He is in Himself infinitely worthy of our love; we love *creatures* because they are reflections of the light of divine love. Through the love of charity (*caritas*) we love with that which is their own value, and beyond it, the infinite value radiating from the divine glory and the eternal love. In this theological virtue of charity the dynamic of our love, its ultimate motive (*objectum formale quo*), is identical in our love for God, for ourselves, for our neighbor (and therewith for the entire moral-religious attitude of the Christian in relation to himself and to others), even though the immediate (material) object is different in the two (as different as God and creation).

8. *Love as Commandment*

Kant and Scheler, though starting from totally different premises, came to the same conclusion, that love cannot be the object of a precept. For Kant love belongs to the "pathological" order, which is to say that it is a sensible appetitive tendency and therefore is not moral but infra-moral. Scheler, on the contrary, says that one possesses love or does not possess it; hence it is futile to impose it as a precept. One cannot prescribe it, nor is there need to prescribe it. Love, which is the highest spiritual reality, is aroused by contact with value as soon as one is aware of the value.

True in this conception of love is the fact that good pleasure over value-in-general (*complacentia boni*) cannot be prescribed. The reason lies in the very character of our spiritual appetite, which, as the power to seek and to love, is drawn to the good whenever the good turns to it and invites it. If one has lost the power to perceive this loving call of value, of the good, he is no longer capable of any moral or religious act whatever.

And yet love in general, and divine love in particular, can be the object of a precept. God has shared everything with us so that we should be able to love. He gave us the capacity to perceive the call of his love, to experience the magnificence of His love and glory and with the aid of His grace to respond worthily. Without this supernatural faculty to know God as the sovereign good and supreme value and to respond in love, any precept to love God supernaturally would be futile.

God revealed Himself to us in Christ as love. Christ made manifest to us, in the incarnation and through His life on earth, the love of the Father and His love for the Father. And He infused into us through the Holy Spirit the power of love. Therefore it is possible that love be prescribed in the imitation of Christ.

Love of God as prescribed means several things: 1) for the sinner it means the obligation to remove the obstacles to supernatural love; namely, the disordered affection for created values. For one in the state of mortal sin, therefore, the command to love God implies the strictest obligation to do all that is in his power to regain God's love. He must demolish the false gods which he has honored heretofore; he must strive for a more profound sense of the love of God. As soon as he can, he must endeavor to make an act of contrition inspired by love. And he must prepare to receive the sacrament which restores him to the state of grace (*renewal of love*). Thus he must remove the obstacles to the re-infusion of the virtue of divine love into his soul.

The great commandment of love demands of us, first, not that we do acts of love, but that we be and remain in the state of love. "Abide in my love" (Jn 15:10). Of course to be in the state of love or abide in love also requires that we keep the commandments, and this is to do acts of love (cf. Jn 15:10).

2) Since only love that is recognized incites love in return, the precept of love presupposes most universally the obligation to meditate on God's love for us. We must ponder the majesty of God, all-good and all-lovable, as revealed to us in Christ; and this we must do with love in our hearts, for value manifests itself only to the eyes of love. The power of divine love, which is the infused virtue of charity, must be effective in our meditation on the marvels of God's love. We may be assured that, if we constantly ponder the motives of love, God's love for us and the blessedness of loving Him in return, we will never fail to keep the command of love. However, it is possible that by constant neglect of meditation on the love of God we lose the love of God entirely. It is a sad truth that one can withdraw from every value through total aversion of one's gaze and by closing one's heart to the thought of the good. Sad indeed is the plight of one who has thus turned from God!

Meditation must also be calculated to foster the sentiments, the passions, and affections which are a manifestation of love or incite the heart to love (such as joy, sadness, etc.). Unto this end one must make frequent acts of love. Of course it is not so much the frequency or number of these acts that is important, but the depth and earnestness of the meditation on the person and the example of Christ. Thus the ardor of our love will be interiorly inflamed.

3) The precept of love demands a free submission of the will. It is true that one cannot evade the impulse to love (insofar as love is good pleasure in value: *complacentia*), once one has been open to the loving rays of the higher value and thus has become aware of it. But God as the Supreme

Good cannot be satisfied with a *good pleasure* of any or every sort. He demands a *good pleasure* that is above all things. If we knew Him directly in His very essence here on earth, as He is known in the vision of the blessed, our *good pleasure* in Him would infallibly be sovereign. But He is known here obscurely by faith, and hence man is not necessarily totally taken up with Him. In consequence a simple love of good will (*amor complacentiae*) which is above all things is possible here on earth only insofar as all disordered pleasure in created values is suppressed by a free and active effort of the will. Finally—and this point is important—the simple love of good will (*amor complacentiae*) is still far from the full perfection of the love-act (above all, love for the person). Essential for such love is the act of freely surrendering the very power which loves to the one loved; i.e., by submission of will (this is *dilectio*).

In effect, the values of the good and the holy (the domains of the moral and the religious) are radically distinct from the value of the beautiful (domain of the aesthetic) precisely in demanding not merely the simple love of good will but also the gift of one's self. This is more than simple love of good will. It is an act of free decision which often requires great effort and struggle.

4) The precept of love demands loving action, the works of love. In fact, love as genuine *good pleasure* and authentic submission of will cannot even survive, much less grow or develop, in a being capable of moral action without the works of love. For we are pilgrims on earthly sojourn who do not merely repose in our love. We must continually pass from repose to action and from action to repose. Love in our hearts must incite us to action, and conversely loving action must unceasingly deepen and enrich the inner sentiment and disposition of love in our hearts.

Here we note again the essential bond which unites love and obedience (religion and morality). The great commandment of love in its classical biblical formulation clearly manifests the totality in the law of love. It claims and engages all the powers and forces of the soul, the purely spiritual as well as the sensible, and also our external efforts. God demands our entire being and our total effort: spirit, heart, and hand: the struggle for ever deeper understanding of divine things, the tender sentiments of our heart, the firm decision of our will, and the external action.

5) The precept of love is unceasing in its demand. It is absolute. We must always and absolutely avoid everything which might destroy love or

gradually lead to its extinction. But it also requires positively that we strive for the highest degree of charity toward God and neighbor as the ideal or goal (the precepted end) of our love. Love requires this as an end toward which we must strive, not as an obligation which we must carry out immediately and at all times (the precepted means) without regard for the degree of charity which we now possess. This means simply that we are bound to strive for Christian perfection, which consists in the fulfillment of the great commandment. But it does not imply that we must always be perfect, even at the very beginning of our spiritual life, nor does it at all imply that we must always and under all conditions do that which is the most perfect (objectively and in itself the most perfect).

9. The Perfection of Charity

The supreme and ultimate perfection of love shall be ours in heaven. Basically and essentially heaven is the tranquil, irrevocable, and perfect communion of love with God. Perfection of love in this world is the possession of Christian perfection (to be distinguished from the "state of perfection," a state which is given this name merely because it is particularly calculated to lead one to perfect love). The gift of wisdom in this life contributes most to the plenitude of charity. Wisdom gives us the savor of the divine love, the intimate sense for God's love. It enables us to penetrate deeply into the loving paternal heart of God and to experience ("taste") with such intimate appreciation the divine love that it captivates us in all our being.

The gift of wisdom in great part coincides with the gift of interior prayer, in particular with contemplation. It is the most important of all the gifts of the Holy Spirit. It not only perfects and completes charity, but all the other supernatural virtues as well. Above all it brings faith and the intellectual virtue of wisdom to fruition. Essentially, however, it is not so much in the intellectual order as in the practical.[70] Contemplation and the gift of wisdom are granted by the Holy Spirit to man not so much to increase his knowledge as to increase the ardor of his love. Contemplation is indeed a *knowing,* but it is rather the *knowing* of St. John, which is *knowing* in the most exalted sense, born of love and leading to love.

Mysticism, though it surely does not exclude private revelations, does not consist essentially in the reception of such favors but in the increase and perfection of charity in the soul. Interior prayer, which cannot progress without the gift of wisdom, and all the stages of mystical life are nothing other than stages of love.

In the gift of wisdom there is manifested most graphically the affinity between knowledge of value and love of value, between living faith and love, between contemplating and loving, between contemplation and beatitude. Under this gift of wisdom we may also include the burning zeal which the love of God enkindles in our hearts, and which in turn is constantly inflamed anew for the love of God by the distress of souls and the concern for their spiritual progress.

10. *Sins against the Love of God*

Every mortal sin is irreconcilable with the divine love. The two cannot exist in the same individual. Venial sin is "only" a momentary opposition to the fervor of charity (*fervor caritatis*). *Laxity* is opposition which has become habitual. The greatest opposition to charity in its essence is the sin of hatred of God. Such a sin would be impossible for man in a state of comprehensive knowledge of God. If man who is inclined to the good by his very nature would have an immediate intuition revealing God as the fulness of all good and the fulfillment of all desire, it would be intrinsically impossible for him to hate God. Even with our supernatural faith we know God only obscurely as reflected in a mirror (1 Cor 13:12). And still it is a perplexing mystery how man, created in the divine image and entirely ordered to God, can hate God even though he knows Him only imperfectly. Here we are at the very heart of the "mystery of iniquity." (2 Thes 2:7).

Hatred of God directly manifests in all its extreme horror what is indirectly and more or less obscurely contained in every mortal sin: hostility to God. One who commits a mortal sin sees in the commandments of God which he violates (ultimately in the holiness and justice of God) an obstacle to his own will. His evil decision manifests his preference for his own will in opposition to the just claim of God. Psychologically and morally there is a vast difference between this sin of weakness, which sees in God's commandments only the momentarily hated obstacle to the sinful love of an apparent, deceptive good, and the bold renunciation of God, the avowed declaration of hostility to God (*odium inimicitiae*).

The usual mortal sin is only opposition to a command or to an attribute of God (*odium abominationis*), whereas actual hatred of God is opposition to the divine person (*odium personae*). The Lord speaks (Jn 15) of this terrible hatred of the world against the Father, against Himself, the Father's own Ambassador, and against His disciples. It is impossible to interpret these declarations of Christ as though the hatred were merely due to a false conception of God, in a measure to a deplorable misunderstanding of some kind.[71] Of course there is a "hatred of God" which in reality is not directed against the true God at all, but rather, if correctly understood, only against an idol or false image of God. It may be no more than a violent rejection of religion falsely conceived or presented or of an unworthy minister of religion (basically therefore it might be a *hidden love* for the true God). But there does exist, according to the word of the Master and the testimony of ecclesiastical history, a veritable hatred of God which is not incited by a false conception of God but is rather itself the cause of a distortion of the true image of God, for hatred perverts and blinds the mind and imagination.

Christ explains the source of this hatred of God: the "spirit of this world" feels that God is its enemy (Jn 15:18ff.). Darkness hates the light. To a great extent even the antireligious hostility directed against the disciples and ministers of Christ does not arise so much from scandal over their frailty as from an enmity of God hidden in their hearts. (Surely it is advisable not to be indifferent regarding the effects of our own conduct, but rather to examine ourselves carefully in order to discover any sins or faults which may be the occasion for scorn of religion.) "If the world hates you, know that it has hated me before you. If you were of the world, the world would love what is its own" (Jn 15:18f.).

The more sharply and clearly the revelation of the *holy* contradicts the enemies of God, the more is their hatred inflamed, since they instinctively sense the opposition to their own spirit of evil. We see all too plainly in the lives of the saints that they were forced to share the lot of the Master. He was destined not only for the rise but also for the fall, the still deeper fall of many, and for a sign to be contradicted (Lk 2:34).

It is totally false to assert that the sins in the Church are entirely responsible for hostility to her. It is most unjust to charge that all opposition to religion, to Christ and the Church, is due to past and present weakness (the human side of the Church) in the Church, more specifically to the frailty of priests and religious. No truthful man will deny they must shoulder much of the blame. However, there is a marked tendency in some quarters today, which is tantamount to a mania, to hold the Church responsible for all hostility against God. These sapient critics might well ponder that Christ, the holiest of men, the wisest, the kindliest, came to live among us; the holiness of God and His loving friendship for men were incarnate in Him, and yet He was made the target of the most dreadful hatred of the enemies of God. And the reason was that they were already hostile in their hearts against His heavenly Father (Jn 15:23ff.).

As the coming of Christ was the occasion of the outburst of malice of sin (cf. Jn 15:22), so must the coming of the Holy Spirit, the Spirit of Love, through the testimony of the saints unmask sin in its vilest and most heinous form (in unbelief and hatred of God). "He will convict the world of sin" (cf. Jn 16:8ff.). Hatred of God is the most malicious of sins. It is the demoniacal sin, the sin which most directly offends the Holy Spirit.

BIBLIOGRAPHY

The Virtue of Divine Love

ADAM, A. *The Primacy of Love.* Translated by E. Noonan. Westminster, Md.: Newman Press, 1958. (Note: in connection with this work of Adam. *See* F. X. Remberger, C.SS.R. "Der hl. Alfons von Ligouri und der Primat der Liebe," *Klerusblatt,* 22 (1941), 273–276.)

ADAM, K. *Glaube und Liebe.* 2 ed., Regensburg, 1927.

ALSZEGHY, Z., S.J. *Grundformem der Liebe. Die Theorie der Gottesliebe bei dem heiligen Bonaventura.* Rom, 1946.

ANGERMAIR, R. *Das Band der Liebe.* Freiburg, 1940.

ASMUSSEN, H. *Das Geheimnis der Liebe.* Stuttgart, 1952.

BALDUCELLI, RUGGERO. *Il concetto teológico di carità attraverso le maggiori interpretazioni patristiche e medievali di I ad Cor. 13* (Catholic University Studies in Sacred Theology, 2d Series, 48) Washington: Catholic U. Press, 1950.

BERNARD OF CLAIRVAUX: *St. Bernard on the Love of God.* Translated by Terence Connolly. Gethsemani, Ky., 1943 (includes *De diligendo Deo,* and fragments from Bernard's sermons on the Ct.).

BORGMANN, K. *Vom Wesen und Walten christlicher Liebe.* Kolmar, 1944.

BRUNNER, A. "Gnade als Freiheit und Liebe," *GeistLeben,* 24 (1951), 429–439.

———. "Indische und christliche Gottesliebe," *StimmenZeit,* 159 (1955/57).

DELHAYE, PH. "La charité reine des vertus. Heurs et malheurs d'un thème classique," *VieSpirSupp,* 41 (1957), 135–170.

DESROCHES, H. C. "Le 'portrait' de la charité: 1 Cor 13," *VieSpir,* 74 (1946), 518–536.

DEUSSEN, A. *Das Geheimnis der Liebe im Weltplan Gottes.* Innsbruck, 1954.

Die deutsche Thomas-Ausgabe. Band 17: Die Liebe (Commentary by H. M. Christmann, O.P.). Heildelberg-Graz, 1959.

Die katholische Glaubenswelt. Vol. 2, 501–563.

EGENTER, R. *Die Lehre von der Gottesfreundschaft in der Scholastik und Mystik des 12 und 13 Jahrhunderts.* Augsburg, 1928.

ENDRES, J. C.SS.R. "Liebe als sittliche Grundmacht," *NO,* 2 (1947), 242–262.

FALANGA, ANTHONY J. *Charity the Form of the Virtues* (Catholic University Studies in Sacred Theology, 2nd Series, 18). Washington: Catholic U. Press, 1949.

GAGNEBET, M. R., O.P. "L'amour naturel de Dieu chez saint Thomas et ses contemporains," *RevThom,* 48 (1948), 394–446; 49 (1949), 31–102.

GALOT, J. *Der Geist der Liebe.* Mainz, 1960.

GARRIGOU-LAGRANGE, R., O.P. "La charité parfaite et les béatitudes," *VieSpir,* 46 (1936), 5–20.

GILSON, E. *Wisdom and Love in St. Thomas Aquinas.* Milwaukee, 1952.

GUARDINI, R. *Die Christliche Liebe. Eine Auslegung von 1 Kor 13,* Wuerzburg, 1940.

HAMM, J. A. *Die Macht der Liebe. Gespraech ueber Eros und Caritas.* Luzern, 1936.

HIRT, P. *Das Wesen der Liebe.* Immensee, 1943.

KAUP, J., O.F.M. *Die theologische Tugend der Liebe nach der Lehre des heiligen Bonaventura.* Muenster, 1927.

KLEIN, J. *Die Karitaslehre des Johannes Duns Skotus.* Muenster, 1926.

LANDGRAF, A. "Caritas und Widerstand gegen die Versuchungen nach der Lehre des ausgehenden 12 und beginnenden 13 Jahrhunderts," *Greg,* 24 (1943), 48–61; 327–346. (Now found in *Dogmengeschichte der Fruehscholastik.* Band II. Regensburg, 1953.)

LAVAUD, P., O.P. *Amour et perfection chrétienne selon S. Thomas d'Aquin et S. Francois de Sales.* Lyon, 1941.

LEMMONYER, A., O.P. "L'amour intéressé et pur amour," *VieSpir,* 58 (1939), 132–145.

MANDERS, H., C.SS.R. *De liefde in de spiritualiteit van Sint Alfonsus.* Bruessel-Amsterdam, 1947.

MERSCH, E., S.J. "Le plus grand des commandements," *NRTh,* 69 (1947), 1009–1026.

MUELLER, M. *Frohe Gottesliebe.* 2 ed., Freiburg i Br., 1936.

NYGREN, A. *Agape and Eros.* Translated by P. S. Watson. Philadelphia, Pa.: Westminster.

OHM, T., O.S.B. *Die Liebe zu Gott in den nichtchristlichen Religionen.* Krailling vor Muenchen, 1950; Titelauflage, Freiburg i. Br., 1957.

OUWERKERK, C. VAN *Caritas et ratio. Etude sur le double principe de la morale chrétienne d'après Saint Thomas d'Aquin.* Nimwegen, 1956.

PÉPIN, A. La Charité envers Dieu. Paris, 1952.

PRAT, F., VILLER, M., LANDGRAF, A. "La Charite," *BSp* (de Viller), Fasc. IX (Paris, 1940), 507–691.

PRZYWARA, E. *Liebe, der christliche Wesensgrund.* Freiburg i. Br., 1924.

———. *Demut, Geduld, Liebe: Die drei christlichen Tugenden.* Dusseldorf, 1960.

RAITZ VON FRENTZ, E. "Drei Typen der Liebe," *Schol,* 6 (1931), 1–41.

REUSS, J. "Die theologische Tugend der Liebe nach der Lehre des Richard von Mediavilla," *FranzStud* (1935), 11–43; 158–198. Separate publication: Muenster, 1935.

———. "Die theologische Tugend der Liebe nach der Lehre des Duns Skotus," *ZKathTh,* 58 (1934), 1–39.

SCHOLZ, H. *Eros und Agape.* Halle, 1936.

SERTILLANGES, A. D. *L'amour chrétien.* Paris, 1919.

SPICQ, C., O.P. *Agápe dans le Nouveau Testament I: Analyse des Textes.* Paris, 1958.

———. *Vie Morale et Trinité sainte chez saint Paul.* Paris, 1957.

STEGMUELLER, F. "Ueber die Moeglichkeit der natuerlichen Gottesliebe," *DivThom* (P) 38 (1935), 306–319.

SUSTAR, A. "De caritate apud S. Joannem," *VerbDom* (1950), 257–270.

TILLMANN, F. *Handbuch der katholischen Sittenlehre.* 3 ed. Vol. III, 143–191.

VAN ROEY, I. E. *De virtute charitatis.* Mecheln, 1929.

VARILLON, F. *Fénélon et le pur amour.* Paris, 1957.

WALTER, E. "Zur Ontologie der Liebe," *GeistLeben,* 22 (1949), 442–456.

————. *Wesen und Macht der Liebe. Beitraege zu einer Theologie der Liebe.* Freiburg, 1955.

————. "Furcht und Liebe," *GeistLeben,* 31 (1958), 443–459.

WARNACH, V., O.S.B. *Agape. Die Liebe als Grundmotiv der neutestamentlichen Theologie.* Duesseldorf, 1951 (with extensive bibliography).

WEINER, CL. *Recherches sur l'amour pour Dieu dans l'Ancien Testament.* Paris, 1957.

WINTERSWYL, L. A. *Mandatum Novum. Ueber Wesen und Gestalt christlicher Liebe.* Kolmar, 1941.

ZIEGLER, J. *Die Liebe Gottes bei den Propheten.* Muenster, 1930.

Additional Works in English

BERNARD OF CLAIRVAUX (Saint). *On the Love of God.* New York: Spiritual Books Assn., 1937.

COLIN, LOUIS, C.SS.R. *Love the Lord Thy God.* Westminster, Md.: Newman, 1956.

————. *Lamps of Love: a Recall to the Principle Source of Love.* Westminster, Md.: Newman, 1959.

D'ARCY, MARTIN C., S.J. *The Mind and Heart of Love.* Lion and Unicorn: a Study in Eros and Agápe. New York: Holt, 1947.

FRANCIS DE SALES (Saint). *The Love of God.* London: B. Herder, 1931.

GILLEMAN, GÉRARD, S.J. *The Primacy of Charity in Moral Theology.* Translated by W. Ryan and A. Vachon. Westminster, Md.: Newman, 1959.

GRAHAM, AELRED, O.S.B. *The Love of God.* New York: Longmans, 1939. (Image Books) New York: Doubleday, 1959.

GREEN, ANDREW, O.S.B. *The Love of God.* St. Louis: B. Herder, 1946.

GROSSOUW, WILLEM K. M. *Spirituality of the New Testament* (Cross and Crown Series of Spirituality, 19) St. Louis: B. Herder, 1961.

JOHANN, ROBERT O., S.J. *The Meaning of Love.* Westminster, Md.: Newman, 1955.

LEFEBVRE, GEORGE, O.S.B. *The Mystery of God's Love.* New York: Sheed and Ward, 1961.

*LEWIS, CHIVE STAPLES. *The Four Loves.* New York: Harcourt-Brace, 1960.

MAGEEAN, ROBERT, C.SS.R. *God's Infinite Love and Ours.* Dublin: Clonmore and Reynolds, 1957.

O'NEILL, PATRICK. *Divine Charity: Its Nature and Necessity.* Dublin: Gill, 1918.

PAUL-MARIE OF THE CROSS, O.C.D. *Spirituality of the Old Testament,* Vol. 1 (Cross and Crown Series of Spirituality, 18). St. Louis: B. Herder, 1961. (N.B. Revelation, Faith, Charity.)

SOLOVIEV, VLADIMIR. *The Meaning of Love.* London: Bles, 1945.

SULLIVAN, JOHN J., S.J. *The Commandment of Love.* New York: Vantage Press, 1956.

THOMAS AQUINAS (Saint). *On Charity* (Medieval Philosophical Texts in Translation, n. 10). Milwaukee: Marquette Univ. Press, 1960.

The Virtues and States of Life (Theology Library, v. 4). ed. A. M. Henry, O.P. Chicago: Fides, 1957. "Faith" (A. Liégé), pp. 1–59; "Hope" (B. Olivier), pp. 61–126; "Charity" (B. Olivier), pp. 127–208; "The Virtue of Religion" (A. Mennessier), pp. 393–444; "The Social Virtues" (M. Gerland), pp. 445–485 (on obedience, piety, liberality.)

Periodical Literature in English

BARROSSE, T. "Unity of the Two Charities in Greek Patristic Exegesis," *TheolS,* 15 (Sept., 1954), 355–88.

————. "Relationship of Love to Faith in St. John," *TheolS*, 18 (Dec., 1957), 538–59.

BURRELL, D. "Indwelling: Presence and Dialogue," *TheolS*, 22 (March, 1961), 1–17.

BOND, L. M. "Comparison between Human and Divine Friendship," *Thm* (Jan., 1941), 54–94.

COOPER, J. M. "Aspect of Perfect Love of God," *AER*, 115 (Aug., 1946), 101–20.

D'AMATO. "One Commandment," *CrCr*, 4 (Dec., 1952), 405–20.

DE LETTER, P. "Perfect Contrition and Perfect Charity," *TheolS*, 7 (Dec., 1946), 507–24.

————. "Hope and Charity in St. Thomas," *Thm*, 13 (April–July, 1950), 204–48.

————. "Sanctifying Grace and Our Union with the Holy Trinity," *TheolS*, 13 (March, 1952), 33–58.

GILL, H. V. "Love, the Philosophy of Life," *IMo*, 68 (March–May, 1940), 131–41, 188–98, 251–62, 310–14, 357–64, 428–33, 468–74, 537–49, 587–91, 655–60; 69 (July, 1941), 21–6, 75–80, 130–33, 193–99, 253–62, 241–51.

GLEASON, R. W. "Charity as the Form of the Virtues," *ITQ*, 24 (April, 1957), 144–53.

GREGORY, T. S. "Eros and Agape," *Mo*, 11 (April, 1954), 221–34. (This is a review of Nygren: *Agape and Eros*.)

GUMBRUGER, C. "Primacy of Charity in Franciscan Theology," *FrancStud*, 24 (Sept., 1943), 209–40.

PHILBIN, W. J. "Scholastic Teaching on the Nature of Charity," *IER*, 42 (July, 1936), 20–46.

SCHNEIDER, J. "Charity, Divine Friendship," *AER*, 104 (June, 1941), 481–91.

Part Two:

THE VIRTUE OF RELIGION

CHAPTER FIVE

WORSHIP IN SPIRIT AND IN TRUTH

I. OBJECT AND NATURE OF RELIGION IN BIBLICAL TEACHING

THE first and highest end and purpose of creation and redemption is the external glory of God. In His external works God Himself manifested His holiness, His majesty, His name to men. Christ is the all-holy God dwelling in our midst. By this very fact He demands loving adoration of His holiness. In Christ creation has received its High Priest with whom it could share in the most tremendous adoration and glorification of the triune God. Christians, sanctified by the Holy Spirit, incorporated in the priesthood of Christ, may and must look upon the glory of God as their sovereign honor and their most consecrated vocation. The zeal of Christ for the honor of His Father consumed Him. He came to seek "the glory of the one who sent him" (Jn 7:18; cf. 8:50). Zeal for the house of God, for the accomplishment of tasks in the divine honor, consumed Him even to the point of sacrificing His life on the Cross. The great and consuming concern of the disciple who through the Sacrifice of the Master participates in the glory of the divine life must be the honor and glory of God. •

Christ brought to us the full revelation of the divine name. With Him and through Him we may call God our Father. And the honor implies the most sacred duty to offer God the filial cult of adoring love. The presupposition, the object, the content of the virtue of religion is expressed primarily in three key concepts: the *Sanctity* (*gadosh, hágios, sanctus, sacer, sacrum*), the *Name* ("*shem*"), the *Glory* (*kabód, dóxa*) of God.

In the following pages we shall pursue our inquiry particularly into this latter biblical concept. But if we single out this one concept, it is always to place it in the light of the holiness of God[1] which forces man to his knees and at the same time beatifies him. And we never fail to view it likewise in the light of the *Name of God*[2] revealed to us with the most intimate and personal of revelations.

1. *The Divine Glory in the Old Testament*

Kabód Yahweh, translated by the expression *dóxa theoû* in the

Septuagint, means the glory and majesty of God manifesting itself, "the divine glory, which reveals the nature of God and His deeds in His creation, which fills the heavens as well as the earth."[3] Wherever God acts and reveals Himself, there His *kabód,* the reflection of His magnificence demanding recognition, manifests itself. On the great day of the revelation of the holiness and love of God Moses and the people see the majesty and glory of God (*kabód Yahweh*) as a "consuming fire." For the people it is an unbearably brilliant light and at the same time a cloud of terrifying darkness, a clouded revelation of the holiness of God (Ex 24:16ff.). Moses was permitted to enter into the "cloud" and harken directly to the word of God. He was permitted to hear the name of God and to perceive the sacred word of grace: "You are my intimate friend" (Ex 33:17). But when his heart welled up within him and he asked: "Do let me see your glory" (*kabód*), the Lord answered him, "I will make all my beauty pass before you, and in your presence I will pronounce my name. . . . But my face you cannot see, for no man sees me and still lives" (Ex 33:18ff.). God Himself holds His hand over Moses to protect him and shield his eyes during the revelation of His glory and majesty (Ex 33:22f.).

This passage, as well as that recording the vision inaugurating the prophetic mission of Isaias (Is 6), shows very clearly how the revelation of the glory and the majesty of God, specifically of the holiness of God, is a mystery which terrifies and at the same time beatifies (*mysterium tremendum et fascinosum*). It brings the bliss of true beatitude and prostrates man in respect and adoration.

The *kabód Yahweh* is not merely the revelation of a truth but a revelation which appeals to the whole man, for it means life or death to him. The glory and majesty of God is a manifestation of the invisible God made really visible, a revelation inciting man to jubilation or to terror (cf. Ex 16:10; Nm 14:10). When God makes known His glory and majesty, he always invites the response of man: "Give glory to my name" (Mal 2:2; Jer 13:16; Is 42:8ff.). To give honor to God is not necessarily offering something which as such is new to God. It means a fitting response which is owing to God, a response in adoring recognition of the glorious revelation and manifestation of the majesty and holiness of God: to the God of *kabód* (glory and majesty) there must be given *kabód* (honor, praise of glory) in return (Jer 13:16).

Wherever the majesty and glory of God is mightiest, where it comes into contact with man because God condescends to approach our hearts:

above the holy tabernacle, in the temple, above the ark of the covenant (Ex 40:32ff.; Nm 9:15ff.; 3 Kgs 8:10ff.), there man must also pay Him honor. There man caught up by His majesty (*kabód*) must prostrate himself before God in praise and cult. The tremendous majesty of creation, the splendor of the storm, all the magnificent manifestations of nature are revelations of the glory of God and a direct summons to adore the infinite holiness of God. This we note particularly in many striking passages in the Psalms (e.g., 17; 18; 28). The presence of Yahweh in the sacred places of cult or wherever He reveals His glory is a demand for the response of adoration due to Him, an absolutely exclusive demand, for God is a "jealous" God. The first commandment lays the sharpest stress on this worship of God: "I, the Lord, your God, am a jealous God" (Ex 20:5). Worship of idols, sharing the majesty and glory of God in the visible creation, awakens the "jealousy," that is the zealous wrath of God (Ez 8:3). "I am the Lord, this is my name; my glory (that is, His *kabód* and recognition of it) I give to no other." No one may erect a throne alongside His (Is 42:8; 48:11, cf. also the words of the *Magnificat*, Lk 1:46ff.).

The judgments of God in condemnation of His people, always mitigated by the promise of salvation to some who shall be spared, flow from God's zeal for His own honor (4 Kgs 19:31ff.; Is 9:7; 37:32). The divine wrath is enkindled like a fire (Ps 78:5). God will be aroused by the fierce and flaming wrath of His jealousy because due honor was denied Him (So 3:8; 1:18; Ez 16:38). Great is the divine concern for God's own people. "I am intensely jealous for Sion, stirred to jealous wrath for her" (Za 8:2). For the glory of His majesty is reflected in His people. The chosen people are His *kabód*, His glory (Za 2:8f.; Is 43:7). Zeal for the chosen race is a type of the providential guidance of God over His Church, which is a far greater manifestation of His loving majesty and the community of those who are sanctified unto His glory.

2. Worship of God in the New Testament

In Christ the glory (*dóxa*), the honor, the majesty of the Father was made visible: "And we saw his glory—glory as of the only-begotten of the Father." The transfiguration on Tabor manifests in splendor the *dóxa* of the Father and Christ to the disciples. It is the anticipation of the glory of Christ in the resurrection and in the parousia. "They saw his glory"

(Lk 9:32). The *dóxa* of God (the divine glory, the divine power revealing the divine glory, the visible reflection of the divine light) and the *dóxa* of Christ are essentially connected in a manner which was incomprehensible in the Old Testament. Not only is God glorified (*doxazetai:* Jn 13.31f.) in Christ through His bloody death on the Cross, but God will uniquely glorify Himself in Him by communicating to Him (in His human manifestation) His own *doxa,* His own proper eternal glory.

Without doubt Christ on earth is in legitimate possession of the *dóxa* of God ("Father, glorify me with thyself, with the glory that I had with thee before the world existed": Jn 17:5), and yet He begs the Father to glorify Him and reveal His *dóxa* in Him (Jn 17:1, 5). And the title of this unique revelation of the glory of God in Him, which is precisely the *dóxa* He possessed from all eternity with the Father, is the glorification of the Father on earth through the work (His death on the Cross) the Father has sent Him to accomplish: "I have glorified thee on earth; I have accomplished the work that thou hast given me to do" (Jn 17:4). The passage in St. John 17:5, "the glory that I had with thee," sheds a very illuminating light on the biblical concept of *dóxa.* This passage, as perhaps no other in the whole Bible, makes clear that all manifestation of the sovereignty of God reflects the invisible glory of the Trinity. But the particular stress not merely in this passage but in the whole Old and New Testaments is on the external manifestation of that glory.

In Matthew and Mark there is mention of the *dóxa* of Christ merely in reference to the parousia (to the exalted Christ). In Luke there is also mention of the *dóxa* in connection with the birth of Christ (the *dóxa* of the Father and the newly-born Infant through the appearance of the angels in the shining splendor of God's light) and in the account of the transfiguration on Tabor. The *dóxa* of the Father and of Christ is revealed in His miracles and His manifestations of sovereign greatness (Jn 1:12, 14; 2:11; 11:4; 11:40) to those who believe. In a special manner the glory and honor of Christ begins with the passion, the supreme priestly work of the glorification of God which inaugurates the eternal, fully visible glory of Christ (Jn 17). Equal honor is given to the Lamb and to Him who sits upon the throne. "Worthy is the Lamb who was slain to receive power and divinity and wisdom and strength and honor and glory (*dóxa*) and blessing. . . . To him who sits upon the throne, and to the Lamb, blessing and honor and glory (*dóxa*) and dominion, forever and ever" (Ap 5:12f.).

The glory (*dóxa*) is revealed in His resurrection and in the full and final completeness (Mk 13:26).

From the biblical teaching on the glory (*dóxa*) of God the following conclusions can be drawn regarding the imitation of Christ: Christ is more than an example or model for the disciple in his attitude toward the glory of God the Father. He is our High Priest through whom and with whom we pay due honor to the Father. As co-possessor of the divine *dóxa* (even in the glorified human nature which belongs to the divine person) with the Father and in the unity of the Holy Spirit, He is the object of our adoration. To the whole Christ in His eternal glory we pay the highest cult (*latria*). We pray in the Canon of the Mass: "Through Him, and with Him, and in Him, is to Thee, God the Father Almighty, in the union of the Holy Spirit, all honor and glory."

Moreover, the *dóxa* passages, referring to Christ in the New Testament in a manner which the Old Testament reserves for the all-holy God (Heb 13:21; 1 Pt 4:11; Ap 5:12f.; 1 Cor 2:8; Jas 2:1; Ti 2:13), are highly significant not only for our Christology but also for our whole attitude toward Christ in our worship. The Christ of our cult is the Lord of power and glory, and nowhere more perfectly than in the holy Mass, which is worship in its supreme perfection, with adoration of the Father in and through Christ. It is Christ's own tribute of glory paid to the Father, for in the Mass He offers Himself to the Father. It is at the same time that heavenly radiance in which the humiliation and obedience of Christ and His disciples is offered in the divine honor. It is glory revealed, glory rendered. Christ who adores is now enveloped with the very splendor of Godhead, a glory given to Him because of His passion and death mystically renewed in the Mass. In the splendor of the Mass the way of humiliation and obedience leading to the exaltation and glory with Christ beckons the disciple who participates in these heavenly mysteries. How magnificently this treasure of grace points to the eternal glories (eschatological orientation of the Mass)!

From what we have just said it is evident that the object of the virtue of religion is the sanctity, the exaltation and magnificence, the honor[4] of God, the splendor of His holiness as it is reflected in creation, in His tremendous epiphanies, and most especially in Christ and through Christ. Christ is our way in the worship of God for we come to the Father through the Son made man. We worship in union with Christ the High

Priest, in union with His interior priestly sentiments, with His prayer, His works and sufferings, above all with His obedience. Intimately united with His perfect obedience, the disciple of the Master gives glory to the triune God.

The Christian looks forward with a great hope of beholding the majesty of God and the Lamb in eternity (Is 35:2; 66:18; Ap 14:1ff.; 15:2ff.; 19:6ff.). But far more awaits him. He is to receive in dependence on Christ, even in his own body, a share in the glory (*dóxa*) of God, which will transfigure him for all eternity. He will share in the exaltation of Christ and in His beatitude forever. God's word in the inspired passage, "I will not give my glory to another" (Is 42:8; 48:11), means that no one may lay claim to honor or glory which does not ultimately belong to God. Hence one who has in all things "given God the honor" will experience in himself a manifestation and reflection of that same glory (the *kabód*, the *dóxa*). "The just will shine forth like the sun" (Mt 13:43). Their ecstatic splendor on the Day of the Lord and in heaven for eternity is a reflection of the glory they have given to God, the wages of their justice attested in their lives: they have sought the honor of God in all things.[5] "The body of our lowliness" will be refashioned by Christ "conforming it to the body of his glory (*dóxa*)" (Phil 3:21) in the resurrection.

The light and warmth of God's love for His elect will be fully revealed in the Second Coming of Christ in His glory (Rom 8:18, 21). But through the Holy Spirit, the Spirit of Holiness and Majesty, infused into our souls by divine grace, the glory (*dóxa*) of God is already active within us (1 Pt 4:14), establishing the "inner man" (Eph 3:16). The Holy Spirit is the pledge and earnest of our participation in the glory (*dóxa*). "But we all, with faces unveiled, reflecting as in a mirror the glory (*dóxa*) of the Lord, are being transformed into his very image from glory to glory (*apò dóxes eis dóxan*), as through the Spirit of the Lord" (2 Cor 3:18).

In his noted passage to Corinthians (2 Cor 3:7ff.), St. Paul makes it very clear that our assurance for the participation and most specifically our hope for a full partnership in the loving majesty of the Lord is our holy service. Our hope rests principally in the *diakonía* (the sacred ministry) or sacred service for the glory of God in the kingdom of Christ. If the splendor of God's glory reflected in the countenance of Moses shone with light, how much more splendid must be the radiance of the glory (*dóxa*) of God and His Anointed in the countenance of the servant of the New Covenant. It is not evident nor immediate in this life, but it is already present and in some way expressed. Even in this life there is something in the countenance of those in grace presaging the splendor of the body in the glory of God which is to come.

Paul was converted through the apparition of the "Lord of glory" on the road to Damascus. Thus began his vocation to the apostolate. Henceforth his apostolic ministry looms mightily in the light of the glorious majesty of God, in the radiance of Christ risen in glory. His theology of baptism and of the indwelling of the Holy Spirit shows every Christian and particularly every apostolic Christian how his life is illumined and caught up by the honor and glory of God.

3. Worship of God and Veneration of the Saints

Adoration in the strictest sense of supreme worship (the cult of *latria*) belongs to God alone. He alone is holy, He alone is Lord, He alone is supreme (from the *Gloria* of the Mass). To him alone belongs supreme honor and glory (*dóxa*). The words of praise extolling the greatness of God (doxologies) found in Scripture and in the liturgy do not ask that the *dóxa* be given to God in the sense that He may possess it, but that He possesses it and that we and all creatures must exult in His greatness. We must recognize His greatness and sing His praises.

Adoration is our response of worship to the revelation of the majesty of God. But since the sovereignty of God is a sovereignty of Love revealed to us in creative and sanctifying love, our response must be an adoring love. And this loving adoration and adoring love must fill all our acts. Love, turning to our neighbor and the world of creation, must always be adoring love.

The sacred humanity of Jesus must be honored with *latria* or latreutic cult, for through the hypostatic union it is filled with the majesty of God, made evident above all in the glorious resurrection. Christ, risen and glorified Lord of heavenly majesty, whose holy passion is the supreme manifestation of the sovereign love of God, reflects the fulness of the Father's might and glory in the splendor of the resurrection and ascension. And therefore there is owing to Him all our adoring love on the title of His passion and death. This is also for us—as for Him—the way to exaltation and heavenly glory. He not only shows us how to adore the Father, He permits us to unite with Him in the true and worthy adoration of the glorious and loving majesty of God.

The immediate object of the virtue of religion is not the intimate glory, the hidden glory of God, but His *kabód*, His *dóxa*, that is to say, the exterior radiance or reflection of His inner divine holiness. It is the presence of His sanctity and loving majesty in the work of creation and sanctification. It follows that God can and must also be honored in His elect, in those whom He has sanctified, in those who have consecrated themselves entirely to the service of His glorious and loving majesty and in whom that glory already radiates with a splendor that can never be lost. These are the saints. To them we may apply the words: "Awesome in his sanctuary is God, the God of Israel" (Ps 67:36).

In the light of this truth we can appreciate more fully the cultal significance of the dogma of the bodily assumption of Mary into heaven. The Mother of God is in heavenly glory with her Son. She is glorified in body and soul. According to the biblical conception of the glory of Christ (the *dóxa*), the body is the term of the glorification, the focus of the splendor of grace reflected from the divine majesty. Wherefore the full glorification of the Mother of God also in her body is the foundation and in a certain sense also the prerequisite of the special solemnity of the cult owing to her (*hyperdulia*): the splendor of the divine glory and the cult due to it should be proportionate to each other. The more the blessed in heaven reflect in their sanctity the loving grandeur of God, the more effectively do they orientate us toward the divine glory. And the more immediately is the honor we pay to them in accordance with their merits a proper act of praise, a hymn of praise to the majesty of "God and the Lamb."

All that which God reserves for His own honor and glory here on earth through blessing or consecration merits a sacred veneration: this includes holy places, sacred articles or vessels; more particularly those who are consecrated for a sacred service or ministry, such as the priesthood, those who dedicate themselves in a special manner to the glory of God and to His love (the state of those consecrated to God, those in vows, the religious). It includes most of all those who in their own lives have entirely realized the fulfillment of the divine consecration conferred on them in the sacraments of baptism, confirmation, holy orders. These are the saints (*sancti*). As consecrated to God (*sacer Deo*), every Christian is an object meriting a degree of reverence or respect. This belongs to him by the very reception of baptism.

II. DIVINE HONOR IN RELATION TO RELIGION AND MORALITY

1. *Meaning of the Term "Religion"*

The term *religion* is derived from the Latin word *religio*. We use it to express worship or cult, honor paid to God, the acts and the virtue of religion, as is evident from the foregoing pages. But the term constantly gives rise to misunderstandings and misconceptions. Thus one may look upon the essence of religion as simply and exclusively the divine worship or cult, only to be perplexed by the fact that St. Thomas and with him most modern moral theologians place this same virtue of religion in the realm of the moral virtues. If in consequence we should form a false impression and reduce religion entirely to morality, how could we continue to look upon religion as the virtue of the divine worship or cult?

The word religion (*religio*) means:

1) Union or community with God. This community or communion with God arises from the ineffable condescension of love on God's part and the response of love which this condescension incites and demands on our part. This community consists of far more than words and love. Through sanctifying grace it becomes a community of supernatural life. The dialog which binds man to God is basically perfected in the theological virtues and their acts. Therefore the essence of religion is found above all in these virtues. Religion is the bond (*ligare, relegere*) uniting us with God through the God-formed life of grace and the personal encounter with God in the acts of the theological virtues.

2) Religion in the more restricted and rather technical sense of the term designates the cult or worship rendered to God, whether it be public or private. By contrast with the previous meaning just given, we may say that the worship of God or divine cult is not the very essence of religion but rather flows from it. Religion is essentially the life in communion with God which demands cult or worship as its direct manifestation. Hence we may say that religion as cult or worship is the first mandate of religion, which is life in union with God. The two notions form the complex or more inclusive concept of religion. Therefore in the integral sense religion is the filial relation with God expressed in cult, giving Him honor and glory.

3) We may add a third note, that of community. Religion in this sense is the community of those who have the same faith and cult. Thus we may ask: what religion do you profess? Summing up, we can give a definition clearly containing all the above: religion is the bond with God mutually joining together in community of faith and worship all those who are thus united with God and acknowledge their union with Him and with one another. Nothing manifests and sustains this common bond more perfectly than community of cult. The Mystical Body of Christ forming one community in the life with God, which is the very essence of religion, offers to God the perfect cult of sacrifice and sacraments.

4) The Church in her canon law uses the Latin term *religio* to designate religious orders or communities or societies. In English we also use the term *religion* in this same canonical sense. More frequently we speak of "entering religion" in the sense of entering a religious community. In this sense of the term we also speak of "life in religion," of "religious," or of "religious men and women," when we are treating of the life or activity or of the members in such communities. Religious are Christians who have consecrated themselves in a special manner by means of a public act (vow) to divine cult, specifically to service in God's honor.

5) Religion in the full and perfect sense of the term is a personal bond of unity with God and a mutual unity in solidarity with all those who are thus likewise united with Him.

2. The Virtue of Religion and the Theological Virtues

In the light of what we have just said, the theological virtues must be looked upon as the foundation and source of the virtue of religion. Religion flows from the divine virtues as a property or essential demand from the essence or nature. Faith is an indispensable prerequisite, love is the very soul and inner form of the virtue of religion. "Charity is the direct and immediate principle by which man gives himself over to God by clinging to Him through a certain spiritual union. But that by which man devotes certain works of cult to God is directly due to religion, mediately however to charity, which is the principle of religion."[6] "The theological virtues have as their proper object the act concerning God Himself and therefore by their command cause the act of religion, which produces certain effects in the order referring to God."[7] "Religion is a certain protestation of faith, hope, and love by which man is basically ordered to God."[8]

The inner spirit of dedication (*devotio,* interior religion or worship) is the very heart of external religion. The interior spirit of devotion as loving disposition for "worship of God in spirit and in truth" is conceivable only as the fruit of divine love. Without charity and the interior spirit and disposition flowing essentially from it there can indeed be external and legal performance of the acts of worship, but not the virtue of religion with the fully worthy and fruitful acts of cult.

It is true that the Christian who is deprived of the state of grace can perform the external acts of cult demanded by the laws of God and the Church. Strictly speaking, he fulfills the law. But since his acts do not flow from the virtue of religion, they have only the value of external legal acts performed with a very imperfect and very incomplete obedience. They fall far short of the true acts of religion which God demands, for God wants the honor and glory flowing from interior virtue. He demands an adoration in "spirit and in truth" (Jn 4:24). There is always present in the cultal act of the Christian in mortal sin the objective sacramental consecration (due to the sacramental mark), but the absence of the interior spirit of consecration constitutes a flagrant contradiction to that same sacramental consecration wrought by the Spirit of God in the sacrament.

To be truly fruitful and pleasing to the infinite majesty and holiness of God, our external acts of religion must be made possible, on the one hand, through the objective consecration to God (by the sacramental mark of baptism, confirmation, holy orders, and the other consecrations and blessings of God and the Church). And, on the other hand, they must be manifestations of faith, hope, and love flowing from a true interior spirit of loving and reverential dedication.

3. The Virtue of Religion and the Moral Virtues

The theological virtues do not of their very nature or essence demand external activity in the world. Of themselves they are rather dialog with God, word and gift of God. And on man's part they are value-response immediately directed to God. Only secondarily do they require an activity in the world which corresponds to the dialog. Only secondarily does there flow from them the value-laden imperative to suitable action in the world. According to the traditional terminology of moral theology these duties imposed mediately in space and time by the theological virtues constitute the proper domain of the moral virtues.

It is sound and reasonable to reckon religion among these moral virtues: this virtue does not directly and immediately give the value-response to the hidden holiness of God as do the theological virtues. Its object is rather the holiness of God as manifested externally. In its content there must be a task for man in space and time, in the body and in the community, a task which belongs to it necessarily and immediately. Such is the nature of the virtue of religion by contrast with the strictly theological virtues. It follows that we may correctly place it among the moral virtues.

This line of reasoning for placing religion and the divine worship under the moral virtues and obligations is not by far as convincing as it might first seem. For that matter even the theological virtues themselves do not exist entirely apart from the visible experiences in this world of time and space. Faith consents to the visible manifestation of God in the flesh, continued in the structure of the Church and the "sacraments of faith." Christian hope turns to the "invisible realities," but still because of the visible pledge in the mysteries of the Incarnation. And divine love for us pilgrims on this earthly sojourn is anchored in the visible covenant of love between Christ and the Church. Nor can it in principle be torn from this sacred basis. From this it is evident that the theological virtues reach out to meet the virtue of religion establishing the foundation for its extension into time and space. This very expansion, of course, is broadened and accentuated progressively by the virtue of religion. But it cannot be denied that the virtue of religion and the divine worship which belongs to it are as closely allied to theological virtue as to the moral.

Moral theology, true to its own traditional principles, never has presented the virtue of religion as moral in the sense of exclusively moral. There never was the slightest connotation of such pure morality as was inaugurated by the divorce of the moral from the religious (in humanism), a divorce which was aggravated by the so-called autonomous morality (Kant), and completed by the modern ethical morality[9] which combated and suppressed religion and sought to supplant it altogether. Unfortunately the wide-spread influence of this baneful attitude in modern times penetrated even into Catholic circles.

According to the Christian teaching morality is not separate from religion. Nor can it be characterized as having perspective and motivation directed to man alone rather than to God. On the contrary, true morality may be said to accept all earthly tasks only in their relation to God. If the *religious* in the narrow sense of the term is *response* directed immediately to God, then the *moral* is *response-ability* as to the spatial-temporal before God and toward God. For the religious man morality is a summons issuing from the immediate encounter with God. It is a call for action in the world. It is not merely a task commanded by God but a task which must be ordered entirely to the glory of God.

From all this it is clear that the virtue of religion, far more than any of the other moral virtues, essentially and immediately directs our acts to God. This virtue flows totally and utterly from inner submission and dedication to the glory of God. But surely the honor and glory of God lays claim to far more than mere inner response to value in holy awe and love. As manifestation of the majesty of God, by its very nature it also claims the recognition of worship carried out in acts of religion, acts which manifest themselves exteriorly and enter into time and space. If "creation is filled with the majesty of God," the virtue which responds to this tremendous reality must manifest itself in external recognition of the divine glory. In adoration and praise man gives expression to it by raising his voice in jubilation. In words that resound, in lights that glow, the thoughts and sentiments of his heart offer praise to God. This is the true content of the virtue of religion. Because man and the world—such is God's part—bask in the light of the divine majesty, but also—such is man's part—because man and the world are stripped of the glory of God through sin (cf. Rom 3:23: "all have sinned and have need of the glory of God"), therefore we are confronted with the task laid down for us by the holiness of God: "Be holy," sanctify yourselves in the Lord, and sanctify the world in the Lord!

The doctrine—we cannot speak of it as absolutely convincing—that religion is a moral virtue implies that acts of religion must enter into the temporal sequence of our lives. They must form the warp and woof of the whole texture of our earthly existence including the communal life among men (thus is the community sanctified). Consequently it belongs essentially to our activity in the world to fulfill the moral tasks imposed by the virtue of religion. In other words we face the world with a moral task which flows from the virtue of religion. This assumption can have only one meaning in the light of the following principle: our entire activity in the world must have a religious formation, for all our acts must be ordered to the loving majesty of God. This means that all our *moral* tasks are at the same time *religious* tasks.

The cultal task of the truly religious man is most intimately bound up with the moral task in its totality, and yet one may rightly distinguish it from the sphere of the moral taken in the strict sense, which requires that man in all his acts observe and fulfill the grand laws of the order of creation.

This division or cleavage between religion and morality in the narrower sense is brought out very clearly by the attempt of the proponents of autonomous morality and of neo-pagan humanism to divorce the domain of religion altogether from the moral domain and to explain and develop the latter entirely on its own principles. In view of this situation and the mentality of contemporary thinkers, we can justify and welcome certain clarifications and distinctions made by some Catholic authors in this area. The effort—something of a departure from the past—is being made to set up distinct boundaries and limits between the realm of the interior moral world and the actual religious sphere. The attempt to distinguish and relate the two spheres is particularly concerned with finding an adequate terminology setting forth both the limits and the mutual relations of the two domains.

The noted attempt of Rudolph Otto has the advantage that his distinctions coincide essentially with the biblical distinction of the two tables of the Law. This author distinguishes between *sacral ethos* and *ethos of sanction*. The *sacral ethos* embraces both the ethos of pure response to value ordered immediately to God (the theological virtues, and with them the cultivation of the right interior dispositions and attitudes toward God) and the ethos of cult which flows directly from it, the cultal recognition of the majesty of God in space and time, in the body and in the community.

The *ethos of sanction* would embrace the common human area of temporal obligation exclusive of the obligation of cult. It would consist in the observance of the laws of nature, that is to say, in obeying the exigencies imposed by the order found in created beings. From the viewpoint of content (*materialiter*), even if not from that of its foundation and direction of purpose (*formaliter*), the *ethos of sanction* can be conceived apart from any appeal to religion—precisely because cult as such lies outside the scope of this ethos. (We say it can be conceived *to an extent* apart from appeal to religion.) But when religion enters into this exclusively moral ethos, it imparts a *sanction*. Religion furnishes a foundation or basis for the duties inherent in the moral realm. It invests these duties with a special vigor and vitality and orientates them to the glory of God. It makes the realm of the moral *sacred*, though it does not (at least not directly and immediately) stamp the domain as interiorly and in essence *cultal*.

Such terminology with its distinction of realms or domains is adapted to the contemporary attitudes. The situation of man today is such that his whole morality is built up on a non-religious basis. It does not bear the stamp and impress of religion. Today man approaches the domain of religion with an entirely profane (as opposed to sacral) morality, a morality which at best is non-religious or pre-religious, if it is not altogether irreligious. If he should enter into the realm of religion, then his ethos, which may well be very earnest and largely in agreement with the laws of nature, would receive a sanction (vigor) and a consecration (orientation toward God) from religion. Even believers in great part have been influenced profoundly by the severance of religion from morality and their moral life is often only superficially affected by the spirit of religion.

Though St. Thomas includes among the moral virtues that portion of sacral ethics which deals with the obligations of worship, with the cultal celebration in the divine honor in space and time, in body and community, this is very far from *moralism* (restriction or suppression of the religious by the moral). It is much more correct to say, on the contrary, that he gives to the whole moral realm the clearest and sharpest religious orientation. Otherwise it would be unthinkable to insert into the realm of moral virtue the obligations and duties which directly and immediately are concerned with divine cult. In Christian ethics not only the virtue of cult but all the moral virtues have God Himself as their end and goal. The immediate object of moral conduct is indeed an *earthly* (that is, a spatial-temporal) task imposed by God and ordered to God. The virtue of cult is therefore to be distinguished from the other moral virtues by a closer and firmer bond of orientation toward God. But we should not forget that our moral theology treats all the moral virtues as supernatural and animated by the virtue of charity.

For this reason I cannot agree with the view of Richard Egenter,[10] who places a natural virtue of religious reverence alongside the theological virtues and subordinate to the virtue of cult. In my opinion any such effort to preserve the essentially religious orientation of Christian morality is not strictly necessary, for in the present supernatural order the religious attitude of man is truly virtue (in harmony with the order of being) only insofar as it coincides with the life in God through the three theological virtues and the correct and proper worship of God. This is possible, of course, only with the assistance of divine grace. Though we agree with Egenter that the attitude of reverence must be present in the acts of worship and in the three theological virtues and that without a natural reverence man is altogether incapable of religion, we see no need for a special and distinct natural virtue of religious reverence.

4. The Cultal Character of Christian Morality

The choir of moral virtues, according to the teaching of Thomas Aquinas, is directed by the virtue of religion. Religion is not merely the most eminent of the moral virtues, but it plays a role of leadership which is analogous to that of charity. While dependent on the theological virtues, particularly on the love of God, it is the religious form of all the virtues.[11] "Every virtuous work belongs to religion, or in other words, to the worship of God (latria), by way of directive or command (imperii), according to which it is ordered to the divine majesty (reverentia), which is the proper end of divine worship. To order acts of other virtues to its own end, however, pertains to the virtue directing or commanding, not to the virtues directed or commanded. And therefore the ordering of the acts of any virtue whatsoever to the service of God, makes them properly acts of religion (latria)."[12]

It follows that this dynamism of religion, animating and orientating not merely the elicited cultal acts properly so-called, but also the whole moral activity of the Christian, directs the entire life of man to the goal of the divine honor and glory. The end and purpose is the majesty and greater glory of God.

But it would be a gross error to conclude that actual cult is rendered superfluous by this orientation and religious motivation which directs all things to the greater honor and glory of God. In fact the very opposite is true, for the Christian must esteem the acts of religion properly so-called above all the acts of the other moral virtues, in order that the firmness and vigor of his inner spirit of worship may effectively direct all else to the glory of God. This is true apart from the fact that the acts of worship are in themselves demanded by the very nature of man and are specifically due to the glorious majesty of God. The majesty and glory of God lays claim to such acts more directly and immediately than to any other moral acts.

The primacy of the virtue of cult (religion) over all the moral virtues corresponds to the cultal vocation of man in the universe in which he is supreme, manifesting both his significance as creature and his dignity as child of God.[13] The holy sacraments, particularly those which anoint us with the Holy Spirit, the Spirit of glory, incorporate us in the high-priestly consecration of Christ and His ineffable mission and set us apart absolutely for the unfathomably exalted cult of God in Christ. (We say that man is deputed interiorly, marked by the sacramental character indelibly, not merely chosen or designated externally.) The Christian is "holy unto the Lord," he is singled out from the ranks of the profane. He is separated from the strangers to God, from those who have not been immediately and directly struck by the rays of the divine majesty and holiness.

In consequence the Christian has the mission first of all to sanctify himself in the service of cult and for the service of cult. In other words, through a personal acceptance of his objective sacral holiness he must consecrate (through devotion or submission to God) himself and all his activity to the service of God. Moreover, he receives the mission of exercising in the created world a priestly service. This means he is to impart to the things of earth a cultal or religious formation through places and seasons set apart for cult, through the oblation of the fruits of his labor, specifically the fruits of the earth itself. Through the holy sacraments and sacramentals and most particularly through the holy Sacrifice of the Mass, human words and the gifts of the earth are placed in the sacred orbit of the divine holiness in a most ineffable manner. It is above all through these acts that the Christian immediately and directly fulfills his cultal vocation and mission.

But since all things are to be consecrated to God in this fulfillment of the priestly vocation, not only formal acts of cult as such, but all human acts are subject to the law of sacral ethos. The total morality of man must bear the stamp of consecration, must "be made holy." The injunction, "As the One who called you is holy, be you also holy in all your behavior; for it is written, 'You shall be holy, because I am holy'" (1 Pt 1:15f.; cf Lv 11:44; 19:2; 20:7), does not demand merely cultal holiness but also moral perfection imbued with the spirit of cult. Thus moral perfection becomes religious morality or holiness, that is, a moral rectitude sustained by the love of God and consecrated to the divine glory.

The cultal sanctification of man, caught up as he is by the loving majesty of the Most High, to which the virtue of religion corresponds as response, demands by its very nature moral holiness in man. The Christian must do far more than merely dedicate his moral efforts to God or subordinate them to the religious. Rightly viewed, the whole moral endeavor, and above all the moral perfection of cultal or religious man, initially flows from his sanctification and is a manifestation of his holiness.

In the moral effort of the Christian, his own perfection may not predominate in the sense that the cultal acts themselves are viewed solely or even primarily as means of self-perfection. The predominant motive of the priestly man must be the glory of God ("All for the greater honor and glory of God!"). The whole moral life of the Christian must be penetrated and motivated by the ideal expressed by St. Peter: "You, however, are a chosen race, a royal priesthood, a holy nation, a purchased people; that you may proclaim the perfections of him who has called you out of darkness into his marvelous light" (1 Pt 2:9). The consecration and sacerdotal dignity of the people of God demands of every Christian that he be formed into a truly priestly structure. "Be you yourselves as living stones, built thereon into a spiritual house, a holy priesthood, to offer spiritual sacrifices acceptable to God through Jesus Christ" (1 Pt 2:5). Even the body of the Christian, or should we say, especially the body of the Christian, also has a share in this priestly dignity and cultal obligation. "Glorify God and bear him in your body" (1 Cor 6:20). Not only the cultal movements and actions, but our whole corporal deportment and our whole attitude toward the body must be a manifestation of honor rendered to God.

Every virtue of every Christian must bear the sacred stamp and impress of worship. This is true above all of the virtues of the ordained priest who has received a special ministry (*diakonía*) for the praise and glory of God (2 Cor 3:7ff.). In all that he does the Christian must be filled with the spirit of praise and adoration.[14] But this is possible only if the virtue of religion occupies its proper place in his moral life. All that belongs to the virtue directly and immediately must be accorded the position of primacy in the Christian life, so that the totality of man's moral endeavor is truly ordered to the glory of God. This means that the virtue must be earnestly and suitably cultivated, and that the explicit acts of worship be given due prominence.

III. INTERIOR WORSHIP AND EXTERIOR WORSHIP

1. *Piety, Devotion, and Worship*

Devotion or the spirit of religion, according to St. Thomas, is not a distinct virtue related to religion. It is rather the most basic and central act of religion, in a sense the heart of religion.[15] "Devotion is nothing other than the ready will to dedicate one's self to those things which pertain to the service of God."[16]

Related to devotion is piety.[17] According to St. Thomas piety as a gift of the Holy Spirit is an interior disposition, a sentiment of filial affection toward God.[18] It manifests itself immediately in the interior life of prayer, in filial protestations of faith, hope, and love addressed to God our Father. Insofar as piety is the interior and exterior life of prayer, we can, in agreement with St. Thomas, call it an act of the virtue of religion, a species of activity belonging to the virtue of religion.[19] But conversely the virtue of religion for its part draws its nourishment from the spirit of piety.

Through the operation of the graces of the Holy Spirit in the gift of piety, the worship which we must pay to the divine majesty manifested in creation and the history of mankind receives the character of a warm and loving homage of a child for its heavenly Father.[20] The piety which is the rich interior life of prayer nourishes charity, the proximate source of devotion.[21]

Only he is truly pious whose heart, enriched by the indwelling of the Holy Spirit, impels him ever and anon to the jubilant chant of divine praise and the exterior acts of religion. Only he truly honors God "in spirit and in truth" whose external worship of God flows from an interior spirit of filial piety and devotion. Piety which lacks the joyous ardor for the praise of God in divine worship is spurious. External cult without the interior spirit of true religion is an abomination to God and calls to mind the hypocrisy of the Pharisees.

2. Necessity of External Worship

External cult flows necessarily from the very nature of man. By his very nature as composed of body and soul, man must render service to God with his whole being. Therefore he must serve Him with both body and soul.[22] It follows that the interior sentiment of adoration must also be expressed exteriorly. In fact it could not long survive without some form of external expression or manifestation.

We moderns with our penchant for the technical and mechanical even in thought and sentiment are only too prone to underestimate the importance of sign and symbol in life. Our appreciation of the ritual and ceremonial symbol as an expression and demand of the psychic and spiritual is often too slight and has need for development through a conscious and earnest effort. A vital form of worship aloof from all formalism can be of considerable service in cultivating it.

But external manifestation of religion is also necessary for another reason. Religion in the heart must essentially find an external expression in word and gesture with a presentation in time and place and community, because its proper object is the *kabod,* the *dóxa* or glory of God, the visible manifestation of the invisible majesty of God. The glory of God is particularly apparent in the mystery of the cross and the blood of Christ, in the mystery of the supreme self-renunciation and in the exaltation of the risen Savior with His glorified body. Therefore, through His willingness to suffer with Christ in His passion (as a means of rendering glory to God and attaining personal resurrection in eternal glory) and through the sacred rites and ceremonies in which perceptible acts and movements manifest the glory of God filling the heart and soul of man, the Christian offers in his very body an essential element of true religion. "Glorify God and bear him in your body," says the Apostle (1 Cor 6:20).

Here we have touched upon one of the theological sources, and not the least important one at that, of the glory and splendor of the Catholic cult. The sacramental consecration of the whole man, including also his body, implies an essential relation to the high-priestly passion of Christ and to His glory in the resurrection, ascension, and the parousia. This relation we find expressed in the sacred signs and symbols of the liturgical cult. Until the great day when the eternal liturgy begins, our liturgy is the manifestation and expression, perpetually renewed, of the glorification of

God through Christ, of the visible glorification of Christ by the Father, and of our participation in both through divine grace.

Finally, external worship of God is demanded by the very essence of religion, insofar as religion is also social, and a necessary bond of the community in giving honor to God. Men must glorify God according to their whole nature, corporeal and spiritual. As individuals and as social beings they must pay honor to the source of their being, for not only the individual but also the community has been created by God for His own honor and glory. Both bask in the sunlight of His majesty and are obliged to acknowledge Him and worship Him. It follows that not only external cult but also social cult, the cult offered by the community, is incumbent upon man.

But external worship, as the expression of the spirit of religion which has laid hold of our hearts caught up by the holiness and majesty of God, may never be a deviation from our true selves. It may not be an alien substance, an antinomy in opposition to our own inner being. It may not be discord destroying the complete harmony of our being in its spontaneous manifestation of reverence and love for God. It must be the very warp and woof of the fabric of our lives as God's honor and glory demands. It must be part of the balanced style of life corresponding to the demands of the divine glory to which it is constantly ordered. Erratic worship is not pleasing to God.

In the Old Testament the prophets bitterly denounced both the externalistic worship which had no inner reverence and filial love for the Lord and also the divorcement of the sacral ethos—or more properly the practice of cult—from true moral formation or virtue. God disdains all cult which is a mere cloak for disobedience in the formation of one's life and lack of love for one's neighbor (cf. Mk 7:7ff.). "Obedience is better than sacrifices; and to harken rather than to offer the fat of rams" (1 Sm 15:22). "What care I for the number of your sacrifices? says the Lord. I have had enough of whole-burnt rams and fat of fatlings; in the blood of calves, lambs and goats I find no pleasure. . . . Bring no more worthless offerings. . . . Your hands are full of blood! Wash yourselves clean! Put away your misdeeds from before my eyes" (Is 1:11ff.; Os 6:6; Am 5:21ff.; Mal 1:6ff.).

The criticism of the prophets is not directed against external worship as such, but merely against externalism and empty formalism in the service of God. Nor did Christ reject external worship of God. In fact He took part regularly in the temple service (Lk 2:22ff.; 4:16ff.). He condemned only the abuses in worship and pure externalism in the honor paid to His heavenly Father. With the greatest insistence he stressed the necessity of the inner spirit of religion. Such is the import of His demand that true worshippers "worship the Father in spirit and in truth" (Jn 4:23). As God Himself prescribed the external worship in the Old Testament through Moses, so Christ in person instituted the holy Sacrifice of the Mass and the sacraments, and conferred on the Church the right to organize the cult with authority and give it external structure and form (cf. 1 Cor 11:17ff.; 14:23ff.).

3. Practical Requirements in External Worship

One must cultivate the spirit of interior prayer and meditation, as well as an earnest concern for the proper performance of the liturgical ceremonies, to the end that external celebration may always be animated by the spirit of piety and the interior sentiment of devotion be truly genuine. Every one, but most of all the ordained priest, must endeavor to appreciate truly the profound spiritual riches of the liturgy. By means of sound instruction the Christian faithful should acquire true insights into the deep spiritual meaning of the divine worship and into the significance of the various ceremonies of the entire liturgy. Since participation in the external worship is demanded of them, they have a strict right to be correctly and fruitfully initiated into the sacred mysteries to the extent of their needs and the measure of their intelligence.

The forms of divine worship must be expressive and adapted to the understanding of the faithful, as are the sacramental signs which express in such a marvelous manner what is wrought in the holy sacraments. Of course we must bear in mind that essentially the sacred ceremonies of worship should not only manifest the closeness or the presence of God, but also proclaim the infinite transcendence of His holiness. The veiled and mysterious has its rightful place, though it never should conceal either what God in His love has manifested or the content of that which all are to hear, and the meaning of the words of the common prayer. The *iconostasis* in the Eastern Churches and the use of Latin, a *dead* language, in the West are largely the result of social and historic developments. They do not spring from an essential demand for obscurity in external worship.

Hence we cannot at all share the view of Dom Guéranger (and his aristocratic concept of the liturgy), who even condemned the use of the translated missal by the faithful, because with it "even the lowliest scullery maid and the simplest workman" might understand what the Church surely wanted to keep hidden from them by her use of Latin in the liturgy.[23] Any position of this kind is altogether outmoded and obsolete in the light of recent developments and our clear understanding of the New Testament worship of God "in spirit and in truth" by the "royal priesthood" of the faithful.

Even the severe reserve which leaves the Latin of the Canon of the Mass and particularly of the consecration unchanged, despite a far-reaching acceptance of the vernacular in our Western liturgy (with considerable encouragement of the Holy See), is not to be ascribed to dogmatic reasons. This is clearly shown by the fact that from ancient times Eastern Catholics, with the explicit approval of the Holy See, have celebrated their entire liturgy in a language understood by the faithful. In the early Church, Greek as the liturgical language gave way to Latin for the express reason that Latin had replaced it as the common idiom among the faithful in the West. Any decision today regarding the adoption of the vernacular in the liturgy is beyond the competence of the individual priest or even of the bishop and is entirely in the hands of the Holy See. Appropriate appeals to the Holy Father for permission to use the vernacular are not a sign of disrespect for the traditional forms but rather demonstrate our respect for the authority of the Church and our trust in her wisdom and prudence.

The celebrated depth psychologist, C. G. Jung, attached very great significance to the religious symbol. Not only did he maintain that there is an affinity in the symbols of all peoples, but his research tends to prove that man today still retains communication with many symbols in the domain of his unconscious life which unfortunately are partially lost to him in his conscious spiritual life. Rather than suppress them, we should seek to restore them to the conscious life again. Correct explanation of the meaning and beauty of religious symbol and the vital celebration of the mysteries in intelligible language should contribute, as far as this is possible, toward making the unknown again known.

Since the divine service is the worship of the entire Christian community, the Church, the individual is obliged to conform to the group as organized by the Church and submit to the forms and directives governing the whole body. Rather than subject the liturgy to his personal criticism, he should seek to profit by submissive use of what is at the service of all. As one individual member he does not have the right to make his personal likes or dislikes the standard for the community ceremonial, much less to revise or modify it according to his own whims. This is particularly true of the ceremonial intimately connected with the essentials of the sacrifice and the sacraments.

Finally, it would be utterly contrary to the spirit of the liturgy to confine our interest in the divine service to a narrow and exclusive concern for our own individual self-perfection. Such anxious effort to make the liturgy a mere means of personal sanctification ignores the central fact that to participate in the divine worship is to serve God's glory and that of His Bride the Church. As a living member of the family of Christ each Christian should edify and assist all the others by vital and joyous participation in the celebration of the holy mysteries. Surely it will accrue to the glory of God and in consequence to his own salvation, if the individual member is first concerned not so much with his own profit and his own individual experience or preference but with the community itself which is the *whole Church*.

Nevertheless, since the interior experience of religion varies to a certain degree according to the individual (and this is altogether legitimate), we should not be impatient with others in such matters. The Church herself has permitted a considerable measure of freedom to the individual in religious forms and liturgical acts, particularly in the area of the sacramentals and popular religious customs and practices.

When the Council of Trent defined that the veneration of the saints and of their images and relics is good and salutary,[24] it did not at all intend to bind or constrain every individual to a fixed and predetermined form of veneration or set a rigid measure for it in this domain of worship. It is quite obvious that for the sake of the community and the community life there must always be a measure of conformity determined by legal norms. But beyond the lines laid down, in areas not affected by the Church's directive, the spirit of liberty guided by a sense of community should prevail. Where the Church herself does not consider it necessary or opportune to make restrictions, her individual members should be allowed complete freedom.

From the Church's very beginnings the liturgy displayed an astonishing adaptability to the needs and characteristics of the various peoples to whom the divine message was brought. The world mission of the Church cannot be effective without a loving and tender appreciation of the diversities of men and races and cultures. How profoundly did the Church sense and feel what was in the heart of men! But never can she compromise the liturgical celebration by transforming it to suit the individualistic spirit of the times. Extensive pastoral-liturgical research has revealed that an individualistic (which is also unfortunately a formalistic) impoverishment of liturgical forms of divine service can in the long run only prove disastrous. The more vitally the community enters into the liturgical participation, the more the faithful join in the chant, the prayer, and in the profounder understanding of its sacred meaning, the greater the participation of the men, the workers, the adults between twenty and fifty years, the more vigorous is the power of resistance to the dangerous and illusory ideas threatening us today. This liturgical community has discovered the defence against the deadly thrust of the "spirit of the times." Such is the evidence of recent studies in this area.

We are in full accord with truth when we assert that only when the community rallies around the altar "in spirit and in truth," only where it is altar-formed, will the Christians in their lives testify to the spirit of community. They will testify to the faith in word and deed, to the salvation of men, the Christianization of the world about us, and thereby to the greater glory of God.

BIBLIOGRAPHY

Worship in Spirit and Truth

BAUHOFER, O. *Das Metareligioese.* Leipzig, 1930.

CARRÉ, A. M. *Sainté, miroir de Dieu.* Paris, 1955.

CATHREIN, V. "Wesen und Aufgabe der Froemmigkeit (Pietaet)," *ZAM* 2 (1927), 239–253; 3 (1928), 28–42.

COHAUSZ, O., S.J. *Die Froemmigkeit Jesu Christ.* 2 ed. Kirnach-Villingen, 1930.

Die katholische Glaubenslehre. Freiburg, 1960, II, 749ff.

DIGNANT, O. E. *Tractatus de religione.* 4 ed., Brugis, 1940.

DILLERSBERGER, J. *Das Heilige im Neuen Testament.* Kufstein, 1926.

DUERING, W. *Pietas liturgica. Studien zum Froemmigkeitsbegriff und zur Gottesvorstellung der abendlaendischen Liturgie.* Regensburg, 1958.

HAERING, B., C.SS.R. *Das Heilige und das Gute.* Krailling vor Muenchen, 1950.

HOFMANN, R. "Gottesverehrung als moraltheologisches Problem," *Der Mensch vor Gott,* Duesseldorf, 1948, 399–416.

JUNG, P. *Das Wesen des religioesen Aktes und der Tugend der Gottesverehrung beim heiligen Thomas von Aquin.* Untersuchung einer moraltheologischen Kontroverse. Dresden, 1941.

JUNKER, H. "Gott und Mensch in ihren gegenseitigen Verhaeltnis in der Sicht des nachexilischen Judentums," *Der Mensch vor Gott*, Duesseldorf, 1948, 11–26.

KIRCHGAESSNER, A. *Die maechtigen Zeichen. Urspruenge, Formen und Gesetze des Kultes.* Basel-Freiburg-Wien, 1959.

*KITTEL, G. UND RAD, G. VON. "Doxa," *ThW*, II, 236–258.

LACKMANN, M. *Verehrung der Heiligen. Versuch einer lutherischen Lehre von den Heiligen.* Stuttgart, 1958.

LANG, A. "Der Mensch im Bannkreis des Heiligen," *Der Mensch vor Gott*, Duesseldorf, 1948, 351–364.

LINSENMANN, F. X. "Ueber den Geist des christlichen Kultes," *ThQschr* 77 (1885), 100–140; 175–215.

LIPPERT, P., S.J. "Fromm sein Koennen," *StimmenZeit* 131 (1936/37), 289–298.

LOTTIN, O., O.S.B. "Vertu de religion et virtus théologales," *Dominican Studies* 1 (1948), 209–228.

LOTZ, J. B., S.J. "Die christliche Froemmigkeit und der Mensch von heute," *GeistLeben* 21 (1948), 418–429.

MARTIMORT, A. G. "Le sens du sacre," *La Maison-Dieu* 27 (1951), 47–74.

OHM, TH., O.S.B. *Die Gebetsgebaerden der Voelker und das Christentum.* Leiden, 1948.

PASCHER, J. "Die 'communio sanctorum' als Grundgefuege der katholischen Heiligenverehrung," *MThZ* 1 (1950), Heft 3, 1–11.

POSCHMANN, B. *Grundlage und Geisteshaltung der katholischen Froemmigkeit.* Koeln-Muenchen, 1925.

PROKSCH, O. "Hagios," *ThW* I, 87–116.

SANCHEZ, M., O.P. "Donde situar el tratado de la virtud de religion?" *Ang* 36 (1959), 287–320.

SAWICKI, F. *Die katholische Froemmigkeit.* Paderborn, 1921.

SCHOELLGEN, W. "Zur Psychologie der Froemmigkeit und der Gottesfurcht," *Der Mensch unter Gottes Anruf und Ordnung.* (Festgabe fuer Th. Muencker). Duesseldorf, 1958, 125–136.

SOBALLA, G., S.J. "Wahrheitsbotschaft und christlicher Wandel. Ein Beitrag zur Theologie der Froemmigkeit nach den paulinischen Schriften," *GeistLeben* 25 (1952), 197–220, 270–284.

STEINBUECHEL, TH. *Religion und Moral.* Frankfort, 1952.

STEINHEIMER, M., O.F.M. *Die "doxa tu theu" in der roemischen Liturgie.* Muenchener Theol. Studien II, 4. Muenchen, 1951.

STORR, R. *Das Froemmigkeitsideal der Propheten.* Muenster, 1936.

THURN, H., S.J. "Seelengrund und Froemmigkeit. Zur Psychologie des Gefuehles und der Froemmigkeit," *GeistLeben* 23 (1950), 346–461.

VAN DER LEEUW, G. *Phaenomenologie der Religion.* 2 ed., Tuebingen, 1956.

VERMEERSCH, A. *Quaestiones de virtute religionis et pietatis.* Regensburg, 1912.

WASMUTH, E. ". . . Nicht der Philosophen! Ueber die Beziehung zwischen Mensch und Gott bei Paschal," *Der Mensch vor Gott*, Duesseldorf, 1948, 119–135.

WEILNER, I. *Gottselige Innigkeit. Die Grundhaltung der religioesen Seele nach J. M. Sailer.* Regensburg, 1949.

WELTE, B. *Von Wesen und Unwesen der Religion.* Frankfurt, 1952.

WIRTHMUELLER, J. B. *Die moralische Tugend der Religion.* Freiburg, 1881.

Additional Works in English

DIEKMANN, GODFREY, O.S.B. *Come, Let us Worship* (Benedictine Studies, 2). Baltimore: Helicon, 1961.

ELLARD, GERALD, S.J. *Christian Life and Worship* (Religion and Culture Series). Milwaukee: Bruce, 1940.

LEFEBVRE, GASPAR, O.S.B. *The Spirit of Worship* (Twentieth Century Encyclopedia of Catholicism, 108). New York: Hawthorn, 1959.

PHILIPPE, M. D., O.P. *The Worship of God* (Twentieth Century Encyclopedia of Catholicism, 16). New York: Hawthorn, 1959.

The Virtues and States of Life (Theology Library, v. 4). ed. A. M. Henry, O.P. Chicago: Fides, 1957. "Faith" (A. Liégé), pp. 1–59; "Hope" (B. Olivier), pp. 61–126; "Charity" (B. Olivier), pp. 127–208; "The Virtue of Religion" (A. Mennessier), pp. 393–444; "The Social Virtues" (M. Gerland), pp. 445–485 (on obedience, piety, liberality).

*UNDERHILL, EVELYN. *Worship*. New York: Harper, 1931.

CHAPTER SIX

THE SACRAMENTS IN THE DIVINE WORSHIP

THE doctrine on the holy sacraments forms an essential element of our moral theological teaching on the imitation of Christ. Nothing is better calculated than this teaching on the sacraments to help us appreciate the significant statement of the Master Himself: "You have not chosen me, but I have chosen you" (Jn 15:16). This teaching shows us very clearly that the discipleship is a grace from Him and is possible only by interior assimilation to Him. The imitation is far more than exterior copying. It is the life in and from Christ which demands a life for Christ and in obedience to Him.

Our most exalted mission in life is to worship God and order the whole of our life to His greater honor and glory. Center and summit of all glorification of God is the Sacrifice of our High Priest Jesus Christ, which offers infinite praise and glory to the Triune God and brings grace and salvation to men. In the holy sacraments we are turned to the Eucharistic Sacrifice and through it to the Sacrifice on the Cross, source of all grace and sanctification.

The first lesson that the doctrine on the sacraments conveys to us is the joyous message from Jesus Christ, our High Priest, who has reconciled us to God by His death on the cross. We are taken up by Christ, we are filled with His life. We are incorporated into His priesthood. Such is the first and basic teaching.

I. Through the sacraments we are sanctified, made holy by Christ the Priest. Sanctified in our innermost being and in the mission to our most decisive life tasks, we are consecrated for a priestly life in Christ, for the praise and glory of God. Such is the consecrated vocation we receive in the sacraments.

II. Through the sacraments our lives are entered into the history of salvation and we are charged with the duty and responsibility of saving our souls. Our lives are spiritually enriched and made fruitful for eternal life.

III. The sacraments are encounters with Christ, most intimate, most personal. Such is this sacred meeting in these sources of grace that it makes possible and demands the response of our whole life to the summons of the Master to the call of discipleship.

IV. The sacraments are the bridal endowment of Christ presented to His Bride, the Church. And for us they are the signs and pledges of membership in the Church and dedication to the service of God in the Church. Through them a sacred claim is placed upon our lives for service with Christ in His kingdom on earth, the Church.

V. The sacraments are obligatory means of grace and sanctification for us.

The study and exposition of the doctrine on the holy sacraments in moral theology involves far more than a mere summation of the positive laws and directives prudently regulating everything which concerns these signs of grace. They are not to be viewed simply and in the first instance as creating sacred obligations to be added to the other moral tasks which we all must perform. We must look upon them first of all as fundamental and formative forces, instruments of grace and salvation. They are forces which take hold of man in his entire being, in the whole of his life on earth. The entire Christian life must be a cultal-sacramental life, if it is to be a Christian life at all.[25]

I. DISCIPLESHIP SACRAMENTALLY CONSECRATED TO GOD'S GLORY

1. *Grace, Sanctification, Worship*

Christ is the One sanctified by the Father, the Holy One, consecrated for His mission as Savior, specifically for His High-Priestly Sacrifice on the Cross (Jn 19:19; Lk 1:35; Heb 7:26). Christ is sanctified through His substantial divine Sonship, that is to say through the hypostatic union of His most sacred humanity with the divine person of the Word. He is the *Messiah*, the *Christós*, the *One Anointed* "with the Holy Spirit and with power" (Acts 10:38; Is 61:1; 11:2f.). He is anointed as the suffering servant of *Yahweh* (Is 42:1ff.). All that He does and all that He suffers is centered in the sun of the majesty of God and is offered in worship to the glory of God for the sanctification of mankind (cf. Is 52:13–53:12).

The assimilation of the disciple to the Master, of the member to the Head, is effected in the holy sacraments, but not in the first instance through the action of the disciple himself. The sacraments give man a share in the divine sonship and at the same time a participation in the sacerdotal mission of Christ. Usually the scriptures place a particular stress on the name they give the Christians. They are the *hágioi*, the *holy ones,* or the *sanctified ones.*

Just as Christ is constituted High Priest by the hypostatic union of His human nature with the person of the Word, so too the Christian becomes priestly through union with Christ in the sacraments which imprint the priestly mark of assimilation with Him. Through baptism, confirmation, and holy order man is given a partnership in the priestly dignity of Christ and is entered into the realm of the majesty and holiness of God. But this is our grace and our task.

Every grace that man receives from God has an essential interior reference to the glory of God (*dóxa*). The operation of divine grace is a radiation from the splendor of God's majesty and holiness. It is the divine enlistment of one so favored for the service of God according to the measure of the favor granted and for the glory of God. Every grace will one day—provided the one favored with this celestial gift has not extinguished the flame lighted for the divine glory—be for him a ray, a reflection of the splendor and majesty of God in eternity. Grace is commitment and promise.

It is precisely the reality and efficacy of the sacraments as causative signs of grace which impresses the Christian mind with a consciousness of God's work through His grace. All holiness is a reflection of the divine splendor. Only because it proceeds from God and is ordered to God can it be truly salutary for men. All the imperatives for the baptized, for the confirmed, for those joining Christ at the sacrificial Banquet are imperatives of grace. They are commands flowing from God's love for us to be transformed into our love for God, flowing from the majesty of God to lead to the glorification of God. Not that it is we who begin to honor God; for it is God who invests us with His own glory. Not that we begin to sanctify our lives; God sanctifies us. The result for the one sanctified is the great imperative, the imperative demanding the Christian life, the life of the discipleship. This imperative is the *Law of Grace.*

In all the biblical concepts dealing with holiness, such as *hágios, hagiázein, hagnízein, hagiosýne, hagiasmós* (holy, to make holy, to form in holiness, sanctification, sanctity), there is a varied stress and emphasis in the mind of the Christian. At one time the words may imply a greater stress on the action of God sanctifying man, and at another, on the moral-religious response of man. But most fundamental and most specifically and properly characteristic of biblical morality is the sanctifying action of God upon man, with its center and most manifest expression in the holy sacraments and its goal primarily in the glory of God.

The visible descent of the Holy Spirit upon Christ at the beginning of His public life was a manifest expression of His exalted consecration, of His sanctification as High Priest and servant of God. Similarly for us the Holy Spirit sent by Christ upon us is the Spirit of sanctification, who consecrates us to holy service, to life and death in union with Christ in the sacred mysteries. Only through sanctification in the Holy Spirit are we made an acceptable offering to God (cf. Rom 15:16).

The Holy Spirit is given to us because of the sacrifice of Christ on the Cross. He is the fruit of that sacrifice, gift of the Christ risen in glory. The Evangelist St. John expressly calls attention to the fact that the glorification of Christ (His exaltation in the *dóxa*) is prerequisite to the mission of the Holy Spirit (cf. Jn 7:39; 16:7). Our enlistment in the service of the divine majesty through the infusion of the Holy Spirit and the communication of grace as effulgence of the holiness and majesty of God in such a manner as to make our whole life sacrificial service—all this is the fruit of the glorious sacrificial oblation of Christ on the Cross. But the full import of the death and the fruits of the death are apparent only in the brilliant light of the resurrection.

The most sacred wounds of the holy passion are resplendent in eternal glory, for the majesty of Christ, the eternal High Priest, is sacrificial majesty resting on the title of His sacrifice on the Cross. Christ is the Lamb that was slain and offered in sacrifice. Now in eternal glory the Lamb that was slain stands before the throne offering the celestial sacrifice in honor of the Most Holy Trinity. His is the sacrificial hymn of praise in the eternal fulfillment of the sacrifice once offered for sin on the Cross (cf. Heb 12:22ff.). The Christian's union with the Christ of glory through the sacramental consecration and the imparting of the Spirit of sanctification is not merely a designation or assignment for divine cult. It is a real bond of assimilation to Christ and His sacrifice. It is an obligation and mission to the sacrificial service of a holy life, a charge engraved into our very being by the consecration of sacramental efficacy. This priestly union with Christ is effected, first of all, through the sacraments which imprint the mark of priesthood, the sacramental character. But each sacrament in its own special way binds us to Christ, so that our prayer, our suffering, our whole life is vested with a new and higher fitness and commitment for sacrificial service in Christ.

By His sacrifice on the Cross Christ founded the community of worship which is His Mystical Body. The Church is essentially the community of the Lord's Supper and therefore also the community in the suffering and sacrifice of Christ. The holy sacraments, according to the trenchant terms of the Fathers of the Church, flowed forth from the riven side of the Crucified in order to bring our whole spiritual life into effective union with the sacrifice of the Cross.[26] It follows that the Holy Eucharist is the center of all the sacraments, their focus and goal, in which the power and love of Christ's sacrifice is imparted to us by the glorified Christ. The sacraments are truly *means of grace* through which the fruits of Calvary are channeled to our souls. But our salvation consists precisely in the acceptance and the reflection of the divine glory. Sacramental piety, the sacramentally nourished and motivated life in Christ, is entirely and essentially theocentric.[27]

Sacramental life flows from the glory of Christ who has triumphed over death through the sacrifice on the Cross and risen in the glory of eternal life. The source of this life in man is the grace of Christ through which we become partners with Christ in His sacrifice. Through this sacramental union we participate not only in the sacramental action of the Church and on the occasion of the reception of the sacraments but in all our moral conduct and throughout our whole life.

For this reason, to cite but one example, the inspired writers conceive of chastity not so much as a perfection of man as glory and honor paid to God. In this sense too the whole life of the Christian should be an oblation or offering (a *prosphorá*, Rom 15:16), and the body a sacrificial gift (*thysía*, Rom 12:1). Even the scriptural terms which denote purely moral excellence have a cultal connotation: as "blameless," "unblemished," "pure" (*ámemptos, ámomos, katharós*). Just as the victim in the Old Testament sacrifice had to be free from blemish or defect, so the Christian must be morally free from stain and fault. If he is morally blameless, the Christian who is sacramentally sanctified as victim and priest is truly qualified for the sacrificial service as victim in union with Christ. This is particularly true of the great works of the Christian apostolate. All apostolic spirit and action is a participation in the sacrificial work of redemption through Christ. All works of Christian zeal are pre-eminently sacrificial.

There is a threefold significance and efficacy in the sacraments: they are *cultal, salutary, social*. They consecrate the recipient for the life of divine worship; they give the individual the graces for his salvation; they unite him by a saving bond in the Mystical Body, the Church, in true solidarity with all the other members of Christ's kingdom. These three facets of significance and efficacy are not separate entities accidentally united but one concordant and efficacious priestly reality. They are the most fruitful source of instruction of the faithful in the divine truths and also the basis of serious obligations in the administration and reception of the sacraments.

Central focus of sacramental instruction and guidance, therefore, must be the Holy Eucharist, the complete and effective initiation of the Christian into the all-holy sacrifice and the sacrificial spirit of Christ the High Priest. Not only are we consecrated to a life for the glory of God: in the holy sacrifice and in the sacraments we offer, we manifest, we celebrate the life which is totally directed to the glory of God. If it is true that the sacraments which imprint a character really and effectively impress upon our souls a priestly mark which affects the totality of our being and our existence, then everything we do, whether it be acts of zeal for others or concern for our own salvation, merges into the adoring love by which we give glory to God.

2. Sacramental Character: Sacraments in the Liturgy

It is an article of our faith that three sacraments, *baptism, confirmation,* and *holy order,* imprint an indelible mark on the soul.[28] Evidence for this teaching is found in all those passages of the inspired pages which refer to a permanent sanctification of man for the sacrificial service by which we honor God through Christ. Significant also are the passages which speak of a permanent seal (*sphragis*) through the Holy Spirit (cf. Jn 6:27; Eph 1:13f.; 4:30; 2 Cor 1:21f.) or express in some other manner the assimilation permanently binding the Christian to Jesus Christ the High Priest (Rom 6).

The noted *Abercius Inscription* suggests how profound was the conviction in the early Christian consciousness that the Christian was permanently consecrated to the divine service. This epitaph, probably the most ancient Christian inscription still in existence, refers to the Christian people of Rome as "people who possess the effulgent seal."[29]

According to the Fathers of the Church the sacramental mark or *character* is the expression of the permanent sanctification and sealing wrought by the Holy Spirit; it corresponds to Christ's own anointing in the flesh as High Priest through the operation of the Holy Spirit: "The Spirit imprints the seal on the soul . . . in order that we, anointed by the Holy Spirit, may approach close to God."[30] "As you according to the spirit have received the pattern of Christ, you became anointed of Christ (*Christoi, Christ's anointed ones*). . . . You are images of Christ. As the Holy Spirit descended upon Him at the baptism in the Jordan in visible form . . . so it is with you, as you arose from the bath of baptism, the anointing was given you as an antitype (that is according to His image and His reality). . . . In the anointing with oil you became members and participants of the Anointed One."[31] "We are stamped with the seal of the Holy Spirit. As we shall die in Christ and again be reborn in Him, so we shall be sealed by the Holy Spirit, so that we may be able to hold fast to the glorious image of Christ and to His grace. It is a spiritual seal. . . . The Spirit imprints upon us the *stamp* of the heavenly pattern."[32]

The apt summation and systematization of the traditional teaching by St. Thomas has become the standard exposition of the doctrine. The Angelic Doctor sees in the character the mark engraved by the risen Christ to whom the sacramental grace directs and orders us. More specifically it is sharing in the priesthood of Christ which is progressively communicated to us by a threefold sacramental character. "It is obvious that the sacramental character is in a special way the mark or stamp of Christ, to whose priesthood the faithful are assimilated (*configurantur*) through the sacramental characters which are nothing less than gradual participations in the priesthood of Christ, derived from Christ Himself."[33]

"As to their function the more recent theologians speak of the sacramental character as a sign which 1) distinguishes, 2) disposes, 3) assimilates, 4) obliges. . . . Insofar as it obliges, it signifies that the bearer must serve in the divine cult."[34] These four determinants of the character must be studied in the light of their relation to their priestly and cultal function. As to the cultal function baptism distinguishes "a chosen race, a royal priesthood, a holy nation, a purchased people" (1 Pt 2:9), i.e., the baptized, from the non-Christian world, but with the obligation flowing from this very same priesthood of zealous concern for the salvation of the non-baptized. Confirmation distinguishes the adult or mature Christians who are soldiers of Christ from those who have not yet attained the fulness of manhood in Christ. The character of the sacrament of holy order distinguishes the priestly hierarchy from the remainder of God's people.

The sacramental character disposes the recipient of the sacrament for the celebration or for participation in the celebration of the divine mysteries and for the cultal orientation of his whole life. It is the basis for the claim to the corresponding graces, sanctifying grace and the actual graces, suited to the priestly endeavors. In this sense the recipient is disposed by the sacramental character for the reception of the magnificent sacramental graces. From this it is apparent that according to our teaching the individual is also spiritually enriched and his salvation furthered through this efficacy in the order of cult. "Character is called a disposition for grace. . . . It prepares the soul directly and immediately for the fulfillment of that which belongs to the divine cult. And since this cannot be effected worthily without the help of grace, according to the words of St. John that 'the true worshippers will worship the Father in spirit and in truth' (4:23), it follows that God grants to the recipients of the sacramental character also the grace which will enable them to accomplish worthily that with which they have been charged (deputed)."[35]

To fulfill this cultal duty we stand in need not only of abundant actual graces as aids in the task imposed by the sacramental character. If our worship is to be truly pleasing to God we must reflect in our souls the celestial glory of God and Christ. This is to say we must be endowed with the life of grace. This sanctifying grace of the sacraments should not be looked upon as something separated from actual grace and the sacramental character. The three are not disjointed and independent realities, but rather diverse forms or phases of the real initiation on our part into the radiant splendor of the divine glory, the *dóxa* of that divine majesty which merits all our honor and praise. The three—habitual grace, actual grace, sacramental character—in their totality and unity give us the capacity and impose the duty of honoring God worthily in Christ.

The sacramental mark is assimilation to Christ. It is an impression of the sacerdotal character of Christ our Head on the souls of the members of His Mystical Body, in whom He carries out His priestly office through their participation in His priesthood.[36] In them He brings to total fulfillment His eternal assignment. As assimilation of our heart to the priestly heart of Christ, the sacramental character assures us of the divine help so that we are formed more perfectly day by day in the priestly spirit of Christ.

Every duty in the Mystical Body of Christ is in a profound sense a work of worship, a task and assignment of cult. The reason is evident:

Christ the Head of the Mystical Body, of which we are members, is the High Priest, and His vital principle is His Holy Spirit. As vital principle of the Church, the Holy Spirit is the Spirit of the priestly anointing. Through Him we are incorporated into the Anointed One from whom we receive our tasks assigned through the sacred signs of cult, the holy sacraments. Particularly, the privileges and duties flowing from baptism, confirmation, and holy order can be understood only in the light of the priesthood of Christ and His Church. God's gifts to earthly pilgrims are pressing *imperatives*. Hence the power and grace of the sacraments bear with them a sacred obligation. Clearly the sacramental character is a sign and consecration to sacred duty; it is assignment to the most intimate partnership in the priestly activity and priestly spirit of Christ and the Church.

This traditional exposition of the doctrine of sacramental character reveals its basic importance for the ideals and goals explained in our moral theology. Through the sacraments of baptism, confirmation, and holy order the whole Christian life is assimilated to the priesthood of Christ and in the degree of that sacred assimilation is penetrated with the glory of God. It is orientated toward the divine glory, with the supreme imperative to work for the glory of God in Christ and His Church.

Not only the three sacraments with the indelible mark or character but also all the others must in some way be viewed on this same level, since they are built up on baptism and are ordered to the Holy Eucharist, sacrifice and sacrament. The sacraments "possess perfectly the nature of sacrament insofar as they are directed to something sacred (sacred in the sense of cultal)."[37] "The sacraments of the new law are directed toward two goals, namely to furnish a remedy against sin and to perfect the soul in those things which pertain to the divine cult according to the rite of the Christian religion."[38] "The sacramental words according to the Catholic teaching have a sanctifying consecratory power."[39] Pointedly and succinctly Paschasius Radbertus says: *"Sacramenta . . . a consecratione sanctitatis* (they are called sacraments because they consecrate to sanctity)."[40] Though in the strict sense of the term only the three sacraments with the indelible mark impart a new cultal power through a permanent stamp of consecration ordered directly to the divine cult, all the sacraments are at least indirectly cultal and place us under the obligation to order our lives to the special glorification of God.

Even the sacrament of *penance*, which may be called a second baptism, is cultal. "Through this sacrament there is not given to man anything new pertaining to the divine cult, but man is restored to his previous state"[41] so that he can again participate in it. The work of reparation performed by the pardoned sinner, all his penitential effort, is united with the expiatory sacrifice of Christ in a special manner and thus has a particular cultal value.[42]

The summit of cultal action to which baptism, confirmation, and order are directed is the celebration of the Eucharistic Sacrifice with the reception of Holy Communion. Though the Eucharist does not imprint a sacramental character, it has the fulness of the priesthood; for it is the Mystical Sacrifice and Sacrament of Christ Himself, Priest and Victim. As such it is the source of the most tremendous graces, the most powerful motives and imperatives for a truly priestly life totally dedicated to the glory of God and the salvation of our fellow men.

The sacramental anointing of the sick (extreme unction) under its cultal aspect is not merely the completion of penance but also a special consecration for death, that is to say, a cultal union of man's final illness and death[43] to the passion and death of Christ. Though every Christian is united to Christ the Priest through the sacramental (priestly) character of baptism and confirmation, and the ordained priest through holy order, the dying Christian is united to the sacrificial passion and death in an altogether special manner which immediately prepares him for the heavenly glory.

In the sacrament of matrimony the cultal power and obligation of the mark of baptism and confirmation are aroused and fortified by means of special graces for the sanctification of conjugal affection and all of family life. It is not the natural bond of marriage itself which creates the partnership and participation in the divine cult but the sacramental consecration, for the sacrament "signifies the union of Christ and the Church which is focused in the Holy Eucharist."[44] Thereby marriage falls under the yoke of Christ the Priest and becomes subject to His influence. It basks in the glow and warmth of the Head of the Church, the Christ risen in glory. And the conjugal bond steeped in the divine cult becomes stronger and firmer as it unites two Christians in the redemptive love of Christ the Head and in the sacrificial service of the Mystical Body. And matrimonial fruitfulness is blessed through the fruitfulness of the redemptive Blood in the sacrament of baptism, in which the offspring of Christian marriage become members of Christ and the Church. (cf. Eph 5:22ff.).

Exalted though it is through the sacramental dignity, radiant as it is in the splendor of the divine glory, Christian marriage is still not superior to Christian virginity, which represents the eternal betrothal of Christ with His Bride, the Church. The virginity of the baptized flowing from an undivided love for Christ and the Church, even without the mediation of any special sacrament, represents and expresses this eternal betrothal through the efficacious grace-giving signs of the other sacraments (baptism, confirmation, Eucharist,[45] and in the instance of priestly celibacy, the sacrament of order). Virginity becomes a consecrated and sacrificial offering only through the sacramental consecration of the dedicated virginal man or woman.

Both marriage and virginity, chosen for God and lived in accordance with His will, are truly special cultal vocations manifesting a loving adoration which flows from the riches of the sacramental life. This concept of itself should convey a better idea of the correct moral-religious attitude to be assumed toward these states than any enumeration of the particular obligations which may arise from them. For that matter the obligations themselves can be properly assessed only in the light of their true cultal grandeur.

II. THE SACRAMENTS AS PLAN AND WAY OF SALVATION

The sacraments are God's plan for the salvation of the world. Through the sacraments "the Christian in his entire existence is entered into the divine plan and the history of salvation."[46] The assimilation of the Christian to Christ is expressly referred to in scriptural passages on holy baptism and the Holy Eucharist (cf. especially Rom 6; 1 Cor 11:23ff.; the latter is the account of the institution of the Eucharist). The Christian is united with the Christ of salvation and glory, the Christ who came to save mankind and who will come again in heavenly glory.[47]

In all the sacraments the *suffering* of Christ is operative in us.[48] What is wrought brings us uniquely in union with Christ so that all our trials borne for His sake mingle with His passion and death. Then we are "united with him in the likeness of his death" and "in the likeness of his resurrection also" (Rom 6:5). In this way the sacraments endow our own suffering and death with a salutary value and assign them a task in the plan and history of salvation through union with His passion and death.

All the sacraments are assimilated to the Christ of glory. The sacramental character, the grace, the reflection of the celestial glory, the seed of beatific vision which once will be ours but is now implanted in our souls through the sacraments—all this is the gift of the risen Savior and the assignment to a life in harmony with the laws of the kingdom of His glory.

The war against sin must still be waged unremittingly despite our configuration in the risen Christ. Under the passion and death we must continue the struggle in deadly earnest, with minds and hearts fixed on the suffering and death and burial of Christ as our model. Our struggle with sin is one with the triumphant combat of Christ, our participation in the total war in the history of salvation. This is the basis of our Christian hope and confidence, but likewise the source of that urgent and pressing obligation depicted so graphically in the sixth chapter of the letter to the Romans. The Eucharistic celebration is the foregathering of the sacred assembly around the risen Christ, who sits on the throne at the right of the Father, and the most intimate communion with Him in commemoration of His Death until He comes again. The figure and force of Christ in His sacramental signs sets us on the way of salvation. It catches us up into the history of salvation, penetrating our lives with it and giving us a partnership in it. The sacraments take possession of man in his totality for Christ and His kingdom which has come down to us and remains ever in anticipation and expectation of the Second Coming.[49]

Even in the Protestant camp today[50] it is conceded that the eschatological attitude of the early Christians was not merely a hyperenthusiastic awaiting of the Second Coming which finally gave way to disillusionment, but an essentially correct Christian attitude. Joyful and resolute anticipation of the end of time is constantly reawakened by the sacraments which order our lives to eternal glory and the Second Coming. The sacraments give form and meaning to the salvific events of the span of time "which is the bridge between the resurrection and the Second Coming of Christ."[51]

Through the sacraments Christians belong fundamentally to a new age, to the "last hour" (1 Jn 2:18). In fact, through baptism they are already seated "in heaven" (Eph 2:6). "The æon which is to come is already pressing upon the ancient æon . . . and still the overwhelming riches of grace will be unveiled only in the age which is to come" (cf. Col 3:3f.).[52] Through the sacraments the tremendous realities and forces of the Messianic Age, beginning with the apostolic mission inspired by the Spirit of Pentecost, take possession of our lives and enrich them with all their fulness. Through the sacred signs, which are the sacraments, the passion, death, burial, and resurrection affect our lives. Such is the efficacy of these signs of grace that the graces of the saving passion prepare us for the Second Coming of Christ and eternal glory.

Sacramental piety and morality are essentially ordered to the Second Coming, for the Holy Spirit sent to us is the gift of the glorified and risen Christ, the grace infused into us is directed to the eternal glory of God to be manifested in the parousia. The eschatological is no longer something alien to the Christian who is inwardly transformed and enlisted into the service of the Lord of glory through the efficacy of the sacraments. Grace within him is the real beginning and anticipation of that which is to come. Miserable as is the current of our existence here below, the sacraments place us in the threshold of a new world. This miserable *now* of ours is nevertheless important, for it has a salutary significance through the sacramental projection into the new and final age opening up before us. The sacraments tear us away from this world (through death and burial with Christ) and hurl us forward with the full weight of our new being into the future, into the orbit of the glory of God. But this tremendous action also burdens us, the redeemed, with the task set by all the new forces of this world which anxiously sighs for its redemption. The holy sacraments lay their claim on us: we must slough off the perishable sinful world and at the same time accept the burden of the sacred mission to sanctify the world.

The Christian who is nourished on the sacraments, with their mission for the life of the spirit, gives testimony to the future which has already taken hold on him. Being witness to the Last Things implies a spiritual life flowing from the loving forces of the passion, death, and resurrection of Christ. Formed in Christ through the sacraments, the Christian must give this testimony throughout his entire life.

The sacraments make this miserable earthly existence of ours the grand interlude in the history of salvation between the decisive victory over death through the cross and the resurrection and the glorious triumph of the Second Coming. They direct our whole spiritual life to this end. Through them we die to sin, resist temptation, and suffer all trials and triumphs in union with Christ. Thus our lives are a twofold testimony to Jesus: the first is the painful testimony to the truth before Pilate and this world; the second is the apocalyptic testimony begun already with the glory of the resurrection and finally manifested in the might and splendor of the Judge of the living and the dead.

From all this it is quite evident that our religious-moral life is truly sacramental and cannot at all be construed as self-perfection in any Aristotelian sense. It belongs to the order and history of man's salvation. It is "bearing witness" in trial and triumph in the kingdom of the Victor over sin and death. In union with Him it is priestly apostolate, worship of God. The sacramental assignment is clear: Be holy! Be perfect! (*téleios*) (Mt 5:48; 19:21; Phil 3:12). Our whole life is directed to this end as its goal (*télos*), to the praise of the infinite holiness of God. An end rich in grace directing our lives and demanding the earnestness of our decision!

Hence our Christian morality is largely formed by this very penetration of the great eschatological realities into the order of time and in this sense is truly apocalyptic. Characterized by a consciousness of ultimate triumph it looks forward to victory with the fullest confidence in the divine promise. It is emancipation from the shackles of the dead world of the past with its slavery of sin and also bond of obligation toward a world still to be redeemed. It is life flowing entirely from the majesty (*dóxa*) of God unto the glorification of God, with the joyous expectation that the majesty will be fully revealed in us so that God will be all in all things. And from the spirit we have received there follows the response of our acceptance: joyously, wholeheartedly, we say *yes* to trial and struggle, even suffering unto death.

Sacramental piety and morality, as essentially bound to the grand interlude between the resurrection and the Second Coming, derive their finality, their absoluteness, their interior emancipation and their surety of triumph from this great apocalyptic reality. It follows that the sacraments mean far more in the Christian life than just another "cycle of duties toward oneself." They can never be deliberately relegated to the mere periphery of our moral system. This significant truth is brought home very strikingly by the new liturgy of Easter. The new ceremonies of the Paschal Vigil with the solemn renewal of the baptismal vows in this most holy night introduce us to the very heart and center of the spiritual life. Here we see very clearly that the sacraments serve above all to draw us more closely to the intimate celebration of the great events of the history of salvation.

Similarly the law of the Church obliging the faithful to receive Holy Communion, and in the event that the recipient is stained with mortal sin, also the sacrament of Penance, at least once in the ecclesiastical year (which is the celebration of the history of salvation), during the Easter period,[53] is evidence of the same relation of the moral life to the historic realities of our salvation. The liturgical celebration of the sacraments, the most basic of which is baptism, with the Eucharist as center, is infinitely more than a commemoration of an historic event: it is the salvific event of the death, resurrection, ascension, and Second Coming of the Lord thrust into the present. It is a commemorative act—"do this in memory of me"—a real act penetrating into the salvation—events here and now. Through it the Christian life is caught up into the meaning and efficacy of the grand realities in the history of salvation. It is submitting the whole Christian life to the yoke of these great salvific realities. These impart objective value and meaning to Christian life through the sacramental signs which are efficacious instruments of the Savior's death and resurrection.

Complete and adequate motivation of the moral act as well as comprehensive judgment of its moral value must embrace much more than relation to the natural reality involved in the created order (consideration of the natural right and natural law). The mighty realities of the order of redemption and salvation must be taken into consideration likewise. We thus penetrate profoundly into the soteriological-sacramental order, viewing all in the light of the eschatological salvific reality.

III. THE SACRAMENTS: PERSONAL ENCOUNTER WITH CHRIST

The sacraments are the most intimate and personal encounter with God. Through the word of faith we are effectively assured of God's gracious concern for us. For the man of faith every subjective uncertainty ceases in the sacrament; here truly is the holy place! Here God works! Here the Holy One lays hold on me, He who heals, saves and sanctifies! We never tire of stressing the point that religion is personal encounter with God. True and effective religion is always a living dialog between God and man. Even pagan religions betray some slight trace of this concept of encounter. But the sacramental encounter is far more than an understanding of this law of "the religious." In the sacraments the Christian experiences the encounter with all its objective and intimate assurance.

We should not at all look upon the sacraments as a species of spiritual medication nor as means of grace severed from their divine source, which alone makes them efficacious. For in every sacrament there is the effective presence of God acting through the sensible sign, assuring us here and now of His healing and sanctifying activity.[54] The Church's doctrine on sacramental causality (*opus operatum*) with its priority over the work of the recipient brings to the fore the gratuitous efficacy of God's presence and the primacy of His grace. The encounter and its efficacy in the sacraments is not from us but from God. But the divine operation is directed to us, it calls out to us, never failing to sanctify and heal us if we are open to the encounter with Him (if we are properly *disposed*).

1. *The Dimensions of Sacramental Encounter*

The sacramental encounter with Christ does not cease after the sacrament has been received, even though the special sacramental action does not continue. But the effect of the word of love remains, a love which addressed to us takes possession of us forever and demands from us a permanent response of obedience and love in return. And God, who wills to complete and perfect what He has begun in us, fills us with assurance through the love He has wrought within us that He will be faithful to His promises. He invites us to continue the life of the sacramental dialog and to deepen and enrich it day by day. The glory and majesty of God (*dóxa*) descending upon us in the sacraments is charged with the divine might and power (Col 1:11). The divine sanctity demands our response. The gift of God lays claim upon our moral life; through it we are *assigned* to the divine service.

As we have already noted, sacramental morality is profoundly religious in its inspiration and as such is essentially a morality of response, a grateful and loving response to the divine gift of grace.

In the clearest terms St. Paul speaks of the basic sacramental realities as of God's present action in us, as gifts received.[55] These realities are the death, burial, resurrection, and exaltation of Christ, with which we are united through our participation in the celebration of the sacred liturgy. Though there is not a moment's doubt in the mind of St. Paul that justification and sanctification, the new being in Christ, is given to us freely, it is equally certain that they place an imperative on our free will. The thought keeps recurring in St. Paul in practically the same words. It is the imperative demanding a holy life, a renewal of justice within us, a life in heaven, a dying with Christ (Rom 6:1–22; 8:9–17; 1 Cor 6:8–11; 2 Cor

5:17–6:1; Gal 5:25; Col 1:9–14). Obviously this morality is totally foreign to the magic of the pagan mystery cults and, likewise, to all quietism or indifference to moral earnestness.

The sacraments do not merely proclaim salvation. They are not merely on the level of the preaching of the word which is calculated to awaken faith and love. Contrary to a certain Protestant conception of the sacrament as the sign inciting to the faith by which one is justified, these sacred signs signify and effect grace. They are not merely words which demand response, but bounteous, creative, salvific words which produce the grace they signify. Objectively they move and incite man in his inner freedom to a newness of being.

The Catholic doctrine is consequently much more than a mere rigid opposition to a one-sided Protestant notion of the sacrament as the divine word which stimulates faith. It would be altogether false and inadequate to stress exclusively the objective efficacy of God's work (the *opus operatum*) and neglect to emphasize the movement of the recipient under the pressing imperative of grace, which rests on the gratuitous act of God in the sacraments. Both must be fully stressed: the creative, sanctifying, and healing work of God and the personal response and responsibility under the impulse of grace. The Catholic concept stresses the personal no less than does the Protestant notion. Precisely because we place clearly in the foreground the creative bounty of the divine action and derive from it the moral-responsive endeavor of man, our concept of sacrament is unsurpassably dynamic, religious-moral, and personal in the sense of the *I-Thou* personalism of the inspired pages.

2. *The Sacramental Word of Christ*

The sacraments are dialog with Christ and, likewise, a participation in real being in and through Christ. The minister of the Church and the sacramental sign (symbol and word, matter and form) are merely the instruments used by Him who makes them effective, Christ. They are His signs and means signifying and effecting grace. In the most Holy Eucharist, the center of all the sacraments, Christ is found not merely in the effect of His power, but also really and permanently, as long as the sacramental species remain. He is "present through His power (*virtute praesens*)" in all the sacraments; but all center in the Eucharist and radiate from it, with Christ working in and through them all.[56]

Christ Himself is the supreme Sacrament. The most sacred humanity of Christ, in a manner of speaking the instrument of redemption, is the invincible cause of all graces. Through it the sacraments have all their power, for they "thrive entirely on the force flowing to them from the sacred humanity of Christ."[57] Sacramental graces are graces of Christ, bonds with Christ, foundation of the life formed in Christ. Accordingly, they constantly call to our attention the significant truth that we meet God only in Christ, that Christ is the "way and the life."

As Christ truly cured the blind, using spittle as a symbol of His marvelous power, so does He truly work through the sacramental signs. He encompasses us effectively with His salvific embrace and binds us to Himself. The sacramental sign in the unity of symbol and word (matter and form) is in the dimension of the personal. It is the Word of Address, the Summons of Christ directed to us personally.

The fact that Protestants in great part cling to the mistaken notion that the sacramental signs and ceremonies surrounding them are mere empty words does not justify us in slighting the true power of the sacramental word and the ecclesiastical ceremonial as personal encounter with the Spirit of God, when we defend, as we should and must, the efficient causality of the sacramental sign which penetrates into the very heart of real being. Unfortunately this important point of the significance of the words and rites, with all their power to move the heart of man, is obscured at times by a thoughtless and slovenly manner of administration.

3. Valid and Fruitful Administration of the Sacraments

The fact that Christ chose as salutary instruments of His sacramental encounter with us expressive actions with audible and intelligible words obliges the minister of the sacrament—under pain of nullity—first of all, to safeguard the sacramental sign instituted by Christ. This is to say that he may never change the matter (element and symbolical action) or the form (the symbolical words). In instances of doubt about the validity of matter he is not permitted to follow an opinion that is merely probable: which is to say that, if there is objectively reasonable doubt about the validity of the matter, he may not use it in the administration. Nor is he permitted to modify or vary the sacramental form. The history of the sacraments shows that the Church does not feel bound by a fixed and determined formula of words and surely not by a sacred language. The formulas she has used vary considerably according to the various rites and periods of history, though the sense or meaning of the words remains the same. The individual minister of the sacrament, however, must adhere strictly to the matter and form prescribed for his rite as found in the approved official books. He cannot at all claim for himself any power which the Church may possess regarding any modification of the sacramental sign. Here we are not speaking of an arbitrary alteration of matter or form on his part which surely would be sinful.[58]

Insignificant variations in the matter or form due to human frailty or to the great need for urgency in emergencies neither endanger the valid administration of the sacrament nor render the minister guilty of sin. However a substantial change in the matter or in the significance of the words is never permitted.

It is not sufficient that the sacrament be validly administered. The sacred sign as instrument of grace must also be administered in a manner suited to its dignity. The minister must observe the norms laid down in the liturgical books for the licit and worthy dispensing of these means of grace. Even though the sacrament is not exclusively the proclamation of the word or declaration of salvation (not declaratory or exhortatory) but rather the effecting of salvation and sanctification (consecratory),[59] nevertheless, Christ chose for that consecration a most suitable sign to which the minister is obliged to give adequate and meaningful expression. As long as the use of the vernacular is not permitted by the liturgical norms, it is a pressing duty of the minister of the sacraments or of those having the care of souls to explain to the faithful the rich meaning of the formulas and rites as found in the liturgical books.[60]

By means of the objectively effective word of the sacramental sign Christ wills to sanctify the heart of man in the Holy Spirit and thereby also speak directly and personally to him. But to be open to this sacred address of the Master in the sacraments requires more than mere comprehension of the significance of the action and the word. It means attention with true faith to all that Christ says to us through the Church about the holy sacraments. It is loving openness to the interior appeal of Christ's unique call of grace. Sign and word are the instrument reflecting the bright rays of the Eternal Word opening itself to us, giving itself to us, demanding from us for itself the response of our love.

Through the ensemble of rites and prayers surrounding the sacramental rite like a garland the Church wishes to interpret for us more profoundly and fully and bring closer to our minds and hearts the in-exhaustible riches and beauty of the sacrament. But even more important is the fact that this rite as prayer and word of power of the Church is a sacramental. The more perfect, the more expressive, the more tender and intimate the manner in which the sacrament is dispensed, the more pleas-ing it is to God and the more fruitful for the recipient, precisely because the sacramentals derive their force from the action and prayer of the Church. And the task of the Church in the person of the minister who prays or proclaims the word can be well performed or, alas, very poorly. Hence the action of the Church in the person of the minister can profit or suffer through decorous or shabby performance. Surely the suffrages and the suffering of the Church compensate to a degree for such defects of the individual minister. But he himself can never shirk the responsibility, if he neglects to dispense sacrament and sacramental with the dignity and impressiveness which their significance and the needs of the faithful demand. It is particularly worthy of note that a hasty and slovenly execu-tion of the sacred rites robs them of their spiritual impressiveness and partially explains why so many Christians fail to appreciate and experi-ence the personal character of the encounter with Christ in the sacraments.

These explanations on the validity and liceity of the administration of the sacraments help to furnish the answer to certain practical questions regarding the matter and form. The matter (the symbolical action or the element and the action) and the form (this is called the *words* and usually consists of words) must be so united as to be morally one. This is to say that the intelligent observer should be able without special study or ex-planation to see that the two belong together and make complete sense in their relation to each other. The matter is informed by the words and together they are the significant and effective sign.

The element or symbolical thing is the remote matter (*materia remota*). The use or application of this remote matter is called the proximate matter, which is the symbolical action (e.g., the water for baptism is the remote matter, the pouring or washing with the water is the proximate matter). In some sacraments there is no material thing used and hence we do not speak of a remote matter, but simply of the matter (e.g. the matter in holy orders is the imposition of hands).

In forming our judgment on the validity of the sacraments it is good to note that in the last century the laudable concern of the moral theo-logians for the greatest possible certainty in matters of validity led to constantly increasing severity. It may be that too great a concern was shown for certain rigid and severe views as to what was required for valid administration. Perhaps it is prudent and opportune for us today to approach the matter with some relaxation of anxiety, particularly in view of the findings in historical theology.

Under normal conditions every conscientious priest will be guided by the usage and prescriptions of the Church. But what shall we say of extraordinary situations or extreme emergencies (such as exist in slave or refugee camps or among deportees and exiles in some parts of the world)? In such circumstances one must first of all be guided by the principle that the validity and suitability of the remote matter of the sacrament is not to be determined according to scientific formulas but according to the direct understanding of the simple ordinary man. Hence what people ordinarily look upon as grape wine and ordinarily look upon as wheat bread is valid matter for the Eucharistic sacrifice. And under the circumstances the use would also be licit.

Let us note that whereas it is never permitted to use any matter which is strictly and objectively doubtful for the celebration of Mass, the same restriction does not hold for administration of the sacraments which may be necessary for salvation. In instances of emergency it may be permitted to use objectively doubtful matter (provided nothing else is available) to administer these sacraments. This is true of extreme unction and even more so of baptism. However in such instances the minister avoids profaning the sacrament and exposing it to nullity by administering it conditionally (e.g. If this is truly water, I baptize you, etc.).

Furthermore it is obvious that the matter should consist of the choicest fruits of the earth, pure clear water, good olive oil, fine wheaten bread, good wine. Vinegar is not wine and therefore not valid matter for holy Mass. Wine that is souring and turning to vinegar, if it is still wine, is valid but not licit matter. Should there be real objective reason to doubt whether or not it is still wine, it may never be used, even in serious emergencies.

4. *The Dispositions for Valid and Fruitful Reception*

From the standpoint of the person receiving the sacrament we must be concerned with the relation toward God in Christ, with the work of Christ in the Holy Spirit, and with the form of words and the efficacy of the sacred encounter itself. As to the dispositions of the recipient there is necessary: 1. the right intention; 2. faith; 3. salutary hope; 4. docility toward the bountiful divine will; 5. sanctifying grace with charity or at least (for sacraments of the dead) the removal of all serious obstacles to the reception of the life of grace; 6. the will to participate in the divine cult; 7. willing disposition to fulfill all the special sacramental obligations.

a. The Intention

It is obvious that without an intention there can be no sacramental encounter. Without the mind and will to approach God in the sacrament, which is to open one's self to Christ in the sacrament, there can be no personal encounter. Of course we must rightly ponder the unique character of this personal approach, otherwise we might draw false conclusions from the personalism of this community of word and response. An infant cannot form an intention, because it has not reached the age of reason; but it also cannot place an obstacle preventing the action of Christ, who can embrace it with His creative-redemptive action and efficacy. The Church herself offers the child and, dependently upon her, the parents present it for baptism to receive the free gift of Christ's sacramental work.

The adult, precisely because he possesses the use of reason, must manifest according to the reason and freedom which is his the positive will to receive the sacrament. For this consent of his will he must possess some measure of knowledge of the significance of the sacrament and a corresponding penetration into its meaning. Should some one seek nothing beyond the performance of the external rite, should he care nothing for personal encounter with Christ, expect nothing from the Church of Christ in the sacrament nor accept any obligation, he does not possess the requisite intention for a valid reception.

It is not necessary that the intention be actually formed interiorly or be renewed at the very moment the rite is administered. It is sufficient that the intention once actually made remain in effect. However, for those sacraments which are the foundation of special states of life with serious obligations (*holy order, matrimony*) it is necessary that an explicit intention to receive them have been made and never revoked. Baptism does not require such an explicit intention, though the intention for this sacrament must be more explicit than the intention necessary for the sacrament of extreme unction, since baptism is the foundation of the whole Christian life with all its rights and duties. Therefore, the adult about to be baptized must have at least the implicit desire or will (this may be included in a more general intention) to become a Christian, if the sacrament is to be valid. Thus a formal decision of readiness to do all that God demands and to accept all that God wills to do in us is a species of all-inclusive baptism of desire and might perhaps be sufficient for the valid reception of baptism, even without any express reference to the sacrament of baptism.

Since the acts of the penitent in a special manner become a part of the matter of the sacrament of penance, it is necessary that the recipient form an explicit intention of some kind. Of course in this instance there is still theological controversy about the nature of the matter of the sacrament, for some authors hold that the entire essence of the sacrament consists in the sacramental absolution which usually is considered the form.

For valid reception of extreme unction the Christian sense may be considered sufficient: this implicitly includes the desire to die as a Christian and to receive the sacraments of the dying. Precisely because of the intensely personal character of this final encounter with Christ it is most important that the Christian in the days of good health awaken the desire to receive the sacraments of the dying fruitfully. In fact the good Christian does this frequently, for he prays with the Church to be spared an unexpected death; he asks for a happy death. It is totally contrary to the Christian ideal to desire a sudden and unexpected death. Only the pagan can say of the sudden and unforeseen death: "what a nice way to die!" The Christian seeks to meet death as the portal to eternal glory!

b. Faith

The very foundation of the personal claim to the holy sacraments is faith. Not without reason does the rite of baptism, particularly in the ancient Church, lay so much stress on the solemn profession of faith. Solemnly taught and inculcated, it was solemnly accepted as a most basic commitment at baptism.[61] Likewise in the very heart of the liturgy, at the solemn moment of consecration in holy Mass, the priest utters the words *"mysterium fidei,"* mystery or sacrament of faith. Thus the whole economy of the sacraments is steeped in the mystery of faith. Wherever the sacrament is, wherever we encounter Christ, there we are called to testify to our faith. St. Thomas calls the holy sacraments "signs attesting to faith" (*signa protestantia fidem, qua justificatur homo*).[62] For him baptism is the "sacrament of faith."[63] The reception of the sacraments is for him the summit of realization of the faith.[64]

Since justification is impossible without faith, the fruitful reception of any sacrament is impossible without faith. It is true that a species of imperfect faith not sufficient for justification may suffice for the valid reception of certain sacraments and therefore for the sacramental character in baptism, confirmation, and holy order, and the establishment of the sacramental bond in matrimony. But in such instances the recipient is still subject to the claim of the faith which saves; these sacraments urgently cry out to him to make the salutary act of faith. And they "revive again," which is to say they confer their graces on the recipient, once he has removed the obstacle to grace. The obstacle is the lack of the right disposition whose basic element is living faith.

A superficial view of the matter might lead to the conclusion that the baptism of infants is totally excluded from the baptism of faith, for the infant surely cannot elicit any rational act. But its tender Mother, the Church, maintains and awakens faith in the name of the infant. Moreover, she demands as condition for permitting the baptism a solid (moral) assurance that the child shall be brought up in the faith. Therefore the baptism of infants is also a baptism of faith: Christ imparts the power to believe through the infused virtue of faith. He grants faith as a permanent gift and with it lays claim to the child for its entire life. He summons the child to the response of faith which the Church in her own solemn and sacred formulas pronounces in the name of the infant. The Church and the parents assume the responsibility that at the proper time the child be made aware of the graces and duties committed to him in the sacrament, so that faith is consciously awakened.

c. Hope

Hope, which as such is reaching out to Christ our Savior, is an essential part of the disposition necessary for fruitful reception of the sacraments. As salvific intervention of God in our behalf, the sacraments are means of grace, earnest money, and pledges of still greater bounty, guaranty of the helps of grace to attain eternal life. In the sacraments the divine generosity holds its rendezvous with its unique claim on our confidence and hope. The fruitful reception presupposes the will to hope, but the virtue of hope is truly vitalized and called to active engagement through the mercy of God active in the sacrament. One who doubts the mercy of God cannot receive the fruits of any sacrament. Even worse, his doubt is a gross injustice to God and the sacrament, which is invitation and assurance of the divine loving-kindness.

d. Docility toward the Divine Will

Indispensable disposition for the fruitful reception of the sacraments is the fundamental willingness to obey the will of God. We might speak of this as "the good or firm resolution to serve God," for one cannot be implanted into the life of Christ without submission to His will. The true docility requisite for the fruitful reception of the sacraments, the obedience which most properly corresponds to these sacred signs is obedience flowing from love, readiness to live according to the law of love: this is to make the bounteous will of God our standard of life. Should the sacrament by its very nature demand this love as prerequisite for fruitful reception, should love be the golden center of the spirit of obedience from which the very fruitfulness flows, then we call the sacrament a "sacrament of the living." But should the sacrament be such that it is intended to impart this true salvific basis of obedience, the divine life of love, to the soul, then we have a "sacrament of the dead."

e. Splendor of Love

The disposition necessary for the fruitful reception of the sacraments of the living so that one worthily encounters the Heavenly Bridegroom[65] is the splendor of divine charity and the divine life in our souls. The sacraments of the dead, baptism and penance, which are sacraments of conversion, introduce this life; the other sacraments, sacraments of the living, presuppose it. Therefore the Christian who has committed a grave sin must follow the way of conversion before he can again approach the sacraments of the living. For the reception of Holy Communion the way of conversion is the sacrament of penance.[66]

Only for very serious reasons (for example, urgent necessity to celebrate Mass or danger of suffering great loss to one's good name by abstaining from Holy Communion or for similar reasons) is one permitted to receive Holy Communion without *previous confession and absolution,* provided, of course, the reception of the sacrament of penance is morally impossible. However, in such cases it is absolutely necessary to make a serious effort to elicit an act of perfect contrition.

The priest who has celebrated Mass under these conditions must receive the sacrament of penance as soon as this is possible,[67] if he is at all able to do so, before he again celebrates the holy Sacrifice. The authors who allow a maximum limit of three days for this confession invariably hold that the confession must precede the very next celebration of Mass. Only if one should not say holy Mass in the interval is he permitted to wait three days before receiving the sacrament of penance.

What we have just said holds, strictly speaking, only for the reception of the Eucharist or the celebration of holy Mass. For the other sacraments of the living it is sufficient to strive earnestly to make an act of perfect contrition before receiving them, if one should have fallen into mortal sin since his last worthy confession. It is always safer and more advisable, however, to receive the sacrament of penance as soon as possible after one has committed mortal sin, particularly if one is to receive any sacrament of the living.

Should any one in good faith and with the spirit of true docility and obedience to God receive a sacrament of the living, even though as a matter of fact he may not be in the state of grace, he will receive sanctifying grace through this reception of the sacrament. Thus it is possible that sacraments of the living, according to the safe and universal teaching of theologians, function as a sacrament of the dead. *Per accidens* they operate as sacraments of conversion, even though the recipient is not aware of it.

f. Disposition for Divine Cult

The spirit of docility and obedience in the reception of the sacraments includes necessarily and in the first place the readiness and proper disposition for true worship of God. It is very important to foster this spirit in the sacramental encounter, particularly in the reception of the sacraments which imprint a character and in the Eucharist, for the very simple reason that the sacraments through their efficacy and their assignment to the spiritual life direct us to the glory of God. The sacraments which imprint a character are the priestly sacraments assimilating men to the priesthood of Christ, and they therefore essentially order man to the divine cult. The most intimate participation in the divine worship is in the celebration of the Mass and in Holy Communion.

g. Gratitude

Our dispositions in receiving the sacraments consist in the necessary readiness to accept the divine action, the effective word of the divine love, rightly in our hearts. In accordance with these dispositions of the recipient the fruits of grace vary. But it is the divine action itself, the mighty word of grace of the holy sacraments, rather than any act of ours, which permanently places us in the dialog with Christ. This word of power so effective in our hearts lays claim to a gratitude which is never satisfied with mere formulas of thanks but manifests itself in deeds. Sacramental gratitude is expressed in a life flowing from the graces received, a life which is the fulfillment of the sacramental assignment. It is formed in the domain and spirit of the sacramental encounter with Christ.

h. Restoration of the Sacramental Efficacy

Particularly consoling is the theological doctrine of the revival or reviviscence of sacraments which are received validly though not fruitfully because of the absence of the dispositions required for worthy reception. According to this teaching, the efficacy of the sacrament is restored and the grace is given on the removal of the obstacle (*obex*) which stood in the way. Such revival of sacramental efficacy must be admitted in the case of the three sacraments which imprint an indelible mark (baptism, confirmation, holy order) and for that reason can never be repeated. The same holds good for the two other sacraments which cannot be repeated during the very period for which the grace they give is intended and necessary. (These are *extreme unction,* which is administered in serious illness, and *matrimony,* in which the bond endures till the death of one of the partners.)

The most solid and attractive reason for this doctrine of the restoration of sacramental effectiveness is the sacral and cultal function of the sacrament. It is the cultal assignment which the sacrament, validly though fruitlessly received, has imposed upon the recipient. Whenever God lays claim to some one for His special service, validly and irrevocably, He will not fail to grant all the graces necessary for the discharge of the task assigned. Such is His mercy that He will give these helps even though the recipient was not properly disposed to receive them at the moment the sacrament was conferred. If God in His holiness still demands the fulfillment of the task imposed, He is ready to grant the required graces to the unworthy recipient, after a true conversion has removed the obstacle to the effectiveness of the sacrament.

If these sacraments have been received not merely fruitlessly—because of ignorance regarding the necessity or the existence of the required dispositions—but also unworthily and sacrilegiously, then we have every reason to fear that the measure of grace restored (the degree of sanctifying grace and the power or abundance of actual graces) will be less generous and less abundant than in the case of the unfruitful reception in good faith. We have reason to hold that God will be more generous in His gifts to those whose dispositions, though inadequate, were at least not sinful or even malicious. On the other hand, we should not be unmindful of the divine loving-kindness which meets sincere repentance with a welcome of infinite love, and bestows grace in the very measure of the spirit of sorrow and overwhelms the most miserable sinner with the wealth of divine favor.

As to the Holy Eucharist, perhaps a kind of reviviscence of the sacramental efficacy may be defended. However, we should limit it to the instances in which the proper dispositions are restored in the recipient (at least to the degree of imperfect contrition) during the time the sacramental species give us the assurance that the Eucharistic Lord is still sacramentally present.[68] But we see no valid reason for holding that the sacrament of penance, which can be received frequently, admits of any reviviscence of sacramental efficacy at all.

IV. THE SACRAMENTS AS SIGNS OF THE ECCLESIAL COMMUNION

The sacraments belong to the very essence of the Church; they are the gifts of Christ who formed her as His Bride. As dowry from the heavenly Bridegroom, they are her gift to her children. As essential to the very nature in which she was fashioned by her Founder, they are the ties of the sacred membership in the Mystical Body in the basic tasks of worshipping God. They are the source of her supernatural life and power. In this sense they are always sacraments of the Church and of Christ whose

Mystical Body she is. Therefore she is their minister on whom they depend absolutely. Not only does she have the power and duty to safeguard the entire substance of the sacraments as instituted by Christ; she has the full authority to regulate their use, to enrich them with ecclesiastical rites, to control those who administer them. Even the validity of their administration is impossible without a true bond with the Church.

1. *The Sacraments in the Community of Worship*

The Church was born on Calvary in the bloody sacrifice of Christ. Says St. Thomas: "Through the sacraments which flowed from the side of Christ hanging on the Cross the Church of Christ is built."[69] Thus the sole community of divine worship which is pleasing to God has its source and support in the sacrifice of Calvary. The most sublime bridal dowry bestowed upon His Bride by the Lord in His sacrifice is the Eucharistic sacrament-sacrifice[70] and the garland of the other sacraments woven about it. Only through the sacraments is the Church truly holy, united with God, sanctified and ordered to the sanctification of men, a community of divine worship in whose liturgy God is glorified through Christ from the rising to the setting of the sun. Through her sacraments she is the temple of God (Eph 2:21; 2 Cor 6:16; 1 Cor 3:16), the true center of worship, the holy community. Through divine convocation (the *ekklesía*) she is summoned in the unity of all the sanctified to chant with Christ the praise of the Father.

The supreme goal of the Church is identical with that of Christ Himself; the glory of the triune God: "that God may be all in all" (1 Cor 15:28). Through her holy liturgy the Church sanctifies her members, who with her and in her give glory to God and thereby really enter into the divine glory. Through the spirit of holiness and majesty which has descended upon her and the divine graces with which God has endowed her, she chants the jubilant hymn of praise in the name of all mankind, glorifying the new creation of man redeemed. The Church with her sacraments is essentially priestly, dedicated to worship. Through the sacrament of baptism which is the portal of the Church men are incorporated into the "royal priesthood" (1 Pt 2:9; Ex 19:6; Ap 1:6). Salvation is in her alone.

From this truth that she is the only saving Church we may never conclude that beyond the visible bounds of the Catholic Church no divine grace is granted. Only the most perverted conception of the divine bounty and mercy could lead to such a conclusion. But it is true that all graces have in the bond of love between Christ and His Bride, the Church, their source and point of reference, just as they all derive from Christ and refer back to Christ. Likewise, we must insist that sanctification and means of holiness ordered to true divine cult are found only in the Church. In her alone can we, in this order of time and space, praise and honor God as is just and right. All honor paid to God outside the Church has value and weight in His eyes only by reference to Christ and "the Church, which indeed is his body, the fulness of him who is wholly fulfilled in all" (Eph 1:23). All those who receive the sacraments validly outside the visible confines of the Catholic Church and, in harmony with these means of grace, lead a good and holy life have some share in the royal priesthood of the one true Church whose sacraments they receive. And even those who receive the grace of justification without the use of these visible signs of grace are at least implicitly and by desire in the sacred choir of the unique community of cult, though they are not strictly members of the Church.

2. The Social Character of the Sacraments

It is no more possible to conceive of the Church without the sacraments than of the sacraments without the Church. Together with the divine commission to rule and teach and preserve the deposit of the revealed truth these holy signs constitute the sacred social order. We can understand them only as gifts of the community of salvation, and we can understand the community only in the light of the sacraments. It follows that they are the sacred bond of its unity and sanctity. Therefore, the spiritual individualist who is entirely preoccupied with his own soul's salvation and follows a solitary path of holiness and perfection even to the point of severing himself from the community in the worship of God outrageously disregards the objective nature of the sacraments and their profound appeal to our mind and heart.

The sacraments constitute for our entire moral and religious life a social imperative because they are essentially a social reality. They form an objectively real bond of all the members of the Church uniting us all in the one Mystical Body. Therefore, they are Holy Assignment to unity and partnership in a responsibility of spirit and deed, to a harmony of hearts and hands. Particularly St. Paul develops this theme with characteristic insistence in his doctrine on baptism (Eph 4:5f.) and the Holy Eucharist (1 Cor 10:16f.).

The Church is founded on the mysterious redemptive solidarity of the Savior with the multitude. By entering us into the salvific work of Christ the sacraments summon us to the community of saints and bid us share the solidarity of salvation, in which the individual no longer lives for himself alone, but one for the other and everyone for the entire community.

The community in its form and spirit arises from the sacraments. From them too comes the vocation and mission to the life of the spirit, first in the unity of worship and then in the solidarity of responsible partnership for salvation. One upon whom God has showered the favors of His graces in the sacraments of the community must realize that his salvation is rendered more secure if the grace received is claim and assignment to apostolic love for the community, particularly for its weakest members.

Since the holy sacraments are the leaven which purges and transforms our entire life, they are also a social ferment and force affecting not only our spiritual attitudes in the social order but even the details of our material existence. One who has partaken of the supersubstantial bread in the community of divine love, who has slaked his thirst on the Mystical Blood of the divine Bridegroom offered in sacrifice by his Mother the Church, the divine Bride, can no longer remain in tranquil possession of superfluous earthly goods while his neighbor and fellow member of the sacred community lives in misery. Rather he will relax his tense grip on material things to offer them open-handedly for pious and worthy causes.

All the sacraments are objective signs of holy fellowship, real ties binding and committing the members of the sacred community. Baptism is the sign of the Covenant, the familial bond and seal. The baptized receives all the rights of the child of God and the Church, particularly the right to participate in the Eucharistic celebration and to receive the sacraments. But it also imposes duties, the duties of sonship, tender love, respect, and obedience toward his Mother the Church. "For in one Spirit we were all baptized into one body, whether Jews or Gentiles, whether slaves or free; and we were all given to drink of one Spirit" (1 Cor 12:13). In the light of the one baptism in Christ all natural diversity or division is insignificant (cf. Gal 3:27ff.; Eph 4:4ff.).

Confirmation bestows upon the child of God, the son of the Church, the gift of the Holy Spirit, who binds us all together in the holy community. It confers the apostolate of profession of faith, "for the confirmed receive the power of publicly professing the faith of Christ in words and, as it were, officially."[71] As adult citizens and as soldiers we are committed to public engagement for the cause of God's kingdom in the spirit of loving harmony. One and the same Spirit bestows a diversity of gifts for the building up of the one Body of the Church (1 Cor 12:4ff.). The law of the Spirit and of the life in Christ Jesus frees us from the law of sin, that is, from the solidarity in perdition (*hamartía*). We are freed indeed through the solidarity of salvation in the Church.

Priestly consecration and sanctity must be accepted as sacrificial service of the community at the altar to continue throughout the whole of life. The exalted dignity of priesthood is not for the priest personally. The priest must turn not to himself but to Christ, who confers with the priesthood the assignment of total and unreserved service for the brethren. The high priestly prayer of Jesus reaches its climax in the petition for unity and concord among the Apostles and their successors, through which the world will be brought to faith in Him, the Ambassador of the Father (Jn 17:6ff.). The priesthood should sustain in unity and solidarity of salvation all those "who through their word are to believe" (Jn 17:20).

Through the priesthood we have the celebration of the communion of salvation in loving solidarity with the Savior. The breaking of bread at the table of love makes us one family in the blood of the same Savior, dedicated to love which is at once oblation, self-sacrifice, and the bond of invincible unity in Christ. It was not by chance that Christ promulgated His new commandment that we love one another as He loved us (Jn 15:12) at the Last Supper. Here above all He prays for harmony and solidarity among His followers. "The bread that we break" forms and founds the community with the Body of Christ. "Because the bread is one, we, though many, are one body, all of us who partake of the one bread" (1 Cor 10:16f.).

In the sacrament of *penance* the Church looses the bond of sin which has held her child captive and enjoins on him salutary and grateful expiation. The baptized sinner has not only offended God by his sin but also the community of worship and salvation which is the Church. And therefore in this sacrament he is given with the word of divine pardon granted by the Church also the duty of reparation and expiation before the community for the hurt his sin has inflicted on her and her children. Extreme

Unction completes the work of penance. In the sacred anointing of her members who are gravely ill, the Church manifests the concern of a Mother for her children by the most powerful assistance in the hour of greatest crisis. But the anointing is also a steeping of our sufferings into those of Christ. Our submissive *yes* to the summons of death and our pain and agony become one with the Mystery of the passion and death and resurrection of Christ, the High Priest, in a salutary union.

The sacrament of *matrimony* does not merely unite the noble love of two human beings by a holy and indissoluble bond. It forms a new community of members and engrafts it onto the tree of the Church. It invites and blesses a human fruitfulness which through baptism, the font of spiritual rebirth, brings new members into the Church. Sanctified by this holy sacramental union, the spouses assume its serious responsibilities. As each is taken up entirely with the other, so both accept lovingly their duties toward the Church.

If we live from the force of the holy sacraments and faithful to the mission they give to us, then the Church is truly the house of divine praise in which we all join, the center of mutual charity and responsibility.

The entire fabric of our social life with its social endeavors should be placed on a higher level than that of natural law and natural right. We must view it in the light of supernatural forces and figures, particularly in the light of Christ as supreme in the whole order of being. Without doubt, in our dealings with non-Christians, which involve cooperative effort in social life, we can certainly appeal to the principles of the natural law as more readily acceptable and as offering a common basis for united effort toward certain desirable goals which all accept as good. But for our own conduct and for the ultimate orientation of our life the forms and the laws of the sacramental life of grace must be taken as seriously as the natural laws. In fact we cannot clearly grasp and correctly carry out these latter, unless we consider them in the light of the totality of the supernatural order in which God has placed them. Thus the sacraments, particularly those which imprint a character, give us not only for the strictly religious or sacred domain but also for the formation of public life itself a social mission, a participation in the mission of the Church in the sanctification of all creation.

Since the sacraments, the Eucharist especially, are "signs of unity, bonds of love and manifestations of harmony"[72] nothing should be lacking in their celebration and administration. Their communal character and spiritual significance should be evident from the beauty and decorum of words and movements in which minister and faithful devoutly participate.[73]

3. Church Membership and Reception of the Sacraments

The sacraments as signs of the ecclesial communion are reserved for the members of the Church. All who are baptized and free from heresy and schism and certain other flagrant sins belong to this community with the right and duty of sacramental reception.

a. Entry through Baptism

All those who have the sincere desire to become members of the Church and live as members have the right to baptism. Even for infants who have not yet attained the use of reason the Church demands as a condition for their admission to baptism previous assurance of a certain minimum of Catholic instruction and training. Therefore, except in danger of death, they may not be baptized without the consent of at least one of the parents or of some other person responsible for their upbringing.[74] However, this principle is not to be insisted upon too rigorously. To demand an absolute assurance that the child will be brought up a Catholic as a condition for baptism might result in the deprivation of the sacrament for many who would die in infancy. Or in some cases the chances for an eventual Catholic upbringing and education might actually be lessened.[75]

In accordance with a well-established principle in the Church, infants are not to be baptized against the will of their parents or guardians. But once they have attained the use of reason, even though they are still minors, children are entirely within their right in making their own decision in this fundamental matter and may rightly and justly be baptized even against the will of their parents or guardians, should they earnestly ask to receive the sacrament.[76] Though prudence surely would urge that parents be asked to give their consent, their refusal would not justify a priest in denying the child's request. In fact it would be a grave injustice to refuse to baptize him.

Any one baptized, no matter by whom, is by the very fact of the reception of the sacrament a member of the Church as to right. Baptism is the sign of the bond and the covenant of union with the one true Bride of Christ. In consequence, infants who have been validly baptized by heretics, even should their parents be non-Catholics, are not strictly required to join the Church as converts, provided they have never by any personal responsible act severed themselves from her. According to the Church law "they are not to be considered non-Catholics, even in the external forum, up to their fourteenth year and therefore can be admitted to the Church's communion without formal abjuration of error or absolution from censures."[77]

In some places this principle might prove very practical in the following instance: a child of non-Catholic parents may not be able to register officially as a member of the Catholic Church because of opposition on the part of its parents or because of some legal restriction, even though his participation in Catholic life and worship and dealing with him as a genuine child of the Church justify the hope that he will remain a loyal son. To refuse the sacraments to such a child merely because bureaucratic officials are hostile and will not register his name officially as a Catholic would constitute a gross injustice to a true child of the Church. In such matters the decision must be dictated by pastoral prudence. The priest or director of souls can make a prudent decision only after he has studied the matter in the light of all the facts.

b. Administering Sacraments to Non-Catholics

Since every sacrament is a sign of real and objective communion with the Church, professed membership in an heretical or schismatical community deprives one of the right to receive the sacraments. Even though every baptized person remains forever orientated toward the Catholic Church through the indelible mark of baptism, the Church, as a matter of principle based on the very nature of the sacraments, must refuse to administer them to any heretic or schismatic. From the moment of their affiliation or profession in the group, the Church must refuse them participation in the sacraments until they are reconciled to her by renunciation of their errors.[78] Nevertheless, if baptized non-Catholics should be in error without fault of their own, and if they sincerely follow their conscience, the Church looks upon them as her true children according to inner disposition. Therefore, in her pastoral tenderness and love for souls she will go as far as she can in this matter, as long as every semblance of approval of heresy or schism is absent. For this reason, in the administration of the sacraments of the dying, she will be content in urgent cases "with an implicit repudiation of error and an implicit profession of faith if no more can be expected in view of the conditions and persons concerned."[79]

For the administration of the sacraments to non-Catholics we are able to determine in a general way certain rules and typical cases. But we cannot set up exact norms of procedure which must be rigidly applied in all instances. In fact each instance must be studied sympathetically and judged prudently in the light of the true spiritual welfare of the individual or the group which deserves our compassion. But one must also safeguard the ideal of love for the true Church and testimony to the true faith.

(1) *In Danger of Death*

Non-Catholics who are unconscious may be given conditional baptism if it is necessary, and even conditional sacramental absolution and extreme unction, provided that there is prudent hope that the sacraments will redound to their eternal salvation. One can ordinarily avoid scandal by a prudent explanation of the circumstances, stressing especially the presumption of the sincerity and good faith of the individual and the tender solicitude of the Church. According to *Arthur Vermeersch, S.J.*, we may hold as probable the opinion that the desire for baptism is contained implicitly in all genuine sorrow for sin. This means that practically the complete openness to God's will and the disposition to accept His grace is sufficient.[80]

As to those who are still in a state of consciousness (though in danger of death) and able to manifest their sentiments, we must distinguish between those actually aware of their separation from the Catholic Church and those who do not realize this fact: "The latter who are not aware of this separation from the Church, may be given those sacraments which they desire to receive worthily,"[81] provided of course that there is no scandal involved. Those who are conscious of this separation from the Church are to be advised in a gentle and loving manner that the Catholic priest is not permitted to administer the sacraments to them unless they profess—also externally—their adherence to the Church according to the circumstances. But should the priest seriously fear that his explanation and admonition might jeopardize the eternal salvation of the sick man by destroying his good faith, then, according to Vermeersch[82] and the noted and respected theologians whom he cites, a much milder decision is indicated. The great Jesuit moralist says that under such conditions he would not presume to condemn the priest who should administer the sacraments, including the Holy Eucharist, to the sick non-Catholic, if the refusal of the sacraments might create a similar peril to his salvation.

(2) *Outside the Danger of Death*

Those who are conscious of their separation from the Church, even though they are sincere and in good faith, may not be admitted to the communion of the sacraments, which is the Church, unless they explicitly abjure their heresy or schism. On the other hand, "those who are entirely ignorant of any rupture with the Catholic Church, but who regard themselves purely and simply as good Christians, are not always, *per se,* and by divine law to be systematically enlightened and instructed regarding the separation of their sect from the true Church. . . . Nevertheless, because of the hazard of scandal or encouragement of the spirit of indifferentism, they should as a rule be reminded of their duty of belonging to the true Church. . . . Sometimes in regions where there is no Catholic community or worship it is more advisable to permit schismatics to practice religion in their own sect in good faith. This seems more prudent than to confront them, after their error has been corrected and they have been formally converted, with the dilemma of falling into sin by participation in a divine cult which they realize is schismatical or of living without the benefit of divine cult at all."[83]

The profound and sympathetic insight and pastoral wisdom revealed in these words of Vermeersch was brought home to the author very vividly by the experiences of four years in Russia. What was the priest to do if schismatic parents, full of trust in him, brought their children to him for baptism? They themselves did not know how to perform the sacred rite. What was he to do if they themselves, so long deprived of the consolation of the sacraments, begged in all humility to receive them from him? Not only did they ask for the sacraments; they would have been overjoyed to keep the priest among them, despite any diversity of rite. Under such conditions not only would the priest have to take into account the danger of death due to war and disease, more or less remote; he would also have to consider what deep resentment might be aroused against the priest who refused them all help and consolation in their need. Perhaps generations would not have been sufficient to erase from the hearts of the Russian people the bitterness against the priests.

We may say truthfully that the attitude of these people was an expressive manifestation of a true Catholic spirit. A false and literalistic application of the decrees of the Holy Office to an entirely different set of conditions not foreseen in these decisions would have been an injustice toward the decisions themselves and against the love of our Mother the Church for souls. Vermeersch, and other authors as well, maintain that the decrees clearly allow for exceptional circumstances and extraordinary cases. Obviously circumstances and conditions must be such that the very events clearly testify to the one, true, holy, catholic Church. And the profession of Christian-Catholic faith, implicit in the action of the Christian externally separated from the Church, must, as far as this is possible, pave the way for the explicit adherence to the true Church through formal rejection of schism.

Evidence for the truly Catholic piety and genuine good faith of many Orthodox people (at least where the Catholic Church is not at all known) and of the Church's maternal love for them is found in the profound and impressive Apostolic Letter of Pius XII, "CARISSIMIS RUSSIAE POPULIS."[84]

The one standard or criterion set up for all cases, even the most singular, must be the simple and unchanging truth that the sacraments of the Church are the signs of the one true community of Catholic cult, of her faith and her love. Precisely in the instances of special necessity and urgency, when the Church comes to the assistance of sincere non-Catholics who are in error through no fault of their own—providing always that indifference to religious faiths is absolutely excluded—do the sacraments clearly bear witness to their real significance as signs of the one holy community of cult, of faith, of love. In these sacraments the community of cult, of faith, and of love, embraces all those whose hearts are open to the reception of the sacred sign and the fruits of the community of divine worship.

4. Exclusion from the Community

The most severe penalty with which the Church threatens the members who inflict wounds on the community is exclusion from the cultal community of the sacraments: excommunication. Such is her tender solicitude for her members, however, that the Church does not impose these severe penalties except as corrective punishments (*poena medicinalis*). She frees the sinner from the punishment as soon as he has given evidence of his conversion and done his best to repair the damage he has inflicted. As an example we may note the evil done by one who has given his children a non-Catholic education.)

5. Refusal of the Sacraments

In some instances the Church refuses to administer the sacraments even to those who seek to receive them. Any one who has dishonored the Church by an openly sinful life or a flagrant public crime is to be excluded from the reception of the sacraments according to the laws of the Church, provided he is not willing to repair the scandal caused by his sin. In many instances the devout penitential reception of the holy sacraments constitutes the minimum demanded by the Church for such reparation of the evil done. In the case of a converted sinner whose public and official admission to the reception of the sacraments could prove damaging to the Church or her members (for example, admission of one to the sacraments who is living in an invalid marriage without the use of the marriage rights), reception of the sacraments in a place where the individual is not known would be a normal safeguard to the spiritual welfare of the community.

If an occult sinner should privately ask a priest to give him Holy Communion, even though the priest is aware that he has not gone to confession or could not be absolved, the priest may and must discreetly refuse the request, for such refusal does not involve a violation of the individual's good name. The matter is different if the knowledge is acquired in the confessional. Respect for the good name of our neighbor forbids the priest to refuse the sacraments publicly to any one except excommunicated, interdicted, or public sinners who have not sincerely renounced their sins.[85]

6. Obligations of the Minister of the Sacraments

Since the minister in the solemn administration of the sacraments is in a unique way the representative and instrument of the Church, there is demanded of him: a) the visible bond with the Mystical Body and its graces; b) the intention which unites him with Christ and the Church.

principal causes of the sacraments, as their subordinate and instrumental cause; c) proper authorization; d) faithful observance of the rites and ceremonies.

a. Membership in the Church

To act worthily the minister of the sacraments must be a living member of the Mystical Body of Christ and therefore of the one visible Church. Undoubtedly the administration of the sacraments by heretics, schismatics, and in the instance of baptism, even by the non-baptized, is valid, provided the minister in some way or other really intends to do what Christ demands and what the Church does. Every validly ordained priest, even though he be separated from the Church, can validly offer the Holy Sacrifice of the Mass and administer the sacraments as long as he conforms to the conditions imposed for validity by Christ and the Church.

Nevertheless, the faithful are strictly forbidden to receive the sacraments from a non-Catholic priest, even though they may not be able to approach a Catholic priest for a very long time. The reason is plain: conscious participation in non-Catholic divine service with reception of the holy sacraments, the signs of unity in the true Church, from the hands of a schismatic or heretical minister must normally and ordinarily be considered proof and testimony against the unity and community of the true Church. And usually it involves serious scandal and danger of apostasy from the true faith. The case is different if in the absence of a Catholic priest, a dying Catholic receives the sacraments from a non-Catholic priest. The Code of canon law[86] in granting to all priests the power and authorization to give absolution to the dying without (at least expressly) excluding non-Catholic priests seems to favor the milder interpretation in this matter.[87]

A different problem confronts us when we inquire into the subjective attitude of Eastern Catholics who receive the sacraments, perhaps after long and painful deprivation of these means of grace, from schismatic priests. We may assume that in many instances they are in good faith and have the best of intentions, even though they are not in danger of death. These individuals, as well as the schismatic groups, are under social and political pressures which make the return to the one true Church very difficult.

Except in danger of death one is not permitted to receive the sacraments from a priest who has been excommunicated by a judicial sentence of the Church. The same holds regarding a priest who is leading a life of sin and scandal and whose exercise of the ministry is unavoidably sinful. He is not a proper minister of the sacraments; and to ask them of him, except in instances of real emergency, redounds neither to the honor of the sacrament nor to that of the Church, and constitutes an act of at least material cooperation in the sin of another. Nevertheless, for a proportionately serious reason such cooperation may be permitted. On this point we should apply the principle that every one is assumed to be good until the contrary is proved. Too strict an attitude in this matter might readily lead to harsh and unjust judgments of our fellow men. At the same time it is a flagrant contradiction for the minister of the Church to function as a sacred instrument of sanctification when he realizes that he is in sin and makes no effort to recover the state of grace suited to his sacred calling.

b. The Intention of the Minister

The minister is a rational instrument of Christ and His Church. Only insofar as he wills to act as such can he administer the sacraments validly. This instrumental dependence on the principal cause is called the intention or purpose to do what Christ and the Church wills, or more simply, to act according to the mind and intent of the Church.

The internal intention of the minister is presumed to correspond to his external action. "The words which he utters (for example, 'I baptize you, etc.') express the intention of the Church which is sufficient for the perfection of the sacrament, unless the contrary is expressed by minister or recipient."[88] For this reason the minister should not manifest any concern about the validity of the sacrament because of his inattention or distraction during the administration of the sacred rite, unless of course in the light of all the circumstances his act is clearly mere exercise or practice (such as we find in the "practice" of seminarians), or he has positively excluded any intention to administer a sacrament.

Surely an actual advertence to one's will or purpose to administer the sacrament or, in other words, an actual intention is very appropriate, but for validity of the act an habitual intention joined with the externally correct execution of the sacred action is sufficient.[89] In this way we are assured of sacramental efficacy (*virtualitatem intentionis*). Even infidelity or heresy on the part of the minister does not destroy the validity of the sacrament if the minister has the intention to do that which the Church of Christ does; for "the minister of the sacrament acts in the person of the whole Church whose faith supplies that which may be wanting in the faith of the minister."[90] It is therefore apparent that there is no reason for anxiety of mind in this matter, although of course the pious priest surely realizes that, as minister of the sacred mysteries, he is bound to consecrate himself with all his heart to the sacramental action, and, as instrument of Christ and the Church, frequently to renew his intention.

c. The Power of the Church

Every man on earth can validly administer the sacrament of baptism. In case of necessity (should the life of a catechumen or of an infant be in danger or, in the case of infants, should no priest be available for a considerable number of weeks[91]) every Catholic has the full authorization of the Church to administer the sacrament to the individual concerned because of the spiritual need. He must consider it a strict duty of religion and love to see that death does not rob the unbaptized of this essential rite, if there is reason to hope that the dying (adult) person is capable of receiving the graces of the sacrament.

The Christian bride and groom administer to each other the sacrament of matrimony. They are both ministers and recipients of the sacrament. They are capable of doing so only if they act in accordance with the power and authority of the Church, as is evident from her legislation. She lays down the necessary conditions for the validity of their consent (presence of an authorized priest, of two witnesses of the Church, and absence of diriment impediments).

A deacon, properly authorized, is permitted for serious reasons to administer solemn baptism and the Holy Eucharist.[92] For the valid administration of the sacrament of penance there is required both the priestly power of order and the power of jurisdiction granted by proper ecclesiastical authority.[93] The reason lies in the very nature of penance, in which ecclesiastical pastoral power is exercised in the act of cultal-juridical reconciliation with God and the sacred community, the Church. In her regulations for the use of this power the Church demonstrates her tender maternal solicitude: she guarantees the greatest freedom to the penitent in the choice of his confessor; she gives jurisdiction to every priest to hear the confession of those in danger of death;[94] she supplies any defect of jurisdiction in all instances of common error or doubt regarding the possession of necessary faculties for hearing confessions.[95]

The administration of the sacrament of order and ordinarily also of the sacrament of confirmation requires the consecratory power of the episcopacy.[96] By force of special papal authorization enlarging the ordinary power of simple priesthood, whether it be through special faculty granted by an indult of the Apostolic See or by the common law of the Church, a mere priest can validly and licitly administer confirmation. Recent legislation grants to pastors and parochial vicars the authorization to confirm their own parishioners in the danger of death if it is not possible to call the bishop. Still more extensive privileges are granted in mission territories.[97] Without such special authorization any attempt of a mere priest to administer the sacrament is invalid.

From the above we can derive some notion of the power Christ has conferred on His Church regarding the more precise determination and regulation of the sacraments.

d. Observance of the Rite

The minister of the sacrament is obliged in conscience to follow the rites prescribed by the Church. He is not permitted to modify them by any omission or addition in accordance with his own whims, for all modifications are within the exclusive competence of the Church's authority. Public cult in its entirety, including the administration of the sacraments, has been entrusted to the Church by Christ.[98] The action of the individual minister is pleasing to God only insofar as he is entirely bound up with Christ and the Church as their faithful instrument. Any arbitrary action on his part is contrary to this bond of union with Christ as is also the mere mechanical performance of the sacred rite. For the minister to carry caprice so far as to tamper with the sacramental matter and form would be a sacrilegious encroachment on the authority of Christ and the Church, even though the Church does have authority to make certain modifications within the essential framework of the substantial significance of the sacramental sign as determined by Christ Himself. This we have already referred to above.

Once the validity of the sacred rite is assured, the minister's next concern must be the devout and decorous celebration which excites the piety of the faithful. Every word and movement of his should be penetrated with the realization that he is announcing and performing the divine mysteries in, with, and through Christ. His every action should be animated with concern for the faithful, whose sacred leader he is in the holy word and chant of the liturgy. To fail in this spirit of reverence for the sacred mysteries and to have no concern for the edification of the faithful is often more regrettable than an occasional slip in the less important rubrics due to inadvertence or thoughtlessness.

The seminarian must make a conscientious effort to inform himself thoroughly on rites and rubrics, and after his ordination never fail to refresh his knowledge in this important area of priestly duty. But pre-occupation with the details of the rubrics should not be carried to excess. Over-emphasis may lead to painful rubrical anxiety and crowd out from the busy priestly schedule pastoral tasks of great importance. The cautions and admonitions of moralists and canonists, which in some instances are very severe, warn us above all against caprice and neglect. Rightly is one condemned if he takes the law into his own hands and by slovenly disregard for the ceremonies shocks and scandalizes the faithful. The prudent priest will devote the greatest care to the rites necessary for validity of the action. He will rank as next in importance the words and actions which are of the greatest symbolical significance. (For example, the mixing of the few drops of water with the wine at the offertory.)

According to the common teaching of moralists, there are preceptive rubrics which are obligatory as such, and purely directive rubrics which are obligatory only insofar as they may be essential for reverence and decorum in the sacred liturgy. The decrees of the Congregation of Rites must be interpreted according to the general principles of law: the ancient decrees are frequently rendered obsolete by living development and practice. It is a deplorable fact that the progress of the liturgical renaissance—a movement of tremendous importance for the life of the Church—has been seriously disturbed by hyperconservatives who are still living in the past. They try to call a halt to every earnest effort to make the liturgy fruitful in the pastorate by brandishing an ancient decree or response of the Congregation of Rites. Some of the replies of the Congregation given a century or more ago applied to situations and conditions in an age totally different from our own. Quite frequently they were intended to bind only the questioner and his circle. One should be constantly on guard against the hazard of matching the dead letter of the law which reflects an historical situation long past and which may not even be clearly understood, against the living, present, forward-looking Church today. The new rubrics of the breviary and missal, decreed by the *Motu Proprio* of John XXIII, July 25, 1960, brought about a long-sought simplicity in the liturgy and also clarified many matters in dispute.[99] Obedience to the Church in this entire sacred area should surely be something obvious for the true Christian, as disobedience would be quite unworthy of him. However, it is far from the spirit of such obedience to fritter away a great part of our energies in controversy over rubrical exegesis, when these energies could be better employed in a joyous use of the pastoral opportunities offered by the new development in the vitalization of the liturgy.

V. SACRAMENTS AS MEANS OF GRACE: THE OBLIGATION TO RECEIVE THEM

The end and purpose of the sacraments is the sanctification of our lives. The sacraments usher us into the light of the divine majesty and most effectively bring home to us the obligation to seek our salvation in the glory of God; they link our lives with Christ and His salvific action in the history of salvation and caution us that our salvation can be wrought only through union with Him; they bind us to the community of cult, the Church, and give to our lives *ecclesial* foundation and assignment. Thus do they sanctify. Precisely insofar as the means of salvation do not leave us entirely to our own resources, they prevent us from clinging to a narrow and one-sided concept of our own salvation. The sacraments manifest the work of our salvation as true sanctification for the glory of God in Christ and the community of salvation, which is the Church. The term *means of grace* should connote for us this deeper concept of the glory of God. But as means of grace they remind us of God's generosity and warn us of our frailty which should constantly induce us to seek a remedy for our weakness. The sacraments are not only means of grace and salvation, they are also remedies for spiritual weakness.

Hence the obligation to receive the sacraments must never be looked upon as a harsh and imperious command but rather as an imperative of grace. Through the sacraments God's will and God's grace invite us to fulfill the divine plan for our sanctification. The duty to receive the sacraments is based on God's will and plan to sanctify our lives. By means of the sacraments He carries out His design to sanctify the world through us, for they give us the mission and the means of saving mankind. They are also our strength in weakness and our healing in spiritual illness.

Baptism is absolutely necessary for our sanctification and healing, for it is the first sacrament of initiation into Christ and His Church. From this necessity there flows the express divine command to receive it (necessity of means and necessity of precept). To receive baptism one must be prepared, if need be, to make the greatest sacrifices. There is also the obligation to offer this way of salvation to others. Every expectant mother must be prepared to risk her life rather than deprive the infant in her womb of the opportunity of baptism even if this means deferring a much needed operation, should that be necessary. In instances of abortion the foetus must be baptized if there is a probability that it is still alive.

The sanctification and the healing which the sacrament of baptism brings to us are the basis for our mission and obligation toward all the unbaptized: we must undertake a zealous apostolate toward the unbaptized.

Confirmation is the second of the two sacraments of initiation. Though theologians are not agreed that the obligation to receive confirmation is serious, they hold that in certain instances special circumstances may give rise to a grave obligation. Surely the sacrament may not be disdained. Moreover in recent times new insights into the nature of its sacramental graces have awakened a new appreciation of its tremendous value as a foundation for the apostolate of the laity and the sanctification of social and public life with the assignment to Catholic Action. When seen in this light, the opinion that one is obliged to receive it under pain of mortal sin is immeasurably strengthened. A close scrutiny of the law of the Church as expressed in the Code of Canon Law[100] suggests that more is involved than concern for one's own salvation. Surely we cannot maintain that the sacrament is necessary for salvation by a necessity of means (*necessitate medii*). But this personal concern is not the only point of consideration, nor may it be made an excuse for failing to receive the sacrament. One can be excused, however, for serious reasons. Even though we are of the opinion that the obligation to receive confirmation is objectively grave, it does not at all follow that we should stress the gravity of the precept principally and primarily when we urge its reception. Quite the contrary, we should first of all create a realization or a sense of the greatness of the sacramental grace through our instruction and through the very solemnity of its administration. There is little point in threatening the risk of damnation to those who have no conception of the grace and the commitment of the sacrament.

Christian initiation in its completion comprises baptism, confirmation, and the Holy Eucharist. Incorporation in Christ and membership in the Church is given in baptism, which essentially looks to the Eucharistic union as its completion.

The law of the Church lays down as a minimum requirement that the faithful receive the Holy Eucharist in the paschal season each year. There is no doubt that ordinarily the law binds under pain of mortal sin.[101] But the pious Christian will feel impelled to respond to the appeal of interior grace inviting him to the community of love with Christ; he will have a sense of his own special needs and will not rest satisfied with the minimum prescribed by the law. He will seek to receive the sacraments of penance and the Holy Eucharist frequently, particularly since he realizes that no more is required for the frequent, weekly, or even daily reception than the state of grace, the proper intention, and the sincere effort to make a good preparation and a good thanksgiving.

We must repeat: it is most essential for the Christian not to view the reception of the sacraments, and particularly the great sacrament of divine love, primarily in the light of *obligation*. He must see them as invitations and gifts of love and approach them in the spirit of loving and grateful response. The reception of the Eucharist every Sunday and, if at all possible, every day should be the ideal goal of every Christian. But it should not be looked upon in the light of any minimum requirement of law. This ideal of Christian zeal attracts only those who have begun to fashion their lives according to the new law of grace (cf. Rom 6:14), orientating them toward the love of God.

If it is universally true that the obligations of the Christian can be rightly grasped only in the light of the *divine generosity,* then surely it is particularly true of the obligations arising from the greatest of the Savior's gifts, His loving offer of the sacraments. The first and greatest obligation regarding the most holy Sacrament of the Altar is to strive with all our might to understand the grand desire of the Savior's loving heart in giving Himself to us in love and nourishing our love in this sacrament.

Therefore priests and others responsible for the spiritual formation of youth must consider it a most sacred trust and duty to prepare the hearts of their charges as soon as possible for the Eucharistic love of the Savior.

Once their hearts are open to this love and they are able to grasp in a manner suited to their age the meaning of the sacramental reception, they have a strict right to receive Holy Communion. Neither parents nor pastors can deprive them of the right without grave injustice.[102] Precisely regarding this point of determining when the child is ready to receive Holy Communion, does the Code of Law stress the sacred and exalted right and the corresponding duty of parents to provide both for the necessary preparation of their children and for the decision that they are to receive the sacrament.[103] The parents have the first care of souls in the spiritual guidance of their children. Of course the pastor in virtue of his office has a supervisory right in the matter. He must "provide that the children who have attained the age of reason and have been adequately prepared be nourished as soon as possible by this divine food."[104] He is obliged to take positive measures to further the preparation and reception of Holy Communion by the children under his care, in conjunction with the family and at the proper time. Should he refuse to permit children who are adequately prepared to approach the Holy Table for a considerable time, he would be guilty of a grave sin by violating a right which the children have through both ecclesiastical and divine law. He would reveal a sad lack of understanding regarding that which is the very heart and core of priestly zeal and action.

Since the whole Christian life centers in the Holy Eucharist, not only must the first education of children who have arrived at the use of reason be directed to this sacrament, but all spiritual education and formation must be orientated toward this goal.

Under certain circumstances the confessor may impose a more frequent (for example, monthly) reception of Holy Communion or of the sacrament of penance as a penance. This means of grace should serve as remedy against sin and as an act of thanksgiving, provided the confessor deem it profitable or necessary for the development of a more profound and vigorous spirit of conversion. But it is of supreme importance that the penitent himself have a true understanding and appreciation of his holy faith. He must realize that reception of the sacraments is not harsh discipline, arbitrary penance in the usual sense of the word, but a gift of the Savior's love to which he must respond in love.

There is an obligation—theologians dispute its gravity—to receive the sacrament of extreme unction in grave illness which constitutes a danger of death. Even though the obligation cannot be proved to be grave, under certain circumstances the neglect of the sacrament may prove to be a mortal sin. Such would be the case if one should despise or scorn this holy means of grace; if one should cause scandal by failing to ask for it; if one should stubbornly refuse to face the danger of death and possible loss of one's soul by such blindness; if one should be guilty of a superstitious and cowardly fear that receiving the sacrament meant that death was inevitable.

As to the attitude of theologians regarding the obligation to receive this sacrament, serious reasons are cited for and against the position that the obligation is grave. Noted theologians are found in both camps. Those who maintain that there is no serious obligation view the problem almost exclusively in the light of the necessity of the sacrament with its graces for salvation of the individual. The other theologians view the question under the aspect of the sanctification of the illness and of the *yes* we are to give to both life and death and the consequent sacramental inclusion of our suffering and death in the sacrificial oblation of Christ on the Cross. This latter opinion, which is far from denying the great value of the sacramental graces for the individual's salvation, holds that the obligation to receive the sacrament is grave. To us it seems the more reasonable teaching.

There is no dispute among theologians regarding the obligation of receiving Holy Viaticum in danger of death. The obligation is certainly a serious one.

Relatives who fail to admonish the dying in due time and with loving tenderness to receive the sacraments of the dying may be guilty of grave sin. It surely is a mortal sin against charity toward our fellow man if the neglect of the sacraments, due to our remissness, endangers the eternal salvation of the individual concerned. Not merely the next of kin but also the closest acquaintances and friends have the sacred obligation to see that one who is dying and unconscious and therefore unable to confess and receive Holy Viaticum be given the sacrament of extreme unction.

The virtue of religion and love of neighbor also demand that the close relatives or others nearest at hand provide for the reception of the sacraments of the dying, even though the sick man is still conscious and possessed of his faculties. This follows from the fact that these sacraments are the greatest consolation and the greatest source of grace for the dying as well as an important act of divine worship.

There is no universal obligation to receive either the sacrament of order or the sacrament of matrimony. These sacraments are at the disposal of those only whom God calls to serve Him in these holy states. One who clearly and unequivocally recognizes the call to either of these sacred states is obliged to follow it. His obligation is as serious as the reasons assuring him that his call is truly from God and beyond the pale of doubt are solid and well founded.

THE SACRAMENTALS

1. *The Sacramentals as Spiritual Symbols*

Man is composed of body and soul, matter and spirit. In body and spirit he stands before God. Because of his spiritual nature he can accept grace and is capable of the most intimate union with God. But man in his whole nature comes from God and is ordered to God; destined for heaven, he is here on earth committed to the divine praise. If, therefore, man wills to honor God with his whole nature and in his entire existence —and such is his duty—then the body must be a partner in the hymn of praise. If with his whole existence he is utterly dependent on God and requires His assistance in his total being, then his body must also sink into the dust before the Lord and raise its hands in supplication to Him. If man in his whole existence is a sinner and as a sinner pleads for grace, then his body too must share in the sorrow and penance of his mind and will.

All of humanity forms a unity before God in Christ and the Church. Christ Himself appeared visibly among men and founded a visible community, the Church, for the salvation of men. Therefore there must be visible adoration through Christ in the Church, perceptible pleas for grace, sensible jubilation and thanksgiving for the divine benefactions. The very heartbeat of the divine praise in the Church, the holy Sacrifice of the Mass, is essentially visible action. Sacrificial action is likewise in the order of a sign, a sensible manifestation of inmost religious emotion and sentiment.

The Church has the mission of sanctifying all things: the material order, time and space, and man. She must take up everything into her Sacrifice which she offers to God in the praise of God. Hence she bids all things to join in her words of sacrificial praise which is holy Mass: human speech forms the word and chant; the human body presents its meaningful gestures and movements; inanimate creatures offer holy signs, images, the matter used in the Sacrifice.[105] The sacramentals continue and expand this sacred plan.

To man composed of soul and body, to the Church visible, Christ channelled His graces in visible signs, the holy sacraments, the consecrated elements, which are both expressive (indicative) and effective (causative) symbols. As Christ loved the beauty and glory of His Father's creation, so He loved symbols. He announced the advent of His new spiritual kingdom in symbols and images of the earthly, visible realities. ("The kingdom of heaven is like a man who sowed good seed in his field. . . . The kingdom of heaven is like a grain of mustard seed, which a man took and sowed in his field. . . . The kingdom of heaven is like a treasure hidden in a field. . . . The kingdom of heaven is like a net cast into the sea." Mt 13:24–47). He announces the dread reality of the judgment by cursing the sterile fig tree and making it wither (Mt 21:18ff.). He uses words and signs as instruments of His miracles. He mixes spittle and the dust of the earth and places them on the eyes of the man born blind as a sign of His power to give sight to the blind (Jn 9:6ff.).

2. The Sacramentals as Continuation of the Incarnation

Christ Himself, the Eternal Word of the Father, assumed human nature and thereby exalted and blessed the whole terrestrial order. The nature which had been created by the Eternal Word as the word from God and made to honor and glorify God was now restored and borne back to the almighty Word of Truth Who had created it. From the beginning man was to express in human words the word resounding in creation. He should shout aloud what nature held dumbly on her tongue. But through the sin of the First Parents nature was profaned. She could no longer proclaim the praise of God loud and clear, because man could no longer lend her the right words of praise. But now the creative Word renews the world, for "the Word was made flesh" (Jn 1:14). The creative Word enters into nature by His presence as the Incarnate One, the God-made-man. In Christ nature is now raised to the dignity of sacred praise of God; the flesh utters words of adoration and praise which are truly acceptable to God.

The Church, since she is the Mystical Body of Christ, must continue to utter this word of her Head. She must take up the word of nature telling of the grandeur and sublimity of God, of His love and condescension, in her praise of God. She must explain and interpret it. All that was created and consecrated by the Word of God must now share in the divine praise and the humble plea for pardon and blessing. The power to speak the praises of God lost by sin is now restored; the elements speak out more clearly and loudly in holy worship, since Christ Himself, the eternal Word, speaks in their voices. Here too the sacred words apply: *mirabilius reformasti* (thou hast more wonderfully restored nature). In the Holy Sacrifice, in the sacraments and sacramentals, the inanimate elements are permitted to sing a song which they could not have sung even before man's melancholy fall.

It is of the greatest practical importance in the explanation of the holy ceremonies and sacramentals that we show how all of nature is drawn into the new creation through Christ. And how as renewed by Christ it must join in the praise-song of redemption.

3. *Man at Home in a Sanctified World*

The above should help us to understand the tenacious defence of the ceremonies and sacramentals carried on by the Church in the sixteenth century against the Reformers. For Luther, and even more so for Calvin, the terrestrial or corporeal domain was alien to God and incapable of redemption. It could not be taken up into the religious and be made to contribute to the divine praise and the dispensation of grace. For Luther the Catholic Church of the Middle Ages was the great *Scandal,* precisely because she was so firmly entrenched in this earthly dwelling. Instead of crying anathema to all that was not spiritual, the Church centered all things in the splendor of the redemption. Instead of expelling the religious man from the confines of earthly culture, she made him feel religiously at home here on earth by elevating and transfiguring through her blessings and ceremonies all earthly realms of being.

The Church was always conscious of what Elizabeth von Schmidt-Pauli expressed so happily: "A child of God does not forsake the earth as it mounts heavenward to bliss."[106] The Church has no desire, when she mounts upward in praise of God, to shuffle off the earth, but rather seeks to draw the earth up with her. This is symbolized by the medieval Gothic spire which ascends to the dizziest heights in a maze of fanciful and fantastic sculptured forms to proclaim the glory of God. Similarly the baroque reacts against the stern harshness of the Reformers with an exuberant display of all earthly forms and figures in the honor it pays to God. The sacramentals of the Church have at all times attested her conviction that nature can be sanctified and can serve the divine honor and man's salvation. The Church blesses everything. She takes up all things into the divine cult. She goes abroad with her holy signs and blessings for the whole universe. She even bears the Eucharistic Lord in solemn procession through cities and towns and out into God's free nature. It was not foreign to her ideals and practices but in conformity with her traditions for Pius XI and Pius XII to introduce new formulas and blessings for technical inventions in the 1925 and 1952 editions of the *Roman Ritual*. Here she applied to contemporary life her traditional principle: nature is to be consecrated and transformed for the service of God.

The religious man should not forsake the earth but should, even as religious man, be at home in it and bear it with him to the Church. His whole life from cradle to the grave should be evidence that all things serve the glory of God and are blessed by religion. Faith must be apparent in his home (in the little holy water font, the crucifix on the wall) and in all his undertakings. The day's work should begin with the holy Sign of the Cross and conclude with the prayer of thanks to God as the mother places her hand upon the brow of her children in blessing before sending them off to bed. Thus man and his whole earthly life is at home in the Church with all her blessings. The home and the field, fruits of farm and industry, all earthly human things are taken up by the Church and placed in the light and warmth of her maternal benediction. Nothing good or useful escapes her blessing. What cannot be taken into the Church she goes forth to bless with solemn chant and prayer or with the Eucharistic Lord Himself.

The homeless man who has no earthly shelter should at least be able to feel at home in the Church with her holy usages and rites, so that he can never fail to recall with nostalgia the warmth of her welcome, even should he be so unfortunate as to desert this home of his Mother.

Significantly there is a bond between the sacramentals and ceremonies of the Church and the religious usages and practices of the people. The sacramentals fashion religious usage and sanctify it. They direct and guide the extra-sacramental activity of the faithful. In the sacramentals there still remains a considerable treasure of ancient pre-Christian usages and customs. What the religious heathen still felt of the closeness of God in nature and manifested, even though with a considerable admixture of error, the Church did not anathematize. She purged and purified it and gave it back to the people with her blessing. The pagan dance and cortege made way for the sacred processions of the Church. Instead of the holy groves and fountains where the heathen thought he heard the whisper of his gods, there arose the shrines of Mary and the saints, the holy places of pilgrimage which proved so fruitful in the cultivation of Christian piety among the people.

Through religious custom and usage the Church entrusted the heritage of the deposit of revelation to the people and brought the sacred truths down to the level of their comprehension. The common people are ordinarily not too conversant with the language of religion; they do not feel at home in the words and phrases of religious thought. But they delight in the idiom of religious signs and practices. This is the language they understand and are not likely to forget. It is passed on from parents to children as a common heritage of Christian families. This language of custom and usage which is such a sturdy guardian of the Catholic faith centers in the Church's sacramentals. They are the very core and heart of religious custom and its firmest support. We need only think of the influence of the sacred customs which took the place of the popular instruction and sermon for centuries in the Eastern churches and served to keep the faith rooted in the hearts of the people.

Bitterly do the enemies of the faith attack popular religious customs and practices, wayside crosses and shrines, images of Mary and the saints adorning the fields and public places and imparting an atmosphere of consecration to our Catholic lands. Because they realize only too well the significance of these signs of faith, they fiercely oppose any such display of religion both in and outside the churches. But though we do not deny that there is considerable superficial or mechanical religious practice involved, possibly even considerable ignorance and misconception or superstition, there are also hidden depths of religious devotion springing from the hearts of the faithful in these religious customs and usages. We must resolutely defend and maintain what is truly and profoundly religious in these pious practices and make every effort to foster them and to prevent their decline or destruction.

The slogan of the enemies of the Church, "Confine religion to the churches!" is an attack also on the sacramentals which presume to sanctify the whole of life. But religion is not a private affair. It must maintain itself also in the cultural domain and sanctify the world of culture. The Bride of Christ has the mission to sanctify all things and to share with all men the treasure minted in the Blood of the redemption. Therefore she may not limit her activity to church and sacristy but must embrace the whole of life, public and private, with her blessings and consecrations. In this too is the Church catholic, that she embraces and blesses all things in our life. The Church in her consecratory acts calls our attention to a like duty on our part; we must transform all realms of life in Christ, fashion them anew in a grand rechristianization of the whole world.

4. *The Purification of Nature: Exorcism*

Though the Church has all the elements join in praising God, and though she blesses all as caught up in the redemptive work of Christ ("All are yours, and you are Christ's, and Christ is God's," 1 Cor 3:23), her sacramentals do not betray any false optimism toward the world. She does not ignore the stern law of salvation: even though all things are redeemed objectively and in principle by the redemptive Death which cost the devil the decisive battle, the individual must still struggle for his subjective redemption. Man and nature must still be brought back, individual by individual, piece by piece, and restored to the kingdom of grace and the following of the Savior.

Hence, even though the devil has lost every right to the nature he desecrated, and all is wrested from him as to right and principle, the Church realizes full well that the *ruler of this world* still casts his sinister shadow over animate and inanimate nature. At every turn sinners are placing nature under his yoke. Therefore the Church blesses everything before it is used or consumed. Above all that which is to serve directly for cult she withdraws in a particularly solemn manner from the devil and even from the domain of the profane[107] by means of her blessings and consecrations.

The Church hears the groans of creation, she recognizes the longing to share in the freedom of the children of God (Rom 8:21). Therefore she blesses all things and purges what has been defiled by sin. For this reason her exorcism is prominent among the sacramentals of the Church. Exorcism is the negative aspect of her work of blessing and sanctifying the whole world. Her first task is indeed to wrest every terrestrial realm from the devil and restore creation to the freedom of the children of God. Since the devil, abusing the form of a creature, blinded Adam and Eve through a glaring mirage of the very creation which surely should speak of God, nature is under the curse of sin: the curse of the abuse wrought by the devil and men through sin, the curse of the seductive power in things of earth.

If the Church applies her powers of exorcism to inanimate nature, it is simply to expiate for the abuse wrought upon this particular thing by man. And the Church calls upon God to stay the spirit of evil so that he will not dare to bedazzle the eyes of men through the deceptive splendor of earthly things and turn them from the path of virtue. She prays that men will rather use them in the service of God and never be drawn by them from the struggle for the heavenly.

Exorcism is a plea made to God to banish the influence of the devil and to grant His servants the grace to use creatures faithfully in His service rather than abuse them by sin. For all nature partakes of the freedom of the children of God when the child of God rightly grasps the meaning of creation and, resisting the wiles of the devil, has all created things turned to the divine praise.

But the Church in her exorcism also turns directly to the devil using her power and authority over him. She commands him to desist from abusing the creatures of God, from blinding and deceiving man or harming him in soul or body. She beseeches God and His holy servants (particularly the angels) to hurl him back to hell and free the children of God from his attacks.

The Church has never forgotten the words of her first Pope: "Your adversary the devil, as a roaring lion, goes about seeking some one to devour" (1 Pt 5:8). From the very beginning of her existence the Church took the measure of the diabolical influence and confronted the devil everywhere with her power of resistance. The forms of exorcism in use in Christian antiquity were as fully developed as the ritual is today. In fact they were much more significant in that early age than they are today. The Church is not only aware of the power and evil zeal of the fiendish antagonist, she is also conscious of her own superiority over him: "Upon this rock I will build my Church, and the gates of hell shall not prevail against it" (Mt 16:18). "I have given you power . . . over all the power of the enemy" (Lk 10:19).

The Church shares in the power of Christ over the enemies He has vanquished:

a. Every just man partakes in the royal dominion of Christ over the evil spirit. He is a member of Christ. The devil can have no claim on him. Moreover, the baptized and confirmed Christian partakes of the kingly priesthood of Christ. On this title and in the measure of his union with Christ in faith and love, he is not simply freed from the slavery of Satan;

he is equipped to combat it as a soldier in the kingdom of Christ with the special spiritual weapons at his disposal, the sacred signs, such as the Sign of the Cross, the use of holy water, and especially the invocation of the sacred names of Jesus and Mary. Thus he is assured that he shall share in Christ's victory over the devil and the world.

b. The special providence of God protects the Church and each of her members, for Christ will not abandon His own. The powerful weapon given her in this combat against the evil spirit is prayer to Christ and His holy ones, especially the angels. If the Church prays well, God will not turn a deaf ear to her petitions and will not permit the devil to score any victory over her.

c. The Church herself exercises—and, after a manner of speaking, in her own name—dominion over demons. She expressly grants this power in her rite of ordination to the cleric who receives the office of exorcist. But it is not absolute for the reason that the Church can act only by participation in the power and authority of Christ. His power is unlimited and infallible; her power rather conditional and moral, effective only to the extent that it is God's will that the vile influence of the devil be restrained at one point or other. In fact God can will to permit the devil to contribute to ultimate good by his evil acts. The power of the Church is further conditioned by the punitive justice of God. He may permit the evil spirit to harass man for a determined period in this world in order perchance to save him for the next. Throughout there is always one condition which holds in the Church's exorcism: "insofar as it is necessary or profitable for the salvation of souls." Ultimately the totality of things will be drawn into the great stream of the redemption, but the first and unconditioned task of the Church is only to save immortal souls. Hence the Church is able to restrain the devil unconditionally and absolutely only in preventing him from overpowering his victim by means of his tortures and temptations to the detriment of his salvation. We have an example in the contest of Job with the devil, the evil spirit who affected his temporal goods and even his body but did not inflict spiritual harm.

The power of the Church is only a moral power. Exorcism does not possess a mechanical or magical force such as sorcerers and medicine men among pagans pretended to have. Nor does it work physically or sacramentally. It is not the divine action of the sacraments, not the efficacious word of divine authority. In the Middle Ages there seems to have been a rather wide-spread notion that exorcism had a kind of medicinal effect on all diseases, a misconception which practically falls in the category of the automatic or mechanical efficacy.

The moral force of the Church against the evil spirits is derived from her mystical union with Christ. But there is a direct proportion between the holiness of the Church herself, the bond of her members with Christ, and the sanctity of the minister, on the one hand, and the efficacy of the sacramental on the other. Hence the power would be effective in proportion to the degree of her actual sanctity, in proportion to the real and effective bond of grace between the totality of her members and Christ their Head, and particularly in proportion to the measure of holiness of the exorcist himself.

Thus we explain the demand of Christ and the Church. Christ said to His Apostles that a certain kind of evil spirit can be cast out only by prayer and fasting (Mt 17:20). Hence prayer and penitential acts are indicated. The Church makes a similar demand. She requires strictly that only a priest strong in faith and of proved holiness may attempt to confront the devil in solemn official form and rite.[108] The act is all the more effective the more the servant of the Church represents the Church and Christ in confident faith and trust. He dare not presume that the power over the evil spirits is something of his own.

This attitude of the Church is not the result of trial and error on her part. Christ Himself taught us through the example of the disciples and their sad experience. Though He had given them "power over the evil spirits," they did not meet with the success they anticipated; and the Lord pointed out the moral of the event for their instruction (Mt 17:16ff.). There is also a pertinent example in the Acts of the Apostles revealing the perils inherent in the efforts of unworthy exorcists (Acts 19:13ff.). In the light of these lessons shown in the sacred pages we see how justified is the Church's demand, noted above, that the priest-exorcist be proved in holiness. One who exercises this power should not himself be a slave of the devil. He must tower above the spirit of unbelief, of pride and mendacity, through a living faith, humility, and the sacrificial spirit of penance.

Concerning the efficacy of the sacramentals we may state the following general rule: The full efficacy of the sacramentals depends very much on the living faith, not only of the recipient but also of their minister. Sacramentals do not act as instrumental causes under the influence of the principal cause, which is God; they do not act *ex opere operato*. Their effects flow from the mediation of the prayer of the Church (*ex opere operantis ecclesiae*). They are sustained and supported by the entire objective and moral sanctity of the Church; but since the Church permits the sacramental to be administered through a human minister, he is first of all the representative of the Church and therefore his faith and sanctity are decisive.

A cautionary note: in all consecrations and all dedicatory blessings the sacral sanctification and dedication of thing or person is entirely independent of the person of the minister. Nevertheless, the abundance of blessing, which should be bound up with the sacral holiness, is dependent on him, although not in the first instance.

It is obvious that the official minister of the sacramental must be in the state of grace, although to administer a sacramental in the state of mortal sin is usually only a venial sin. It should be added that the very nature of the sacramental demands a decorous and worthy execution of the sacred rite with correct enunciation of the words. The entire rite should be executed with attention and devotion.

In conclusion we note that in the liturgical and religious life the sacramentals are indeed "ontologically only on the periphery, but psychologically often in the foreground,"[109] according to an essential trait in man who presses forward from exterior to interior but only too often remains clinging to the exterior. Hence it is imperative to root such psychologically important values as the sacramentals in the center of Catholic dogma (above all, in the dogma of redemption and of the plenitude of salvation in the Church). The priest should treasure the abundance of blessings entrusted to him no less than do the Catholic faithful and should dispense them with generous heart and hand.

BIBLIOGRAPHY

The Sacraments in Divine Worship

AHRENS, CL. "Sakramentale Froemmigkeit," *GeistLeben*, 25 (1952), 296–304.
AQUIN, THOMAS VON. *Deutsche Thomasausgabe* Bd. 29: "Die Sakramente."
*ASMUSSEN, H. *Das Sakrament*. Stuttgart, 1949.
BISER, E. *Das Christusgeheimnis der Sakramente*. Heidelberg, 1950.
BOUYER, L. *Life and Liturgy* (London); American edition: *Liturgical Piety*, Notre Dame Press, 1955.

CHENU, M. D. "Les sacrements dans l'économie chrétienne," *La Maison-Dieu,* 30 (1952), 7–18.

DANIÉLOU, J. *The Bible and the Liturgy,* Notre Dame Press, 1956.

DONLAN, TH. C., O.P., F.L.B., CUNNINGMAN, ROCK, A. *Christ and His Sacraments.* Dubuque, 1958.

GICKLER, D., O.P. *Das 'Ja' zum sakramentalen Mysterium.* Koeln, 1955.

Initiation sacramentelle. LumVit, 9 (1954), Nr. 1.

KRAUTWIG, N., O.F.M. "Sittliche Tugend und Sakrament," *WissWeish,* 9 (1942), 100–109.

KIRCHGAESSNER, A. *Die maechtigen Zeichen. Urspruenge, Formen und Gesetze des Kultes.* Freiburg, 1959.

———. *Heilige Zeichen.* Aschaffenburg, 1959.

LANZA, A.-PALAZZINI, P. *Sacramenti e vita sacramentale.* Roma, 1957.

MENOUD, PH. "La définition du sacrement selon le Nouveau Testament," *RThP,* 38 (1950), 138–147.

O'NEILL, C. "The Role of the Recipient and Sacramental Signification," *Thm,* 21 (1958), 257–301, 508–540.

PASCHER, J. *Form und Formwandel sakramentaler Feier.* Muenster, 1949.

———. *Die Liturgie der Sakramente.* Muenster, 1951.

PHILIPON, M. M. *The Sacraments in the Christian Life.* Translated by John A. Otto, Westminster Md.: Newman Press, 1954.

PINSK, J. *Die sakramentale Welt.* 2 ed., Freiburg i Br., 1941.

PIOLANTI, A. *I Sacramenti,* Firenze, 1957.

RAHNER, K. "Persoenliche und sakramentale Froemmigkeit," *GeistLeben,* 25 (1952), 312–429.

ROGUET, A. M. *The Sacraments: Signs of Life.* Translated by Carisbrooke Dominicans. London: Blackfriars, 1954.

SCHMIDT, H. *Introductio ad liturgiam Occidentalem.* Romae, 1960.

SEMMELROTH, O. *Vom Sinn der Sakramente.* Frankfurt, 1960.

STEINBUECHEL, TH. "Sakramentales Mysterium und personales Ethos," *Religion und Moral,* Frankfurt, 1951, 55–152.

TAYMANS, F., S.J. "Les sacraments et la vie du chrétien," *NRTh,* 69 (1947), 1027–1034.

VAGAGGINI, C., O.S.B. *Theological Dimensions of the Liturgy.* Translated and adapted by J. Doyle. Collegeville, Minn., 1960.

VILLETTE, L. *Foi et sacrement. Du Nouveau Testament à saint Augustin.* Paris, 1959.

WALTER, E. *Quellen lebendigen Wassers. Von der Fuelle der sieben Sakramente.* Freiburg i Br., 1953.

WARNACH, V. "Wort und Sakrament im Aufbau der christlichen Existenz," *Liturgie und Moenchtum,* 20 (1957), 68–90.

WINKLHOFER, A. "Kirche und Sakramente," *TrThZ,* 68 (1959), 65–84.

Discipleship Sacramentally Consecrated to God's Glory

BENOIT, A. *Le baptême chrétien au second siècle des Pères.* Paris, 1953.

DURST, B., O.S.B. *De characteribus sacramentalibus.* Romae, 1924.

KRAUTWIG, N. "Sittliche Tugend und Sakrament," *WissWeish,* 9 (1942), 100–109.

LAMPE, G. W. H. *The Seal of the Spirit. A Study in the Doctrine of Baptism and Confirmation in the New Testament and the Fathers.* London, 1951.

LEEN, E., PÉGHAIRE, J., C.S.S.P. *La Pentecôte continue.* Paris, 1952.

MCCORMACK, S., O.P. "The Configuration of the Sacramental Character," *Thm,* (1944), 458–491.

OULTON, J. E. L. *Holy Communion and Holy Spirit.* London, 1951.
THILS, G. "Le pouvoir cultuel du baptisé," *EphThLov,* 15 (1938), 683–689.
THURIAN, M. *La confirmation. Consécration des laïcs.* Neuchâtel, 1958.
TYCIAK, J. *Der siebenfaeltige Strom aus der Gnadenwelt der Sakramente.* Freiburg, 1954.

The Sacraments: Personal Encounter with Christ

BACKES, I. "Die Sakramente als Zeichen Christi," *TrThZ,* 65 (1956), 329–336.
BISER, E. *Das Christusgeheimnis der Sakramente.* Heidelberg, 1950.
BOUYER, L. "Le baptême et le mystère de Pâques," *La Maison-Dieu,* 2 (1945), 29–52.
D'AVIGNON, J. *Sous les voiles des sacrements.* Tournai, 1949.
DE BACIOCCHI, J. "Les sacrements, actes libres de Seigneur," *NRTh,* 73 (1951), 681–706.
DIACRE, A. *Les baptèmes en danger de mort. Traité théorique et pratique.* Louvain, 1951.
DONDAINE, H. F. "Le baptême est-il encore le 'sacrement de la foi,' " *La Maison-Dieu,* 6 (1946), 76–88.
DORONZO, E., O.F.M. *De baptismo et confirmatione.* Milwaukee, 1947.
GARNIER, M., O.P. *La grâce de mon baptême.* Paris, 1950.
GRABER, R. *Christus in seinen heiligen Sakramenten.* Muenchen, 1937.
GRAIL, A. "La place du baptême dans la doctrine de saint Paul," *VieSpir,* 82 (1950), 563–584.
HOFINGER (and others) *Worship: the Life of the Missions.* Notre Dame University Press, 1958.
HUGON, *Les sacrements dans la vie spirituelle.* Juvisy, 1936.
KOROLEVSKI, C. *Liturgie in lebendiger Sprache.* Klosterneuburg, 1958.
KOSTER, D. "Symbol und Sakrament," *NO,* 2 (1947), 385–403.
KUEHLE, H. *Sakramentale Christusgleichgestaltung. Studie zur allgemeinen Sakramentenlehre.* Braunsberg, 1943.
MARTIMORT, A. G. *Les signes de la Nouvelle Alliance.* Paris, 1959.
NUENHEUSER, B., O.S.B. *Taufe und Firmung (Handbuch der Dogmengeschichte,* Band IV, 2), Freiburg, 1956.
PARIS, P. *Initiation chrétienne. Leçons sur le baptême.* Paris, 1948.
PITTENGER, W. N. *Sacraments, Signs and Symbols.* Chicago, 1949.
SCHILLEBEECKX, H. "Sakramente als Organe der Gottesbegegnung," *Fragen der Theologie heute* (J. Feiner, F. Boeckle). Einsiedeln (1957), 319–335.
———. *Christus Sakrament der Gottbegegnung.* Mainz, 1960.
SEMMELROTH, O. "Wortverkuendigung und Sakramentenspendung als dialogische Zueinander," *Catholica,* 15 (1961), 43–60.
SOEHNGEN, G. *Symbol und Wirklichkeit im Kultmysterium.* 2 ed., Bonn, 1940.
WARNACH, V. "Die Tauflehre des Roemerbriefes in der neueren theologischen Diskussion," *Archiv fuer Liturgiewissenschaft,* 5 (1958), 274–332.
ZERBA, C. *Commentarius in decretum "Spiritus Sancti munera."* Citta del Vaticano, 1947 (Decree of Sept. 14, 1946, on the Administration of Confirmation to the Dying).

The Sacraments As Signs of the Ecclesial Community

ALGERMISSEN, K. "Das 'Sakrament' im oekumenischen Gespraech," *MThZ,* 9 (1958), 296–298.
BACCARI, R. *La volontà nei sacramenti (de intentione ministri).* Milano, 1941.
BAYART, P. *Les sacrements dans la vie de l'Église.* Paris, 1947.

CHANSON, A. *Pour mieux administrer Baptême, Confirmation, Eucharistie, Extrême Onction.* Arras, 1952.

CONGAR, Y. "L'Eucharistie et l'Église de la nouvelle alliance," *VieSpir,* 82 (1950), 347–372.

CULLMANN, O. "Le baptême agrégation au Corps du Christ," *Dieu Vivant,* 11 (1948), 45–66.

Directoire Épiscopale pour la pastorale des sacrements à l'usage du clergé. Paris, 1951.

GIBLET, J. "Le baptême, sacrement de l'incorporation à l'Église selon saint Paul," *LumVie* (May, 1956), 83ff.

GRAIL, A. "Eucharistie, Sacrement de la charité, dans le Nouveau Testament, *VieSpir,* 85 (1951), 369–387.

HAERING, B. "Die gemeinschaftsstiftende Kraft der Liturgie. Liturgiesoziologische Beobachtungen und Probleme," *Liturgisches Jahrbuch,* 7 (1957), 205–214.

———. "Die Bedeutung der Sakramente fuer das Leben der Gemeinschaft," *ThD,* 1 (1958), 228–236; *LumVit.,* 13 (1958), 446–455.

"Le baptême, entrée dans le peuple de Dieu," *La Maison-Dieu,* 32 (1952). (*See* entire volume.)

LIEBHART, L., C.SS.R. "Der Sakramentenempfang Zivilgetrauter," *ThPrQschr,* 98 (1950), 47–54.

OPPENHEIM, PH. "Vom Wesen und sozialen Charakter der Sakramente," *Lit Leb,* 4 (1937), 189–204.

RAHNER, K. *Kirche und Sakramente.* Freiburg, 1960.

RAMBALDI, F., S.J. *L'oggeto dell' intenzione sacramentale nei teologi dei secoli XVI et XVII.* Roma, 1944.

RENWART, L. "L'intention du ministre des sacrements, problème mal posé," *NRTh,* 91 (1959), 469–488.

ROGUET, A. M. "Sévérité ou vérité dans l'administration des sacrements," *La Maison-Dieu,* 6 (1946), 92–106.

SCHNACKENBURG, R. *Das Heilsgeschehen bei der Taufe nach dem Apostel Paulus. Eine Studie zur paulinischen Theologie.* Muenchen, 1950.

SCHOELLIG, O. *Die Verwaltung der heiligen Sakramente unter pastoralen Gesichtspunkten.* 4th ed. Freiburg, 1952.

SEMMELROTH, O. *Die Kirche als Ursakrament.* Frankfurt, 1953.

WAGNER, J. *Erneuerung der Liturgie aus dem Geiste der Seelsorge unter dem Pontifikat Pius XII. Akten des Ersten Internationalen Pastoralliturgischen Kongresses zu Assisi.* Trier, 1957. [*Assisi Papers,* Collegeville, Minn.: The Liturgical Press, 1957.]

For the address of the pope on the close of the Congress, *see* "The Liturgical Movement" in *The Major Addresses of Pope Pius XII,* edited by Vincent a. Yzermans, Volume one, 373 ff. St. Paul: North Central Publishing Company, 1961.

WINKLHOFER, A. "Kirche und Sakramente," *TrThZ,* 68 (1959), 65–84.

The Sacramentals

BAUHOFER, O. *Die Heimholung der Welt.* Freiburg, 1927.

DOERFLER, P. "Das liturgischen Symbol," *Ho,* 34 (1936/37), 198ff.

DUDLI, N. *Das Segensbuch der Kirche.* 1936.

FRANZ, A. *Die kirchlichen Benediktionen im Mittelalter.* Freiburg, 1909.

GASQUET, A. C. *Sacramentals.* Saint Paul, Minnesota, 1928.

GUARDINI, R., *The Church and the Catholic,* and *The Spirit of the Liturgy.* Translated by Ada Lane. Sheed and Ward, London, 1935.

———. *Sacred Signs.* Translated by Grace Branham. Pio Decimo Press, St. Louis, 1956.

HOLTUM, G. VON. "Die Sakramentalien," *Pastor Bonus,* 32 (1919), 27–33; 33 (1921), 303–310; 34 (1922), 281–284.

JANSEN, N. *Die Kirche segnet die Menschen.* 1935.

KOETTING, B. *Peregrinatio religiosa. Wallfahrten in der Antike und das Pilgerwesen in der alten Kirche.* Muenchen-Regensburg, 1950.

MICHEL, A. "Sacrementaux," *DTC* 1, 465–482.

PROBST, F. *Sakramente und Sakramentalien in den drei ersten christlichen Jahrhunderten.* Tuebingen, 1872.

SCHAUERTE, H. *Volkstuemliche Heiligenverehrung.* Muenster, 1948.

SCHMID, F. *Die Sakramentalien der katholischen Kirche.* Brixen, 1906.

SCHMIDT-PAULI, E. VON. *Elemente und Naturalien in der Kirche.* Paderborn, 1937.

SCHREIBER, G. *Wallfahrt und Volkstum in Geschichte und Leben.* Duesseldorf, 1934.

VEIT, A. "Der Heimat- und Brauchtumsgedanke in den Benediktionen der Kirche," *Gestaltkraefle Lebensnaher Seelsorge,* Edited by W. Meyer und P. Neyer, (Freiburg, 1939), 265–284.

WIESEHOEFER, F. *Das Weihwasser in der Fruehzeit und bei den Klassischen Voelkern des Altertums.* Muenster, 1933.

Additional Works in English

BOUYER, LOUIS. *Liturgical Piety* (Liturgical Studies, 1). Notre Dame, Ind.: Notre Dame Univ. Press, 1955.

———. *The Word, Church, and Sacraments in Protestantism and Catholicism.* New York: Descleé, 1961.

CALLAHAN, DANIEL. *Christianity Divided: Protestant and Roman Catholic Theological Issues.* New York: Sheed and Ward, 1961. "The Sacraments: Encounter with God" (E. Schillebeeckx), pp. 245–275.

Christ in His Sacraments (Theology Library, 6). ed. Antione M. Henry, O.P. Chicago: Fides, 1958.

Christ's Sacrifice and Ours (Proceedings National Liturgical Week, 1947) Conception, Mo.: Liturgical Conference, 1948.

DE SALVO, RAPHAEL. *The Dogmatic Theology on the Intention of the Minister in the Confection of the Sacraments* (Catholic University Studies in Sacred Theology, 2nd. Series, 26). Washington: Catholic Univ. Press, 1949.

HANLEY, PHILIP, O.P. *The Life of the Mystical Body: the Church, Grace, and the Sacraments.* Westminster, Md.: Newman, 1961.

HASTINGS, CECILY. *The Sacraments.* New York: Sheed and Ward, 1961.

JUNGMANN, JOSEPH A., S.J. *Liturgical Worship: an Inquiry into Its Fundamental Principles.* New York: Pustet, 1941.

KELLY, BERNARD J., C.S.Sp. *The Sacraments of Daily Life.* New York: Sheed and Ward, 1943.

KING, JAMES I. *Administration of the Sacraments to Dying Non-Catholics* (Catholic University Studies in Canon Law, 23). Washington: Catholic Univ. Press, 1924.

MURPHY, GEORGE L. *Delinquencies and Penalties in the Administration and Reception of the Sacraments* (Catholic University Studies in Canon Law, 17) Washington: Catholic Univ. Press, 1923.

PASCHANG, JOHN L. *The Sacramentals According to the Code of Canon Law* (Catholic University Studies in Canon Law, 28). Washington: Catholic Univ. Press, 1925.

PERKINS, MARY E. *The Sacramental Way.* New York: Sheed and Ward, 1948.

PHILIPON, MARIE MICHEL, O.P. *The Sacraments in the Christian Life.* Westminster, Md.: Newman, 1954.

PINSK, JOHANNES. *Towards the Center of Christian Living; a Liturgical Approach.* New York: Herder and Herder, 1961.

ROGUET, AIMON M., O.P. *Christ Acts Through the Sacraments.* Collegeville, Minn.: Liturgical Press, 1954.

The Church Year (Proceedings of the National Liturgical Week, 1958). Elsberry, Mo.: Liturgical Conference, 1959.

The New Man in Christ (Proceedings of the National Liturgical Week, 1948). Conception, Mo.: Liturgical Conference, 1949.

The Precious Blood Study Week. *Proceedings of the Second Precious Blood Study Week,* August 2–4, 1960. Rensselaer, Indiana: Messenger Press, 1962.

Periodical Literature in English

BULARZIK, R. "Liturgy in Relation to Life," *OF,* 6 (April 16–May 14, 1932), 248–54, 299–307.

CRICHTON, J. D. "Mass and the People," *LiSp,* 11 (June, 1957), 548–60.

———. "The Parish: the Assembly of God's People," *Lit,* 29 (July, 1960), 53–60.

CUNNINGHAM, F. L. B. "Spirituality for All. Christ's Sacrifice and Ours," *CrCr,* 11 (March, 1959), 95–108.

DAVIS, C. "The Mass as the Assembly of Christians," *Fur,* 12: 549–63.

DE LETTER, P. "Encounter with God," *TH,* 36 (Sept., 1961), 5–24.

DITTOE, J. T. "Sacramental Incorporation into the Mystical Body," *Thm,* 9 (Oct., 1946), 469–514.

ELBERT, A. "Holy Eucharist, the Center of Catholic Worship," *AER,* 82 (June, 1930), 600–611.

FITZGERALD, T. "Sacraments and Grace-Life," *Sursum Corda,* 4 (June, 1958), 313–319.

GILLEMAN, G. "Divine Life and Christian Community," *LumVit,* 14 (1949), 613–620.

GILLIS, J. R. "Spirituality for All: Sacramental Beginnings," *CrCr,* 10 (June, 1958), 313–319.

HENNRICH, K. J. "Liturgical Piety," *HPR,* 39 (May, 1939), 804–13.

KIESLING, C. "Faith, Sacraments, and Calvary," *CrCr,* 8 (Dec., 1956), 430–41.

———. "Spirituality for All: Channels of Grace," *CrCr,* 10 (March, 1958), 87–107.

LEEMING, B. "Recent Trends in Sacramental Theology," *ITQ,* 23 (July, 1956), 195–217.

McAULIFFE, C. "Unworthy Ministers of the Sacraments," *RR,* 10 (Jan., 1951), 25–32.

McMANUS, F. "The Law, the Liturgy, and Participation," *Jur,* 20 (Jan., 1960), 42–54.

McREAVY, L. L. "Ministering to Dying Non-Catholics," *ClerRev,* 40 (Feb., 1955), 79–90.

MOONEY, D. "Love in Sacrifice," *OF,* 18 (Jan. 23, 1944), 114–22.

O'NEILL, C. "Role of the Recipient and Sacramental Signification (Reception as Worship; the Faithful and the Mass)," *Thm,* 21 (Oct., 1958), 508–40.

PEPLER, C. "The Sacrament of Faith," *LiSp* 11 (Oct., 1956), 163–72.

PRUEMMER, D. "Conditional Administration of the Sacraments to Non-Catholics," *HPR,* 30 (Oct., 1929), 234–41. *See also* 31 (Oct., 1930), 17–31.

REYNDERS, B. "Religious Value of the Sacramentals," *OF,* 15 (Feb.–March, 1941), 168–174, 219–24.

SCHLITZER, A. L. "All Sacraments Are Social," *WOR,* 28 (Sept., 1954), 398–407.

SMITH, G. D. "Church and Her Sacraments," *ClerRev,* 33 (April, 1950), 217–31.

WESKAMM, W. "Formation and Life of the Parish Community," *WOR,* 28 (Feb., 1954), 138–52.

WINZEN, D. "Born of God," *OF,* 20 (Feb.–March, 1946), 153–166, 217–26.

————. "Formation in Christ; Born of God. Baptism," *OF*, 20 (Jan.–Feb., 1946), 111–19, 153–66.

Woywood, S. "Penal Law of the Code: Offenses in the Administration of the Sacraments," *HPR*, 38 (Sept., 1938), 1277–86.

————. "Penal Law of the Code: Unauthorized Administration of the Sacraments," *HPR*, 38 (May, 1938), 843–50.

CHAPTER SEVEN

SINS CONTRARY TO THE NATURE OF RELIGION

B Y WAY of supplement to the explanation of the nature and essential requirements of religion we now propose to study the doctrine on the sins which are contrary to this virtue. But religion also has its own special modes of activity (prayer, use of the divine name, the vow, the sacred rest, and the celebration of the holy mysteries) and there are also sins contrary to these special modes. We these shall discuss after we have studied the activities themselves, even though they are also contrary to the nature and essential requirements of religion in general.

I. IRRELIGION: DIRECT VIOLATION OF GOD'S HONOR

1. *Blasphemy*

Blasphemy is an injury against God expressed in words or signs. In its gravest form it is the deliberate and intentional insult and scorn attacking the divine honor and sanctity (diabolical blasphemy). Blasphemy turns against God directly or against His work, more specifically against the friends of God in relation to God. Forms of speech, expressions, actions which are blasphemous in their meaning or implication are sins of the same nature as direct and intentional blasphemy to the extent that one is aware of the insult they imply and acts freely, even though he does not have a blasphemous intent. Though blasphemy is usually manifested in speech, certain signs and gestures are clearly blasphemous. To cite some examples, one may clench one's fist in gesture of defiance toward the heavens or toward a sacred image, or one may desecrate a sacred thing in various ways. Blasphemy may likewise be purely internal.

Blasphemy may take the form of wishing evil to any one with reference to the mysteries of divine love (cross, sacraments, Blood of Christ). This is blasphemous cursing, associating the sacred mysteries with evil (e.g., one asks a just God to inflict unjust punishment, or the sacred mysteries to redound to evil, etc.). Blasphemy may also be heretical (one may attribute something to God contrary to His divine nature or attributes or specifically repudiate His truthfulness by rejecting articles of faith, etc. Thus one may say: some men are predestined to hell; God does not give all men sufficient grace; if there were a divine providence, innocent children would not suffer; etc.).

Particularly in regard to purely internal blasphemy, the confessor should proceed with the greatest caution. There may be merely question of temptation or perhaps disturbed imagination or at worst compulsive thoughts. One who leads a sincerely devout life does not readily commit this sin. Compulsive thoughts and images should not be suppressed with vehemence but rather disregarded calmly with occasional recourse to a simple prayer of divine praise.

Blasphemy is in its entire nature (*ex toto genere suo*) a dreadful mortal sin. It is a grave sin regardless of the motive which occasions it, be it impatience, outburst of temper, or hatred and scorn for God. Habitual blasphemy is the language of hell and a sign of reprobation.[110]

Frequently distress and mental depression caused by the trials and afflictions of life are so profound that men complain of their lot in terms of blasphemy. However, one should not readily accuse the individual concerned of grave sin. The very intensity of his emotion diminishes the attention and deliberation to such a degree that he may not even be fully aware of what he is saying. There is no certain evidence, in such instances, that the evil disposition of blasphemy and grave guilt of conscience is really present. (Examples of such violent utterances: "Can there still be a God?" "Don't talk to me of the justice of God!" "How can God be so cruel?")

In instances of doubt about the meaning and implication of an apparently blasphemous utterance the confessor should decide in the light of the milder interpretation. The penitent, however, who uses such expressions must follow the more safe and certain view and avoid such expressions under all circumstances.[111] He may not run the risk of actually and objectively insulting God and damaging the divine honor before men.

It is not *in itself* blasphemy to use sacred expressions intemperately in order to vent one's anger and impatience by means of forceful utterance. But such language lies dangerously close to this terrible sin. And if the deliberate surge of passion or impatience rises directly against God, the evil intent is blasphemous. Such anger is blasphemy.

The vulgarization of holy names in the free and easy manner of conversation with reference to things sacred and the manifestations of God's love is commonly considered insulting to God. The blasphemous disposition and intent is implied in the attitude which deals with sacred terms as though they were common or vulgar. However, uncouth men may not be aware of the implications of their common speech. The confessor, though he should not in every instance (in the confessional) accuse his penitent of blasphemy, should correct him and point out to him how grossly unsuited such language is to the Christian. Earnest and enlightened instruction should go far in correcting this evil among the faithful.

As already noted, scorn and insult directed to God's friends, the saints, and particularly to the Mother of God, is surely blasphemy. As friends of God who live in intimate relation with Him they reflect the honor and glory of God which is indirectly attacked when they are scorned or insulted. However, to curse other free creatures of God, to wish them evil (in actual desire, not merely in words), is rather a grave sin against love of neighbor and contrary to the spirit of prayer and the obligation to pray for our fellow men. Only in this latter sense is it contrary to the virtue of religion, although it might also become blasphemy obliquely insofar as insulting reference is made to God or some divine attribute.

Blasphemous language spoken in drunkenness is *culpable,* provided the individual in his normal state is aware that he uses such language when he is intoxicated and makes no serious effort to avoid intoxication. If, despite his clear understanding of the dire effects of drink, he does not have the good will to abstain from it or at least control his use of it and thus shun the sin of blasphemy, he gives evidence that he is not really sincere in his protestations that he hates the dreadful sin he commits in his drunken state.[112]

In the Old Testament the sin of blasphemy was punished by death in accordance with an ordinance of Moses: "Whoever blasphemes the name of the Lord shall be put to death. The whole community shall stone him; alien and native alike must be put to death for blaspheming the Lord's name" (Lv 24:16). Jesus regarded the accusation that He cast out devils with the help of Beelzebub as blasphemy against the Holy Spirit, a sin which would not be forgiven in this world nor in the next (Mt 12:24ff.).

Ancient pagan peoples proscribed and shunned blasphemy, and Justinian in his Code of Law prescribed capital punishment for the sin.[113]

2. Tempting God

The sin of tempting God approaches that of blasphemy or direct injury to God. One who tempts God calls on Him to work a miracle or manifest

His power in some extraordinary manner not included in the divine promises or in the course of divine providence. One who manifestly tempts God irreverently and insolently demands that He intervene. The reason may be unbelief or doubt regarding a divine attribute (heretical tempting of God) which he seeks to put to a test. Or he may be so presumptuous as to demand that God resolve his difficulties or show His will by some extraordinary sign. Tempting God is a caricature of true prayer. It is an insolent request addressed to the Most High.

Christ Himself condemned the sin of tempting God in His rebuke of the evil spirit. Satan sought to lead Him astray, to induce Him to call on God to display His almighty power miraculously and protect Him as He boldly hurled Himself down from the pinnacle of the temple: " 'Thou shalt not tempt the Lord thy God' " (Mt 4:7).

To tempt God openly and expressly is a grave sin in its entire nature (*ex toto genere suo*). The implied tempting of God, hidden in the context of words and actions (interpretative tempting of God), is a grave sin if the matter is grave. Hence this sin may in some instances be only a venial sin. What is actually sought is not tempting God but rather something else in which the tempting of God is more or less implicitly included. An example would be the simple arrogance of the preacher who does not prepare his sermons, on the assumption that God will inspire him with the right thoughts and words "if He is really concerned about His kingdom and its progress." (This is usually not tempting God but simply falling victim to laziness and false self-confidence.)

To beseech God for extraordinary favors is not necessarily tempting Him. To demand of God in all humility an extraordinary sign in an urgent or exceptional necessity with only the divine honor and the salvation of souls in mind is not at all to tempt Him. Rather it is an act of great confidence in the divine bounty and mercy. On the other hand, to beg for a miraculous cure of a serious malady while refusing medical guidance and human remedies would be tempting God. Finally, to neglect the ordinary means and the simple tasks demanded in the fulfillment of our duty to promote the kingdom of God in the hope of extraordinary divine intervention because of an unfounded reliance on an alleged private revelation or personal *inspiration* is not so much tempting God as culpable credulity and neglect of duty.

The so-called Judgments of God (*ordeals*) in the Middle Ages were nothing less than tempting God, even though at the time men may not have been aware of it. They were based on the presumption that God would in every instance safeguard and manifest the innocent by a miraculous sign, if men should seek it. The accused would have to undergo the trial-by-combat which was a judiciary duel; or the ordeal-by-fire in which he would seize a red-hot iron or walk with bare feet over burning coals; or the ordeal by water in which he would immerse his hand in a cauldron of boiling water. His innocence was presumed to be proved if he was the victor in the duel or emerged unscathed from the ordeal by fire or water.

In His mercy God might have rescued some innocent victims of vicious accusations in these trials, but it was not because of the effrontery of the judges themselves. Though we may excuse many concerned with these so-called trials as invincibly ignorant because of the false conceptions prevailing in man's conscience at the time, objectively and as such the ordeal was the sin of tempting God. It was also a grave sin of injustice to accuse individuals of great crimes without a shadow of evidence that they were guilty, a double injustice to torture them and endanger their lives to prove innocence or guilt. Surely those who falsely accused innocent people of crimes could not lay claim to invincible ignorance because of the false notions prevalent in those ages.

Only gradually and with great difficulty could the Church suppress these barbarous travesties of true religion and legal justice. Pope Nicholas I forbade the judiciary duel; Stephen V, the ordeal by water. Innocent III strictly prohibited the attendance and assistance of the clergy at these judgments of God.[114]

3. Sacrilege: Desecration of the Sacred

As blasphemy attacks God Himself, the all-holy Lord, sacrilege wounds His honor in that which is sacred to Him or sanctified by Him. Sacrilege and simony are sins against the *holy;* they profane that which is sacred. (Here we use the word not in the ethical sense, the *sanctus,* but in the sense of *sacral,* consecrated by God, set apart for God.) Simony is a special form of profanation of the holy; it is traffic with that which is sacred.

God alone is substantial holiness ("Thou alone art holy!"). A ray of His glory falls on all that He has created, and nature reflects His holiness. But we do not say that every being participates *analogously* in the holiness of God in the same way that all creation is one, true, and good by analogy with God. The holy is not a transcendental. Rather holiness points to the absolute otherness, the exaltation of God over all creatures. The splendor of the holiness of God forces the creature to his knees and to joyous confession that God alone is worthy of honor. But what God selects directly for His cult, that is to say, what the Church by divine assignment singles out for cult and places in the orbit of the glory and glorification of God, that is caught up in a special way by the holiness of God. Therefore, it merits a reverence in proportion to the greatness of its consecration.

Persons, places, and things can be holy and consecrated to God (times or seasons may be holy in an improper sense of the term, insofar as they are reserved for special cult). Corresponding to these three there are three kinds of profanation: a. desecration of *sacred persons* (*sacrilegium personale*); b. desecration of *sacred places* (*sacrilegium locale*); c. desecration of *holy things* (*sacrilegium reale*).

Later on we shall treat explicitly and at greater length of the profanation of sacred days and seasons. Such profanation is not ordinarily looked upon as sacrilege in the strict sense of the term by present day moralists. One sins against the sacred seasons or holy days set apart for the special worship of God through refusing to offer worship on such days or by disturbing the sacred rites. Rightly the old traditional moralists considered desecration of sacred days, dedicated to divine cult, through actions in themselves sinful as graver desecration than mere violation of the commandment of sacred repose.[115] The simple faithful today react similarly, particularly regarding very heinous sins committed on the great feasts of the redemption.

By the way of critical appraisal, we add that the sin of sacrilege in each of the three areas indicated above is a very grave sin in itself. However, the sin is not mortal *ex toto genere suo*. Sacrilege may be a venial sin because of slightness of matter or object.

a. Personal Sacrilege

Persons can be sacred (sacral) because of sacramental consecration or blessing of the Church or public vows. Consecration carried out or confirmed by the Church makes the following sacred (sacral) in various degrees: first, those who have received Holy Order; secondly, all clerics in general; thirdly, members of religious communities. All these persons are *separated* from the rest of the faithful by the Church insofar as she admits them to sacred orders or the clerical state, grants them clerical privileges, or accepts their public vows, so that they are set apart for the service and glory of God. The objective consecration, which is essentially imparted by the Church, is interiorized and perfected by a personal act of dedication, most fittingly by a vow. In the case of the public vows of the religious state or of the major cleric the Church intervenes (in a solemn or non-solemn manner), confirming the act of religion by which men are dedicated to the divine service and glory. As to the private vow, the person is not consecrated to God in this same full sense of the term. For this reason there are theologians who hold that a sin against a private vow of chastity, though it is a sin against the virtue of religion, is not strictly a sacrilege. This opinion may be considered truly probable.

Sacrilege against a consecrated person is committed: 1. by violation of the vow of chastity on the part of the consecrated person himself, or by violation in reference to such a person even though it be only through a sin in thought; 2. by physical violence inflicted on the person consecrated to God (this is a violation of the *privilegium canonis* which protects clerics and religious against violence); 3. by interference in the sacred preoccupation of the consecrated person in the service of God (this is a violation of the *privilegium immunitatis,* the privilege of immunity, which exempts the consecrated person from all service and employment incompatible to a greater or lesser degree with the divine service). From the standpoint of canon law a violation of the *privilegium fori* or of legal immunity is a sacrilege (an example would be the citing of a cleric before a secular court). But it is sacrilege only from the standpoint of Church law, as is apparent from the fact that the Church does not always recognize the privilege and does not insist upon it universally.

Because of the cultal consecration of the Christian (through baptism and confirmation) and his essential ordering to cult, every sin against his dignity as a Christian, particularly profanation of his body, seduction, and abuse of neighbor for evil ends merits in a broad but real sense the name of sacrilege. Though the distinction on this level should not be of practical importance for integrity in the accusation of the sacrament of penance, it should be seriously considered in the religious-moral judgment of the sin of the Christian in general. With his whole moral life and being the Christian must be taken up entirely into the divine cult for the service of God, and in this sense he is sacred. By his sin he refuses this fulness of cult and worship and to this extent becomes profane.

b. Local Sacrilege

According to the law of the Church those places are holy or sacred which through liturgical consecration or blessing have been set apart for the divine service or for the burial of the faithful.[116] Every act in direct or immediate contradiction to the sacredness of these places must be looked upon as sacrilege. The following acts are sacrilege: 1. All objectively grave sins which seriously violate or offend against the sacred character of the place: thus in particular, murder or suicide, criminal bloodshed, external sins against chastity. 2. Use of the church for profane activities and purposes which are evidently contrary to its sacred character. Surely it is profanation to use the sacred place for sheer worldly entertainment, as balls, revels, banquets, or for commercial purposes such as sales, bartering, auctions, or to indulge in noisy demonstrations or quarreling in the sacred precincts. The episode of the vendors in the temple whom Jesus rebuked so severly (cf. Mk 11:15ff.) is proof that the all-holy God is angered through such disregard for the sacredness of the places dedicated to Him.

The quartering of soldiers or the housing of refugees, particularly the sick or wounded, in the sacred edifices in cases of urgent necessity arising, for instance, from the inclemency of the weather is not a profanation of the sacred place. It is rather using the means at hand for works of Christian charity. 3. Forceful entry into a church and likewise, according to canon law, the violation of the right of asylum[117] are sacrilegious transgressions against the place dedicated to God.

Use of the church for impious or sordid purposes, murder, serious shedding of blood, burial of an infidel or one excommunicated by judicial sentence all constitute not mere sacrilege but canonical violation of the sacred place.[118] These violations are so abhorrent and shocking as to demand a reconciliation, or ritual expiation, of the sacred place, before sacred functions can be performed there.[119] Reconciliation is required, however, only if the act of desecration is of a notorious nature and has been committed in the interior of the church or sacred place itself.

c. Real Sacrilege

Those things are sacred which serve the divine cult exclusively: the sacraments—we include them here under this term because of their matter which may be a real thing (though in some instances it is only an action), and their form; the relics of the saints; and the words of Sacred Scripture. All these are in their very nature holy things. Other things become holy, that is, reserved for cult, by being set apart through consecration or constitutive blessing. Among these we must mention first of all the sacred vessels, the vestments, and the altar. The more sacred a thing is, that is to say, the more essentially or intrinsically it is ordered to cult, the more culpable is its profanation.

Among the most heinous forms of sacrilege is the unworthy reception and unworthy administration of the sacraments, above all, the unworthy celebration of Holy Mass and reception of Holy Communion. "Therefore whoever eats this bread or drinks the cup of the Lord unworthily will be guilty of the body and the blood of the Lord . . . for he who eats and drinks unworthily, without distinguishing the body, eats and drinks judgment to himself" (1 Cor 11:27ff.). Not to distinguish sacred from profane is of the very essence of sacrilege; but here we have the Holy *par excellence* since the Sacred Species of bread and wine are the immediate sign of the presence of the most holy humanity of Christ.

Grave though the sacrilegious communion may be, we may not say that it is absolutely the greatest of all sins. The sins against the theological virtues are directed against God much more immediately, and even subjectively they ordinarily have more of the nature of a decision against God. Apart from an excessive and almost morbid sense of human respect, the principal cause of unworthy communions in very many instances is a weak and superficial faith.

The most heinous form of real sacrilege is the deliberate desecration of the Sacred Species through which sacrilege is compounded by the sin of irreligion, the contempt of Christ in the sacrament of His love. One guilty of this crime incurs the penalty of excommunication whose pardon is reserved in a most special manner to the Holy See (*specialissimo modo*).[120]

There is also more or less of sacrilege in the act of dishonoring relics and holy images, in the unseemly or irreverent presentation of sacred persons or objects in art, in the abuse of the inspired words of the Scriptures. The latter may assume various forms: the sacred words may be turned to ridicule or be used as sparkling witticisms for the purpose of vain display of learning. Or they may be used to flatter, to insult, to revile, or even to serve superstitious purposes.[121] Here we also include the profane use of sacred vessels, vestments, and church appointments.[122] The mere absence of respect for holy things is not sacrilege though it springs from the same source, which is the failure to distinguish the holy from the profane.

Theologically (the classifications of canon law are not considered here) the unjust acquisition of ordinary Church property is not to be considered sacrilege though it is a particularly grave act of injustice. It inflicts great harm on the solemn celebration of the Church's cult or on the pastoral exercise of charity. The crime is punished by serious ecclesiastical penalties for this reason.[123]

d. Simony: Traffic in Holy Things

Simony[124] is an especially dangerous form of sacrilege. Simony (the name derives from Simon the magician mentioned in Acts 8:18ff.) consists in the criminal effort to turn the holy (a purely spiritual thing: for example, the power to consecrate and bless; or a temporal thing essentially bound up with something spiritual: for example, a benefice attached to the office of care of souls) to material advantage or gain, above all, into monetary evaluation. The malice of simony consists in this: the holy is not merely equated with the profane in one's mind and inner desire, but even selfishly recruited to the service of the temporal and placed under the yoke of the earthly. And this may even assume the crassest form in the barter of the earthly for the spiritual. The simonist seeks to exploit the piety of others and their esteem for the spiritual (the holy) for temporal gain, to capitalize on their regard for what is sacred. A particularly fatal form of simony is bribery aimed at obtaining an ecclesiastical office.

Allied to simony is nepotism and the advancement of unfit candidates to spiritual dignity or office for personal or party reasons. Classical nepotism, if we may use the unsavory term, consisted in the promotion of one's family or relatives in both wealth and honor by placing spiritual offices in their hands. First concern was not the good of souls but the good of the family despite the detriment to spiritual interests. Spiritual power was a mere tool for the advancement of material interest. Not only is the record of simony and nepotism in the injury inflicted on the Church a tragic one, insofar as unworthy men were raised to spiritual office, not excluding bishops and even some popes, but by their very nature these sins tend to destroy the sense of the holy and, thereby, religion itself.

As far as ecclesiastical usage and, more particularly, as far as penal law is concerned, it is important to delineate the confines of actual simony very clearly. We distinguish what is strictly simony according to the divine law and what cannot be proved to be such. And then we draw a line between simony according to divine law and those acts and actions which the Church forbids in her attempt to fend off every hazard of simony. This latter is simony according to ecclesiastical law. These distinctions must be kept clearly in mind.[125]

Our moral theology, which is the doctrine of the following of Christ, is concerned with the discovery of the spiritual dispositions and attitudes in the background of simony itself. It deals with the interior dispositions and their control, insofar as it sets up the most lofty and exacting ideal: in the midst of any necessary solicitude for material advancement and for the economic means necessary for ecclesiastical purposes, the ecclesiastic should never place the spiritual, the holy, at the service of the earthly. He should do precisely the opposite; in reverence for the holy he must place the very essential means for his own livelihood and the apostolate entirely and utterly in the service of the sacred office, in the service of the kingdom of God.

One who enters a sacred state (the priesthood or any position with the care of souls) or accepts a spiritual charge in a worldly frame of mind or even for worldly reasons may conceivably hold himself aloof from simoniacal conduct, but he will always be motivated by a selfish desire which is fundamentally identical with the simoniacal. He will always subordinate the spiritual interests of the Church and his office, the sacredness of cult, and the salvation of souls to his desire for gain, ambition, or at least a craving for ease and comfort. The disposition and will to subordinate the spiritual to the temporal is culpable.

One who aspires to a spiritual office because of his love for gain or because of an earthly-minded attitude toward the spiritual has already gone beyond the borderline which separates the sacred from the profane. The words of Yahweh to Moses apply to any one who enters the sanctuary of the priesthood or takes up any other spiritual charge: "The place whereon thou standest is holy ground" (Ex 3:5). The faithful rightly abhor nothing so much as pastors of souls who in the very exercise of their spiritual office betray their craving for wealth or honor.

Simony in violation of the divine law is in all its forms and degrees (*ex toto genere suo*) mortal sin. It is not merely the actual sacrilegious traffic in sacred things or offices that is gravely sinful. The very intent and resolution, every open or hidden effort to buy, to sell, or to grant holy things, offices, or privileges (authorizations, faculties, etc.) for money or temporal value or advantage is sinful. The laws of the Church which are aimed at the utter exclusion of any semblance or species of simony and every danger of the sin (simony according to ecclesiastical law) are gravely binding in conscience. Violations of the laws are according to their category (*ex genere suo*) mortally sinful. Sad experience reveals how necessary such laws were in times past and still are today.

The giving of alms voluntarily or in accordance with the regulations concerning such gifts is not simoniacal. The offering is intended as a contribution to the sustenance of the clergy and the defrayal of expenses incurred in the Church's pastoral and charitable endeavors. Obviously it is not simoniacal to give or accept these offerings on the occasion of certain spiritual work. But even when there is not the slightest question of simony, false notions and misleading expressions should be shunned. Under no circumstances should one tolerate the query, "What does a Mass cost?" Instead we should insist on an unexceptionable form such as, "What is the usual offering for a Mass?" or "What is the required stipend?"

The diocesan regulations regarding stipends and *stolae* and *taxae*, etc., are in themselves absolutely free from simony. The Church's express purpose above and beyond her concern for the decent sustenance of her ministers is to avoid every semblance of simony. She does not leave the decision in such matters to individuals who might be guided by less noble motives. Nevertheless, the minister of the sanctuary readily exposes himself to the taint of simony if he clings too tenaciously to temporal possessions, even though he may be altogether correct in his external actions and may keep the Church's regulations very exactly.

Refusal to contribute to the Church according to ecclesiastical custom and regulation or, more specifically, not to recognize the need for material help in the divine worship and the pastoral work for souls is not simony if we judge the act by the external conditions and circumstances. But inwardly such niggardliness usually arises from the same source as simony; namely, from a lack of understanding and esteem of the importance of religion and religious values.

II. FALSE CULT

Contrary to the virtue of religion as it should be practiced in the adoration of Almighty God are these sins: 1. false worship of the true God in cultal forms which are unworthy of the true God; 2. irreligious cult, a pseudo-divine worship paid to fictitious deities, to the devil, or to other creatures; 3. quasi-religious adherence to impersonal forces and powers by way of divination, superstition, and magic.

1. *False Worship of the True God*

The worship of the true God must correspond, insofar as this is possible, to His utter transcendence and holiness, and therefore it must bear the hallmark of the pure Christian faith. It must reflect the inaccessible splendor of His own revelation of Himself. To fall short of this lofty ideal is a natural consequence of human frailty. However, there are also forms of worship of God which are positively unworthy,[126] in fact superstitious, and therefore in direct opposition to the very meaning and essence of religion. These are practices of piety vitiated by superstition. Note the following: 1. a great reliance on the number or form of the rites and prayers which one hopes will be efficacious, not so much because of the loving-kindness of God and His fidelity to His promises, as because of rigid adherence to prescribed human forms and formulas. Here we have a quasi-magical conception of the divine worship. A practical example is the trust in "chain prayers" (often there is a threat of curse on those who refuse to rely on them, do not recite them, fail to copy them and forward them to others), in "infallibly efficacious" formulas of prayer, ridiculous prayers, inane and unseemly devotions combined with rare promises (as an example: devotion to the "hair of Christ" or to the "sacred stature" of Christ). Even the so-called "Gregorian Masses" (for which it is essential that a Mass be said for a deceased person daily without interruption for thirty days, in the light of an alleged revelation and promise of St. Gregory the Great) might readily be the occasion of a superstitious exaggeration of number and unbroken sequence, even if confidence in their efficacy have the warranty of such a promise of the saint. In view of the danger of superstitious trust and of the weak historical foundation of the claim to a special private revelation, the practice of the Gregorian Masses does not merit any special encouragement.

The Council of Trent admonishes the bishops to watch over the Christian cult zealously lest it be defiled by the stealthy introduction of superstitious practices which are "a counterfeit of true and genuine piety." The Council, likewise, demands that the practice of celebrating holy Mass according to a pattern of "a fixed number of days and candles be entirely removed from the Church for it is more an invention of superstitious cult than true service rendered to God."[127]

Faith-healing has been developed into a veritable cult by the Christian Scientists and some other sects, but it is by no means limited to these followers of Mrs. Eddy. It must be considered a particularly crass form of devotion to words and numbers. Certain formulas, which are often ridiculous, must be repeated a specific number of times in order to prove infallibly effective against various maladies (to stop the flow of blood, to heal wounds, to destroy the venom of serpent bites, etc.). Guarding the secrecy of the formula from the uninitiated is usually considered a condition for its effectiveness.

This method of "prayer" is directly condemned by the word of the Lord: "But when thou prayest, go into thy room, and closing thy door, pray to thy Father in secret; and thy Father, who sees in secret, will reward thee. But in praying, do not multiply words, as the Gentiles do" (Mt 6:6f.). In regard to prayer-healing each instance must be subjected to the most careful scrutiny to ascertain whether trust is placed principally in the exactness of the formula itself or whether there is a real charism (*gratia curationum* or the gift of healing, 1 Cor 12:28ff.).

Conscientious observance of the rubrics of the liturgy has nothing in common with the superstitious reliance on mere formulas of prayers and texts. In the observance of the rubrics there is no preoccupation with words and movements as possessing a kind of magic power, but a question of obedience to the Church and of conformity with the prescribed forms in union with other members for worthy celebration of divine worship. However, the priests who manifest a major concern for mere external performance in rite, rubric, or prayer formula and consequently seriously neglect to make them intelligible and meaningful to the faithful are culpably responsible for many false notions among non-Catholics. They cannot be excused from guilt if people of other faiths manifest constant misgiving and suspicion about Catholic cult, as though it were akin to magic in concept and attitude.

a. Allied to such superstitious adherence to precise forms and often bound up with it is the purely mechanical use of religious objects (holy images or relics used to bless the faithful, imposed upon them, placed about one's neck, sewn into one's clothing, etc.). We condemn as inordinate in all this not the actual use and veneration of the objects as something *holy,* but reliance on the effectiveness of the material thing itself rather than on the interior devotion to God which perhaps may be entirely neglected. Not far removed from such material-mechanical conception of the effectiveness of prayer is the practice of swallowing tiny religious objects as holy pictures, threads (relics of cloth), etc., which is rather widespread in a number of countries. Even though we may be too severe if we brand it as outright superstition—for the interior spirit of piety and devotion to the saints is not altogether excluded—any practice of this kind is very unseemly in form. Not only could it readily degenerate into superstition, it cannot fail to be misunderstood by many and lead to harsh criticism of the devotions of the Church. The practice surely should be discouraged.

The use of objects of devotion inspired by true interior piety and confidence in the prayer of the Church, whose blessing is upon them, is not superstition.

Objectionable and improper in cult is either the unworthiness of certain external forms or the interior attitude of the superstitious individual who, by an unwarranted analogy with the sacraments, attributes to formulas, rites, and objects arbitrarily chosen by men an infallible efficacy. The sacraments contain and produce grace. These signs and symbols established by Christ infallibly cause the divine effect in the souls of those who receive them with the proper dispositions (place no obstacle in their way). Superstitious cult by means of formulas and objects chosen arbitrarily by men presumes to have a similar efficacy by doing a kind of violence to God.

There is no doubt that superstitious cult is prejudicial to true worship of God. It is illogical and confused and a source of endless scandal. It surely is a grave sin in its general class (*ex genere suo mortale*). Hence the practice of superstitious cult by one who is fully aware of its unworthiness and realizes its shocking effect upon those who have neither faith nor piety must be gravely culpable. However, in many instances the individual is not aware of the malice of the sin and hence is excused because of His ignorance, at least from mortal sin.

The wise director will not be satisfied with a negative attitude concerned merely with guilt or its absence. He will realize that even superstition indicates a certain depth of the religious and spiritual in the heart of man. With all his power he should aim to instruct and enlighten those who cling to false forms and deepen the true piety present in their souls and to initiate them in the practice of religion in spirit and in truth. In the same constructive spirit the priest is well advised if he desist from stigmatizing every shallow and superficial form of devotion in vogue among the faithful as superstition. Rather than attempt to destroy root and branch all religious practices which seem to him lacking in religious significance and rich doctrinal or moral content, the wise pastor will seek to re-animate all that can be corrected and elevated, destroying only what cannot be made a part of true religion. Formulas and rites which are so false as to be equivalent to false worship, or perhaps even actually idolatrous or ungodly, must of course be completely eliminated.

2. Worship of False Gods

All superstition is the very antithesis of true worship. It is false cult. But the most extreme form of false cult (cult directed against divine worship) is payment of divine honor to mere creatures, to idols, or to fictitious deities (idolatry), or even the worship of the enemy of God, the devil (devilolatry). Let us note the serious implication in the episode of the third temptation of our Lord. The devil says to Jesus: "If thou wilt worship before me, the whole (world) shall be thine" (Lk 4:7).

For a clear and well-ordered presentation of this subject with an explanation of the various types of sin we must make a five-fold distinction of *idolatry:* 1) Idolatry may spring from conscious apostasy from the true God, which in reality is a more or less conscious service of the devil. Satan, too, has his forms of cult. All the religious instincts and tendencies can be placed in the service of sin and the devil. Note the teaching of the Sacred Scriptures (Dt 32:17; 1 Cor 10:20) and of the Fathers of the Church that the gods are devils.

2. Idolatry may have no real cultal object at all. The cult of *nothing* is evident in the feigned worship of deities by mere external acts of cult

due to human respect and desire for some earthly advantage, without any actual belief or disbelief in the superstition. Nevertheless, it is idolatry in the strict sense of the term, a real denial of the true faith, which may be more culpable than the idolatry which is offered to idols with interior conviction.

The scriptures emphatically state in many passages that the gods are *nothing,* that therefore idolatry has no real object and idolaters adore nothing.[128] Reason also makes man aware, and men could not fail to know that the gods do not really exist; therefore idolatry is always in itself a denial of the true God. But the malice of the servants of false gods is not always so great that they would be willing to adore in person the enemy of God the devil.

3. Idolatry may be based on a dualistic concept of the world: besides the good God, Source of all good, there is also an evil spirit, the adversary of God, a power independent of God. Instead of following the teaching of revelation and faith and paying honor to God alone, such dualists also pay tribute to the evil spirit, attempt to appease him or even win his favor and invoke his help.[129] Students of comparative religions discovered a cult of this kind in honor of the wicked and jealous deities among many tribes of the primary and secondary cultures. Often the good spirit, simply because he is good, is ignored and offered no sacrifice or scarcely any prayer, whereas the evil spirits are placated by a rich cult because their evil influence is feared. This practice gives us some insight into the false cults of Israel. There was a cult of the evil gods in the persistent idolatry among the Chosen People: to a degree they still believed in the God of the Covenant, Yahweh, yet they cultivated the local and tribal deities which might after all be still in existence and possessed of some power to harm them.

All these forms of idolatry imply an attack on the exclusive sovereignty of God (Ex 20:2ff.). In the graphic imagery of the prophets it constitutes adultery, because Israel, the chosen bride of the Lord in a covenant of love and worship, turned away from Him to honor and worship, if not to love, the horrid local deities. It is not far-fetched to associate all superstition with this type or form of idolatry, at least insofar as the superstitious man constantly reckons with all sorts of mysterious powers and forces besides God (today God is often excluded altogether). There is concern for such forces; they are feared by many superstitious minds even in the most civilized countries today. Even Christians who are in constant dread of the devil and see him at work in all things show an excessive and one-sided awe for Satan, as though he were not completely under the dominion of God. Though we should never underestimate his evil power, we should neither fear him nor honor him as a spirit independent of God.

4. There is, or perhaps it is more accurate to say there was, a kind of idolatry which may more truthfully be called a yearning for the true God through purity of inner disposition and spirit. St. Paul found traces of this among the Athenians who had dedicated an altar "to the Unknown God" (Acts 17:23ff.). Truly pious pagans, particularly if they were not actual polytheists but rather adorers of one supreme being (henotheists), looked upon the gods rather as names and symbols through which they sensed the goodness and majesty of the true God, even though masked and hidden.[130]

Objectively every form of idolatry is a mortal sin (*ex toto genere suo*). However, the form just referred to above (under No. 4) is subjectively not a sin of idolatry, although it may in great measure be attributable to the consequences of the sins of mankind.

5. In a broader but truly significant sense Sacred Scripture designates as idolatry the perverted attachment or subjection which makes a created thing the supreme and final good. St. Paul calls fornicators, the unclean, and covetous persons "idolaters" (Eph 5:5). In the sin of pride man exalts and defies his own self: "Because it is like the sin of witchcraft, to rebel: and like the crime of idolatry, to refuse to obey" (1 Sm 15:23). Every gravely culpable orientation of one's life implies apostasy from the living God, the erection of an idol which the impious frequently serve with a devotion and fervor suggesting a religious—or we might say more accurately, a pseudo-religious—attitude of mind and heart.

As religion decays, superstition and vicarious religion thrive. The religious impulses seek a vicarious satisfaction in an idolatrous cult of form and fitness with athlete, movie star, and songster as the idols of the masses. Even love of one's fellows is reduced to supreme concern for bodily needs, and the cult of progress is measured by the production and enjoyment of the fruits of material wealth. In the ethos of classical capitalism the ideal was unlimited production and acquisition of wealth, with the "ascetic" totally devoted to the service of gain. The fierce zeal for production exacted tremendous sacrifices from the worker while spending the vital energies of the employer. Masked though it may be, our Western civilization has become de-christianized in the idolatrous cult of wealth.

Infinitely worse is atheistic communism, which demands renunciation of the joy and peace of the present in the confident hope of building a workers' paradise in a classless society of the future. When man becomes totally immersed in the material and carnal, he betrays his religious and cultal orientation precisely by investing with the halo of the divine the very goal of the good which he has perverted. It has been said that man is incurably religious. So ineradicably religious is he that he betrays this tendency even in his denial of the God of majesty, even in the horror of the decline and decay into the vileness of counter-cult.

A new idol has been placed in our current world of industry and exchange, the dangerous idol of the "higher standard of living," which submits even the loftiest values to its goal.

3. The False Cult of Superstition

In a broader sense of the term, superstition also includes irrational worship of God and frivolous concern for private revelations and visions. Actual worship of idols and forming pacts with the devil in a way are also based on superstition (false religion or false faith), on stupid or silly notions and expectations, but basically they are irreligion, counter-cult rather than superstition. Superstition in the stricter sense of the word, of which we are here speaking, is the confused and irrational attitude toward imaginary and impersonal powers or forces, an attitude which borders on the religious and yet is contrary to religion.

Superstition has its roots in the innate urge of man to penetrate the mysteries of life, to peer into the future and master the secret forces of nature and solve the problems of man's existence. In part it is created by the avid reading of superstitious literature which for purposes of greed cultivates the artistic superstition (in contradistinction to the grass roots superstition of simple folk). We may not ignore the devil's share in this. However, the principal source of superstition is the decline and decay of true religion, leaving a vacuum in the human heart which superstition only too readily fills. Thus it becomes a substitute, an *Ersatz* for religion (as it may be called an *Ersatz* for science, flattering man that he has secret knowledge and even secret power, giving him control over the very destiny of man, his fortune, his health, his love, his relations with others), an improper development of the ineradicable religious tendency of man. For this reason we designate superstition as erroneous or misdirected cult.

Many serious pitfalls await man's dealing with the occult. Superstition constitutes a danger to man's body, to his spiritual balance and harmony, to his morals and his faith. The utter disregard of fact or science in the exercise of occult powers by one who presumes to predict the actual course of events or influence them often results in neglect of essential medical care by those who are duped. This is particularly the case in those who trust in faith and prayer healing of the Christian Science practitioners. (A similar disregard of prudent care of one's bodily health is found in certain groups whose misconception of the meaning of the text of Sacred Scripture leads them to deny to their own children essential medical care.)

Reliance on the efficacy of superstition places the victim in a very unreal world: Why should one go to any pains to plan and work for a future which is already fixed and determined or if one can by occult means attain the object of one's desire without laborious effort? The superstitious person is often the victim of fixed ideas which make him incapable of facing the realities of life. His decisions will be formed on the basis of an utterly false conception of things and even the most obviously prudent course of action will be paralyzed because of all sorts of superstitious fears. In this way superstition seriously mars the whole outlook on life, destroys true Christian optimism which rests on the virtue of hope.

The moral life suffers seriously by an impairment of the sense of freedom and personal responsibility. Trust in the astrological propaganda of the literature of superstition (horoscopes) may be an incitement to immoral conduct. Statements as the following found in many newspapers can only be inducement to evil: "The following week is favorable for love and passion for all who are born under Aries. Love ventures will turn out well. Enterprises will fail. . . ." "If the woman born under Capricorn meets a man born under Libra, her marriage will be wrecked."

Superstition always weakens and endangers the faith. Particularly destructive are Spiritism and other forms of occultism which claim to communicate with the other world. If superstition is placed consciously in the service of false religion (yoga, spiritism, theosophy are examples), almost inevitably faith in God's omnipotence and all-embracing providence, in human liberty and the efficacy of the sacraments and prayer, in the true state of the future life is weakened or even destroyed. Some Catholics, seduced by the organizations of the "occult," have left the Church to join heretical and unchristian groups where the influence of the evil spirit may be very great. The warning of the inspired pages is still valid: "If there arises among you a prophet or a dreamer who promises you a sign or wonder urging you to follow other gods, whom you have not known, and to serve them: even though the sign or wonder he has foretold you comes to pass, pay no attention to the words of that prophet or that dreamer." (Dt. 13:2ff.).

On the basis of knowledge and action we may divide superstition into divination which is concerned with knowledge and magic which is concerned with action.

a. Divination

Divination is the attempt to foretell by means of certain signs and manifestations future events, even those which depend on the free decisions of men. Should one appeal to the evil spirit to obtain this result, his act would be idolatry, cult of the devil, rather than simple superstition. Ordinarily, at least in our day, the devil is not invoked at all. But this does not prove that the spirit of evil is not deeply involved in some way and does not take his devilish delight in the game. Nevertheless there is an essential distinction between divination which springs from a pact with Satan and divination which is simply superstition. The latter may not so much as include a belief in a devil and may even exclude it altogether.

When the moralists of former times attempted to prove by simple "logic" that divination resulting from a pact with Satan and simple divination were essentially and equally diabolical and therefore equally culpable, they failed to take into account the "illogicality" of superstition. Their argument is as follows: where the natural causes are not adequate to explain the revelation of the future, it must have been effected either with the help of God or the help of the devil. (The same argument can be given for any extraordinary effect.) However, in cases of true divination there is no natural explanation nor can there be question of divine intervention. (God would not intervene in a special way to assist any one moved by greed and using evil means and possibly leading others to grave sin.) Therefore only the devil can be at work whether he is actually called upon or not. The reasoning is in itself logical and does prove the objective evil of divination. But psychologically there is a vast difference between explicit traffic and pact with the spirit of evil and an act motivated by a craving for hidden knowledge and guided by a chimerical notion of occult powers operative in the world. This point must be borne in mind in our times, for today many superstitious people would be amazed at the very suggestion of any diabolical influence. Either alternative, God or devil, at work in their area of superstition is utterly foreign to them.

Conjectures about the future, based on purely natural causes and reasons, should not be simply dismissed as superstition. To cite an example, it is not impossible to hazard a guess regarding the character of a man and the direction of its development from a scrutiny of the lines in his palm. Similarly the moods and disposition, and even more so the vigor of health of extraordinarily sensitive persons may be influenced by climatic and atmospheric conditions and the position of the moon. Atmospheric conditions may be very exhilarating or depressing.

Should a true prediction be made regarding a specific and clearly determined event which is dependent in the last instance on the free decision of man, we might pursue an investigation of the fact along these lines: is it perhaps a genuine prophecy due to a divine illumination? Circumstances, for example, the irreligion or greed of the "prophet," may exclude this possibility a priori. Is it due to clairvoyance ("second sight")? Here the relevancy of prediction must be restricted to events close at hand, to what is nearby and in the immediate future. Going beyond the purely natural we may ask: is there evidence of direct influence of the devil? Obviously the devil, despite all the cleverness and astuteness of his spiritual nature, can only make a very shrewd surmise of the future which is contingent on the free decision of men. Or the whole affair may be a hoax, which surely is the simplest and most probable explanation of the usual prediction of the future (fortune telling). The superstitious query is cultivated and encouraged by cleverly planned deception. Again, the diviner (fortune teller) may be the victim of his own false notions.

Divination may not be dismissed lightly. It is an irreligious counterfeit of genuine prophecy and the announcement of the truths of faith, just as magic or sorcery is a counterfeit of genuine miracles and the efficacy of the holy sacraments. Every seriously intended divination is a very great sin against the virtue of religion. It is mortal sin in all degrees and forms (*ex toto genere suo*). The guilt of this sin is incurred by the one who practices divination in any form and by those who are the subject or interested party in the procedure (e.g., by having their fortune told). Even though the diviner does not accept his own claims to occult power but perpetrates a hoax and exploits the superstitious credulity of others, he is guilty of superstition and violation of fraternal love, for he seduces them and cooperates in their superstition.

Holy Scripture condemns divination and sorcery with equal severity (cf. Dt 18:9–14; Ex 22:17; Lv 19:31; 1 Sm 28:3, 7ff.; Is 2:6; 44:25; Jer 27:9f.; Za 10:2; Mal 3:5; Acts 8:9ff.; 19:19; Gal 5:20; Ap 21:8). The Church from her very beginning has consistently condemned both divination and witchcraft unequivocally and annexed severe sanctions to her prohibitions of these sins.[131] Emperor Constantine even forbade them under pain of death.

Often subjective reasons, such as simplicity of mind, ignorance, lack of reflection diminish the gravity of the fault. To practice this "art" manifestly as a joke for the plain amusement of others is not sinful, provided scandal is entirely avoided and there is no danger that any who take part in the game put stock in the "occult" powers of the performer at all. In fact one may expose the hoax of a fortune teller by having one's fortune told under circumstances which reveal the fraud.

The commonest forms of divination are: 1) necromancy, or communication with the dead; 2) astrology; 3) cartomancy, or reading of cards; 4) chiromancy, or palm reading; 5) magnetic reading; 6) interpretation of dreams. After discussing these forms of divination we shall briefly treat various types of false beliefs and popular superstition.

(1) Necromancy or Conjuring of Spirits

Necromancy is the attempt by means of magic to conjure up the spirits of the dead in order to obtain through them the secrets of the future or other occult knowledge. The Mosaic law forbade under capital punishment the evocation of the spirits of the dead by the people of Israel, a practice which was common among Israel's neighbors (Lv 19:31; 20:6; Dt 18:11). The episode of the conjuration of the spirit of Samuel by the witch of Endor for Saul (1 Sm 28) poses a difficulty for the exegete. But it is certain that Saul was quite aware of the illicitness of his action and that he was acting in defiance of the will of God, for the Lord had refused to give him any hint of the future through the lawful sources of information. Was it Samuel who really appeared to Saul in response to God's command in order to announce to the sinful king the punishment he merited, or some clever conception of the witch herself contrived to frighten the king, because he had persecuted all diviners of spirits and had them killed? The text is not altogether clear on this point nor are exegetes agreed in their explanation of it. Nor does the text in any way state that Saul actually saw the spirit of Samuel (1 Sm 28:13ff.).

The spiritualistic seances of our day are a modern form of the ancient evocation of the spirits of the dead. The Spiritualists maintain that through the mediation of certain specially endowed persons (the mediums are a modern version of the ancient pythonesses or sybils) contact can be established with the spirits of the departed and hidden truths, including future events, learned from them. To accept the authentic spiritualistic interpretation of the spiritualistic phenomena as actually due to the presence of the spirits of the departed is superstition. God in His all-wise providence will not permit the souls of the dead to be forced to appear before us at the beck and call of such disedifying individuals as the mediums usually are. Both the character of the mediums, who usually are the worst of charlatans, and their method of procedure in such a profoundly important matter totally exclude the divine approval. The very attempt to conjure up the dead under these conditions is frivolous and wanton.

The hypothesis of a diabolical intervention in view of the great prejudice to faith and morals implicit in the whole spiritualistic enterprize cannot be dismissed as wholly superstitious and unfounded. But the greater part of the significant phenomena can be explained as very artful deceit practiced by clever prestidigitators. The tiny fragment of real phenomena transcending such obvious natural explanations awaits the scientific exploration with which parapsychology (and often pseudoscience as well) deals.

The Holy Office has forbidden attendance at, and more especially, active participation in spiritualistic seances.[132] The hazards to faith and good morals and even to health and the scandal caused are usually the determining factors which make participation in seances unlawful. However, true research for scientific explanation of the spiritualistic phenomena by competent Catholic savants, exercising the essential prudential caution, is naturally not forbidden.

To hold that the spirits of the dead may occasionally appear to men with the divine permission in order to warn the living and beg for their prayers does not in the slightest savor of superstition. But credulity regarding alleged appearances of the dead is very far from praiseworthy and very likely will expose our faith to ridicule.

(2) *Astrology*

Astrology is a superstitious practice which attempts to read the meaning of earthly events and the destiny of man in the stars. It is a very ancient superstition spread among many peoples and seems to be irradicable, for it is found today among the most cultured and civilized. Two possible sources of relationship between terrestrial events and the course of the stars may be suggested. The one is a causal relationship: the destiny of man would be causally dependent on the course of the stars. Such a dependency would necessarily and obviously imply a fatalistic absence of freedom. It would mean that the course of events on earth is strictly determined. The other possible relationship is that of parallel and harmonious courses: the course of the heavenly constellations would have a fixed relation to the life course and destiny of man. There would not be the relation of cause and effect but of mutual representation and assimilation: there would be a kind of "pre-established harmony."

The basis for this latter view is the Ptolemaean cosmology according to which all the stars rotate around the earth and ultimately around man. By any standard of consistency the scientific rejection of the Ptolemaean astronomy should mean the collapse of this form of astrology. In any instance such "representative" astrology with its gross classifications according to constellations can never harmonize with the unique individuality and countless variations in man and his course of life. We must note, likewise, that it is impossible that the destiny of man, which in decisive points follows the law of human freedom, pursue a course parallel to that of the stars, whether in virtue of a causal dependence or merely exemplary parallelism. Science today leaves no room for doubt that the stars are governed by a law of necessity.[133]

Neither astrologer nor fanatical devoteé of horoscopes (which predict the course of life according to the position of the stars at the time of birth or the course of married life by the position of the constellation at the time of the wedding, etc.) is much concerned with evidence for the system. They are simply credulous, astrology-minded, though the astrologer may be a simple fraud. It is the earmark of superstition that it requires no rational basis for its origin and growth. The superstitious man blithely subscribes to the irrational.

Combination of pseudo-science and vague religious sentiment, heir of an abandoned astronomy and a vitiated astral cult, astrology by its practical negation of human freedom and the loving providence of God must exercise a most baneful influence on the entire life of its devoteés. Evil in its basis and the atmosphere it creates, it readily destroys the Christian faith and the Christian moral life. Therefore astrology in its various phases, the reading of the horoscope for others, the consultation of the astrologer, and particularly the propagation of the vile cult through the spread of its literature is a grave sin. If, however, contrary to the present vogue, "astrology" is clearly and plainly made a game or a species of symbolism which is not taken seriously, it cannot be objectionable, unless it becomes an occasion of scandal. But such grotesque symbolism, with all its cosmic overtones and its susceptibility to endless misconceptions, should not be given the name *astrology,* so suggestive of superstitious ignorance and error. Possibly another name might be found for it.

Scientific astronomy today sharply repudiates the current astrology. It is looked upon as vapid and pseudo-scientific. But we have already noticed that logic has little impact on the superstitious.

The system of seven planets and twelve signs of the zodiac, which have been used from time immemorial by the astrologers, is repudiated by science. On the one hand, we have discovered many other planets beside the ancient seven. And the twelve signs of the zodiac are not at all cosmic unities, much less real and effective unities. They rather constitute, from the stellar point of view, an arbitrary ensemble of stars separated from one another by vast worlds of space. Likewise, the signs of the zodiac, traditionally established for the various seasons of the year according to the astronomical observations of the past, are no longer in accord with the corresponding constellations, for they are constantly displaced in their relation to the seasons. Around the year 150 A.D. the signs of the zodiac bound to the months of the year and the effective constellations in the heavens corresponded fairly well. But since that time they have gotten so far out of harmony that today, to cite an example, one born "under the sign of the ram" would in reality fall under the stars of the pisces at his birth and not under the ram. Nevertheless, by the rule of the astrologers who construct the horoscopes, if they follow any rule at all, he would still be under the ram.[134]

Our condemnation of the superstition of astrology does not mean that we may not admit some influence of the stars on man's health and psychic life and activity. But this influence, like that of the climatic and meteorological conditions, is rather indirect and never predetermines or necessitates the decisions of the will. St. Thomas, though a stern and uncompromising critic of all astrological forecasts of free acts of men, concedes (possibly with tongue in cheek) that astrologers are able to make some very startling predictions (*in multis vera prenuntiant*) not merely through the help of the devil but also through natural means. He is speaking of predictions which we might call statistical today (*in communibus eventibus qui dependent ex multitudine*). Such predictions are true, because men in general do not utilize their freedom but permit themselves to be carried along by their urges and passions, which can be affected by cosmic influences.[135] Such is the position of the Angelic Doctor.

Even though we might concede that cosmic influences could affect the psychic life of man, the critical problem still facing the astrologer is: how can the millionfold influences of uncounted stars and their constantly varying constellations be even remotely measured? And even more difficult to answer: by what right does the astrologer presume to ascribe the influence affecting and determining the whole of human life precisely to one constellation?

As to the actual proof that the supra-terrestrial has an influence on men, there is some evidence of the influence of the moon on certain hypersensitive people who become "moonstruck." But this is a very far cry from the claim of those present-day astrologers who persist in setting up the most minute and detailed horoscopes for human actions which depend on the free decisions of the human will, insisting all the while that the stars do not coerce but merely influence and dispose men. If we should assume even for a moment that they are correct, then the most normal men would be altogether "starstruck." In fact this position leaves nothing of human dignity. Not only should any normal man feel outraged at the picture of himself presented by our current astrologers; the very notion of an astrological forecast of life destiny which is both free and real in the stars should be repudiated as an offense to sound reason and human dignity.

(3) *Cartomancy*

Cartomancy or the superstitious reading of cards[136] (this form of divination was introduced into Europe only in recent times) is on a par with the reading of tea leaves and coffee grounds. They are among the most vulgar forms of divination. On the part of the Madame (for it is usually a woman who performs this "service") the reading is more an exploitation of the naive and a diffusion of superstition than an actual belief in occult powers. Astrologers and cartomancers are quite astute in their perceptions and clever in their methods of procuring background information on the life and character of their clients. Often they have an organized system of espionage to supply them with information. As professionals in their field they may be masters of the art of association, so that they can construct a fairly accurate picture of the certainties and probabilities in a man's life on the basis of an incidental fact or a slight innuendo. Even at that much of their success is due to the obscurity of their pronouncements which remind one of the Delphic oracles.

(4) *Palm Reading (Palmistry or Chiromancy)*

Chiromancy is a very ancient "art." Man as essentially composed of body and soul reveals his interior self through his bodily actions and movements, particularly through his hands and his countenance. In this connection the noted painting of Dürer, *Praying Hands,* comes to mind. Therefore, it is not at all superstition to look for clues to character in the lines of the hand, provided one has a serious knowledge of the forms of expression found there. Both the lines of the hand and handwriting are significant objects and factors in the practical study of characterology. But the future cannot be more evident in the lines of the hand and in the handwriting than in the character itself, and the traits of character only restrict the potentialities of the future. They do not entirely specify and determine them, for character leaves room for the exercise of liberty. Moreover, there are other essential factors entering into the formation of the future decisions. In addition to character there is also the environment with its influence, deliberate or indeliberate, upon all that we do.

(5) *The Divining Rod and Magic Pendulum*

The use of a divining rod or magic pendulum for such purposes as water and mineral dowsing, the discovery of lost or hidden objects (e.g., treasure), the learning of certain hidden facts (whether a missing person is still alive, where he may be, as in the case of service men or others in time of war), or the diagnosis of disease and prescription of remedies cannot readily be branded as superstition, even though the merit of such a course of action is questionable and reliance upon it otherwise objectionable.[137] The very attempt to provide a scientific or natural explanation (through magnetic rays, the extraordinary sensitivity of certain individuals, as in telepathy or clairvoyance, etc.) for the accepted phenomena distinguishes it from superstition strictly such. But to seek occult information regarding the present condition of a departed soul, the moral character of an individual, and especially unknown and future facts and events which depend on the free decisions of men, is, if not actual superstition, open to suspicion of superstition.

In order to safeguard the dignity of religion and true piety, the Holy Office[138] obliged ecclesiastical superiors to strictly forbid clerics and religious from using *radiaesthesia* (with or without the usual devices such as pendulum or rod) for the purpose of discovering occult facts and future events regarding human persons (*ad personarum circumstantias et eventus divinandos*). But the Church did not have in mind to decide the scientific merits of radiaesthesia. At any rate, abstracting from any positive law or regulation, right reason and Christian faith in divine providence forbids us to hold that future free decisions of men can be learned by such means.

(6) *Interpretation of Dreams*

God may speak to us through dreams, as the Sacred Scriptures frequently testify. If the dream comes from God, the meaning and fulfillment is apparent to the one concerned. Some dreams arise from sane premonitions of the subconscious and point to the immediate future somewhat after the manner of so-called "second-sight" or clairvoyance. Particularly for people with sound and healthy natural instincts the dream may be the expression of many true premonitions of this kind, of well-founded fear or hope. Perhaps this is a normal function of the subconscious.

In the Middle Ages it was not uncommon for sincere Christians, even for saints, to search for norms in the discernment of dreams, with distinctions between the futile and the meaningful, and to interpret the latter. In fact the interpretation of dreams according to the present-day depth psychology (note the work of Carl Jung) is an earnest scientific effort as long as it does not presume to forecast the future by means of dreams, but investigates psychic traumas and depressions and their remedies. It is quite another question whether or not the psychoanalysts read too much into dreams.

Most dreams, particularly those of the present day hypercivilized man, whose subconscious has been so strangely disturbed, have no value for the discernment of the future. Prudence dictates, therefore, that we place little or no trust in them as signs of what is to come. Already the Old Testament writers warned against "dreamers" and "dream interpreters." This form of superstition, like all attempts to "reach out to the future," usually so conspires with fraud and deception as to make even the modest kernel of truth they may possess inacceptable for religion. "Therefore harken not to your prophets, and diviners, and dreamers, and soothsayers, and sorcerers. . . . For they prophesy lies to you" (Jer 27:9f.; cf. Jer 23:25–32).

(7) Various Forms of Popular Superstition

In many parts of the world superstition and superstitious practices are almost second nature in the lives of the masses. (Often they are remains of old pagan customs.) The simplest ways were found to "discern" the future. First of all, there was the superstition of the "first contact" (the first object encountered was an omen) which was widespread among the ancient Romans. They would break off important affairs of state, if at the inception of the task or at the break of day they failed to encounter the right animal or see the proper omen. Tacitus tells us that among the ancient Germans, likewise, much attention was paid to portents of ill fortune or disaster and to the auguries of good fortune. Omens were taken into consideration before journeys were begun or important tasks taken up. It is interesting to note that a bad omen in one region might have been a good omen in another (examples: a black cat, a hunchback, a crow, magpie, wolf, etc.). We consider especially ignoble the superstition which makes meeting an old woman a bad omen. In many places country folk associate the events of the twelve holy nights between Christmas and Epiphany with good or bad fortune, good or bad weather, for the whole year. Similarly the weather on certain feasts is an omen of the rain or ice and snow for weeks to follow.

Very common is the superstitious dread of numbers, for example, the number *thirteen*. There is also a superstition regarding Fridays. The fear of the number thirteen is so widespread that some hotels skip the number altogether for fear that room thirteen will usually remain unoccupied. Many consider the combination of Friday and thirteen especially unlucky.

It is evident enough that such delusion is opposed in a greater or less degree to the dignity of the divine faith. However, these phobias and practices, even though found among devout Christians, usually are not seriously culpable. It is closer to the truth to say that they are usually due to an unreasoning timidity which cannot simply ignore foolish practices if they are widespread. They are rather the tribute weakness pays to conformity. Usually people are only half in earnest, and among religious people some of the "signs" of future events are looked upon as coming from God or as resting in nature. In this class we may place some of the almanac predictions of the weather. The prevalence of such forms of superstition, despite the simplicity and good faith of many, is alarming. A revitalization of true faith is indicated. Moreover, neglect of serious duties because of superstitious omens or placing greater reliance on vain observances than on the commandments of God and the sacraments cannot readily be considered as only venial sin.

b. Magic (Sorcery)

Whereas divination seeks knowledge in a manner forbidden by God, magic seeks power. There is an ancient distinction between "black" and "white" magic. The latter is the attempt to obtain a mastery of the forces of nature by recourse to secret practices of a more or less irrational nature. The classical example of this white magic is alchemy. "Black" magic and "black" art attempt to inflict harm (evil sorcery) or to reap advantages, honor, riches for oneself through the aid of the devil. Witches have always been accused of practicing black magic. So grave is this sin that Old Testament Law and Roman Law punished it with death. (This ancient severity accounts for the harsh procedure against the "witches" in later times.) The gravity of the sin is not altered by the fact that although the devil has been called upon to further the evil work there may not actually be any diabolical influence exerted at all.

More widespread than the actual practice of black magic itself is the credulous or superstitious dread of its effects, which often is carried to the extreme of undermining filial trust in the omnipotence of God and His providential protection. The Church herself, as her rites of exorcism reveal, is fully aware of the power of the evil spirit and his accomplices among men. She never fails to take them into account, but she places her trust entirely and without reserve in the power and love of God.

Without divine permission the devil can harm no one. For this reason it is superstition to look upon maledictions, execrations, spells, enchantments as infallible instruments of sorcery which of their own vile power bring harm to others (Prv 26:2). The devil can do his evil work only if man places himself in his service. He can enter with his baneful influence only if God permits him, either to prove man's virtue—in which case special graces to resist evil will not be absent—or where sin has already cleared the way for him. Directors of souls should warn the faithful against false suspicion of others regarding black magic and black art and just as sternly against false dread of the power of the evil spirit. Obviously where hatred and enmity, unjust exploitation, seduction, cursing, and blasphemy prevail, there is good reason to fear both God and devil; those who breath this vile atmosphere of sin are slaves of the devil.

Witch baiting and witch phobia and the "legal" prosecution of witches from the late Middle Ages down to the eighteenth-century are among the most shameful events in the annals of Christian history. Without doubt, among the "witches" burnt at the stake or put to death in some other way there were disturbers of the peace, sectaries, criminals, and sorcerers who actually did evil through diabolical means. But the fanatical and superstitious imagination created the most preposterous world of crimes in justification for the cruel persecution (witches' sabbath, the riding of witches through the air to attend witches meetings, transformation into animals, sexual commerce with the devil, etc.). Most dreadful of all was the execution, by burning at the stake, of very many innocent persons whose worse crime was eccentricity (old women or men who may have looked odd or strange). If those suspected of black magic were not executed, they were at least tortured into admission of the most horrible and appalling crimes. All of which merely added fuel to the flames of hatred and fear of witchcraft. Eventually the penal legislation against superstition and sorcery itself developed into the most shameful superstition.

From the very beginning of Christianity (note particularly Hippolytus and Chrysostom) the Church took a defensive position against the terror and phobia of sorcery coming in from the Orient. But toward the end of the Middle Ages the waves of mass superstition proved too powerful and even bishops and popes were swept along in the dreadful movement. Disastrous was the effect of the approval of the use of the rack and torture in the Inquisition—though it was not at first directed against witches— by Innocent IV (1252) and the publication of the fatal Bull against witchcraft by Innocent VIII (*Summis Desiderantes,* 1484) due to the insistence of the two inquisitors, Institoris and Sprenger. The persecution raged first of all in Switzerland and southern France. In Germany the resistance of priests and laity proved a check to the worst excesses for a time. But Martin Luther's work, *Daemonologie,* contributed much toward breaking down these barriers, and the pest of superstition raged in Germany also. In fact fanaticism was carried to the excess of mass persecution of alleged witches in the various countries recently won over to Protestantism. In the Catholic countries similar unsavory practices prevailed until the stern action of the Church intervened. A decree of Gregory XV and an instruction of the Roman Inquisition (1654), inspired by the German Jesuit Friedrich Spee, eventually halted the persecution.

White magic has also played a considerable role in the history of religion: totemism, taboos, and many complex rites govern the social life of whole tribes (note the *mana* cult of the Melanesians, the *orenda* and *manitou* of certain American Indians). The complex hocus pocus of the sorcery and witchcraft of many primitive peoples with their fetishes, talismans, and amulets forms a notable element of tribal life down to our own times. Mingling with the fanciful creations of fables and legends are the marvelous accounts of wizards and magicians with magic mirrors and wands and strange potions and powers. In all this there is no appeal to diabolical intervention though the devil's influence and surely his interest cannot be altogether excluded, for white magic demonstrates too much of human folly and results in much damage to religion.

Some writers have attempted to trace the origin of religion to magical and other superstitious practices. But the history of religions offers evidence that magic is a perverted offspring of religion and is hostile to true religion. It is not in evidence in the most ancient and primitive tribes in whom a true religious sense is deeply rooted. But we find it later on a very wide scale among the patriarchic hunters (especially totemism) and also among the matriarchic husbandmen.

White magic is essentially an effort to influence the forces of nature and the course of history by totally insufficient means or instruments (such as ritualistic mimicry, intricate formularies in precise number, etc.).

Belief in mysterious, impersonal powers and forces evokes belief in other contrary powers and forces, equally occult and mysterious, which men, or at least certain men, can control and use. Very often only abysmal ignorance of the forces of nature or dread of their influence is responsible for the most naive attempts to keep them in check and control them with ease. Only when man attempts to coerce or restrain the power of God by these controlling powers, or when the latter reveal themselves as the power of God's great adversary (Satan), does the malice of magical practices become evident.

The judgment of moral theology on current magical practices may be summed up very briefly: all vain observances (all use of charms, amulets, talismans, or magical formularies of any kind) are strictly forbidden even though they may not be taken too seriously or at least not recognized in all their true opposition to God. But, as we noted above, we cannot fully agree with the severe condemnation based on the "logical dilemma" set up by some writers: "either the means used and the effect are natural and then there is no magic or superstitious observance and objectively no sin, or there is diabolical influence and a very great sin. There is no middle way between these two." According to this reasoning there is no distinction between the so-called white and black magic (compact with the devil, etc.) and both are placed on the same evil level. Of course we may be guided by this rigorous logic when we instruct the faithful. Where natural means are totally excluded and there is no question of divine intervention because of the manner and method of the art and practice, only diabolical influence can be present. Therefore, not only the virtue of religion but also respect for right reason and the dread of evil spirits forbids all these superstitious observances. (Cf. what was said above under a) Divination, regarding the "logicality" of the superstitious.)

The moral malice or moral defect in this practice does not lie so much in association with the devil. Usually he is not so much as considered. It lies rather in the irrationality and folly of the practices which are a clear indication of the weakness of the religious penetration of thought and life. Instead of turning whole-heartedly to God in loving trust of His providence, one attempts, even though it may be only half-heartedly, to seek his good fortune in stupid practices. The rational and religious man descends to the impersonal and absurd.

The Church combats these superstitious practices by exhorting us to have confidence in prayer. In a manner of speaking, she concretizes in consecrated objects the power of her prayers and blessings which she bids us use. She gives us special heavenly patrons in the saints whom she begs us to invoke. In our needs and cares we should turn to the sacred means she points out to us. Though the use of any material thing or sign, even the most sacred, may degenerate into the mechanical and externalistic, we should never attempt to destroy an institution in order to suppress its abuse. The result would only be to make place for even worst types of real superstition. But we should not do the very opposite and dismiss all magic and folly of superstitious observance with a sympathetic chuckle over human stupidity or frailty, for these practices do supplant true religion. They vie with true religion for a place in man's heart and life. Superstition in every form is irreligion. It is either actual cult of the powers hostile to God or at least refusal to give true and proper service to God.

The Protestant reproach against Catholic sacramental piety, as a form of superstition much like magic, either betrays a woeful ignorance in certain circles of the actual nature of magic or manifests very palpably a wrong notion of the holy sacraments and their true import. As we stated very clearly in the above discussion, magic is an attempt by use of occult or even diabolical forces to produce an effect on God or, more specifically, to come to an easy and independent control of the world and even to direct it against God. The sacraments are the very opposite. They are rich and meaningful signs instituted by the God-man Himself in which God brings His grace to one who in faith, humility, and submission opens himself to God. God works in us through the sacraments. In the sacramentals of the Church we humbly implore the protection of God by uniting ourselves loyally with the prayer of the Church for the divine blessing in all phases of our earthly life.

Sacraments and sacramentals are the expressive signs of the virtue of religion and of grace, the signs of the most humble attachment to God and of recognition of His majesty. Magic on the contrary is aversion from a personal God and a turning to impersonal forces, perhaps even attachment to the enemy of God in person: it is therefore false cult and counter-cult.

BIBLIOGRAPHY

Direct Violation of God's Honor

BAECHTHOLD-STAEUBI, H. *Handwoerterbuch des deutschen Aberglaubens.* 10 Baende, Berlin, 1942.

BLINTZLER, J. "Gotteslaesterung," *LThK*, 2. Aufl. IV, col. 1117 ff.

BURI, F. "Glaube und Aberglaube," *ThZschr*, 12 (1956), 206–236.

CONTENAU, G. *La divination.* Paris, 1940.

DE MARTINO, E. *Il mondo magico.* Torino, 1948.

GREGORY, TH. *The Unfinished Universe.* London, 1935.

HEDLEY, G. *The Superstition of the Irreligious.* New York, 1951.

KLOPPENBURG, B., O.F.M. "Adivinhaçôes supersticiosas," *Rev. Eccl. Brasileira*, 18 (1958), 944–970.

LA ROCHE, R. *La divination.* (with supplement *La superstition en Afrique centrale.*) Washington-Quebec, 1958.

LEITMAIR, CH. *Die Kirche und die Gottesurteile.* Wien, 1953.

MAURA Y GAMAZO, G. *Supersticiones de los siglos XVI et XVII.* Madrid, 1943.

MELLOT, J. *La superstition, ersatz de foi.* Paris, 1959.

MELLOR, A. *Le problème des guérisseurs. Étude historique et critique.* Paris, 1958.

NOTTARP, H. *Gottesurteilstudien,* Muenchen, 1956.

PRESSEL, W. "Moderne 'Glaubensheilungsbewegung.' Wahrheit oder Schwaermerei?" *Wege zum Menschen,* 11 (1959), 65–77.

SÉJOURNÉ, P. "Superstition," *DTC* 14, 2764–2824.

———. "Sorcellerie," *DTC* 14, 2394–2417.

SCHAUERTE, H. "Neuzeitlicher Aberglaube," *ThG,* 47 (1957), 40–42.

SCHMIDT, PH. *Dunkle Maechte. Ein Buch vom Aberglauben einst und jetzt.* Frankfurt, 1956.

VOLKER, G. D. *History of the Crime of Blasphemy.* London, 1928.

ZUCKER, C. *Psychologie de la superstition.* Trad. de Vaudou. Paris, 1952.

False Cult of Superstition Necromacy

ALFANO, G. B. *Piccola enciclopedia di scienze occulte.* Napoli, 1949.

BICHLMAIR, G. *Okkultismus und Seelsorge.* Innsbruck, 1926.

BJOERKHEM, J. *Die Verborgene Kraft. Probleme der Parapsychologie.* Olten-Freiburg, 1954.

DESSOIR, M. *Vom Jenseits der Seele.* 6th ed. Stuttgart, 1931.

Herderkorr. 13 (1959), 489–495; "Der Spiritismus in Brasilien."

HOHENWARTEN, P. "Forschungen im Reiche des Uebersinnlichen," *Der Seelsorger,* 30 (1959/60), 150–160.

JAFFÉ, *Geistererscheinungen und Vorzeichen. Eine psychologische Deutung.* (With a preface by C. G. Jung.) Zuerich, 1958.

KLOPPENBURG, B. O.F.M. "Der Brasilianische Spiritismus als religioese Gefahr," *Social Compass,* 5 (1959), 237–255.

———. "Attuacâo de demónio no espiritismo, *Rev. Ecclesiastica Brasileira,* 17 (1957), 301–320.

KOEBERLE, A. *Evangelium und Anthroposophie.* Bern, 1939.

MAGER, A. *Theosophie und Christentum.* 2nd ed. Berlin-Bonn, 1926.

MARTIN, B. *Von der Anthroposophie zur Kirche.* Speyer, 1950.

MOSER, F. *Der Okkultismus, Taeuschungen und Tatsachen.* 2 Baende. Muenchen, 1935/1936.

OMEZ, REGINALD, O.P. *Psychical Phenomena.* (Twentieth Century Encyclopedia of Catholicism, 36). New York: Hawthorn, 1958.

REITERER, A. *Bruecke zum Jenseits.* 6th ed. Graz, 1928.

SCHMIDT, PH. *Vom Tischruecken und Geisterbeshwoeren.* Berlin-Dahlem, 1952.

SCHNEIDER, W. *Der neuere Geisterglaube.* Paderborn, 1913.

SCOTT, C. *An Outline of Modern Occultism.* New York, 1936.

THURSTON, H. *Ghosts and Poltergeists.* Edited by J. H. Crehan. Chicago: Regnery, 1956.

WIESINGER, A. *Okkulte Phaenomene im Licht der Theologie.* Graz, 1949.

Astrology

BERGLES, A. E. "Astrologische Leistungen," *StimmenZeit*, 126 (1933–34), 398–406.

FAERY ET AURELIUS, T. *Interprétation rationelle de l'astrologie.* Paris, 1937.

HENNEMANN, G. "Kritik der Astrologie," *Neues Abendland*, 10 (1955), 33–41.

KOCH, A., S. J. "Um die astrologie," *StimmenZeit*, 149 (1951/52), 308 ff.

REINERS, L. *Steht es in den Sternen? Eine wissenschaftliche Untersuchung ueber Wahrheit und Irrtum der Astrologie.* Muenchen, 1951.

SCHMIDT, PH., S.J. *Astrologische Plaudereien.* Bonn, 1951.

———. "Die Stellung des heiligen Thomas zur Astrologie," *StimmenZeit*, 156 (1955), 65–69.

———. "Schmutz und Schund im astrologischen Schriftum," *StimmenZeit*, 163 (1958/59), 228–230.

STEINLEIN, S. *Astrologie, Sexualkrankheiten und Aberglaube.* Muenchen, 1915.

TOPITSCH, E. "Steht es in den Sternen? Zur Geistesgeschichte der Astrologie," *WW*, 11 (1956), 279–288.

ZINNER, E. *Sternglaube und Sternforschung.* Freiburg-Muenchen, 1953.

Divining Rod and Magic Pendulum

KOEBERLE, A. "Radiaesthesie in christlicher Sicht," *Wege zum Menschen*, 11 (1959), 411–418.

———. "Probleme der Ruten-und Pendelkunde," *Wege zum Menschen*, 11 (1959), 424–429.

LUCCHINI, CHAN. *La Radiesté.* Paris, 1957.

Magic (Sorcery)

ANHOFER, H. *Aberglaube und Hexenwahn heute.* Freiburg, 1960.

AUBIN, H. *L'homme et la magie.* Paris, 1952.

Die katholische Glaubenswelt. Freiburg, 1960, II, 777 (Bibliography).

LEPROUX, M. *Medicine, magie, sorcellerie.* Paris, 1956.

LIENER, J. "Die neue Bewegung des Gesundbetens im Urteil der Seelsorge," *Der Seelsorger*, 27 (1956/57), 387–393.

SCHAUERTE, H. "Totbeten und Totenmessen fuer Lebende," *ThG*, (1959), 141–144.

SCHMIDT, PH., S.J. *Daemon Aberglaube.* Saarbruecken, 1938.

———. *Talisman und Zauberwahn. Ein Buch vom Aberglauben—einst und jetzt.* Einsiedeln, 1937.

———. *Froemmigkeit auf Abwegen. Besprechen, Gesundbeten, Zauberbriefe.* Berlin, 1955.

———. "Das Archiv zur Bekaempfung des Hexenwahns," *StimmenZeit*, 164 (1959), 389–392.

SELIGMAN, K. *Das Weltreich der Magie. 5000 Jahre Geheime Kunst.* Stuttgart, 1958.

SIEGMUND, G. "Magie und Religion," *ThG*, 49 (1959), 124–134.

WEBSTER, H. *Magic. A Sociological Study.* Stanford, California, 1948.

ZWESLOOT, H., S.J. *Friedrich Spee und die Hexenprozesse.* Trier, 1954.

Additional Works in English

BLACKMORE, SIMON A., S.J. *Spiritism: Facts and Frauds.* New York: Benziger, 1924.

COAKLEY, THOMAS F. *Spiritism, the Modern Satanism.* Chicago: Extension Press, 1920.

GARESCHE, EDWARD F., S.J. *Communion with the Spirit World.* New York: Macmillan, 1925.

HARRIS, WILLIAM R. *Essays in Occultism, Spiritism and Demonology.* St. Louis: B. Herder, 1919.

HEREDIA, CHARLES M. DE, S.J. *Spiritism and Common Sense.* New York: Kenedy, 1922.

———. *True Spiritualism.* New York. Kenedy, 1924.

LANSLOTS, ILDEFONS, O.S.B. *Spiritism Unveiled: a Critical Examination of Some Abnormal Psychic Phenomena.* St. Louis: B. Herder, 1913.

LEPICIER, ALEXIS H. (Card.) *Unseen World: Catholic Theology in Reference to Modern Spiritism.* New York: Sheed and Ward, 1929.

LILJENCRANTS, CARL J. *Spiritism and Religion.* New York: Devin-Adair, 1919.

McEVOY, W. VINCENT, O.P. *Spiritism's Two Failures.* London: Catholic Truth Society, 1921.

MESEQUER, PEDRO, S.J. *The Secret of Dreams.* Westminster, Md.: Newman, 1960.

O'DONNELL, ELLIOT. *Menace of Spiritualism.* New York: Stokes, 1920.

OMEZ, REGINALD, O.P. *Psychical Phenomena* (Twentieth Century Encyclopedia of Catholicism, 36). New York: Hawthorn, 1958.

O'NEILL, HERBERT V. *Spiritualism as Spiritualists Have Written of It.* New York: Kenedy, 1945.

PRATT, (Sister) ANTOINETTE. *Attitude of the Catholic Church Toward Witchcraft and the Allied Practices of Sorcery and Magic.* Washington: Catholic University Press, 1915.

RAUPERT, J. GODFREY. *Facts and Fallacies of Modern Spiritism.* St. Louis: Catholic Central Verein, 1920.

———. *Modern Spiritism: a Critical Examination of its Phenomena, Character, and Teaching in the Light of Known Facts.*

———. *The New Black Magic.* New York: Devin-Adair, 1920.

———. *Spiritistic Phenomena and Their Interpretation.* Buffalo: Catholic Union Store, 1916.

———. *Christ and the Powers of Darkness.* St. Louis: B. Herder, 1915.

RYDER, RAYMOND, A. *Simony: an Historical Synopsis and Commentary* (Catholic University Studies in Canon Law, 65). Washington: Catholic Univ. Press, 1931.

THURSTON, HERBERT, S.J. *The Church and Spiritualism* (Science and Culture Series). Milwaukee: Bruce, 1933.

———. *Modern Spiritualism.* St. Louis: B. Herder, 1929.

———. *Superstition: a Backward Glance over Nineteen Centuries.* New York: Benziger, n.d.

TONQUÉDEC, JOSEPH DE, S.J. "Metapsychic Phenomena and Christian Miracle," in *New Problems in Medical Ethics,* 4th Series, ed. Dom Peter Flood, O.S.B. Westminster, Md.: Newman, 1960, pp. 137–225.

VAN ANTWERP, EUGENE I. *St. Augustine: The Divination of Demons and Care for the Dead* (Catholic University Studies in Sacred Theology, 2nd Series, 86) Washington: Catholic Univ. Press, 1955.

WALSH, JAMES J. *Spiritualism a Fake: Can We Communicate with the Dead?* (bound with: *Spiritualism a Fact,* by Hereward Carrington). Boston: Stratford, 1925.

WEBER, NICHOLAS A. *A History of Simony in the Christian Church . . .* (Catholic University Studies in Sacred Theology, 8). Baltimore: J. H. Furst, 1909.

WIESINGER, ALOIS, O.C.S.O. *Occult Phenomena in the Light of Theology.* Westminster, Md.: Newman, 1957.

Periodical Literature in English

DOOLEY, E. A. "Religion and Superstition," *RUO,* 6 (March, 1936), 41–62.

DRISCOLL, J. J. "Spiritism Today," *AER,* 117 (Oct., 1947), 276–83.

ELLISON, R. C. S. "Blasphemy and the Law," *Mo,* 158 (Oct., 1931), 308–14.

JOHNSON, H. J. T. "From Witchcraft to Spiritualism," *ClerRev,* 32 (July, 1949), 1–13; 32: (Sept., 1949), 156–70; 32 (Nov., 1949), 299–314; 33 (March, 1950), 145–62.

McDonnell, T. "Stipends and Simony," *IER*, 53 (June, 1939), 593–612; 54 (Aug., 1939), 35–57, 159–75.

Murphy, J. P. "Science and Seance," *DubR*, 188 (April, 1951), 299–312.

Thurston, H. "Bodily Elongation: A Curious Mystical Phenomenon," *Mo*, 168 (Dec., 1936), 537–48.

————. "Do Poltergeists Invade the Tomb?" *Mo*, 171 (March, 1938), 220–30.

————. "Lithobolia: New England Poltergeist," *Mo*, 169 (May, 1937), 406–16.

————. "Medium 'Margery,' " *Mo*, 163 (March, 1934), 248–59.

————. "Poltergeist in Westmorland," *Mo*, 165 (March, 1935), 242–52.

————. "Poltergeists before the Law Courts," *Mo*, 163 (April, 1934), 337–44; (May, 1934), 433–43.

————. "Rare Type of Poltergeist," *Mo*, 167 (Jan., 1936), 52–62.

————. "Some Knotty Points for Spiritualists," *Mo*, 172 (Aug., 138), 118–28; (Sept., 1938), 210–219; (Oct., 1938), 312–23.

————. "Spiritualism for the Masses," *Mo*, 164 (Oct., 1934), 323–34.

————. "Talking Mongoose," *Mo*, 167 (May, 1936), 438–48.

————. "Three New Poltergeist Tales," *Mo*, 167 (March, 1936), 242–51.

————. "Spiritualism Today: a Survey of the Movement as a Religion," *Mo*, 164 (Sept., 1934), 240–50.

————. "Spiritualism and the War: Unreliability of Their Predictions," *Mo*, 174 (Oct., 1934), 333–43.

————. "Case of Doyle vs. Houdini," *Mo*, 156 (Aug., 1930), 97–109.

————. "Case of Mollie Faucher," *Mo*, 156 (Dec., 1930), 527–38.

————. "New Theory of 'Raps,' " *Mo*, 159 (Jan., 1932), 47–57.

————. "Phenomenal Mediumship," *Mo*, 161 (June, 1933), 532–41.

————. "Spiritualists in Adversity," *Mo*, 158 (Nov., 1931), 427–37; (Dec., 1931), 529–39.

————. "The New Rodriguez," *Mo*, 154 (Nov., 1929), 420–8.

CHAPTER EIGHT

SPECIAL WAYS OF HONORING GOD

I. PRAYER

1. *The Place of Prayer in the Imitation*

WITH a prayer of love Christ made His entry into the world: "Behold, I come . . . to do thy will, O God" (Heb 10:7). The prelude to His public life was a great prayer of forty days. The Gospel informs us that He prepared for all the important events in His life by means of prayer. His passion, finally, as the sacrifice of His life for the salvation of the world, unfolds as liturgical prayer, beginning with the high-priestly prayer in the cenacle at the Last Supper and continuing to the prayer of the bloody tears and sweat in the Garden, unto the last breath of His soul at prayer in the death of the Cross: "Father, into thy hands I commend my spirit" (Lk 23:46). He prayed in the utter stillness of solitude as well as in the presence of His disciples and with them. Jubilant prayer flowed from the innermost depths of His soul, prayer such as the world had never heard. But He did not disdain the consecrated formulas of prayer of His own people. He used them as did every zealous Israelite and in using them brought out the full perfection of their meaning.

As no other, Christ taught us and showed us how to pray; for He is the Supreme Teacher and Model of prayer. Fascinated by the interior depth and majesty of His prayer, His disciples begged of Him one day: "Lord, teach us to pray" (Lk 11:1). Not only did He teach us the most beautiful prayer, a prayer which embraces all the grand interests and needs of the Kingdom of God and the soul; He taught us above all the right approach to the Heavenly Father and true familiarity with Him through His word and example. He taught us the Our Father, the Lord's prayer, the heart to heart prayer, the loving dialog between man and God to which the Holy Spirit Himself gives the words.

He inculcated upon His apostles nothing more earnestly and emphatically than prayer. Nothing did He impress upon them and bid them take to heart more seriously than prayer, persevering, humble, suppliant, penetrated with the spirit of gratitude and jubilation. And in imitation of Him His great apostles, Peter, Paul, John, and James used it and stressed it in their letters. And following them the great saints taught the same lesson. In fact, to be a saint means, in the judgment and mind of the Church, to be a great man of prayer, constantly and intently a man of prayer. Nothing plays so important a role in Christendom, in fact nothing plays so important a role in the lives of all truly religious men in the whole history of the world as prayer. The words of St. John Chrysostom are a classical expression of the mind and conviction of the Church: "Nothing is more powerful than prayer, nothing is comparable to it."[139]

That a man can speak with God is the noblest evidence of his resemblance to God and, in the order of grace, a most adorable mystery. The prayer of the Christian is not merely an external imitation of the prayer of the Savior. It is inner attachment to Christ, constantly enkindling itself anew, constantly penetrating more deeply into the soul. It is in truth a participation in the eternal dialog between the Word of God with God the Father in the Holy Spirit. Is it not the Holy Spirit Himself who prays within us and pleads "for us with unutterable groanings (Rom 8:26)?"

As Christians we can pray well only through the Holy Spirit of Christ in our hearts or at least only through the graces which His Spirit grants us for our conversion and sanctification, that is, in preparation for His coming. Our prayer does not have its true value and dignity, its full power of intercession except through our confident participation in His prayer and His merits. This is what is meant by praying in the name of Jesus (Jn 15:16).

As such the imitation of Christ means attachment to Christ through grace, love, and obedience. But it also means attachment to Him in the practice of His virtues and in the imitation of His holiness. Similarly the prayer of the Christian must be not only the surge of his love and trust toward Christ Himself, but likewise the participation in Christ's own prayer to the Heavenly Father. Not only do we pray to Christ, but also with Christ to the Father, according to the doctrine and example of Christ.

Our entire imitation of Christ depends on our union with Him in prayer. Eternal union with Christ (the grace of perseverance in love) can be secured only through prayer. (It is especially St. Alphonse who ceaselessly stresses this truth.) The adult can never attain to everlasting happiness except through persevering prayer, which in fact is already the very beginning and preparation for the blessed vision of God, the prelude here below to the blessed colloquy of love in heaven.

2. The Essence of Prayer

Prayer presents man on his knees in an attitude of the most profound reverence. In prayer man recognizes his own pettiness before the infinitely great and holy God. But at the same time prayer also elevates man above the whole material creation and places him face to face with this Infinite. In prayer man speaks with God. It is the greatest act of which he is capable. When St. John Damascene says, "Prayer is raising the heart to God,"[140] he enunciates a tremendous truth indeed, but not all the truth. What is greatest in prayer, the reality which is most its own, is not merely pondering on God, nor detaching one's self from all created things in mind and heart, nor even contemplation of the created in the sole light of the divine. The most tremendous truth about prayer is that it is real converse with God. Not merely our thoughts are with God, but we ourselves are really with Him in prayer because God really bends down over us, addresses us, responds to our response. The best definition of prayer is that of St. Augustine: "Your prayer is speaking with God. In spiritual reading God speaks to you; in prayer you speak to God."[141]

Prayer is not a unilateral act but bilateral: it is God's word and man's word. It is an encounter of God and man in word and response, in word of love with response of love, in incitement of grace and cooperation with grace. Prayer is colloquy, dialog.

For this reason reflecting on God is not really prayer, unless the divine truths which we have pondered bring us in some way to a realization that through them God says something to us. Pondering on God must convince us that the divine truths are addressed to us and that we must turn not only our minds and thoughts to God but also set our hearts and our whole person in motion toward Him (in acts of submission, admiration, supplication, prayer for pardon, and gratitude).

The study of theology, spiritual reading, harkening to the divine word, contemplation of the beauties of nature—all these become prayer if God Himself approaches us in their truth. They become prayer when through the Holy Spirit they speak to us vitally, and we in turn permit ourselves to hear and to be moved thereby toward God. Spiritual reading, preaching (or harkening to) the word, the study of theology can be carried on properly only in an atmosphere of prayer.

Not man but God opens the dialog of prayer. How could man presume to approach God, how could he actually extend his hands to Him unless God Himself first bent down over him and in accents of love bade him respond to God? This is strikingly brought to mind by the prefatory prayer of the Our Father in Holy Mass: "Directed by saving precepts and schooled in divine teaching, we make bold to say, Our Father, etc." If the one who prays were not truly convinced with all his heart that God harkens to his prayer and is ready to answer Him (through gracious acceptance of his adoration and thanksgiving and lending a favorable ear to his supplication), there could be no colloquy or dialog with God. Prayer is rooted in the word of God, draws its life from the word of God, and in its growth and development constantly turns again to the divine word.

The dialog of Christian prayer blossoms with unique perfection and beauty in the sacraments. In them God's word and love come to us, immediately experienced in faith. Our prayer is response to the incomprehensibly great gift God bestows upon us in His sacraments. But it is a response which is made possible through the divine capacity given us in the sacraments themselves. Not only is all the love which was manifested to the world in Christ, the basic and primordial Sacrament, now offered to us in the sacraments; but in these sacred signs we are also placed in the orbit of Christ's own response of love, thanksgiving, adoration, expiation, the response which He as the new Head of mankind offered the Heavenly Father on the cross. Through sacramental sanctification in the Holy Spirit our prayer, caught up in mystico-real union, joins in the eternal dialog of love in the Trinity itself.

The dialogical character of prayer is most fully realized in the so-called *passive* or mystical prayer, in which the divine motion is in the foreground of consciousness and divine love stirs the heart, and the loving majesty of God manifests itself in infused contemplation. Though the prayer is called passive, man is not purely passive in it. On the contrary, one is never so completely and utterly active as when God moves him by the graces of mystical prayer. But in this mystical experience the "divine partner in the dialog" is in the foreground rather than the human response. In mystical prayer the soul experiences the life in grace and from grace as a gift of divine love. It is the experience of faith in its most exalted realization.

In active prayer our own self is more in evidence, and our personal share in the dialog is brought into sharper focus; but the impulse of divine grace inciting and moving us is not directly and immediately experienced. And yet in its essence it is awakened in the soul precisely as is mystical prayer. It is as dependent on the divine motion and appeal, on the assurance of the divine response, as is mystical prayer. The more keenly conscious we are of the divine word addressed to us and of the assurance of the divine response, the better and more perfect is our prayer. This is to say that prayer is more perfect the more lively is our faith which places us in the presence of God to whom we pray. The very moment that our words and reflections center in soliloquy with ourselves and our own interests (however spiritual) rather than centering in God, they cease to be prayer.

Prerequisite to prayer—or should we say, the principal elements of prayer—are, first, faith in a personal God, in a divine *Thou;* second, faith in His actual presence, in His closeness to us. This is far more than the closeness of the divine omnipresence. It is faith in the intimacy of presence through His loving will, the faith that He is Yahweh for us, the God "who is." This means He is present to our prayer and favorable to it. The final essential is the dynamic converse with God whereby God enters into communion with man and man into communion with God.[142]

3. *Prayer in Relation to the Virtues*

Prayer is *par excellence* an act of the virtue of religion. In fact, next to sacrifice and united with sacrifice it constitutes the most characteristic and the most important act of that virtue by which we pay God the worship due to Him. Without prayer religion cannot survive, for without prayer all cult becomes a meaningless and futile gesture. All prayer is cult or divine worship, pre-eminently so the prayer of praise, adoration, and thanksgiving, but also the prayer of supplication and propitiation. We can say that the prayer of adoration, praise, and glorification centers directly on the glory of God as the prayer of eternal fulfillment. In itself, therefore, it is a more perfect act of religion than the prayer of petition and expiation and must be practiced even in this earthly sojourn, for here we yearn and strive for the final consummation. We must aspire to the most perfect prayer of praise and exultation. Nevertheless, since we are still pilgrims who have not yet reached the perfection of our goal, the prayer most suited to us here below is the prayer of supplication and propitiation.

The worth of our prayer of petition depends on the object for which we pray. As such it is calculated to arouse the virtue of hope. And insofar as it focuses our attention on our total need for God and our utter dependence on Him, it is an indispensable element of religion corresponding to the realities of our life here below. But precisely because of the object for which we pray it may be even more perfect than the prayer of praise. Prayer for the divine love, for the advent of the Kingdom of God is directed toward a loftier object than a prayer of praise for the bounty of God shown to us in earthly things. In this way the prayer of petition may be more excellent than some prayers of praise.

To consider prayer solely under this aspect of the virtue of religion would be to restrict its full significance and importance. It is a vital manifestation of religion in its totality, in its fullest and richest sense. "Prayer is the religious life explicitly elevating itself to God and expressing itself in His sight. It is an effective exercise of all the religious virtues in the divine presence. They all unfold in prayer before God."[143] These religious virtues are, above all, the theological virtues. "Faith, hope, and love pray."[144]

Prayer draws its life from the theological virtues, and they in turn live on prayer. Without prayer faith would at best be a mere conceptual or philosophical faith. And prayer without faith would be vain and empty. Hope without prayer would be hollow presumption, and prayer without hope a mockery. Love could not express itself without prayer, for it would be deprived of all impulse or motivation, of all sense of intimacy with God or submission to Him. Love without prayer would not be love at all. Prayer gives expression to all three theological virtues, and they in turn through prayer become cult or the exercise of the virtue of religion: they adore God in His infinite truthfulness, fidelity to His promises, and His loving-kindness. They recognize the dependence of man on God, his sinfulness before the just and merciful God. They offer themselves in homage to the goodness and majesty of God. Finally prayer is the exercise of religion insofar as it is the prayer of the religious community, the Church. Religion is indeed the holy community, the family of Christ, which unites in the prayer of adoration and praise and common supplication for the needs of all the brethren. In prayer and sacrifice the community joins in the most intimate bond expressing its faith, hope, love, and worship.

Prayer gives expression also to the other moral virtues. In the prayer of contrition the sinner, mindful of the divine presence, turns again to the moral values he has violated by sin. In the prayer of petition he wrestles for that perfection of love which is the fulfillment of the commandments in obedience to the loving will of God[145] and for the grace of loving compliance in the practice of all the virtues. Far from last in importance in the value of prayer is the resoluteness or at least the earnestness of the desire to fulfill the will of God in every domain. One who prays and at the same time still has the intention of transgressing the commandments of God in important matters acts as though he were turning to God, whereas in reality he merely directs words to Him but keeps "his countenance," that is, his heart and will, averted from God. Therefore, the most urgent prayer and the only good prayer from one who is still held captive by the bonds of mortal sin is the petition: "Lord, turn thy countenance toward me! Lord, grant that I may be able to turn my face to thee! Lord, rescue me from my sin!"

4. Species of Prayer

a. Cultal, Apostolic, and Mystical Prayer

In the prayer of cult man turns principally to the divine glory itself. He gives glory to the holiness of God. As expression of the virtue of religion it hallows the divine name: "Hallowed be Thy Name!" Apostolic (prophetic) prayer flows from zeal for the honor of God and the spread of His Kingdom among men. "Thy Kingdom come!" This prayer expresses the desire for the fulfillment of the will of God on earth. "Thy will be done on earth as it is in heaven." Mystical prayer (here we are using the term somewhat broadly insofar as it rises from the depths of self-absorption in God) is repose in the love of God. It is being overwhelmed by the intimate closeness of God before whose holiness one trembles in awe. Often it does not go further than the "Our Father" (the intimacy of the divine love) and the "who art in heaven" (the holiness and transcendence of God).

It is obvious that cultal prayer (the entire ensemble of prayers used in cult) can embrace all things, all needs, all interests, but primarily in the light of the glory of God. The same holds true of the apostolic (prophetic) prayer whose most characteristic mark is the ardent zeal for the kingdom of God. Mystical prayer, to the measure in which it is authentic, as well as the cultal and apostolic prayer, embraces all things, but focused in the foreground is the intimate movement of the soul by God (*Deus et anima,* God and the soul). And in this mystical prayer the soul experiences above all the saving love of God. It experiences truly that its salvation is in and through God. Trembling in awe before Him, it begs for salvation. But it proves that it is genuine precisely by shunning the narrow circle of its own needs, even spiritual needs, and touched by the divine love, opens itself with ever increasing love to all the needs and interests of the honor of God and His Kingdom.

b. Active and Passive Prayer

Mystical prayer in the proper sense of the word is not active prayer, although active prayer can readily share some of the characteristics of the three kinds of prayer we have just treated. Mystical prayer is really passive prayer or the prayer of contemplation, the exercise of the virtue of religion in the most sublime and exalted sense of the word. It is truly the triumph of the soul in its submission to God, the most profound experience of the glory of God. In a manner hitherto undreamed of man experiences the love of God drawing nigh to him, enkindling the zeal for the divine honor and the spread of His Kingdom. Active interior prayer is called meditation (*meditatio,* discursive prayer and prayer of affection). Passive prayer is called contemplation (*contemplatio*).

c. Interior Prayer and Vocal Prayer

From the standpoint of the manner of its expression we speak of interior and exterior prayer. Interior prayer is the encounter with God experienced in the spiritual part of the soul, or the inner impulse toward God. Of course if this movement toward God is genuinely human, it must in some manner be associated with mental words and images. Exterior prayer expresses itself in exterior movements and words, for which reason it is also called vocal prayer. If it is to be truly authentic, it must be sustained by interior prayer or at least by a desire to awaken interior prayer.

As such, interior prayer is superior to external prayer in the sense of the exclusively external prayer proceeding from without and not from interior ardor of spirit. Such vocal prayer bears little relation to the inner movement of prayer. Nevertheless, for man taken in the totality of his nature it is not the interiority itself which is the more perfect. It is rather the prayer of the heart which expresses itself spontaneously in forms of external prayer more or less frequently, more or less warmly, and which is constantly renewed and re-enkindled in such manifestation.

To repudiate external prayer or to refuse to offer it to God on the pretext that interior prayer is more profound and sublime in dignity and value betrays a gross misconception of human nature. "Oral prayer is as much the natural expression of interior devotion as it is incitement to it."[146] St. Augustine says, "The spirit of prayer is enkindled anew through the expression of the words of prayer."[147]

d. Common Prayer and Private Prayer

In the sacraments we have the most intimate personal experience of being called by name (*klethoí*). But this personal call is also a collective summons of love by which Christ draws the Church (the *ekklesía*, from *kaleîn, to call*) and each individual to Himself. Only in Christ and His Church do we possess individuality and personal rights before God. In consequence individuality and solidarity are as inseparable as two mutually attractive poles in our prayer life with God: common prayer and individual prayer must mutually complement and enrich each other. Just as man himself may not be totally absorbed in the community to the loss of his individuality nor, on the other hand, hold himself aloof and isolated from the community, so must his prayer bear the mark of individuality and of community. It must take place in his own heart and in the privacy of his chamber (this means it must be altogether and entirely individual prayer suited to each individual and in conformity with his distinctive individuality and with his needs and interests as they may arise). It must likewise have the constant assurance of the community of those who pray and help to sustain and support their fellows in the community of prayer. The thought is expressed very pertinently in the words of the Savior Himself: "When thou prayest, go into thy room, and closing thy door, pray to thy Father in secret; and thy Father, who sees in secret, will reward thee" (Mt 6:6). And: "Where two or three are gathered together for my sake, there am I in the midst of them" (Mt 18:20). If collective prayer is in no wise nourished and enriched through individual prayer, it soon becomes externalistic, mechanical, or at best entirely vapid and impersonal. Without the support of the prayer in common the individual prayer becomes narrow and egotistic, a mere routine totally isolated from the right manner and correct forms of prayer which we must constantly learn anew through our community with the Church.

e. Informal Prayer, Formal Prayer, Prayer Formulas

Informal prayer flows spontaneously from the fulness of the heart and supplies its own form of words after the manner of conversation, when men speak freely with their fellow men. Such free and informal prayer must absolutely be considered the goal and ideal of prayer formation even in the spiritual training of children.[148] Of course in periods of spiritual aridity we must have recourse ever and anon to formal prayer and the fixed formula. The same is true of our constant effort to renew ourselves spiritually in the great images and models of prayer, Christ and the saints. But the formula may in no instance suppress free and spontaneous prayer; it should rather stimulate and shape it.

Even in collective prayer the free and spontaneous outpourings of the soul to God, as we note particularly in the practices of the early Church, occupy a prominent place. In the early Church the one who presided in the assembly had the right to lead in prayer freely and spontaneously without the restraint of prayer texts, as the situation itself and his own heart might inspire him to do. This form of free prayer still plays a significant role today in the good sermon which must constantly ascend to the heights of inspiring prayer. Moreover, since there is no ecclesiastical law to the contrary, spontaneous prayer is altogether to be recommended for certain situations and occasions when the priest leads in prayer. We should not underestimate the importance of this free form of prayer, particularly in the task of forming and educating the faithful in the spirit of prayer. It is the most direct and effective means of setting the heart on fire for God, and therefore is especially calculated to awaken in us a proper appreciation for the stations of the cross, the rosary, and above all for holy meditation. However, the dignity of the holy liturgy and the necessity for regularity and conformity in its use made it imperative for the Church to substitute and require her own well-fixed and typical prayers for official use in the divine worship instead of the spontaneous utterances of the officiating priest or bishop. Common prayer cannot permanently uphold its dignity and precision without some fixed formulas of prayer.

Formal prayer, that is, prayer expressed in fixed and established formulas, is necessary not merely for the community prayer service in God's honor but also for the individual exercise of piety. Even in the hours of greatest exaltation in His earthly life Christ Himself used the sublime traditional formulas of prayer used by His own people. At the Last Supper and at other rites in which He participated, Christ recited the ritual prayers of the Israelites. His words on the Cross are in part derived from the psalms.

Though Christ Himself taught His Apostles and us the Our Father, the words were not intended as a mere formula of prayer. It is much more than a rigid formula. It is a model and example of the ideal prayer, a lesson teaching us the right kind of prayer. It teaches the disciple of Christ the form and manner of prayer and the great concern of his prayer. Now the disciple of Christ should know the kind of prayer, the manner of prayer, the objectives of prayer suitable to him in the imitation of the Master. If He had taught no more than a formula of prayer in the Our Father, it would be incomprehensible how Matthew (6:9–13) could have left us a different and more detailed version of the Our Father than does St. Luke (11:2–4).

The Church expressly reserves the right to safeguard the formulas of prayer.[149] But a soulless recitation even of the correct formulas is a great evil contradicting the spirit of the New Testament (cf. Mt 6:5ff.). Nor has prayer recited in an alien and totally unintelligible idiom any great value if it is assessed in the light of prayer as colloquy or dialog with God. A completely unintelligible formula is not truly word and speech but merely sound, although it can in some way become expressive through an appropriate melody or a fine community recitation. Nevertheless, interior prayer can be bound up with unintelligible formulas of prayer, even though the two cannot merge into a perfect unity.[150] The recitation of unintelligible formulas of prayer can be made a valuable and meritorious act of obedience or of penance. The legislator who requires such a recitation must have a reason for his act sufficiently serious to justify the imposition of an act which is not in itself intelligible.

Moreover, the lawmaker who imposes the obligation to recite such prayers must make some provision which will prevent those who are obliged to recite lengthy prayers in an alien tongue from forming false concepts of prayer because of such practice. It is certainly not the mind of the Church that women of active religious institutes, above all nursing sisters, who have a strenuous schedule of work filling the day, be required to occupy a great part of their prayer time with the recitation of Latin formulas of prayer, if they do not know any Latin. They forget the very art of prayer. We note in this connection that in her choice of a religious community a girl with a religious vocation should above all ponder the prayer forms of the order or congregation she is considering. As the prayer in common, so the community!

However, the demand for intelligibility of the prayer formulas does not justify the conclusion that holy Mass can be celebrated properly only in the vernacular.[151] But the conclusion that the priest himself who celebrates Mass in Latin and also recites the canonical hours in Latin must be conversant with the language is absolutely justified. The laity who may not know Latin must be made familiar with the thought-content of the liturgical prayers so that they grasp their meaning, or more specifically, that they learn to accompany the sacred prayer and rite in their own language, so that they say in their own tongue that which the priest at the altar prays in the name of all. The holy Council of Trent expressly admonishes priests who have the care of souls that they make the sublime content of the liturgical prayers accessible to the faithful, "so that the lambs of Christ do not go hungry and the little ones do not cry out for bread, whilst there is none to break it for them (Lam 4:4). Therefore frequently during the celebration of holy Mass they should explain something of that which is read and interpret a mystery of this all-holy Sacrifice."[152] The very laudable desire that the prayers and the instruction parts of the liturgy be recited in the vernacular is vain if we do not use the opportunities that are already available.

f. Prayer of Praise, Thanksgiving, and Petition

According to the content of prayer we distinguish prayer of praise or adoration, prayer of thanksgiving, and prayer of petition.[153] The prayer of praise is the manifestation of wonder or admiration, joy and jubilation of one who is caught up with the grandeur and goodness of God. Joined with praise is the adoration which is the declaration of our utter dependence on God and the recognition of His absolute holiness and loving majesty externally manifested in words or signs.

St. Thomas uses the word *adoration* in the precise sense of homage paid to the majesty of God through external movements or gestures, as a genuflection or bow. The current use of the term has a more comprehensive meaning.

Genuine piety is essentially characterized by the prayer of thanksgiving. All petition is basically lacking in piety, lacking in the filial spirit, if there is not present also the offering of thanksgiving for the favors granted in response to our prayer of supplication and in general for all gifts and graces we have received from the divine bounty.

St. Thomas is entirely correct in his comment that we must not look upon the prayer of praise, thanksgiving, and petition merely as so many distinct species of prayer, but rather as phases or component parts of the one perfect prayer.[154] Only the harmonious union of all these elements constitutes the perfectly good prayer. Should thanksgiving be lacking, then the praise of God is artificial and unreal, for the one who prays does not have a true heart for his prayer and God is praised as a kind of stranger. What would the prayer of contrition, of repentance, of expiation be, if the heart of the pardoned sinner would not leap up in thanksgiving for the gift of pardon? And what would the prayer of thanksgiving and praise avail if one should, in opposition to the commandment of the Lord, refuse to recognize through humble prayer of petition one's own personal dependence on the supreme goodness of God?

The significance and importance of prayer of petition is explained more extensively in the doctrinal course on grace. Since the present order of salvation is an order of grace, it is likewise an order of the prayer of supplication or petition which is made possible only through the bounty of divine grace.[155] Every adult receives the grace to pray. This prayer is absolutely essential for him if he is to keep the commandments, and above all, if he is to obtain the great gift of final perseverance.[156] Since the Church, on the one hand, clearly teaches that the gift of perseverance cannot be merited[157] and, on the other, that God wills all men to be saved, it follows that the grace of perseverance depends primarily on praying rightly. Such is the conviction of Catholic teaching and practice. In his famous booklet "On Prayer as the Great Means of Grace," St. Alphonse establishes the spiritual axiom: "He who prays will certainly be saved; he who does not pray will certainly be lost."[158]

If petition is essential by a necessity of means to attain eternal salvation, it is apparent how urgent is the precept to use this means and to pray. Our Savior never tired of inculcating this precept. "He who does not pray with insistence, with confidence, with perseverance and humble submission has no sense of his own particular moral needs, has no impulse to turn to God and to holiness, experiences no desire to cooperate with divine grace, has not placed his own earthly existence and all good and all hope in the hands of his Creator, and is not His child."[159]

Our prayer of petition must also include the petition which the Lord taught us all: "Forgive us our trespasses as we forgive those who trespass against us!" Hence the prayer of sorrow, the prayer for forgiveness and expiation must accompany the prayer of supplication for grace and favors;[160] any petition which slights the prayer of sorrow is utterly lacking in humility and truth.

The petition we direct to God must embrace all that the virtue of hope encompasses; first the eternal goods, then the temporal goods in the service of the eternal,[161] one's own salvation and that of one's neighbor. The communal prayer of petition and the prayer for one another in the Mystical Body is an expression of our common hope.

In the communion of saints it is possible for the individual members of this community to intercede for one another. The great commandment of love transforms this mere possibility into an obligation. The saints in heaven can pray for us earthly pilgrims (of course there is a question of the degree of the efficacy of their intercession in the instances in which we neglect to call on them for their help). We ourselves can pray for all earthly pilgrims and for the holy souls in Purgatory. Should one fail altogether to pray for one's own who may be in great need or perhaps in the state of mortal sin, or for one's closest relatives who have just departed this life, one might readily incur grave guilt. Under certain circumstances such neglect might be a mortal sin against the commandment of love and piety.

5. Prayer Prescribed? Prayer Meritorious?

Rationalists and deists dismiss prayer as waste of time and neglect of duty, whereas devoteés of false mysticism (Quietism) and even more so many Protestants take offense at any suggestion of prayer of precept. They object vehemently to the notion that prayer can be imposed as obligatory work, specifically as a sacramental penance, or that prayer can be meritorious.

It is true that the Church expressly teaches that prayer is meritorious and, furthermore, that it possesses an expiatory value;[162] but it is not the intent and import of this doctrine that merit or the gaining of an indulgence should be the principal or even the exclusive object of one's prayer. Nor is it the Church's mind that merit be foremost in our minds when we pray and that God be secondary or incidental. What the Church desires to inculcate in us, first of all, is the simple fact that prayer has a most exalted value for time and eternity, and secondly, that oftimes it may be difficult and laborious, demanding effort and a wrestling with the frailty of human nature. In consequence it has expiatory value and is most suitable as a work of satisfaction which can be offered in atonement for neglect of duty and for the lessening of temporal punishment due to our sins. And finally, if prayer is actually performed with joy and without any concern for hardship which may be involved in it—something most desirable, though unfortunately far beyond our grasp—then the merit of the prayer is not lessened and its expiatory value is not diminished. It is rather augmented.

That prayer must be imposed at all by law or command is simply due to our sorry fallen state. But the very fact that it is so sublime and eminently appropriate for the child of God renders the precept of prayer reasonable and suitable to fallen man. To require a specific minimum of prayer cannot be contradictory to the nature of prayer or the dignity of man. Moreover, since the priestly state and the religious life are voluntarily chosen as states of prayer, it cannot be opposed to the dignity of prayer nor the true freedom of the Christian to demand an even higher standard of prayer for priest and religious than for other Christians (such is the precept requiring the daily recitation of the canonical hours). But it would be an egregious error to place prayer principally or—something far worse—exclusively in the class of mere legal acts, or perchance view them solely in the light of their meritorious or penitential value.

Prayer must be the loving and winsome speech of the child with the heavenly Father, of the loving disciple with the Master, of the members of the Church in this earthly sojourn with their glorified brethren and most of all with their heavenly Mother. Prayer should not flow primarily from the incidental or secondary purposes of prayer, but from the spirit of love.

It would be an error, as worthy of condemnation as the one indicated above, to look upon prayer as something residing in the feelings so that we should wait for the proper mood or inspiration to pray, wait until the sentiment of prayer prevails. The spirit of prayer may not be made the slave of sentiment and emotion. The Christian is not permitted to hold aloof from prayer merely because he is not in a proper frame of mind. He must even submit to the threat and pressure of law and its sanction if this is necessary. Prayerfully he must overcome the frailty arising from original sin by dwelling on the thought of duty and fear of punishment. He must have the firm will to pray.

6. Necessary Qualities of Prayer

The Church suggests that we should pray *"digne, attente ac devote."* Usually this is expressed in the simple condition that we should pray with "devotion." Devotion is the will, ordered to God, which promptly and gladly dedicates itself to the service of God.[163] The English word *devotion* should not be equated with simple attention, which surely is essential to prayer, nor looked upon as the exact equivalent to the Latin *devotio.* As commonly used, the word means the heart-felt fervor which is aroused by meditation on the divine truths. Nevertheless, in its strict theological sense devotion does not essentially include or demand the sensible elements or the "feelings" of devotion. It is rather the interior dedication of the will itself. Thus viewed devotion is a spiritual attitude reconcilable with spiritual dryness. However, such is the nature of man that the interior disposition and dedication of the will tends to manifest itself also in the intensity of the emotions, and conversely genuine feelings or affections usually react in a deepening of the spirit of dedication. This is particularly true of dedication or emotion which is sustained over a considerable period of time.

Attention consists either in ordering the spiritual activity immediately toward God, toward the divine presence or some particular divine truth, or toward the spoken word itself in the prayer formula. In recitative or oral prayer it is not essential that every single word or even every sentence be caught attentively. It is sufficient that in a general way our attention be riveted on God Himself. Oral prayer which is thus recited without attention to the meaning of the words is not altogether empty and futile, for it can always stimulate interior prayer if this tends to ebb and weaken. It also may serve to encourage others and particularly to promote the solemnity and common bond of unity in the divine worship.

All this suggests the serious query: is prayer performed in complete wilful distraction deserving of the name prayer at all? On this point Hirscher[164] says: "Every prayer that is purely external is not worthy of the name! God is spirit and they who worship Him must worship in spirit and in truth" (Jn 4:24; cf. Mt 15:8). That interior prayer immediately ceases to be present when one is entirely distracted is evident from the nature of prayer and must be apparent to any one who knows what true prayer really is. However, merely external prayer, the prayer of the lips without this interior spirit, is no real prayer. It follows that one who has neither devotion nor attention at prayer does not pray at all; at best he parrots empty formulas of prayer. To him the word of the Lord applies: "But in praying, do not multiply words, as the Gentiles do; for they think that by saying a great deal, they will be heard" (Mt 6:7). It is not the external word itself that constitutes prayer but the lifting of the mind and heart to God. Better a single devout ejaculation than hours of wilfully "distracted prayers." We say "wilful" distractions, for involuntary distractions do not simply destroy the value of prayer. The one who is involuntarily distracted still maintains the dedication of his will to God. He is not entirely lacking in devotion.

The following are the effects of devout and attentive prayer:[165] 1) There is the vivifying effect on the soul, the spiritual refreshment of the heart through actual converse with God. This spiritual effect is utterly absent in "distracted prayer" for the obvious reason that wilful distractions turn the mind away from God. One who prays with wilful distractions is not in the presence of God. 2) There is in the prayer of petition the actual capacity to be heard. God can of course harken to the prayer offered in distraction, provided there is an earnest will on the part of the petitioner. God can look with favor upon such a good will though wilful distractions surely mar the earnest disposition. 3) The value of the prayer itself in God's sight as a meritorious good work, the value which expiates and satisfies for faults, which gives glory to God. This third value is also found in distracted prayer, entirely or at least partially, in proportion to the good will and the desire to pray well.

Attention and devotion at prayer are not altogether compatible with every type of occupation which might be carried on during prayer. Purely mechanical tasks permit the attentive and coherent recitation of vocal prayer. But it is not permissible to recite obligatory prayers (such as the breviary) while occupied with a task which claims a great part of our mental attention. On the other hand we should make every effort to turn all our tasks to prayer by constantly recurring to the thought of God and raising our mind to Him while we are working. Basically no task which is morally unobjectionable is incompatible with the prayer of the mind and heart while it is being performed. Hence it is true without qualification that one can and always may pray at his work. But it is not valid without qualification to say that one may work while one prays (namely, during obligatory prayer).

Trust in the goodness of God and His fidelity to His promises is indispensable for true prayer, precisely because prayer of petition is an act of the virtue of hope. Whoever prays with mistrust offends God and may not hope to be heard (Jas 1:5ff.). When we pray as we must "in the name of Jesus," we place our hope and trust in the redemptive love of Jesus and in the power of His merits. This confidence is expressed in the prayers of the liturgy in which the Church concludes all her prayers with the words "through Christ our Lord." Likewise our private prayers must be inspired by that same confidence which should be constantly renewed as we turn lovingly to Jesus. When we are thus inspired and pray "for Christ's sake, for the sake of Thy most beloved Son," we are able to touch the heart of the heavenly Father and solemnly beseech Him to harken to our entreaties. Confidence in Christ, however, is actually powerful in us only if we ourselves are in Christ through the grace of His loving friendship, for only when we are in the state of grace and animated by divine love can we pray worthily and truly "in the name of Jesus."

To this confidence there must be joined utter abandonment of self to the providence of Him who loves us. We may not hold that by our prayers we have first to dispose God to be favorable to us. It is we who must, by the attestation of our dependence on God and our total abandonment to His loving will, make ourselves capable of receiving His love and His favors. Hence our prayer of petition must necessarily include the manifestation of our submission to the will of God.

If we pray for the goods necessary for salvation and for the most excellent of graces, the grace of final perseverance, we know that God, as far as it depends on Him, wills to grant our request. And hence our prayer is no more than an incessant effort to abandon ourselves to the gracious and saving will of God. It is an appeal to God, a cry for help that He remove all the obstacles in us to the designs of His love.

If we ask God for temporal things, we may do so with the confident expectation that God will grant the favor if it is truly profitable for our salvation. This confidence in the disposition of God's providence must be such that we ask for nothing that does not redound to God's glory and the salvation of our souls.

Abandonment of ourselves to God in prayer, submission of our will to His, is one of the essential elements of interior devotion by which we are dedicated to God. This is the very heart of the virtue of religion. This submission of our will implies reverence for the transcendent greatness of God which creates in us sinners the spirit of humility and repentance in our prayer (note the publican in the Gospel). How would it be possible for a miserable sinner to approach reverently transcendent Holiness Itself without being overawed at the dissimilarity between himself and God? A contrite and humble heart is pleasing to God (Ps 50:19).

Prayer demands a reverential deportment and recitation of the formulas. A sense of fitness regarding the manner and means of manifesting reverence for God is determined by a general sense for the fitting and beautiful in human association. Thus prayer which is attentive and devout also becomes gracious and worthy in its externals (*attente, devote, digne*).

Prayer which is converse with God, the earnest entreaty for the greatest gift of God, abiding love, demands of us above all the sanctification of the spirit within us and absence of all hatred and defect of love (cf. Mk 11:25f.; Mt 5:23f.). This does not mean that the sinner cannot pray and is not obliged to say the prayers prescribed by the law. Rather it is certain that he can and must fulfill these obligations regarding prayer. But his prayer has full value only if it represents an effort toward his conversion and the abandonment of his faults. True prayer is either the prayer of the friend of God or of the contrite sinner searching for the return to friendship with Him. Whoever has the evil will to persevere in grave sin averts his gaze, the very depth and core of his spirit, away from God. How can he at the same time engage in prayer which surely means lifting the mind and heart to God? "When one turns away his ear from hearing the law even his prayer is an abomination" (Prv 28:9; cf. Os 6:3; 10:12).

Prayer must be persevering. "They must always pray and not lose heart" (Lk 18:1ff.; 11:5ff.; 21:36). "The unceasing prayer of a just man is of great avail" (Jas 5:16). This perseverance in prayer should not be confused with mere length of prayer. Perseverance does not refer to the length of our vocal prayers or to the time spent in praying. It is better to say short prayers frequently and devoutly than long prayers that lack devotion. St. Thomas lays down the rule that prayer of petition should last as long as may be necessary or profitable to enkindle the interior fervor of prayer.[166]

When our Lord says that we must pray always, this does not mean literally uninterrupted prayer. It means, first of all, that we should never presume that we no longer have need for prayer, that we have prayed enough or done enough—as though our salvation is altogether assured.[167] We are never permitted to relax in our prayer for perseverance in love until the very hour of our death. Nor are we allowed to lose confidence and grow remiss in prayer if we are not promptly granted a favorable response regarding the other true needs and interests of our life. Finally, to pray always means, in the beautiful words of St. Augustine, that "in faith, in hope, and in love we pray always by a continuous and truly persevering desire. And therefore at specific hours and seasons we also pray with words to God, so that by these signs of reality we may admonish ourselves, so that we may render an account of the progress we have made in our inner desire and bestir ourselves with greater enthusiasm to increase it."[168]

The warning of Sirach, "repeat not the word in thy prayer" (Sir 7:15) and the admonition of the Lord not to multiply words (Mt 6:7; 23:14) are directed against vain and idle repetition and false confidence in mere abundance of words and formulas. They do not forbid the earnest, incessant appeal which finds an expression of urgency in repetition of the words of prayer. In fact the very prayers of Sacred Scripture often are a rhythmic repetition of the self-same words forming a beautiful litany in praise of God, as in Psalm 135.

Our prayer must be catholic. It must embrace the universal interests of the kingdom of God and serve as a vital bond of communication in the great family of God which includes also the saints in glory. We need not fear, as do the Protestants, that in our dialog with the saints we abridge the rights of God.[169] Our prayer must be orientated toward the prayer of the Catholic Church, both toward her liturgical prayer and toward the magnificent prayers of her great saints.

7. Sins against Prayer

The sins against prayer are culpable defects in the qualities of prayer which we have just enumerated. In addition to these we must mention the "exhibitionist" type of prayer, a particularly offensive form of prayer condemned so vehemently by our Lord: "When you pray, you shall not be like the hypocrites, who love to pray standing in the synagogues and at the street corners, in order that they may be seen by men" (Mt 6:5). In contrast to this pretense of prayer there is the prayer of seclusion in one's chamber or behind closed doors where one prays to the "Father in secret" (Mt 6:6). This is really the prayer of purity of heart which may be said anywhere, but is directed solely to God. Such is the prayer demanded of us by our Lord. It does not at all imply a condemnation of community prayer or even rate it as lower in value. Closely allied to the prayer of ostentation is purely external and mechanical prayer which is the vapid utterance of formulas without the spirit of prayer. This, we have repeatedly mentioned, is a sin against prayer.

Purely formal prayer, exclusively and entirely formal, is defective rather than sinful. It is the result of inadequate and even false formation in the science and art of prayer, to be corrected by pious meditation on the sacred mysteries and the serious reading of the Sacred Scriptures. Similar to merely formal prayer is the "legalistic" approach to all required prayer. Due to this attitude the required prayers may degenerate into mere legal endeavors. Thus, for example, if a priest "gets the breviary out of the way" merely in order to avoid transgressing the law, without any interior penetration into the prayers themselves, he falls short of fulfilling the essence of the law of prayer. The danger of mere legal fulfillment in the recitation of the canonical hours, without genuine inner appreciation of the text and the purpose of the law, is particularly great if one is totally indifferent to distribution and sequence of the hours according to their intent and import, or if he is led to the other extreme by a false dread that he is violating the law in seeking even the most reasonable exemption from it. Even in recitative prayer which is prescribed by law (as is the breviary) our first concern must be joy in praying and praying well.

There is undoubtedly a grave obligation to recite the entire breviary. Even careless neglect of so much as one canonical hour is generally held to be a mortal sin. However, it is true that in view of the limitations of human nature, rigorism as to the details of the law may have fatal consequences in this matter. One's psychic energy may be entirely spent in a mechanical recitation which fulfills the law externally, but in which the joy of prayer and inner devotion suffers, and spontaneity in the divine service, the simple openness to the call of grace when it comes, disappears. On the other hand, chafing under restraint may gradually lead to spiteful grudge against the recurring onus of recitation, and finally to brutal in-difference and total neglect of the prayer.

Surely the priest is strictly obliged, in principle and at all times, to provide that prayer, and especially the breviary prayer, have the place of preference in his daily program. It is true, practically all authors hold that the priest may readily be excused on occasion from the recitation of parts of the office. Nevertheless, there is always the unconditional duty to examine himself anew regarding his whole attitude toward prayer: does he always make the necessary effort to fulfill piously and consistently this sacred duty of reciting his breviary?

It is scarcely possible to insist that the diocesan clergy say the office recitatively, i.e. with the movement of the lips, since Mother Church has exempted the regulars from such an obligation. As essential as is the worthy utterance of all the lofty texts for common or choral recitation, for private, silent recitation the all-important point is the thoughtful and pious completion of the prayer.

In principle the breviary prayer must be recitated by priests in the liturgical idiom prescribed by the Church. If, however, to cite an example as exception, a priest has lapsed into a spiritless and uncomprehending manner of reading the text, he might be advised to resort to the following mode of correction. In a sincere effort to reform he could be permitted to use epiky; that is, the earnest effort to attain the primary intent of the law. He could recite the office for a time in his mother tongue. We consider epiky justified in such an instance because we are dealing with the avoidance of very great evil.

We do not consider it edifying that priests silently and with dour persistence finish their breviary prayer at a common divine service at which the faithful participate actively. Even if no other time is available for the canonical hours, it is advisable for them to participate devoutly and joyously in that common divine service at which they are expected or required to be present. In such cases the one divine function takes the place of the other.

Should a priest binate or even trinate on Sunday, he must have time for quiet recollection, so that he can worthily and devoutly carry out the noble rites and utter the lofty words of the Eucharistic celebration. In view of our limited psychic energy, it may be counselled in many instances that the priest do not attempt to recite his entire office on such days. For in no instance may we violate the command of the Gospel: "In praying, do not multiply words, as the Gentiles do" (Mt 6:7). It would seriously offend our Mother the Church to interpret her positive law regarding the breviary recitation in such a way as to violate the prayer in spirit and in truth. The effort for a meaningful prayer must always be first. The Church does not demand mechanical spiritless obedience, but childlike trustful submission which penetrates to the innermost purposes of the law.[170]

The Christian has the obligation to strive for the perfection of prayer, just as he has the obligation to strive for perfection in his whole spiritual life. Christian perfection and the perfection of prayer go hand in hand, and neither is possible without the other. Only by striving for perfection in prayer will the Christian be assured that he shuns sins and faults in his prayers.

It is not easy to determine what is required under pain of sin in the matter of prayer. Ordinarily the voluntary lack of attention and devotion is only a venial sin, for we cannot readily assume that one would deliberately offend God gravely at the very time one has turned to prayer. But the permanent habit or disposition of being indevout at prayer is the manifestation of a basic disesteem of prayer itself. It reveals an utterly indifferent attitude toward God, an attitude which might readily be seriously offensive to God. Similarly, if we deal with strict requirement, it is not easy to determine when neglect of prayer becomes a mortal sin. St. Alphonse and many noted authors with him hold that to neglect prayer altogether for a month and surely to neglect it for two months is a mortal sin. This judgment is based on the obligation to practice religion arising from the virtue of religion and the theological virtues,[171] abstracting altogether from any special reasons which might make more frequent prayer obligatory. In many cases neglect of prayer even for a shorter period may involve one in grave sin for the simple reason that neglect of more frequent prayer leads to neglect of serious moral duties which can be performed only with the aid of prayer.

The minimum requirement of prayer, as determined specifically by law and binding under pain of mortal sin, is the devout participation in holy Mass on Sundays and Holy Days of obligation. For the priest and cleric in major orders there is the obligation to recite the canonical hours daily. Priests and religious have also a number of additional duties[172] with obligations, more or less grave, attached to them.

"The Christian moral spirit has created and established a custom of prayer among Christian people, such as the morning, evening, and table prayers. Though not expressly commanded, these prayers are so intimately and beautifully bound up with the Christian concept of the life and attitude of the child of God in relation to His heavenly Father that the Christian deems it a matter of course, something self-evident, that he should not fail to say them. It follows that they may not be entirely neglected or disregarded for a considerable time without hurt to the inner life and consequently without sin."[173]

It is false to assert that, since these prayers are not imposed by any specific law, they do not bind under pain of sin; the obligation arises without any positive law from the relation of the child of God to his heavenly Father. Even though there is no command to do so, the good child realizes full well that it would be most unseemly to fail to speak to its parents for days or even weeks on end, to neglect to thank them for anything, to neglect to greet them. Similarly the pious Christian is not in need of a positive law to convince him that he cannot refuse to give God a morning and evening greeting, to offer thanks for the daily gifts and benefits without being guilty of offending Him.

In this connection the words of Hirscher are much to the point: "The neglect of prayer is not merely the omission of a duty of religion; it is also the manifestation of a heart averted to a greater or lesser degree from God, an expression of a heart falling prey to sin or already the victim of sin."[174] Obviously an occasional lapse due to forgetfulness is not sinful, but one who no longer says his morning and evening prayers, whether it be by interior dialog of the heart with God or at least through some memorized formula, is in a very bad spiritual way. Experience proves that such a man is in a state of spiritual decline. His fervor is rapidly waning because even the barest minimum of vital manifestation essential for the interior life is absent. When the spiritual life ceases to manifest itself in prayer, it loses its vigor altogether. Similarly, if a family has lost its contact with common prayer at meals or perhaps with all forms of common prayer, the family community spirit, the contact at meals, and all the other family contacts, will gradually grow more and more profane and estranged from God.

Only through prayer can the Christian satisfy the obligation of the virtue of religion to sanctify the whole of his life and the community in which he moves. However, there is no specific length set for these prayers nor any required formula which he must use. In the matter of the daily prayers it is not easy to determine the exact time for prayer or their length. We are dealing with the new law of the children of God, with the law of grace and love. Consequently there is no question of sin if one should find his own time and place for his daily converse with God in prayer. If one's daily program does not readily admit of adjustment to the morning and evening prayers, or there is no quiet place for them at the usual hours, the individual may surely set aside a time or find a place which suits his particular needs. But the normal and usual thing must be the prayer at specifically determined times, ordinarily in the morning and evening, for without such a program men would soon forget to pray altogether.

The Psalmist (Ps 118:164) speaks of praying seven times a day. The early Christian work, the *Didache,* which dates back to the days of the Apostles, demands of the Christian that he offer prayer to God at least three times a day.[175] The devout Hindu leader, Mahatma Gandhi, says very wisely: "Prayer must be the key of the morning and the latch of the evening."

II. REVERENCE FOR THE HOLY NAME OF GOD

1. *Religious Significance of the Divine Name*

a. The name is the expression of the essence or of the pre-eminent characteristic of that which it designates. The people of antiquity, particularly the Israelites, felt very keenly that names should not be arbitrary designations but expressions of something essential. Homer sees a sign of our human limitations in the fact that the names bestowed by men do not fully express the nature of the individual things to which they are given. For this reason many things had a different name among the gods than among men. Plato points this out in reference to the names of the gods: only the gods themselves can know their own proper names because they alone know their own true essence. "The true names of the gods are those by which the gods designate themselves. Since we men cannot know these authentic names we must be satisfied with the names we use to invoke the gods in prayer."[176] When God Himself condescends to make His name known to men, He reveals His true name to us, a name which is characteristic of His essence and His attributes.[177]

The revelation of the divine name, *Yahweh,* is a most solemn moment in the history of salvation (Ex 3:13ff.). Through the name, "The God of your fathers . . . ," God reveals Himself to Moses in His uniqueness and unequivocally as the God of sacred history and the Lord of the ages. With the supreme name of Yahweh, God reveals that He Himself is the "Mighty-Helper." The prophetic names of the Messiah ("Emmanuel," Is 7:14; cf. Mt 1:23; "Wonder-Counsellor," "God-Hero," "Father-Forever," "Prince of Peace" in Is 9:5; "Jesus" in Mt 1:21) focus attention on the most characteristic qualities and activities of Christ, the "Anointed One." To invoke the name of the Lord is to call upon Him as present.

b. The name is the basis of a new relationship, of dependence and protection. According to Genesis 2:19f., Adam gave the names to all the animals as they appeared before him. This means, in the first place, that he correctly discerned the nature of things and, secondly, that he fulfilled the divine mandate to "have dominion over" all the beasts of the earth. Designating lands or cities by new names is often attestation of their subjection through conquest or submissive acceptance of protection (cf. 2 Sm 12:28). In times of public disaster every woman would desperately seek a husband, begging to become his by receiving his name (Is 4:1).

Yahweh calls Israel by name and on this act bases his title to her love and fidelity to Him (Is 43:1). The name of Yahweh is invoked over Israel to express the divine dominion and protection (Is 63:19; 2 Par 7:14). The holy name of Yahweh is invoked over the temple (Jer 7:10ff.), over the ark of the covenant (2 Sm 6:2), and over Jerusalem (Jer 25:29; Dn 9:18f.).[178] Thereby they become "holy," consecrated to the Lord; they belong to Him. The invocation of the divine name is the source of the confidence in the special protection of God (cf. Jer 14:9: "thy holy name is invoked over us;" *nomen sanctum tuum invocatum est super nos,* the Church prays in her evensong). "Whoever calls upon the name of the Lord," that is to say, whoever places himself under the dominion and protection of God, "shall be saved" (Acts 2:21; cf. Rom 10:13).

With the new creation the victors will receive a "new name" and "they shall see his face, and his name (i.e. the name of the Lamb) shall be on their foreheads" (Ap 3:12; 14:1; 22:4). This means the inauguration of a new world order. To receive a new name from God implies an entirely new relation of dependence, of sovereign protection and interior assimilation. This sheds light on the custom of choosing a new name at baptism, and in many instances at the time of religious profession, as an expression of new allegiance and loyalty. But the baptismal name should not be cast aside at religious profession, for the evangelical counsels practiced in religion are a special mode and manner of realizing more fully the relationship with Christ established in baptism.

c. In revealing His name God manifests His love for us and His desire to enter into communion with us.

All the divine names in the Old Testament point to the providential offer of God's tender care and love for man. But this revelation of the divine name reaches its climax in the manifestation of the name of God as Father brought to us through Christ: "Father . . . I have manifested thy name to the men whom thou hast given me out of the world" (Jn 17:1-6). The fact that God Himself has revealed His name to us and invited us to invoke it gives to our prayer an assurance which is absolutely unique.

To know one by name and call him by name is a sign of trust and familiarity. Jesus the Good Shepherd knows and calls His sheep "by name" (Jn 10:3). Similarly it is a sign of our intimacy with God through grace that we are so much as allowed to call Him "by name." And since the name is that of Father, there is enclosed in the name the incomparable gift of intimate trust by which we are admitted to the inner community of divine love which is the Trinity itself.

d. The name (*shem*) in the Old Testament often designates the person of God. The name of God stands for God Himself. His name is assurance of His presence and His help. "Behold I will send my angel, who shall go before thee . . . my name is in him" (Ex 23:20f.).

e. The name of God stands for the honor and glory of God. "My name (i.e. my honor) is great among the nations" (Mal 1:11). The words in the Our Father are similar: "Hallowed be thy name." Here *name* is practically equivalent to *honor,* but it connotes something further, above all the loving will of God. The words in Malachias, "Everywhere they bring sacrifice in my name, and a pure offering" clearly reveal the bond between the name of God and the divine worship. This corresponds to the intimate relationship between the two concepts, honor and glory of God and the divine cult or worship of God.

Already the skeptical Democritus referred to the names of the gods as "articulate images of cult."[179] The divine names revealed by God Himself are cultal images of insuperable force and clarity. The divine name, which is an epitome of all that God has revealed about His essence and activity, is a hymn of praise of God's goodness, presence, power, and majesty. Therefore the proper use of the divine name is an important act of the praise and worship of God.

The term "in the name of God" (*beshem Yahweh*) is used rather commonly to designate an action accompanied by solemn invocation, specifically the invocation of the name of God, hence as an attestation or indication that the action is to take place in honor of God, as mandate from God and under the divine protection. To act "in the name" of some-one means to represent his person. The Apostles preached the word, healed the sick, "in the name of God" and "in the name of Christ," that is, as representatives or ambassadors of the One who sent them, with the power and authority of the One who gave them their mission and mandate.

The name of God, which is associated essentially with the love of God for men and the revealed will of God inviting men to a community of fellowship with Him, also connotes something of the honor and glory (*dóxa*) of God. This is particularly apparent in the Gospel according to John.[180] "Father, glorify thy name!" "I have both glorified it, and I will glorify (*doxázein*) it again" (Jn 12:28). The heavenly Father glorifies His name most of all through the manifestation of His Fatherly love in Christ, particularly in the passion and resurrection. Tenderly and lovingly He reveals His glory and honor by showing and proving that He is truly our Father. Hence, the proper use of the name of God implies homage to the majesty of God. If that which is ultimate in the revelation of the divine name is the manifestation of God as our Father, it must follow that every divine name can be properly spoken and truly honored only through the expression and inner spirit befitting the name of one's Father. In every name of God we must honor Him as our Father: this means, pro-nunciation with loving reverence. We pronounce every divine name, including the names which reveal the loving majesty and glory of God (particularly the words, *Cross* and *Holy Sacrament*) with this veneration and love.

The intimate association between the name of God, the honor and glory of God, and the worship of God is graphically expressed in the inspired passages which speak of the name of God in the temple, "that my name might be there" (3 Kgs 8:16ff.). While God dwells in the heavens in inexpressible grandeur and majesty, He permits His name to dwell in His temple, that is, in the center of cult. This means that He is really present, but in a manner that is suitable to the glorification of God in human worship, a manner clearly distinct from the celestial manner of presence. Here God is present with His grace in order to be adored and praised and invoked. Here he harkens most graciously to the entreaties of men. This dwelling of the name of God in the temple is fulfilled in the most marvellous manner in the Eucharistic Sacrifice and the abiding presence of the Eucharistic Lord on our altars.

We pray "in the name of Jesus," because the Father manifests in His Incarnate Son all His loving majesty. Through our union with Jesus He gives us the power to respond worthily to His love. We can pray "in the name of Jesus," only if we abide in the love of Jesus and truly believe that He has gone forth from the Father as the Word of the Father addressed lovingly to us. We must believe, if we are to pray "in the name of Jesus," that the Father will hear our prayer and love us as He loves His own Son, if our prayer is offered in union with the prayer of Jesus (Jn 16:23f.). Praying in Jesus' name is to be caught up with the glory of Jesus. This is the glory of the paschal mystery in which He gives honor to the Father, the glory which He received from the Father and in which He was exalted above all creatures. Finally, it means a participation in the love and glory of the triune God, in the eternal processions of infinite love in the bosom of the Godhead. Thus we share in eternal loving cult, for the name of God is in us forever.

2. Specific Ways of Honoring the Divine Name

a. Invocation of the Divine Name

An explanation of the meaning of the divine name indicates the various ways and means of paying honor to it. We must invoke the name of God and also appeal to the divine mandate and mission committed to us. We must profess the name of God by bearing it as a mark of allegiance and openly confessing it before men. This we do specifically when we bear the name of Christ as "Christians." By accepting the divine name we acknowledge and honor the divine dominion over us and the divine love for us. Above all, we must call on God in prayer, since it is the principal import of the revelation of the divine name that God permits us to invoke it. In the true worship of the name of God there is particularly the prayer of the heart, for the revelation of the divine name imposes on us the duty that we turn to God in an ever growing intimacy of reverential love. The basis of such reverence and love is the "thou-to-thou" relationship between man and God. Every approach to God, every mention of His holy name in loving address is the most unique adoration and worship of God.

Particularly emphatic and expressive is the invocation of the divine name in the solemn appeal called "adjuration." We adjure God by His holy name, "for thy name's sake." Precisely because the name of God reveals His majesty and His will to help us, the solemn adjuration which calls on God as Father (or invokes Him under any other name expressing His love) is a most efficacious prayer. To pray "in the name of Jesus" is a penetrating adjuration addressed to the paternal heart of the Father, beseeching Him by the might of His love expressed in that loving name.

A most tender and trustful manner of invoking God, which is at the same time solemn and exalted, is calling down blessings through the divine name. It is evident that such a "cultal" adjuration has absolutely nothing in common with magical adjuration, for the blessing expresses most forcefully the personal relationship with God. This is clear from the loving and personal use of the sacred name. In direct antithesis to the invocation of God's name in blessing is the malediction of the enemies of God and their expulsion through the invocation of the love and power of God in the Church's exorcism.

b. The Oath

Just as God confirms His promises and His threats with His name ("Whose name is the Lord of hosts": Is 47:4; 51:15; 54:5; Jer 46:18; 48:15) so that in a sense the name is the endorsement and the solemn "Amen" for His word, so too man in critical and important situations can confirm his word and his promises with the solemn pronouncement and invocation of the name of God. Through the oath the truthfulness and fidelity of God embraced in His name are to be honored insofar as man, after a manner of speaking, offers as witness and pledge of his own truthfulness and fidelity God's own name, which is to say he pledges the divine truth and fidelity as assurance of his own sincerity.

In the declaratory oath God is called to witness to our sincere concern to tell the truth (I swear to tell the truth, the whole truth, etc.). In the promissory oath God is in a sense made the guarantor of the pledge or promise which has been given (I swear that I will return the money, etc.). In either instance the name of God as embracing the attributes of truthfulness and fidelity is actually referred to and invoked; otherwise there would be no true oath. The formal declaration which in some legal documents takes the place of the oath is a forceful and explicit attestation of one's truthfulness and therefore has some importance, but it is not an oath because it is not intended as an act of religion which every true oath must be.

Just as it is obvious from the very meaning of the oath, as we have just explained it, that it is an eminently religious act, so it is evidently a very serious act which should never be considered something trivial. An oath may be taken only with full and clear consciousness of its truth, after the formation of a prudent judgment on the fitness of the circumstances (and with sincere and honorable appraisal of the possibility of fulfillment, if it be a promissory oath), and with full preservation of justice. "Then you can swear, 'As the Lord lives,' in truth, in judgment, and in justice" (Jer 4:2).

An oath may be in the best interests of the individual or of the community. If it is necessary or profitable for either individual or community, it should be taken as an act of religion in honor of God. But in itself the oath savors of evil insofar as even the word of the Christian may require confirmation. The Christian's word should be so carefully measured by the standard of the truthfulness and fidelity of God that no oath should be necessary. In a sense the word of the Christian should be as acceptable and reliable as an oath. (cf. Mt 5:33ff.).

The Sacred Scripture calls certain solemn assurances of God oaths and compares them with the oaths of men (Lk 1:73; Acts 2:30). The letter to the Hebrews (6:13–18) compares the oaths of men with the "oaths" of God. "For men swear by one greater than themselves, and an oath given as a guarantee is the final settlement of all their disagreement" (Heb 6:16). This proves that the oath is both a religious and a social act. Jesus Himself confirmed His most tremendous testimony, the testimony of His divine Sonship, by a most solemn oath when He was adjured by the High Priest to respond to the question whether He was truly the Son of God (Mt 26:63f.).

The false declaratory oath (perjury) and the false or insincere promissory oath, which one has no intention of fulfilling, are both among the gravest of sins against the virtue of religion. They are grave in all their forms and degrees (*ex toto genere suo*). Imprudent or useless oaths usually are no more than venial sins. In this they are similar to the profane use of holy names. An oath which is not false but used as an instrument of sin (for example, to testify to detraction) is gravely sinful. Promising something sinful under oath is seriously sinful, and the oath itself is null and void. To fail to keep what one has promised under oath is grave sin if the matter promised is of a weighty or serious nature. If the matter is petty or slight the sin is usually only venial, always provided there is no manifestation of disesteem for the divine honor. The promissory oath must be fulfilled because of the honor due to the name of God, even though the oath was made insincerely and dishonorably, again provided that what has been promised is not evil. An oath which is the result of palpable, unjust deception or extorted by force usually is not binding.

3. Misuse of the Holy Name

Apart from inculpable imperfection in the degree of love and reverence owing to God in His holy name, there are various stages or degrees of dishonor shown to the sacred name of God, ranging from profane language (using the name "in vain") to diabolic disdain or scorn for it.

It is contrary to the reverence and love due to the name of God to refer to Him and the loving majesty of His holy name in the same vein as one speaks of profane sciences. It is not reverential to refer to God lightly as "he" or "it." Sometimes we note the use of such terms as "the deity," as though God were some far-off thing. If we must not only speak to God in prayer but also about Him, for the simple reason that the very enunciation of His holy name is a special tribute of honor paid to it, then surely our speech must be filled with loving reverence. There must always be something of sacred jubilation, of tender and reverent intimacy, of loving friendship implied in the direct address which refers to God as "Thou."

In this matter the theologian himself is confronted by a danger which he must take seriously. Because of his great familiarity with them, he may fall into the habit of using the holy name and speaking of the divine mysteries in the purely scientific manner in which the savant or research worker often discusses the phenomena of his science or specialty. From this casual and matter of fact type of speech about his sacred subject the theologian can be preserved only through intimate converse with God in prayer. For one can properly speak the name of God prayerfully only in an atmosphere of adoration, with an attitude of profound respect and filial love. Then even though the theologian should speak of God as "He," it is always with the same tender and loving accents of adoration and praise which address God as "Thou."

If the "unconcerned" and indifferent use of the holy name is opposed to the holiness and splendor of God's love and majesty as manifested in His name, how much more objectionable and offensive is the frivolous or flippant and disrespectful use of the divine name to express mere natural sentiments or emotional disturbances? Often the holy names are bandied about as mere emphasis or exclamation, as vehicles of profane and worldly excitement, or as expressions of surprise, fright, fear, wrath, feelings and emotions which, if not sinful in themselves, are not at all related to God nor indicative of any reverence for God. Such use of the sacred names is the "vain" use in the stricter sense of the term, which is in a special manner forbidden by the second commandment of the decalogue (obviously the more evil forms are also included in this prohibition). Even the use of the name of God in justifiable and inculpable wrath must be included among the "vain" uses for an angry and vexatious tone of voice is evidence that the name is used irreverently.

The sin of "vain use" of holy names, often called profane language, is in all its forms a venial sin (*ex genere suo veniale*). But the forbearance of theologians for human frailty, evident in the mildness of their censure of this species of abuse of the holy names, does not warrant the conclusion that it is not important to fight against the evil of profane language or to overcome the habit if one has fallen into it. A truly interior reverence for God, perfect worship of God in spirit and in truth, is utterly incompatible with any misuse of the holy names.

It is essentially more malicious to misuse the name of God as an expression or manifestation of emotions which are in themselves disordered and sinful, as for example feelings of vexation and impatience, unrestrained or unjust anger. Nevertheless, we must make a distinction: the sacred names may be uttered merely on the occasion of sinful emotion or violent outburst of feeling. They may be blurted out without thought or reflection or by force of habit. But, on the other hand, they may be consciously and intentionally employed for the very purpose of venting base emotions or even to give vile passions a kind of hypocritical respectability or sacredness.

The unreflecting utterance of holy names in moments of culpable excitement (for example in anger) is certainly no more than a venial sin in individual instances. Possibly the same is true—at least as a general rule—

of the deliberate utterance of sacred names in culpable agitation, provided the holy name is not used as a direct manifestation of the sinful frame of mind. Note the judgment of St. Alphonse: "It is a venial sin of particular seriousness (*inter venialia grave*)."[181] But he expressly adds: "However, because of the danger of falling into the sin of blasphemy, and because it rarely happens that these terms are used without giving scandal, and because those who hear them get the impression that God and holy things are dishonored, there is seldom an excuse for such expressions." From the context it is evident that he means one can rarely be excused from the charge of mortal sin. Finally he advises: "With good reason the faithful should be warned against such language and be taught to shun it with horror." It is very important to note that the danger of scandal is particularly great if parents show so little restraint in their conduct as to give vent to their passion in the presence of their children through outbursts of profanity and other misuse of the holy names.[182]

Objectively the habitual misuse of holy names in sinful anger is to be characterized as a gross (that is, gravely sinful) disorder, a serious violation of the honor due to God, even though the individual act in many instances must be judged more mildly because of the absence of freedom and deliberation. Anton Koch, noted moral theologian of Tuebingen, speaks of this fault as "a display of anger with scornful utterance of the name of God or other holy names. As a sin both of anger and irreverence it is in itself a grave offense."[183] Koch's conclusion cannot readily be refuted. He says that every one is required under pain of mortal sin to fight strenuously against the rise and development of such a habit. The teaching of Franz Xavier Linsenmann differs little from that of Koch: "Quite often misuse of God's name appears as thoughtless and altogether unreflecting exclamation due to habit and without any specific evil intent. In such instances its malice is surely lessened. And yet at the very least such acts are a revelation of an interior spiritual moral coarseness. Nor can the evil be entirely excused because of the habit since the beginnings and growth of the habit itself must be considered a grave sin."[184]

When one who has acquired the evil habit of misusing the holy names in anger and vexation shows his approval of the wicked practice by deliberate and conscious refusal to correct it, by yielding to it constantly and renewing it on every occasion (even though he realizes he is giving scandal), it follows that the individual acts themselves can no longer be considered indeliberate and merely habitual. They rather assume the character of premeditated offenses against God. Nor can the individual claim that he does not act freely, for in this instance the freedom essential to the commission of grave sin is present basically and "in cause," insofar as he is responsible for the origin and continuation of the bad habit. In fact failure to struggle against a conscious evil habit betrays indifference to its existence and growth and a grave absence of reverence for holy things. Such an attitude is indicative of a gravely sinful disposition in all instances in which the evil habit itself and the serious obligation to combat it is sufficiently evident to one's conscience. Should one actually detest the habit and at least with some degree of earnestness combat it, then we are not to assume that the individual acts are grave sins.

There are Christians of good will who, to their deep regret, frequently give vent to vexation and anger through the use of holy names. Either due to an unfortunate habit which they have acquired or to the prevailing usage in their surroundings the divine name or the names of saints will inadvertently fall from their lips. It is sound spiritual practice for these Christians not to abstain from frequent communion even though they have not previously gone to confession, always assuming that their disordered temper or excitement is not a grave sin in itself. In their case the misuse of the sacred names, though most regrettable, surely should not be construed as gravely culpable.

Should one so abuse the holy name as to make it the express and intended vehicle of one's sinful passion, the malice of the act is still greater. There is but a short step from such a sin to blasphemy. The sin is blasphemy if culpable passion seizes upon the sacred names to attack what is holy; that is, to strike at God Himself. The habitual misuse of the name of God creates an atmosphere which readily disposes one to blasphemy not merely in the sense of objectively blasphemous utterances but also in thought and desire. Thus one who habitually misuses the holy names may readily become a blasphemer. Torrents of profanity are occasions of far greater sins, a fact which confirms our thesis that there is a grave obligation to combat and overcome the evil habit of angrily misusing the holy name of God.

It is very important for the proper theological appraisal of "cursing" and "swearing" (all abuse of the holy names) to understand its psychological basis. Very often the use of these names arises from the desire to confirm and strengthen one's assertions rather than from any desire to insult or dishonor that which is holy. In youth it may be due to a swaggering boldness based on a feeling of inferiority or sense of inequality which must be vehemently denied. "As far as the basic origin of this habit is concerned, there lies at its root an element of blasphemy or at least a conception of divinity which is pagan and unworthy of God. We find that pagan peoples on a low cultural level not only adore their gods and beseech their help, but also revile and strike them if their petition is not granted. In such a debased mentality there is rooted the instinct to blurt out sacred names in wrath as often as an obstacle interferes with one's work or desire. . . . Once the abuse of sacred names becomes habitual the individual utterance is altogether unrestrained and indeliberate, in fact almost unconscious. But the habit itself is sinful in its origin and formation, in the tolerant indifference to its entire existence."[185]

In the matter of appraisal of guilt in this difficult area authors seem at first sight to be very much in disagreement. However, closer scrutiny reveals that many an author who judges abuse of holy names uttered in moods of passion as simply no more than a venial sin, is, if possible, really more severe than other theologians who qualify their teaching by more careful distinctions. Many of the "mild" authors look upon the abuse of the holy name in the sense just described as actual blasphemy, an insult directed against God. And one must concede that the conscious utterance of holy names to express profane sentiments, sentiments which have nothing at all to do with holy things, does psychologically open the flood gates to blasphemy itself. But man is frail and imperfect and quick to anger. His abuse of the holy name is often due to thoughtless impulse, which rarely is carried to the horrible extreme of scorn and insult for God Himself.

It is a most appalling contradiction of the loving will of God, as manifested in the holy names, to use these same sacred names in order to give vent to hatred of others by cursing them. To curse someone is to invoke the name of God, or another sacred name, in the expression of the hateful desire that he be afflicted with some temporal or even eternal evil. In a manner of speaking, God is called upon to carry out our evil will. The All-Holy is made an instrument or accomplice of human hatred and malice. Hence cursing one's neighbor by calling on the name of God or on the devil as the enemy of God is a grave sin against love of neighbor and the virtue of religion. To ask the all-holy God to inflict unjust punishment on any one is in itself a sin of blasphemy. Cursing is the extreme antithesis to the prayer of petition. Even the cursing of irrational creatures of God—if seriously meant—is in itself a grave sin. But here also the severity of judgment is somewhat tempered by the realization that lack of deliberation or of serious evil intent may free the individual's conscience from the charge of grave sin in the single acts. But the obligation to correct the habit is a serious one, and the conscious failure to do so is gravely sinful.

"In some places a rather naive religious conception of the efficacy of prayer is responsible for an attitude of mind which puts cursing, at least in practice, on a par with prayer of petition. . . . Underlying this attitude is the assumption that God must harken to the curse as He does to prayer, for the oppressed and helpless victims of injustice were granted the right to curse as a weapon of defence against the power of oppression."[186] Obviously this crude concept is unworthy of God, for we cannot say that He will harken to a curse or fulfill a curse as He harkens to prayer or fulfills prayer. Nevertheless, the anguished cry of the victims of cruel oppression, the piteous cries of parents driven almost to desperation in love and grief over the hideous injustice to their children will not fall upon deaf ears. As they pour out their hearts to God in a prayer for justice, the guilty may well tremble because their sins themselves cry to heaven for vengeance.

Any and every form of cursing is opposed to Christian love of neighbor. Even the desire that the sinner be afflicted by some temporal (never an eternal) evil, which surely may flow from a heart filled with fraternal love and governed by the loftiest moral motives, may never be allowed to descend to the level of the curse. Only evil itself and evil in person, the devil, who is forever fixed in evil, may be cursed. Never the poor and miserable sinner!

III. WORSHIP OF GOD THROUGH THE VOW

1. *Meaning of the Vow*

a. Not only in the Old Testament but in the entire history of religions we find that the vow is often a most forceful prayer of petition and thanksgiving. A strictly binding promise of a gift in gratitude for favors received, an offering or sacrifice, makes the prayer of petition more pressing and insistent and the manifestation of sentiments of gratitude more secure and solid. An example in point is the vow of Jacob (Gn 28:20ff.) and that of Anna (1 Sm 1:10ff.). Though prayer is itself an act of worship which bespeaks our dependence on God, its religious character appears more explicit when it is accompanied by a vow. One who makes a vow obliges himself by his very prayer of petition to thank God in a special way for harkening to his request; namely, by offering to God the consecrated gift or thanksgiving which he promised. The psalmist also speaks of vowing and offering a hymn of praise. Consequently, by these vows accompanying the prayers of petition God is promised all praise and thanks, all honor and glory for the bounty of loving-kindness which we confidently expect from Him. And there is the assurance that the promise will be fulfilled and God will be given praise and thanks.

The vow bound up with the prayer of petition is called a conditional vow because its fulfillment does not oblige unless the request has been answered favorably. If the prayer is not heard, there is no obligation of fulfillment. But this does not necessarily imply that the promise springs from imperfect dispositions, as though one were haggling or bargaining with God. On the contrary, the petitioner can be so confident that God will hear his prayer that, even before it is answered, his sense of gratitude impels him to oblige himself by vow to do the good work. Nevertheless, the promise is conditional, because it derives its value and significance through the anticipation of a specific favor in response to prayer.

A vow which is made unconditionally is not attached to a prayer of petition or at least is not dependent on the answer to our prayers. It has its meaning and significance as an autonomous form of religion, arising from a profound sense of gratitude for favors received from God or from an interior spirit of desire to consecrate self and one's gifts to God. Only the unconditional vow reveals the true depth and beauty of the Christian vow, for it alone is rooted in the complete and unconditioned devotion to God.

b. What man seeks to express and is able to express by the vow—from the very depth of his being—is the consecration of his God-given gifts or himself in a personal consecration to the glory of God. In this sense the vow participates in the significance of sacrifice and at its profoundest depths can be fully understood only in the light of sacrifice. In order to make the gift one has vowed acceptable to God and its offering pleasing to Him, the vow, like sacrifice, must be sign and symbol of the offering of one's self and one's service to God. It must represent not only man's personal oblation of self to God and the pledge of what he promises to Him but also in general his engagement in the divine service.

Since the three great vows of voluntary poverty, chastity, and obedience offer man's deepest and most personal gifts to God, they surpass in dignity and value all real vows in which the personal is not offered but only a specific real gift, a particular symbol of a total personal oblation.

It would be superficial indeed to judge the vow merely from the juridical point of view and see in it no more than self-imposed obligations to do certain things or offer certain gifts to God. Such a point of view ignores entirely the "priestly" dignity and consecration of the Christian and his comprehensive cultal vocation. Ultimately in this basic cultal vocation is rooted the possibility for the Christian to honor God truly in his vows, to transform the promised gifts into consecrated gifts, into sacrifices. Therefore at the summit of all vows is the baptismal vow. Hence when the newly-baptized is anointed with the chrism of the priesthood of the faithful, his solemn baptismal promises attain a new depth of meaning: they become consecratory promises of one anointed for divine cult. The Christian—the very name calls our attention to Christ, the Anointed One, whose followers we are—is obliged to carry out his baptismal promises by the very fact of his baptismal character and his cultal enlistment into the universal priestly service in the glorious assignment of Christ the Priest. Hence the constant stress on the unity of the baptismal vow with all the vows of the Christian must lead to a more realistic appreciation of this sacramental foundation of our promises to God. Every vow is a renewal in depth, in extension, in interior acceptance of the promises made in baptism, a renewal of the priestly consecration given in the baptismal character for the perfect worship of God.

It is in virtue of this priestly consecration in baptism and the spirit of interior and voluntary renunciation founded in it that the three principal goods of man (free power of disposal of one's material goods, of one's right to found a family, and of one's own person) become in the three great personal vows of poverty, chastity, and obedience truly sacrificial offerings to God. They are freely added to the general Christian duties arising from baptism, and precisely as surest and most direct means of fulfilling them. They are made with the explicit priestly purpose of rendering glory to God in the confident hope, justified by the baptismal chrism, that God will be pleased to accept such a gift as a consecratory offering. From what other source could we derive so great a trust as from the assimilation to the priesthood of Christ, attested and guaranteed by the character of baptism and confirmation. It is this bond of priesthood which makes all our gifts truly gifts of Christ, gives them immeasurable cultal value so that they are acceptable and agreeable to God.

In the light of this priestly perspective the vow of virginal chastity implicit in the sacred order of the subdiaconate is far more than an extension and enrichment of the baptismal promise. United with the order of priesthood to which it is directed, this vow penetrates to the profoundest depth of the person in the offering of self as preparation for the most exalted sacrificial vocation in the most intimate association with Christ the Priest. This vow makes plain that the priest must be not merely one who offers the sacrifice but also one who is offered. From the very inmost center of that which is human within him, he must be both priest and victim. One who embraces this holy state must do so in obedience to the call of grace and resolutely make the sacrifices necessary to preserve virginal chastity. Then, from his union with the Sacrifice of the Cross, a constantly more intimate union shall grow, union with the sacrifice of praise, with the heavenly liturgy.

Though the private vow is not the same as the public vow, it is nevertheless an act which transcends the merely private sphere and extends into the "priestly" community of the baptized. The public vow as such, even in its external form and legal formulation, is dependent on the community which is the Church. She authorizes, accepts, and confirms the public vow. In consequence, the cultal signification is derived not only from the person who makes the vow on the title of his baptism but also from the Church officially and as a cultal institution. Her action also has an influence on the effect of the vow in the divine cult.

The conception of the vow which does not place an exclusive emphasis on the obligation freely imposed, but stresses as of equal if not primary importance the priestly character of the Christian who makes the vow (and accordingly stresses also the "consecration" of the gift or the person to God), sheds considerable light on the current and practically common teaching of theologians that the object of the vow is not limited to the supererogatory. According to this doctrine, that which is already obligatory can become the object of an additional obligation through the vow.[187] That to which the Christian is already obliged by some virtue or law he can single out with a fuller realization and decision by viewing it under a new aspect in its total relation to the glory of God. On the basis of his baptism and under the title of the virtue of religion he can consecrate himself to such duties with a far greater appreciation and devotion.

There is a wealth of meaning in the term *marriage vows,* which, according to an old Christian usage, refers to the matrimonial consent given by the bridal couple before the altar of sacrifice. This consent is much more than a simple contract. It is a sacred promise of fidelity placed in the hands of the Church, a religious act of mutual submission to the consecrated order of marriage ordained by God to the service of Christ and His Church. It is the will and the duty of the spouses to bear witness to themselves and their surroundings; they are witnesses of the faith in the God of truth, of life, of love.

2. *Conditions for Validity and Liceity*

a. *On the part of the one making the vow:* he must act freely and with full deliberation, for God does not welcome a consecratory gift which is wrested by a kind of force from His creature. Since the vow must be the freest of gifts, any vow induced by external force is invalid; but not a vow one is induced to make because of wholesome interior dread of sin and God's punishment.

The vow must be the object of prudent reflection and decision (cf. Prv 20:25). Any one who lacks prudence must seek counsel and be guided by prudent advice. As a general rule, vows should not be made without the advice of one's father-confessor. An obviously imprudent vow (for example, the vow to do something clearly beyond one's ability, something which is an obstacle to a higher good or even the source of damage to one's neighbor) is not valid. A doubt in this matter can best be resolved by means of a dispensation from the vow or a commutation into something more prudent, granted by one having proper authority (usually the father-confessor).

Essential to the vow is firmness of decision. There can be no indecisive vow; for the vow, unlike the mere resolution, which allows of various degrees of firmness and as such does not bind in conscience, consists of a promise made to God with the firm will to oblige oneself in conscience. Just as liberty is essential to the making of the vow, so is the obligation contracted in full liberty absolute after the vow has been made. "When you make a vow to God, delay not its fulfillment. For God has no pleasure in fools: fulfill what you have vowed. You had better not make a vow than make it and not fulfill it" (Eccl 5:3f.). "When you make a vow to the Lord, your God, you shall not delay in fulfilling it; otherwise you will be held guilty, for the Lord, your God, is strict in requiring it of you. Should you refrain from making a vow, you will not be held guilty. But you must keep your solemn word and fulfill the votive offering you have freely promised to the Lord" (Dt 23:22ff.).

If one really doubts whether he has made a vow or only a simple resolution, he is free; for liberty is in possession. If there is serious question regarding the validity of a vow because the necessary freedom may have been lacking when the vow was made, dispensation from obligation surely may be sought. The probabilists say simply there is no obligation. As to public vows, the decision of the Church is decisive.

As to the gravity of obligation: since the vow arises from one's own will to bind one's self, gravity of violation depends on the intention one had in making the vow. Should one have had the intention of assuming a grave responsibility or obligation, the vow binds under mortal sin. Generally speaking, a petty matter is not capable of "bearing" an obligation under pain of mortal sin.

b. *On the part of the object:* the thing promised must be possible and better than its contrary.[188] This implies that it must be more than merely good in itself or in theory or in general agreement with the law of perfection. In the concrete circumstances it must be truly such as to promote Christian perfection. The vow is strictly not legitimate if one can foresee that he will most probably not be able to keep it or that in his effort to do so he will be in constant danger of violating the vow. It ceases to be valid as soon as it becomes evident that the opposite of what has been promised would be better in the sight of God for the individual concerned than what has been actually vowed. However, when there is question of a public vow, the final decision must be left to the authority of the Church.

c. *The role of the Church:* since the Church is the community of divine cult in which the Christian participates in the priestly dignity and activity of Christ, every vow must be in harmony with the nature and will of the Church. The vow is simply participation in the sacerdotal vocation of the Church and conversely the Church is in some way a participant in carrying out the vow. She even assumes the private vows in her perpetual ministry of consecration and sacrifice. And the public vow must be expressly placed in her hands, accepted and ratified by her. For this reason it is entirely within her right to lay down conditions essential for her participation and cooperation. Hence the ecclesiastical effects of vows depend exclusively (not arbitrarily) on the will of the Church. She alone has the right to determine which vows are to be recognized as public and what are to be their legal or juridical effects. (Note the distinction between *solemn* and *simple* vows, a distinction which is related principally to their effects, the former invalidating marriage, the latter merely making marriage illicit; the former removing the very capacity for ownership of property, the latter making certain species of possession or ownership and use illicit).

The Church enjoys the competence to test, regulate, and adjudicate matters regarding the acceptance and continuation of individuals in the state of the vows (the religious state). Because of her pastoral authority she is obliged to guide men prudently and wisely in the making of vows and in their fulfillment. In virtue of her priestly office the vows in a sense are made her own, so that they receive from her (ultimately from Christ) their value and merit. Because she has the jurisdiction by which she binds and looses, the Church has the right, vicariously and in the name of God, to interpret vows in His name. She has the right to free men from them, or as the case may be, to insist on their observance.

3. *The Religious and Moral Value of the Vow*

The value of the vow is first of all a religious value. Making a vow and fulfilling it are both special acts of the virtue of religion. "To vow is to direct those things which one vows to the divine cult or homage. And hence it is evident that to make a vow is properly an act of *latria* or religion."[189] Because it is made freely without the obligation of law, the vow has the special value of a spontaneous sacrifice which ultimately can only be the will to respond to the love of God bestowed upon us.

The value of the good is greater if it is vowed and fulfilled under the vow. Surely one can live according to the three evangelical counsels and practice virtue of a very high order in pursuit of the ideal which is not the object of the vow. But by adding the vow to the effort one adds to the value of the virtues themselves the merit of the special worship of God, so that his acts become in a special way acts of religion. The virtue of religion based on the vow imparts the character of consecration to the gift already presented to God. It becomes a consecrated gift.

So sharply does Thomas stress the consecration arising from the solemn vow of perfect chastity that he arrives at the extreme conclusion that even the pope cannot dispense from it.[190] If he concedes the possibility of such papal dispensation from the vow of chastity annexed to the major orders, it is because the solemn consecration belongs directly to the order and indirectly to the vow of chastity which is annexed to it by the free disposition of the Church. Today we admit that the Church can also dispense from the solemn religious vow of chastity. But this does not detract at all from the cogency of St. Thomas' argument regarding the consecratory nature and power of the public vow itself. Giving one's self totally and forever by this public act to the service of God is to realize fully the essence of the vow. There is the special consecration which accompanies it: any one whose life is consecrated to virginity (or perfect chastity) through a public act of religion, approved and authorized by the Church, is in the fullest sense of the word "consecrated to God."

The religious and moral value of the vow consists primarily in the firmness of the obligation arising from such a promise to God. This firmness is an antidote to human inconstancy, particularly evident in our resolutions which do not oblige by any universal law. The vow erects a barrier against a grossly legalistic mentality which is loath to recognize or accept any norm except that of impersonal universal law. But the vow is concerned not so much with general law viewed impersonally as with God's good pleasure.

Since the vow binds under sin, it creates a wholesome fear of offending God, and thus, when laxness tends to weaken the will to good, it firms our resolution and prevents us from abandoning our sacred enterprise. Already St. Augustine made mention of this point: "Do not therefore regret your vow; rather rejoice that you are no longer free to do that which would have been allowed only for your harm. Proceed therefore intrepidly to your task and complete words with acts: He will help you who accepted your vows. Happy indeed the necessity which impels you toward better things."[191] To vow correctly as well as to fulfill the vow is a grace. This gives the one who vows great confidence. "Do not therefore be slothful in making vows, for you will not fulfill the vows with your own powers!"[192] "He who invites you to make a vow, gives you the grace to fulfill it."[193]

St. Thomas stresses three special sources of the singular value of the vow. First, every act performed in fulfillment of the vow becomes in a special way an act of religion. Second, the vow confirms the will in the good one is to perform in accordance with the vow.[194] Third, through the vow not only the single act but even more so the faculty or power itself, "not merely the fruits but the entire tree with its fruits" is offered to God. This last point does not hold for every vow but surely it does hold pre-eminently of the three vows of religion.

Through the three vows in religion the three great obstacles to holiness are attacked in their very roots: the lust of the eyes through the vow of poverty, the lust of the flesh through the vow of perfect chastity, the pride of life through the vow of obedience.

St. Jerome, St. Bernard, St. Thomas, and others speak of religious profession as a "second baptism" which deletes all guilt and all punishment for past sins.[195] This view derives its plausibility from the very nature of the religious profession. The day of profession is a great occasion of grace, on which one can most readily rise to the heights of perfect submission to God. The very act of profession through the holy vows is a most direct and immediate effort to give one's self entirely to God. On this occasion the grace of baptism and the baptismal vow, by virtue of the cultal power of the baptized, are uniquely renewed. Hence it is altogether probable that one is freed from all guilt and penalty of sin on this holy occasion.

The vows, most particularly the vows of religious profession, have a great value for the ecclesial community. They assure the Church of the necessary stability, promptness of submission, and readiness of engagement in service on the part of her religious communities, societies, and priests. They safeguard the thoroughness and permanence of the work of the Church; here too the tree and its fruits are assured for the divine service.

4. Fulfillment of the Vow

The conditions which are laid down in the vow when it was made must be fulfilled as they were promised. One must carry out a vow as to

time, manner, form, or other conditions, as one has made it. Postponement which endangers fulfillment or lessens value is not permitted. Thus,
for example, one would not be permitted to defer for years on end one's
vowed entry into a convent. Such delay would be a serious infraction of
the vow unless the time of entry was expressly left to one's free discretion.

Real vows, or the promise of real things to God, are attached as a right
to the property of the one who makes the vow. If he himself cannot or
does not carry out the vow in his own lifetime, the obligation of fulfillment encumbers his estate and is passed on to his heirs.[196] But the
obligations binding in justice and piety must be honored first. The Savior
sharply rebuked the teaching of the rabbis according to which one might
justly evade the duty of providing for one's parents by a sacred pledge of
the needed sum as a gift consecrated to God (*Corban*, Mk 7:11ff.). In
judging the obligations arising from vows we follow the rules and norms
of law itself (and the rules of prudence). The vow is a species of "law"
by which the individual, with the sanction of the Church, has bound
himself.[197]

5. Release from Vows

The vow no longer binds if there is such a substantial change of circumstances that the work promised is either morally impossible or ceases
to be the "better" work. In instances in which the fulfillment of the vow
would clearly and evidently prove an obstacle rather than a help to perfection, fulfillment of the vow would be actually forbidden.

In the case of public vows (the vow of religious profession, of clerical
celibacy) only the Church can pronounce judgment. The decision is
never left to the free discretion of the individual, for there is question not
merely of the private good of the one who made the vow but of an
ecclesial act affecting the Church as such. Moreover, we do not have the
right to assume that God will refuse to harken to the humble and penitential appeal for grace necessary to fulfill the vow. Surely he will assist
the individual to continue on the way of the evangelical counsels without
prejudice to his spiritual good, once he has prayerfully chosen this way
with the counsel of his lawful guides and superiors and the approval of
the Church. Still, there are cases in which a serious morbid condition
would advise a release from the vow even after such a decision of the
Church.

One who has culpably brought things to such a pass that he can no longer fulfill his vow or fulfill it properly and adequately (for example, through negligent delay in performing the promised work) is obliged by virtue of the vow itself to do penance for his culpable disregard of the vow. Such is the express doctrine of St. Thomas: "Should one culpably render the fulfillment of his vow impossible, he has a special obligation to do penance for the sin he has thus committed. If, for example, a woman who has vowed perpetual viginity should later on sinfully lose it, she must not only continue to preserve what she is still able to preserve, namely perpetual chastity, she must also do penance for that which she has lost through her sin."[198] This principle is also valid in those instances in which the dispensation from the vow in religion was brought about because of the guilt of one who made the vow and was later freed by dispensation from it.

Release from the bonds of the vow may be effected not merely through altered circumstances, but also by exercise of legitimate power, namely, by annulment, dispensation, and, to a degree, commutation.[199]

a. Annulment (*Irritatio*)

"One who lawfully exercises dominative power over the will of the one who makes the vow [parents over their minor children, religious superiors over their religious subjects within the limits of their rule] can validly and, for a good and sound reason, also licitly invalidate the vow of their subjects with the result that the obligation never will revive."[200] Obviously this power may not exceed the legitimate bounds of dominative authority over the wills of the subjects. This principle is valid apart from any regulation of positive ecclesiastical law. It holds universally that parents have the moral right to direct and guide their children under seven years of age (and to a considerable extent even children who have attained the age of puberty) also in religious and moral decisions such as are in question when vows are made. In all such matters they have the right to direct their children and guide them effectively.

It would not be correct to conclude from the canon just cited above (1312) that superiors who possess dominative authority, by contradistinction to merely domestic authority, have the right to declare all the vows of their subjects invalid directly. Surely husbands do not possess such a right over their wives, nor parents over their children who have reached spiritual majority. At least the right is not theirs by the very nature of their position.

The clearest position on this subject among moral theologians is that of St. Thomas.[201] He bases the competence of superiors to invalidate the vows of their subjects universally on the principle that the subject cannot vow something which lies outside the area of his competence and within the competence of another.[202] "The man who has attained the age of puberty . . . is master over his own acts in regard to things pertaining to his own person; for example, he can oblige himself by a vow to enter religion or he can contract matrimony. But he does not have the power over domestic arrangements (*quantum ad dispositionem domesticam*). Hence he cannot make a final decision by vow regarding such things without the approval of his father."[203] "The subject does not have the power to do what he chooses regarding the things in which he is subject to another, but he depends on the will of another. Therefore he cannot oblige himself strictly by vow regarding those things in which he is a subject without the consent of his superior."[204]

This clear teaching of Saint Thomas destroys the very basis of the notion that the husband can nullify any vow which his wife may make during their marriage.[205] Such a notion does not rest on theological principles but is rather derived from an ancient, absolutistic, and patriarchal concept of marriage now outmoded and outdated. There is an interior domain in the life of any wife which must be totally divorced from the power and authority of her husband. Only in matters of the marital life and, in general, of the common life is there a right of one spouse to invalidate the vow of the other spouse because it limits or restricts his or her rights. We must hold the same for parents in relation to their children who are mentally mature and spiritually developed. Hence the vow of an eighteen year old youth who has unconditionally obliged himself by a sacred pledge to God to enter an order with solemn vows or to perfect and perpetual chastity does not require the consent or ratification of his parents. It is entirely valid, and release from it is not within their competency but must be sought from the Holy See.[206] Hence the teaching that parents or guardians have the right to nullify directly the vows of their children who, though minors, have attained puberty is entirely indefensible, particularly if their vows in no way interfere in the domestic or family life.[207]

Surely the text of Numbers (30:2-17) may not be cited to prove that husband or parents can annul vows concerned with purely interior acts. The text at least in part is only a positive regulation for the people of Israel. And it expressly denies the right of the father of the family and the husband to nullify any vow of wife or children which they had previously explicitly or implicitly ratified. In the light of this text it is difficult to see any basis for the claim that religious superiors or heads of families in the New Testament should have the legal power and authority to invalidate the vows which they have previously confirmed.[208] The text states very clearly and pointedly that the husband (the same would hold for any superior) who should act in such a manner "is responsible for her guilt" (Nm 30:16).

But in the event that any superior should act in this way, we do not concede that he has acted "validly." The contrary is true, for he simply does not possess the competence. However, it is reasonable for the subject to submit insofar as the domestic and familial order is concerned. The force of the vow in consequence of the unjustified intervention may be suspended but the vow itself does not cease to exist. Though God does not expect the subject to disturb domestic peace by carrying out the vow, the husband or father or religious superior, as the case may be, must accept the full responsibility, the burden of the debt, if he arbitrarily interferes with the carrying out of a vow which he once ratified and which is still in force. Obviously our judgment would be entirely different if the subsequent intervention of the one in authority is based on prudent deliberation: such would be the case if there were evidence that the vow had become harmful to the one who made it, to the family, or to others. In such a case the vow which under different circumstances would still remain in force would cease to be something "pleasing to God."

b. Dispensation From Vows

There can be no doubt about the power of the Church to dispense from vows. But she does not exercise this power in her own name. Her jurisdiction in this matter is vicarious, for as it is God Himself who accepts the vow and is therefore the "lawgiver," so the Church can dispense only in His name. For this reason every dispensation from a vow which is granted without sufficient reason is not merely illicit but also invalid, even though it has been granted by the pope himself.

Just reasons for dispensation: the spiritual security and progress of the soul of the individual who has made the vow (for example, the desire to lift the burden of anxiety and scrupulosity or spiritual compulsion, to remove the imminent danger of breaking the vow because of physical or moral weakness); defect of true moral insight at the time the vow was made; and finally the good of the Church. Particularly in dispensing from the vows of religious profession it is not rare that the one dispensed has no just ground for being released from the vow as far as he personally is concerned. But the Church herself may have ample reasons to release him, because in the last instance the welfare of the Church and the religious community itself must be seriously considered. The member of the community may have lost all zeal for the spiritual life; he may be a perpetual malcontent, personally unhappy in his religious life and constantly stirring up disorder and dissatisfaction to the scandal of his fellow religious and people in the world. But all this, rather than being a just reason for release from vows as far as the religious himself is concerned, is merely a very grave reason for him to turn to prayer and penance in an effort to regain his original fervor. But alas, if by his ill-motivated request he instead demands of God and the Church the return of his sacrificial oblation (the vows), once placed so solemnly on the altar of God, then he indeed sins against his vows. But the ecclesiastical superior, for the sake of religious discipline and the honor of the community, is permitted to grant the dispensation. In fact he may even be obliged to do so if there is no hope for the spiritual betterment of the unfortunate religious.

It goes without saying that the superior may not accede to the request for dispensation until all other means to remedy matters have failed. But if all hope for betterment has vanished, he must assume that God can no longer take pleasure in a vow which at best is observed only in a material sense and under constant surveillance and moral constraint.

The one who is dispensed or dismissed is really released from his religious vows since he actually leaves the religious state which was the end and motive of the vows.[209] But one who is released because of the good of the Church and the religious community cannot be excused from the sin of disloyalty. Nor is he dispensed from the obligation of special expiation for his renunciation of the sacrificial offering once made to God. Now that the vow can no longer be observed, he is obliged by the same virtue of religion to do penance which is permanent and, in some measure, corresponds to the meaning and the constant service of the vow he once made but failed to fulfill.[210]

Such expiatory work taking the place of the vow wrested from the altar of sacrifice is particularly binding upon the priest-member of a religious community, who, secularized through his own fault, seeks to carry out his priestly vocation at the altar of sacrifice, in the administration of the sacraments and in preaching the divine word. If he fails in the spirit of penance and does not plan to expiate his past failure, it would be better for him and the Church if he should renounce the sacred ministry altogether. Obviously the case of one who seeks a dispensation because of sound reasons is quite different, though he too should attempt to compensate for what he has lost.

Who has the power to dispense? For a good and just reason the local ordinary can dispense his own subjects; the superior of an exempt clerical religious society can dispense those under his jurisdiction (using the term in a broad sense).[211] In either instance the Church insists that the dispensation may not prejudice the rights of others.[212] The local ordinary and religious superior just referred to also have the power to dispense from vows which are confirmed by oaths and from promissory oaths.[213] Father-confessors of the medicant orders and the religious who share their privileges on this point have the same power in this matter as the bishops for their subjects and can dispense any of the faithful in and outside the sacramental forum.

Vows made previous to religious profession are universally suspended by law for the duration of the time spent in the religious state. This dispensation through law rests on the assumption that the religious vow pre-eminently contains the good of all the other vows, or that the vows of religion plus these other obligations would prove too great a burden or would disturb the religious life.

Dispensation from the vows of religious profession is reserved to the one designated by universal and particular law, usually to the Holy See or the highest superior of the religious institute. The dispensation from a vow to enter an order with solemn vows or from the private vow of perpetual and perfect chastity, provided these vows have been taken unconditionally and after completion of one's eighteenth year, is reserved to the Holy See.[214] Should there be reasonable doubt about any of the conditions or requirements set down in the law, or should any of these conditions not be verified, the vow is not to be considered reserved.

The good work promised in a non-reserved private vow can be commuted into a better or equivalent work by the one who has made the vow.

The right to commute the work into something of lesser value is restricted to those who have the power to dispense from the vow,[215] for the simple reason that such commutation is nothing less than a partial dispensation. Should there be adequate reason for a partial but not for a total dispensation, one may not simply dispense from the vow but must commute the work promised into some other work. In any instance of such commutation there must be a serious effort to do that which is spiritually the most advantageous for the individual concerned.

Practical comment for the confessor: he should forbid the scrupulous to make any kind of vows. In advising them regarding entrance into religion he should be very cautious and reserved, unless there is reasonable hope that they will be cured of their weakness. Penitents who are constantly under compulsion to make vows, whether they actually attempt to make them or think that they have made them, must be told with all clarity that their vows are all null and void. Nor should one permit youths—unless there are altogether singular signs of God's will in this regard—to make the vow of perfect chastity or virginity for life or for a very extended period of time without a long and serious probation. On this point the confessor must respect the opposition of parents who may take exception to such a vow for good and weighty reasons.

IV. THE LORD'S DAY

Our entire life, days of work and days of rest, private life and public, all that belongs to man in his priestly reality must be transformed into the service of God. Since man is priestly by association with Christ, all that he does and has must be made to serve God and to worship God. The task is never completed. It will be fulfilled only in the future in that perfect state which is still to come. The New Jerusalem on which we build in the here and now, but which in its completeness and perfection can come only from heaven, will be "the holy city" in which there is no longer need for a temple; for the "Lord almighty and the Lamb are the temple thereof." "And the city has no need of the sun or the moon to shine upon it. For the glory of God lights it up and the Lamb is the lamp thereof" (Ap 21:2, 22f.). This is the state of perfection and completeness in which everything is an eternal temple service, a worthy hymn of praise, a sinless reflection of love. "There shall be no night there" (Ap 21:26; cf. 22:5). Nothing defiled, nothing accursed shall be there. No lies, no abominations shall be there; but only those "who are written in the book of life of the Lamb" (Ap 21:27; cf. 22:3).

In this earthly time and tide, however, there is still the profane and sinful. And even the Christian cannot escape the persistent danger of being completely immersed into the profane (into that which is not ordered to cult, that which is not encompassed by the virtue of religion) and the sinful, unless holy hours and holy days enter into the rhythm of his time. Surely all the activity and work of the Christian should be worship of God, practice of religion. But only too easily would he fall short of this ideal if holy seasons, holy feasts and ceremonies, cultal days of repose did not encompass everything, encircle everything.

As of now the world has simply not yet become "holy." It is not entirely devoted to the glory of God, which surely is its ultimate purpose. It must first be drawn into the holy cult through "holy places" (houses of God), which are not merely "places of retreat or seclusion," but rather centers, points of departure, in a sense sally ports for the conquest of the world for the glory of God. Houses, farms, towns, and cities which do not have the houses of God for their center, which do not join up with the parish, have no holy center at all and soon fall prey to the profane. The towers soaring up to the heavens carry aloft with them the houses nestling under their pinions in a magnificent *sursum corda* of praise to God.

The whole order of time in this world is taken up with the sacred beginning, for God Himself called it into being; it is caught up by the holy "center of the ages" since Christ appeared. It must look to the "end of the ages," since Christ will draw to Himself all the temporal which has turned to Him. The leavening of all time and its transformation from these cardinal points is the task of Sunday and the Church year. We here speak of the Lord's Day above all as the perpetual mystery of the Pasch, the passing of the Lord through passion and death to resurrection. Insofar as this mystery becomes a reality for us Sunday after Sunday, our whole earthly existence joyfully awaits the Second Coming of Christ.

The central point of all places is Golgotha with the Cross and the altar where the Cross is a constantly renewed reality. The high point of the worship of God, which is sanctification of the world, is the Sacrifice of the Cross and its perpetual renewal in presence through the Holy Eucharist. From this central point all time and every community must be made holy, must be caught up into the praise of God. The sacraments and sacramentals of the Church (the sacramentals amplify and extend the sacra-

ments through sacred usage and custom) are radiations of the sacrifice of
Calvary (the Mass) for the sanctification of every man, every community,
indeed every creature. Through the Sunday and its holy Mass all the
trial and effort of the Christian is immersed into the suffering and death
of Christ. Sunday is repose from all work in the glorification of the
resurrection in which we participate and which shall one day be revealed
in us also on the title of our own toil and trial.

1. Origin and Meaning of the Lord's Day

Sunday is specifically Christian, essentially different from the Jewish
Sabbath, although it is the perfect fulfillment of all that was typified by
the Sabbath. It is not in the first instance a day of repose, although it frees
us from every "servile work" more truly than does the ancient Sabbath
with all its severity. It frees us from sin and the perilous snares of earthly
things and permits us to look with more perfect assurance to the eternal
participation in the blessed repose of the Lord in glory. What makes
Sunday the Lord's Day is the Eucharist, the presence of the resurrected
Savior among us in commemoration of His death. Sunday, "the day
after the Sabbath," is eternally marked and consecrated by the resurrection
of Christ (Mk 16:9; Mt 28:1). Since the days of the Apostles Christians
have foregathered "on the first day of the week" "for the breaking of
bread" (Acts 20:7) and to celebrate the day in the community of love at
the banquet of love (cf. 1 Cor 16:2). Not on Thursday (some scholars
hold that the actual day was Tuesday), the day of the Institution, but
very definitely on Sunday, "on the day of the Lord," the early Christian
communities already commemorated the death of the Lord through the
Eucharistic celebration; for through the Eucharistic celebration of His
death the resurrected Christ is among us. "For as often as you shall eat
this bread and drink the cup, you proclaim the death of the Lord, until
he comes" (1 Cor 11:26). The Eucharist is the "Lord's Supper" (1 Cor
11:20). Note that when Paul speaks of the "Lord," he always has in mind
the One resplendent in the glory of the resurrection, Who sits at the right
of the Father.

The Apostles were mindful that they "ate and drank with him after
he had risen from the dead" (Acts 10:41; cf. 1:4; Mk 16:14; Lk 24:42f.).
Memory of the Lord's Supper and of these apparitions of the risen
Savior only too readily would suggest to the Apostles that they should

commemorate the mystery of His death and resurrection "on the first day of the week." The evangelist John particularly stresses that Jesus appeared to the Apostles on the very day of the resurrection, "that same day, the first of the week" (Jn 20:19). "After eight days" (Jn 20:26), therefore on the same day of the week, He again appeared to them, this time with Thomas in the group. All this would seem to indicate that Jesus Himself determined the rhythm of the Sunday recurrence for the celebration of His resurrection, or at least He intimated it.

The Holy Spirit was also sent on Sunday. Should we not say that the promises of Maundy Thursday were fulfilled on Pentecost: "I will not leave you orphans; I will come to you. Yet a little while and the world no longer sees me. But you see me. . . . The Advocate, the Holy Spirit, whom the Father will send in my name, he will teach you all things" (Jn 14:18–26). On that Pentecost the Apostles conceived in an altogether new way what the resurrection of the Lord means in the history of the world and how He is present among us in the vast interlude between the resurrection and His Second Coming. Now they recalled the word which the Lord spoke at the promise of the Eucharist: "What then if you should see the Son of Man ascending where he was before? It is the spirit that gives life; the flesh profits nothing" (Jn 6:63f.).

When St. John wrote the Apocalypse the concept of the "Lord's Day" was already fixed. He writes: "I was in the spirit on the Lord's day" (Ap 1:10). And the risen Lord appeared to him in all the radiance of His glory and said: "I was dead, and behold, I am living forevermore" (Ap 1:18). This apparition in the glory of resurrection sanctions the Apostles' choice of Sunday: it shall always be the day on which we celebrate with the risen Christ His sacrificial death and the triumph of His resurrection, "until He comes again," and cry out with deepest yearning, "Come, Lord Jesus!" (Ap 22:20; cf. 1 Cor 16:22).

In the early Christian Church the character of the Lord's Day, as that of the resurrection, is very apparent. Tertullian calls the day simply "The Lord's day of the resurrection" (*dies dominica resurrectionis*).[216] The Greek Fathers use the same term for the feast of Easter and for each Sunday of the year, "the day of resurrection" (*anastásimos*). Jerome gives the sense of an unbroken apostolic tradition in sharp words: "The Lord created all the days, but the other days may belong to the Jews, the heretics, and even the pagans. But Sunday, the day of the resurrection, is our day. It is called the day of the Lord because on this day the Lord

returned victoriously to His Father."[217] Similar is the thought of St.
Augustine: "The day of the Lord is not revealed to the Jews but to the
Christians through the resurrection of Christ. And therefore we celebrate
it."[218]

Since Sunday is essentially the commemoration and celebration of the
resurrection of Christ and our participation in it through baptism, it is
basically a feast of joy. "We pass the eighth day on which the Lord arose
from the dead, in joy."[219] "Whoever is sad on this day commits sin."[220]
In order to stress the joyous character of Sunday the early Church forbade
kneeling at prayer on this day. "We celebrate the day of the Lord as a
day of joy, because Christ arose from the dead on this day; hence according to our tradition we are not to kneel."[221]

Among the Greek Fathers the usual designation for Sunday was
either *day of the resurrection* or *The Lord's Day,* and among the Latin
Fathers simply *The Lord's Day.* (This is still the usual term in the Ro-
mance languages.) Nevertheless at times even the Fathers took over the
name in use among the pagans, *Day of the Sun* (Sunday), in order to associate it with the commemoration of the resurrection. Thus, for example,
Maximus of Turin: "The day of the Lord is solemn and worthy of veneration, for on this day our Savior arose and shone as the sun after He had
dispelled the darkness of hell in the splendor of the resurrection. Therefore
among the children of this world the day bears the name *Day of the Sun,*
for Christ, the risen Savior, the Sun of righteousness, enlightens it."[222] The
traditional explanation, dating from the patristic age, is succinctly stated
by St. Thomas: "The Church chose this day; for she wished to have us
keep in true remembrance the resurrection of Christ to which we must
conform our lives."[223] Thus he stresses the day as commemorating first of
all the resurrection of the Lord.

The Christians keep holy the Sunday not merely in remembrance of
a past event in the history of salvation but in the celebration of a present
salvific mystery of the death and the resurrection in the mystical renewal
of the eternal Sacrifice. In the unity of the Mystical Body the risen Christ
is truly present and is offered for us. With Him the Mystical Body offers
and is offered as He leads it to the glorious festive assembly of the
heavenly Jerusalem. On this day it honors and glorifies Him above all
through this manifestation of unity. Already in the Acts of the Apostles
(20:7) the Christians are spoken of as gathering for the breaking of bread
on the first day of the week. Beginning with Ignatius, disciple of the

Apostle John, the Fathers constantly admonish the Christians to maintain this bond of unity and to assemble regularly. The *Didache* commands: "Assemble on the day of the Lord for the breaking of the bread and thanksgiving after you have first confessed your sins in order that your sacrifice may be pure."[224] The *Didascalia* stresses the same point: "Order and admonish the people to gather faithfully, so that no one weakens the unity of the Church, that no one remains aloof and thus robs the Body of Christ of one of its members."[225]

By renunciation of sin and through unity and community in the commemoration of the death of Christ we participate in the joy of the risen Christ and await in faith "the resurrection of the dead and the life of the world to come" (*Credo*).

In addition to the joyful celebration of the resurrection and the mystery of unity and love in the festive assembly, tradition never fails to stress the eschatological orientation of the Lord's Day. The thought is beautifully expressed in the classical lines of Augustine: "As on that seventh day God shall rest, having us rest with Him for we are that seventh day. . . . This seventh day will be our Sabbath. Its end will not be evening, but the day of the Lord, that eternal octave which is sanctified by the resurrection of Christ, the eternal repose not only of the spirit but also of the body. There we shall be free and we shall see; we shall see and shall love; we shall love and praise. This is end without end. For we have no other goal than to attain to the Kingdom which shall never end."[226]

2. Sanctification through the Sacrifice of Christ and the Church

a. Sacrifice of the Cross and the Christian Life

Sacrifice is the most perfect expression of the virtue of religion. We have no better way to show God that we recognize Him as our Creator and Sovereign Lord. The man who is conscious of the meaning of his act when he offers sacrifice has discovered the ultimate meaning of his life. Like a flash of lightning it looms up before him as adoration of God, as submission of all that he has, all that he does, all that he is, for the glorification of Him who has given it to him.

The symbolical meaning and value of the visible sacrificial offering lies in its power to express the interior spirit of sacrifice and submission of the person. The sacrifice of first fruits which prevailed among all the primitive peoples is the oblation of that which is first (fruits or first-born) and best to God, in order to show that it and all else comes from God and therefore in all instances must be given back to Him by His creatures as a return gift of adoration and love whether in form of sacrificial oblation or through a grateful and worthy use.

Among all peoples, most particularly among the Israelites, the type and form of sacrifice reveals its expiatory and propitiatory significance: man groaning under the burden of his sins acknowledges by his holocausts in which the whole victim is consumed, and above all by bloody sacrifices (the life is offered, and among the pagans in some cases a human life) that he deserves death because of his sins. But God graciously accepts in his sacrifice the very confession of sin and frail will as expiation and accordingly grants pardon.

Surpassing all human conception is the fulfillment of all sacrificial offering and inner spirit of sacrificial oblation among the peoples of antiquity in the holy Sacrifice of Christ on the Cross. Here on Calvary that which is noblest and best, the flower of the human race, is offered. The divine *agápe* ("God so loved the world that he gave his only-begotten Son": Jn 3:16) in all its rich abundance bestowed upon man makes possible the fulfillment of his profoundest need and yearning for sacrifice to God. Here God's noblest gift of love (the *agápe* in the person of the beloved Son) is offered by creation as its sacrifice to the heavenly Father. Christ as our Head offers Himself as the Victim vicariously representing all of mankind to the Father, as grateful tribute of praise to the triune God, as condign satisfaction for all sins of men. He offers Himself in petition for all the supernatural gifts, pleading so eloquently that the Father cannot resist His appeal. He offers Himself in praise, satisfaction, and petition for the salvation of the human race, in order that it may again become an acceptable offering to God and again capable of offering to its heavenly Creator and Father truly worthy adoration and praise.

The Sacrifice on the Cross endows us with unbounded love for God the Father and our neighbor. As gift of God's love for us it demands in return our love for God and man, even for sinners. In His Sacrifice on the Cross Christ manifests the new law of love which is taken up entirely with the loving majesty of God and at the same time is mankind's response to the heavenly Father. Here the "new law" of unbounded love is both the sundering of the law of mere human justice bounded by the potentialities and limitations of human fulfillment and the transcendent fulfillment of divine justice with infinite mercy. Here is the new law in whose fulfillment love and obedience mingle. The Sacrifice of the Cross is the culmination of the high-priestly life of Christ offered as Victim of love and obedience unto the honor and glory of the Father and the salvation of all the brethren.

The fullest and deepest realization of the imitation of Christ is made possible through the Sacrifice of the Cross in which mankind is redeemed and freed from the servitude of Satan and reconciled to God with the dignity of children of God. The Cross is the supreme manifestation of the loving power of the Master to draw all hearts to Himself. As He wins every sympathetic heart by the power of His love, so He speaks to them in compelling accents of His holy life which is the Master's pattern for all His disciples. Calvary is the wellspring for the whole life of the imitation with all its force and vigor, its value and merit. Through the Sacrifice of the Cross the life of the imitation becomes the hymn of love and praise for the Father in heaven.

The Sacrifice of the Cross teaches us the spirit and pattern of the imitation: Christian life is imitation of the Crucified; it is following His example in trial, suffering, humility. "If any one wishes to come after me, let him deny himself, and take up his cross, and follow me" (Mt 16:24; cf. 10:38). Christian morality stands in the shadow of the Cross with all the deadly earnestness of partnership with the Crucified. But precisely because the Christian life has its roots in the Sacrifice of Calvary, it also reflects the splendor and dignity of priesthood. Union with the Crucified means bond with His priesthood and the supreme sacrificial act on the Cross. To follow Christ on the way to the Cross for the consummation of His priestly Sacrifice, to be partner with Him on this priestly path, we must be ingrafted in His sacrificial power and sacrificial dignity through holy baptism. The baptized Christian who humbly and loyally accepts his cross day by day submits freely to the spirit of sacrifice and merges his sentiments with the sacrificial sentiments of the High Priest, Jesus Christ. He is united with the High Priest of Calvary for the fulfillment of the priestly assignment which flows from assimilation to Him (particularly through the sacramental character of baptism, confirmation, and holy order).

Such participation in sacrificial oblation means utter renunciation of sin. Just as Christ died for sin once and for all, so also those who have been ingrafted through baptism into this tremendous reality of Christ's act and who freely grow in it, renounce sin. Once and for all and in deadly earnest they say *no* to sin (Rom 6). In an incomprehensible solidarity Christ took upon Himself the burden of us all in order to lead us to the beatifying fellowship of love with God. So also His true disciples by virtue of the law of the spirit, which endows us with participation in the life and manner of Christ, break the chains of egoism and solidarity of perdition (Rom 8:1ff.). They wage a war in unity and solidarity against sin in their own hearts and in their surroundings.

In the light of Calvary the following of Christ means readiness to expiate for one's sins and the sins of our brethren by daily bearing the Cross (cf. Col 1:24). The Cross brings home to the disciple the dreadful seriousness of sin and its unholy power in the world, which power he is made to realize can be overcome only through partnership in the death of Christ and the power of His resurrection. Once he has associated himself with the priesthood of His Master and sought to imitate His life, he is bathed with the waters of divine justice, borne aloft by the divine *agápe* to which he responds by a readiness for expiation for sin and a fruitfulness in the growth of love.

The Master whom we are to follow is the High Priest sacrificing Himself with infinite love on the Cross. He is Love crucified. Therefore the imitation is imitation in Christ's priesthood; it is following the "priestly way," the way of the Cross, the way of utter love. This is to say that our bond with Christ is the bond of worship of the heavenly Father, of divine cult. This implies partnership in offering, in being offered, partnership with the High Priest and the sacrificial Lamb, Jesus Christ. It demands a readiness to offer ourselves and permit ourselves to be offered, as Christ offered Himself and permitted Himself to be offered, manifesting the loving majesty of God to His brethren.

The Sacrifice of Calvary is the culmination of the life of Christ and the abundant wellspring of all the graces of the imitation. For this reason the whole Christian life must be viewed from the lofty heights of Calvary and enriched through the graces flowing from its Cross. Christ began His life with the sacred Introit of the Sacrifice of the Cross: "Sacrifice and oblation thou wouldst not, but a body thou hast fitted to me—Then said I, 'Behold, I come . . . to do thy will, O God' " (Heb 10:5ff.). Sacrificial submission marked His whole life to His last dying breath on Calvary. Wherefore the life of His disciple must be orientated as that of the Master: it must look to death in constant willingness to offer one's self, to live totally for God and the brethren.

Christian morality, rooted in Calvary and flowing from its graces, is not first of all self-perfection but rather self-submission, cult, glorification of God in brotherly unity and solidarity. The very idiom of the sacrificial sign leaves no room for the barren concept of personal profit. In the liturgy of sacrifice everything aspires upward to God, is utterly intent on Him, adoringly and jubilantly sinks to its knees before Him. Even the cry of petition in the Holy Sacrifice is a yearning for holiness of life, flowing from the divine grace and lived for the divine honor and glory in union with the risen Christ.

For Christ sacrificial death in honor of the Father was the path to His own exaltation. Similarly the Christian must find his sole hope in the way of self-denial and submission, the way of life with a view to death, but with the radiant assurance of hope rooted in the death and resurrection of the risen Christ.

b. Renewal of Calvary in the Mass and the Imitation

Not only is the Sacrifice of Calvary pattern and obligatory norm of genuine discipleship, it is also the never failing source of the graces which enable the disciple to follow the Master. Ceaselessly the graces of Calvary flow into the souls of men in holy Mass and the sacraments. They are the focal points, the area of concentration in which Christ transforms and sanctifies the whole of Christian morality and summons it to the glorious service in the divine honor. The Mass is the inexhaustible fountain of all assimilation to Christ. Only through the efficacy of the Holy Eucharist, center of all the sacraments, and through vital participation in its tremendous drama (in its life-giving movement) does the disciple truly enter into the innermost depths of the life, death, and resurrection of Christ.

The celebration of the Lord's Day through commemoration of the sacrificial love of Christ in His paschal mystery, a love which constantly offers itself and constantly triumphs, uniquely represents and embraces us in our situation as earthly pilgrims. Our gaze extends from the resurrection to the Second Coming, but we never lose sight of the commemoration of the death. Our cult consists in the Sacrifice of Good Friday and the jubilation of Easter Sunday. From the force of this cult we obtain readiness for sacrifice and the assurance of victory in our assignment which is to sanctify all domains of life and gather them up in a tribute of praise of God. We build on the victory of Christ insofar as we enter the sanctuary of His death and sprinkle ourselves with the Blood of the New Covenant and give our adoring and prayerful *yes* to the sacrifices destined for us.

We are baptized in the death, in the resurrection of Christ, and in joyous anticipation of the great day of the Lord's Coming. But we are still far from possessing the intoxicating presentiment of blessed repose. The resurrection of Christ, our baptism, the Sunday celebration are for us still a beginning and pledge: Sunday after Sunday we "proclaim the death of the Lord" (1 Cor 11:26) and by force of His death and resurrection we die daily to the old man and proclaim the universal dominion of God and the Lamb.

The living fountain of sacramental piety is the Holy Eucharist. It is the center of the whole spiritual being and formation of sacramental man, for the sacraments and all supernatural efficacy revolve about it. The inexhaustible riches of the mystery of salvation which we encounter there is unfolded before us in the mysteries celebrated in the Church year. All the sacred days which commemorate our salvation through Christ, all the feast days of the Church are celebration of the sacrificial death of Christ leading us to the final resurrection and the great day of the Lord's Second Coming. The Eucharistic Sacrifice bears in itself the fulness of all feasts, sombre and joyous. All the festal mysteries are caught up into the high-priestly devotion of Christ, into its continuous oblation which begins with His sacrificial prayer at the Incarnation: "Behold, I come to do thy will, O God" (Heb 10:9) and culminates in that final commitment of all things into the hands of the Father so that God will be all in all (1 Cor 15:28).

Even the Old Testament Sabbath gave us an inkling of this. It presented to man the vast panorama of human history, spanned by a luminous arch extending from the very morning of creation to the blessed repose in God. If the Old Testament Sabbath was a pledge of this sacred rest which would be fulfilled in the end of time, then surely the celebration of the Eucharistic Sacrifice Sunday after Sunday and in concert with the rhythm of the Church's calendar in a very mysterious but altogether true and real sense ushers us into the sacred salvific work of Christ and the Church, and bears us on toward the final revelation and consummation of all things in God.

The entire week must be viewed in the light of the meaning of the Lord's Day. Even the work day of the Christian must be sanctified and become a holy day (*feria*). To sanctify the work day as well as Sunday through participation in Holy Mass and the reception of Holy Communion is to place the stamp of *sanctification* on our Christian life. The entire week is seen in its relation to the obligation to sanctify all the days in the spirit of the Lord's Day. But if this is not possible, then at least the Lord's Day with its saving Sacrifice must give the tone to the whole week with all its tasks. The whole week must be sanctified by Sunday.

In the foregoing pages we frequently stressed the New Law of the life in Christ Jesus in relation to grace and sacraments, as expressed preeminently in the gifts of grace and the commitments of the sacraments with their source in Calvary and the Mass. It follows that we must now point out, at least summarily, how the whole of the spiritual life is formed and fashioned by the sacraments through their very relation to the Eucharistic Center.

The Sunday celebration resounds with the paschal jubilation of the baptized, with the hope of Christian victory yearning in anticipation of the consummation of all things at the end of the world. But it is also the grace-bearing assignment from God and the *yes* of Christianity to the transformation of life through these mysteries of salvation. The Eucharist is the Gift and Feast of Love (the *agápe*) of the sacrificial Lamb shedding His Blood for us and also our close partnership with the priestly sentiment of Christ offering Himself in love. It means our voluntary and intimate association in the death of Christ, our ceaseless readiness to give ourselves over to the transforming power of Christ, so that through the Eucharist the tremendous reality is verified: "It is now no longer I that live, but Christ lives in me" (Gal 2:20).[227]

Christ instituted the sacrifice of the Mass so that His oblation would become our offering and that of the universal Church. But holy Mass is our Eucharist (our tribute of praise, prayer of praise, thanksgiving, expiation) only if He who is the Eucharist lives in us. In baptism He gives us not only a share in His life but also the stamp of His priesthood; in confirmation, a richer and more vigorous life and a new priestly seal which is enforcement of the mark of baptism with the special qualification for vigorous apostolic assignment. The sacrificial Victim of the Eucharist nourishes the supernatural life in us and imparts Christ's own sacrificial spirit. The Eucharistic graces draw us to Christ in the most intimate and vital union of sacrificial life in which we are both victims, the lambs of sacrifice offered to God, and the priests who offer.

Even though only the ordained priest can offer the sacrifice through consecration (transubstantiation) of the gifts (of the people) in the name and person of Christ, the people truly participate. The entire priestly race of Christians, the "holy priesthood," the "royal priesthood," the "holy nation" (1 Pt 2:5, 9) not only offers the gifts for the actual consecration but also actively shares in offering the Lamb of God and with it all other things as "spiritual sacrifices acceptable to God through Jesus Christ" (1 Pt 2:5). Only because the baptized, and even more so the confirmed, are truly partners in offering the chalice filled with the Blood of the New Covenant, are all their good works "spiritual sacrifices."[228] The bond which links the baptized with the offering of the sacrificial Blood makes them and all their works sacrificial.

Only if Mass is in truth the center of the Christian life,[229] do baptism, confirmation, and holy order attain their true fulness; only then does the Eucharist receive fitting honor and come to full fruitfulness; then do we ourselves arise above the lowliness of our nature. Only with the holy Mass as spiritual center can our entire life be wrested from the narrowness and pettiness of self and elevated and transformed for the divine praise in sacrificial service in the Church and for the brethren.

Even illness and death are sources of force and splendor for the Christian through the anointing in the Holy Spirit; for in extreme unction illness and death are totally taken over into the priestly grandeur of the passion, death, and resurrection of Christ.

Not merely the "consecratory" sacraments are to be looked upon as cultal and sacrificial. Any one who fails to see penance in the light of Calvary, from which it derives, and in the light of the Mass, toward which it is essentially ordered, fails to grasp its staggering depth and its cultal blessing. Penance is the conciliatory power of the sacrificial Blood and, for the well-disposed recipient, the tremendous earnestness of Christ in saying *no* to sin. It gives release from all that is "unholy" so that the pardoned sinner can again freely enter the sacred orbit of sacrifice through which he directs his whole life to God.

Marriage and family (the tiniest but most important society) are sanctified by their own special sacrament and thereby become a community in sacred sojourn with Christ, a sacrificial community in the Church (the family is a "church in miniature"). Just as the power and holiness of marriage derives from Calvary's Sacrifice, so the family must be centered in the Eucharist for the formation of its life in the service of the Church and the honor of God through Christ.

To celebrate the Eucharist means to join in the alliance of love between

Christ and the Church. Since sacramental marriage is modeled on this same covenant and signifies grace-giving participation in it, the family too is a salvific community nourished on Eucharistic piety. It takes over, first of all, the Eucharistic education of the offspring, which is preparation for the reception of the Sacrament of the Altar at the appropriate time. The child's reception of the Sacrament should ordinarily be in the company of its father and mother who share the Sacred Banquet with their family.

"Mass as center" invests our Christian life with the ineffably exalted seriousness of the "theology of the Cross"[230] and commits us to the uncompromising struggle against sin. But it likewise brings to us the jubilant hymn of the eternal liturgy breaking through the barrier of time. The Sacrifice of Calvary, which is the vital source of this heavenly Sacrifice, constantly turns us toward it and bears us on into its celestial orbit.

c. Sunday: Day of Fellowship in the Breaking of Bread

"Mass as center" means above all a life with the Church, for the vital center of the Church is the Eucharistic Sacrifice: this is the whole Sacrifice of Christ and of His Holy Bride, the Church. *Sentire cum ecclesia* (a bond of feeling with the Church and work in union with her and for her) presumes a partnership in her life.

Participation in the celebration of the holy Eucharist and reception of the sacraments is never exclusively private sanctification (surely it is not simply "self-sanctification"). The truth is, it is always sanctification through God and for God for the community which in baptism embraces a sanctified member, in confirmation a "lay apostle," in holy order an official celebrant of the liturgy. As the Mass is the Church's Sacrifice, so the sacraments are the sacraments of the Church, to whom they are entrusted for the salvation and blessing of the community.

Not without reason is the celebration of the Lord's Sacrifice perfected in the sacrificial Meal which symbolizes both life and unity of the faithful. Christ offered Himself on the Cross "that he might gather into one the children of God who were scattered abroad" (Jn 11:52). He was offered for the destruction of sin with its disruption, for He "was delivered up for our sins, and rose again for our justification" (Rom 4:25). He was sacrificed to reconcile us with the Father and unite us in one great family, "that of the two he might create in himself one new man, and make peace and reconcile both in one body to God by the cross, having slain the enmity in himself" '(Eph 2:15f.). This unity in community is wrought in us by the Holy Spirit whom the risen Savior gives to us (Eph 2:18, 22); it is wrought in the essential principle of unity which is the Eucharistic Body of the resurrected Savior. Thus Sunday is the day of unity and of community, the day of "communion of the breaking of the bread" (Acts 2:42; 20:7).

The foundational sign and symbol in which the Church as community is rooted is the Mass with the sacred community Banquet. "As essential assembly of the Christian community, the Mass characterizes, postulates, and completes with ever increasing perfection the unity which Christ willed and merited."[231] "And the bread that we break, is it not the partaking of the body of the Lord? Because the bread is one, we though many, are one body, all of us who partake of the one bread" (1 Cor 10:16f.). As the old covenant was founded in the blood of sacrifice (Heb 9:18f.), so in the new the bond of covenant and holy community is the sacrificial Blood and the sacrificial Banquet which is the Eucharist.

The Fathers of the Church and the great theologians never tire of stressing this grace and this mission of the Eucharistic celebration, which is also rightly called *communion* (that is community). The blissful experience of faith lived in the liturgy breathes through these words of Augustine: "O mystery of piety! O sign of unity! O bond of love!"[232] No less striking are the words of Thomas in his usual sober accents; "What the sacrament immediately signifies and effects, is the unity of the Mystical Body . . . it is love."[233]

As efficacious signs the sacraments signify what they effect and effect what they signify. Immediate goal and purpose of the Eucharist is the unity and community of the Body of Christ. Such is its sacramental sign. Or, in the words of some writers, it is "the unity of the faithful people," the People of God! Consequently it is imperative that the celebration of Mass attain this end and purpose, bear this gift to the people of God and bring this essential mission to fulfillment and realization. One who wills the true realization of Christian love and community spirit, the Christian formation of a closed community in the apostolate and the common resistance to the collective forces of evil, one who wills that love and community be vital assignment of grace truly experienced, rather than naked and futile imperative, must make every effort to realize the true meaning of Holy Mass. He should devote all his strength and talent to give to the celebration of Sunday Mass its full force of expression as a salutary work of the community, as joyous celebration of the "community of the breaking of the bread."[234]

That the Christian Sunday should descend to the level of mere fulfillment of a commandment to attend Mass is one of the saddest tragedies in the whole domain of spiritual life. And such a misfortune cannot be averted if the Eucharistic celebration is choked in dead formalism, if it is becalmed by an atmosphere of individualism or the fashion of private preference, or if the faithful are to be merely "entertained" with baroque Latin choirs. Sunday must again become the day of the Lord with all the joyous experience of the community joined in the breaking of the Bread.

No one may doubt that every Mass, even though it be celebrated privately by priest and single server, bears the essential and perpetual character of community. It is "community of the faithful with Christ and of Christians with one another." But the very nature of the Eucharist as "a truly living and wonderful symbol of the unity of the Church," suggests that the faithful celebrate with the priest "in common petition and prayers."[235]

The immemorial practice of concelebration of the Eucharist by priests of the Oriental rites undoubtedly is a more adequate expression of the ideal of the Eucharist as sign of unity among the people of God and the priestly generation than is the celebration of many priests individually at the same place and time. In fact, in the multiple celebration there is often the disturbance and distraction due to the restriction of space, or the saying of Mass entirely in subdued whispers. But the law in vigor today does not permit the individual priests who may be present in numbers at community spiritual exercises or other events to dispense with the individual celebration of Mass in order to participate actively with the other faithful through reception of Holy Communion. Positing the gradual awakening of a new sense of spiritual community and a deeper understanding of the Eucharist as a grace-giving and obligatory sign of unity and harmony, the greater part of the priests of the Western rite may soon be ready for real concelebration. Then changed attitudes should justify our confidence that the Holy See may look favorably upon an appeal for modification of the present practice.

At the celebration of the sacrificial Banquet the Church directs to all her children the invitation of Christ: "Take and eat" (Mt 26:26), "Do this in remembrance of me" (1 Cor 11:24). "For this reason the Council of Trent . . . has earnestly exhorted 'the faithful when they attend Mass, to communicate not only by a spiritual communion but also by a sacramental one.' "[236]

Pius XII, in agreement with Benedict XIV before him, proposed the ideal that the faithful receive the sacred hosts which have been consecrated in the very Mass in which they participated.[237] Although for good reasons the Church permits Holy Communion to be distributed outside of Mass, nevertheless she urges the faithful not to disregard the liturgy, and as long as there is no reasonable difficulty, to do everything by which the living unity of the Mystical Body is manifested more clearly at the altar. Thus the actions of the faithful reflect the unity of the Mystical Body.[238]

Once we have referred to these clear and emphatic utterances of ecclesiastical authority, must we still repeat that the Christian community has a sacred right, fully documented in these statements, that the Bread be not merely broken but also distributed at the celebration of the Sacred Banquet? What is to become of the "community of the breaking of bread" and of Sunday itself if the pastor or priest in charge of souls refuses to distribute Holy Communion in the parochial Mass because he finds the task "disturbing"? And should it be true that the faithful do not make any request to receive Holy Communion in accordance with their undoubted right, because they have not been enlightened by proper instruction nor brought to a living realization through fruitful celebration of this great sign of unity in community, then there is another right to be considered: the right to kindly and patient instruction.

Not only the Eucharistic Bread but also the bread of the divine word must be distributed to the faithful assembly on Sunday (Acts 20:7). The Logos, the Second Person who is the Word of the Father, gives both to us through the Church. He it is who says that man lives from the Eucharistic Bread (Jn 6:51) and also "by every word that comes forth from the mouth of God" (Mt 4:4). The group acceptance of the word of God creates the spirit of community. It is a part of the correct preparation for participation in the celebration of the Holy Sacrifice, which is the most vital communal profession of the faith, and therefore must share in the nature and form of the liturgical celebration.[239] Faith, basis and root of the whole supernatural life, must wither away unless it is constantly nourished on the word of God: for "faith . . . depends on hearing" (Rom 10:17). The Eucharist as "Mystery of Faith" (*mysterium fidei*) means the Word of God come to us and the response of faith made by the believing community. "For with the heart a man believes unto justice, and with the mouth profession of faith is made unto salvation" (Rom 10:10).

The entire Lord's Day should bear the stamp of the "community of the breaking of bread" and be made a day of loving fellowship. Paul exhorts the Christians of Corinth to "put aside" some gift for those in need "on the first day of the week," that is, on the day of the community celebration of the Eucharist (1 Cor 16:2). In the early Church the day of the breaking of bread was also the day of the *agápe,* the love feast, at which rich and poor should mingle in loving fellowship. The day of Christian love, it was the day on which the lonely and sick of the community were visited and consoled by their fellow Christians.

d. Specific Obligations regarding Sunday Mass

As already noted, much more is involved in the observance of the Sunday rest than a mere law of the Church. *A fortiori* the obligation to assist at holy Mass is not merely a matter of ecclesiastical law. It is more than a requirement of natural law that a certain time be reserved for divine worship. Here we are concerned with the very heart of the Christian life, with the necessary union with Jesus Christ our High Priest and the holy community which is His Church, a union which, growing constantly stronger and deeper, must be solemnly proclaimed to the world. The Sunday Mass is an invitation—and surely no offer could be more exalted and sublime—coming from the loving Savior and His holy cultal fellowship in the New Jerusalem. We are asked to participate in the heavenly worship. "He who is of God hears the word of God" (Jn 8:47; cf. 1 Jn 4:6), the word of love. There is something of "not hearing" in clinging to the bare minimum requirement of the law.

This very negative attitude suggests a serious responsibility on the part of priests. Some, on the one hand, will stress with unrelenting repetition that there is a grave obligation to attend Mass on Sundays, but, on the other, do precious little to vitalize the Eucharistic service. In fact they may oppose with open hostility all efforts made by others in this direction. Such priests incur greater guilt than the marginal Catholics who simply refuse to believe they have a Sunday obligation—or to be disturbed by it! Why should God require that they participate in the Sunday Mass about which they understand nothing, at which they feel the priest does not welcome them or consider them seriously. In fact they carry away the impression, when they do attend, that the priest proceeds with words and acts at Mass as though it meant no more than the performance of another task. Nevertheless, they are not permitted to ignore the law. Here we must clearly deliniate the minimum requirements regarding participation in Sunday and Holy Day Mass:

1. Every Christian who has reached the age of seven years is obliged to participate in the celebration of an entire Mass on all Sundays and feast days of obligation.[240]

This obligation is by its nature grave (*ex genere suo gravis*). Anyone who is knowingly and inexcusably absent from the entire Mass or from a notable part of it, thereby neglecting the Eucharistic grace and duty, commits a grave sin. A part is notable either because of its quantity (a third part of a full Mass rite would certainly be notable) or because of its relation to the essential sacrificial action (thus, the Consecration itself, the Canon of the Mass, or the Communion with its preparatory prayers). There is dispute over the gravity of the sin of absenting one's self culpably from the first part of the Mass, the so-called Mass of the Catechumens, which extends from the very beginning to the Gospel and *Credo* inclusive. Surely it reveals a woeful lack of reverence to attempt to participate in the celebration of the all-holy mystery of the altar and yet scorn the preparatory prayer and instruction service whose whole purpose is to dispose one for the reverential assistance at the Mass of the faithful. Still, if one comes late because of a degree of negligence or slovenliness rather than deliberately or of set purpose, the neglect is not readily assumed to be grave.

One is obliged to attend one integral Mass and is not permitted to add fragments of Masses to form one Mass. But should one have attended the Consecration and Communion of one Mass and supplied the remainder from another, he should not be disturbed in conscience, particularly if this was inadvertent and not deliberately planned.

The rite of the celebrating priest in no wise affects the precept. Every Catholic is permitted to attend Mass in any of the Eastern Catholic rites and also to receive Holy Communion in both species.[241]

A pastor who refuses to admit a seven-year-old child to Holy Communion while at the same time insisting on the grave obligation of attending Sunday Mass under pain of mortal sin, is himself in danger of mortal sin. The law of the Church requiring that children of seven years or more attend holy Mass on Sundays and Holy Days is not separable from the law requiring that they receive their First Holy Communion at the proper time. The contradictory attitude of directors in these matters must bear some of the responsibility that many Christians from early youth learn to look upon attendance at Mass as exclusively or at least principally a legal obligation and burden.

2. *To participate* at holy Mass means to be present bodily. Surely to follow a broadcast or telecast of the Mass devoutly on radio or television may prove very fruitful for shut-ins and to a degree serve as a consoling substitute for actual presence at the Sacrifice. But the obligation to participate with the visible community assembled about the altar is not fulfilled by following the sacred ceremonies transmitted over the airways. As to the Sunday sermon, under certain circumstances one might do better by listening to a good sermon over radio or television rather than to a mediocre effort in church, provided no scandal is involved. Though there is no strict obligation in law regarding the sermon preached at the Sunday Mass, the complete and perfect celebration of the Lord's Day calls for liturgical proclamation and instruction of the community in attendance at the preaching of the word.

It is obvious that Christians who openly tarry outside the doors of the church, gossiping and entertaining one another, while Mass is going on in the church cannot even claim to be bodily present at Mass, not to speak of spiritually participating in it. They not only fail to attend the Sunday Mass but are guilty of irreverence and scandal as well. The case is quite different for those who cannot find room in the church or who for some other valid reason follow the sacred ceremonies devoutly outside the house of God. Both in spirit and in its bodily manifestation they participate in the celebration together with the community in the church.

Naturally most appropriate for the Mass, as the divine service of the community of God's people, is that form of participation which is the maximum expression of the unity of priest and people in and with the one High Priest, Jesus Christ. This is manifested by community unison in prayer, chant, response, common attitudes and postures such as standing and kneeling. But even more fundamental is the sentiment of love embracing all the Church and her members. "Man for man, you should become a choir which resounds in perfect harmony of spirit as it takes up the divine melody and in one voice chants the praises of God the Father through Jesus Christ."[242]

Excommunicates, those who are "shut off from communion," do not possess the "right" to participate in the celebration of the great mysteries of love and community,[243] but only to hear the word of God exhorting and summoning them to penance. Still, apart from those who are excommunicated as *vitandi* (to be shunned), their presence at holy Mass is practically tolerated, particularly as long as they have not been condemned by a judicial sentence (hence have incurred the excommunication only automatically or *lata sententia*). However this principle of law that the excommunicates have no right to participate in the sacred mysteries does not at all justify the conclusion that they are therefore free from the obligation to attend Mass. On the contrary, the obligation arising from the virtue of religion is all the more urgent. The obligation binding in religion that they participate in the celebration of the community of love very specifically demands that they strive earnestly to free themselves from excommunication and properly dispose themselves for fruitful participation.

3. The duty of participation in the sacred mysteries on Sunday arising from the law of the Church and from the essential orientation to worship on the part of the baptized Christian cannot be fulfilled without an earnest effort to attend Mass devoutly. Authors are all agreed that one who makes no effort to be externally attentive (by avoiding every external activity conflicting with attention, such as study, reading of fiction, gossiping, sleeping) in no way fulfills the positive command of the Church.

Even though serious theological writers maintain that purely exterior attention is sufficient for the fulfillment of the letter of canon law, they do not at all assume that simple exterior bodily presence and absence of distraction is adequate for worship "in spirit and in truth" (Jn 4:24) as demanded by the baptismal character and the divine precept. The precise delineation of the positive legal obligation has as its very purpose the clearing of the vision for the more essential obligation of moral theology. Still, a proper appreciation of the pastoral solicitude of the Church, which specifies and delineates the divine law, and even more so a genuine esteem for the "new law" of the Christian bids us place first the essential obligation of the baptized to worship in spirit and truth, and from this lofty point of vantage study the delineation of obligation as laid down by the Church. The Christian who forms his life "not under the Law but under grace" (Rom 6:14) is aware of the hazard of relapse into sin under the deadening weight of an alien law which threatens him if he attempts no more than external compliance with the pastoral laws and regulations of the Church. One who lives "under grace" perceives in the Church's determinations of the divine commandments the same accents of love as he discerns in the voice of grace of the Holy Spirit telling him of the "new law" within him. In this spirit he must at least endeavor to penetrate into the sense of the ecclesiastical law which is fulfilled by the sincere will to be devout and attentive even though with little success or perhaps no success at all.

Voluntary distractions during Mass are by their nature venial sins (*ex genere suo veniale*), provided they do not consciously extend over the entire Mass or the principal parts of the Mass. One who does no more than attend Mass as a visitor or tourist for the sake of the music or the art, without any actual mind to pray, cannot be said to have fulfilled his "priestly baptismal assignment." Nor has he responded to the Lord's invitation to worship as defined by the Church.

Obviously the performance of essential tasks contributing to the solemnity of the sacred service does not conflict with the fulfillment of the obligation to hear Mass. Those who play the organ, direct the choir, ring the bells, take up the collection, or discharge similar functions fulfill their Sunday obligation, even though interior recollection is rendered more difficult by such activity. Reception of the sacrament of penance is certainly not an ideal form of participation in the divine services. Nevertheless, if some attention is given at least to the principal parts of the Mass, then a humble confession of sins can be meaningfully caught up with the sacred liturgy of the altar as a prolongation of the Confiteor of the Mass, as a tribute of praise to the mercy and justice of God. Such is the exalted cultal significance of the sacrament that, particularly for the faithful who cannot confess at any other time or at least not without great difficulty, going to confession during the Sunday Mass is admissible. But the pastor should provide ample opportunity for confession at other times.

4. Worthy participation as adoration of God "in spirit and in truth" in the Sacrifice for the sins of the world is possible only for one who is in the state of grace. The sinner who desires to fulfill the obligation as he truly should must make every effort to reinstate himself in the divine friendship before or during Mass.

Genuinely pious and fruitful participation in the sacred celebration demands far more than attentive following of the parts of the Mass or an impeccable adherence to the text of the missal. Most essential is the action by which we enter into the spirit of the High Priest and immolated Lamb,

Jesus Christ Himself, who offers and is offered on the altar. Thus we participate in the sacred action by the resolve to form and transform our whole life through the power of the Sacrifice of Calvary by merging ourselves and our entire life with the Eucharistic offering. Active participation in community exercise and in reception of Holy Communion must also be a *yes* to the commandment of love. It is the great commandment of love and harmony announced at the Lord's Supper!

5. As to the place, there is no longer any obligation to attend Sunday or feast day Mass in one's own parish church. The obligation can be satisfied elsewhere, though the ideal is to attend in the parish or community in which one lives and works. The reason is evident: our sanctification should flow from the altar around which we assemble in sacred fellowship. And special preference should be given to the parochial Mass which the pastor offers for the parish.

The positive ecclesiastical law obliging us to assist at holy Mass on Sundays and feast days may be fulfilled in any church, in any public or semi-public oratory[244] or cemetery chapel, though not in a private oratory unless this right is granted by apostolic indult.[245] This last restriction is evidence of the will of the Church that the Sunday celebration should display externally the bond with the community of God's holy people. For a sufficient reason one may lawfully and worthily assist at Mass in a private oratory.

6. Reasons which excuse one from attending Sunday Mass. a) As in the instance of other positive laws, one is freed from the obligation if attendance involves a disproportionately great hardship or disadvantage. We say disproportionately great, by which we mean that the difficulties must be greater than one is normally expected to face in carrying out such a precept. From this it is apparent that a difficulty sufficient to excuse one from the obligation on one or other occasion may not be adequate excuse for habitual or almost habitual absence. Here too the reason is plain: there is a positive divine precept as well as the essential cultal obligation of the baptized underlying the commandment of the Church. Very great sacrifices must be made to maintain in our hearts a vital bond with the Sacrifice.

The sick who cannot attend Mass without actual or probable harm to health are simply excused. In serious doubt about the point in any individual instance the natural law requiring us to care for our health takes precedence over positive ecclesiastical law. However, if absence from Mass jeopardizes the faith or at least threatens to disrupt the vital bond of communion with the Church, the greater evil must be avoided at the price of the lesser. Loss of health is a lesser evil than loss of faith.

Those who live at a considerable distance from Church are excused from the regular attendance at Sunday Mass but not from attendance altogether. In the judgment of moral theologians a distance requiring over an hour (possibly an hour and a quarter) of travel is sufficiently great to excuse one from attending Mass sometimes. However, a number of factors must be taken into consideration, such as one's age or state of health, one's physical vigor, the condition of the weather, the character of the terrain or road, the means of conveyance, even the protection offered by one's clothing. At times even a short distance may prove very difficult for those who have no means of conveyance.

Modern conveyances, which make attendance at Mass relatively easy even for those who live at some distance from church, render obsolete the computations of miles and kilometers found in the older moralists. However, even in our times poor people surely are not obliged to avail themselves Sunday after Sunday of means of conveyance which involve burdensome payments for bus or carfare. Surely they would not be obliged to attend regularly at Mass. On individual occasions one may also be excused because he must undertake a journey which cannot be postponed readily, or because piety and charity require that he visit his sick relatives. In some instances even the lack of decent or proper attire may be an excuse.

b) Urgent works of charity toward our neighbor are likewise valid reasons excusing from attendance at Sunday and Holy Day Mass. Such are: care of the sick, assistance to the needy in emergencies, prevention of sinful deeds which might cause scandal. The disturbance of devotion may also be the basis for excuse: frequent or prolonged attacks of coughing, the painful wheezing of asthmatics, strong and offensive body odors, and similar problems might prove very disturbing to the faithful and their reverence for the liturgy. In such cases the excuse is as valid as reasonable concern for others would demand.

c) Unavoidable conflict between one's work and the attendance at Mass is the basis for excuse from the obligation to attend Mass. They may be the duties of one's office or profession (for example, the physician). They may be tasks which by the nature of the case cannot be postponed: a laborer may be assigned to Sunday shift in an industrial plant or other place of employment; workingmen or domestics who are kept from Mass occasionally through assignments to tasks by their employers may in good conscience consider themselves excused in individual instances. But should the conflict occur frequently or regularly, the employee must, if such a course is reasonably open to him, seek other employment as soon as possible. Farmers are excused if they must remain at home because of some unforeseen mishap among their livestock.

Where several holy Masses are offered, it is usually possible to arrange one's work so that one is neither forced to miss Mass nor neglect the work, by a staggering of tasks and church attendance among the members of the family. Surely parents and others in authority have an obligation to make provision for such arrangements so that their employees or dependents are able to attend holy Mass without prejudice to any serious duty.

d) Even reasons which are not sufficient in themselves to excuse from attending obligatory Mass may be considered sufficient if an approved custom makes them such. As an example we cite the custom prevailing in certain regions that a mother for a time before and after childbirth remains at home, even though she could go to church.

e) The reasons we have just enumerated are considered sufficient in themselves to excuse one from the obligation (*excusatio*). However, should these reasons not be adequate, one may still request a dispensation from proper authority. In this matter the same rules apply as in dispensation from the law of Sunday rest. A very common reason, to cite an example, is the occasional need for escape from the hectic life of the crowded city by excursions into the country or resort places. If under the circumstances it is not possible to attend Mass on the Sundays which the city dwellers choose for such excursions, a dispensation may reasonably be requested, provided the occurence is not too frequent. For that matter, should conscientious Christians who ordinarily do not absent themselves from Mass feel that they are justified to join in such an outing occasionally, even though they do miss Mass and are not dispensed, we should not pass too severe a judgment on them under these circumstances. But it must not be forgotten that what may be sufficient reason for one or other occasion would not be sufficient to justify frequent abstention from the sacred mysteries. Moreover, it is most advisable for the one who has been excused, or even more so if he has been dispensed, to compensate partially for the loss of the Sunday Mass by attending holy Mass on a weekday.

f) The Church no longer attaches penalties to the law of Sunday Mass and Sunday rest. In former days there were instances of great severity in her legislation. The Council of Elvira (about the year 305) threatened with temporary excommunication all those who culpably missed Mass on three consecutive Sundays.

The confessor may find it difficult at times to accept at face value the profession of sincerity from a penitent who continues to break this law very frequently, especially if he has more than once been absolved of the same offense after due warning and promises of amendment. It might be advisable in the more serious cases of this kind to postpone absolution until the penitent demonstrates a greater firmness in his good resolution. But such postponement of pardon must be the result of a prudent and thoughtful decision of the confessor, not merely the application of a mechanical rule without deeper understanding of the spiritual condition of the penitent and the reasonable hope for his moral betterment.

3. Work Sanctified by Cult and Sacred Repose

The greater part of the life of most Christians is taken up with work. Therefore it is very important for a Christian doctrine of morals to present the correct religious-moral conception of work. The best approach to such a Christian understanding of work is to study it in the light of the sacred cultal repose of the Sabbath (established by God the Creator as a day of worshipful rest) and in the light of the Sunday celebration of the mysteries of the passion, death, and resurrection of Christ in holy Mass. No Christian evaluation of work is possible without reference to these fundamental religious realities.

In the light of these realities there is all the difference of night and day between work which is sacred, grasped and accepted in the light and spirit of cultal repose and holy worship, and profane work which is not thus sanctified and does not spring from love of God and is not ordered to the divine service but is intrinsically and totally enclosed in this world. We shall briefly indicate in the following pages how the Lord's Day is the decisive factor in determining the heights to which labor can ascend or the abyss to which it can sink and draw men down. When we speak of the significance of Sunday in this fashion, we include everything that tends to sanctify the day. We include everything that makes work sacred, all that is implied in the Benedictine *pray and work:* the celebration of holy Mass, the cultal repose (what is called *vacare Deo*), the liturgical cycle, the feasts, the sacraments and sacramentals, all that gives our life a religious orientation and motivation. All this we include in *Sunday;* all this centers in Sunday and is implied when we speak of the Lord's Day.

Our Sunday determines: 1) whether we are to remain masters in our work as worshipping participants in the creative majesty of God, or through refusal of worship descend to the level of serfs of labor and technique. 2) Whether the weekday labor oppresses us as the yoke of slaves, or is constantly made more acceptable as the "sweet burden of Christ." 3) Whether the trial of work means for us the malediction of sin and eternal sterility or blessed imitation of Christ, the Worker, Christ crucified.

a. Master or Serf

God made man to be the servant who is the master, serving God as the master of the earth. By dominating the earth through work man was to manifest his likeness to God: "God said, 'Let us make mankind in our image and likeness; and let them have dominion over the fish of the sea, the birds of the air, the cattle, over all the wild animals and every creature that crawls on the earth.' . . . Then God blessed them and said to them, 'Be fruitful and multiply; fill the earth and subdue it. Have dominion over the fish of the sea, the birds of the air, the cattle and all the animals that crawl on the earth'" (Gn 1:26ff.). "The Lord God took the man and placed him in the garden of Eden to till it and to keep it" (Gn 2:15). These texts clearly show that even before his fall man was to be a worker. Cultivation of the garden of paradise, which means to subdue and subject the earth, was to be a special manifestation of man's likeness to God.

God, the Sovereign Lord of the Universe, reveals His absolute dominion in the creation of the world. He spoke and the world was created. Man should do likewise, though the distance between him and God is infinite. He must be active by "creatively" forming and shaping the world. The creativeness of the human spirit, man's work, reflects the continuous operation of God in the world.

Work means "self-mastery in purposeful activity."[246] Not only does man sustain himself bodily by work; he also develops both bodily and spiritual powers. Without well-ordered work man will never become "master of himself." Through bodily and spiritual work "man acts upon himself," he fashions with ever greater perfection the divine likeness which is his own being. Those who work the earth or labor with material things (farmers, craftsmen, artisans, artists) place the stamp of the human spirit on matter. In the pattern of his Creator man leaves the mark of his spirit on all material things.

Work is the most primitive and most noble title for the acquisition of property. Rightful possession is another manifestation of our likeness to God. Work, however, manifests and perfects the true image of God in us only in the measure in which it is consciously placed under the dominion and in the service of the one Sovereign Lord and Creator. Wherefore, there must be a holy rhythm of work and prayer; for these are the binding forces which master the things of the world. Through work coupled with sacred relaxation the dominion of God is recognized in adoration and praise of worship.

Even the natural economy of human force and energy calls for the rhythm of work and rest, of day and night, and surely also the turn from workdays to Sunday repose. This rhythm becomes a sacred movement insofar as the day of repose becomes the day of sacred and restful cult (a holy day), with the result that work in the whole rhythmic movement of life becomes sacred. It becomes consecrated work insofar as man, in his worship on the day of rest as well as in his weekday work, recognizes the sovereignty of God. Through his worship on the day of rest man not only subjects the royal domain of his work to the service of the One who alone reigns over all, His Lord and Creator; he also acquires and proclaims thereby a new likeness to God, which far surpasses the divine likeness in his work itself. He partakes of the blessed repose of God.

Greatest in God is not His creative action in the world but His own absolute transcendence over all things. God is totally His own transcendent being, totally happy even without creation. He is pure act (*actus purus*), the most perfect Life precisely in His blessed repose. Precisely because God has no limitation or potentialities, never moves from possible to actual, because He is not Life seeking further life, but infinite living, infinite possessing, infinite enjoying of all-perfect Life, His eternal Life Stream is also His infinite blessed repose. From eternity to eternity even without creation God celebrates the festal movement of His own Love-Reality in the Holy Spirit. Creation is no more than an echo, result of God's free act, an echo of this eternal ecstasy and repose in fulness of life and love, a fulness which knows no increase, no diminution.

The sacred writer who juxtaposed the Sabbath command with the command to work (Gn 1–2) derives the Sabbath of man from the Sabbath repose of God, just as he views the work of man under the aspect of the creative dominion of God. We note how emphatically the writer stresses the six works of creation (*days*), in each instance repeating in almost identical terms: "And there was evening and morning, the sixth (or first, second, etc.) day" (Gn 1:31). But of the seventh day the writer says tersely: 'And he rested on the seventh day from all the work he had done" (Gn 2:2), indicating that the work of God is work in time with "evening and morning" (category of time). But his repose is without beginning or end, a "day" without morning and evening.[247] In this description the sacred writer presents a concept of God the Creator which is totally removed from that of the creation myths of the surrounding peoples. In the Babylonian myths the world and mankind came into existence by a process of fission and the destruction of the gods themselves, which means that they are a part of the world and share the tension of its torment and unrest. They have no "day of rest without morning and evening" but are merged entirely in creation. They are "deities of nature" in a world of nature, and when we compare them with the God of Genesis, we must exclaim: As his God, so is man!

The man who has lost all sense of the repose for worship which should be joined with his days of work and carry him above the grind and tension of his occupations becomes entirely immersed in the turmoil of secular life. He is completely taken up in the worldly and profane. He assumes the image not of the God of Genesis, creative in blessed repose, but of the Babylonian deities, Thiamat and Marduk. But the man who keeps the "Sabbath," who receives from God the mission and blessing for his work in the world, who has found in the divine cult the center of repose lying beyond his work, rises serenely above the turbulent combat of the world of toil and care. It is true, he has not yet entered into the eternal Sabbath of God's rest, but, insofar as he is essentially on the way to it, his participation in the divine repose has already begun here below. "Happy is the man who does this . . . who keeps the Sabbath free from profanation (Is 56:2).

The Sabbath and more so the Sunday of the Christians bears the stamp of the Last Things. These special days are eschatological. If the Lord's Day is not to prove an anticipation here on earth of the verdict of man's final condemnation, then it must ever and anon direct man's gaze to his final destiny: work is not the ultimate; it is the way and the trial. In order to remain worthy of man it must point beyond all that is earthly to man's participation in the eternal jubilee of the divine Sabbath, in the glory of the risen Christ who after the fulfillment of His work among men entered into the fulness of eternal repose.

To the degree that man acknowledges that his rights of dominion over created things and his own work are God's loan and to the degree that he adoringly places them at God's feet, he participates in a much more magnificent way in the power and majesty of God. Through participation in the feast the working man rises above material creation. Let him refuse, however, to pay the tribute of the "seventh day" for the patent of nobility ennobling his work and this very day will wreak its revenge on him; like the deity of the Babylonian myth he will fall completely under the spell and ban of the world's agony. Without the sacred time of repose and worship man becomes a mere slave of work.

The "robot-genius" of our decade repudiates prayer and celebration of sacred feasts as insufferable superstition and waste of time in his fretful march toward cultural development and world domination. Totally absorbed in technique, he has succeeded in unleashing the hidden forces of the elements. The unveiling of the secret powers of nature no longer awakens the awe and wonder which forces man to his knees before his Creator. And yet he is unhappy to the very core of his being, precisely because through sheer work and progress he has forfeited the key to the deeper likeness to God, to participation in the blessed repose of God. He has made work his idol and perverted the divine image which lies in it; and in the abasement of his idolatry he has fashioned himself into an image of technique, into a soulless machine. He has become like his god.

The climax is mass enslavement of labor. Men are driven from their homes, farms, and families to build the earthly paradise of the workers, of the men without a Sabbath, men who despite shorter hours and better working conditions have become men without rest. Confronted by this condition we may well ask: what is more diverse than the soul of work? On the one hand it can be lordly service under God. It can be the means to fulfillment by participation in the Sabbath repose of God. It can be anticipation, a beginning here and now of the enjoyment of the eternal repose of the blessed Creator enthroned above the world. But on the other hand it can also be the most appalling instrument of enslavement which assumes absolute dominion over the world and denial of the sacred repose consecrated to the worship of God.

b. Work: Intolerable Burden or Sweet Yoke of Christ?

Even after the fall of man work undertaken in the spirit of adoration still bears the stamp of the divine. But it also has something oppressive about it since God spoke these words to our First Parents: "Cursed be the ground because of you; in toil shall you eat of it all the days of your life; . . . In the sweat of your brow you shall eat bread, till you return to the ground" (Gn 3:17ff.). In our present state we must wrest from the earth in laborious effort our daily bread. Many a man must strain every nerve, often working beyond his strength, merely to support himself and his family. Every man is under the law of work. The obligation to perform manual labor applies only to the race as a whole, but the law of labor is directed to every individual man and woman. It is an individual precept[248] affecting all who are not incapacitated by illness or old age (i.e. by special trial or suffering).

Some may not be under the necessity to work in order to support themselves and their families. But even though there is no necessity (cf. Prv 6:6–11), there is the obligation arising from the virtue of temperance and mortification, penance and expiation. "If any man will not work, neither let him eat" (2 Thes 3:10). This universal obligation to work, whether manually or intellectually, is imposed upon all, even upon contemplative men and women in religion. It is based not only on the law of nature (Gn 2:15; 3:17ff.). It also flows from the duty to do works of penance and expiation (Gn 3:17ff.). Moreover, work is a universal means of avoiding spiritual pitfalls and raising our minds and hearts to higher things. It makes it possible for us to cooperate in both the natural and supernatural order in the designs of Providence through the exercise of charity toward our fellow men.[249]

Labor is a stern taskmaster for fallen mankind. Without the discipline of work fallen man cannot maintain the true dignity of a well-ordered life, as is all too evident from the moral evils which beset the masses of unemployed. It follows that the unemployed are bound to use their enforced leisure as prudently as possible by keeping occupied in such times of trial. But there is also an obligation on the part of "superfluous wealth" (those who possess it) to create work or conditions which offer opportunity for work in time of wide-spread unemployment. Surely public authority cannot be indifferent to these evil conditions.

Though work is a burden divinely imposed, it is not God's will that man be oppressed by labor. Hence, for the child of Adam, weighted down by the heritage of sin and groaning under the burden of oppressive toil, the Sabbath has a further meaning: it serves to make the yoke of work bearable. The law of the Sabbath rest becomes God's social legislation for the easing of the burdens and trials of labor. At least on one day of the week God wishes to remove the yoke from man's shoulders, so that he may breathe freely and raise his eyes heavenwards. As the body relaxes and recuperates its strength by rest from toil, the spirit should receive new vigor from God through the celebration of divine cult for the proper bearing of one's burdens.

The Old Testament attitude toward manual labor is totally different from the Greek disdain—note the words: "Hate not laborious tasks, nor farming, which was ordained by the Most High" (Sir 7:15). But it is also profoundly imbued with the thought of the harshness of the yoke to which man must submit. It is God Himself who imposes the wholesome burden, which is not merely a burden, and which God gives us the grace to bear. This is particularly true for the socially lower classes who are most oppressed by human toil. "Remember to keep holy the Sabbath day. Six days you may labor and do all your work, but the seventh day is the Sabbath of the Lord, your God. No work may be done then either by you, or your son or daughter, or your male or female slave, or your beast, or by the alien who lives with you" (Gn 20:10).

The social aspect of the law of Sabbath rest is particularly stressed: "For six days you may do your work, but on the seventh day you must rest, that your ox and your ass may also have rest, and that the son of your maidservant and the alien may be refreshed" (Ex 23:12). This injunction is explicitly repeated, "Your male and female slave should rest as you do. For remember that you too were once slaves in Egypt, and the Lord, your God, brought you from there with his strong hand and outstretched arm" (Dt 5:14f.). The social establishment of the Sabbath rest was to serve as a grateful memorial of the liberation from the serfdom of Egypt. The ecclesiastical prohibition of servile work has something of this historic significance. Work should not prove oppressive to anyone. Above all, it should not hinder anyone from celebrating the "festivals of the Lord" with joy (Lv 23:2).

One who permits the Lord to lift the burden of work for one day in the week by that very fact accepts the toil of the coming week as assignment from God. Each week he accepts it anew as a task from the altar of sacrifice, as his share of the toil of Christ, as a yoke that is sweet and a burden that is light (cf. Mt 11:29f.). In the spirit of love for Christ and through His grace he takes up the yoke of the Master who bore the hardship of labor and sanctified it by His passion and death.

The social character both of the sanctification of the cultal repose with its consequences and of its violation and desecration is very evident in our times. Man and his day of rest are sacrificed to ruthless passion and greed in the acquisition of wealth. Mad competition in the production of material goods and the dreadful arms race make man and his sacred times their victim. (Particularly significant is the stress of the double-time compensation for work on the Lord's Day.)

Work and sacred rest are equally obligatory under the divine social law. Social history shows how work has created class warfare among men instead of forming the bond of unity between man and man. As yoke of Christ it should bring men together in the common acceptance of toil as divine assignment carried out in a community of love. The hope that work will prove itself to be the yoke of Christ, a loving bond of unity among men, will be fulfilled only if men learn to bear the burden of work for themselves and their neighbors and seek earnestly to lessen the oppressiveness of labor for mankind. The men of power must cease to shirk their share of the common task and cease to shift their burdens to the shoulders of the socially weak. Each man capable of work must bear the portion of labor (as the yoke of Christ) which is essential to support the one incapable of work[250] Then and only then will man be able by means of his work to carry out his vocation of dominion over the world without failure or catastrophe. Only if these ideals are realized will work become the bond of unity among men.[251]

In the Old Testament transgression of the law of Sabbath brought down the curse of God on the offender. Such a curse must fall particularly upon one who oppresses the weak beyond their strength, so that even the repose of the Lord's day is crowded out of their lives, the day on which we should all join in the celebration of the Sacrifice of Christ.

An attitude toward work and rest inspired by Christian social legislation can attain to full fruitfulness only if, ordered to God as its last end, the day of rest through its holy cult sanctifies the days of work.

c. Work: Curse for Sin or Eternal Portion with Christ?

Through the fall of man work became not merely a harsh, though salutary, yoke; but for mankind refusing to pray, work became a curse. The malediction placed on work still stands: "Cursed be the ground because of you; in toil shall you eat of it all the days of your life; thorns and thistles shall it bring forth to you" (Gn 3:17f.). Without doubt Christ lifted the curse from the earth and from work by His labor and His passion and death. But individual men and nations are still confronted with the alternative: either sanctify work or work under the curse. Eternally fruitful and holy is work performed in partnership with Christ the Worker who bore the pain of the Cross. The curse of work is upon selfish labor for one's own exclusive profit or self-aggrandizement, upon work forced upon others through the indolence or arrogance of those who shirk the tasks which duty imposes upon them.

Cursed is the toil and trial which knows no Sunday repose, which has no motive but self and serves only selfish interests. Only fulfillment of the meaning of Sunday can free man from the naked and exclusive thought of self, and this is always a hazard for the man who merely works; for selfishness makes man dour toward others and spiritually barren. The worker who attends Mass on Sunday brings bread and wine with hands dampened with the sweat of his labor. He offers to God a gift free from all selfish interest. (The very sacrifice of the profits accruing from the work which one gives up for the worship of God is an oblation.) One who refuses to offer the first fruits of his labor, the first day of the week and its gifts to the glory of God will inevitably fall victim to the curse of the profane which makes work the source of schism and conflict among men in the whole area of human relations and makes much of labor itself sterile.

The worst curse befalls the man whose work estranges him from God. One who ignores Sunday repose will soon find that he has become a slave of work with no allotment of sacred rest and no opportunity even to strive earnestly for repose in God. Though the weight of toil falls heavily upon those who must labor at menial and strenuous tasks for long hours, paradoxically enough those who groan under such a yoke do not bear as great a curse as the victims of the capitalistic mania for production in modern times. The creed of "progress" with its motivation of greed, unlimited acquisition of wealth, and idolization of technique has driven men to ignore both the value of divine cult and the human value of the worker himself. This latter evil pressed from the paternal heart of Pius XI the anguished cry: "And thus it was that manual labor, decreed by the fatherly providence of God for the good of man's body and soul even after the fall, has been made the source of a strange perversion: for dead matter leaves the factory transformed and ennobled, whereas men are corrupted and degraded."[252]

"Ultimately man is faced with but one alternative in his work: he may direct his work to God or merely to things (matter). If work is ordered solely to things, then man himself is excluded. If it is ordered to God, then man is included. Work orientated entirely to matter (the conception of work in the "capitalistic" ethos) is essentially non-religious and non-social . . . should man succumb to the craving for things, he will in the same measure be possessed by the demon of work."[253]

In the present century the baneful light of tremendous apocalyptic events has revealed the sterility of human labor. A veritable curse has descended on the labors of a humanity which no longer seeks its center in the repose of divine worship. With ever increasing tempo the forces of destruction annihilate the fruits of the frantic and unsanctified work of peoples. Loss of life and liberty has been accompanied by total economic devastation through crises of inflation, wide-spread unemployment, and insane wars of destruction. "Vanity of vanities!" Vainest of all is the seven-day workweek unsanctified by worship and repose of the Lord's Day.

The utter futility of work which serves only selfish ends (which becomes one's god) is brutally manifest in death. The Lord points this out in the parable of the rich farmer (Lk 12:15ff.). "For what does it profit a man, if he gain the whole world, but suffer the loss of his own soul?" (Mt 16:26). The "woe" pronounced over the evil rich by our Lord strikes at the passion for possession and also at the obsession for work which leaves no time for prayer or sacred repose and worship.

Groaning under the weight of his tasks, the Christian in this world is profoundly distressed over the utter futility of earthly trial and effort. But he knows that beyond earthly failure there is the eternal promise. In the midst of all hardship the Cross of Christ looms large with its blessed promise of a rich and fruitful eternity to the Christian worker who constantly renews his pledge and effort of unity with the Crucified. Sanctification of Sunday with celebration of holy Mass transforms the curse, places work under the blessing of the Cross. With this ideal in mind, the Christian performs his tasks as penance and expiation, as discipline and instruction, in which day by day he is transformed into the image of Christ. Not least in the discipline and instruction is the trial and failure which beset him in his work.

Sunday possesses this value for our labor only if repose means *"vacare Deo,"* a cultal rest, a relaxation leaving us free for God. Sheer profane rest, mere chase after relaxation and indulgence (and the divine worship viewed as boredom and interference with one's freedom) does not lift the curse from work, does not relax the stranglehold of the addiction to work, but merely leads to other forms of enslavement. A certain physician very pertinently refers to the "Sunday neurosis" as a form of escape from God and one's self into the cacophony of self-indulgence. Such a Sunday might indeed restore the physical energies, but it cannot at all serve "to maintain spiritual and mental balance and spiritual health."[254]

The proper celebration of Sunday makes work a vocation in the religious sense: we encounter God Himself and accept from Him our work in imitation of the crucified Christ and for the glory of His heavenly Father. Thus our work is steeped in the mystery of the redemption. More simply: work is sanctified and made fruitful for the kingdom of God and the salvation of souls. As Christ accepted trial and toil not only for Himself but also for the brethren, so work as a vocation (in imitation of Christ) must have a social orientation. All this is implied in the religious connotation of the word *vocation.* Every genuine vocation (*munus, officium, office* or *charge*) is a service to the group based on a divine summons and mission.[255]

The theology of terrestrial vocation with its express denial of the superior vocation of perfection according to the evangelical counsels derives from Martin Luther. In Calvinism there was an extensive development and transformation of this position into rich significance and influence in the history of economic capitalism.[256] But to esteem and cherish every type of work to which one is called as social service and glorification of God according to the designs of Providence is a venerable Catholic concept. In fact, not the least effect of this higher esteem for the special spiritual vocation is the correct adjustment of secular vocations through proper balance and religious motivation. The *yes* to the evangelical counsels arising from awareness of the eschatological fulness of salvation and the dazzling force of the absolutizing of the world of work and technique imparts to terrestrial vocation the final submission to the "things of the Lord" and to the kingdom of His love: this is also the ideal and goal of the Lord's Day (cf. 1 Cor 7:30f.).

For the Christian work is a vocation and not mere occupation or avocation. It is mission, because it is an assignment from God which concerns everybody, because it can and should become a manifestation and fulfillment of the likeness of God within us and imitation of Christ the Worker who suffered and died for us. It is a vocation for the reason and in the measure in which the Christian looks upon his tasks as appointed and assigned to him on the basis of social needs and special gifts from God (signs of vocation).

The celebration of the seventh day primarily recalls that God grants to the harassed working man at the end of each workweek, and finally at the end of his life of toil, a participation in the divine rest and the eternal liturgy. On the other hand the celebration of Sunday as "the first day of the week" stresses worship more than any work. It is, first of all, the day of the Lord's resurrection. And from this vantage point the celebration looks forward to our own resurrection with triumphant joy. But since the celebration of the resurrection in the holy Sacrifice of the Mass places in the foreground the celebration of the passion and death of Christ as a pilgrimage to resurrection and ascension, the character of work as a burden and hardship is not hidden in the joy of the Lord's Day. The celebration of Sunday through holy Mass is a sacred acceptance of the trials and toils of life in union with Christ in the pilgrimage to eternal glory.

Sunday as the "eighth day" is the completion and perfection of the Sabbath week which heralds the apocalyptic dawn of the Second Coming. At the same time it is the "first day" which proclaims the great inception of the victory of Christ over sin, death, and pain. The Christian week, with Sunday and workdays, and the whole Christian life, is thus united with Christ. Through the sacrament of baptism the Christian with all his effort is given the stamp of the death and resurrection. However, the baptized must constantly testify anew to this union with Christ, constantly strengthen its bonds. Without such renewal the ponderous attraction of the profane world will draw our work down from the high plane of vocation and imitation to the debased level of arbitrary pursuit of power and other selfish ends. Through celebration of Sunday the Christian is constantly taken up with the truth-giving and life-sustaining graces of the passion and resurrection of the King of heavenly glory who transforms the frustrating curse of work into the service of love, the holy service of the blessed pilgrim whose eyes are turned to the celestial liturgy.

d. Divine and Ecclesiastical Law regarding Sacred Rest and Cult

Man as a creature ordained to cult must have a certain period of time set aside for sacred repose and worship in virtue of his natural and supernatural relation to God. The specific choice of the seventh day was, by force of positive precept, valid only in the Old Testament. Though the newly-formed Christian community took over and observed this seventh day as the day of rest, the day of worship commemorating the death and resurrection of Christ was determined already in the time of the Apostles. This day of commemoration, the "Lord's day" (Ap 1:10), the day selected "for the breaking of bread" and for instruction in the word was the "first day of the week" (Acts 20:7). Paul pronounced the law of the Sabbath as no longer binding on the Christian conscience (Col 2:16).

As to the celebration of the cult on the first day of the week we are certain it was determined by an apostolic, perhaps even by a positive divine command. The Apostles who made the ruling were "organs of revelation" in union with Christ and in subordination to Him.[257] Of course many points remain unclear, and we might inquire in what sense an ordinance of the Apostles could be a permanently binding divine command. It should not be assumed that the celebration of the first day of the week would be entirely irreconcilable with an apostolic order or command.

The establishment of obligatory feast days and more detailed regulations regarding worship and rest is a positive ecclesiastical determination of the more generic and less accurately defined divine law. Interpretation of the duties arising from these positive ecclesiastical regulations must be primarily concerned with safeguarding the values of the positive divine law. They may never prejudice the vigor of the divine law and its cultal values in relation to God. In this light we must interpret the freeing of conscience from obligations of Church law in the whole area of Sunday precept. The universal principles regarding exemption and dispensation are valid only to the extent that the substance of the law of worship deriving from God Himself is left intact. Since a divine law underlies the more specific requirements regarding sacred rest and cult, the exempting causes must be more serious and urgent than for release from those which are merely positive ecclesiastical laws. However, exemption or dispensation for one or other occasion does not directly involve the divine law, and hence the excusing reasons or causes need not be as serious as those required for a considerable period of time.

The law of Sunday rest was not as clearly specified in the early Church as it is today. The tiny persecuted Church had neither the power nor the opportunity to impose strictly and rigidly upon her members a law so profoundly bound up with social and economic conditions. Repose was largely dictated by the simple need for released time from work for the purpose of attending the liturgical service. Since the celebration of the divine cult on Sunday necessarily demanded some cessation from labor for the purpose of worship, the practice of Sunday rest developed more or less spontaneously. Already in his time Constantine made Sunday a day of rest for the entire empire.[258]

Through the course of her history the Church has established a number of feast days. The obligation attached is the same as for the Lord's Day, participation in the celebration of Mass and abstinence from servile work. The number has varied considerably and in modern times only comparatively few remain. We have already listed them above (cf. note 240).

The obligation of sacred repose is grave by its nature (*ex genere suo gravis*). Reliable authors hold that performance of manual labor which does not exceed one hour (or possibly two) would not at all be more than a venial sin, provided there is no disturbance of the public sacred rest directed to divine worship (cultal repose) and the work does not cause serious scandal.

(1) *Works Prohibited on Sundays and Feast Days*

Ecclesiastical law forbids the performance of all servile work on Sundays and holy days of obligation, the holding of court and trying of cases, and various types of buying and selling. This latter includes the public operation of grocery stores and markets, stock and commodity exchanges, downtown department stores and suburban shopping centers, auctions and bargain sales, in a word, all *public* buying and selling. In some localities lawful custom may permit certain forms of buying and selling.[259]

By positive law of the Church only servile work, but not the work of the liberal arts, is forbidden. But it is not easy to determine what is actually servile work in the sense of the law. The matter must be studied under various aspects: 1. Historically and socially that work is looked upon as servile which was performed by servants and slaves in former times. Hence servile work is primarily manual labor. 2. The aspect of wages or hire enters in. We might ask is it work for wages, for livelihood? The point must be considered but is not in itself the deciding factor. 3. From the point of view of the purpose of the law there is the aspect of disturbance of divine worship and conflict with it. This point is particularly significant and decisive. Does a particular type of work disturb the public sacred rest of the feast day or Sunday; does it disturb public worship and conflict with it? Occupations and activities interfering with public cult or disturbing the faithful in the celebration of the divine mysteries are particularly forbidden by the law of Sabbath rest.

Works of the liberal arts which are not forbidden by the positive law include all intellectual activity whose primary purpose is to cultivate the mind and foster spiritual culture rather than to produce material values. Artistic efforts, insofar as they are carried on without typical manual labor, sports and similar activities whose main purpose is relaxation and recreation are not forbidden. However, even intellectual and artistic occupations and recreational activities or sports in general, though not forbidden by positive law, may not be permitted to frustrate the purpose of the Sunday rest, which is to release one for the repose in God (*vacare Deo*) and for sacred worship. For this reason, even though ecclesiastical law may not expressly prohibit it, the intent and spirit of the law is particularly violated by the carrying on of sports or other forms of recreation which involve the roof-raising clamor of the crowd or of cheering sections in immediate proximity to the church and at the very time the sacred mysteries are being celebrated. Even more reprehensible, the game may lure youth from the duty of divine worship while it is disturbing the faithful at Mass.

The explanation and interpretation of the law prohibiting servile work must be free from every species of rigorism. The Lord's own words are our guide: "The Sabbath was made for man, and not man for the Sabbath" (Mk 2:27). The law is not end in itself but a means to guard and guide man in his essential relation to divine worship. For this reason the Church herself has approved of local custom and the conscience of her devout members as an acceptable form of interpretation of her own positive law. By the same token there can be no comprehensive casuistic catch-all, offering a solution for all points in the minutest detail and valid for all places and conditions. The very attitude of Christ toward the Sabbath observance itself and the rigorous interpretation of the Pharisees is a warning to us that any petty casuistry regarding Sabbath repose is simply out of place. Such an approach to the problem merely leads to anxiety of conscience and confusion regarding the meaning of the commandment itself.

A case in point is the fine distinction made consistently by some writers of manuals of moral theology between embroidery, which is looked upon as simply in the area of the permissible work because it is included in liberal arts, and simple knitting which is frowned upon as servile work. Such a distinction, according to reliable authors, does not in any way destroy the validity of a custom to the contrary. Quite often conscientious women sitting around and leisurely chatting with their neighbors on Sundays and feast days will "take out their knitting" without in any way feeling they have broken the law. In fact the ordinary faithful will find the distinction between embroidering and knitting and other fine distinctions made by some authors rather perplexing. The important point always to be borne in mind and stressed is the ultimate meaning of the law and its basic purpose. A right grasp of the meaning of Sunday repose and the correspondingly correct attitude of mind and heart might at times bid us avoid many things not forbidden by the letter of the law.

(2) *Corporeal Work Which is Permitted*

a) All essential work in and about one's home or establishment is permitted. This includes the necessary tasks which must be performed in stables, barns, and garages. Cooking, laundry work, patching, sewing are permitted insofar as they may be necessary and cannot be readily done on weekdays. Petty jobs about the house of whatever kind are always permitted. Provided there is no occasion of scandal, the laborer who has worked elsewhere all week may cultivate his little garden on Sunday. However, to make a practice of mowing the grass and gathering in hay or feed on Sunday morning can hardly be considered a lawful custom or beyond the restriction of the law.

b) Cases of emergency, threats of serious damage or loss always excuse one from the precept. Hence the poor man who cannot support himself and his family unless he works on Sunday is excused from the law, as is the subject who is constrained to work and cannot free himself from the constraint without great damage. The same holds for the workers in industries or factories which cannot be closed or shut down without great loss (for example, railroads, furnaces, etc.). Farmers and others may protect their crops and fruits against the hazards of the weather. For example, they may harvest the crops before a threatening storm, irrigate their fields in drought, smog their fruit trees when frost threatens, etc. To protect themselves from great loss they may use heavy machinery, such as combines to harvest their grain on Sunday. If, however, the loss were minor or merely incidental to the contract, this would not be permitted. But in every instance the use of noisy machines during the very time of divine services should be avoided.

c) Not merely one's own need or threat of loss to oneself offers sufficient reason to free an individual from the obligation of Sunday rest. The necessity of others who require the help of our Sunday work is often sufficient reason for the performance of the work. In fact, at times there may be an obligation to do the work for them. Physicians or nurses or druggists must provide essential service even on Sundays. The obligation to come to the rescue of men in misfortune and even of animals was evident to the Pharisees despite their over-refined conception of the law of the Sabbath (cf. Mt 12:11f.). Repairing machinery or vehicles for necessary travel or for journeys already begun, finishing, altering, or otherwise preparing urgently needed articles of clothing for oneself or for others is universally conceded to be lawful. However, neither individual producer nor craftsman is permitted to accept such an abundance of orders that Sunday work becomes a necessity for him while other craftsmen are kept in idleness.

d) Lawful custom not only makes the work at markets or fairs and public buying and selling legitimate but even other activity which in itself may be classed as servile work. These activities, however, may never be permitted to crowd out the exercises of religion. Our tasks must always leave room for sacred rest and the celebration of worship. No work may totally exclude the freedom to serve God, the *vacare Deo*.

Should one doubt whether or not he is allowed to perform certain tasks on Sundays or feast days, or should he doubt about the validity of the reasons which might excuse him from the law, he may always seek a dispensation. Probable cause is always sufficient for him to seek it. But he should note that, wherever there is a clear and certain case of lawful custom contrary to the law, or of necessity for performing the work or danger of great loss or damage, no dispensation is necessary. In doubt whether the reason for exemption is sufficient, the dispensation can still be granted by proper authority. This holds both for the law of Sabbath rest and for the obligation to attend holy Mass. But it must be noted that the more frequent the claim or request for dispensation the more serious must be the reasons presented. One may not jeopardize the substance of the law.

The local ordinary and the pastor have authority to dispense their subjects, individual persons and families, and within the geographic limits of their jurisdiction outsiders also, from the positive law of Sabbath rest and attendance at holy Mass.[260] Religious superiors have the same power in regard to their subjects as do pastors. Their subjects include all, even laymen, who live in the religious houses of their order.[261] But none of the above-mentioned have authority to dispense entire communities, parishes, or dioceses.

Emergencies which affect an entire parish are usually such that the exemption from the law is automatic. In such cases there is not so much question of dispensation by authority as simple declaration that the subjects are free from obligation of the law. The purpose of the declaration is to free the subjects' conscience from possible confusion and anxiety. Obviously, where the exemption from law is clearly evident, the pastor does not have the right to pretend that he is dispensing or that exemption depends on his decision. Nor does he have the right to summon each member of the parish to appear before him for a declaration of exemption. One must trust the adult conscience of the Christian to form such a decision in individual cases for himself, particularly in view of the insight of the individual into his own daily problems. The farmer surely knows more about the weather hazards and the need for work in the fields than his pastor, despite the latter's theological understanding of authors. Therefore it is advisable for the pastor to consult prudent men before he makes a ruling from the pulpit about the presence or absence of exempting causes.

BIBLIOGRAPHY

Prayer—Its Essence and Its Place in the Imitation

BAMS, K. "Das Gebet zu Christus beim heiligen Hieronymus," *TrThZ*, 60 (1951), 178–188.
CERFAUX, L.-COGNET, L., etc. *La Prière*. Paris, 1959.

CLOSEN, G. E. *Die Heilige Schrift und das Beten des Christen.* Wien, 1949.

DIETZEL, A. "Beten im Geist," *ThZschr,* 13 (1957), 12–32.

DOELLER, J. *Das Gebet im AT.* Wien, 1916.

FENTON, J. C. *The Theology of Prayer.* Milwaukee, 1939.

FONCK, A. "Prière," *DTC,* 13, 169–244.

GEBETSERZIEHUNG. *LebS,* 7 (1956), H. 3.

GRAEF, R. *Macht des Gebetes.* Regensburg, 1957.

GREIFF, A. *Das Gebet im AT.* Muenster, 1915.

GUARDINI, R. *Prayer in Practice.* Translated by Leopold Loewenstein-Wertheim. New York: Pantheon, 1957.

HAMMAN, A. *La Prière. I. Le nouveau Testament.* Tournai, 1959.

HARDER, G. *Paulus und das Gebet.* Guetersloh, 1936.

HILLMANN, W., O.F.M. "Vom Wesen des Betens," *WissWeish* (1949), 129–137.

LOTZ, J., S.J. *Meditation. Der Weg nach innen.* Frankfurt, 1954.

MARITAIN, J. and R. *Prayer and Intelligence.* Translated by Algar Thorold. New York: Sheed and Ward, 1943.

MOREL, CH., S.J. "Das Gebetsleben des heiligen Augustinus nach seinen Briefen," *Anima,* 4 (1949), 66–77; 177–179.

NIELEN, J. M. *Gebet und Gottesdienst im NT. Eine Studie zur Biblischen Liturgie und Ethik.* Freiburg, 1937.

PIUS XII, "De natura et efficacia orationis" (Allocutio) *AAS,* 35 (1943), 105–116.

RAHNER, K. *Happiness through Prayer.* Translated by T. Henning and M. Carroll. Westminster, Md.: Newman, 1958.

――――. "Sendung zum Gebet," *StimmenZeit,* 152 (1953), 161–170.

ROHR, I. *Das Gebet im NT.* Muenster, 1924.

SCHNEIDER, O. "Gott und Mensch im Gebet," *ZAM,* 14 (1939), 157–185.

SOIRON, T., O.F.M. *Das Geheimnis des Gebetes. Betrachtungen zu seiner theologischen Sinndeutung.* Freiburg, 1937.

STEIDLE, B. *Das Gebet des Herrn.* (With selected patristic texts.) Leipzig, 1938.

TILLMANN, G. *Das Gebet nach der Lehre der Heiligen.* Freiburg, 1874/77.

WULF, F., S.J. "Vom Wesen und der Einuebung des Gebetes," *GeistLeben,* 21 (1948), 231–236.

Cultal, Apostolic, and Mystical Prayer

GUARDINI, R. *Die Anbetung.* Wuerzburg, 1940.

HAERING, B. "Liturgical Piety and Christian Perfection," *Wor,* 34 (1960), 523–535. [Valuable discussions in this number.]

HOPHAN, O. "Liturgie oder Volksfroemmigkeit?" *Anima,* 14 (1959), 72–81. (Note the entire: Heft 1, 1959).

JAMBOIS, L. "Adoration et prière," *VieSpir,* 88 (1953), 134–140.

MARITAIN, J. and R. *Liturgy and Contemplation.* Translated by J. W. Evans. New York: Kenedy, 1960.

RAITZ VON FRENTZ, E. "Mystisches und liturgisches Beten," *ZAM,* 14 (1939), 48–60.

ROESER, E. *Liturgisches Gebet und Privatgebet.* Wien, 1940.

VAGAGGINI, C. "Liturgy and Contemplation," *Wor,* 34 (1960), 507–523.

Active and Passive Prayer

GARRIGOU-LAGRANGE, R., O.P. *Christian Perfection and Contemplation According to St.*

Thomas Aquinas and St. John of the Cross. Translated by Sr. T. Timothea Doyle. St. Louis: Herder, 1937.

Hock, K. *Der Wandel in Gottes heiliger Gegenwart.* 11th ed. Vechta, 1936.

Lindworsky, J. "Vom Wandel in Gottes Gegenwart," *StimmenZeit,* 98 (1920), 41–56.

Mager, A. *Der Wandel in der Gegenwart Gottes.* Augsburg, 1921.

Tillmann, G. *Der Wandel vor Gott.* Limburg, 1920.

Interior Prayer and Vocal Prayer

Boelaars, H. "Het moeilijke mondgebed," *Nederl. Kath. Stemmen,* 45 (1949), 235–242; 277–287.

Bomm, U., O.S.B. "Der Leib im Gebete," *Anima,* 9 (1954), 131–138.

Ohm, Th. *Die Gebetsgebaerden der Voelker und das Christentum.* Leiden, 1948.

Common Prayer and Private Prayer

Mersch, E., S.J. "Christengebet ist Gliedgebet," *ZAM,* 16 (1941), 109–126.

Informal and Formal Prayer
Prayer of Praise, Thanksgiving, and Petition

Edwall, P., Hayman, E., Maxwell, W. D. *Ways of Worship. The Report of a Theological Commission of Faith and Order.* London, 1951.

Guerard, des Lauriers, M. L., O.P. "Tu adoreras le Seigneur ton Dieu," *VieSpir,* 83 (1950), 417–445.

Morandi, L. *La sorgente delle grazie. La preghiera.* Rovigo, 1948.

Philippe, P., O.P. "La prière d'adoration et de louange," *VieSpir,* 70 (1944), 490–504.

Necessary Qualities of Prayer

Beckes, G., O.S.B. *De continua oratione Clementis Alexandrini doctrina.* (Studia Anselmiana, 14), Romae, 1952.

Bieder, W. "Gebetswirklichkeit und Gebetsmoeglichkeit," *ThZschr* (1947), 40–54.

Eller, E. *Das Gebet. Religionpsychologische Studie.* Paderborn, 1937.

Kerkhoff, R., O.S.B. *Das unablaessige Gebet. Beitraege zur Lehre vom immerwaehrenden Beten im Neuen Testament.* Muenchen, 1954.

Max M., O.S.B. *Incessant Prayer in Ancient Monastic Literature.* Rome, 1946.

Moschner, F. *Christisches Gebetsleben.* Freiburg, 1949.

Pinard, de la Boullaye, H., S.J. "L'oraison diffuse," *RAM,* 24 (1948), 31–59.

Plus, R., S.J. *How to Pray Well.* Westminster, Md.: Newman, 1948.

———. *How to Pray Always: Principles and Practices for Attaining to Union with God.* Translated by Irene Hernaman. London, 1942.

Poggi, A. *La preghiera dell' uomo.* Milano, 1944.

Tilmann, K. *Taeglich beten, aber wie?* 5th ed. Recklinghausen, 1950.

van Veghel, S., O.F.M. *Het gebedsleven.* Haarlem-Antwerpen, 1948.

Wunderle, D. "Ueber die Wesensfrage der inneren Gebetshaltung in der Ostkirche," *ZAM,* 18 (1943), 150–163.

Invocation of the Divine Name

Criado, R., S.J. "La investigación sobre el valor del nombre divino en el Antiguo Testamento," *Estudios Ecclesiasticos,* 26 (1953), 313–352; 435–452.

Giesebrecht, F. *Die Alttestamentliche Schaetzung des Gottesnamens,* 1901.

The Oath—Honoring God's Name

BAUERNFEIND, O. *Eid und Freiden.* Stuttgart, 1956.

EBEL, W. *Der Buergereid.* Weimar, 1958.

GOEPFERT, F. A. *Der Eid.* Mainz, 1883.

GUIDON, B. *Le serment, son histoire, son caractère sacré.* Ottawa, 1957.

HAPPEL, I. *Der Eid im AT.* Muenster, 1908.

HOFMEISTER, PH. *Die christlichen Eidesformen.* Muenchen, 1957.

MUELLER, H. *Zum Eidesverbot der Bergpredigt.* Padenborn, 1913.

PRIBILLA, M. *Der Eid nach der Lehre der katholichen Moraltheologie.* Muenchen, 1956.

SCHOELLGEN, W. "Der politische Eid," *Ho,* 40 (1948), 242–251.

SCHULZ, F. "Der Eid als wesentlich religioese Tatsetzung," *ThG,* (1936), 703–716.

Misuse of the Divine Name

FRANCESCHINI, G. *La bestemmia in Italia.* Venezia, 1938.

NOHARA, G. *La bestemmia.* Udine, 1941.

VAGLIA, G. *La bestemmia,* Torino, 1942.

Worship of God through the Vow

Acta et documenta Congressus de statibus perfectionis. 4 vol. Romae, 1950.

AUXENTIUS A ROTTERDAM, O.F.M. "De obligatione canonica religiosorum tendendi ad perfectionem," *Commentarium pro relig,* 31 (1952), 250–275.

BOUYER, L. *Meaning of the Monastic Life.* Translated by Kathleen Pond. New York: Kenedy, 1955.

GANSEWINKEL, J. v. *Die Grundlage fuer den Rat des Gehorsams in den Evangelien.* Moedling bei Wien, 1937.

GRIBOMONT, J., O.S.B. "Obéissance et évangile selon saint Basile le Grand," *VieSpirSupp,* 21 (1952), 192–215.

HEUFELDER, E. M., O.S.B. *Die evangelischen Raete.* Wien, 1953.

HOLSTEIN, H. "La mystère de l'obéissance," *Etudes,* 278 (1953), 145–157.

KIRCHBERG, C. *De voti natura, obligatione.* Muenster, 1897.

MALONE, E. E., O.S.B. *The Monk and the Martyr. The Monk as the Successor of the Martyr.* Washington, 1950.

MENNESSIER, I., O.P. "Donation à Dieu voeux de religion," *VieSpirSupp,* 49 (1936), 227–301.

———. *Obedience.* Westminster, Md.: Newman, 1953.

PHILIPPE, P., O.P. "La portée du voeu d'obéissance," *VieSpir,* 86 (1952), 509–524.

PIUS XII. "Address to Religious Superiors Aug. 12, 1950," *AAS,* 43A (1951), 26–36.

SCHMITT, A., S.J. "Vaeterliche Gewalt und Geluebde Minderjaehriger," *ZKathTh,* 60 (1936), 244–248.

SÉJOURNÉ, P. "Voeu," *DTC,* 15, 3182–3224.

SNOEK, C. *De idee der gehoorzaamheid in het Nieuwe Testament.* Nijmegen, 1952.

THALHAMMER, D., S.J. *Jenseitige Menschen. Eine Sinndeutung des Ordensstandes.* 2nd ed. Freiburg, 1953.

The Lord's Day—Sanctification through the Sacrifice of Christ and the Church

Anima, Heft 4, 1949: "Unsere seelsorgliche Verantwortung fuer den Sonntag."

AUER, A. "Der Eucharistie als Weg der Welt in die Erfuellung. Von der Bedeutung der Eucharistie fuer die christliche Laienfroemmigkeit," *GeistLeben,* 33 (1960), 192–210.

BARBEL, J. "Der christliche Sonntag in der Verkuendigung," *TrThZ*, 60 (1951), 17–30.

BECKER, K. *Wahrhaft selige Nacht.* Freiburg, 1952.

BOEHMER, I. *Der christliche Sonntag nach Ursprung und Geschichte.* Leipzig, 1930.

BREUNING, W. "Die gesitliche Kommunion—Froemmigkeitsuebung oder Grundhaltung des Christen," *TrThZ*, 69 (1960), 224–236.

CASEL, O. "Art und Sinn der aeltesten Osterfeier," *Jahrbuch fuer Liturgiewissenschaft*, 14 (1938), 1–78.

CULLMAN, OSCAR. *Early Christian Worship.* Naperville, Ill.: Allenson, 1954.

DANIÉLOU, J. *The Bible and the Liturgy.* Notre Dame Press, 1956.

DREHER, B. *Die Osterpredigt von der Reformation bis zur Gegenwart.* Freiburg, 1951.

DURRWELL, F. X. *The Resurrection: a Biblical Study.* Translated by Rosemary Sheed. New York: Sheed and Ward, 1960.

EBERLE, A. "Unsere christliche Sonntagsfeier," *ThPrQschr*, 105 (1957), 116–123.

FISCHER, B. AND WAGNER, J. *Paschatis Sollemnia. Studien zur Osterfeier und Osterfroemmigkeit.* Freiburg, 1959.

GRELOT, P. AND PIERRON, J. *Osternacht und Osterfeier im Alten und Neuen Bund.* Duesseldorf, 1959. (Sammlung: Die Welt der Bibel, Nr. 4).

GUARDINI, R. *Der Sonntag gestern, heute und immer.* Wuerzburg, 1959.

HILD, J. *Dimanche et vie paschale.* Tournhout, 1949.

JUNGMANN, J. A. "Beginnt die christliche Woche mit dem Sonntag?" *Gewordene Liturgie*, Innsbruck-Leipzig, 1941, 206–231.

KUHAUPT, H. *Die Feier der Eucharistie.* Muenster, 1950.

Lebendige Seelsorge, Heft 2, 1953: "Feier des Sonntags."

Le huitieme jour. Cahiers de la Vie Spirituelle, Paris, 1947.

LOUIS, PETER. *Der Christ und sein Sonntag. Ursprung und Geschichte, Segen und Ziel des Herrentages.* Wuerzburg, 1950.

NIELEN, J. *Das Zeichen des Herrn. Sabbat und Sonntag in biblischer und urchristlicher Bezeugung.* Freiburg, 1940.

PASCHER, J. *Eucharistia. Gestalt und Vollzug.* Muenster-Freiburg, 2 ed. 1952.

PEICHL, H., O.S.B. *Der Tag des Herrn. Die Heiligung des Sonntags im Wandel der Zeiten.* Wien, 1958.

Pro mundi vita. Festschrift zum Eucharistischen Weltkongress 1960. Herausg. von der theol. Fakultaet Muenchen. Muenchen, 1960.

REUSS, J. M. *Opfermahl—Mitte des Christseins.* Mainz, 1960.

RUDOLF, K. *Der Christliche Sonntag.* (Wiener Seelsorgertagung, 1955), Wien, 1956.

SCHMIDT, H. A. *Introductio in liturgiam Occidentalem.* Romae, 1960 (Excellent bibliography on the Eucharist in this work).

SCHNITZLER, TH. *Eucharistie in der Geschichte.* Koeln, 1960.

SCHULTE, R. *Die Messe als Opfer der Kirche. Die Lehre der fruehmittelalterlichen Autoren ueber das eucharistische Opfer.* Muenster, 1959.

Theologie der Gegenwart in Auswahl, 3 (1960). Heft 1: Zum Eucharistischen Weltkongress 1960 (Beitraege von M. E. Boismard, J. Dupont, B. Haering, E. Rideau, V. Schurr).

VOLK, H. *Sonntaeglicher Gottesdienst. Theologische Grundlegung.* Muenster, 1956.

Vom heiligen Pascha. Ein Osterbuch. Published by Abtei Herstelle. Paderborn, 1950.

WAGNER, J.-ZAEHRINGER, D. *Eucharistiefeier am Sonntag.* (Erster deutscher liturgischer Kongress.) Trier, 1951.

WALTER, E. *Die Euchariste. Das Sakrament der Gemeinschaft.* 3rd ed., Freiburg, 1940.

Work Sanctified by Cult and Sacred Repose

*Bienert, W. *Die Arbeit nach der Lehre der Bibel. Ein Beitrag zur evangelischen Sozialethik.* Stuttgart, 1956.

Borne, E. and Henry, F. *A Philosophy of Work.* Translated by Francis Jackson. New York: Sheed and Ward, (no date).

Brunner, A. "Macht die Arbeit menschwuerdig!" *StimmenZeit,* 140 (1947), 321–336.

Chenu, M. D. *Pour une théologie du travail.* Paris, 1955.

Dessauer, F. *Streit um die Technik.* Frankfurt, 1956.

———. *Seele im Bannkreis der Technik.* 2nd ed. Olten, 1954.

Die Kirche und die Welt des Arbeiters (Wiener Seelsorgertagung). Wien, 1957.

Doncoeur, P. *L'Evangile du travail.* Paris, 1940.

Grimm, W. "Mehr Kontakt zur Welt der Arbeit," *LebS,* 11 (1960), 78–85.

Guenther, A.-Janes, J. *Die Arbeiterpriester* (Dokumente). Heilbronn, 1957.

Haering, B. "Der Geist des Technizismus und der Liturgie," *Liturgisches Jahrbuch,* 8 (1958), 194–204.

Haessle, J. *Das Arbeitethos der Kirche nach Thomas von Aquin und Leo XIII.* Freiburg, 1923.

Hauck, F. "Die Arbeit im Heidentum und Christentum," *RACh,* 1 (1942), 585–590 (with bibliography).

Hoeffner, J. "Menschenwuerde und Betriebsverfassung," *TrThZ,* 59 (1950), 364–373.

Holzapfel, H. *Die Sittliche Wertung der Arbeit im christlichen Altertum.* Wuerzburg, 1941 (with bibliography).

Koessler, P. *Christentum und Technik.* Wuerzburg, 1959.

Legendige Seelsorge, 7 (1956), Heft 6: "Seelsorge in der industrialisierten Welt."

Lotz, J. B., S.J. *Mensch, Wirtschaft, Sonntagsfeier.* Salzburg-Koeln, 1958.

Mahr, F. *Der Christ in der Welt der Apparate.* Wuerzburg, 1958.

Mounier, E. *Be Not Afraid: a Denunciation of Despair.* London: Rockliff, 1951.

Nattermann, Ch. *Die moderne Arbeit soziologisch und theologisch betrachtet.* Dortmund, 1933.

Nell-Breuning, O. von "Arbeit und Musse," *StimmenZeit,* 160 (1957), 93–99.

Ohm, Th. O.S.B. *Ruhe und Froemmigkeit.* Koeln-Opladen, 1955.

Pietsch, M. *Von Wert und Wuerde menschlicher Arbeit.* Frankfurt, 1952.

Selected Letters and Addresses of Pius XII: The Dignity and Prerogatives of Labor. Catholic Truth Society, London, 1949, pp. 291f.

"Réflexions sur le travail," *LumVie,* 20 (1955), 143–146.

Reinermann, W. "Um das Ethos der entseelten Erwerbsarbeit," *GeistLeben,* 25 (1950), 266–279.

Rondet, H. "Elements pour une théologie du travail," *NRTh* 77 (1955), 27–48, 123–143.

Scheler, M. "Wert und Wuerde der christlichen Arbeit," *Jahrbuch der deutschen Katholiken,* Augsburg (1920/21), 75–89.

"Technische Werte und Seelsorge," *Anima,* 15 (1960), Heft 2.

Teichtweier, G. "Versuch einer Theologie der Arbeit," *ThQschr,* 138 (1958), 307–328.

Valiente, F. "Sentido y valor del trabajo," *CiTh* 78 (1951), 104–123.

Weber, Max, *The Protestant Ethic and the Spirit of Capitalism.* Translated by Talcott Parsons. London, 1930.

Wyszynski, S. *Work.* Chicago: Scepter Press, 1960.

Divine and Ecclesiastical Law regarding Rest and Cult

BERTE, P., S.J. "A propos des oeuvres serviles. La recherche du gain influe-t-elle sur leur determination?" *NRTh*, 63 (1936), 32–56.

DELHAYE, PH. "Le repos domicial," *AmCl*, 68 (1958), 225–234; 241–249. Cf J. R. Connery, *TheolS*, 19 (1958), 522 ff.

FISCHER, H. "Um den Sonntag in der Industrie," *NO*, 14 (1960), 29–40.

GECK, A. "Arbeitszeitentwicklung und Seelsorge. Ein Beitrag zur sozialen Moral," *Koelner Pastoralblatt*, 9 (1957), 111–114; 135–140.

GINTHOER, A. "Die Moraltheologie der Aufklaerung und die Sonntagsheiligung," *Erbe und Auftrag*, 35 (1959), 357–370; 453–471.

HOEFFNER, J. "Der Tag des Herrn und die gleitende Arbeitswoche," *TrThZ*, 65 (1956), 277–283; also *Die Kirche in der Welt*, 10 (1958/59), 353–359.

HUBER, H., C.SS.R. *Geist und Buchstabe der Sonntagsruhe. Eine historisch-theologische Untersuchung ueber das Verbot der knechtlichen Arbeit von der Urkirche bis auf Thomas von Aquin.* Salzburg, 1958.

McREAVY, L. "The Sunday Repose from Labour. An Historical-theological Examination of the Notion of Servile Work (from the Era of the Apostles to the Advent of Charlemagne)," *EphThLov*, 12 (1935), 291–323.

———. "Servile Work. The Evolution of the Present Sunday Law. Criticism and Suggestions," *ClerRev*, 9 (1935), 270–284; 453–466.

MICHAUD, H. "Les oeuvres serviles interdites le dimanche," *RevApol*, 62 (1936), 290–303; 462–473.

MOSER, G. "Die Automation und ihre Probleme," *ThQschr*, 137 (1957), 187–206.

NIEMEIER, J. "Die rechtliche Problematik der Sonntagsarbeit," *NO*, 14 (1960), 358–370.

PETTIRSCH, F. "Um eine sinnvolle Kasuistik der Sonntagsruhe," *Die Kirche in der Welt*, 9 (1957), 129–134.

———. "Aktuelle Probleme um die Sonntagsruhe," *ThQschr*, 106 (1958), 105–113.

———. "Das Verbot der opera servilia in der Heiligen Schrift und in der altkirchlichen Exegese," *ZKathTh*, 69 (1947), 417–444.

PIUS XII. Address on Automation to the Christian Association of Italian Workers (ACLI). Cf *Major Addresses of Pope Pius XII*, edited by Vincent A. Yzermans, vol. I, p. 408ff. St. Paul: North Central Pub. Co. 1961.

Revolution der Roboter, Untersuchungen ueber Probleme der Automatisierung. Muenchen, 1956.

Sonntag kann Sonntag bleiben. (Hattinger Gutachten zur Gleitenden Arbeitswoche.) Essen, 1957.

STEINMETZER, F. "Arbeitsruhe," *RACh*, 1 (1950), 590–595.

VEREECKE, L. "La théologie du dimanche selon Henri de Gorkum (1431), *MelScRel*, 14 (1957), 167–182.

———. "La théologie du dimanche selon saint Antonin de Florence," *ScEccle*, 11 (1959), 345–363.

WALLRAFF, H. J., S.J. "Ordnungsethische Aufrufe aus dem Vollzug der Automation," *StimmenZeit*, 160 (1956/57), 1–12.

———. "Die Fortenwicklung der Sonntagsruhe," *NO*, 14 (1960), 40–49.

WELTY, E., O.P. "Durchlaufende Arbeitsweise mit betontem Wochenrhythmus," *NO*, 11 (1957), 277–283.

WINGEN, N. "Die Sonntagsarbeit im Rahmen der Arbeitszeitfrage," *NO*, 11 (1957), 350–356.

ZEMANEK, H. "Automation und die Folgen," *Ho*, 49 (1956/57), 297–311.

Additional Works in English

ALPHONSUS LIGOURI (Saint). *Prayer, the Great Means of Salvation.* St. Louis: B. Herder, 1922.

BALTHASAR, HANS URS VON. *Prayer.* New York: Sheed and Ward, 1961.

BOUYER, LOUIS. *Introduction to Spirituality.* New York: Desclée, 1961.

CABROL, FERNAND, O.S.B. *Prayer of the Early Christians.* New York: Benziger, 1930.

CLAUDEL, PAUL. *Lord, Teach Us to Pray.* New York: Longmans, 1948.

D'ARCY, MARTIN C., S.J. *Success in Work.* Eastcote (Middlesex), England: Grail, 1947.

FENTON, JOSEPH C. *The Theology of Prayer.* Milwaukee: Bruce, 1939.

GIRARDEY, FERREOL, C.SS.R. *Prayer: Its Necessity, Its Power, Its Conditions.* St. Louis: B. Herder, 1916.

GUARDINI, ROMANO. *Prayer in Practice.* New York: Pantheon, 1957.

GUINIVEN, JOHN J. *The Precept of Hearing Mass* (Catholic University Studies in Canon Law, 158). Washington: Catholic Univ. Press, 1942.

JUNGMANN, JOSEF A., S.J. *The Meaning of Sunday.* Chicago: Fides, 1961.

KELLY, VINCENT J., C.SS.R. *Forbidden Sunday and Feast-day Occupations* (Catholic University Studies in Sacred Theology, 70). Washington: Catholic Univ. Press, 1943.

LOWRY, JAMES M. *Dispensation from Private Vows: Historic Synopsis and Commentary.* (Catholic University Studies in Canon Law, 237). Washington: Catholic Univ. Press, 1946.

McNABB, VINCENT, O.P. *Faith and Prayer.* Westminster, Md.: Newman, 1953.

MARITAIN, JACQUES-MARITAIN, RAISSA. *Prayer and Intelligence.* New York: Sheed and Ward, 1928.

MOORE, THOMAS V., O.S.B. *Prayer: Instructions and Addresses for Religious and Laity.* St. Louis: B. Herder, 1921.

MORRISON, ROBERT B., S.J. *In Touch With God: Prayer, Mass, and the Sacraments.* (Religion and Culture Series.) Milwaukee: Bruce, 1943.

PERRIN, JOSEPH M., O.P. *Living With God.* St. Louis: B. Herder, 1961.

REGAN, FRANCIS A. *Dies Dominica and Dies Solis, the Beginnings of the Lord's Day in Christian Antiquity* (Catholic University Studies in Sacred Theology, 2nd Series, 125 A). Washington: Catholic Univ. Press, 1961.

Restore the Sunday. Loveland, Ohio: Grailville, 1949.

Sanctification of the Sunday (Proceedings of the National Liturgical Week, 1949). Conception Mo.: the Liturgical Conference, 1949.

VAN ZELLER, HUBERT, O.S.B. *Approach to Prayer.* New York: Sheed and Ward, 1958.

Periodical Literature in English

BALSAM, B. M. "Value of Mental Prayer," *CrCr,* 5 (June, 1953), 169–81.

BELFORD, J. L. "Let Us Pray," *HPR,* 32 (Sept., 1932), 1241–9.

DE JAEGHER, P. "Towards Continual Prayer," *RR,* 11 (Sept., 1952), 231–41.

DONOVAN, C. F. "Faith and Prayer," *RR,* 6 (Nov., 1947), 335–41.

DUFFY, D. "Sunday Rest," *Fur,* 11 (June, 1960), 364–71.

GRAF, E. "Prayer: Definitions, Kinds," *HPR,* 34 (Sept., 1934), 1321–25.

———. "Excellence of Vocal Prayer," *HPR,* 40 (July, 1940), 1129–31.

KELLY, G. "How Often Must We Pray?" *RR,* 8 (Nov., 1949), 289–96.

KLAAS, A. "In Praise of Prayer," *RR,* 6 (Nov., 1947), 363–71; 8 (July, 1949), 139–50.

KNOX, R. A. "Prayer," *ClerRev,* 16 (June, 1939), 485–98; 17 (July, 1939), 2–17.

MacIvor, D. "Sunday Worship," *Fur,* 11 (June, 1960), 372–79.

McREAVY, L. L. "Sabbatarianism and the Decalogue," *ClerRev,* 20 (June, 1941), 498–508.

MARTINDALE, C. C. "Sanctifying Sunday," *Mo,* 170 (Aug., 1937), 118–25.

PETTIRSCH, F. X. "Theology of Sunday Rest," *TD,* 6 (Sept., 1958), 114–20.

——. "Prayer of the Church," *CrCr,* 5 (June, 1953), 127–40.

PUTZ, J. "Liturgical and Private Devotion," *RR,* 7 (Jan., 1948), 23–33.

TIERNEY, C. "Doctrinal Aspects of the Sunday," *Australasian Catholic Review,* 33 (July, 1956), 239–45.

UTZ, A. F. "Nature of Prayer," *CrCr,* 5 (June, 1953), 154–62.

Book Two

Love in Human Fellowship

SURVEY

Christian moral teaching places the total devotion of our life to Christ above all things. The very rhythm of the divine life is in us through the divine virtues by which we are united to God in faith, hope, and love. Through them in the virtue of religion we worship God and sanctify our whole life by divine cult. This is the religious life (or the sacral ethos) prescribed in the first part of the great commandment (love of God) and the first table of the Law of Sinai. Next to this and flowing from it is the vast moral domain which embraces the second part of the great commandment and the second table of the decalog: love of neighbor and the moral tasks (taken in the strict sense of that word) in all realms of terrestrial life.

The two great cycles of life, our life in God and our commitment in the world, are not merely contiguous to each other without interior bond. They belong together in the highest possible form of unity, despite any conceptual distinction we might make. The more perfectly we live the Christian life, the more do we realize and manifest this ideal unity. The destruction of the unity, in fact its reduction to a mere external bond by which the two life circles exist merely side by side would be the clearest evidence of the caducity, the frailty, or at least the superficiality of both our moral and our religious life.

It is the task of the disciple of Christ to base his moral action in the world on the vital religious foundations in such wise that its goals and motives are entirely religious—that it is transformed by the religious virtues, though retaining fully its own unique characteristic formal structure and objective conformity to reality.

The decisive basic power through which the supernatural religious life communicates to the moral life its primal formation is charity. Charity is the divine love reaching out into love of neighbor. As the love of God, so Christian love of neighbor is sustained and upheld by the foundation of divine faith. It is borne aloft by the dynamism of the divine virtue of hope. It is steeped in priestly humility and elevated to the heights of religion or divine worship. The basic model and dynamic life force of Christian love of neighbor is the sacrificial death of Christ and the oblation of the Eucharist.

Love of neighbor is therefore to be placed at the apex of all moral virtue. Love must forge the connecting link between the religious and the moral life. Moreover, the whole moral mission of the Christian (obedience, sense of family and community, the preservation of human life, its sustenance and motivation, justice and right use of property, cultivation of truth, loyalty, and honor) must be hedged in with charity. Charity must be the light and warmth, the very sinews of the Christian commitment, its firmness and source of unity.

CHRISTIAN LOVE OF NEIGHBOR

CHAPTER NINE

POSITIVE CONTENT OF THE LOVE OF NEIGHBOR

I. INNER UNITY OF DIVINE LOVE, LOVE OF SELF, LOVE OF NEIGHBOR

1. *Essential Triad in the Mystery of Love*

THE *I* of person and personal being signifies the subsistent being spiritually conscious of self. But being spiritual and being a person can become articulate only through words and love. The word in turn is meaningful and deals meaningfully in speech only when confronted by a *Thou,* by a spiritually other one to whom as correlative the *I* is directed. Depth and earnestness of the word can be sounded only in accents of love, in taking the *Thou* earnestly and understandingly. A Thou, a real independent spiritual other, can be found only in word and in love. In every attitude which is defective in love (as in passion, or mere motive of personal profit), we do not perceive the being in its true reality, the Thou of the other. (Hatred takes the being of the other seriously indeed, but completely rejects him as Thou, as partner in word and love, so utterly in fact that it relishes the thought of destroying him.)

Discovery of the Thou in love is essential. If we fail to discover and recognize the Thou in love, we shall not discover the essential level of our own person, the I in ourselves which manifests itself essentially only in word and love. The person as objective spiritual reality, as life, signifies both the I as independent and self-possessing and the relation to a Thou in a movement of recognition and submission.

The so-called *egoism* of the self-in-being and self-preservation is no more essential in the realm of the personal (the living personal being) than is the *altruism* of the movement to the Thou. Only if there is the movement of love from the I to the Thou, which takes the Thou as seriously as the I itself, are both firmly fixed in themselves. If love does not draw its warmth from the Thou, or if the sinister fire of passion and self-seeking envelop and exploit one's fellow man, then the I is not firmly fixed in itself as lived being. It is not the person in lived being, but is rather like an undeveloped situation or a burnt out shell!

As created persons we are in the objective reality of our being orientated to God. The most profound reality of our being, our personal being, is first experienced when God's splendor is reflected in our words, when we abandon ourselves to love of God. We are really I, only ourselves fully, when we face the Thou of God. The immense span of the bridge of love of God reaches the shores of eternity only if it is supported by the pier on our own shore, the love of neighbor.

The I-Thou relation to God can be realized here in this earthly sojourn only if we in some measure have activated word and love in relation to our neighbor. How drear is the consequence in the religious life of a child who does not learn to love, does not master the dialog of love because it has not had love's experience! It is true of natural love—and all the more of supernatural love—that we cannot love God unless we love our neighbor: "How can he who does not love his brother, whom he sees, love God, whom he does not see?" (1 Jn 4:20).

Word and love for neighbor obviously grow deep and strong only if our word and our love flow from God as their source and turn to Him in ultimate motivation. From Him come their beauty and charm. For Him they are fashioned and destined. So it is that man's I-Thou relation is possible only through participation in the unique character of God's being which is personal and triune. We must be linked with that Triad of person which rests in the I-Thou relation of the Eternal Word and of the Eternal Love, the Word eternally coming forth from the Father as His Son, the Holy Spirit proceeding eternally from Father and Son as Infinite Love.

The word and the love between man and man, flowing from the I to the Thou, is in a measure always conditioned by a third, because God is already in our midst when there is a real communication between person and person.[1] It follows that man cannot truly love if he has not discovered in love the Thou of his neighbor. Love of self and love of neighbor cannot reach the depth essential for preservation and fulfillment unless both seek and find in God their origin and their center. "Only those who love themselves for God's sake love themselves as they should. Therefore in order that they truly love themselves they must love God.[2]

Natural love of self and self-preservation is nothing other than the dignity of human partnership in the love of God, by which man is created in the divine image and conserved. Submission to neighbor and the self-movement toward him is the clearest reflection of the love of God, the love by which God gives Himself to man, the divine I-Thou, self-giving love. Only to a consciousness, fully aroused to the meaning of love, fully astonished at one's neighbor, and fully puzzled by the unfathomable riddle of the I-Thou relationship, does the primordial basis of the movement of word and love make itself known as proceeding from God. Only to such loving awareness does the ultimate meaning of end and goal of these spiritual realities unfold itself and reveal their orientation toward God.

The deep natural love of self and of neighbor is rooted in the natural value and dignity of the person (and personality), in man's natural likeness to God. Even in the natural order man is the image of God. But the supernatural love of self and neighbor is far loftier than any mere natural love, for it rests in our supernatural likeness to God. It has its foundation in the participation through grace in the divine nature (2 Pt 1:4) and in the divine call of all men to this participation. In charity or supernatural love we are allowed not only to love God as our Creator but as our Father, and indeed with the rich warmth of His own love, with the love with which in His intimate divine life He knows and loves Himself in the Word of Truth and the Breath of Love. The love of God for us, transcending all mere love of Creator for creature, is caught up in His own infinite love of Self in this triune intimate life of eternal self-communication: thus also the Christian love of self and of neighbor in the life movement of charity is a partnership in this incomprehensible love of God for us.

In Christian love we love ourselves and our neighbor as the "beloved of God," within the sacred orbit of the divine love. Christ prays for us: "That the love with which thou hast loved me may be in them, and I in them" (Jn 17:26; cf. Jn 13:34; 15:9).

2. *Unity and Diversity of Charity*

According to St. Thomas, charity as love of God and of neighbor is one self-same virtue: "for the end of charity is one, namely the divine goodness. And there is also only one fellowship or participation (*communicatio*) in the eternal bliss, on which this friendship is founded."[3] Aquinas is quite aware that the material object of the love of God and the object of the love of neighbor (including love of self) are poles apart; they differ as much as God and creation. But the formal object, the end and motive, namely, the fellowship and participation or, more specifically, the call to participation in the beatifying love (*beatitudo*) of God is only one. In God we love His love which beatifies Himself and us. And we love in ourselves and in our neighbor the inconceivably exalted title of nobility granted through participation in the beatifying friendship of God.

It is not at all irrelevant to speak of the diversity of the material object: love of God, love of neighbor. To disregard this distinction would lead to pantheism and complete obliteration of the diversity between religion and morality. But the identity of formal object and, above all, the oneness of the supernatural basis and motive for love of God and neighbor imparts to the love of neighbor and with it to love of self the immediate supernatural religious value, and guarantees the unity of the supernatural religious and moral life as a life in God.

In the infused virtue of divine love we love God. And rooted in Him and His divine love, we love ourselves and our neighbor in and with Him. As partners in His love, sharing in His loving paternal embrace of the children of His predilection, we love with the same embrace of divine love ourselves and our neighbor. Consequently when we speak of the love of God and the love of neighbor as one, the meaning in relation to the divine virtue is not at all the same as in reference to love in a merely natural order. In all our supernatural love we are caught up in the stream of the divine love which flows eternally between Father and Son in the Holy Spirit. This perfect fusion of the love for the Father and the love for the adopted children of the Father in one same Source, the Holy Spirit, is the inexpressible mystery of the Sacred Heart of Jesus. An inexpressible mystery indeed and yet transparent in all His words and acts!

Scripture stresses both the unity and the diversity of the supernatural love of God and love of neighbor. The unity we note particularly in the hymn on charity in the first Letter to the Corinthians, chapter 13, and in the Lord's response to the lawyer, in which he placed the two together (cf Lk 10:27); the diversity, in the twofold character of the commandment of love, as seen in the same passage. As St. Thomas pertinently notes, the commandment of love for one's neighbor is in itself already contained in the first commandment.[4] It is explicitly formulated only because of our limited human intelligence. For our clearer understanding it is articulated as the *second* which is like the first (Mt 22:39).

One who places the major stress on the radical diversity of material object (the person who is loved) insists on the advantage of duality and diversity of the commandments of love in the unity of the supernatural gift. One who, with St. Thomas, focuses attention on the unique fellowship and friendship in the divine love—the objective element of love[5]—as the common formal object of the one same supernatural dynamic of love, must accentuate the unity. "With one unique love we love God and our neighbor; God for Himself, ourselves and our neighbor for the sake of God."[6]

3. *Blending of Natural and Supernatural Love of Self and Neighbor*

Supernatural love of self and neighbor far transcends in value and motivation all natural or merely human love. But to be efficacious and fruitful, it must be rooted in natural love, using its dynamic force and profiting from its motivation. All this is possible only to the degree that natural love is rightly ordered. And, in turn, this natural love can often be directed and grasped, only if it begins with the narrow circle close at hand, in which the celestial can take hold from its very inception. Thus supernatural love enters into the ceaseless struggle between well-ordered love and the self-love which is self-seeking, or, more specifically, false self-abandonment. Here we have a case analogous to that of the relation between spirit and the body-soul forces: as the spirit directs and unifies these powers and derives vigor and vitality from them, so too charity remains largely impotent until it lays hold of the sensible powers and forces for its drive and vigor.

In the ultimate analysis all sin flows from the disordered seeking of self, a self-seeking which is not open to charity.[7] In like manner all the supernatural, permanent values are set in motion by charity. "The two kinds of love have produced two states: the earthly, produced by self-love to the extreme of disdain for God; the heavenly, produced by the divine love to the point of renunciation of self for God."[8] Whereas false self-love is the great enemy of love for God and of Christian love for self and neighbor, "the basic demand of the imitation of Christ is self renunciation."[9] Christian love of self has nothing in common with self-infatuation, but is the fulfillment of love for the Crucified; it is sacrifice of self in the will to live only for the brethren. The goal of self-abnegation (with and alongside the love for God) is the better, the genuine love of self in God. "He who loses his life for my sake will find it" (Mt 10:39; 16:24f.; Lk 17:33; Jn 12:25).

Supernatural love of neighbor must penetrate and animate every naturally good inclination toward our fellow men: our love of friends, of

children, of parents; wedded love, marital love. Not solely spiritual love of
spouses, but also the erotic-sexual love of husband and wife directed to this
spiritual love must be animated by the celestial love, by the charity which
approaches the erotic through the spiritual. In this domain charity is both,
and effects both: now it will be self-denial and agonizing renunciation,
now submission and ecstasy in true love. The ultimate norm and standard
for eros (love passion) and sex (for body-soul inclination and bodily
union) is the totality of all these movements of love in charity. Thus it
is that either the lesser love can and must be embodied in the higher, or
it must be sacrificed as the price of charity. What cannot be absorbed in
charity as imitation of crucified love is by that very fact condemned. What
is absorbed in charity is incomprehensibly ennobled and exalted.

II. THE COMMANDMENT OF LOVE OF NEIGHBOR

("Thou shalt love thy neighbor as theyself." Mt 22:39)

1. *The Motive and Obligation* (*"Thou shalt"*)

The dynamic of Christian love of self and of neighbor is not the naked
command. A tremendous impulse to love of self exists in the natural
instinct and desire for self-preservation. In fact, if man were perfectly in
order, love of self would not at all need to be formally or specifically
prescribed. Every man necessarily loves himself. However, because of
original sin man is in constant peril of loving himself badly. Therefore
the first great duty of love of self is the sharp curbing of our native
egotism. But once the supernatural order is established, man also loves
himself badly if he does no more than love himself naturally. A purely
natural love is not enough. He must love himself above all as a child of
God and as the "new man" in Christ. Hence the second, and the greater,
duty of love of self is: love yourself as a Christian with Christ in God.

There is a ready natural ally of love of neighbor in the force of innate
altruism (in the I-Thou urge, in the social instinct). The conscious
realization that man is fully I only in the measure in which he serves as a
Thou in love constitutes a powerful and correct impulse for love of
neighbor. But once the authentic love of neighbor is perfected, the merely
natural tendency must recede into the background absolutely, if masked
self-seeking is not to assume control and the genuine Thou in deferential
love is to be discovered.

Christian love has its own true and proper motive, its sustaining impulse, in the charity of God, in his love for us and for our neighbor. In the supernatural order we cannot love ourselves without including in our love and motivation our neighbor who is called with us to the divine likeness and the imitation of Christ. The motive of love for ourselves and for others is absolutely the same. It is unique and indivisible. The most eloquent and most pressing command and invitation to this twofold and unique love comes to us from the example of Christ, from His divine-human love for us and for all the brethren. God commands us to love by the very love He bestows upon us, a unique love which reaches out to us before we love Him.

It is God's very love, the unique love with which He loves Himself and us, which is the proper motive of supernatural love of self and of neighbor. God is love (1 Jn 4:8). Therefore the power to love in and through God is the supreme gift; being permitted to love and obliged to love, the chief commandment. God's own love, which is poured forth in 'our hearts through the Holy Spirit (Rom 5:5), is the ineffable bond which links us together and impels us to love (2 Cor 5:14). Christ in His glory, through all His acts which are manifestations of His infinite love for each of us and all of us, bestows upon us His Holy Spirit who is His Love in person, thus forming us in an ineffable divine unity and inciting us to mutual love. In this way the mystery of charity coincides with the Church in which Christ engraves the law of love in our hearts through the sacraments.

Through holy baptism we are made members of the one Body of Christ, and as members we are intimately related, members one of the other in this Mystical Body (Eph 4:1ff.; 4:25). Through confirmation we are given the Pentecostal flame of apostolic zeal for one another, transcending every division of race and culture. The sacred powers for loving service in the interests of souls are conferred in the sacrament of order. At the shores of eternity the sacrament of extreme unction prepares us for entry into the Church triumphant and the celestial liturgy. The Church steeps our mortal illness and our penance and pain into the high-priestly passion and death of our Savior, so that we are enabled in a truly priestly spirit to offer our life as sacrifice of love in union with Christ for our neighbor. In the sacrament of matrimony the natural love of two human beings for each other and for the children of their desire forms a partnership in the unselfish love of the Savior. They are made witnesses to each other and to all men in the world of the love of Christ and His Church. The efficacious word of pardon is spoken in penance, the love-gift from Christ and His Church. Through it there is restoration and re-introduction of the lapsed into undiminished membership in the loving fellowship of the sacrificial community. The supreme sign of love of the Savior for all of us is the Holy Eucharist, in which sign of His love we are most intimately and perfectly drawn together in fraternal love.

Authentic supernatural love of neighbor which includes necessarily true love of self, both as to inner spirit and external act, has as basic requirement this objectively real union of togetherness in Christ. Signified and effected by the sacraments, this inner bond of unity and participation in Him is also the mightiest incentive to our love. All the sacraments orientate us efficaciously to the great object of our common hope, to the triumph of love in God's eternal Kingdom, the ultimate union in the Spirit of love, in the triune God. Succinctly St. Paul sums up all these motives for love of neighbor: "I . . . exhort you to walk in a manner worthy of the calling with which you were called, with all humility and meekness, with patience, bearing with one another in love, careful to preserve the unity of the Spirit in the bond of peace: one body and one Spirit, even as you were called in one hope of your calling; one Lord, one faith, one baptism; one God and Father of all" (Eph 4:1ff.).

The Church, likewise, in her Postcommunion prayer for the feast of Easter sums up the fundamental motives for the fraternal fellowship of Christians: "Pour forth upon us, O Lord, the Spirit of thy love. In thy goodness unite us all in mind and heart, whom Thou hast nourished with Thy paschal sacrament."

The love of Christ is not an extrinsic motive acting upon us from without. It is a vital and overwhelming love-force, a force impelling us from within (cf. 2 Cor 5:14). With this in mind, the Apostle jubilantly refers to the marvelous works of God's love in Christ and to the incomparable gift of His love for us, the Spirit of Love Himself. Flushed with the sense of utter triumph he cries out in exultation: "Who shall separate us from the love of Christ?" (Rom 8:35). In this same spirit all Christians must feel impelled to love one another, with a firm invincible love; for in and through the sacraments they have received the love triumphant of the resurrected Christ. The overpowering impulse of this great love of neighbor should move them since they are surely united vitally in the bond of celestial love. But the sinner is not excluded even though he is bereft of sanctifying grace. We are linked with him through the Holy Spirit whom we have received. The love-force of the sacraments urges us to love him with redemptive love, for through them we are steeped in the redemptive love of Christ, through them we grow into it and are in a way identified with it.

The chief motive of Christian love of neighbor is not the simple commandment as such. Even less is the motive sheer menace and dread of the judgment for those who refuse to love. Much rather is it God's own love and the marvellous Gift of Love, which is His Spirit, embracing us all in its sweep and generosity. The more the Christian grows in love, the more does his awareness of joyful and grateful acceptance of God's love in ever-deepening partnership of love grow strong within him, the more does he enter into the divine love, into the example and force of Christ's love creating in him the impulse and motive for love of neighbor and himself.

In countless ways God announces His commandment of love: it is transmitted in every tone of voice among men. It has been tenderly carried by the song of harps, tumultuously proclaimed by clang of bells and blare of trumpets. In mercy, in judgment, in joyful triumph God's love has been told to men in a vast and varied message committed to all mankind. And thus should be man's response to love, a splendid orchestration of a thousand instruments in accompaniment, each according to degree or growth of love proclaiming the full and rich accord of the motives of Christian love for the God Who has first loved us. Surely there is no ambiguity regarding the gift of love which commits to us also the most pressing command of love. Many passages of Old and New Testament prescribe it in an explicit formula. It is the golden gift bestowed upon man. But there is also the unconcealed threat of eternal exclusion from the divine community of love for those who are without love.

The most pregnant form of the commandment reads: "Love your neighbor as yourself!" (cf. Lv 19:17f.; Mt 5:43f.; 22:39; Rom 13:8). The content of this law is explained diversely (cf. Dt 22:1ff.; Sir 17:12), particularly in the maxim of the "golden rule": "See thou never do to another what thou wouldst hate to have done to thee by another" (Tb 4:16).

For all its negative formulation in Tobias, the commandment of love of neighbor in the Old Testament required a positive manifestation of love, as does the commandment in the New Testament formulated positively in the maxim of the "golden rule": "Therefore all things whatever you would that men should do to you, even so do you also to them; for this is the Law and the Prophets" (Mt 7:12; Lk 6:31; Rom 13:8ff.).

The commandment of love of neighbor belongs to the chief commandment. In union with the commandment of love of God, it is the most pressing and the greatest commandment (Mk 12:31; Lk 10:27ff.). Love of neighbor, though obviously now raised to utterly new heights, is the "new commandment" (Jn 13:34f.; 15:12ff.). It is the "royal law"; "If, however, you fulfill the royal law, according to the Scriptures, 'Thou shalt love thy neighbor as thyself,' you do well" (Jas 2:8). The moral exhortations of the apostles are repeatedly summed up in this one great commandment (Gal 5:6; Col 3:14; Heb 10:24; 13:1; 1 Pt 1:22; 2:17; 4:8; 2 Pt 1:7ff.).

The very form in which this commandment is presented, in all its precision, reveals the Christian moral of grace. 1 Cor 13 and also the letters of John are a unique hymn of praise and a tremendous imperative of love: "And this commandment we have from him, that he who loves God should love his neighbor also" (1 Jn 4:21). The commandment is both terrifying and beatifying, as Jesus' own description of the judgment clearly reveals (Mt 25:31ff.). After the enunciation of the commandment of love the judgment follows. It is based on this commandment of love, for the whole law is comprised of love. And love bears within it all blessing.

2. "Our Neighbor"

a. Whom Must We Love?

Our Lord Himself in a most dramatic fashion answered the question: who is "our neighbor"? (Lk 10:29ff.). Our neighbor is in any instance the one who here and now is in need of my love and my help. The man whom the Lord describes as the victim of brigands is obviously a Jew. He came from Jerusalem. The Samaritan could have shrugged off all responsibility, "He is a stranger; I don't know him at all." Or more likely, contemptuously, "He is a Jew, and we hold no truck with them." But instead the Samaritan, "seeing him, was moved with compassion. And he went up to him and bound up his wounds." He did not restrict his kindness to first aid, but extended his responsibility until the victim was completely out of danger.

In the parable of the Good Samaritan the helpless Jew robbed and wounded was the neighbor. But the parable does not deny at all that there are natural relationships or circumstances which draw us more closely to one person than to others. In fact the precarious condition of the poor Jew demanded the attention of the priest and then of the Levite of his own race. The alien was finally the "neighbor," because the people closest to him through bonds of race and religion had despised and neglected him. It is entirely consonant with the spirit of the parable to hold that ordinarily parents are the neighbors to their children, children to their parents, the wife to her husband, neighbor to neighbor. Stating the matter simply, we can say in principle those bound together by the closest ties are neighbors to one another. This means that their needs have the first claim on the good will and generous impulse of those closest to them. But in principle there can be no barrier or limitation of relationship or friendship or race or nation: every human being in any concrete situation can become our "neighbor," if God in His providence leads him to us in his misfortune and opens our heart to him and grants us the necessary means to assist him.

Whoever wishes to come to the assistance of a stranger in the hour of misfortune, in the manner of the Samaritan who rescued the hapless Jew, must in mind and spirit embrace and receive all men with loving kindness. It is essential that such interior attitude precede any particular contact with those in distress. And the spirit must be far more than a humanistic sentiment of esteem or affection for humanity, more than an expansive philanthropic generosity. It must be a true sense of love ready for action and flowing from a faith deeply conscious of the most intimate and profound solidarity between us and our neighbor.

Christian love of neighbor excludes no creature enjoying the friendship of God or at least still capable of this beatifying friendship. Our neighbors, therefore, are all the saints and angels in heavenly bliss, all the holy souls in purgatory and all men on earth. The friends in heaven lay claim only to our sense of love and its cultal expression in our worship. The holy souls and, above all, men still on earth—the latter are still in state of trial—are our neighbors with a claim to our love. And this love implies constant readiness for action: it must be love in action.

The damned have eternally shut themselves off from the community of fellowship in the divine love. Hence they can no longer be the object of Christian love of neighbor. They have utterly ceased to be our neighbor, for they are severed from us by the chasm of irrevocable estrangement from God.

Brute animals and all irrational creation are objects of our wonder. In a sense we cherish all of God's creatures for their Creator's sake, but strictly speaking nothing irrational can be the object of the Christian virtue of neighborly love, charity. Nothing irrational is capable of the beatifying friendship with God which is the bond of Christian love of neighbor.

The blessed in heaven and pious souls here on earth, because of the possession of the love of divine friendship, the formal motive of supernatural love, are nearer to us than the sinners who have forfeited the divine friendship. But if the saints draw closer to us because of the divine intimacy, sinners by their very estrangement from charity in their hostility to God demand our loving pity. Their very misery and the loving-kindness of the Savior for all sinners has a special appeal to our charity and brings them closer to us. The divine love in us which makes us like to God turns actively to sinners in the effort to bring them back to the Savior. In fact the sinner whom we can help here and now in the misery into which sin has plunged him is our *neighbor* more uniquely than the saint who has no need of our help. This we can understand only in the light of the divine love (*agápe*), which is not primarily esteem and benevolence based on human merit but the bounteous love of self-giving wherever a heart opens itself humbly. For this reason zeal for souls preferring to seek out the most miserable sinner is here in our earthly pilgrimage the finest participation in the divine *agápe* which converts the sinner into the child of God.

After the final fulfillment of all things in heavenly glory love no longer can look to poverty or misery. It rejoices over the rich bounty of divine glory in every saint. Here in our earthly pilgrimage, however, the most significant and impelling motive for the love which presses into action is the very misery of our mortal state calling for love and pity.

Most profound and touching is the appeal of our dear ones in their distress, our close relatives, our parents, children, brothers, or sisters. But it is not only the bond of natural relationship which calls out to us for love; all men as children of God, actually or at least potentially, are bound to us most intimately. Hence every man's need is a claim to our kindness whenever we are confronted by it, particularly if we alone can help or we alone can best care for his needs in loving pity.

b. The Order of Love

In practical situations the old question constantly recurs: "Who is my neighbor?" "Who of these two or three or of this group of people, all in need of my help, is my neighbor?" As the Lord indicated in the parable, it is not easy to discern beforehand who is to be considered my neighbor as particular instances of need may arise. Still less possible is it to form a universal rule by which we can predetermine who among many has the first claim on our love. We can do no more than provide a general outline of this order:

1) As to inner esteem saints should be closer to our heart than sinners.

2) As to the effective engagement of charity the magnitude of the distress which confronts us is decisive. The first concern is for spiritual or moral need, which takes precedence over material or bodily necessities.

3) Should we be confronted by a situation in which equal need or equal misfortune calls for our work of love, we must first help those who are more intimately related to us by natural bonds (blood relationship, friendship) or who are entrusted to our care. It is not easy to determine who has the prior claim in instance of equal necessity, one's own parents or one's own children, one's wife (or husband), or one's parents. In this instance, wife or husband takes precedence. On an equal footing as to love and demand for care in need are one's parents and one's children. As a rule the bond of blood relationship in the first degree (father, mother, brother, sister) takes precedence over every bond of friendship in this matter of responsibility and obligation to assist our neighbor in his need.

Basically and in principle the order of charity binds under pain of sin. In certain instances or under certain circumstances the violation may even be a grave sin. Such might be the case, should one offer assistance to those whose misfortune is slight or whose need is not extraordinary but refuse to aid others who are in great distress or perhaps even in extreme necessity. The same holds for the case in which one displays a strange love for his fellows by neglecting his own parents or close relatives and helping his ordinary neighbors or more distant kin, although they are in no greater need than the closer relatives.

The deep love of affection and the love in action rightly shows a preference for blood relatives and close personal friends over others who are really nearer to us in the order of grace. St. Bonaventure offers a very plausible explanation for this preference: heavenly love, says the saint, is not merely loosely related to the natural love as though it hovered over it daintily. It must penetrate and animate the whole natural urge and movement of love. Accordingly, there arises necessarily from this natural source the obligation that, given the same conditions, we are to prefer those who are nearer to us by nature.[10]

c. Our Enemies as "Neighbors"

The love of enemies is an essential part of the "royal law" of love of neighbor. It is the acid test of our attitude toward our neighbor: does our conduct really spring from and correspond to the divine love. God's love for us is not merely love of friendship ("I have called you friends," Jn 15:15) but also, and in an entirely true sense, love of enemies. "But God commends his charity toward us because when as yet we were sinners, Christ died for us . . . when we were enemies we were reconciled to God by the death of his Son" (Rom 5:8ff.). In its point of departure God's own love turns first to enemies (rather than sinners). The objective of the divine love of enemies is the destruction of the enmity. God wishes to make friends out of enemies, and the price is the death of His Son.

Similarly Christian love of enemies is not primarily directed to the enemy as such; it is rather turned to the "enemy" insofar as he is called by the love of God to the same friendship as we. Love of enemy in its root, its profoundest source, is this invincible good will, the love of benevolence, which seeks to bring to one's enemy the highest of all good things: fellowship in a common divine friendship with ourselves, hence friendship in its most tremendous sense. It seeks to turn the enemy into a friend in God. Our external approach to the "enemy" must be fashioned in such a manner as seems best calculated in each particular situation to draw him closer to this goal of our Christian love of enemies.

The admonition of our Lord to turn the other cheek to one who strikes us (Lk 6:27ff.) inculcates the most constant interior restraint and the most loving patience. However, we must be ready for the external, literal fulfillment of such a lofty ideal only when it is necessary or at least useful for the conversion of our enemy. But such restraint is not required or even permitted when our forbearance would merely confirm insolence and intransigence. Our Lord's own example in His conduct toward the servant of the High Priest is the best illustration of the passage about "turning the other cheek." With the most exalted and quiet dignity he bears the insult in patience, but His expiatory death for His enemies is the very apex of the fulfillment of its supreme demand. It is infinitely more than any literal turning the other cheek.

Of this love of enemies which invites our neighbor to the community of divine friendship the very first manifestation must be prayer. "But I say to you, love your enemies, do good to those who hate you, and pray for those who persecute and calumniate you" (Mt 5:44). Here we have not only the renunciation of revenge and reprisal, what might be called the negative phase of love of enemies, that is, pardon, but also the positive effective disposition of love in God and through God. The Lord's demand that we love our enemies goes far beyond simple pardon. It demands that we do good to those who hate us (Mt 5:44). This love of enemies, utterly disinterested and oblivious of self, totally averted from the I, distinguishes the charity of the Christian from the love of the pagan who loves only his friends. This love and only this love shows that we are truly God's children, this love makes us "children of the heavenly Father," whose universal love alone can be for us the model of our love and its decisive motivation (Mt 5:45ff.).

Love of enemies as manifested in action, St. Paul teaches, must above all be directed toward the salvation of neighbor. The Apostle cites the emphatic text of Proverbs 25:21f.: "But 'if thy enemy is hungry, give him food; if he is thirsty, give him drink; For by so doing thou wilt heap coals of fire upon his head.' Be not overcome by evil, but overcome evil with good" (Rom 12:20f.).

Had Max Scheler[11] not slighted the last verse of this letter of St. Paul, "overcome evil with good," he would not have arrived at the grotesque misconception that the attitude of Paul is the expression of a hidden resentment which compensates inner frustration over the impossibility of revenge by obtaining at least the satisfaction of shaming the enemy and perverting this attitude into a "love of enemies." Quite the contrary, the admonition of Paul does not represent a masked gloating over another's misfortune but a lofty "shaming" of the enemy, in order to convert him and, through a love which is totally oblivious of self, raise him from the low state of hostility.

The admonition of St. Paul, "Be not overcome by evil," directs our attention to a further profound insight into the correct exercise of love of enemies. The hatred of an enemy is a perilous focal point of infection which one can avoid only by resorting to the most vigorous of antidotes, active love. In the tendency to harbor hatred there lurks the danger of the desire to destroy or devour the object hated. By sentiment and act of love one must counteract this danger. The disposition of love and the act of love protects and safeguards one's self, the I, disarms and enkindles the truculent Thou, by seeking to bless those who do evil to us, by striving to do good to all men (cf. Rom 12:14; Thes 5:15). Even before the close of day, before the sun sets, the Christian should overcome the instinctive impulse of anger which the offense of his enemy has aroused within him (cf. Eph 4:26).

Since we are all called to "inherit a blessing" from God, so too we must bear the word of blessing to our neighbor, even our enemy (1 Pt 3:9). As we stand daily in need of pardon for our sins from God, so too must we continually pardon those who offend us (cf Sir 28:1ff.; Mt 6:14f.; 5:24ff.; Mk 11:25f.).

Only a very paltry love would go no further than to abstain from sentiment of hatred and revenge for our enemy. We must show a genuine and loving concern for him. Such is the teaching of the well-known passage of St. Matthew. These are the Lord's words: "If thou art offering thy gift at the altar, and there rememberest that thy brother has anything against thee, leave thy gift before the altar and go first to be reconciled to thy brother, and then come and offer thy gift" (Mt 5:23f.). The very one who is the object of disdain and hatred, even should he be the innocent victim of another's injustice, cannot approach God with gifts of love. Though he himself is not guilty, he first must make a loving effort to remove the hatred and bitterness from the heart of his brother. The Lord does not say, "if you have anything against your brother, but rather if "thy brother has anything against thee."[12]

With a most compelling sense of urgency our enemy becomes our "neighbor." His enmity urges us to act precisely when and where only our effort of love can be effective in lifting the dread weight of his bitterness and hate. The more extreme the estrangement due to an attitude and disposition of hatred, the more must the misery of soul which it creates appeal to us since only our generous and alleviating love can soften hatred. God's love to us is our model. How often have we become victims of distress and misery in the sight of God through our own hostile acts of sin! From this only God can deliver us. Our sin has cast us down totally and utterly, making us entirely dependent on the mercy of God. Similarly any one who is caught in the net of hatred awaits the pardoning love of the one whom he has offended.

Every stinging word, every hostile glance or action revealing animosity toward us is a word—albeit a distorted one—directed precisely to us. We cannot refuse or turn away from the answer, for unavoidably we are living in a word-response relationship to our neighbor: every word demands an answer. We can correct the distorted word of animosity only through the correct counter-word of love. The word of hate gnaws at the very root of the I-Thou relationship which consists of the word joined with love. Wherefore, as this word corrodes the relationship, so the response of love must heal the hatred, awaken love instead. Without this response of love both the I and the Thou are seriously imperiled.

We are obliged to love our enemies. The commandment, truly binding our conscience, is repeatedly stressed in the Old Testament (Lv 19:17; Jb 31:29f.; Prv 25:21f.; Sir 28:1ff.). The loftiest examples of love of enemies are the tender solicitude of Joseph of Egypt toward his brothers who sold him into slavery and the magnanimity of David toward Saul. The Old Testament nowhere says, "thou shalt hate thy enemy" (cf. Mt 5:43), but texts which commanded love of enemies were interpreted by the rabbis as mere counsels with the result that they were made to mean, "you shall love your neighbor, but you may hate your enemy." By contrast Jesus not only broadened the Old Testament concept of love of enemies, but stated very emphatically that love of enemies was a duty. In fact, unless we love our enemies we cannot be accepted as God's children: "Love your enemies, do good to those who hate you . . . so that you may be children of your Father in heaven, who makes his sun to rise on the good and the evil" (Mt 5:44).

1) Forgiveness must always be more than a formula of words; it must be truly inward and from the heart, even though the offender has not so much as begged for pardon. This is the condition God Himself lays down before He will forgive us our sins against Him (Mt 6:12ff.). Spite and revenge in spirit cannot be harmonized with Christian ideals. Sincere and genuine pardon of one's enemies may not erase the smarting memory of the offense and injustice committed; but to cherish the memory is to create a temptation constantly endangering the spirit of forgiveness. Noblest safeguard against the temptation is prayer for the offender. Even those who sincerely desire to forgive their enemies may find it difficult to forget, particularly if the injustice of others has brought great and permanent harm to themselves and those they love. If on their lips the somewhat trite "I can forgive, but never forget!" implies determination never to forget or to keep the offense ever in mind, they would be lacking the true spirit of forgiveness.

2) Sincere forgiveness does not remove the obligation of the offender to restore what he has destroyed or damaged. Nor does the most genuine pardon cancel one's right to demand restitution of one's good name unjustly tarnished or of one's property unjustly seized or damaged. However, justice may not be confused with the spirit of spite and reprisal. On this point Christians are well-advised against the masking of hatred in the guise of justice.

In instances of gross injustice against one's name or property it is too much to expect the ordinary Christian both to pardon the offence and at the same time act with restraint in demanding his just rights. There is an ever present danger of lapsing into sentiments of bitterness and even hatred. In such instances there is no other recourse but to forego for the time being the demand for restitution. It is psychologically necessary to await a calmer moment when the memory of the outrage is less vivid and the passions are brought under control, when a just course of action can be pursued with the necessary restraint and moderation. As to legal action, one may justly demand punishment according to law if he has been victimized by others; but the motivation must always be love of justice itself (for the sake of the common good) and genuine concern for the true welfare of the offender. Here too St. Alphonsus warns, "Love of justice is only too readily made a cloak hypocritically masking the spirit of revenge."[13] Nevertheless, should the common good or inalienable rights of an individual demand justice, prayer and good will can effect true harmony in one's interior attitude. The sentiment of love of neighbor can be reconciled with a moderate and restrained insistence on justice and punishment for the evil committed.

3) We must freely acknowledge all that is good in those who have offended us. We must wish them well. Most of all, we must avoid all rejoicing in evil which may befall them, and wish them the great good of eternal salvation. Gloating over the misfortune of others is like a worm gnawing at the root of love of neighbor; against this frame of mind men were sternly warned even in the Old Testament (cf. Prv 24:17f.). Job enjoyed a special peace of conscience because he never exulted over the misfortune of an enemy (Jb 31:29f.). To wish that misfortune or divine retribution befall an enemy (or any evil person) as a means of his conversion does not conflict with our love for him. But it harbors the lurking danger of self deception. Our desire may be profoundly influenced by

personal dislike, by a disguised spirit of hate. Moreover, it is not for us to prescribe the ways of grace for the providence of God.

4) One must show the customary signs of respect and love to his enemies. All men have a right to such a manifestation of good will on the part of all others. A special tie of relationship or proximity demands a particular sign of recognition. According to general usage among men we must show our special love and respect to those closer to us. The common universal signs of love and regard surely include the response to greetings and inclusion in prayer. Not merely responding to greeting, but greeting others is a special or particular sign. By way of exception, however, justice and love may permit one to refuse these signs of respect and love. For serious reasons (of correction or instruction of those who have offended) one may temporarily refuse not only the particular signs of respect and love but even the most ordinary and universal signs. Husband or wife might well show his or her deep displeasure in this way toward one who has seduced the other spouse. Parents could act in the same fashion toward those who corrupted or harmed their children. And this could (and perhaps should) continue until the evil individuals have mended their ways. Surely there is no question of enmity but of prudent defence in all this. Parents are permitted to show their displeasure to their children in a similar manner if prudence dictates such procedure as a wholesome means of correction and improvement. But refusal to show the usual signs of love and respect may never be permitted to degenerate into a manifestation of dislike and even hatred.

As already indicated, directors and spiritual guides should not make excessive demands from one who has been very deeply hurt. One should not demand complete and utter forgiveness in one brief moment. Without doubt the Apostle admonishes us not to let the sun go down on our anger (Eph 4:26), but the words indirectly suggest the simple psychological fact that tempers cool slowly. Always allowing for variations in temperament, every man requires a certain amount of time to master his emotions and to learn to live with distress and pain. In many instances the director or confessor will have to rest content for the time being with the first or perhaps second step on the part of the penitent who has become embittered over the offenses of others. He should endeavor to induce him to overcome his hostile spirit through prayer for those who have offended him, through prayer for the grace of pardoning love, through the resolution to forego all unfavorable criticism or comment about the "enemy." But what should one advise if several efforts at reconciliation have been frustrated? What is to be done if one of the parties refuses stubbornly to respond to a sincere greeting by the other? In such instances prudence would require that the other patiently wait for a more opportune moment for reconciliation, maintaining all the while a sincere openness for reconciliation in his heart.

There are tragic instances of deeply rooted enmity between close relatives or close neighbors. In such cases we usually demand that both parties make a decisive step toward reconciliation. This is all the more obligatory if both have for years received the sacraments without any effort at suppression of their mutual ill will or hatred. Most favorable occasion for reconciliation is the time of the parish mission or retreat. It may happen that only approaching death itself can stir the conscience from its dreadful torpor. Superiors of religious houses or other institutions under ecclesiastical direction are well within the bounds of prudence if they vigilantly inquire regarding the existence of enmity among their charges, not to speak of actual hatred continuing for months or even years in an atmosphere which should be one of mutual love of God and neighbor.

5) The offended party must under all circumstances struggle for the interior resolution and readiness of will to assist his enemy in necessity (as the Lord Himself required already in the Old Testament; cf. Ex 23:4f.). And should it prove necessary for the salvation of his offending neighbor's soul, the offended party must also be prepared to show not merely general but also particular signs of respect and love to him. Willingness to come to the assistance of one who has offended him in instances of special necessity is conclusive evidence that he is sufficiently disposed for absolution in the sacrament of penance. Despite this sufficient disposition, the offended party may still be filled with bitterness of spirit to the degree that he even says he can never forgive the offense. It is closer to truth to say that he cannot be reconciled to the hurt and pain of his injury.

6) The offending party or the one with greater guilt is obliged in justice to take the first step toward reconciliation. And in justice and charity the offended party is bound to respond favorably and accept a reasonable restitution for the injury inflicted. In accordance with the command of love of enemies he too must be prepared to cast aside animosity. He must seriously desire to end the enmity, as far as this is

possible, and keep open his heart for sincere reconciliation at the opportune moment.

Consummate prudence is often required when dealing with man's hatred for his fellow man. If one can assume that the offender, despite all his injustice, will only remain obdurate in his vicious position and that any attempt at reconciliation on the part of the innocent man will only confirm him in injustice, prudence surely dictates a delay in our efforts to a more propitious time. The same is true, of course, if the offended party will harshly rebuff any offer of conciliation. In this connection we note also that where no injustice involving restitution has been committed—and this includes injustice in matters spiritual—we have no obligation to seek reconciliation with one who is no longer connected with us by any tie, whether it be because of great distance or for some other reason.

Finally, beyond the domain of obligation there still lies the area of counsel in this matter of love of enemies. The love which characterized the saints is our model: with the great abandon of sacrificial love they concerned themselves with the temporal and, even more, with the eternal welfare of their enemies. According to the measure of His gifts of grace God requires of us the fruits of grace in our love of enemies. This is especially true of priests and religious.

d. Our Friends as "Neighbors"

Love, abiding and faithful, and resting on mutual esteem and mutual interior affection is friendship. As on the natural plane friendship is the summit of noble love,[14] so too on the supernatural level friendship must be formed through Christian love of neighbor. The Old Testament furnishes us with touching examples of love and loyalty among friends (David and Jonathan, Chusai and David, Elias and Eliseus). The sapiential books particularly never tire of extolling the value of true friendship: "A faithful friend is a sturdy shelter; he who finds one finds a treasure. . . . A faithful friend is a life-saving remedy, such as he who fears God finds" (Sir 6:14ff.).

John the Baptist boldly calls himself the friend of Christ. He is the "friend of the bridegroom" (Jn 3:29). The Savior Himself cultivated intimate friendship with the family of Lazarus. Even more intimate was His attachment to His own Apostles, among whom He singled out as disciples of His special love Peter, James, and John. Though He calls them all "his friends" (Jn 15:14f.; Lk 12:4), His tender love for John made him the "beloved disciple," the disciple of special predilection.

Even Aristotle held that true friendship is essentially based on virtue and mutual quest for virtue. All other attachments to which we sometimes give the name friendship are merely unions based on personal profit or advantage or the expression of emotional enthusiasm and sympathy. Among evil men there can be no friendship.[15] Prerequisite for friendship with Christ is concord of wills, according to His own words: "You are my friends if you do the things I have commanded you." As signs of our friendship He mentions the common possession of the truths which save and beatify, participation in the Father's mysteries of the heart. The most exalted sign and mark of friendship is sacrificing one's life for one's friends (Jn 15:13ff.).

True friendship among Christians rests in the common participation of divine friendship which it preserves and enriches. In the absence of the divine friendship there can be no well-ordered friendship at all. For, at least among Christians, either all lofty natural love is animated with charity or, should charity be absent, it loses the nature of true friendship. Therefore all love of parents, love of children, love of husband and wife, and love among friends must be penetrated with supernatural love. Christian love is not something which hovers above nature. Rather, if it is to be effective, it must transform and invigorate all that is tender and noble and strong in natural love. It must enter into the rhythmic unison of human hearts in their aspirations and sentiments. No realm of natural love, if it is to survive as true love, may be shut off from the formative power of charity. Without charity natural love necessarily descends to the low level of self-containment and personal profit or to the indulgence of hazardous, unrestrained passion.

It is an indispensable sign of Christian friendship that it is not exclusive and restrictive. On the contrary, as Christian friendship deepens, it constantly becomes more open and inclusive, reaching out to every one who stands in need of love. (Only wedded or married love as such is exclusive; yet it does not exclude true friendship.) Wherever *friendship* closes itself in and seals itself off from the community and lives at the expense of the all-embracing love of the fellowship of community, it no longer draws on the immense resource of supernatural love but feeds on the barren husks of petty egotism. In fact, even within a family or religious community special intimate friendships may spring up. But they are only focal centers of deep warmth and power from which the familial spirit and the love which embraces all in true friendship expands and grows rich and strong.

Wedded love and marital love must also be animated by the spirit of Christian friendship. The nuptial relationship itself and, even more so, the sacramentally sanctified conjugal society must be a conscious loving pilgrimage to eternal life, a sacred rivalry in the love for God. Every disturbance of the divine love or even mere indifference toward the sacred presence of divine friendship in one of the marriage partners mars the love of the two for each other.

Friendship is possible between man and woman even outside the area of nuptial love and beyond the radius of the sexual and erotic. It may be within the family circle or beyond it. But if the principle is universally valid that the aloofness of reverence must restrain the closeness and intimacy of love, it is particularly valid in this instance. Quite often the hazard of erotic or even sexual temptation proscribes any intimate friendship between man and woman. Often the danger of scandal forbids it. The example of St. Paul must be our norm of action in such instances: "if food scandalize my brother, I will eat flesh no more forever, lest I scandalize my brother" (1 Cor 8:13). Wherever man and woman, outside marriage, are drawn to each other in a friendship which is not orientated toward mutual furtherance of divine friendship nor mindful of the salvation of the weak, who see in such friendships a justification of their own frivolous "friendships," they embark on a course filled with peril for Christian love of neighbor.

3. The Essence, Characteristics, and Effects of Love of Neighbor

Love is first of all sentiment and disposition which precedes every motivation to act.[16] It is interior response to value and inclination to the beloved Thou. The soul-body affection may be present with love, but it is not necessarily bound up with it. But of course, if it is absent, the inner spirit of love loses much of its immediate vital force. Love for a person must be rooted in the serious acceptance of and esteem for the unique and immutable value he possesses. In the sentiment of genuine personal love reverential aloofness akin to shyness is delicately balanced with the spiritual sense of attraction toward the other. No sooner is the one pole in this tense polarity outbalanced by the other than the love is essentially dissolved. Every one-sided preponderance jeopardizes true love.

Attraction without aloofness or reverence would result in a fusion or blending (the very contrary of personal community) and therewith in an undermining of the Thou or a dissolution of the autonomy of the I. Reverence without attraction would lead to aloofness and flight. The highest love, friendship with God, is centered in a togetherness with the most intimate attraction and immeasurable reverence. Contrary to what one might expect, this relation of tension in no wise ceases to exist in the most intimate form of Christian love of neighbor, in conjugal love. Rather, at every deepening of self-submission, at every intensification of the mutual union, the sacred ramparts of reverence must be fortified if the love of neighbor and of one's self is to be effectively safeguarded, protected, and elevated—in fact, if it is to continue to exist as Christian love at all.

Christian love has its center in the sentiment and disposition of man. In this it is similar to lofty natural love. It is rooted in the "heart of man," in the natural sentiments of love to which it imparts a new and loftier direction. The supernatural sentiment of love, similar to the natural, has its own proper urge to flow forth actively in the manifestation of love. Nevertheless, the force and the motivating impulse of the Christ-formed love are from another world. In its nobility it is infinitely superior to the mere humanistic love of men from which the deepest values of one's neighbor, his call to divine friendship, remain hidden. Love of enemies, which is uniquely Christian, shows that Christian love of neighbor based on the divine bounty and the supernatural motive can exist even where the harmony and sympathy based on nature is absent. Christian love is not nourished by the graces of natural sentiments of love, though it will triumphantly awaken them as it transforms and directs to its ends those which are already present.

Love is not only esteem of value, respect and inclination toward another, but also wishing him well. Such is the nature of the sentiment of love's response to value, such its quality in the heart of man that it is the essential source of a force reacting upon the will, already prone to act, so that man turns not only to the object of his love but also wishes him all good. Love not only wills that things go well with the one we love, but love itself wishes to do the good to the one loved, to do for him all good that is possible. The sentiment and spirit of love tends always to active love.

To benevolence, or well-wishing, and wishing to do well, flowing from love as such, there must be added in Christian love of neighbor also the recognition of the obligation to be prepared to act. This is the will to intervene actively in behalf of those we love, arising from the consciousness of essential solidarity with our neighbor. For by dint of the divine love reigning in our hearts we are bound up with our neighbor in fellowship of life, love, and destiny. The one same kingdom of love from which we draw our supernatural life and in which we live demands of us concern and care for the preservation and increase of the love, not merely in the individual himself but likewise in all the members of the family of the kingdom. Awareness of the most intimate bond of unity in the one Body, in Christ, makes of our natural sentiment a real and effective sympathy for our neighbor in his suffering and distress. It creates in us a true willingness to suffer for him. "If one member suffers anything, all the members suffer with it, or if one member glories, all the members rejoice with it" (1 Cor 12:26). From sympathetic suffering arises the effective readiness for atonement to which Paul refers so strikingly: "What is lacking of the sufferings of Christ I fill up in my flesh for his body which is the Church" (Col 1:24).

The greater and purer the love with which the Christian cherishes his neighbor, the less likely it is to fill him with a pride of achievement as though he did something out-of-the-ordinary. Though it is superabundant, filled with joyous action for good, self-sacrificing, and steeped in vicarious atonement, this love from the profoundest depths of its life creates the sense of responsibility for others. We are truly our brother's keeper, fully conscious that the callous attitude expressed so tersely in the phrase *Am I my brother's keeper?* is rooted in hatred and murder. Aware of our solidarity in love, the Christian realizes that true Christian solidarity implies concern for one's neighbor and an elemental sense of the need for intervention by working for his good, especially for his salvation. Paradoxically, the richer and deeper the interior love within us, the more tensely do the poorest and weakest of our brethren lay a claim upon it: love is merciful.

Human mercy is a singular imitation of God's love. It is the unique characteristic of divine love to bestow itself in the measure of created needs. The greater the misery of man, the greater the condescension and abandon of divine love. The deeper the debt toward God, the greater is the divine generosity in forgiving it. The most unique—though not the only—sphere of mercy is love of enemies, which turns graciously to the need and misery of the enemy, measuring the love of pardon by the very hostility which irritates the wounds it has inflicted.

The characteristics and fruits of love are rich gems set in a golden crown. The classic text is that of St. Paul: "Charity is patient, is kind; charity does not envy, is not pretentious, is not puffed up, is not ambitious, is not self-seeking, is not provoked . . . bears with all things, believes all things, hopes all things, endures all things" (1 Cor 13:4ff.).

Love is just and fiulfills all demands of justice superabundantly. With clear and unobscured vision love discerns all that is demanded of her. Love is agonizingly just and equitable in fulfilling obligations, though long-suffering and merciful in exacting fulfillment in return. Any one who is motivated by supernatural love considers it just to pardon every sin committed against him by his brother: does not God pardon far greater sins?

Love is truly prudent and wise. If prudence is tact of conscience in a situation, then a fine sense of tact regarding one's neighbor is the fruit of love. There can be no perfection of prudence without the perfection of love. For only love leads us into the heart of the good. Says Augustine, "Love, and then do what you will." This is to say, "Do what love wills." For it is love that unerringly points out the good.

Love is stouthearted, brave. Love "endures all things" (1 Cor 13:7). Love has inner stamina to bear patiently the weakness of one's neighbor and endure great trials and suffering for him. This inner strength of soul flowing from the force of love is matched by the courage which never despairs of one's neighbor, which ventures all for an apparently lost sinner, ventures and hopes. Love is patient, but the patience of true love has nothing in common with the irresoluteness which yields to every pressure and concedes to every demand, and worst of all, constantly confuses pampering with true love.

Love is temperate and disciplined. It is primarily love which orders and disciplines the emotions and drives within us and thus brings forth the virtue of temperance and moderation. Love "is not pretentious." This indicates both the delicacy and tact which are akin to prudence and the shunning of all that is passionate and undisciplined. Christian love does not blind man as does sensual infatuation, but rather imparts a great sensitivity to the danger of a fall from genuine love into the pitfall of passion. From love likewise flows the strong force of self-control.

Love is humble. The movement of attraction to the beloved is accompanied by submission before the inner value present there. Love is indeed participation in the perfection of God's own loving condescension to His creature. Add to this the reverence found in the polarity of love and we have humility. Humility is founded in this reverence of loving submission.

4. The Standard: "As Yourself"

a. Love of Christ, the New Standard

The Old Testament sets the standard of our love of neighbor in the so-called Golden Rule. Though formulated negatively, the counsels which explain the precept indicate the positive obligation. The words, "See thou never do to another what thou wouldst hate to have done to thee by another" (Tb 4:16), are immediately followed by counsels such as "Eat thy bread with the hungry and the needy, and with thy garments cover the naked," etc. (Tb 4:17ff.). Thus clearly is indicated the positive nature of the Old Testament "Golden Rule."

The New Testament precept is couched in positive terms: "All things whatever you would that men should do to you, even so do you also to them; for this is the Law and the prophets" (Mt 7:12). Both the negative and positive conceptions of the Golden Rule are explanations of the words: "Thou shalt love thy neighbor as thyself" (Mt 22:39; Rom 13:9; cf. Lv 19:18). Ultimately the standard is the commandment of love of neighbor seen in the light of the words of Christ Himself: "A new commandment I give you, that you love one another: that as I have loved you, you also love one another" (Jn 13:34; 15:12; cf. 1 Jn 3:11; 3:16ff.).

Love is meek. "Love is inexorable." Meekness is the concentrated force of love. Meekness gathers all the energies of love. "Blessed are the meek, for they shall possess the earth" (Mt 5:4).

These passages of the Scriptures splendidly illustrate the meaning of the standard of love, love thy neighbor as *thyself*. The noble-minded man must look upon love of neighbor as a duty which is as important, as self-evident, as much a part of his nature—a second nature indeed—as natural and lofty love of self. And yet the final standard or measure of Christian love of neighbor is not at all the unenlightened, passionate, or even the naturally noble or lofty love of self. It must be the holy love of self in God, made possible by the example and redemptive death of Christ, a love of self which is a participation in Christ's own love for us. Ultimate in Christian love of neighbor is not our self-love, but love of neighbor and self measured by the standard of Christ's love for us. The motive and basic power of supernatural love, of self and of neighbor, is the Savior's own sweet love for us and for our neighbor. The inescapable conclusion is that our love for self as well as for neighbor must have the same basic motive, the same direction to ends or goals.

When we spoke of the love for God, we stated that as to appreciative esteem (*appretiative*) one must love God more than one's self and all other creatures. Similarly, the precept of love of neighbor requires that as to esteem, serious acceptance, and wishing well (benevolence), we must love our neighbor in the same full measure as we love ourselves. We might go so far as to say that humble love looks even more gladly to the value of our neighbor than to our own.[17] Of course, as far as the primary motive of supernatural love, namely, the value of the call to God's friendship, comes into question, this is to be seen and loved just as expressly in the I as in the Thou. Ultimately we find this in God who is the source of its love-value.

Equality of love of self and of neighbor as to intensity of affection is not required by the law of love. Such an exact emotional equivalence at all times and in every instance is not even possible for fallen man. And still we should in some measure strive for this goal. Love of neighbor must be more than an abstraction thought out in the mind. It should be lived in pondering and acting, with the sentiment of the heart, so that we may say the Christian lives and feels with his neighbor as with himself. That this lofty ideal is possible is proved by the example of the saints whose love of neighbor was heroically oblivious of self in sacrificial service for others. It is the fruit of the gifts of the Holy Spirit who is Love.

As yourself does not mean that the individual is prior, that he must first see to it that he loves himself sufficiently and then turn to his neighbor. Christian love of self and of neighbor can only thrive together, one with the other, each into the other. If it is correct to say—and this is surely true—that one cannot rightly love his neighbor unless he rightly loves himself because of the virtue of divine love, it is equally true that one cannot love himself in a truly Christian manner unless he sees and loves in his neighbor as in himself the child of God, the redeemed in Christ.

Some writers refuse to admit an obligation of strict equality. They maintain that one is not even permitted to love his neighbor as himself according to this commandment.[18] They contend that we are to love our neighbor not strictly in the same way as ourselves, but only in a similar manner. According to this view the heroic sacrifice of one's life for others, set forth by the Savior as an example of the fulfillment of the precept, in itself and as such, conflicts with the precept of well-ordered love. But since such an act of love brings with it the increase of virtue and in the first instance redounds to the advantage of self, it is clear that in the final analysis one really loves self more than one's neighbor. And this is the right order.

We feel that this interpretation of the precept is a distortion of the true meaning of loving one's neighbor as one's self. One cannot simply and without qualification deny that we must love our neighbor as ourselves. At most we concede that the position just explained possesses some elements of truth. However, it is based on an ethical position which is closer to the ideal of self-perfection than to that of submission, of the *agápe*. Nor is the argument that one is never permitted to commit the slightest sin as a means of helping one's neighbor possessed of any validity in this instance. One is never permitted to commit any sin, for one's own advantage or for any other reason whatsoever. Sin is first of all directed against God and not against ourselves. Therefore it offends against love of neighbor as well as against love of self. "If you fail to observe equality in love between your neighbor and yourself, but make a distinction, you do not possess well-ordered love; your love is not in the correct order."[19] "You should not hate any one. Rather, you should win some over to truth; for others you should pray; and, moreover, you should love them more than your own soul."[20]

b. Measure of Love and Responsibility

The difficulties created by the problem we have just referred to can be solved by means of a clear distinction between love and responsibility: the Christian is in duty bound to strive to love his neighbor as himself according to interior sentiment and spirit of sacrifice. Even though the commandment is not a pressing, prescriptive one, it is nevertheless obligatory. It binds universally and unconditionally as an ideal to be striven for, as a precept of goals which the one advanced in virtue can and must approximate more perfectly than the beginner. However, when we deal with responsibility, we make a distinction. Responsibility for one's own self, which practically of course is easier to carry out, in many ways takes precedence over participation in responsibility for one's neighbor.

The spirit of solidarity in the salvation of men is nourished above all by the Sacrament of the Divine Love which draws us all to an ever growing intimacy in the unity of the one Body of Christ. This spirit of unity demands that we take the salvation of our neighbor as seriously as our own. Any one who participates in the sacrificial offering of the redemptive Blood and is nourished on the Eucharistic Food in the sacrifice, and is thus united with his neighbor in the fellowship of worship, must be ready to engage in the task of his neighbor's salvation in word and deed— as gladly and as readily as for his own!

Nevertheless, in the order of the attainable our own salvation depends more on our own responsible acts than does the salvation of our fellow men. That this is our more immediate obligation follows logically. As free and responsible persons we have received from God an immediate dominion in freedom only over our own self with its spiritual and bodily goods. It is true that we can exercise a considerable influence on others, particularly in the realm of supernatural salvific solidarity. But dominion over the free will of others is excluded. Only insofar as one is the free and responsible master or the administrator of an object can one dispose of it freely and be held immediately accountable for it. From this arises the duty that we must have a greater care for the goods which are directly placed in the control of our freedom than for other objects over which, in the first instance, other free beings have a responsible control.

The conclusion is evident. Clearly, to love one's neighbor as one's self cannot imply that we must consider ourselves immediately responsible for the health, life, bodily and spiritual goods of every fellow man exactly as for our own values and goods. These latter are entrusted to us; and if we are more concerned with them than with our neighbor's goods, it does not follow that we necessarily prefer ourselves to him. It does not mean that emotionally and in sentiment we love ourselves more than we love our neighbor. To a certain extent there is a serious truth in the saying—often uttered flippantly—that every one is his own neighbor: our salvation is entrusted more to our responsibility, and our neighbor's to his own free decision. Only a perverted attitude would lead us to be concerned about the mote in our neighbor's eye, and all the while to disregard the beam in our own. In this sense too charity may be said to begin at home.

But once the goods of our neighbor are entrusted to the solicitous care of our freedom and responsibility, which means whenever our fellow man is really in the special situation as "our neighbor" (as the man who fell among brigands in the parable of the Good Samaritan), then we must be prepared to accept him with the same earnest and loving solicitude with which we accept our own selves.

We must constantly endeavor to make our love of esteem and benevolence for our neighbor equal to our love for ourselves. Active and responsible engagement in the affairs of our neighbor, however, is demanded only in special situations, in those situations, namely, in which we according to God's will can provide for our neighbor in his need as earnestly as for ourselves! Or it may be that in certain instances and situations our neighbor is striving helplessly against fearful odds and we are able to do more for him than he is able to do for himself; for example, when our free activity under the influence of divine grace would be able to cope with his distress better than he in the impotence of his freedom!

Cultivation of one's own values in preference to those of one's neighbor conflicts with the royal commandment *love your neighbor "as yourself"* only if we appear in our own eyes as more valuable and important than our neighbor, and are consequently unwilling to relinquish goods of lesser value in order to preserve the higher values of our neighbor in his need or distress. The evidence of our sincerity is apparent whenever our own interests conflict with those of our neighbor. The spirit of Christian love and our sense of co-responsibility or solidarity is apparent in the manner in which we resolve the conflict. If one ruthlessly advances his own interests, even though equal or even higher values of his neighbor are at stake, one reveals that he loves himself in a sinful way more than he loves his neighbor: he loves himself too passionately, and too little in the divine love.

c. The Basic Norms of Co-Responsibility

1) When we are concerned with equal values (with goods of the same order, equal needs, etc.), responsibility for one's own goods enjoys a practical priority of right over the co-responsibility for the goods and needs of others. In spiritual values, one's own interest rightly viewed cannot conflict with the spiritual needs of one's neighbors. Salvation rests entirely in love. We can never further the spiritual good of others by inflicting

hurt on our own souls. In fact, harming one's own salvation is spiritually hurtful also to the soul of our neighbor. "There is no moral movement, not even the slightest moral gesture, which does not set endless reverberations in motion; it is much like the pebble dropping into the water, creating endless circles of rippling waves."[21]

Anyone whose concern for the salvation of others involves him in grave and imminent danger of sin must first concern himself with his own weakness. He must first make the effort to grow strong in virtue. Otherwise his spiritual labor in behalf of his neighbor will prove fruitless. The exclusive spiritual activism of the spiritual director who neglects his own sorely sick soul calls to mind the conduct of the priest and Levite in the Gospel parable. They saw the victim. His needs made a special appeal to them. But they ignored him in his necessity and passed on (Lk 10:30ff.). In this context the spiritually endangered director is himself in greater necessity. He is his own neighbor, most in distress and need. He must concern himself first with his own need, so that he is not a dead member or even a source of spiritual infection in the Body of Christ. For the time he must leave to others the hazardous spiritual care.

Obviously, solid spirituality is foreign to all petty concern for one's own spiritual advantage in preference to the spiritual need of others. One who combines trust in divine providence with the spirit of true love of his fellows and tranquilly gives up a hypothetical spiritual progress (a position of quiet contemplation, many exercises of piety), because he is aware of a call to the pressing spiritual needs of others, will truly find his own soul (Mt 16:25). He will be enriched spiritually before God. However, all this does not hold good for one who exposes himself to great spiritual hazards for the sake of his neighbor without compelling reasons, and without having first made every effort to fortify himself spiritually.

2) In instances of conflict between spiritual and temporal values, our temporal or material advantage must yield to the spiritual good of our neighbor. The reason is evident: the spiritual good, the salvation of others, the glory of God must be the first object and motive of Christian love.

a) One must be prepared to come to the assistance of one's fellow man, even at the risk of life, in instances of extreme spiritual necessity (such as danger of eternal damnation). However, one cannot be obliged to incur the loss of one's own life (or great risk of its loss) unless there is a well-founded hope for the salvation of the individual whose soul is gravely imperiled. Without such a hope it would not be right to expose one's life to serious hazard. It may even happen that a consideration for the common good or other very urgent spiritual duties would forbid such an heroic sacrifice. A great dearth of priests, just to cite an example, might forbid a priest from risking his life (so essential for the spiritual good of Christians) in order to baptize a single infant if he could foresee that he might by that very act deprive many souls of the boon of baptism and all other spiritual care.

b) Should one's neighbor be in extreme temporal need (he may be starving or in danger of losing either his life or his mind), his fellow man must come to his rescue even at the cost of considerable material sacrifice. However, one is obliged to sacrifice relatively great material values only if there is an obligation of justice or piety (the latter would require coming to the assistance of close relatives or benefactors). Under certain circumstances a very generous spirit of love would prompt one to go much beyond what is here laid down as obligatory, even though it should demand very great sacrifices.

c) Great spiritual necessity (as danger of loss of faith or of the state of grace) on the part of our neighbor requires that we come to the assistance of our fellow man to the extent of our power and resources. However, one is not strictly obliged to risk one's life or suffer great material loss in rendering this assistance unless in a special instance the common good demands it, or unless there is a special obligation arising from one's state of life or office (parents toward their children, children toward their parents, spiritual directors toward their charges).

By his ordination and, more particularly, by his acceptance of a spiritual charge with the care of souls, the priest assumes an especially pressing obligation to help his fellow men in their spiritual necessity. As a good shepherd he undertakes to help the flock placed under his care or immediately directed to his attention, all the while seeking those who have strayed from the fold. This task should be accepted and carried out even though it may call for a spirit of sacrifice and involve great hardship. If a conflict of interests or of values arises, the priest is obliged to sacrifice his own temporal or material advantage within the limits of the possible for the salvation of souls committed to him. In consequence he may be obliged to forego many stole fees or other economic advantages in order to avoid scandal or to find a way to soften the hearts of sinners. Sometimes only heroic priestly sacrifice can open an embittered heart to God. The priest is strictly obliged to hazard the dangers of contagious or infectious disease in order to administer the sacraments to the seriously sick and dying insofar as the salvation of souls committed to him demands it. Nevertheless, pastor or director must always view the welfare of the entire congregation or group in relation to that of the individual soul. He is not permitted to consume himself for the one or for a few to the serious neglect of the many. But petty calculation in numbers is likewise not in place: the Good Shepherd forsakes the ninety and the nine, trustfully, in order to bring the lost sheep back to the fold.

The special obligation of the priest arising from ordination and spiritual office or assignment (in fact, ultimately even in virtue of the income derived from his official position) charges him with the salvation of the souls entrusted to him. Even at the cost of temporal or material interests, he is committed to this spiritual concern and care. But the duty of zeal for souls is not at all limited to the priest. Every Christian has spiritual obligations arising from the commandment of love of his fellowmen, due to the sacraments of holy baptism and confirmation and the active Eucharistic membership in the Mystical Body of Christ. The salvation of his neighbor must concern him seriously, more seriously indeed than his own temporal interests. His love of neighbor is not well-ordered if he is not at least basically disposed to suffer material loss for the saving of his fellow man's soul. The Christian must be prepared to endure temporal disadvantage for such spiritual gain of neighbor (to cite some examples, he may have to forego legal prosecution where it may redound to his material advantage and result in spiritual hardship to others; he may have to exercise social justice and social charity to alleviate the needs and remove the bitterness of the poor). Catholics possessed of wealth may not be indifferent to the misery of the poor and the needs of the Church.

d) One must come to the assistance of his fellow man in time of need even at the cost of considerable material sacrifice. However, extreme or very grave sacrifice is not required. One is obliged to make great sacrifice of one's own material goods to avert or relieve great need of very close relatives. This surely holds for parents and children, and to an extent also for uncles, aunts, cousins. The virtue of gratitude requires that we include benefactors also in this list.

e) No Christian may deprive himself (and ultimately the company of the redeemed) of important spiritual values in order to obtain temporal advantage or profit for his neighbor (who is not in great need). It follows that a child is not allowed to disregard the call to religion or priesthood for the mere reason that his parents (we assume they are not in urgent need of his help) would be deprived of the comfort of his presence. But one would be permitted to turn aside from the apparent call to religion or priesthood in order to carry out an important apostolic work in the world (an example: to save the soul of a specific sinner who depends almost entirely on our zeal). The priest is not obliged to renounce the work of spiritual care of those in danger of eternal perdition because of temptations that assail him in the discharge of the task, provided the temptations are not gravely dangerous and he uses the necessary spiritual precautions and means of grace as safeguards. However, if there is grave reason for him to fear spiritual shipwreck, he would be obliged to relinquish his spiritual office.

BIBLIOGRAPHY

Inner Unity of Divine Love, Love of Self, Love of Neighbor

Bopp, L. *Zum Lobe der Liebe. Von der christlichen Caritas und den Richtungen ihrer Entfaltung.* Freiburg, 1952.

Cohausz, O. "Wohlgeordnete Selbstliebe und ungeordnete Eigenliebe," *ZAM,* 2 (1927), 113–128.

Deman, Th. "La charité fraternelle comme forme des vertus," *VieSpir,* 74 (1946), 391–404.

De Lubac, H. *Catholicism: a Study of Dogma in Relation to the Corporate Destiny of Mankind.* Translated by Lancelot C. Sheppard. New York: Sheed and Ward, 1958.

de Puybaudet, J. "La charité fraternelle est-elle théologale?" *RAM,* 24 (1948), 117–134.

Gilen, L., S.J. "Selbstwertstreben und Entwicklung zur Persoenlichkeit," *StimmenZeit,* 163 (1958/59), 42–53.

Haering, B. "Die Kirche ist die Liebe," *Der Christ und die Wirklichkeit* (hrsg. von von K. Rudolf), Wien, 1960, 21–31.

Hausherr, I., S.J. *Philautie de la tendresse pour soi à la charité selon saint Maxime le Confesseur.* Roma, 1952.

Henry, A. M. "Charité et communautés," *VieSpirSupp,* 2 (1948), 363–393.

Houtryve, I. v. *L'amour du prochain selon saint François de Sales.* Paris, 1944.

"L'amour du prochain," *Cahiers de la Vie Spir,* 1954.

Nothomb, D. M. "Amour du prochain, amour du Christ, d'après saint Jean Chrysostome," *VieSpir,* 87 (1952), 364–375.

Ratzinger, J. "Christliche Bruederlichkeit," *Der Seelsorger,* 28 (1958), 387–429.

———. *Die Christliche Bruederlichkeit.* Muenchen, 1960.

Vieujean, J. *L'autre toi-même.* Tournai, 1952.

Voelki, R. *Die Selbstliebe in der Heiligen Schrift und bei Thomas von Aquin.* Muenchen, 1956.

Vogel, G. L. *Tiefenpsychologie und Naechstenliebe.* Mainz, 1957.

Woehrmueller, B. *Das koenigliche Gebot.* Muenchen, 1949.

Love of Neighbor: Motive and Obligation

BEUMER, J. "Die Naechstenliebe als universelles motiv des religioesen Lebens," *ZAM*, 13 (1938), 140–146.

BREMOND, A., S.J. "La raison et la charité," *Greg*, 21 (1940), 17–33.

NOTHOMB, D. "Le motif formel de la charité envers le prochain," *RevThom*, 52 (1952), 97–118; 361–377.

SPICQ, C., O.P. "Die Liebe als Gestaltungsprinzip der Moral in den Synoptischen Evangelien," *Freiburger Zeitschrift fur Phil. und Theol.* 1 (1954), 394–410.

WARNACH, V. *Agápe. Die Liebe als Grundmotiv der neutestamentlichen Theologie.* Duesseldorf, 1951.

Whom Must We Love

BRAUN, F. "La charité et la fraternité des peuples," *VieSpir*, 46 (1936), 21–30.

DEMAN, TH. "Ceux que nous devons d'abord aimer," *VieSpir*, 75 (1946), 678–709.

MUSSNER, F. "Der Begriff des *Naechsten* in der Verkuendigung Jesu," *TrThZ*, 64 (1955), 91–99.

RADE, M. *Der Naechste.* Tuebingen, 1927.

ROULLET, A. "L'amour du prochain loi de l'Homme et de la Société," *VieSpir*, 46 (1936), 128–145; 247–262.

STURZO, L. "La charité chrétienne et la politique," *Vielntell*, 42 (1938), 409–436.

Our Enemies as "Neighbors"

BACH, E. *Die Feindesliebe nach dem natuerlichen und uebernatuerlichen Stittengesetz.* Kempten-Muenchen, 1914.

CALO, G. *L'odio e l'amore.* Roma, 1958.

COLNAI, A. "Versuch ueber den Hass," *PhJb*, 48 (1935), 147–187.

DE MONTCHEUIL, Y. "Le ressentiment dans la vie morale et religieuse d'après M. Scheler," *Melanges theol.,* Paris, 1946, 187–226.

GICHON, A. M. *Le pardon.* Paris, 1948.

REGAMEY, R., O.P. "Un amour des ennemis réel et sage," *VieSpir*, 96 (1957), 379–400.

SCHELER, M. *Ressentiment.* Edited by L. A. Coser and translated by W. W. Holdheim. N.Y.: Free Press of Glencoe, 1961. ("Das Ressentiment im Aufbau der Moralen," *Gesammelte abhandlungen und Aufsaetze;* later entitled *Vom Umsturz der Werte,* vol. 3 of Gesammelte Werke. Bern: A. Francke Verlag AG.)

STEINMUELLER, F. *Die Feindesliebe nach dem natuerlichen und positiven Sittengesetz.* Regensburg, 1909.

WALDMANN, M. *Die Feindesliebe in der antiken Welt und im Christentum.* Wien, 1902.

Our Friends as "Neighbors"

BOND, L. M., O.P. "A Comparison between Human and Divine Friendship," *Thm*, 3 (1941), 54–94.

BOUTON, J. "La doctrine de l'amitié chez saint Bernard," *RAM*, 29 (1953), 3–19.

DANDER, F. "Grundsaetzliches zur Auffassung der Fruendschaft nach der Lehre des hl. Thomas von Aquin," *ZAM*, 6 (1931), 132–145.

DE GUIBERT, J., S.J. "Les amitiés dans la vie religieuse," *Greg*, 21 (1941), 171–190.

FABRE, P. *Saint Paulin de Nole et l'amitié chrétienne.* Paris, 1949.

GILLON, L. B. "A propos de la théorie thomiste de l'amitié," *Ang*, 25 (1948), 3–17.

HENN, L. *Freundschaft.* 4 ed. Duelmen, 1950.

MUELLER, M. *Die Freundschaft des hl. Franz von Sales mit der hl. Johanna Franziska von Chantal.* 3 ed. Muenchen, 1937.

NOLTE, V. *Augustins Freundschaftideal in seinen Briefen.* Wuerzburg, 1939.

ODDONE, A. *L'amicizia. Studio psichologico e morale.* Milano, 1936.

OTTEN, K. *Die heilige Freundschaft. Des seligen Abtes Aelred von Rieval Buechlein 'De spirituali amicitia' uebersetzt.* Muenchen, 1925.

PHILIPPE, P. *Le rôle de l'amitié dans la vie chrétienne selon saint Thomas d'Aquin.* Rom, 1938.

ROUZIC, L. *Essai sur l'amitié.* Paris, 1945.

SCHWERTSCHLAGER, R. *Lob der Freundshaft.* Heidelberg, 1947.

VISCHER, L. "Das Probleme der Freundschaft bei den Kirchenvaetern," *ThZschr,* (1953), 173–200.

The Essence, Characteristics, and Effects of Love of Neighbor

GUIBERT, J. *On Kindness.* Paterson, N.J., 1947.

SCHELER, M. *The Nature of Sympathy.* Translated by P. Heath. New Haven: Yale Univ. Press, 1954. London: Routledge & Kegan Paul, 1954.

SOROKIN, P. A. *The Ways and the Power of Love.* Boston, 1954.

STAKEMEIER, E. "Hoeflichkeit als Tugend," *ThG,* 34 (1942), 289–292.

"Wege zum Bruder," *LebS,* 3 (1952), H. 4.

Additional Works in English

DANIEL-ROPS, HENRI. *Of Human Love.* Chicago: Fides, 1960.

D'ARCY, MARTIN C. *The Spirit of Charity.* New York: Benziger, 1929.

GUITTON, JEAN. *Essays on Human Love.* New York: Philosophical Library, 1951.

Love of Our Neighbor. Albert Plé, O.P., ed. London: Blackfriars, 1955. (Springfield, Ill.: Templegate.)

Love and Violence. Bruno de Jésus-Marie, O.C.D., ed. New York: Sheed and Ward, 1954.

MEYER, BERNARD F., M.M. *Lend Me Your Hands.* Chicago: Fides, 1955. (C.F.M.)

MONTCHEUIL, YVES DE, S.J. *A Guide for Social Action.* Chicage: Fides, 1954.

MOUROUX, JEAN. *The Christian Experience: an Introduction to a Theology.* New York: Sheed and Ward, 1954.

VIEUJEAN, JEAN. *Your Other Self.* Westminster, Md.: Newman, 1959.

Periodical Literature in English

BALSAM, B. M. "Value of Mental Prayer," *CrCr,* 5 (June, 1953), 169–81.

BELFORD, J. L. "Let Us Pray," *HPR,* 32 (Sept., 1932), 1241–9.

DE JAEGHER, P. "Towards Continual Prayer," *RR,* 11 (Sept., 1952), 231–41.

DONOVAN, C. F. "Faith and Prayer," *RR,* 6 (Nov. 15, 1947), 335–41.

DUFFY, D. "Sunday Rest," *Fur,* 11 (June, 1960), 364–71.

GRAF, E. "Prayer (Definitions, Kinds)," *HPR,* 34 (Sept., 1934), 1321–25.

———. "Excellence of Vocal Prayer," *HPR,* 40 (July, 1940), 1129–31.

KELLY, G. "How Often Must We Pray?" *RR,* 8 (Nov. 15, 1949), 289–96.

KLAAS, A. "In Praise of Prayer," *RR,* 6 (Nov. 15, 1947), 363–71; (July 15, 1949), 139–50.

KNOX, R. A. "Prayer," *ClerRev,* 16 (June, 1939), 485–98; 17 (July, 1939), 2–17.

MACIVOR, D. "Sunday Worship," *Fur,* 11 (June, 1960), 372–79.

McReavy, L. L. "Sabbatarianism and the Decalogue," *ClerRev,* 20 (June, 1941), 498–508.

Martindale, C. C. "Sanctifying Sunday," *Mo,* 170 (Aug., 1937), 118–25.

Pettirsch, F. X. "Theology of Sunday Rest," *TD,* 6 (Sept., 1958), 114–20.

"Prayer of the Church," *CrCr,* 5 (June, 1953), 127–40.

Putz, J. "Liturgical and Private Devotion," *RR,* 7 (Jan. 15, 1948), 23–33.

Tierney, C. "Doctrinal Aspects of the Sunday," *Australasian Catholic Review,* 33 (July, 1956), 239–45.

Utz, A. F. "Nature of Prayer," *CrCr,* 5 (June, 1953), 154–62.

CHAPTER TEN

THE TWO PRIMARY MANIFESTATIONS OF
LOVE OF NEIGHBOR

ITHOUT doubt no part of our life may be excluded from love: our whole life must be an expression of love for our neighbor. In this sense special moral theology in its entirety is a presentation of the expression and realization of love of neighbor in the various realms of life. Here we are specifically concerned with the meaningful content of active love of neighbor and its immediate extension to the twofold area of the bodily and the spiritual needs and concerns of our neighbor and the community.

I. LOVE OF NEIGHBOR AND BODILY NEEDS

1. *The Imitation and the Corporal Works of Mercy*

"The attempt to limit oneself to the simple proclamation of the tidings of salvation and in the process to pass over in silence its practical implications, particularly those which focus attention on the Christian social teaching, would be a betrayal of the Gospel. True love demands that we love our neighbor after the manner of Christ who did not wish to dismiss his hearers—who were so eager to harken to the news of salvation—without first giving them food to eat, so that they would not faint from hunger on the way (cf. Mk 8:3)."[22]

We know that Christ did not come to found an earthly kingdom or to promote material welfare. But far from ignoring the bodily suffering of men, he showed the most profound and most heartfelt sympathy for the sick and the crippled and even worked many miracles to cure them. Christ is not only the Savior of men's souls, but the Redeemer of the whole man.[23]

The soul's salvation (which consists in the bond of friendship with God and in God) is the goal and principal object of Christian love. But the bodily needs of our neighbor may not be treated without sympathy and action. We must love man, and man is not simply a spirit; he is mind and body. His bodily needs are real and inseparably interwoven with his spiritual, his supernatural life. Nothing so readily embitters the heart and paralyzes the spirit of man as to suffer bodily ills helplessly in an atmosphere of indulgence and indifference to all human misery. To ignore the bodily suffering of one's neighbor, to make no effort to relieve other men's own undisturbed ease and quest for material enjoyment despite the call and the opportunity to help those in need is to close one's heart to the good. The result is growing spiritual impoverishment in love, progressive incapacity for divine love.

Active love of the true Christian for the poor and the poorest is a grand and visible sign of God's loving dominion among men, a sign made effective through divine grace. For those to whom the redemptive signs of God's love, the sacraments, are still hidden, this love of the Christian is a kind of "sacrament of the love of God." The thought is from Augustine who says very dramatically: "The sacraments of baptism and Eucharist are concealed in the Church. They are not public and manifest. But our good works are evident even to the heathens, whilst the sacraments are kept hidden from them: that which they do not see is the source of that which they do see. It is like the base of the Cross sunk deep in the earth, but bearing aloft the entire Cross which is apparent to all."[24]

On the other hand, the poor and the miserable are to those who can help them "sacraments of love." In sign and guise of human misery Christ comes to us, the Christ who wills to draw the whole world redemptively into His sanctifying love. The physical misery of the pauper arouses us from the smugness of self-satisfaction and spurs us on to unselfish love. It is the instrument of a more vital, concrete premonition of the love of the Crucified for us than is the sacrament of the Church alone without the poor or the love of those in distress. Similar to the sacraments in their symbolism, the effective giving of alms in assistance of the lowly is an incorporation, an embodiment of the interior spirit and the word of love. Through this charity to the poor, love in its inner spirit and in its word or expression is safeguarded and deepened. The sacrament is personal encounter with Christ which demands the most loving affection for our Savior. Similarly, encountering Christ in the lowly calls for the most reverential personal warmth of Christian love. The result can only be fruitful for both unto eternal salvation.

Already in the early centuries Lactantius enumerates six *corporal works* in connection with the Last Judgment (Mt 25:35ff.): to feed the hungry, to give drink to the thirsty, to befriend the homeless, to clothe the naked, to visit the sick, to console the captive (or to liberate prisoners and slaves). To these he then added the seventh work from Tobias 1:20:

"to bury the dead."[25] The works enumerated correspond to the bodily needs of the social world of the Gospel period. Love must always sense the special needs of the age and find a remedy for them.[26]

We epitomize the entire work of material assistance to the poor in the spirit of love in the term *almsgiving*. In this wide sense of the word the entire bounty for the welfare of our neighbor is comprized. In this bounty the alms of the lean purse, produced by the sweat of one's own brow, is far more meritorious than the gift of our superfluities. Since almsgiving includes also the material gifts for sacred cult and for the care of souls, it is both a corporal and a spiritual work of mercy. If we use the term in the widest sense as including any material assistance given the needy in the spirit of love, almsgiving is a universal obligation. After we have discussed this general obligation, we shall take up the special duties and lay down the particular norms and limits for the more specific obligations.

2. Universal Obligation

Repeatedly and emphatically Scripture and Tradition stress the merit and duty of giving alms. Most impressive are the words of the Lord Himself, starkly stating the duty of almsgiving in the glorious promises and the dire threats in the account of the general judgment. This final decision of judgment will set up as a standard the doing of bodily works of mercy to determine who is the true disciple of the Master. The final test for us all: did we really and effectively see and love Christ Himself in our neighbor. To feed the poor, to clothe them, to provide for them in our homes means to feed, clothe, embrace Christ Himself. To neglect the needy and show them no mercy means to fail in mercy toward Christ Himself (this is to ignore the historic Christ in our sentiments and attitudes, to really slight in deed and effect the "mystic Christ") (cf. Mt 25:35ff.). Even those who are still ignorant of Christ, because they do not have explicit faith in Him, possess a saving bond with Him through a firm and unshaken love for their neighbor.

True love in spirit is inseparable from tender mercy for those in need. "He who has the goods of this world and sees his brother in need and closes his heart to him, how does the love of God abide in him?" (1 Jn 3:17). "For judgment is without mercy to him who has not shown mercy; but mercy triumphs over judgment. . . . If a brother or a sister be naked and in want of daily food, and one of you say to them, 'Go in peace, be warmed and filled,' yet you do not give them what is necessary for the body, what does it profit?" (Jas 2:13ff.).

The Old Testament prophets repeatedly contrasted the bodily works of mercy with the oblations which lacked the spirit of sacrifice. They constantly prescribe efficacious love and mercy as preparation for the true worship of God: "For it is love that I desire, not sacrifice, and knowledge of God rather than holocausts" (Os 6:6). Fasting without mercy is worthless, and the prayer of one who fasts in this manner is vain and will not be heard: "This, rather, is the fasting that I wish: releasing those bound unjustly, untying the thongs of the yoke; setting free the oppressed, breaking every yoke; sharing your bread with the hungry, sheltering the oppressed and the homeless; clothing the naked when you see them, and not turning your back on your own. . . . Then you shall call, and the Lord will answer" (Is 58:6ff.). "He who shuts his ear to the cry of the poor will himself also call and not be heard" (Prv 21:13). Indeed Sirach, the wise, threatens the hardhearted with the divine wrath. The wail of anguish and despair rising from the oppressed hearts of the poor who have been rejected with contempt and disdain is an imprecation to which God will harken (Sir 4:1ff.). The most splendid sermon on the blessings of almsgiving in the entire Old Testament is the book of Tobias (Tb 2:1ff.; 4:7ff.; 12:8ff.; 14:11). The story throughout is a paean of praise of the merit of almsgiving. The elder Tobias says to his son: "Give alms out of thy substance, and turn not away thy face from any poor person. . . . According to thy ability be merciful. If thou have much give abundantly: if thou have little, take care even so to bestow willingly a little. For thus thou storest up to thyself a good reward for the day of necessity. . . . Alms shall be a great confidence before the most high God, to all them that give it" (Tb 4:7ff.).

The first Christian community held almsgiving in high esteem. The rich at Jerusalem distributed all their superfluous possessions among the poor of the community, at first through the Apostles, and later through the newly established diaconate (Acts 2:44f.; 4:32ff.). The Apostles formed an official and well-regulated organization to care for the needy (Acts 6). The assemblies at the suggestion of Paul collected alms in the various communities of the Church for the community of Jerusalem (2 Cor 8–9 may be considered the oldest extant sermon on charity).

The Fathers take up and continue this earnest train of scriptural thought with undiminished vigor. St. Cyprian has a special work on the value of efficacious almsgiving (*De Opere et Eleemosynis*). For him the right use of wealth, which pays rich dividends before God, is to "nourish Christ" by feeding the poor.[27] Clement of Alexandria treats almsgiving in his noted little book, *What Rich Man Shall be Saved?* (*Quis Dives Salvetur?*). Clement does not condemn riches as in themselves evil, though they may surely prove a hazardous snare of injustice. But wealth can also be an aid to salvation if it has "justice for its guide" and is placed at the service of the poor. Wealth can be spiritually profitable if the rich man forms of the poor whom he has assisted in this life a kind of peace corps with which to assail the kingdom of heaven.[28] Jerome does not hesitate to place the loving use of wealth for the poor before the construction and adornment of churches.[29] Augustine cannot bear to see a Christian rolling in superfluous wealth while others live in squalor. He appeals to the rich to cast off at least a portion of the wealth which is too cumbersome for them by giving to the poor who have nothing. Thus shall the rich sustain the poor and lighten their own burden.[30]

The Fathers base the obligation of performing the corporal works of mercy in the mystery of the Eucharist. They delight in pointing out how all mercy toward one's fellows, all love of neighbor rests in the mystery of the Savior's Eucharistic love. The words of John Chrysostom are very telling: "How can we justify ourselves if we are nourished on this Food and still perpetrate such sins; do we eat of the Lamb and turn into wolves? For this sacrament not only forbids rapine but prescribes the purging of every uncharitable sentiment. This mystery is the mystery of peace: it does not permit man to set his heart on riches. If He did not spare His own (Son), how great a punishment shall we incur if we cherish and hold fast our wealth to the neglect of souls. This is the sum and center of all good things, that God did not spare His own Son in order to break the bonds of slaves. No Judas, no Simon may approach this table, for both perished through avarice. . . . Have you a desire to honor the Body of Christ? Do not pass Him by disdainfully when you see Him naked and exposed to the shame of the streets. Do not glorify Him in the Church with garments of silk if you slight him without pity in the streets where He is perishing in cold and nakedness! For He who spoke the word of power, 'This is my Body' (Mt 26:26) also said, 'I was hungry, and you did not give me to eat . . . as long as you did not do it for one of these least ones, you did not do it for me' (Mt 25:42ff.). Therefore let us learn to grasp the truth with love and to honor Christ as He wills it. Show Him the honor which He has prescribed: give your riches to the poor."[31]

The entire course of her history is evidence that the Church has never failed in loyalty to this commission of her Lord. She built splendid temples in His honor. But she bestowed no less of her substance and solicitude, wherever it was necessary, upon the poor and the needy. For many centuries this solicitude and care for the sick and poor was almost exclusively her concern.[32] In the mission lands in the past and also in our own time the Church has pioneered in the care for the sick, the crippled, the homeless, the orphans. She has brought to men an understanding of mercy and new means of caring for those in need. She has relieved the misery she has had no share in causing, the misery due in large part to the pride and ambition of leaders who persecuted or at least ignored the Church. And she has done so without the aid of immense funds from the state, often indeed despite the deprivation of funds owing to her and her faithful in distributive justice on the part of the state. In our own time vast networks of Catholic charity are a practical realization of this Christian ideal. In the United States the National Catholic Welfare Conference is an example of worldwide effective engagement in the relief of human misery wherever it may be found. The Roman pontiffs have also shown in this our age how profoundly and effectively they have been moved by the charity of Christ whose vicars they are. Following in the footsteps of the Master who went about doing good, the Church in caring for the salvation of souls has never neglected man's bodily needs.

3. Charity: Private and Organized

Private charity and publicly organized charity must be parallel efforts mutually assisting each other. Because of the intimate personal contact of man with man, private charity has the advantage which derives from immediate and direct action. In this instance more readily does tender love accompany the gift of charity with the warmth and inner sympathy of the one who gives, enriching both giver and receiver. "The profound moral influence on the poor is not the work of boards and committees but of personal love. No one can rightly discharge his duty of almsgiving by donating a carefully calculated sum of money to a community chest and then close his eyes to the poverty which it might relieve and also to the sincerity of thanks which it might merit. Though this is not the motive of Christian charity, there is an ennobling result flowing from it upon the benefactor, an elevating, purifying, sustaining element."[33]

Benevolence as a work of Christian love does not have as its sole and exclusive purpose the alleviation of bodily needs and ills. Even this purpose would fail in accomplishment, were there no loftier motive. Christian benevolence seeks to go far beyond the bodily need or misery. Its higher objective is to open the inner fountain of love, to open the heart of the recipient to the divine love, and to make the giver like to God. Its lofty objective is the formation and enrichment of the divine friendship in those who give and those who receive.

One who has no sense for this richness of love flowing from the heart and back to the heart will never penetrate to the depths of true Christian mercy. He will never be able to understand how a Catholic nun can spend herself utterly in the care of the poorest and lowliest of men: the aged, the incurably diseased, the lepers, the mentally retarded and deranged. He has never been awakened to the realization of the effects of sacrificial love on those who seem to evoke only repugnance or pity. He has not seen the effect of love on a retarded child who once felt totally excluded from the warmth of love. Through charity the greater riches, heavenly riches, are scattered like precious seed which bears a harvest far more abundant for the benefactor than the most lucrative investment in stocks and bonds.

Private charity, the gift from individual to individual, since it is personal, not only corresponds better to the idea of Christian love, the *agápe,* but is also in many ways indispensable. It has a special quality by which it is most calculated to remove the hatred of the dispossessed. Only private charity seeks out the poor who are too proud or ashamed to beg or admit their need to any public relief agency.

Despite its obvious superiority to the organized forms of relief of human need, private charity is not equal to the task of caring for all the bodily and mental needs which exist. For the greater tasks which deal with widespread misery we must have organized charitable work. Again, there are certain types of charitable activity which can be carried out only in institutions. Many cripples, mentally retarded persons, the feeble-minded, endangered youth, and certain others in need of specialized help or treatment ordinarily cannot be cared for properly except in institutions equipped for such purposes. Only some type of organization can assure a sound and stable basis for works of this kind. For this reason the Church, beyond her constant endorsement of private charity, has from her very beginning organized and stabilized her works of mercy in the more comprehensive areas. In this way Christian hospitals, hospices, institutions of special care were established and entrusted to particular communities of charity. Thus the great ecclesiastical orders and societies of charity arose.

Organized charity in its innumerable forms and institutions has the advantage over private (in itself indispensable) initiative that help and relief are not made to rely totally on the individual. Rather the aid is placed on a broader and firmer basis for which there can be organized planning as well as special education and training of administrators and workers. Only in this way can we cope not only with individual or incidental needs, but also with pressing social ills and hazards. Moreover, in the religious charitable orders and societies personal tenderness of approach in works of mercy is not at all suppressed. Rather, it is enlarged and expanded, incited and encouraged in a splendid fellowship and coordination of loving mercy. A fine example is the hospital sisterhood in its care for the sick and needy: only God knows the extent of loving devotion manifested in endless acts of sacrificial mercy. More significant is the relief of mental and spiritual suffering, the consolation of mind and spirit brought to those in bodily need: in these acts of tenderness toward our neighbor the love of God is eternally praised in the Christian love of His suffering creatures.

Priests and spiritual guides have the obligation to encourage the collection of funds for the charitable works of the Church. Even greater is their obligation to be concerned with the vocations through which the work is to be carried on. They must further in every good way the call to the institutes of mercy.

In our age, preoccupied with physical and social welfare, there are many free social institutions and agencies under secular control. In large measure they are not sustained by the Christian concept of supernatural love but by purely humanitarian or philanthropic ideals of human welfare or social betterment. As a general rule the Christian should support the organizations under the Church's administration (orphanages, hospitals, etc.) rather than the neutral institutions. This is not to endorse a species of total opposition to secular or civil institutions in a world which is largely nondenominational and even dechristianized. Surely the immense movements of relief which seem to draw from the deep reservoirs of human kindness and generosity have their hidden sources to a large extent in Christian ideals. They draw from the attractive force of the example of Christ and Christian influences in our civilization. We cannot approve of the merely temporal approach and attitude, nor of the decline of true love of God as basic motivation for all charity, much less of any conscious attempt to supplant the Christian charitable endeavor. Nevertheless, Catholics should be covered with shame if this extra-Christian, or at least extra-Catholic, charitable activity were to surpass the Church's own charitable endeavor in sacrifice and extent of effectiveness. It would be small consolation to excuse our failure by stressing the superiority of our motives. Small consolation indeed; for the very loftiness of our motives should create a joyous sacrificial endeavor. But we should not engage in any species of rivalry which would place our great ideals in the background and fail to fix our attention on the grand spiritual works of mercy and the use of temporal resources for worship and the care of souls.

In dealing with the various organizations concerned with relief of human misery and need, the Catholic is often confronted by the problem of cooperation with non-Catholic welfare societies. A prudent cooperation, even of an organizational type, with such societies is permissible, provided unobjectionable ends are pursued.

The relation of the Church-supported beneficence and the state welfare endeavor requires a more detailed discussion. The new age has brought about an unfortunate tension in this area between the state welfare concern and activity and the Church's supernatural beneficence. Theoretically speaking the two are not contradictory, but rather necessarily complement each other. The state should make every effort to remove social inequalities and show its concern for the socially weak and defenseless. But all responsible leaders should clearly realize that, after the state has reached the limits of its powers, there still remains a vast area of need which only voluntary action by the individual and the community in the spirit of love can rightly care for. The Church is far from condemning any genuine concern on the part of the modern state for the socially distressed. On the contrary, no one realizes so well as the Church that the prevalence of a high standard of social justice is the best presupposition for fruitful charitable activity. Christian love never can and never will dispense with justice nor ignore it. It is not the first purpose of the Church to rush to the defense or leap into the breach when justice has been violated, though unfortunately she is often constrained to do so. She rather wishes to go beyond justice and heal men's wounds with loving charity as she opens and warms their hearts.

The attempt on the part of infidel states to suppress Christian charitable endeavor or, more specifically, to control it and take it over, is due to a basic misconception of the distinction between law and love. It is a mad attempt to legalize the activity of love. Human welfare has a legal side but also a charitable one, which is no less significant. Only the legal phase and only that which is strictly the obligation of justice can and should be legislated by the state according to norms of law. Even though the state should temporarily be able through legal pressures to take over by some external control and operation a portion of the Church's charitable activities, this very intervention would repel that which is best, the free movement of love. But should the spirit of voluntary charitable endeavor wane, then the minimum measure of love would also disappear from society. The love which is prerequisite for the clear knowledge and realization of legal social duties would cease to be effective. This is obvious from the many misconceptions prevalent among the leaders in pagan states. (There is little realization of the duty of the state to protect the rights of the unborn child, no understanding of the evils involved in certain types of birth restriction, little grasp of the duty of the state to avoid educational monopoly and to treat all children equally in the distribution of state funds for educational purposes, etc.)

The state by seeking to take over the charitable institutions of the Christian communities, even only externally, while permitting the communities to operate them, would involve itself in an absurd contradiction; for the inner vitality of the very communities placed under duress would be sorely constricted. Moreover, for the state to force such massive control in every area is most destructive of all human right and freedom. The more the Church is excluded from the works of charity, the more she is forced to withdraw from the work which is proper to her as the institution of love, the more exclusively will mere impersonal and purely legalistic concepts and, eventually, merely pragmatic motives enter into what was once the abode of love. Thus the state, far from promoting justice, will eventually destroy charity, and ultimately be the source of the gravest social injustice.

Not only should the state shun all unjust interference in the work of the Church; it should welcome the service of love performed by her through the communities of love, welcome and in some manner include it in the grand project of human welfare promoted by public authority. This inclusion, however, must always allow for that indispensably free action of the Church's charity and, paradoxically, also for unimpeded acceptance of material means to further her work. For this reason public funds should not furnish all the means for the Church's institutions, since the gifts which she herself procures through free love for charitable activity are in every way more precious and fruitful than the money obtained by pressure of taxation—which scarcely anyone looks upon as a gift of love.

Except for the actual dechristianization of the schools nothing is so destructive of the care of souls as the undermining and cramping of the charitable work of the Church, particularly through the expulsion of Catholic sisterhoods from hospitals and institutions of care for the needy. Countless men have opened their hearts to divine love in the sacred moment when human misery met with the tenderness of Christlike love, when divine grace turned sinners to a Christian life or at least prepared them for a Christian death.

4. Obligations in Justice as Distinct from Charity

The obligatory nature of almsgiving can be studied correctly only in the total context of the universal obligation of the social use of material goods, from which use it must be clearly distinguished.

Charitable endeavor bereft of a sense of justice cannot be genuine love. Nor is it effective and fruitful. It may even prove very baneful. This is not to deny that love is queen in the hierarchy of virtues, but to make plain the inescapable fact that charity rests on justice. Justice is an essential support for the right order of love.[34]

First Principle: Commutative justice demands compensation for work according to the principle of exchange, like value to be given for like value. An employer who does not pay wages according to this principle does not redress his wrong conduct by giving the equivalent of the defrauded wages in the form of alms. He must restore the amount to the worker who earned it, as a recompense for the work itself, and not as alms or other form of gratuity.[35]

Second Principle: Legal justice obliges us to pay the tax which the state justly levies for the general welfare. Only in instances of great need in which the state cannot or will not render necessary assistance is one permitted, under certain circumstances, to substitute for the tax imposed or other payment required a form of direct contribution under the guise of alms to the individual concerned.

Third Principle: Social justice (this means the social direction inherent in the earthly goods themselves as God created them, and even more emphatically in the sum total of created reality as saved and redirected by Christ who offered Himself in Sacrifice for all men) requires that all property be used with a sense of social responsibility. Superfluous goods must be so used as to contribute to the good and welfare of society. This is the same as to say they must be used for the good of our neighbor.

Only a thorough understanding of the social and economic situation can determine in individual instances the most appropriate use of superfluous goods in the social order. Suggested as more effective in promoting the general welfare than indiscriminate or massive distribution of gratuities are the following: construction of adequate housing, promotion of widespread employment, furnishing of loans interest free or at a low rate of interest for construction of homes. In general it is socially and morally more advisable to create a sound economic and social order in which the individual is encouraged to work, to save, to exercise thrift, and to care for himself and his family.

Fourth Principle: In determining concretely and in individual instances what goods are to be classed as superfluous, strict social justice will prove less flexible than expansive and generous love of neighbor. After a manner of speaking, we may set up a doubly relative standard. On the one hand, we must look to the vast acquisition of wealth far beyond the individual and family needs of the possessors, and on the other, to the appalling misery of countless human beings the world over. In the light of these two extremes one must form the sincere judgment: how much of my wealth is superfluous, unnecessary for me, capable of relieving human misery and distress?

A standard based on the concept *station in life* must meet with many difficulties. It is entirely too relative and too readily misapplied. In a world saturated with passion for self-indulgence, egoism, cupidity, the Christian can scarcely find a valid standard, particularly if he is dealing with the wealthier classes on the basis of the customary standard of living among our rich. In fact, experience proves that the very rich rarely, if ever, are disturbed in conscience by the realization that the *station in life* is also to be gauged by the general condition of human needs, not merely by the life to which one is accustomed. It is contrary to social justice that one social class should lay claim to an affluence and luxury suited to its so-called rank and station in life while vast masses do not have the minimum essential to sustain health. Nothing could be more perverted than to have moral theology confirm an erroneous conscience through false teaching regarding the standard of living in accordance with one's station in life. True Christian life is not to be judged by its conformity to the special privileges or prerogatives of a station in life, but rather by conformity to the teaching and example of Christ. Nevertheless, there is a correct sense in which we may use the term, *station in life.*[36] For example, one's office or one's position in life or society has a bearing on the education of one's children. One's position may determine the type of education and training which is to be provided for them. The cultivation of one's home life, the cultural activity of individual and family, all the efforts for cultural progress depend very largely on one's social attainments and status.

Fifth Principle: Not even charity (not to speak of social justice) requires that one devote all one's superfluities to almsgiving. A socially sound and fruitful use of material goods in other ways may frequently prove more advantageous to the furtherance of the true welfare of our neighbor than the distribution of alms. The sharp utterances of many Fathers of the Church declaring that there is an obligation in charity, or even in justice, to give all one's superfluous goods in alms may reasonably be interpreted to mean that there is a real obligation to devote the total superfluity to the welfare of one's neighbors, primarily in the form of alms. Ambrose's statement directed to the rich almsgiver, "You return to the poor something of his own,"[37] is according to all theologians literally true if the poor who receive the gift are in desperate need. As to other instances Ambrose means merely that the goods of this earth have an absolute and immutable destination to the welfare of all, and therefore also of those who are in need through no fault of their own. Augustine repeatedly stresses that all superfluities of the rich exist in order to serve the poor in their misery.[38] Particularly sharp in this context are the following words: *Res alienae possidentur, cum superflua possidentur* (One who possesses superfluous goods is in possession of another's property.) "The superfluity of the rich is necessary for the poor. Hence to cling to superfluous wealth is to possess the property of others."[39] These bold assertions of Augustine are not at all pious rhetorical exaggeration. St. Thomas also says that the refusal to give alms from one's superfluity in instances where our neighbor is in great need is a violation of legal justice.[40]

In weighing the gravity of these words of the Fathers or similar expressions we must always bear in mind that in the economic system of the period, the superfluous goods to which Augustine directly and immediately referred were not productive, but unproductive, amassed, inherited wealth. Augustine and the Fathers did not have in mind the alternative between a use of wealth in the social order through almsgiving and the consequent relief of distress and the use in some other responsible form. The only alternative in mind was either the use of superflous wealth for the alleviation of distress by almsgiving or clinging to amassed wealth which had no social value or very little social value at all. In any instance the position of Augustine is quite clear. He holds that the withholding of superfluity by refusal to contribute to the alleviation of the misery of others is a violation of the right order in the use of material goods. It is not easy to determine whether the great Doctor has in mind the violation of legal (or, more specifically, social) justice, or perhaps a violation of charity. But the saint surely refers to the objective order inherent in the material values as such and in their relation to us, not merely the order of our love to our fellows. With this thought of Augustine in mind, we may assert that no earthly possession is free from the claim of social justice. Every earthly possession is stamped with this claim. And the possession of the disciples of Christ bear the mark of yet another claim in the social order. Christ Himself by His example has placed upon them the special mark of His redemptive possession: He Who has the right of ownership to all earthly things and Who redeemed all things with the price of His Blood kept nothing, not even His garments, when He died naked on the Cross.

Very sharp are the words of St. Gregory the Great in reference to the rich man in the Gospel: "No one should feel secure even though he can say, 'I have not stolen anything belonging to others, and what belongs to me I use lawfully.' For that the rich man (Dives of the Gospel) was delivered into hell because he used the wealth given him for luxury and closed his heart to the misery of the poor."[41]

No one who studies the passages just cited—and there are many others in the Fathers—can escape the conclusion that, at the very least, there is an obligation to use all one's superfluous goods in a socially responsible way for the needy. The sharp stress of almsgiving by the Fathers, however, is also conditioned by the sociological factors of their time, and must be so understood.

Sixth Principle: From what we have just said it is clear not only that there is an obligation to make a social use of the entire superfluity we may possess, but that a certain portion must be distributed as alms. The amount depends on the greatness of the necessity and the extent of one's wealth.

In the Old Testament a tithe for worship and a tithe for the poor was prescribed. Every seventh year the poor were allowed to reap the harvest. They also had a claim to the annual gleanings (Ex 23:11; LV 19:9f.; 23:22). But beyond all this, the generous loan without interest or profit and the giving of alms are particularly stressed (Dt 15:7ff.).

Even though the state should demand and expend huge sums for welfare in many forms, even though wealth is used intelligently and with great vision for the common welfare, there is still a constant need related to the care of souls and divine worship for various types of charity, all of which call for almsgiving. Little appeals are always directed to us wherever we may be. So many are the demands on the charity of every openhearted man, due to extraordinary distress ("The poor you have always with you." Jn 12:8), that total refusal to give alms must be considered sinful.

5. *Practical Norms in Charity and Almsgiving*

First Principle: The natural and positive divine precept to give alms from one's superfluous possessions binds under penalty of mortal sin by its nature (*ex genere suo*). Proof for this assertion is contained in scriptural and patristic teaching and in the very nature of earthly goods in relation to us and to the order of redemption. The proof is found in the previous paragraphs.

Second Principle: The measure and degree of the obligation is determined by the amount of one's wealth or income and the extent of the need or distress. In periods of great and widespread disaster or misery this precept is graver and more urgent than in times of prosperity; but it never ceases to oblige, for we always have the poor with us. The unheard-of assumption that one can scarcely ever find a man who has a real superfluity in view of his rank and station has been condemned by Innocent XI.[42] But unfortunately it is true that, where love is dead, scarcely anyone will possess the true insight into his own relative superfluity. The man without charity will not realize that by comparison with the poor he does possess superfluity which he must relinquish. In one lapidary sentence the bible tells what is really *superfluity* for the true disciple of Christ: "Let him who has two tunics share with him who has none; and let him who has food do likewise" (Lk 3:11). By comparison with a man in naked tatters, two suits of clothes are a superfluity—which would hardly be the case were there no such appalling poverty.

Third Principle: To assist our neighbor in his extreme necessity (for example, in danger of death or in a very serious illness) we are obliged to use not only our superfluous possessions but also a portion of that which seems necessary for the maintenance of our station in life. But we are not strictly obliged to do more than relieve the extreme distress. As a rule there is no obligation to make an extraordinary effort or undergo extraordinary expenses in such instances. To cite an example: one is not required to procure expensive medication, treatment, or hospitalization unless there are special reasons demanding such action on our part (e.g., to save the life or health of a man or woman who is the sole support of a very large family). Magnanimous love, however, is generously active in a vast area without the constraint of any universal commandment.

Fourth Principle: In instances of great need there is a grave obligation to relieve the distress of our fellow man by use of one's superfluous goods. There is no actual obligation to contribute to this end by means of alms or gifts if the same purpose can be attained by means of a loan (under certain conditions this should be interest-free or at a low rate of interest), provided this will tide the man over in his need. Or one may provide employment to relieve the distress. In fact, the loan or employment may be the better approach to solution of the problem as more calculated to further the moral integrity of the individual.

Fifth Principle: If it is evident that the distress places our neighbor in serious moral jeopardy from which he can be saved only by the intervention of material assistance, then we are obliged under penalty of mortal sin to render such assistance. We are certainly obliged to use something of our superfluous goods and, to an extent at least, also some of the goods necessary for maintaining our station in life.

Sixth Principle: There is no obligation to give alms from the goods indispensable for the support of our own life. The reason is that every man has the obligation and the right above all to care for his own life and health and that of his dependents.

Seventh Principle: Scripture and tradition propose for us a most exalted ideal, not by way of universal commandment, but rather by way of counsel: "If thou wilt be perfect, go, sell what thou hast, and give to the poor" (Mt 19:21). One following this lofty ideal gives all he has to the poor, so that he can live entirely from the work of his own hands and then give some of his earnings to the needy (cf. Eph 4:28; 2 Thes 3:8). Throughout the centuries the lofty ideal of the Franciscan family was: sell all one possesses, work for others without recompense, and live entirely on alms. Even should one not own or possess any real property but live exclusively on a fixed income from one's work, there is still something of an obligation to do what one can toward helping those who are still poorer, by saving a mite for them and for the spiritual and charitable work of the Church. The petty gifts of the common people are a principal source of charity.

6. Almsgiving in the Christian Manner

a. Essential and decisive in almsgiving is the right Christian motive. Without the supernatural attitude of mind the gift of love is of no avail to the giver. "If I distribute all my goods to feed the poor . . . yet do not have charity, it profits me nothing" (1 Cor 13:3). Through the right disposition we enter into the love of Christ, we join with Him in His love and participate in its efficaciousness: "Whoever gives to one of these little ones but a cup of cold water to drink because he is a disciple . . . he shall not lose his reward" (Mt 10:42; cf. Mk 9:40; Mt 25:35ff.). Christ will reward those who see Him in the poor and are tender and kind to Him through the manifestation of love to them.

Selfish and hypocritical motivation should never be allowed to insinuate itself into the giving of alms. "Do good, and lend, not hoping for any return, and your reward shall be great, and you shall be children of the most High" (Lk 6:35). "When thou givest alms, do not let thy left hand know what thy right hand is doing" (Mt 6:3). The words of our Lord should not be distorted. We are not prohibited from prudently pondering on the object of our almsgiving, to whom we are giving, how the gift is to be used. But the admonition of the Lord warns that our motive must be pure in God's sight. Human vanity and worldly prestige destroy the pure motivation of genuine charity.

b. Not merely disposition and spirit of the giver must be correct, but also the manner and mode of the giving must be in right order. Loving reverence for the poor, gentle words of comfort, delicacy, and tact in the actual giving of assistance are far more effective in opening the hearts of the distressed to the love of God than the most munificent largess which is bereft of this spirit. Rather than look with patronizing condescension upon the poor, the man of wealth must be mindful of Christ who became the servant of the poorest. To him wealth should be a commitment obliging him to service toward his brother in Christ. A sour and impatient attitude toward the poor mars the most generous giving, as though the poor were not worth the effort of personal concern. "God loves a cheerful giver" (2 Cor 9:7; cf. Rom 12:8). "In every gift show a cheerful countenance and sanctify thy tithes with joy" (Sir 35:11). "If thou have much, give abundantly: if thou have little, take care even so to bestow willingly a little" (Tb 4:9).

c. Almsgiving must above all be governed by prudence. The *logion* (saying) of our Lord handed down in the *Didache* brings out beautifully the need for prudent concern in the giving of alms: "Let your alms sweat in your hand until you know to whom you should give it." The teacher of the book of Sirach, wise even in his day, admonishes us that alms should not be diverted to the support of evil (Sir 12:1ff.). When he says "refuse the sinner" and "give nothing to the proud man," it does not mean that evil persons are to be totally excluded from our almsgiving, but only that we should not bestow gifts in such a manner nor with such abandon as to endorse and further their evil conduct. Christian charity may not be confined to a narrow circle of the good and pious. Nor should those of other faiths or unbelievers be excluded, so long as our good deeds are not tantamount to a practical support of heresy or unbelief or of evil conduct. Prudence demands that we be circumspect, that we consider all the circumstances connected with our almsgiving: the age, the capacity for work, the position in life, the motive, the innocence or guilt of the prospective recipient of our generosity.[43] Those who are too lazy to work should receive nothing at all or very little. "If any man will not work, neither let him eat" (2 Thes 3:10). His family, however, should not be made to suffer, but should be assisted in the spirit of genuine prudence.

II. LOVING AND ACTIVE CONCERN FOR THE SALVATION OF OTHERS

1. *A Universal Obligation*

There is in the Church a specific office for the care of souls with its own special consecration which places the recipient entirely and utterly in the service of immortal souls, in the service of the kingdom of God. To be a priest means to be "appointed for men in the things pertaining to God" (Heb 5:1). The priest stands at the altar not only for himself, but above all for the people. He has received his pastoral charge not in order to enrich himself (Ez 34:8), but to nourish the souls of his brothers and sisters by announcing the doctrine and administering the sacraments, to preserve them and stimulate them to good through word and example. With his ordination and office he must also accept the charge expressed in the words of the Good Shepherd as his own ideal: "The lost I will seek out, the strayed I will bring back, the injured I will bind up, the sick I will heal (but the sleek and the strong I will destroy), shepherding them rightly" (Ez 34:16).

Woe to the director of souls who allows the exalted gifts of his consecration to lie fallow and unused, who lives indeed from the altar but does not work for the salvation of souls with the total devotion of his love and the unrestricted employment of his official capacities. As official ambassador of divine love, he is doubly guilty of violating the law of love, and guilty also of violating justice.

Parents and educators must care for the bodily welfare and the intellectual development of their children; but the eternal salvation of their offspring or charges must be a matter of even greater concern. In fact, parents are commissioned by the very nature of the sacrament of matrimony to this great duty; they receive a commission at the altar to be a "church in miniature," which admonition includes most particularly the duty of caring for the souls of each other and of the children God entrusts to them.

The discharge of any public office wields an influence in the formation of public life, in some manner accentuating its pace and rhythm. The journalist, the public official or civil servant, the politician, the statesman are obviously not designated administrators in the kingdom of God on earth. But their conduct is surely to be judged by its relation to the kingdom, and this judgment is not a secondary matter. Does their conduct redound to the profit of the spiritual kingdom or is it an evil influence on the kingdom of God and the salvation of souls? The greater the influence of the public servant in public life on his fellow citizens or subjects, the greater is the obligation to exploit that influence for the salvation of others.

But nothing would be further from truth, more hazardous to our spiritual welfare and more unchristian in its implications than to think that the obligation to care for the salvation of souls with active effort depended solely and utterly on a special or specified office, or that such commitment derived exclusively from a special office. Quite the contrary! There is a most sublime precept obliging every Christian according to his endowments and capacities. By a thousand titles every Christian must be concerned with the salvation of his neighbor's soul. He must further the work of salvation by active engagement wherever and whenever he can.

1) First of all, the virtue of Christian love infused into our souls impels us (2 Cor 5:14) to love our neighbor actively "in God." This implies that we must help him to love God so that God can embrace him and accept him in His eternal realm of love. And it is not at all a rare thing that only the solicitous love of one particular individual, a love that is in every way warm and personal, can open the heart of a certain fellow man to God. It follows that this particular individual is precisely the one whom God calls and obliges to do this work of love.

We all are aware that priests are called in a special manner to seek the way of salvation and holiness in zeal for souls. We know that religious strive for perfection in following the evangelical counsels. But this should not create any doubt in the mind of any Christian living in the world or in the cloister. We know that all are called to the fulfillment of perfection in love. And this implies active work for the salvation of souls on the part of all those who are capable of the task, for there can be no progress on the way of perfection without progress in loving action for the salvation of souls.

What does it mean to dedicate one's self to the apostolate? It is to yield to the impulse of love and to strive that the divine love which animates us fulfill its mission, that it become the bearer of glad tidings to others, assist them to discover the love of Christ and also, for their part, surrender to Him in a consummation of divine love.[44]

2) The totality of this divine gift of love we have in the Mystical Body of Christ which by its very nature calls us to love through living fellowship of the many members in one body and one love.[45] Analogously to the natural body, in the Mystical Body of Christ all the members must "have care for one another" (1 Cor 12:25).

The official priesthood and the official magisterium of the Church alone are not adequate for the carrying out of the great task of the salvation of souls, the full realization of the kingdom of God on earth. One is tempted to say that the cooperation of all individuals is in many ways still more important than the official activity of the shepherds of the flock. "The eye cannot say to the hand, 'I do not need thy help'; nor again the head to the feet, 'I have no need of you.' Nay, much rather, those that seem the more feeble members of the body are more necessary" (1 Cor 12:21f.).

"Because the position of Christ as Head is so eminent, we should not think that He does not require the help of His Body. What Paul said of the human body is to be applied also to the Mystical Body. It is obvious that the faithful need the help of the divine Redeemer. . . . Yet this too must be held, marvelous as it may seem: Christ requires His members . . . Our Savior does not rule the Church directly in a visible manner; therefore in carrying out the work of redemption He chooses to be assisted by the members of His Body. It is not because He is weak and helpless, but rather because He has so willed it for the greater glory of His unspotted Spouse. . . . This is indeed a profound mystery, the subject of inexhaustible meditation: the salvation of many depends on the prayers and voluntary penances which the members of the Mystical Body of Jesus Christ offer for this intention and on the assistance of pastors of souls and of the faithful, especially of fathers and mothers of families, which they must offer to our divine Savior as though they were His associates."[46] "To us it has been granted to collaborate with Christ in this work of salvation, 'from one and through one saved and saving!' "[47]

For compelling reasons the noble popes of our times have made us aware of the Christian principles underlying the apostolic mission and obligation of all members of the Mystical Body of Christ. To a great extent the world today has become estranged from the Church and her magisterium. Often contact with the Church extends no further than the association with Catholic neighbors merely "as individuals." And for this reason it is so very important that the Christian Catholic layman arrive at a clear understanding of his mission and fully realize that he possesses both apostolic endowment and commitment. In fact, he has a special mission which the priest cannot carry out: the Christianization of the world, penetration of the Christian spirit into the centers of influence.

Surely the virtue of obedience manifested in subordination to the Church's magisterium is essential for the members of the Mystical Body. But to make of this virtue of submission to authority a negation of all Apostolic effort and initiative by limiting it exclusively to the official Church would be as baneful as subordination to authority is virtuous.

"The member of the Mystical Body genuinely aware of his membership does not look upon himself as a mere object of the Church's action, as though she were exclusively hierarchy. He rather thinks of himself as a subject who cooperates through positive and constructive action in the Church's life. . . . The faithful member thrives on the Church as he strives for supernatural holiness. In this sense we may say he lives on the Church. But he also lives for her."[48]

Each member of the Mystical Body has his special gift from the Holy Spirit (his charism) for the building of the entire Body (1 Cor 12). Each gift implies also the commission which he—and only he—is called to fulfill in the Church and for his neighbor.[49] As persons we are so fashioned by God that only by engagement for the Thou and by cooperation in solidarity can we safely follow the path of progress.[50] This law of progress in solidarity which is basic for the individual is even more effective when applied to the entire Mystical Body of Christ: The more intimately we become "members one of another," "mutually one of another," the more closely shall we be united with God, with Christ. And on the other hand the more ardent the love that binds us to God and our divine Head, the closer the bond of union with one another in charity (cf. Rom 12:5 and 1 Cor 12:25f.).[51]

Each member of the Mystical Body must form the image of Christ within himself in accordance with his station, his talent, his character. In this fashioning according to the pattern which is Christ, let us not fail to note, however, that Christ our Head is above all the "Savior of the body," that he "also loved the Church, and delivered himself up for her" (Eph 5:23ff.). In like manner every member of the Mystical Body who bears within himself the spirit of the Head must make the love of Christ for souls present among men. His apostolic prayer, work, and pain must be a unique concrete realization and continuation of the love of Christ for souls.

3) Finally, the sacraments—such is the significance of the sacred signs —tell us that the grace and sanctification which they effect essentially bear the commission of the apostolate within them. The Eucharistic celebration is the dynamic source of power and the ever insistent mission[52] to our neighbor in loving and effective care for his salvation. By participation in holy Mass the "priestly" man (baptized, confirmed) experiences the sense of urgency for the apostolic effort in the splendor of the loving majesty of God, in unison with the sacrificial will of the Redeemer, for whom the

honor of His Father and the salvation of men is one sole mystery. In this Eucharistic celebration the Christian receives for himself the infinitely precious fruits of the redemptive love of the Savior. Not only does he partake of the fruits of celebration; he shares in the celebration itself, participating in the sacrificial and redemptive dispositions of the great High Priest Himself. "In this act of sacrifice through the hands of the priest, by whose word alone the Immaculate Lamb is present on the altar, the faithful themselves with one desire and one prayer offer It to the Eternal Father—the most acceptable Victim of praise and propitiation for the Church's universal needs."[53]

Active participation in the Sacrifice of the Church is itself a response to the life mission and apostolate: action for the great concern of the Church, salvation of souls. Whoever partakes of the Eucharistic Food, which is the Body of Christ offered for the salvation of the world, must be inflamed with zeal for the salvation of all men. The great object and concern of Christ's Sacrifice on the Cross, the salvation of all mankind unto the glory of God, must also be the object and concern of those who partake of the sacrificial Body of Christ in the Eucharist. Any one who becomes one with all the members of Christ through holy baptism and, even more consummately and sublimely, through Holy Communion must realize a true solidarity of salvation with all the redeemed throughout his whole life. This solidarity must be a living reality, which he experiences as the sublimest and holiest commitment to work for the salvation of souls.

The sacramental character of baptism and confirmation[54] impresses indelibly on the soul of the Christian the sacred commission of participation in the high-priestly concern of Christ for the salvation of men unto the glory of God. Sacramental character is a sacral gradation from baptism to ordained priesthood in a progressive participation in the sacerdotal office of Christ the Priest, which has the honor of God and the salvation of men as its one indivisible goal. It follows that the baptized and, even more so, the confirmed Christian and the ordained priest must realize that the salvific will of God directed to them in the sacrament is an authoritative commission for the salvation of their fellow men in and through the glory of God's love.

In classical simplicity St. Thomas states his doctrine on the character of confirmation. Through this character the confirmed is granted the gift and committed to the task of participation in Christ's own redemptive zeal: "The sacramental character in a special way is the mark of Christ, in whose priesthood the faithful are formed by means of the sacramental characters, which are naught else but a certain participation in the priesthood of Christ derived from Christ Himself."[55] "The confirmed receives the power to proclaim publicly and in words his faith in Christ, as it were, in an official manner."[56] The Thomistic teaching on the task to which the confirmed is committed can be summed up in the following words: "Confirmation imparts the plenary power for priestly actions which refer to the entire Church."[57] "In baptism man receives the power to do those things which pertain to one's own salvation . . . in confirmation one receives the power of doing those things which pertain to the spiritual combat against the enemies of the faith."[58]

The objective of baptism is priestly-mindedness. The baptized must be a priestly-minded man who, primarily through progress in his supernatural life in Christ, honors God in the realization that concern for his own salvation should be directed in a priestly manner to the honor of God and the salvation of the entire Church. Confirmation, on the other hand, means a progress characteristic of the new life of love. The expansion through confirmation of the priestly participation in Christ imparted in baptism manifests the basic lines of supernatural growth: the Christian grows into Christ and His kingdom of love in the measure in which he realizes that his individual salvation is only a radiation of the loving majesty of God and of the total fulness of salvation in the Church.

With increasing clarity and consistency we must follow the first and fundamental law of the kingdom of God which starkly and simply calls for consuming priestly zeal for the glory of God and the salvation of our neighbor. If the baptized are nourished on the new heavenly life, then they will live for God's honor and the increase of the fulness of salvation in the divine kingdom. But once they have grown to full maturity through confirmation's spirit of Pentecostal fire, the conscious impulse which totally dominates them must be active zeal for salvation of neighbor, for increase of the kingdom of God, for the revelation of the loving divine majesty.

In confirmation the Pentecostal spirit of love imprints on us with its gift of grace our assignment for the kingdom: we must be constantly concerned with the entire kingdom of God. Care for our own salvation may never be such as to permit us to ignore our share in the responsibility for the whole kingdom and for our neighbor. Confirmation's grace imparts a new perception, the insight of the mature Christian who now sees his own eternal salvation in the effort and action for the salvation of his neighbor.

"This is new in the character of confirmation by contradistinction to the mark of baptism: the confirmed is qualified and obliged to act as a mature member of the Church. Through independent and responsible decision he is to participate in the priestly and royal action of Christ by publicly cooperating in the building of the kingdom of God despite the obstacles and difficulties which hamper his work and conflict with the growth of the kingdom."[59]

In the apostolic period there was a very astonishing combination of confirmation with charismatic gifts. These gifts were not granted to individuals in the first instance for their own salvation or perfection. They were rather in the nature of an assignment or commitment to the task of building up God's kingdom. Hence, not the least of the purposes of the seven gifts of the Holy Spirit imparted in confirmation is the spiritual combat which the confirmed must wage for the Kingdom of God. In consequence, insofar as the Pentecostal spirit animates all the natural powers, the individual who is confirmed is under a double obligation: not only his supernatural but also his natural powers and his special natural endowments must be placed in the service of God's Kingdom.

The confirmed must be a protagonist for the kingdom of God and the salvation of his fellow man. "The nature of the struggle against evil is to be determined by the nature of the struggle of Christ whose features are stamped upon the confirmed. Through loving submission unto death Christ conquered the sins of the world. Similarly, one is Christ-formed through the seal of the Holy Spirit. To be sealed with the Spirit is to be sealed with love."[60] From this it is evident that the confirmed is equipped and committed by the Spirit of love to carry on the struggle of love for the soul of his brother and sister, for the kingdom of divine love, with all his natural and supernatural gifts. His is the struggle of Christ, a struggle unto death against sin. It is waged in the spirit of love.

Noblest school of the lay apostolate is the sacramentally sanctified family. As joint ministers and recipients of the sacrament of matrimony, the spouses hold a decisive position throughout their married life as spiritual guides of each other. Indissolubly united in the solidarity of salvation in Christ, they also have a primary duty to care for the spiritual formation of their children. And since marriage is a grace-giving participation in the all-embracing bond of love between Christ and His Church,

the sacred sacramental realm of marriage does not shut out the external
world from their care of souls. Rather, it imposes a new and pressing
obligation and offers a new motivation for the married to participate
intimately with Christ and the Church in the salvation of all men.

Consecration to Christ through the vows of religion is evidently not a
sacrament. But the public vow in religion binds one even more than sacramental marriage with the saving union between Christ and the Church.
And therefore it imposes a still more pressing obligation to bear witness to
love. The purer and more compelling the zeal for souls flowing from the
submission of the consecrated person to Christ, the more effective is its
influence also on those who are married. The greater the zeal of the individual whose religious vow has consecrated him to God, the more readily
also do the married come to realize that their love to one another and
their witness to love before the world around them must be fashioned
in Christ who will "present to himself the Church in all her glory, not
having spot or wrinkle . . . that she might be holy and without blemish"
(Eph 5:27).

The vows in the religious orders and congregations and the vow of
celibacy in sacred Orders are most intimately bound up with the nature
of the Church as Society and Fellowship of divine worship. Through
these acts of religion God is indeed worshipped. In the Church the consecrated person offers himself in the relinquishment of rights of earthly
possession, of powers of his body, together with the submission of his will.
The public vows are indeed essentially "ecclesial," for they are bound up
with the very cultal honor men pay to God in the Society of the Redeemed,
giving supreme glory to God.

Two predominant types of participation and cooperation in redemptive
love are open to the individual who follows the call of the apostolate,
endowed as he is with the Pentecostal spirit of love and fortitude through
the sacrament of confirmation. First is the individual engagement granted
him in his own position and in the hour of grace; second is the organized
action of the Catholic laity (the lay priesthood) under the direction of the
hierarchy. This is Catholic Action. We may not assume that there is a
universal obligation to participate in this latter form of apostolate.

2. Universal Forms of Active Zeal for Souls

The general obligation binding all Christians to concern and care for the salvation of their fellow men in a positive form includes the following: prayer, the will to do works of expiation: good example, the work of Christian instruction, encouragement, correction. There is a general obligation, negatively, to shun all that could imperil the salvation of others. This includes scandal and cooperation in the sins of others.

a. The Apostolate of Prayer

The prayer of the Christian must be apostolic. This implies that our prayer must be an expression of loving concern for the salvation of our neighbor. Accordingly, it must be a prayer in the spirit of Christ. "In the days of his earthly life, with a loud cry and tears, [he] offered up prayers and supplications to him who was able to save him from death, and was heard because of his reverent submission" (Heb 5:7) who continues unceasingly to pray for us in heaven and in the Sacrifice of the Altar as Mediator between us and the Heavenly Father.

The prayers of the Apostles were totally and utterly sustained by this loving concern for the salvation of others. Such, too, should all our prayers be: "I urge therefore, first of all, that supplications, prayers, intercessions and thanksgivings be made for all men. . . . This is good and agreeable in the sight of God, our Savior, who wishes all men to be saved and to come to the knowledge of the truth" (1 Tm 2:1ff.).

Normally we should particularize the objectives of our prayer and with special fervor pray for those who are near and dear. St. Monica in her incessant prayer for the conversion of her son, Augustine, is a model in this petition for one's own. So too we should pray for this or that particular individual because of his special closeness to us or his special need. But Catholic prayer—the grand prayer, the Mass, is our model—is always a missionary prayer in the most comprehensive sense, "for the Holy Church throughout the world," for the Holy Father, for all bishops, for the return of all Christians to unity and for the conversion of the heathens. "Prayer of petition is essentially bound up with the apostolate, has the apostolate for its origin, its constant impulse, and motivation for action. But prayer also prepares for the apostolate, accompanies it, and is itself a form of apostolate."[61]

It is not as though the prayer of Christ is in any way inadequate for all souls; but the salvific economy of the kingdom of God takes into account our participation with Him. Through the all-sufficient prayer of

Christ our prayer is fruitful for the attainment of special graces for our fellow men. So too we hold in loving faith that Mary as Queen of the Apostles in her prayer on earth and its incessant continuation in heavenly glory is all love toward us: she is taken up entirely in the prayer of our Savior for the good of our souls.

b. The Apostolate of Expiation

Not merely our prayer but also our mortification and patient acceptance of the trials and suffering of this life must be drawn into the redemptive prayer and redemptive pain of the Savior. "Since we can love God only with the love with which He first loved us in Christ, every entry and growth in the life with God is growth into the redemptive love of Christ, a union with His bleeding and atoning Heart."[62] Loving penetration into the redemptive love of Christ, particularly through the devout participation in the Sacrifice of Christ, will not only reawaken the spirit of penance but also the realization that in the Mystical Body of Christ all suffering must likewise be caught up into love of neighbor, borne for love of our fellowmen, even for the most miserable sinner. The liturgical renaissance and the newly stressed consciousness of solidarity in salvation, by which our concern for our own soul implies responsibility for our neighbor also, would not be genuine and profound if expiation were excluded. The whole order of the Mystical Body of Christ is the salvific order of vicarious atonement of the Head for the members and—in the Head—of the members for one another."[63]

This concern is expressed especially in certain phases of the devotion to the Redemptive Blood and in the devotion to the Sacred Heart of Jesus and the Heart of Mary. It is essentially bound up with these devotions: the lover of the Precious Blood and the Sacred Hearts of Jesus and Mary stands with Mary at the foot of the cross as the Savior sheds His Blood.[64] And he beholds with pain not only the riven Heart from which flowed Blood and water; he looks also upon those for whom the Blood was shed. With a bleeding heart, a heart ready to endure any pain, he turns to those for whom the Savior suffered and whom He has entrusted to the Mother of Sorrows and, in a lesser degree, also to us.[65]

With that unique apostolic fervor so characteristic of him, St. Paul reveals this spirit of sacrificial expiation: "I rejoice now in the sufferings I bear for your sake; and what is lacking of the sufferings of Christ I fill up in my flesh for his body, which is the Church" (Col 1:24). "This is why I bear all things for the sake of the elect, that they also may obtain the salvation that is in Christ Jesus" (2 Tim 2:10; cf. 1 Cor 4,9ff.). Ignatius of Antioch, in his letters and in his heroic acceptance of a martyr's death, gives a most dramatic expression to this faith in the solidarity of salvation.[66]

All Christians must possess the sense and spirit of expiation. All must be prepared to accept their daily trials and sorrows in expiation for sin. But beyond this universal obligation there is the higher call for some Christians to become victims for Christ. As total victims with Christ they make of themselves expiatory oblations for the salvation of sinners. Zeal for souls and readiness for suffering is the basic motive of their entire life.

c. The Apostolate of Good Example

Prayer and expiation are immediately directed to God. Only through unity and solidarity of salvation in the whole Mystical Body of Christ are they efficacious before God and fellow men. Yet good example and fraternal correction are directed to our neighbor in a more immediate and psychologically experiential manner. Most effective and constant in this immediate influence on one's fellows is good example, the power of an exemplary personality.

1) *The Significance of the Model in Christian Moral Teaching.* a) Man is made in the divine image (Gn 1:27). Christ is the perfect "image of God" (2 Cor 4:4; Col 1:15). Our likeness to God can be understood only in relation to Christ. In Him the invisible Father becomes visible to us. "He who sees me sees also the Father" (Jn 14:9; 12:45). Since Christ is the perfect image of the Father and the Model of our likeness to Him, and since our earthly task consists in bringing to full realization the natural and supernatural likeness to God in us, there is no other way to perform our earthly task than through the following and imitation of Christ. To follow Christ, to be made like to Him, to put on the new man means to form in ourselves the image of Him who created the new man (cf. Col 3:9f.).[67] Insofar as we are formed in the living image of Christ, we are in Christ a manifestation of the glory of God which indeed will be

revealed in us with all its splendor only in the future life (2 Cor 3:18). All God's grace working in us has as its goal that we "become conformed to the image of His Son" (Rom 8:29).

Of course it is true that Christ teaches us the way to this goal a'so through general laws and norms. But the focal point around which His whole doctrine radiates is His own Personality as Supreme Model. Christian morality is not concerned merely with abstract legality.[68] It is above all concerned with the right relationship to absolute Person, to God, to Christ, and for this reason the Model presented in the person of Christ is much more central and basic than all individual laws and norms.

The incomparably exalted ideal of the disciple of Christ is to be perfect as his heavenly Father is perfect (Mt 5:48). Since Christ represents the Father to us, only He can lead us to the Father: "He who sees me sees also the Father" (Jn 14:9). Therefore, Christ can point with equal emphasis to His own example and to the work of the Father: "I have given you an example that as I have done to you, so you also should do" (Jn 13:15). "The Father dwelling in me, it is he who does the works" (Jn 14:10).

The Father, the Ultimate Pattern, was brought to us by Christ. In Christ, the Incarnate Son, the Apostles and men of all subsequent times could recognize the Father. Thereby the true character of the supernatural likeness of men to God is revealed. In a similar manner the great saints, each in his own time and for his own contemporaries, are visible reflections of Christ and guides leading to Him. Though by comparison with Christ the reflection is faint indeed, nonetheless the image of Christ is clearer and more vital to those who have seen Him in His saints. This is one of the reasons—there are others—why veneration of the saints is so significant in the Church. Since Christian morality in its living perfection is fashioned much more immediately through example than by abstract utterances, the model and exemplary personality of the saint is the most effective moral exhortation. The saints reflect the bright rays of the true Light, Christ, the perfect Ideal and Model. As in a prism the sun is reflected in many rays, so in each of the saints (each, that is, in the setting of his own special gifts and the spirit and the call of his age) Christ is reflected for us. Fully aware of such special gifts of grace, St. Paul admonishes his Christian disciples in this vein: "I beg you, be imitators of me, as I am of Christ" (1 Cor 4:16; 11:1; Phil 3:17). With all a father's tenderness he writes to his beloved assembly at Thessalonica: "You became imitators of us and of the Lord" (1 Thes 1:6; cf. 2:14). The Apostle realizes that the call to the apostolic office brought with it the grace and duty to preach Christ not only in words but by example as well (cf. 2 Cor 10–12). This is also in his mind when he admonishes his two favorite disciples, Timothy and Titus, that they should present themselves as living models in word and deed (1 Tm 4:12). In this manner the teaching of Christ is to prove effective (Ti 2:7ff.).

That the Gospel has not yet penetrated all hearts is due only in a degree to the fact that it has not been adequately announced or preached. In greater measure it is due to the fact that it has not been lived adequately. The exemplary conduct of the first Christians was largely responsible for the incomparable triumph of Christianity in that period. Even the pagans exclaimed, "See how they love one another!" The blood of the martyrs was the seed of Christians.[69] St. Peter taught the Christians to conduct themselves in such a way as to shame into silence those who reviled the Christian way of life (1 Pt 3:16). He tells the Christian wives that their example, even without a word of preaching, can win their husbands to the Gospel (1 Pt 3:1).

b) This significance of example, or rather of the exemplary person, in the order of salvation is fully appreciated by present day psychologists who explain the value of example with sound reasons and considerable insight. Obviously the merit of a model lies first of all in the concrete and vivid appeal. Example awakens and arouses the imagination to an appreciation of the values presented, whereas mere enunciation of good couched in abstract terms scarcely gets beyond the conceptual and ideal. Deep and undisclosed is the wealth of the potential realization of good in the hour of grace. Least of all does the abstract concept lay immediate hold on the power of love, but only mediately through sheer unaroused intelligence. In general it is quite correct to say that a clear perception of value, and especially a fervent appreciation of value, is enkindled only through the presence of a concrete model or pattern which we can actually see before us.[70]

The inimitable warmth of the Gospel account presents Christ as our incomparable Ideal. In the Gospels (and in St. Paul), with the help of grace, we can see Him as the true Model of our lives. And yet in a certain respect the picture of Christ in the Mystical Body is more immediate: we see Him in the holy assembly, in the people of God, in the actions of all His saints, each in his own unique way pointing to the supreme Law and Model.

A heart-warming knowledge of values (to an extent also the easy and practical knowledge of law) is enriched even as to content and comprehensiveness in a manner that can scarcely be overestimated through the contact with the moral genius, the saint. But, above all, the model that merits our love stimulates the warmth and power of our religious and moral life. "The greater life force dwells not in doctrine but in a model and exemplary life."[71] "The religious life is enkindled much more by men than by books."[72] Religious life does not thrive so bountifully on books or on instruction as on intimate contact with religious personalities. Youth, particularly with its unspoiled and ingenuous aspirations and its openhearted freshness of mind, is much influenced by such personalities, provided they are understanding and sympathetic.[73] Max Scheler is not guilty of exaggeration in his assumption that "the principle of the pattern of conduct exemplified in a model is everywhere the primary vehicle of all transformations in the moral world."[74]

2) *Conscious Attitude toward the Models:* From all this we draw the simple practical conclusion for our moral teaching that each one should hold fast to the models of holiness. With full awareness of value we should open our hearts to the pattern of good, above all to Christ, but also to the saints, and not the least important, to the examples of holiness one has himself known and experienced in his own life. Everyone sets up his own heroes and ideals, known or unknown. Wrong impressions regarding the heroes youth sets up for imitation may well prove disastrous to the developing personality. The models or heroes may not be really models at all but rather creations of youthful imagination. Some, sincerely convinced of the existence of the ideal or model, find it worthy of imitation, whereas the reality is utterly devoid of merit for imitation. Often the ideal or model is really an antitype or countertype. It may happen that sad experience, let us say with a teacher or guide, consciously or unconsciously sets up in the mind of youth a contrary ideal: "I want to be anything except an imitation of this individual!" In such instances the whole moral effort is negatively slanted. Consciously or unconsciously it is formed and fashioned in the mold of spite and contradiction. On the other hand, the fully wise and deliberate choice of a model in the spirit of love is truly an emancipat-

ing force, drawing the individual from the attraction of the masses and the ideals, more or less conscious, of his surroundings.

Turning lovingly to Christ in response when He graciously opens His Heart to us and in consequence developing enthusiasm for one of His favorite saints or for a winning religious personality should preserve us from fatal submission to the sinister powers of the spirit of the times and the milieu. It is no mean achievement in the training of youth to discover the true ideals and models they strive to imitate. We do well to point out the heroes they may have followed. Often the evil lies not in direct disobedience or rebellion but rather in an excessive "obedience" to false models, to vicious companions on whom they pattern their lives. To free them from the slavery of perverted heroes or a poisoned atmosphere is the task of noble guides and educators in wholesome surroundings.

3) *The Obligation to Give Good Example:* Such is the power of example that our responsibility regarding the salvation of souls imposes on us a serious obligation to give a good example. This implies much more than the duty to perform individual acts which are exemplary. It means that we have a comprehensive obligation to endeavor to become model personalities calculated to attract and influence others for good.

Concern for the salvation of our fellow men may and also should be the motive for specific exemplary actions. Many things may be good and lawful as far as the individual Christian himself is concerned, but consideration of the effect which they might have on others forbids us to do them.[75] Similarly, one may be obliged to perform many actions which are not in themselves preceptive, simply because of the influence they have on others. The incentive they furnish for our fellow man's welfare and the advancement of a good cause may oblige us to perform them. Nevertheless, if there is a constant repetition of such positive acts with no further objective than the giving of "good example," with no interior penetration into the actual value of the act itself, the eventual result will be to stamp the personality as fraudulent and the "good example" as futile. For this reason the "giving of good example" by particular acts ordinarily must be only a subsidiary motive contributing to the mastery over inner resistance to good which would otherwise be scarcely possible. In consequence the inner worth of the action will even be enhanced because of the loving and tender consideration for the salvation of others (the "weaker" brothers).

The practical effectiveness of good example does not consist in the individual acts insofar as we might weigh their value and influence—though they may at times be very essential—but in the attraction for good in the personality itself. Therefore for the apostolic-minded Christian—not merely for the priest—the sustaining motive building up his personality must be the ideal of attracting souls to God. "I must be a saint in order to garner many souls for God."

There is a special obligation to live an exemplary life binding those, above all, who are in the religious or clerical state.[76] However, no individual, regardless of his state of life, is exempt from this obligation if he is responsible for the education and spiritual formation of others. Parents and all those who are in a public position where their conduct may readily influence others are above all obliged to give a good example. To them the words of Christ apply in an altogether special way: "So let your light shine before men, in order that they may see your good works and give glory to your Father in heaven" (Mt 5:16). But the motivation for good example is not exaltation in men's eyes. The glory of the heavenly Father and the salvation of souls must be the actual motive for the effort to give good example, to become an exemplary personality.

Weight of authority and power of example conspire to produce an overwhelming effect upon men, a tremendously internal emancipating effect. In parents a winning exemplary character furnishes the very foundation for the early moral formation of the children. Perhaps a child cannot quite fathom the value of individual parental precepts, but a morally significant sense of trust is already taking shape in its little heart. Those who command are good. "What the parents ask is good because they themselves are surely good." This simple loving trust makes the care of the child even in the tenderest years something of moral worth. It also makes moral obedience easy and beautiful.

4) *Necessary Characteristics of Good Example:* "Good example to be effective must be joined with loving kindness of nature (1 Cor 13:4); it must possess earnestness unmarred by any puritanical harshness or pharisaical posturing (Mt 6:16)."[77] Nothing is so ineffectual, in fact so repulsive, as the hyper-sensitive person who is constantly grumbling about the need for "cautious" conduct and for good example in order to impress others with a sense of his own moral superiority. It is as though "we" are "superior," "exemplary."

Truly model or exemplary conduct must always be loving conduct.

Wherefore, an exemplary character must be a loving and winning personality.[78] In consequence, the very first requisite for all those who aim at full apostolic effectiveness of personality is to hold fast to the confidence of those entrusted to them. To forfeit their love is to forfeit one's influence. It is indeed most fitting that parents and superiors make a valiant effort to deserve and win the love of their subjects. Such an attempt can be completely free of false egoism if the actual motivating impulse is the ideal to win one's neighbor for the love of God and not merely a craving for popularity. Only a kindly personality, a personality truly kind and free from all dissimulation and affectation, possesses the tremendous attractive power to draw men to the divine love. When the Savior on the great evening of His love called attention to His own example (after the washing of the feet), He clearly implied that His disciples who had experienced His love should lead men to a similar experience. By their example they should draw men to the experience of their own beneficent, self-effacing love in turn. The same is true for all followers of Christ. This is not the least of the lessons taught by the Savior at the Last Supper.

Whoever has merited the love of a fellow man is doubly bound to give a "good example." Love which has merited a response of love makes the good example much more effective, bad example all the more hazardous. Noble friendship—most of all wedded love—must express itself principally by hastening the effort to become an exemplary personality, a personality directed to the ennobling of one's fellows.

d. Fraternal Correction

In the traditional list of spiritual works of mercy (to instruct the ignorant, to counsel the perplexed, to console the sorrowing, to correct the erring, to forgive injuries, to bear wrongs patiently, to pray for the living and the dead) fraternal correction occupies a prominent position.

(1) *Meaning and Obligation*

Fraternal correction (the term is derived from 2 Thes 3:15) signifies any direct influence on our neighbor guided or directed by love, which has as its object to confirm him in the way of virtue and to turn him from evil. It may consist of instruction, advice, encouragement, rebuke, warning. Perseverance in the efforts of fraternal correction (should they appear fruitless or futile) depends on the cooperation of others, principally on reporting to superiors.

Here we are primarily concerned with brotherly or fraternal correction and reporting, in contradistinction to the canonical (juridical or strictly authoritative) correction and reporting with a view to official correction. It has as its principal purpose the salvation of the individual himself who has committed the fault or sin, whereas juridical correction has the common good in mind. The latter's direct concern is the restoration of the right order which has been disturbed, the betterment of the sinner in relation to the common welfare.

Correction of others is often counseled in Sacred Scripture as a great work of love; in fact, it is even specifically commanded. "He who causes a sinner to be brought back from his misguided way, will save his soul from death, and will cover a multitude of sins" (Jas 5:20; cf. 1 Pt 4:8). "We exhort you, brethren, reprove the irregular, comfort the fainthearted, support the weak, be patient towards all men" (1 Thes 5:14). The sapiential books are particularly insistent in stressing the loving duty of correction of neighbor: "Admonish your neighbor—he may not have said it; and if he did, that he may not say it again. Admonish your friend—often it may be slander; every story you must not believe" (Sir 19:13f.).

Fraternal correction is not restricted in its purpose to the prevention of mortal sins. It also aims positively at the advancement of others in the way of good wherever this is possible. But the strict obligation to correct others in individual instances exists only when the following conditions are *all* present: 1) when the salvation of another's soul is in serious peril; 2) when there is a reasonable hope that the instruction or correction will prove fruitful; 3) when the admonition is the sole means of averting the evil according to one's prudent judgment.

As to point one: it is not the sin or fault already committed which justifies or demands the correction, but the danger which threatens. We are not the judge of the sin or fault of our neighbor. It is better to assist one's fellow man by judicious and timely intervention to prevent or forestall a fall than to await actual commission of sin. For this reason it is advisable to act whenever the proximate occasion of sin creates a danger for others, even though they may not at all be aware that they are spiritually in danger. However, only parents and directors of souls would be obliged to investigate as to the existence of spiritual hazards endangering those committed to their care. In fact, any distrustful or suspicious approach in such matters relating to others' conduct might very easily prejudice or even jeopardize the position of confidence essential for any success in admonishing them. But if one does enjoy the fullest confidence of the individual who is thought to be in spiritual peril, he is well advised that delay may be fatal. Reticence or hesitation until the danger is apparent to all may prove spiritually disastrous to one whom we could have saved by timely intervention. In such instances it is most prudent to act freely in what seems a probable danger. Even an honest inquiry about the matter might itself prove to be an effective form of admonition, should the spiritual peril be real (cf. Sir 19:13ff.).

As to point two: one is obliged to admonish or correct others only to the degree that there is reasonable prospect of success. But even should there be no such hope, one may still be obliged to make the correction in order to avert the scandal which might arise from our apparent indifference or neglect. Our intervention would then be in the interest of a third party and for the divine honor. Should there be no danger of scandal caused by our non-intervention and no other good at stake except the salvation of the individual who is in error or is sinning, there can be no obligation to act in a cause which is futile. *A fortiori* there is no obligation to correct the faults of others if there is reason to anticipate more harm than good as a result of our endeavors. On the other hand, if no harm is in prospect but rather some hope of success despite our misgivings, we do not have sufficient reason to omit the correction.

In some instances one who is obliged to correct another knows from past experience that he is not likely to succeed because of personal reasons. He may be inept or unfit because he does not have the proper approach or persuasive forms of speech or he may be a *persona non grata*. Any correction would create ill will instead of promoting the good. Ordinarily these personal reasons are sufficient to excuse one from any personal correction of others. But they suggest finding someone, preferably a friend of the individual in need of correction, who is qualified and willing to undertake the task. Parents, superiors, spiritual directors have a special duty of admonishing those in their charge. The source of the obligation is not merely their special responsibility for the spiritual welfare of those for whom they are spiritually accountable, but also because success of their effort is more likely due to their authoritative position and its bond of love. As a rule, therefore, parents and superiors have the very special obligation to admonish and correct those under them.

As to point three: baseless and even contrary to charity is the follow-up criticism of faults. Once the sin is corrected and our erring brother has seen the evil of his ways and amended his fault, there is neither need nor excuse for further correction. Only in the event that reference to past faults or sins forms a part of prudent spiritual guidance for the future may it be considered pedagogically sound and sincerely charitable. One who is truly converted bears his former frailty in mind as a constant caution against future falls—and a warning to be grateful and humble!

If the spiritual danger others might incur is not extremely grave and the hope of success in the matter of correction rather doubtful, one is not gravely obliged to correct others at considerable risk of harm to himself. The matter assumes a different aspect in cases of extreme danger. Should a dying person be in extreme danger of losing his soul, every one has the obligation to assist him, even though very considerable temporal loss may be involved, provided there is some hope that our action will result in his salvation. There is a special obligation incumbent on parents, educators, and spiritual guides or directors; by their advice and correction they must assist those who are entrusted to their care if they are in serious spiritual danger, even though a risk of serious material hurt or loss is involved.

As a matter of principle the scrupulous do not incur the obligation of fraternal correction. Experience shows that a great part of their mental torment is centered precisely in this sensitive area. The persistent harassment and fear regarding the correct fulfillment of such an obligation leads to the unsound judgment that it is found everywhere in their relation to others. In consequence correction is often given at the wrong time and in the worst conceivable manner, so that no one is helped and the poor monitors themselves placed in a most painful position. For this reason the confessor should explain clearly to his scrupulous penitents, unless it is evident to him that they are altogether normal in this matter, that they are not to be concerned at all with correcting others.

(2) *The Right Procedure in Correcting Others*

There is no legitimate motive for correction of others except zeal for the divine glory and the salvation of souls. To admonish others because of personal pique or resentment is always evil. Nor is there any prospect for success of our admonition or correction of others if we are influenced even slightly by personal bitterness or irritation. Our attitude, our bearing, our manner in admonition and correction must be kindly and earnest. Only in altogether exceptional circumstances would a sharp or harsh demeanor be permitted. Dealing with persons who are very insensitive morally and who would not be moved seriously by any species of gentleness is a case in point. But even for these the exhortation of St. Paul should be kept in mind. The correction must be made "in a spirit of meekness" (Gal 6:1). Only the full and restrained force of love "shall possess the earth" (Mt 5:4), that is, lead to the triumph of the good.

St. Paul gives a splendid and very pertinent directive to his disciple, Timothy: "Do not rebuke an elderly man, but exhort him as you would a father, and young men as brothers, elderly women as mothers, younger women as sisters in all chastity" (1 Tm 5:1ff.). Only if the offense has been public and it is necessary to guard against scandal, is public correction in place "that the rest also may have fear" (1 Tm 5:20).

The occasion chosen for correction is not without importance. It is better to wait for an opportune time, even though new faults be added to old, assuming of course that the common good is safeguarded. One must always be on guard against imprudent and unseasonable admonition which may frustrate the best of intentions and defeat every prospect of success. No one will deny that ordinarily it is far better to correct evil in its very inception than to wait till it has waxed strong and obdurate in its hold on our neighbor. It is a gross violation of prudence to nag those in our charge for every petty failure due perhaps to oversight or remissness. Nagging—itself a fault which demands correction—creates such bitterness and irritation of spirit that it hardens its victims against correction even though they may be guilty of serious faults. The Lord Himself teaches us a method of procedure in fraternal correction: "If thy brother sin against thee, go and show him his fault between thee and him alone. If he listen to thee, thou hast won thy brother. But if he do not listen to thee, take with thee one or two more . . . if he refuse to hear them, appeal to the Church; but if he refuse to hear even the Church, let him be to thee as the heathen and the publican" (Mt 18:15ff.).

The Latin text and our English translations of Matthew 18:15 read: "If thy brother sin against thee . . . ," whereas the best Greek manuscripts and the parallel passage in Luke 17:3 do not have the "against thee." St. Luke says simply, "If thy brother sin, rebuke him." But even if we should have to include these words, "against thee," one is still not permitted to think of one's own interest in this matter. One must have in mind those sins of our neighbor which in a special way concern the one who should make the correction. They cry out precisely to him because he is aware of them and can and must come to the assistance of his neighbor in spiritual need. The words of St. Matthew cited above, "If he listen to thee, thou hast won thy brother . . . ," clearly show that there is not a question of one's own interest, but only of the salvation of another's soul. Obviously the passage refers only to serious faults which are a great hazard to the soul's salvation. If such were not the case, so serious a corrective procedure including public denunciation could not be demanded.

The duty of instructing the inculpably ignorant is the same essentially as the duty of fraternal correction. The obligation of instructing one who errs, though in good conscience, is incumbent upon those who are entrusted with his education. Others incur the obligation only if the error redounds to the dishonor of God, to the harm of the erring man himself, or to others. A striking instance of this we find in the person of St. Paul. Paul thought it his duty to call St. Peter's attention—and he was most insistent—to the effect of his attitude toward observance of the Old Testament ritual law. Surely there was no guilt nor evil intent on Peter's part, but the conduct of the Prince of the Apostles could not fail to prove very prejudicial to the cause of the apostolic mission among the heathen (Gal 2:11ff.).

It is the universal teaching of moral theologians, based on the Pauline passage just cited, that there is a greater obligation of charity toward superiors than towards others in the matter of fraternal correction, provided they are actually in need of the spiritual assistance.[79] However, correction or admonition in nowise justifies any defect of reverence in one's approach and procedure (cf. Tm 5:1). A public correction is in place only if public and very scandalous faults have been committed, only if the resultant spiritual evil cannot be averted except by such forthright action.

(3) Reporting Faults

The logical consequence of fraternal correction is the "reporting" of the sinner to the superior as to his "father." It is permitted, and obligatory, when it is necessary for the salvation of his soul or at least when it is spiritually more profitable for him than direct correction. Such is the case for a worthy reason, but not for the small purpose of spite or impish delight.

Facts the superior has learned through reports of this kind, brought to him for the spiritual good of others, he may never use as occasion for punishment or discrimination against the individual who has been reported. Only if the common good clearly demands it, or, in rare instances, if the salvation of the individual himself requires it, may and must denunciation be made to the superior in his capacity as judge. To a report of this category the superior may respond and act with a juridical intervention. If a sin which requires such juridical intervention has been first brought to the superior's attention only in his capacity as father, he often can and must demand that an authoritative juridical report of the same matter be relayed to him and that he be permitted to act in his capacity as judge of the fault.

We must allow for an exception, however. The obligation to make the denunciation does not bind in the case in which an evil which might befall the one who should make the report is greater than the evil affecting the common welfare. In all this it is well to bear in mind that faults which are publicly known may not be kept from the superior even though he may be the last to hear about them. Anonymous denunciations should not be acknowledged at all, for the simple reason that acceptance of such charges encourages a dangerously vicious procedure against which there is no defence. The assurance that the subject's identity will be kept rigorously secret and that there will be no reprisals against those who report to superiors should go a long way toward eliminating anonymous reporting.

In every community, especially in institutions of training for youth, all petty reporting or informing must be severely proscribed. On the other hand, everyone in the institution should be well aware that seducers and all those who make it a point to undermine the right order, the good spirit, or the good repute of the institution or community must be duly reported to the lawful authorities if they fail to respond properly to admonition and correction. Subjects should be instructed in this duty, particularly since so many entertain the erroneous notion that every kind of reporting is dastardly, even though it may be essential to prevent great evils.

The superior must carefully weigh the statements and the character of those who report to him. He must clearly distinguish between a report based on clear evidence and mere suspicions. Often the most innocent acts are reported by hypersensitive individuals as serious faults. If possible, the superior must also grant the accused opportunity to defend themselves.

According to the norms governing secrecy, he may not as a rule divulge the names of those who report to him. The report of a secret fault or sin may not be made the basis of a public accusation or of punishment, for such procedure would reveal the secret and expose the offender to public shame. But for serious reasons he is permitted to discuss the matter with one or other advisor strictly committed to secrecy. In consequence of the denunciation he must keep an eye—surely in a very unobtrusive way—on the offender if there is any danger that the fault will be repeated. But he may never relay the report to a higher superior if it has already been corrected.

e. The Apostolate and Tolerance

What is the proper attitude of the Catholic Christian toward the erroneous conscience of the non-Catholic? We reply in the form of a set of principles dealing with this matter, which is very important in our time:

First Principle: No one may tolerate error in principle. This form of tolerance, which we call dogmatic tolerance, is evil. We must defend dogmatic intolerance, the intolerance directed to error as such and in principle. 'Total hostility to error" (*Errores interficite*).[80] The Christian may never act as though he places errors in faith on the same level practically as the Catholic truth, or even worse, as though he considers errors in faith condemned by the Church as a matter for free and open discussion. Of course we are far from denying—and we must concede this point if our dialog with non-Catholics is to prove fruitful—that underlying practically every error there is a kernel of truth. And not only is there some truth underlying the error; there is even a genuine need and concern on the part of those in error. This partly explains their acceptance of it. The error may be an attempt to safeguard this earnest and even fearful concern for something which is true and good.

But every genuine and sincere conviction creates an impatience with error, is intolerant of error as such. Theoretic or dogmatic tolerance implies as much as indifference, scepticism, total absence of conviction, denial of the faith. But authentic intolerance demands a humble and honest investigation of one's own cherished convictions. Are they truly matters of faith, and do we formulate them with due prudence and circumspection? Every tenacious presentation of doctrine as truth of faith or certain teaching which represents no more than the views of theological schools discredits true dogmatic intolerance.

Second Principle: Personal and civic tolerance of those in error is a Christian virtue. "Love the erring!" (*Errantes diligite*).[81] One should not attempt to form any judgment regarding the sincerity of non-Catholics in matters of religion. The domain of subjective convictions is entirely beyond our power to judge. Here we should follow the directive of our Lord: "Do not judge, that you may not be judged!" (Mt 7:1).

Even though he may be in objective error, we must respect the sincere convictions of every individual and give evidence of our respect. Until the contrary is evident—and who would presume to anticipate the divine judgment—we may impute to the non-Catholic the sincerity of conscience, which we must respect in the same manner as God Himself respects every honorable conscience. Our attitude toward an apostate Catholic creates a very delicate problem for us. If he has been properly instructed and is mentally entirely normal, he is indeed in a very sad state. But since it is simply impossible to arrive at absolute certainty on all these points in concrete individual instances, in the final analysis we must suspend our judgment regarding the actual state of his soul.

The Christian virtue of tolerance is that love-force through which we truly and with all our heart wish the non-Catholic the inestimable good fortune of the Catholic faith. Because of this power of love, we trust the good faith and sincere good will of those who differ with us. Even when we endeavor to win them over, we sincerely try to avoid violating any religious convictions which they hold sacred.

Even in his conflict with error, one who possesses this tolerance with the spirit of love for the individual conscience and person shuns every species of unkindly polemic against the individual himself. The conflict is directed to the error. The truly tolerant Christian is concerned sincerely with the salvation of souls, and does not exploit an intellectual or spiritual discussion for personal triumph with the weapons of rhetoric and dialectic. Just to cite one example: Martin Luther has been a very controversial figure for centuries; but in our day, discussion of Luther and Protestantism has become far more objective and irenic. What advantage could a Catholic gain if he merely presented one side of Martin Luther—only the unfavorable—and neglected or ignored all that is good and favorable? One might conceivably win an argument and thereby destroy all possibility of a better understanding.

The more objective we are, sincerely objective, clinging to truth and avoiding all extremes, the more likely we are to gain the respect of others. As to the old historic quarrels: the more willing we are to concede that personal faults and human frailty are not all found on one side, the more readily we admit the good in non-Catholics, the more graciously will they open their hearts to us. Even though we may not be able to win them to the Catholic faith, we shall at least help to create an atmosphere of mutual respect and love for a noble form of interdenominational charity and peace.

We teach, of course, and we believe that the Catholic Church is the only saving Church. But in full accordance with the spirit of this basic truth we can call to the minds of men of other faiths that we link them with this only saving Church, insofar as they are of good will in striving for the truth and living according to their consciences. Even though they are not members of the Church, they are bound up with her saving mission in the attainment of eternal salvation. On the very basis of our faith we look upon all disciples of Christ as belonging to us.

The Christian virtue of tolerance is opposed to all forms of false proselytism which is concerned not with salvation of the brethren of other faiths, but with statistics and the power image of the Church. The Church's own law explicitly commands that "no one may be forced to embrace the Catholic faith against his will."[82] *A fortiori* no one may be misled to an external acceptance of the faith against the conviction of his conscience. This would be a violation of freedom of conscience and in contradiction of the teaching of St. Paul: "All that is not from faith is sin" (Rom 14:23).

A problem of great consequence is suggested by the teaching we have just enunciated: how shall we deal with non-Catholics in the matter of mixed marriages? We require that the non-Catholic partner agree to permit all the children of the union to be brought up as Catholics, even though this may conflict with his conscientious subjective convictions. There is only one recourse: either we must convince him that the action we ask is objectively sound and correct and therefore not sinful, or we must persuade the Catholic party to give up the marriage. Should the non-Catholic party still remain unconvinced, the Catholic party must be made to realize that he cannot enter a contract under conditions which leave him no alternative but to violate a conscience: either that of the non-Catholic whom he sincerely esteems and loves, or his own.

Finally, as to sincere attempts to convert non-Catholics to the Catholic faith, once it is evident that every endeavor of ours is futile and serves only to irritate and offend them, love (the virtue of true tolerance) forbids such a vain effort. Prudence suggests rather that we turn with all the greater fervor to the apostolate of prayer and good example.

Third Principle: Civil (political, legal) tolerance is necessary within proper limits. Civil and juridical tolerance in matters of religion has had an extremely varied history. Absolute freedom of creed and religious practice with complete equality of all religious groups which are not hostile to the state itself is a recent development in Church-State relations, and is found only in modern pluralistic society. The heathen states of antiquity were openly intolerant. From the times of the Apostles to the Constantinian era the Church rarely enjoyed the barest minimum of freedom which would allow her to preach the Gospel to all and to celebrate the divine mysteries in peace. Though there were some periods of considerable liberty, there was also bitter, prolonged, systematic persecution, particularly after the middle of the third century. The great turn of events under Constantine with his Edict of Toleration brought her freedom. And eventually with freedom and increasing privileges she assumed the role of the established Church. And in the wake of establishment followed the grim heritage of civic religious intolerance.

The civil and juridical intolerance of the Middle Ages shocks and scandalizes our present-day sensibilities largely because it is almost in direct antithesis to the tolerance of our time. To arrive at a balanced and temperate judgment in this difficult matter we must study the principles involved and the totally different cultural and legal situation of the age. For centuries there was practically unanimous acceptance of the truth of the Catholic faith in the countries of Europe. To rulers and people the Catholic religion seemed so obviously and certainly true that only a perverted conscience would rebel against it. Such an attitude was in harmony with the contemporary setting. But we now live in a society in which the most diverse forms of religion mingle with complete denial of religion, every form of scepticism and atheism.

However, we are not so naive in our appraisal of historic realities as to consider this basic attitude toward the Catholic religion as a full and adequate explanation of the medieval harshness toward heresy. Nor was the religious unity as complete as it is sometimes thought. Very disturbing heresies trace their beginnings to the medieval period and are largely due to scandalous conditions in the Church herself. The very terror of heresy is also due to the simple starkness of the age, the dreadful and almost unbelievable anti-social character of some of the doctrines (often they were a species of social war essentially subversive and destructive of the very civilization in which they existed). The cruel insistence on uniformity derived from the heritage of Roman Law also must bear its share of the blame.

Even though we take into account all the sociological and historic factors, we cannot fully justify—nor would we wish to justify—the official religious intolerance of previous centuries. The temporary attempt of the Inquisition to resort to force and torture to extort the inmost convictions of its victims and to employ in the process the legal intolerance of the state must be looked upon—as we turn to the matter in retrospect—as a sign of the "impotence of religion" in this domain. The environment and the forces at work in that age proved far stronger than the love-power of revelation.

The official intolerance which was part and parcel of the whole social order developed with appalling cruelty during the period of Reformation and Counter Reformation. Christians of diverse religious groups fought one another bitterly on account of their faith and burned one another as heretics. The cruel alternative, enforced by authority, of embracing the religion of the ruler or migrating to other regions, robbed of one's property, was a gross injustice to the members of nonconforming groups. Today all denominations which have a history must share the shame of the age-old maxim: *Cuius regio, ejus et religio.*

The situation is altogether different today. In many nations there is legal toleration of all religious groups on the basis of equality before the law. No attempt is made to interfere with the free profession and exercise of any religion. There is not only complete freedom of religious activity but also the liberty of being undisturbed in the complete denial of religion or non-exercise of religion. Even states which recognize and support an established church usually do not interfere with the freedom of other groups. International law, which is gradually being formed and to some extent implemented, is also directed toward official toleration in matters of religion.

Apart from historic and social considerations the Catholic has two beacons guiding him in his judgment on the nature and degree of civil tolerance in matters of religion: on the one extreme is the rejection of error, on the other reverence for the conscience of the erring and the desire for freedom of conscience in matters of faith on the part of all citizens. However, it is preposterous to look upon error and false doctrine as equal to truth; as such, error cannot be the basis of right nor can it lay claim to protection as though it should be placed on a par with truth, except in the minds of those who look upon truth as beyond man's grasp.

Pius XII in his address to the Fifth National Convention of Italian Jurists, December 6, 1953, clarified many points on this difficult question. Regarding the right or duty of authority to interfere with error, the Pope says: "Could God, although it is possible and easy for Him to repress error and moral deviation, in some cases choose not to interfere with it without contradicting His infinite perfection? Could it be that in certain circumstances He would not even communicate the right to impede or repress what is erroneous and false? A look at things as they are gives us an affirmative answer. Reality shows that error and sin are in the world in great measure. God reprobates them, but He permits them to exist. Hence the affirmation is not absolutely and unconditionally valid that religious and moral error must always be impeded when it is possible because toleration of error is in itself immoral. Moreover, God has not given even to human authority such an absolute and universal command in matters of faith and morality. Such a command is unknown to the common convictions of mankind, to the Christian conscience, to the sources of revelation, and to the practice of the Church. To choose among scriptural texts which are adduced in support of this argument consider the parable of the cockle in which Christ gives the following advice: let the cockle grow in the field of the world together with the good seed for the good of the harvest (cf. Mt 13:24ff.). The duty of repressing moral and religious error cannot therefore be an ultimate norm of action. It must be subordinate to higher and more general norms which in some circumstances permit and perhaps even counsel, as the better policy, the toleration of error in order to promote a greater good."

The Pope then laid down two basic principles for the jurist, the statesman, and the sovereign Catholic state in regard to religious and moral toleration: "First: that which does not correspond to truth or to the norm of morality objectively has no right to exist, to spread, or to be activated. Secondly: failure to impede this evil through civil laws and coercive measures can nevertheless be justified in the interests of a higher and more general good."[83]

Within reasonable limits civil toleration of religion is a practical necessity at any time, but particularly today in our pluralistic society. Among
other reasons, such toleration is a prerequisite for the open and uninhibited
profession of faith by the believing community which itself is thus im-
mune from worldly sham and hypocrisy. To a certain degree civil tolerance also creates favorable conditions for the more effective practice and
manifestation of the faith on the part of many. The appeal to civil authority to suppress errors which are not themselves supported by any force
nor likely to be sustained by any coercive measures arises from a lack of
confidence in the persuasive power of the truth we proclaim, or at least
must create the impression in the minds of many contemporaries that
our truth is impotent.

Civil tolerance, in the last analysis, must also be an expression of the
virtue of tolerance for the Christian statesman. It must be the manifestation of an enlightened zeal for the divine kingdom of love which is filled
with respect and consideration for the convictions of others. Nevertheless,
civil tolerance is not directly concerned with eternal salvation but with
cordial coexistence in a religiously mixed society or some other form of
pluralistic community.

Catholics living in a country in which many Christian (and non-
Christian) groups are represented can rest quite content with their position as one group equal to the others before the law. This type of legal or
juridical equality does not necessarily create an atmosphere which covertly
nourishes an unbearable indifferentism. The modern state does not even
attempt to make a decision regarding the objective truth. It is concerned
with domestic tranquility and ultimately with the protection of the complete freedom of individual conscience throughout its domain. In consequence, the state guarantees this domestic freedom of the individual and
protects him against any illegal interference in the propagation and
exercise of his religious beliefs. This solution is not without its advantages
to Catholics. It surely should remove from their minds any temptation to
place their trust in external privileges rather than in the power of truth.
Even in a country in which the Church does enjoy special privileges, her
growth and effectiveness must depend on the demonstration of the truth
in love rather than on the "privileges" to which she is rightly entitled.

Upright and consistent civil tolerance is most favorable to truth. But
error by its very nature begets intolerance, for it is hostile to truth and
disposes men to be impatient with the truth. But it also must be borne in

mind that civil toleration is constantly in jeopardy in a pluralistic society which makes no distinction in legal structure and procedure between any one religious group or belief and the other. The reason is apparent: the "liberal" who has no absolute convictions will never fail—for despite all his boasting of liberty, he is essentially intolerant—to find a way of robbing the Church of her inalienable right to preach absolute truths and norms. There will also be other forces at work which will bend every effort to pervert universal civil tolerance into a dictatorship of their own ideology. We have a patent example in the tactics by which dialectical materialism is being promoted today in those countries in which the Communists have not yet taken over.

One should never be so naive as to imagine that the modern state can never reach the stage when its vital interests and concern for domestic tranquility among citizens of different groups will demand intervention and even a degree of coercion. There is a point where restraint of ideological propaganda directed to destructive political interests and subversion of the whole civil order is unavoidable. The state may not permit its protection of individual freedom to be turned against its own existence and well-being. Nor can those who abuse the exalted prerequisites of tranquil coexistence for the very purpose of suppressing every freedom of faith appeal to the honesty and sincerity of their conscience as just defense of their actions. The state must restrain their subversion as it restrains mayhem or murder.

In order to form a fair and dispassionate judgment of the alleged civil intolerance of certain Catholic countries, we must first study all the facts and seriously ponder the many historic and sociological factors present in a very complicated situation. There are countries in which the Church has collaborated with the people for over a thousand years in achieving a national culture and welfare. Surely it is asking altogether too much to demand from such a "Catholic" country that it suddenly yield to certain sects (often imported from hostile states where they often do not enjoy any great prestige among their own people) and place them on a par with the Church, despite the fact that in the same breath with which they scorn the Church they also disdain the national culture. On the other hand, preservation of the rights of the Church—which are justly hers by her very nature and her achievements—does not at all require a restriction of the freedom of conscience and worship of other denominations.

No matter what the special situation may be, enactment of legislation which does violence to the conscience of any adherent of a religious community is never permitted. Nor may the state resort to sanctions or coercion to force an individual to accept any particular religious faith. There is an added obligation affecting the Catholic politician in this age in which international relationships are so close and international communications so intimate. In carrying out a policy of civil tolerance in his own country he must also consider the effect his action may have on the Catholic minorities in non-Catholic countries. In shaping the image of civil tolerance in his own country he must exemplify the Catholic norm which forbids forcing anyone to enter the Church against his will. The result should be that no non-Catholic state or statesman will be able to point to the Catholic politicians or the Catholic countries as justification for discrimination against Catholic citizens.

f. The World Mission of the Laity

Many are the indirect approaches and methods available for the apostolate of our neighbor's salvation, which are as important as the direct apostolate. We have in mind, above all, the daily cultural and economic contribution of Christians to the humanization and Christianization of the environment in which they live and move. We are indebted to the modern sociology of religion for a better understanding of the tremendous influence the structures of our environment exert on the spirit of faith and morality of the great mass of men. Our knowledge of the influence of the milieu, both in its immediate and its more remote contacts with individual and group, directs us to study with heightened anticipation that portion of the "care of souls in the environment," which belongs to the world mission of the laity.[84]

The father and mother of the family, who in their own home concern themselves with healthful sustenance and clothing, with a reasonable regimen of home life, with play and song, joy and earnestness, thereby also serve indirectly the eternal salvation of their children. Workers and managers, employers and employees, all who rise above the clash of petty material interest and class partisanship, who concern themselves seriously with social peace and social justice, who work harmoniously for sound labor conditions and a wholesome atmosphere in every area of human employment, all these directly further their world mission. But indirectly they also serve the kingdom of God's redemptive love. This holds even though they may not at all be aware of the religious influence which their correct conduct has on the terrestrial realm. It is impossible to calculate the influence for weal or woe which politicians, writers, journalists, teachers, jurists and attorneys, physicians, nurses, artists, and program directors of radio and television indirectly wield on the souls of others merely through the correct or incorrect exercise of their calling.

If all this is an expression of supernatural love for others, it truly becomes an apostolate. The motives, of course, must be "missionary" motives by which the work is directed in love to the salvation of souls. And the task must be performed in such a consciously reflective manner that the actions performed in response to one's vocational duty are by circumstance and intention directed to this goal. Of special value are the vocational societies, cultural and political. In our pluralistic society they often prove more effective in their endeavor to promote the good than exclusively Catholic societies or ecclesiastical organizations. The layman who cooperates in the moral and religious betterment of public life and its social structures through organizations which do not bear the stamp of ecclesiastical formation is not an official representative of the Church. Nor does he receive his world mission from the ecclesiastical hierarchy. But his position among the people of God basically obliges him to direct his world mission to the service of the kingdom of God and salvation of men. He is "the church in the world."[85]

To discharge such an important office correctly in a world as extensively dechristianized as our world today the Christian layman must, as a living member of the people of God, be profoundly penetrated with the doctrine and spirit of the Church. He is not permitted to sit idle and wait for particular directives given in each instance by Church authority. He is himself responsible for the right interpenetration of the Gospel into the vocational and cultural life. On his own initiative and with mature judgment he must set forth the Christian spirit in the context of his own life. We expect of him the thorough and objective competence of a true master. A decisive test of authentic Christian maturity in this matter is the solidarity, the readiness to cooperate with all good men and women and to be ever aware of the total order of things.

3. *The Official Apostolate of the Church*

The universal or common forms of apostolic activity, which we have just treated, arise from the very nature of Christian existence. They do not require an official organization or assignment. This is reserved for the official apostolate which we intend to present in its nature, its tasks, and its fulness of power, the while considering the type and manner of participation of various states of life in the mission of the Church.

a. The Power and the Duty

The Church possesses an official apostolate. It is exercised by those who have received from the Lord the magisterial power by mission and consecration and by those whom they in turn expressly or implicitly commission by a communication of their power.

The Church is the People of God on earthly pilgrimage. As an all-embracing community of salvation and mediatrix of salvation, the Church has been furnished by her divine Bridegroom with a fully adequate magisterium by which to guide and direct mankind. The subjects of this power are the pope and the bishops. Together they form the hierarchy of the Church. They are in the strict sense of the term a hierarchy of jurisdiction.[86] The Church is established by the Lord to serve officially and authoritatively for the salvation of the Christian people and to bear the responsibility for announcing the tidings of salvation to all men. The hierarchy, and the hierarchy alone, has the commission and the fulness of power to rule the Church of God. The entire public life of the Church falls under their supervision. Hence there can be no official apostolate without her approval and her (at least implicit) commission.

From the plenitude of authority which the hierarchy possesses flows their obligation to foster the apostolate. With all care and circumspection they must further this apostolate, encourage spontaneous private initiative, protect it and, if occasion arise, confirm it expressly and impart to it fixed form so that its effectiveness is guaranteed. To direct a community means to summon all its energies and direct them collectively toward their essential goal. And the Church is essentially apostolic, missionary. She is the People of God, the assembly of the saints, which unfolds and develops, from the days of her divine origin in Christ and His chosen Apostles down to the day of the Second Coming of our Lord. If we call the Church apostolic and Catholic, this means far more than a designation of her origin and present constitution. To say she is Catholic and apostolic is to make an essential pronouncement on her dynamism, on her vocation and destiny. These flow from her inmost essence by which she is constantly to expand and manifest herself everywhere through her apostolate as the Catholic, all-embracing community of salvation and love. Built on the foundation of the Apostles whose mission she continues, the Church may never repose or rest as long as there are Christians who are severed from her unity and men anywhere who have not been caught up by the tidings of salvation.

When we speak of the office and authority of the Church (ultimately, of the hierarchy of jurisdiction), we must always keep in mind the bond between the power of ruling and guiding in the Church and her sacramental, priestly character. The Church is sacramentally rooted in the mystery of the redemption; chosen in the Blood of Christ, the Church must bring the love and salvific concern of the Redeemer to the perception and experience of all men in all times. Made one through the unbreakable covenant of love with Christ, she participates as servant and bride in his plenitude of power to teach all men and make them disciples. This supreme jurisdiction first assumes form in the authority of Peter and the college of the Apostles and their successors. To them Christ said: "All power in heaven and on earth has been given to me. Go, therefore, and make disciples of all nations, baptizing them in the name of the Father and of the Son and of the Holy Spirit, teaching them to observe all that I have commanded you; and behold, I am with you all days, even unto the consummation of the world" (Mt 28:18ff.).

From this text and other passages in Scripture it is evident that the center of commitment and plenary power of the Church is in her priestly office. Through participation in the priesthood of Christ she is to redeem and sanctify all things in the triune love of God.[87] Unto this end the authoritative proclamation of the Gospel is directed. From this also flows the authoritative announcement of the moral message and the whole exercise of the Church's authority.

Hierarchical jurisdiction is a grace-giving participation in the mission of Christ by the Father: "As the Father has sent me, I also send you" (Jn 20:21). It is a mission flowing from the loving divine power and supreme rule of love. And what is the goal? To bear the message of love through the witness of a faith aglow with love. To bear the message of love in the power of the Holy Spirit who is Love in person. It is participation in the witness of love which Christ has bestowed on His Church and the whole world in the paschal mystery. Unto this end Christ grants the Church His assistance, His Spirit. "You shall receive power when the

Holy Spirit comes upon you and you shall be witnesses for me . . . even to the very ends of the earth" (Acts 1:8).

The ruling authority of the Church and its official character are directed essentially to serve an all-embracing unity in faith and love.[88] Here the decisive question arises: how does this faith come to souls and how does it take firm hold and assume fixed form? It is with the aid of three forces which the Church can bring to bear through her mediation: 1) through the word of God whose power and efficacy is climaxed, centered, and concretized in the liturgy; 2) through the celestial signs which accompany and authenticate the word; 3) through the grace of God which opens men's hearts. Only through the concurrence of these three principles can there be both an authentic expression of faith in the community of faith and love (which is the Church) and also a genuine and effective evangelization.

This basic task of the Church is carried out through the plenitude of power imparted by Christ. It is entrusted to the authority He has established. It is performed not only by those who primarily bear authority and are its source (the jurisdictional hierarchy), but also by the entire Mystical Body according to the degree of participation in the threefold office of Christ the Priest, who is also Prophet and King. However, there exists in the Church a dual manner of participation in these three offices of Christ: first, a generic, common, or universal participation because of the very fact of being a Christian; secondly, an official participation through proper directive or mandate of the hierarchy.

Through the life of grace our whole existence is most intimately bound up with Christ, the Head of renewed and redeemed mankind, and His established authority. Through participation in the grace of His Headship and through the infused virtues flowing from the life of grace all our capacities and faculties are directed according to the plan of salvation. Through the sacramental character which is not severed from the visible sign of the sacrament and from visible membership in the people of God the dignity of the Christian estate is in some manner made perceptible in the orientation to external cult and visible witness of love. It is first of all —though not exclusively—the sacramental mark which designates or establishes the diversification of participation in the three offices of Christ. Through the sacrament of order the hierarchical priest is officially elevated from the status of baptized and confirmed, from membership in the people of God, and deputed to the special service of sanctification, to service of the Word and the sacrament. The authority of jurisdiction which was committed to St. Peter and the college of the Apostles and their successors, the pope and the bishops, must (at least according to the conception prevalent in the Eastern Churches) be viewed in intimate union with the fulness of the official priesthood despite the necessary distinction between the power of order and the power of jurisdiction. Even the pope is, first of all, a bishop occupying the episcopal See of Peter with the corresponding unique position in the college of bishops.

The governing authority in the Church, consisting of the pope and the bishops subject to him, represents the threefold office of Christ. It is special, plenipotentiary, and at the same time dedicated to total service. Subordinate to it, all the baptized and confirmed participate in a general and unofficial way in the Church's worship and work. Nevertheless, the three offices of Christ are visibly proclaimed only through the various states in the Church: *the hierarchical priesthood* with its ministry of word and sacrament centering in the sacrament-sacrifice of the Eucharist; *the states of perfection* manifesting the prophetic office of Christ and, by prophetic witness wrought by God for the final plenitude of grace at the end of time, being "insofar as it is now already possible an anticipation and imitation of the celestial life;"[89] *the laity* serving the royal dominion of Christ the King over all realms of life, serving pre-eminently through the organized apostolate or Catholic Action. Thereby the sanctification which flows from priesthood and the ultimate eschatological witness of the evangelical counsels is projected into the terrestrial realm. Thus Christ the Savior and Lord of the "new earth and the new heavens" is rendered true homage.

The supreme responsibility for the harmonious exercise of these three foundational forms of the official apostolate rests with the jurisdictional hierarchy of the Church. By fulfilling the threefold office of Christ in perfect harmony they carry out the great commission of love and salvific concern for men. The following pages are an explanation in detail of the special commitments of each of the three basic forms.

b. The Official Apostolate in Its Basic Forms

(1) *Hierarchical Priesthood*

The first arm of the official apostolate in the Church is formed by the clergy. Included are all those who have received the clerical tonsure. The hierarchical priesthood in the clergy embraces episcopacy, presbyterate, and diaconate, all of which are sacramental by divine institution. The hierarchy of order also includes the subdiaconate and the minor orders which are usually considered as ecclesiastically instituted. According to present custom, which is subject to the decision of the Church and susceptible of modification, the four minor orders and the subdiaconate are received in preparation for the priesthood. In the early ages of the Church these orders, as blessings of the Church and not of divine origin, were conferred on men who without planning to be priests placed themselves by reception of an order at the service of the Church in some special manner. It would be quite in harmony with the spirit of the early Church if our lay catechists and instructors in religion, women parish helpers, and leaders of both sexes in Catholic Action would be given such an ecclesiastical blessing for similar duties.

The fulness of priestly power, unlimited and unrestricted service of word and sacrament, is conferred on the bishops of the Church. As "priests of the first hierarchical rank," they select "priests of the second hierarchical rank," who are simply called priests, to collaborate with them in their sacred tasks. Since these latter do not have the power to raise others to the priesthood, they do not have primary jurisdiction. They must be empowered by the bishop through some form of delegation according to the conditions and terms of the Church's law. The power to confer confirmation as ordinary minister is a prerogative of the bishop, but simple priests can be specially delegated by proper authority.

According to the testimony clearly presented in the Acts of the Apostles (chapter 6ff.) the diaconate constituted a distinct office in the Church (as is still the case in the Eastern Churches) and not merely a preliminary step toward the priesthood (as is the case in the Latin Church). The deacons were chosen by the Apostles in conjunction with the whole community; by prayer and the laying on of hands they were officially empowered to discharge the duties of their office (Acts 6:6). They were chosen officially for the service of the poor and also charged by the Apostles with the duty of preaching the word of God (cf. Acts 6:8ff.; 8:5ff.). The twofold service of charity and the word is strikingly expressed in their participation in the Eucharistic celebration.

Today there is a widespread movement, especially in mission lands, toward the restoration of the diaconate in the Western Church as a distinctively permanent state with full exercise of functions. This movement, which holds out a very promising and fruitful activity in our modern age, envisages a diaconate as a transient stage in preparation for the priesthood, but of longer duration and with a variety of spiritual tasks according to the needs of time and place in the Church. It has also been seriously suggested that this sacred order might with great spiritual profit be conferred upon married men who would be chosen because of special qualifications to exercise the functions of the order permanently and without the promise or hope of receiving any higher order.

In my opinion the establishment of married deacons for special service would result in an enrichment of the apostolate. Moreover, it might well prove that only those truly called should choose the celibate life with the result that the celibacy of the priests should be a more convincing testimony in the Church. There may be many very clear instances of a call for unselfish cooperation in the service of the Church without a correspondingly unequivocal call to celibacy. Fathers of families, who by an exemplary Christian life have proved themselves in virtuous living and in the lay apostolate, if ordained to the diaconate, should be able to bring to their tasks in this order a special effectiveness because of their very closeness to all the realities of life. The Church's care for souls should profit much by these contacts.[90]

It is an object of constant emphasis and exhortation that the priestly order by its very nature implies a solemn acceptance for the official apostolate. It is a *"diakonía* of the spirit" (2 Cor 3:8) which in manifold gifts of grace seeks to express the visible unity of love of the Body of Christ. The priestly service is a "ministration that justifies" (2 Cor 3:9) for the glorification of the loving majesty of God. The Eucharistic Sacrifice which is the center of the priestly service is offered for the salvation of souls, for the salvation of the entire world. Priestly piety is in consequence genuine only if it is totally formed and exercised in unity of faith and love and turned to the praise of God. The zeal and purity of the priestly apostolate must be nourished with the Eucharist, as must the priestly meditation. The canonical hours should likewise echo the Eucharistic celebration through the whole day of the priest at prayer and work. It is sad indeed if there is a chasm between the sacred celebration of the divine worship and the active apostolate. Even the examination of conscience should focus attention on this point: that everything in the external service of God should be the form and fashion of that which is professed in the celebration of the divine mysteries.

The Eucharist expresses uniquely the unity of the priesthood just as the

very words *hierarchical priesthood* sum up the unity in the one sacrament of order. Recent studies in this area do full justice to the concept
of the Christian priesthood as collegiate in character.[91] Priests are not
"solitary warriors" or isolated apostles, but form an apostolic body in a
living unity, which is guaranteed through loving, spiritually motivated
obedience to the bishops and the pope. Not to individual Apostles did the
Lord entrust His Church, but to the Apostolic College. The first part of
the Lord's own high-priestly prayer is climaxed in the petition for the
Apostles: "Holy Father, keep in thy name those whom thou hast given me
that they may be one even as we are" (Jn 17:11).

By His exercise of priesthood in the celebration of the paschal Mystery,
Christ made known His absolute unity of love with the Father—"all
things that are mine are thine, and thine are mine" (Jn 1-7:10). Similarly
will He be glorified in the Apostles, in the priestly hierarchy, by their
unity in love and apostolic labor. The unity of the priests is a necessary
condition for the unity of all those who by their word are brought to faith
in Christ. And finally this unity is a basic prerequisite for the fulfillment
of all the apostolic work of the Church: "The glory that thou hast given
me, I have given to them, that they may be one . . . that they may be
perfected in unity, and that the world may know that thou hast sent me,
and that thou hast loved them even as thou hast loved me" (Jn 17:22f.).

The author has had the extreme good fortune to devote many years to
the study of pastoral sociology and to have conducted over sixty pastoral
spiritual exercises for the clergy of various dioceses and regions. In the
light of this experience he is able to corroborate—with allowance of course
for some significant exceptions—the judgment expressed by many well-
informed men that the clergy of our day is most zealous in its spiritual
apostolate. But in great measure, unified and coordinated planning is
with the bishop and his ordinariate. The abundant natural and supernatural endowments and gifts do not come to full and rich fruition because awareness of the absolute necessity of solidarity in cooperation in
the apostolate and solidarity in striving for holiness is not at a maximum.
Nor is there a general realization of the impious nature of group-egoism.

The concelebration of the Eucharist, still practiced in the liturgy of
the Eastern rites, is a profound manifestation of priestly unity in the
mystery of faith. We suggest the same liturgical expression of the unity of
the priesthood: on appropriate occasions the group of priests concelebrat-
ing the mystery of the Eucharistic Sacrifice could give visible evidence of

a unity of mind and spirit in the apostolate. At least on occasions such as the diocesan retreats for the clergy, when the bishop celebrates the Eucharist together with his priests, all could join in one holy Mass at which the ordinary is the celebrant. Obviously, in accordance with the present legislation in the Latin Church concelebration in the strict sense of that term is excluded. But a Mass in common, with the bishop himself celebrating and all the priests participating, should deeply impress the entire body of the clergy. Such living experience of the mystery of unity in love should unite them all more effectively in their pastoral apostolate.[92]

Should unity not be centered primarily in the Eucharistic celebration, in lived fellowship of love, but depend too exclusively on the exercise of administration, the consequence might well be tragic in many instances. It often assumes that carping form of criticism which is most destructive. Or the conformity to the specifications and directives of the bishop and his ordinary may be largely obedience to the letter of the law with precious little interior conformity and harmony of spirit. No one denies that priestly unity also demands a certain degree of uniform prescriptive regulation and administration; but in the first instance unity must flow from the celebration of the Eucharistic mystery of love and from the interior working of the gifts of the Holy Spirit.

Next to unity and harmony of spirit the institution of the Eucharist and the New Testament priesthood stresses nothing so emphatically as the special need for humility in the priest. The sacramental washing of feet was designed as a lesson for all the faithful. It is an altogether special lesson for bishops and priests. The more exalted the service in the celebration of the Eucharist and in the apostolate, the more must the priest realize that the bounty of grace through participation in the mystery of Christ depends on his ready willingness to perform every humble service symbolized by the washing of the feet. With full consciousness of His divinity and His royal office (cf. Jn 13:3ff.), Christ fulfills his priestly office in self-renunciation and through the most menial service so that he could say of Himself: "I am in your midst as he who serves" (Lk 22:27). It follows that the force of testimony and the fruitfulness of the priestly office draw profoundly on humility, on absolute selfless dedication to the service of others. With humility absent and self-denial non-existent, harmony disappears! And without harmony in love and service there is no effective testimony to the faith (cf. Jn 17).

A very pressing task, a real task of pastoral care today in the face of the blasphemous slogan, "Religion is a private affair . . .," is to proclaim the royal dominion of God over all realms of life. This message and the parallel pastoral care for the world around us would still prove unacceptable to the modern man who is not persuaded of the humility and unselfishness of the priests, of their spirit of total renunciation of prestige and dominion. More than ever before the clergy today must take the laity seriously, and with absolute earnestness guard against every unpriestly tutelage over them. Only in this way can the priest win mature apostles for a fruitful cooperation in the apostolate. And only in this manner can he be an example to the laity whose testimony for the royal dominion of God likewise presupposes humility and unselfishness.

Since priestly service means an apostolate that is total and outstanding, saying *yes* to the call of God and the Church by embracing the priesthood is the loftiest or at least an outstanding unfolding of the universal call of Christians to the apostolate. As in ancient Christian times the community often had a predominant share in the calling of men to the priesthood and the episcopacy, so today it is the lot of the laity to face and share the responsibility of providing true vocations to the spiritual life in sufficient numbers. Fathers and mothers particularly have a great responsibility in this matter; for the Christian home, the Christian family, is the hearth at which the vocation is first nurtured. They furnish the foundation stones for our seminaries. Vocations to the priesthood can best mature in an environment in which an exemplary apostolic spirit prevails. Any conscious effort to frustrate the vocation to the priesthood is a gross injustice and a violation of love toward all those for whose salvation God awakened this vocation. All Christians pray and act in accordance with the admonition of the Lord: "Pray therefore the Lord of the harvest to send forth laborers into his harvest" (Mt 9:38; Lk 10:2).

(2) *The States of Perfection*

The orders, congregations, religious societies, and "secular institutes" are officially recognized by the Church and established and governed according to her law. Basic to all of them is the rule of perfection, the striving for perfection by a community effort according to the evangelical counsels. We cannot form a true and appropriate picture of the Church's apostolic task if we ignore the significance of religious organizations. The point was clearly stated by Pius XII: "The Church, the Bride of Christ, would not fully respond to the mind of her Divine Bridegroom, and men would not fix their eyes on her as on the 'signal unto the nations' (Is 11:12) if they did not find in her men who reflected the splendor of the Gospel more through the example of their life than by means of words."[93] Those who are members of these communities are *apostles* in the original sense of the term, for they possess an official and public mission from the Church. Though on a lower level than priests (except for congregations of priests), they still possess their mission in a solemn manner as members of Catholic Action.[94]

In our inquiry into the special function of the "states of perfection" in the framework of the apostolate of the Church, it is best to begin with the basic point of their testimony. To what do these "states of perfection" in the Church testify? By resolutely pursuing the way of perfection, striving at all cost to increase in holiness, those who are dedicated to the evangelical counsels in the religious life testify unmistakably that every Christian must strive for perfection, albeit not necessarily through the evangelical counsels or religious vows. The life of the religious vows is a renunciation of the full life of earthly possession and free disposal of property, of marriage and children, and of complete independence in personal decision. The vows of poverty, chastity, and obedience not only strengthen the religious himself, but impart strength to all in the untiring struggle men must undertake against the lust of the flesh, the lust of the eyes, and the pride of life. Obedience and life in community point to the meaning of unity in the exercise of the apostolate and to the price demanded if we are to obtain it: self-denial.

The full apostolic import of the testimony of the evangelical counsels must be seen first of all in the countless vocations to the religious life and in the tremendous unity of polarity with the testimony of the Christian who is witness in marriage and in the world as the religious is in the convent. The witness of the religious stresses above all the one eschatological aspect: "This world as we see it is passing away" (1 Cor 7:31). Such being the case, this testimony enjoys its full validity of unity only in conjunction with the characteristic witness of those who in marriage and in the world follow Christ radically and thus bear the witness of faith to the redemption of all creation, sighing and yearning for participation in the blessed freedom of God's children.[95]

The states of perfection should bear witness to the truths of faith which decide human destiny. To the validity of the faith they bear witness by their activity, but even more by the fulfillment of the purposes of their existence. And the testimony is immensely rich and varied. The hidden life in the contemplative orders teaches silently but impressively that prayer and sacrifice are an essential and pre-eminent portion of the Church's apostolate. Contemplation is the most complete expression and exercise of the intimate consecration to the Lord, but in its very totality of dedication to God it is also devotion to the salvation of souls. Since the Church herself approves this form of religious life and solemnly accepts the dedication to God, we have in contemplation an official form of apostolate in the full sense of the term. We see clearly the pattern of its spiritual efficacy: St. Therese of Lisieux, though a cloistered Carmelite, was officially chosen as the Patroness of the foreign missions.

The apostolate and testimony of the contemplatives is complemented and perfected and safeguarded against every misconception through the active orders. Here too we have the perfect polarity of contemplation and action. In the active orders there is a spiritual response to special needs and also a special call to every species of external apostolate. In answer to these needs and this call the members of the active orders turn to the primacy of the contemplative life as the basis and source of a fruitful apostolate. The actual retirement to strict *clausura* is testimony in the religious life of the renunciation of false attachment to worldly things; it is a concrete example of the spirit of renunciation essential to every form of the apostolate. Besides the religious orders and the congregations there are the more recent secular institutes which by their form of life, open to the world, testify to the sincere conviction that it is possible even "in the midst of the world" to preserve the *clausura* of the heart. Especially do members of the secular institutes bear witness through the pattern of their lives that men in secular vocations and in secular garb can fully realize the evangelical counsels. Such being the case, they are value-laden bridges to the perfection of the laity in the world and in the married state; for the laity and the married should also follow the spirit of the evangelical counsels in the depths of their heart, in radical interior detachment, and in total dedication to "the things of the Lord" (1 Cor 7:29ff.).

In addition to the numerous orders and religious institutes dedicated explicitly and immediately to the apostolate, the countless members of orders and of secular institutes devoted to charitable and cultural tasks are singularly significant evidence that the Church is thoroughly in earnest about the terrestrial order and realizes that earthly things are indissolubly bound up with the salvation of souls. Through the charitable active orders the testimony of the holiness and love of Christ and His Church assumes flesh and blood in earthly things. Should the religious orders in the Church cease to exist or lose their effectiveness, the faith itself would suffer immensely in its power to influence mankind.[96]

The humble and retired life of Jesus at Nazareth is a model and ideal for Christians in the world. Life in the world, interiorly animated by the fulness of the Christian spirit, has a profound apostolic value and is testimony to faith in Christ. To stress this testimony and apostolic value the Little Brothers and Sisters of Father De Foucauld seek to imitate the humble presence of Christ in the home of the Holy Family at Nazareth.[97] In all these instances the fully authorized commission by which they are charged to do the work of Christ takes complete and utter possession of men in order to emancipate them for many tasks.[98] Dedication to God and the apostolic service of the Church form a most perfect unity.

(3) The Apostolate of the Laity and Catholic Action

Our current theological and practical-pastoral literature[99] clearly reflects the special upsurge of interest we are experiencing in the lay apostolate. Though the layman has played a great and essential role in the apostolate from the very beginning of the Church, in our times his position and duty have been stressed with increasing emphasis since the time of Pius XI. To present the doctrine of the layman in the Church with all the areas still open for discussion would go far beyond our purpose. The subject is too vast for a work attempting to cover the whole field of moral theology. We can do no more for the present than throw some light on the more significant features of the complex problem, not going beyond the points which are entirely clear or at least almost universally admitted.

(a) THE UNIVERSAL AND PRIMAL APOSTOLATE OF THE LAITY

The "ordinary" apostolate of the laity derives from the state of being a Christian. Without any kind of special commission or form of organization, merely by virtue of the Christian reality (by force of the inner capacity and "mission" given in baptism and confirmation, and in virtue of the sacrament of matrimony for the married), one exercises this apostolate. The Christian simply works for Christ in his station or vocation through word and deed. The sacramental character imparts to the Christian a grace-giving participation in the redemptive vocation of Christ so that in Christ and with Christ he cooperates in the salvation of the world.[100] There is no special precept. The mere fact that one is a Christian, a member of the Mystical Body of Christ, lays down the obligation. The very heart of the Law of Christ, the love of God and of others, obliges the Christian to be an apostle.[101] Place and position of the apostolate are dictated by the existential situation in which one finds himself.

It follows that we can justly speak of the spontaneous apostolate and the fulfillment of one's duties in the world as the primal lay apostolate. The stress is on the word *lay.* And the word is not a mere negation. A layman is not simply a "non cleric." We are to think in the positive sense of one who is an active member of the people (the Greek word is *laós*) of God.[102] The primal apostolate of which we speak, flowing simply from being-a-Christian, includes every cooperation or collaboration in the "building up of the Body of Christ" through prayer, expiation, good example, individual instruction, and admonition. What marks the layman as layman is his station and position in the world and the form of apostolate flowing from it. In this sense it is occasional and largely indirect. "The interpenetration of the entire life of the family, of the social, economic, and political life with the Christian spirit! . . . The consecration of the world (*consecratio mundi*) is essentially a task of the laity itself, the task of men who have the greatest participation in the economic or industrial and social life, who take part in the government and the legislative assemblies."[103]

Pius XII does not consider all the forms of primal apostolate of the laity enumerated here as "lay apostolate in the strict sense."[104] But here the stress is not on the *lay* but on the word *apostolate,* insofar as it implies a special official mission, a mandate to a specific missionary task.[105]

The layman announces in his own way the tidings of salvation simply by fulfilling his civilizing vocational task with objective fitness and with the force and spirit of his Christian faith. He cooperates in a transformation of the arena of his life which redounds to the honor of God and the salvation of souls. "The law of God is engraved through the instrumentality of the layman's conscience on the earthly realm."[106] As the occasion dictates and the specific situation which confronts him demands, the layman will expressly and concretely announce the glad tidings of salvation—and this also belongs to the immediate primal task of the laity—and thereby he will also confirm the testimony of his faith through the word. He is empowered not directly by superiors but immediately through the efficacy of the sacraments: "The confirmed receives the power, as it were officially (*quasi ex officio*), to profess the faith in Christ."[107]

Fr. Congar maintains that theological writers are practically in agreement in the understanding of the manner and mode of the layman's position in the world. They agree on its extent and confines so that we are able to determine what is strictly and properly the lay apostolate. The layman is the Catholic Christian whose share in the work of salvation and in the spread of the kingdom of God is realized in and through his entry into the world structures, into the whole terrestrial domain."[108]

(b) THE APOSTOLATE IN MARRIAGE AND THE FAMILY

The sacrament of marriage "is in its essential act apostolic."[109] The spouses in marriage are in the administration of the sacrament of matrimony mutually efficacious causes (instrumental causes) of the divine life. By their whole life they should be to each other witnesses of the divine love and at the same time spiritual directors and guides of their children by virtue of the plenitude of power of the sacrament which imparts to them full authority in the familial society. On condition that they are in perfect conformity with the teaching and authority of the Church, the pastoral word of spouses to each other and the pastoral word of parents to their children has a fulness of power analogous to the word of the bishop for his diocese. Their apostolate in the family is in a pre-eminent sense official, but it is without a special mandate. Commission and full power comes to the married for the wedded and marital society by the sacrament of matrimony itself.

(c) LAITY IN OFFICIAL CARE OF SOULS

Tens of thousands of laymen and laywomen are principally or incidentally engaged officially in the service of the care of souls. There are sacristans, organists, choir directors,[110] administrators of Church property, and above all catechists. They are officially commissioned for this task by ecclesiastical appointment to a limited area of activity. For the regular and continuous giving of religious instruction a canonical mission (*missio canonica*) is necessary. This is an express commission to proclaim and teach sacred doctrine, something which must be clearly distinguished from the doctrinal magisterium which by divine institution is strictly the prerogative of pope and bishops. All others, priests as well as laymen, cannot claim any official teaching status except "in virtue of the mission which they receive from the legitimate teaching authority."[111] A limited or qualified teaching status may be granted priests and laymen in religious matters in virtue of a mandate "which indeed can be the same for both as far as the mandate is concerned. But they are distinct in this, that the one is a priest and the other a layman; and in consequence the apostolate of the one is priestly apostolate, that of the other is the apostolate of the laity. The value and the effectiveness of the apostolate depend on the capacity of the individual and his natural and supernatural gifts."[112]

It is altogether possible that the spiritual contribution of a capable laity who are well instructed and profoundly animated with the spirit of faith under certain conditions may far surpass the work of many priests. Nevertheless, abstracting entirely from the fruitfulness of the task communicated to them, from their ecclesiastical position, and from their readiness for service in the Church, they still retain the status of laymen. And their apostolate in this instance is not the typical apostolate of the laity. However, it may not be considered intrinsically foreign or alien to them since they too have received the Holy Spirit in richness and depth in the sacrament of confirmation (cf. Ti 3:5f.).

As a matter of fact laymen can take over from the short-handed clergy many functions which are still performed by priests. Pius XII explicitly exhorts: "Here too the Church authority can apply the generally valid principle of subsidiarity and mutual complementation: one can entrust those tasks to the laity which they can perform as well as priests, or perhaps better than priests."[113] The same Pontiff poses this question: Can those laymen "who place themselves at the service of the hierarchy and accept from them, for a specific or undetermined time, certain tasks for which they receive a mandate" by that very fact alone belong to Catholic Action in the strict sense?[114]

(d) THE ORGANIZED APOSTOLATE OF CATHOLIC ACTION

To the essence of the hierarchical apostolate of the Church there belongs, as we have already noted, a fraternal unity with its ultimate visible summit in the papacy. This unity is a demand resting in the essence of supernatural love for a corresponding unity and harmony in life and in the communication of the good tidings of salvation. It also pertains to the essence of the lay apostolate that it coordinate its forces and energies and, if need be, make use of organized forms and methods. Thus there arise in our time as in the past new groups and new movements in the lay apostolate. As long as these groups do not possess any express or implicit ecclesiastical recognition or ecclesiastical mandate to a special apostolate, the activites must still be classified as the spontaneous and primal apostolate of the laity. Through ecclesiastical approval and, in a still higher sense, through a special mandate these forms of the apostolate receive an official character.

From time immemorial pious unions, confraternities, Marian sodalities, and various third orders have assumed an official place in the Church. The time-tested criterion by which we can judge the value of the efforts made by these organizations in striving for holiness is their zeal for the honor of God in the salvation of souls.[115] These pious organizations are official indeed, but they are not—at least not in the first instance—official organs of the external apostolate. At any rate they cannot at all attain what is properly their essential goal, the formation of the perfect Christian, without at least drawing close to the primal apostolate of the laity and awakening a readiness to participate in organized apostolate when the opportunity presents itself.

In contrast to these pious organizations, Catholic Action as presented and developed by Pius XI, and more precisely defined since his time, is an organized official form or structure for the very purpose of concerted apostolic action. Pius XI used the term *Actio Catholica* officially for the first time in his encyclical of December 23, 1922, *Ubi Arcano*. He specified it in his letter to Cardinal Bertram of Breslau on November 13, 1928,[116] and used it repeatedly thereafter as "participation in the hierarchical apostolate." His successor to the See of Peter, Pius XII, usually substituted for the expression *participatio,* the obviously neutral term *cooperatio*. He, likewise, makes a clear distinction between the apostolate of the laity with its special mandate (Catholic Action) and the hierarchical apostolate. The former is always the "lay apostolate" even though formed by special mandate; the latter, "the hierarchical apostolate."[117] Note the same clear concept in the following definition of Catholic Action given in the recent Roman Synod: "Catholic Action is a union of laymen who in accordance with their regulations place their service of cooperation at the disposal of the hierarchy. Catholic Action is directly and in a special manner under the guidance of the hierarchy in the fulfillment of its task, the establishment of the dominion of God in souls, in families, and in human society."[118]

Catholic Action is essentially Church Action in contradistinction to the primal apostolate of the laity which can be termed "action of Catholics." Since Catholic Action is an organized ecclesiastical endeavor, it cannot be conceived except as being under the guidance of the hierarchy without whose commission and supervision there can be no fully official apostolic service. Nevertheless, this guidance of the hierarchy in no way means that the task of the layman is limited throughout to mere responsive and effective instrumentality. It should be much more than a mere execution of directives handed down from above. The individual in Catholic Action should develop the greatest possible initiative and the finest sense of Christian maturity. This close affinity between true obedience and independent contribution to the apostolate is expressed very clearly and pointedly in the definition of Catholic Action: "Catholic Action is an organization of laymen 'with its own responsible domain of operations in necessary submission to the guidance of authority' in such a way that the laity themselves hold positions of leadership. For this it is essential that men be chosen who will be able to inspire the various associations with apostolic spirit and lead them to the full development of their vigor."[119]

"The mandate—specifically, the mandate to teach—is, moreover, not communicated to Catholic Action as a whole, but in accordance with the free decision of the hierarchy, to its specially organized membership."[120] Catholic Action is a richly structured organism with a multiplicity of tasks and offices. One of the most important tasks is to lead its membership to full maturity, to a more profound appreciation of the faith, to the development of more effective methods of apostolic procedure, but most of all to cultivate those arts and skills which help effect the concerted penetration of the environment. Obviously, laity, priests, and religious must all cooperate harmoniously. Each must contribute according to his special capacity. Priests, however, are not the leaders but only spiritual counselors of the units of Catholic Action.

The hierarchy of the Church looks to the layman in Catholic Action not merely for effective activity as instruments. He is not merely to follow and carry out the designs placed before him. The Church expects much more of him: he is to act as a mature and full-time cooperator in the vineyard of the Lord. But to guarantee the effective cooperation of all the forces, the harmonious orchestration of the vast diversity of gifts of grace, there must be obedience to the directive of the hierarchy. All must dutifully follow the lines of action laid down by Church authority.

The bishops, as should be evident to everyone, grant to the societies of Catholic Action their commission and lay down the decisive course of action they must pursue and from which they may not deviate. But the laity are much closer to the scene than the clergy; often they possess a better knowledge of the objective realities when dealing with the Church's spiritual-temporal problems and appraising the vital events in the terrestrial area. In consequence, the laity are counselors in addition to being implementary organs of the hierarchy. It is likewise the will of the Church that the individual pastor in his parish should gladly make extensive use of the skill and service of the advisory activity of Catholic Action (particularly in the parish committees). They need not fear that their own prestige and authority will suffer diminution in consequence.

We consider as mistaken and misguided the efforts made in some quarters to cultivate, parallel to the theology thus far developed largely by priests, a distinctive type of independent theology for the laity.[121] But we cannot welcome too heartily the effort of laymen, versed in theology, to cooperate closely with priests in cultivating those parts of the one science and wisdom of theology which in a particular way deal with the encounter with the modern world.[122] Laymen, of course, are required—and in this their problem is not a whit different from that of priests and all clerics— to submit their writings on theological problems for ecclesiastical approbation. (Nor are they exempt from the Church's law regarding the keeping and reading of forbidden books.) Conversely, it is desirable that priest-theologians try to meet on common ground with the laity and obtain their advice and criticism.

(e) ORGANIZATIONAL PRINCIPLES OF CATHOLIC ACTION

The forms in the organization of Catholic Action are not uniformly the same throughout all parts of the world. There is a considerable diversity in the various countries and regions. And to a point this is surely absolutely necessary since Catholic Action must essentially promote the encounter of the Church with the modern world in all its great diversity.[123] The entire tendency and development is in the forward direction indicated by Pius XII to the Second World Congress: "All groups will belong to Catholic Action and keep their name and independence; but as Catholic Action they will form a federated unity."[124] Accordingly Catholic Action forms a framework organization for all the organized activities of the laity. And these activities should be of such a nature that they arise and prove most fruitful only through cooperation with the hierarchy and the established organs of Catholic Action.

The framework organization (the various centers of the "federated unity") has its structure in accordance with the hierarchical organization of the Church: according to parishes, bishoprics (between the two there can be regional or deanery groupings and various social groupings), and countries. They may also be grouped according to "episcopal conferences" or in some other recognized way.[125]

According to the original concept of Pius XI, Catholic Action is built first of all according to the four natural states occupied in life by men, young men, women, and young women. This structure obtains also in the overall organization. But it would be fallacious to conceive it as antithetical to a structure arranged according to the diversity of environment. The attempt—there never was an all-out effort in this direction—to group the vastly rich structure of Catholic social forms into a Catholic Action built up exclusively according to the four natural states is now conceded to be a complete failure.

Catholic Action turns toward specialization in individual or particular organizations to the extent that special apostolic needs may require. The determining principle of division in this matter is the milieu, the diversity of the realms of life. The reason is obvious; the environment is the principal area of the care of souls for which the laity are responsible.[126]

There is also an apostolate of the neighborhood.[127] It flows from the sociological meaning of the place in which we live, as the industrial apostolate flows from the center of business and place of work. In this field the guiding principles are those laid down by Canon Cardijn for the Young Christian Workers he founded. His principle ("To observe, to decide, to act") entails knowledge of environment, concerted effort to arrive at a fitting appraisal of the command of the hour, and prompt action according to a common plan. This approach furnishes a solid foundation for mission activity. The immense contribution this group has made toward the development of pastoral sociology in the care of souls is proof of the merits of the plan.[128] In a message to Cardinal Van Roey of Mechlin on the occasion of a convention of the YCW at Brussels, Pius XI calls this a genuine form of Catholic Action.[129] Christian trade unions and, to a lesser extent, other groups, who promote a common Christian educative and cooperative endeavor in the field of labor among the working classes, follow a similar pattern of operation. For true effectiveness the action group must be drawn from the milieu and be orientated toward the Christianization of the milieu. Worker organizations, whose members in industry are not united in an apostolic effort and which do not seek any contact with the forces ready to further the apostolate, do not fulfill the requirements or measure up to the ideals of Catholic Action and the lay apostolate enunciated by the late pontiff.

In many places, particularly in France, the small family circles have proved exceedingly effective. In the USA the Christian Family Movement was organized in Chicago in 1947. Its aim is restoration of family life to Christ and the creation of a community atmosphere conducive to Christian living. Family and community problems related to Christian living are taken up in informal and practical discussions in regular meetings. The movement employs the techniques and practices of specialized Catholic Action. Small groups or cells of married couples form parochial sections under priest-chaplain guidance, whereas larger units are formed into regional groups and diocesan federations. The movement numbers 50,000 couples in the USA and Canada. Spreading throughout many parts of the world, CFM is contributing tremendously to the advancement of the ideals of Catholic Action.

In many countries, including the USA, a very elaborate system of societies and organizations, rich and varied in their social structure and in many instances ante-dating the formal constitution of Catholic Action, can readily be embodied in Catholic Action as participating societies associated in a federation. The attempt to regroup and reconstruct them on a wide scale along present-day sociological lines is surely worthwhile. Obviously reconstruction will dictate in many instances an inner reorientation reflecting the powerful currents of present-day life or a transformation of the constitutions and statutes governing these organizations. However, most important is truly effective unity.[130]

That many organizations of Catholics of set purpose reject any formal incorporation into Catholic Action is not in itself deserving of censure. Under certain conditions there may be sound and valid reasons for pursuing cultural objectives and carrying on cultural—and even semi-political —activities in the full spirit of the Catholic faith, but entirely on lay responsibility. Preference may be honest and sincere for moving without implicating the hierarchy of the Church. But a degree of mutual cooperation under federated auspices with formally recognized branches of Catholic Action is not thereby excluded.

In opposition to certain endeavors, above all in Italy, Pius XII very expressly declared that "Catholic Action in itself cannot lay claim to a monopoly of the lay apostolate." He refers to the bad atmosphere which is created in many places through too restricted a use of the term *Catholic Action*. In consequence of this rigid concept "all organizations which do not find a place in Catholic Action so-conceived are made to appear somewhat unauthentic or of inferior rank. They seem to enjoy less favor in the mind of the hierarchy and to be relegated to the outer fringe of the essentially apostolic endeavors of the laity. . . . In practice this attitude has become so extreme as to exclude from some dioceses all apostolic endeavors which do not bear the label of Catholic Action."[131]

It is altogether correct and normal to recognize, besides the specialized organizations of Catholic Action which are built up according to the various milieus, other parallel apostolic forces which in a similar way turn to people of every situation and social state. Thereby in union with the federated organizations of Catholic Action, they discharge the important task of testifying to and guaranteeing that unity of apostolate in the Church which transcends all social divisions. In this regard, to cite just one example, the Legion of Mary occupies a prominent position.[132]

(f) CATHOLIC ACTION AND POLITICS

Catholic Action draws a very clear line of cleavage between itself and political organizations. Nevertheless it does not at all abdicate its right to make Christian principles effective even in political life. But according to the directive of the Roman pontiffs, Catholic Action must be fully independent and completely aloof from political parties.[133] The reason is inherent in the political party as such. It does not receive its directive from the hierarchy but must assume its own responsibility on the political level. In present-day society the political party is in no way the projected organ of the hierarchy. It is specifically a portion of the typical service performed in the world by the laity. Therefore, politically capable and intellectually-morally equipped laymen who are called to political activity should enter this important area. Thereby they discharge a task which under certain conditions is more significant than the work of Catholic Action. But note the difference: political activity is performed in their own name, not in the name of ecclesiastical authority.

"Responsible leaders must do everything in their power to keep Catholic Action completely divorced from political parties. For this reason the leaders of Catholic Action who are in higher positions may not assume office in any political party. Nor may they accept any other position which would place upon them responsibility of a political or administrative nature."[134]

(g) UNIVERSAL AND PARTICULAR VOCATION

The preceding pages are no more than a sketch of the organizations concerned with the lay apostolate. We do not have space to give a detailed account of all the varied and elaborate forms. But in the face of such multiplicity we cannot fail to ask a question which must arise in the mind of every Christian: "Am I also called to cooperate in a specific type or form of the apostolate? Does any specific movement make a claim upon my loyalty? Does it demand any degree of earnest affection and support?"

In any instance each one of us must be fully aware that the very fact of being a Christian obliges us to be apostles, witnesses of the all-embracing kingdom of divine love, to the extent at least of exercising this apostolate in its most universal forms. Concern for one's neighbor and his salvation is the first and most basic prerequisite of this supernatural love. Though it is the first and most important, we should still not overlook the second requisite. We must come to the assistance of our neighbor in his temporal needs. Even though this concern does not attain immediately to the exalted peak of the first demand of love, nevertheless, in concrete situations concern for our neighbor's material needs might often be the more elementary and pressing.

The Lord Himself gave us the signs which should precede the coming of the kingdom of God: "The blind see, the lame walk, the lepers are cleansed, the deaf hear, the dead rise, the poor have the gospel preached to them" (Lk 7:22). The Christian works of charity, considering the callousness of unredeemed man, are a continuation of our Lord's cures and miracles of love. Such active love is also a portion of the glad tidings of salvation announced to the poor. How could one preach to them the powerful kingdom of heavenly love without at the same time assisting them as far as possible in their earthly needs. Since the kingdom of divine love is all-embracing, every manifestation of Christian love of others is at least indirectly also a work of service for man's salvation.

Each man has his task. It is given him through the call and the summons of the hour, the call of the *kairós*. "To each one of us grace was given according to the measure of Christ's bestowal" (Eph 4:7). And since it is the one same Lord, the One who governs the world through His providence and the One who comes to men with the riches of His grace, we must recognize in their unity both our neighbor and our God. "What does my neighbor need here and now that I can give?" "What return shall I make to the Lord for all that He has given me?"

BIBLIOGRAPHY

The Two Primary Manifestations of the Love of Neighbor
Bodily Needs and the Corporal Works of Mercy

ANGERMAIR, R. "Seelsorge und Caritas in ihrer inneren Beziehung Zueinander," *Festschrift fuer Kardinal Faulhaber*, Freising, 1949, 91–118.

———. *Schutzaufsicht, eine Pficht der christlichen Geselschaft*, Freiburg, 1935.

AUER, J. "Gedanken zu einer Theologie der Barmherzigkeit," *Jahrbuch fuer Caritaswissenschaft und Caritasarbeit*. (Editor: K. Borgmann), Freiburg, 1958, 7–24.

BARGELLINI, LAZZARINI, *La carità nella vita professionale*. Roma, 1943.

BERG, L. *Christliche Liebestaetigkeit in den Missionslaendern*. Freiburg, 1935.

BOLKESTEIN, H. *Wohltaetigkeit und Armenpflege im vorchristlichen Altertum*. Utrecht, 1939.

BOPP, L. *Zum Lob der Liebe. Von der christlichen Caritas und den Richtungen ihrer Entfaltung*. Freiburg, 1952.

BORNITZ, M. *Erbe der Heiligen. Vom christlichen Armendienst in Vergangenheit und Gegenwart*. Freiburg, 1940.

GEBSATTEL, V. v. *Not und Hilfe. Prolegomena zu einer Wesenslehre der geistigseelischen Hilfe*. Freiburg, 1947.

GOERRES, I. F. *Des andern Last. Ein Gespraech ueber die Barmherzigkeit*. 4th ed. Frankfurt, 1951.

L'Assistance charitable et l'hygiène sociale. Actes du VIe Congrès Catholique de Malines Tom. VI.

L'EgLise éducatrice de la charité. Congrès national de Lyon 1950. Paris, 1951.

MARSOT, G. "Bienfaisance," *Dict. de Sociologie* (Jacquemet), 1936, III, 864–883.

MICHEL, O. *Das Gebot der Naechstenliebe in der Verkuendigung Jesu. Zur sozialen Entscheidung*. Tuebingen, 1947.

NOPPEL, C. *Einfuehrung in die Caritas*. Freiburg, 1938.

PANK, W. *Der Hunger in der Welt* (Herder-Buecherei Bd. 38), Freiburg, 1959.

PAUPER, A. *Die Werke der Barmherzigkeit.* Freiburg, 1937.

ROESLER, J. B. *Der naturgerechte Aufbau der freien und der staatlichen Hilfeleistung.* Heidelberg, 1954.

SEVERUS, E. v. *Fremde beherbergen.* Hamburg, 1947.

SVOBODA, R. "Oeffentlichkeitsaufrag und Oeffentlichkeitscharakter der kirchlichen Liebestaetigkeit," *Caritas* (Freiburg), 60 (1959), 178–185.

UHLHORN, G. *Die christliche Liebestaetigkeit.* Neukirchen, 1959.

VON DEN DRIESCH, J. *Geschichte der Wohltaetigkeit. I. Wohltaetigkeit im Altertum.* Paderborn, 1959.

WOLKER, L. *Die Werke der Barmherzigkeit.* Freiburg, 1946.

WOLLASCH, H. "Die Stellung der Caritas im oeffentlichen und kirchlichen Raum," *Caritas* (Freiburg), 50 (1949), 103–115; 148–158.

Charity: Private and Organized. Justice as Distinct from Charity

BORGMANN, K. "Das Siechtum der Barmherzigkeit," *Caritas,* 56 (1955), 166–172.

DAMEN, C., C.SS.R. "De recto usu bonorum superfluorum," *Miscellanea Vermeersch,* Roma, 1935, I, 63–79.

DICHGANS, G. "Das Siechtum der Barmherzigkeit," *Ho,* 47 (1955), 452–455.

DE SANCTA TERESA, SILVERIO, *El precepto del amor. Estudio históricocrítico de la caridad cristiana y sus relaciones con la justicia legal y la filantropía.* Burgos, 1941.

GARRONE, MGR. "La justice revêtue d'amour," *VieSpir,* 84 (1951), 70–80.

GIERS, J. *Gerechtigkeit und Liebe. Grundpfeiler gesellschaftlicher Ordnung in der Sozialethik des Kardinals Cajetan.* Duesseldorf, 1941.

GUARDINI, R. *Der Dienst am Naechsten in Gefahr.* Wuerzburg, 1956.

KLEIN, F. *Christ und Kirche in der sozialen Welt zur Stellung der Caritas im Spanungsfeld von Liebe und Recht.* Freiburg, 1956.

KROPP, A. "Macht Almosen den Mammon gerecht?" *NO,* 4 (1950), 400–411.

LIO, H. "Determinatio superflui in doctrina Alexandri Halensis eiusque scholae," *Antonianum,* 27 (1952), 75–168; 253–296; 429–498.

———. *Estne obligatio justitiae subvenire miseris? Quaestionis positio et evolutio a Petro Lombardo ad S. Thoman ex tribus S. Augustinii Textibus.* Roma, 1957

SCHILLING, O. "Die alttestamentlichen Auffassungen von Gerechtigkeit und Liebe," *Festschrift fuer Meinertz* (1951), 9–27.

VYKOPAL, A. *La dottrina del superfluo in S. Tommaso.* Brescia, 1945.

ZALBA, M., S.J. "Destino natural obligatorio de lo superfluo, *Fomento Social,* 3 (1948), 293–306.

Practical Norms in Charity and Almsgiving

BORGMANN, K. "Christliche Verantwortung gegenueber der heutigen Not," *Caritas* (Freiburg), 51 (1950), 112–117.

BOUVIER, L., S.J. *Le précepte de l'aumône chez saint Thomas d'Aquin.* Montreal, 1935.

DEURINGER, K. *Probleme der Caritas in der Schule von Salamanca.* Freiburg, 1959.

DOSCOCIL, W. "Wie steht es heute mit der Almosenpflicht?" *Caritas* (Freiburg), 51 (1950), 57–63.

LOTTIN, O., O.S.B. "La nature du devoir de l'aumône chez les prédécesseurs de saint Thomas d'Aquin," *EphThLóv,* 15 (1938), 613–624.

ZALBA, M., S.J. "El motivo de la limosna," *Fomento Social,* 3 (1948), 421–426.

Universal Obligation: Concern for the Salvation of Others

ARNOLD, F. X. "Bleibt der Laie ein Stiefkind der Kirche?" *Ho,* 46 (1954), 401–412; 524–533.

AUER, A. "Die Eucharistie als Weg der Welt in die Erfuellung. Von der Bedeutung des eucharistischen Mysteriums fuer die christliche Laienstandes in der Kirche," *Geist-Leben,* 33 (1960), 192–205.

CAMELOT, P. TH. *Spiritualité du baptême.* Paris, 1960.

CARRÉ, A. M. *Le sacerdoce des laics.* Paris, 1960.

CHAVASSE, A. *Eglise et apostolat.* Paris-Tournai, 1953.

CONGAR, YVES M. *Lay People in the Church: a Study for a Theology of the Laity.* Translated by Donald Attwater. Westminster, Md.: Newman, 1957.

DABIN, P. *Le sacerdoce royal des fidèles dans les livres saints.* Paris, 1942.

HAMER, J., O.P. "Le fondement biblique de la théologie de l'apostolat des fidèles," *Evangel-iser,* 13 (1959), 416–436.

HANSSLER, B. *Das Gottesvolke der Kirche.* Duesseldorf, 1960.

JEDIN, H. "Laietheologie im Zeitalter der Glaubensspaltung," *TrThZ,* 64 (1955), 11–24.

LECUYER, J., C.S.Sp. "Essai sur le sacerdoce des fidèles chez les Pères, *La Maison-Dieu,* 27 (1951), 7–50.

LOCHET, L. *Die Sendung der Kirche im 20. Jahrhundert. Eine Theologie des Apostolates.* Freiburg, 1958.

LOMBARDI, R., S.J. *Per un mondo nuovo.* Roma, 1951.

PIUS XII. Encyclical "Mediator Dei," *AAS,* 39 (1947), 552–560.

PLÉ, A., O.P. "La sainteté de l'apôtre," *VieSpir,* 78 (1948), 198–226.

PRUEMM, K. *Diakonia Pneumatos. Der zweite Korintherbrief als Zugang sur Apostolischen Botsschaft.* II, 1: "Apostolat und christliche Wirklichkeit," Rom-Freiburg-Wien, 1960.

RAHNER, K. "Die sakramentale Grundlegung des Laienstandes in der Kirche," *GeistLeben,* 33 (1960), 118–132.

REINHARD, W. *Der Laie im uebernaturlichen Organismus der Kirche,* Freiburg, 1932.

SCHERER, R. *Christliche Weltverantwortung.* 3rd ed. Freiburg, 1949.

————. "Die Eucharistie und der Christ in der Welt," *GeistLeben,* 33 (1960), 206–218.

SCHURR, V. *Seelsorge in einer neuen Welt. Eine Pastoral der Umwelt und des Laientums.* 3rd ed. Salzburg, 1959.

WULF, F., S.J. "Ueber die Herkunft und den Ursprung und den Sinn des Wortes 'Laie,'" *GeistLeben,* 32 (1959), 61–63.

"Zweiter Laienweltkongress in Rom," *HerderKorr,* 12 (1957), 110–137. (Cf *The Major Addresses of Pope Pius XII,* vol. I, pp. 152ff for the address of the Pope at the First World Congress of the Lay Apostolate, October 14, 1951. For the texts of the Second International Congress of the Lay Apostolate, Rome, 5–13 October, 1957, Rome, Palazzo delle Congregazione, 1958. Cf. AAS (1957) 922ff.)

Fraternal Correction

COSTELLO, Jos. A. *Moral Obligation of Fraternal Correction* (Catholic University Studies in Sacred Theology, 2nd Series, 27) Washington: Catholic Univ. of America Press, 1949.

NISIDEI, U. *Correzione fraterna e superbia.* Montegiorgio, 1941.

The Apostolate and Tolerance

*ASMUSSEN, H.-BRANDENBURG, A. *Wege zur Einheit. Zur Praxis interkonfessioneller Zusam-menarbeit.* Osnabrueck, 1960.

AUBERT, R., BOUYER, L., L. CERFAUX. *Tolérance et Communauté humaine.* Tournai, 1952.

BARION, H. "Ueber die Begrenzung der Staatsreligion durch die Toleranz," *NO,* 8 (1954), 65–71.

BORGMANN, K., SCHMIDTHUES, K., THIEME, K. u.a. *Freiburger Rundbriefe.* (Beitraege zur Foerderung der Freundschaft zwischen dem Alten und dem Neuen Gottesvolk im Geiste beider Testament, Freiburg.

CONGAR, YVES M. *After 900 Years: the Background of the Schism between the Eastern and Western Church.* New York: Fordham Univ. Press, 1959.

EGENTER, R. "Staat, Toleranz un Konfession," *Ho,* 46 (1954), 305–312.

GALLI, M. "Zur Toleranz des Staates," *Orientierung,* 20 (1956), 125–127; 147–151.

GAMBERONI, J. *Der Verkehr der Katholiken mit den Haeretikern. Grundsaetzliches nach den Moralisten von der Mitte des 16. bis zur Mitte des 17. Jahrhunderts, Brixien, 1950.*

HARTMANN, A., S.J. *Toleranz.* Frankfurt, 1955.

HIRSCHMANN, J., S.J. "Konfession und Toleranz in katholischer Sicht," *Zeitenwende,* 26 (1955), 159–166.

HOLZAMER, K. *Grundriss einer praktischen Philosophie, Freiheit, Toleranz, Sittlichkeit, Ressentiment.* Frankfurt, 1951.

KARDINAL SEGURA Y SAENZ, KARDINAL OTTAVIANI, J. COURTNEY MURRAY, S.J. "Kontroverse ueber die Religionsfreiheit in Spanien," *HerderKorr,* 6 (1951/52), 495; 7 (1952/53), 106; 8 (1953/54), 213–215.

KARRER, O. "Der Streit der Konfessionen," *Ho,* 49 (1956/57), 22–33.

KLETT, H. *Die religioese Intoleranz.* Meisenheim/Glan, 1948.

KUEHNELT-LEDDIHN, E. VON. "Katholische Toleranz," *WW,* 4 (1949), 342–353.

———. *Zwischen Ghetto und Katakombe.* Salzburg, 1960.

LECLER, J. *Tolérance religieuse et tolérance civile. Les controverses depuis la Réforme.* Paris, 1951.

———. *Histoire de la tolérance au siècle de la Réforme.* 2 vols. Paris, 1955.

LORTZ, J. "Sind wir Christen tolerant?" *Ho,* 50 (1957/58), 430–445.

MARITAIN, J. *Truth and Human Fellowship.* Princeton, 1957.

MONZEL, N. "Das Probleme der toleranz," *Solidaritaet und Selbstverantwortung,* Muenchen (1959), 223–245.

PIUS XII, "Ansprache vom 6.12.1953 zum Probleme der Toleranz in einer Ueberstaatlichen Gesellschaft," *HerderKorr,* 8 (1953/54), 173–176. [For a fine summary of papal teaching cf. Cardinal Lecardo, "Religious Tolerance in Catholic Tradition," in the *CM* J-F 1960, p. 12ff.]

RAHNER, K., S.J. "Ueber Konversionen," *Ho,* 46 (1953), 119–126.

SIEWERTH, G. "Von der Toleranz," *Erbe und Entscheidung,* 10 (1956), 73–98.

VERMEERSCH, ARTHUR. *Tolerance.* Translated by W. Humphrey. New York: Benziger, 1913.

The Official Apostolate of the Church—the Hierarchical Priesthood

BOUYER, L. *Le sens de vie sacerdotale.* Tournai, 1960.

CACCIATORE, G. *Enciclopedia del sacerdozio.* 2nd ed. Firenze, 1958, 1531–1636: Bibliografia generale delle opere attinenti al sacerdozio.

DILLENSCHNEIDER, C. *L'Unique Prêtre et nous les prêtres.* Paris, 1960.

DOMS, H. "Die Froemmigkeit des Weltpriesters," *GeistLeben,* 31 (1958), 424–442.

GREINACHER, N. (ed.) *Priestergemeinschaften.* Mainz, 1960.

GUYOT, J. (ed.) *Das Apostolische Amt.* Mainz, 1961.

KORSTEN, W., FROTZ, A., LINDEN, P. *Die Kirche und ihre Aemter.* Koeln, 1960.

SCHELKLE, K. H. *Juengerschaft und Apostelamt. Eine biblische Auslegung des priesterlichen Dienstes.* Freiburg, 1957.

SEMMELROTH, O. "Das geistliche Amt. Theologische Sinndeutung," Frankfurt, 1960.

WULF, F. "Die Spiritualitaet und Froemmigkeit des Weltpriesters," *GeistLeben,* 32 (1959), 38–48.

Universal and Particular Vocation

ALVAREZ. *In fremden Land. Wege zur Laienspiritualitaet.* Colmar, 1958.

Anima, 14 (1959) Heft 2: "Der Laie als Sendbote der Kirche."

AUER, A. *Weltoffener Christ. Grundsaetzliches und Geschichtliches zur Laienfroemmigkeit.* Duesseldorf, 1960.

BAUER, J. B. Die Wortgeschichte von "laicus" in *ZKathTh* 81 (1959), 224–228.

BEDOYERE, MICHAEL DE LA. *Christianity in the Market Place.* Milwaukee: Bruce, 1944.

———. La promotion des jeunes travalleurs, ferment de l'apostolat jociste, Masses ouvrières, 16 (1960), 2–44.

BRUNNER, A. "Die Frage der Laienaszese," *GeistLeben,* CB (1959), 190–204.

CARPENTIER, R. "Theologie des Ordensstandes und Heiligkeit des Laien," *GeistLeben,* 32 (1959), 433–441.

CONGAR, YVES. *Lay People in the Church: a Study for a Theology of the Laity.* Translated by Donald Attwater. Westminster, Md.: Newman Press, 1957.

———. *Si vous êtes mes témoins.* Cerf. Paris, 1959.

Der grosse Entschluss (Vienna newspaper devoted to lay piety).

"Der Laie und die Heiligung der Welt. Eine europaeische Rundfrage," *WW,* 13 (1958), 573–593; 661–680.

Die Katholische Aktion (Das katholische Laienapostolat) in den deutschen Dioezesen. Published by the *Bischoefliche Hauptarbeitsstelle Duesseldorf.* Hildesheim, 1935 (Utterances of the German bishops, and extensive bibliography).

DUMÉRY, H. "Les trois tentations de l'apostolat moderne," Recontres, 28 Paris: Cerf, 1948.

EGENTER, R. *Die Aszese in der Welt.* Ettal, 1957.

———. Christliche Laienfroemmigkeit. Erwagungen zu ihrem Begriff und ihrer Aufgabe *MThZ,* 10 (1959), 7–18.

FISCHER, A. *Seelsorgehilfe. Werkbuch fuer apostolische Schulung und Arbeit der Laien.* Freiburg, 1952.

GeistLeben, 23 (1950), Heft 4: Laienfroemmigkeit.

GLORIEUX, P. *Le laïc dans l'Église.* Paris, 1960.

GOERRES, I. F. *Die leibhaftige Kirche.* 3 aufl. Frankfurt, 1951.

HAERING, B. "Die Froemmigkeit des Laien. Wege der Nachfolge Christi in der Welt," *WW* 14 (1959), 179–189.

HAMMAN, A., O.F.M. *L'Apostolat du chrétien. Réflexions sur les données bibliques.* Paris, 1956.

HANSSLER, B. *Das Gottesvolk der Kirche.* Duesseldorf, 1960.

HEIMERL, H. *Laien im Dienste der Verkuendigung.* Wien, 1958.

HIRSCHMANN, H. "Die evangelischen Raete im Weltstand der Christen," *GeistLeben,* 26 (1953), 101–105.

KELLER, J. *You Can Change the World.* New York: Longmans, 1948.

KLOSTERMANN, F. *Das christliche Apostolat. Idee und Problematik.* Innsbruck, 1961.

———. Laienapostolat und Katholische Aktion, *ThPrQschr,* 100 (1952), 249–270; 340–357.

———. Der Laie in der Kirche, *Der Seelsorger,* 29 (1959), 259–269.

L'apostolato dei laici. Bibliografia sistematica. Milano (Vita e Pensiero), 1957.

LAROS, M. *Volk im Heiligen Geist.* Regensburg, 1937.

Lebendige Seelsorge, 6 (1955), Heft 1: Laienverkuendigung.

Lebendige Seelsorge, 9 (1958), Heft 6: Helfermangel-ungerufene Reserven.

LOTZ, J. B. *Meditation, der Weg nach innen.* Frankfurt, 1954.

————. "Laienchrist und neue Froemmigkeit," *GeistLeben,* 26 (1953), 304–308. *See also* 21 (1949), 418–429.

NEUHAEUSLER, E. "Ruf Gottes und Stand des Christen. Erwaegungen zu 1 Kor 7," *Bibl. Zeitschrift,* 3 (1959), 43–59.

PERRIN, J. M. *L'heure des laïcs.* Paris, 1954. 55–147: Spiritualité apostolique.

————. *Geist und Aufgabe der Saekularinstitute.* Mainz, 1960.

PHILIPS, G. *The Role of the Laity in the Church.* Translated by Gilber and Moudry. Cork: Mercier, 1955.

PIUS XI. *Ubi Arcano. AAS,* 14 (1922), 673–700. (*See Paepstliche Weisungen und Erlasse,* Mainz, 1933).

PIUS XII, For teaching on Catholic Action, cf. Utz-Groner, *Soziale Summe Pius XII,* Band II 1493–1554; cf. also *HerderKorr.*

RAHNER, K. "Regarding the Lay Apostolate," *Schriften zur Theologie,* II. Einsiedeln-Koeln, 1955, 339–373.

————. "Paul Apostel heute," *Sendung und Gnade.* Innsbruck-Muenchen, 1953.

————. "Bemerkungen zur Theologie der Saekularinstitute," *Orientierung,* 20 (1956), 87–95.

Ruf und Reich. Gestalt und Werk des Laien in der Welt (F. Lorenz ed.) Recklinghausen, **1959.**

SCHMID, M. "Bemerkungen und Fragen zur Spiritualitaet der Laien," *Der Christ und die Weltwirklichkeit* (K. Rudolf ed.). Wien, 1960, 65–110.

SCHOISWOHL, V. SCHURR, F. KLOSTERMANN. *Der Laie. Rechte und Pflichten.* (K. Rudolf ed.) Wien, 1959.

SCHULTE, B. "Die byzantinisch-slawische Theologie ueber den Dienst der Laien in der Kirche," *Ostkirchliche Studien,* 5 (1956), 243–284.

SCHULZ, H. J. *Froemmigkeit in einer weltlichen Welt.* Stuttgart, 1959.

SCHURR, *Seelsorge in einer neuen Welt. Eine Pastoral der Umwelt und des Laientums.* 3 aufl. Salzburg, 1959.

SEMMELROTH, O., HOFMANN, L. *Der Laie in der Kirche. Seine Sendung, seine Rechte.* Trier, 1955 (appeared first in *TrThZ,* 64 (1955), 332–362.

SVOBODA, R. *Bilder der Liebe. Erwaegungen fuer den Dienst im Caritas- und Pfarrapostolat.* Regensburg, 1958.

————. *Der Laie in der Krise der modernen Welt* (II World Congress for the Lay Apostolate. ed. Svoboda). Koeln, 1958.

SUAVET, TH. *Der Weltauftrag des Christen.* Augsburg, 1961.

TRESE, L. *Many Are One.* Fides (Dome Books), 1961.

TROMP, S. *Actio catholica in corpore Christi.* Romae, 1936.

URS VON BALTHASAR, H. *Der Laie und der Ordensstand.* Freiburg, Einsiedeln, 1949.

WELTE, *Vom Geist des Christentums.* Frankfurt, 1955.

————. *Ihr sollt mir Zeugen sein. Der 76 Deutsche Katholikentag in Fulda.* Paderborn, 1955. (Note especially pp. 441ff.)

WOLTER, H. "Bernhard von Clairvaux und die Laien. Aussagen monastischer Theologie ueber Ort und Berufung des Laien in der erloesten Welt," *Schol,* 34 (1959), 161–189.

WULF, F. *Geistliches Leben in der heutigen Welt. Zur Geschichte und Uebung der christlichen Froemmigkeit.* Freiburg, 1960.

————. "Der Laie und die christliche Heiligkeit," *GeistLeben,* 20 (1947), 11–26.

————. "Ist die Bergpredigt fuer Christen in der Welt realisierbar?" *GeistLeben,* 31 (1958), 184–197.

ZEIGER, I. "Katholische Arbeit im oeffentlichen Raum," *StimmenZeit,* 144 (1949), 7–15.

Additional Works in English

A Guide to CFM. Chicago: Christian Family Movement, 1958.

BOYLAN, MARGUERITE T. *Social Welfare in the Catholic Church.* New York: Columbia Univ. Press, 1941.

BLUNT, HUGH F. *The Quality of Mercy: Thoughts on the Works of Mercy.* (Religion and Culture Series). Milwaukee: Bruce, 1945.

CARDIJN, JOSEPH. *Challenge to Action.* Chicago: Fides, 1955.

CATHOLIC STUDENTS MISSION CRUSADE. *The Lay Apostolate: Some Fundamental Principles.* Cincinnati: CSMC, 1960.

CERFAUX, LUCIEN. *Apostle and Apostolate.* New York: Desclée, 1960.

CHAUTARD, J. B. *Soul of the Apostolate.* Gethsemani, Ky.: Abbey of Gethsemani, 1946.

CLEMENS, ALPHONSE H. *The Cana Movement in the U.S.* Washington: Catholic Univ. Press, 1953.

CLUNE, GEORGE. *Christian Social Reorganization.* Dublin: Browne and Nolan, 1940.

CONGAR, YVES M. J., O.P. *Laity, Church and World.* Baltimore: Helicon, 1961.

————. *Lay People in the Church: a Study for a Theology of the Laity.* Westminster, Md.: Newman, 1957.

COSTELLO, JOSEPH A., S.M. *Moral Obligation of Fraternal Correction* (Catholic University Studies in Sacred Theology, 2nd Series, 27) Washington: Catholic Univ. Press, 1949.

CRONIN, JOHN F. *Catholic Social Action.* Milwaukee: Bruce, 1948.

GEANEY, DENNIS J., O.S.A. *Christians in a Changing World.* Chicago: Fides, 1959.

————. *You Are Not Your Own.* London: Chapman, 1958. (Catholic Action.)

GIESE, VINCENT J. *The Apostolic Itch.* Chicago: Fides, 1954.

GIORDANI, IGINO. *The Social Message of Jesus.* Paterson, N.J.: St. Anthony Guild, 1943.

————. *The Social Message of the Early Church Fathers.* Paterson, N.J.: St. Anthony Guild, 1944.

HESBURGH, THEODORE M., C.S.C. *The Theology of Catholic Action.* Notre Dame, Ind.: Ave Maria Press, 1946.

HUECK, CATHERINE DE. *The Story of Friendship House.* New York: Friendship House, 1940.

INSTITUTE OF SOCIAL ORDER. *Social Orientations.* Chicago: Loyola Univ. Press, 1954.

KAVANAGH, WILLIAM A. *Lay Participation in Christ's Priesthood* (Catholic University Studies in Sacred Theology, 41). Washington: Catholic Univ. Press, 1935.

KELLER, JAMES G., M.M. *Change the World from Your Parish: a Christopher Handbook.* New York: Guild Press, 1961.

LECLERCQ, JACQUES. *Christians in the World.* New York: Sheed and Ward, 1961.

LYNCH, SISTER MIRIAM, O.S.U. *The Organized Social Apostolate of Albert de Mun* (Catholic University Studies in Sociology, 36) Washington: Catholic Univ. Press, 1952.

MONTCHEUIL, YVES DE. *For Men of Action.* Chicago: Fides, 1951.

MURPHY, JOHN F. *The Moral Obligation of the Individual to Participate in Catholic Action* (Catholic University Studies in Sacred Theology, 107) Washington: Catholic Univ. Press, 1958.

N.C.W.C. (National Catholic Welfare Conference): a Description of its organization and Activities. Washington: N.C.W.C., 1950.

N.C.W.C. *The Lay Apostolate Today.* Washington: N.C.W.C., 1950.

PERRIN, JOSEPH M., O.P. *Forward the Layman.* Westminster, Md.: Newman, 1956.

———. *The Fundamentals of Catholic Action.* Chicago: Fides, 1959.

———. *Secular Institutes: Consecration to God and Life in the World.* New York: Kenedy, 1961.

PHILIPS, GÉRARD. *The Role of the Laity in the Church.* Chicago: Fides, 1956.

PUTZ, LOUIS J., C.S.C. *The Modern Apostle.* Chicago: Fides, 1957.

RIGUET, MICHEL. *The Charity of Christ in Action* (Twentieth Century Encyclopedia of Catholicism, 104) New York: Hawthorn, 1961.

RULAND, LUDWIG. *Pastoral Medicine,* ad. by T. A. Rattler, ed. by A. Preuss (Pastoral Theology, vol I.) St. Louis, B. Herder, 1934.

———. *Foundations of Morality,* ad. by T. A. Rattler, ed. N. Thompson (Pastoral Theology, vol II.) St. Louis: Herder, 1936.

———. *Morality and the Social Order.* ad. into English by T. A. Rattler, ed. N. Thompson (Pastoral Theology, vol III.) St. Louis, Herder, 1942

SALIEGE, JULES G. (Card.). *Who Shall Bear the Flame?* Chicago: Fides, 1949.

STURZO, LUIGI. *Spiritual Problems of Our Times.* New York: Longmans, 1945.

———. *The True Life: Sociology of the Supernatural.* Paterson, N.J.: St. Anthony Guild, 1943.

SUENENS, LÉON J. *The Gospel to Every Creature.* Westminster, Md.: Newman, 1957.

———. *Theology of the Apostolate of the Legion of Mary.* Westminster, Md.: Newman, 1954.

SUHARD, EMMANUEL (Card.). *The Church Today: His Collected Writings.* Chicago: Fides, 1953.

SZAL, IGNATIUS J. *Communication of Catholics with Schismatics* (Catholic University Studies in Canon Law, 264) Washington: Catholic Univ. Press, 1948.

The American Apostolate. Leo R. Ward, C.S.C., ed., Westminster, Md.: Newman, 1952.

The Catholic Church. U.S.A., Louis J. Putz, C.S.C., ed., Chicago: Fides, 1956.

The Lay Apostolate: Papal Teachings Selected and Arranged by the Benedictine Monks of Solesmes. Boston: St. Paul Editions, 1961.

The New Ritual; Liturgy and Social Order (Proceedings of the National Liturgical Week, 1955). Elsberry, Mo.: Liturgical Conference, 1956.

The Virtues and States of Life (Theology Library, v. 4). A. M. Henry, O.P., ed. Chicago: Fides, 1957. "Faith" (A. Liégé), pp. 1–59; "Hope" (B. Olivier), pp. 61–126; "Charity" (B. Olivier), pp. 127–208; "The Virtue of Religion" (A. Mennessier), pp. 393–444; "The Social Virtues" (M. Gerland), pp. 445–485 (on Obedience, Piety, Liberality).

WALSH, MARY E., and FURFEY, PAUL H. *Social Problems and Social Action.* New York: Prentice-Hall, 1958.

WARD, LEO R., C.S.C. *Catholic Life, U.S.A.: Contemporary Movements.* St. Louis: B. Herder, 1959.

Periodical Literature in English

BEDOYERE, M. DE LA. "Catholic Action and the Layman," *Mo, 174* (Sept., 1939), 233–40.

BENARD, D. "Cardinal Newman and the Lay Apostolate," *AER, 109* (Jan., 1944), 17–23.

BOYD, W. "Cell: Technique of Catholic Action." *HPR, 39* (June, 1939), 898–906.

BRUEHL, C. "Pius XI and Catholic Action," *HPR, 39* (June, 1939), 898–906.

BUDDE, G. H. "Christian Charity: Now and Always: the Fathers of the Church and Almsgiving," *AER, 85* (Dec., 1931), 561–79.

CAHILL, E. "Catholic Social Movement," *IER, 36* (Dec., 1930), 572–87; 37 (Feb., 1931), 113–23.

CAMPBELL, J. I. "Catholic Action and Politics," *IMo*, 64 (Jan., 1936), 10–17.

DALY, J. J. "Catholic Action among the Cultures," *HPR*, 35 (Aug., 1935), 1208–16.

DAVIS, H. F. "Priesthood of the Faithful," *DR*, 69 (Spring, 1951), 155–70.

DE BLACAM, A. S. "Christianity in the Market-place," *IMo*, 71 (Sept., 1943), 389–97.

FEREE, W. "Role of the University in Catholic Action," *National Catholic Educational Association Proceedings* (1939), 186–98.

FITZSIMMONS, J. "Institutional Apostolate," *CM*, 48 (Feb., 1950), 93–100.

———. "Pius XII and the Apostolate of the Laity," *ClerRev*, 43 (Sept., 1958), 530–39.

FLYNN, V. J. "Other Sheep: Proper Attitude toward Non-Catholics," *AER*, 84 (Jan., 1931), 45–51.

FOLEY, A. S. "Cell Technique of Specialized Catholic Action," *RR*, 2 (May 15, 1943), 164–75.

GOODE, B. "Catholic Action for Young Workers," *ClerRev*, 14 (June, 1938), 485–97.

GRAF, E. "Catholic Action and the Liturgical Life: Mystical Body: Beatitudes," *OF*, 9 (June, 1935), 360–71.

GRIFFIN, J. "Catholic Action and the Liturgy," *HPR*, 40 (Nov., 1935), 154–63.

HENNRICH, K. J. "Leadership in Christianity," *HPR*, 40 (Dec., 1939), 387–99.

———. "Leadership in Labor and Economy," *HPR*, 40 (Dec., 1939), 258–73.

———. "Leadership in Training," *HPR*, 40 (Oct., 1939), 18–25.

LAFARGE, J. "Some Questions as to Interdenominational Cooperation," *TheolS*, 3 (Sept., 1942), 315–32. *See also* 4 (June, 1943), 314–16.

McLAUGHLIN, M. "Catholic Action and Catholic Education," *HPR*, 41 (Sept., 1941), 1174–82.

MAHONEY, E. J. "Christian Cooperation: with Texts of Papal Directives Touching on the Question," *ClerRev*, 22 (July–Nov., 1942), 294–311, 521.

MEYER, B. F. "Lay Vocation," *AER*, 124 (Jan., 1951), 41–8.

MILLET, J. H. "Catholic Action Rural Movement," *AER*, 117 (Nov., 1947), 348–60.

MURRAY, J. C. "Christian Cooperation: Summary of Recent Thought on the Subject," *TheolS*, 4 (Sept., 1942), 413–31.

———. "Current Theology: Cooperation: Some Further Views," *TheolS*, 4 (March, 1943), 100–11.

———. "Intercredal Cooperation: Its Theology and Its Organization," *TheolS*, 4 (June, 1943), 257–86.

PALMER, P. F. "Lay Priesthood: Real or Metaphorical?" *TheolS*, 8 (Dec., 1947), 574–613.

PARSONS, W. "Intercredal Cooperation in the Papal Documents," *TheolS*, 4 (June, 1943), 159–82.

ROCHE, G. K. "Duties of the Church towards the Poor," *IMo*, 66 (Feb., 1938), 75–85.

ROPE, H. E. G. "Catholic Intolerance," *Mo*, 158 (Sept., 1931), 203–10.

RYAN, L. A. "Charity and the Social Order," *Thm*, 3 (Oct., 1941), 539–63; 4 (April, 1942), 70–120.

TODD, J. M. "Apostolate of the Laity," *DR*, 70 (Spring, 1952), 150–62.

———. "Apostolate of the Laity," *CrCr*, 2 (Spring, 1952), 27–34.

WRIGHT, L. "Apostolic Role of the University Graduate," *DR*, 70 (Jan., 1953), 43–60.

CHAPTER ELEVEN

SINS AGAINST LOVE OF NEIGHBOR

M ost sins against love of others consist of omission of the positive duties of love. But the sharpest conflict with the "royal law" nevertheless exists in attitudes and acts of hostility against oneself or one's neighbor and in any conduct which hurts one's own and others' welfare in a positive way. The principal sins of this kind are: hatred and hostility toward the person of an other (by contrast with hatred of his sins, which as such is good); diabolical hatred, which is consciously directed against another's spiritual good or salvation, against his friendship with God; envy, which begrudges one's neighbor the good he possesses and which becomes diabolical envy if one begrudges him the good of divine love. It is from hatred and envy that flow controversy and discord, unjust conflict and war. Through these it is that peace, which is both the flower and root of love, is undermined. There is also, of course, a harmless scolding rising from a sudden flare of opposition or passion; prompt readiness to be reconciled shows that it does not flow from hatred. In an unjust war the defect of love in many swells up and bursts forth in vile fury. The most dreadful concomitant of war is the widespread and systematic sowing of the seeds of hatred for foreign nations and their citizens.

Inconsideration of others has a thousand ways of manifesting itself. The defect of love is apparent from the manner in which the thoughtless and inconsiderate utterly disregard the consequences of their actions. A thoughtless man rarely realizes how deeply he wounds his fellows. Typical today is the mad orchestration of cacophony in many city neighborhoods: the honking, the screaming sirens, the screeching motors, not to mention the blaring radios and stereo sets. Even worse is the utter disregard of traffic regulations and the sacredness of human life. The highway fatalities cannot be excused as the result of mere thoughtlessness; the thousands of fatalities are evidence of criminal carelessness.

As the love of others is realized in the virtues through which charity is exercised, so the violation of these virtues is always indirectly a violation of the love of others. Here we can merely indicate this point, since we treat of the matter in the next volume of our special moral theology. In the following paragraphs we are concerned only with those sins which are in direct opposition to the inmost essence and nature of Christian love of others, that is, to the loving concern for his salvation: seduction, scandal, and cooperation in the sins of others.

I. SEDUCTION

Seduction (*scandalum directum*) is the deliberate effort to lead others into sin. The seducer lays a trap, a snare (*scandalum*), which is expressly designed to bring about the fall of another. Seduction can take place not only through direct persuasion, advice, or command, but also through carefully suggestive actions which convey to another one's will and intent in order to create in him an attitude leading to evil action.

The insidious form of seduction places the hazardous snare in such a way that the victim is entrapped without being aware of the evil intent of the seducer. The tempter does not wish to become externally involved in the matter in order to escape accusation of evil or recognition as a servant of evil. Such covert enticement to evil is in no way to be judged more leniently than the overt efforts in which the tempter makes no effort to conceal his purpose. The obligation of reparation is the same in both instances.

Seduction is a mortal sin according to its nature (*ex genere suo*). In fact, it is a twofold sin, one violating the virtue of charity, the other violating the particular virtue which one induces others to violate. The accusation in the confessional must include mention of both sins, the sin of seduction and also the mortal sin which one has induced or sought to induce another to commit. The success or lack of success in the evil design does not alter the guilt of the tempter, but may be very significant in the matter of the reparation which is demanded for the serious temporal or eternal damage inflicted by the successful seduction.

To entice others to commit venial sin is a grave sin in some instances. Such should be the case if one were to induce others to commit venial sin who in virtue of their station are particularly obliged to shun venial sin— or if the tempter sees that his act leading another to venial sin will eventually result in mortal sin—or in any instance when the act is a manifestation of hatred or very patent indifference to the salvation of others.

Usually tempting others is due to sinful self-interest or to a craving for companionship in attitudes and actions. The deliberate effort to pervert someone spiritually, to tear him away from God is, however, the great sin of diabolical seduction (cf. Jn 8:44: The devil "was a murderer from the beginning."). It is grave in all its kind (*ex toto genere suo*).

The Lord is stirred to wrath by this sin. Like a lioness whose cubs have been attacked, He turns on seducers with great anger: "Whoever causes one of these little ones who believe in me to sin it were better for him to have a great millstone hung around his neck and to be drowned in the depths of the sea" (Mt 18:6). The meaning is: "It would be a good fortune for him to suffer the most gruesome death in order to avoid incurring so great a guilt."[135]

II. SCANDAL

1. *The General Concept*

In Scripture and tradition seduction is included in the concept of scandal which in turn comprises many things.[136] In a very broad sense scandal is the occasion of the fall into sin, a block or trap which causes one to stumble or fall. Whereas in the instance of seduction the trap is laid with evil intent, this does not hold for scandal in the strict sense (*scandalum indirectum*) although the evil is in some way permitted. Between seduction and indirect scandal there is the same distinction as between deliberate murder and careless homicide, though of course on a different level of justice. Scandal and seduction deal with spiritual loss or hurt.

Scandal is any deliberate act which is calculated to become a hazard or snare for another—taking him as he actually is—on his way to salvation. Corresponding to the giving of scandal (*scandalum activum*) is the taking of scandal (*scandalum passivum*). Taking scandal, stumbling, may be due to a snare sinfully laid (*scandalum datum et acceptum*), or, for that matter, even to a good act another has performed, or to an act which is at least subjectively good (*scandalum mere acceptum*).

We must distinguish between "scandal" and shock or anger." By comparison to real scandal this shock is essentially rather superficial. Scandal in the strict sense of the term, however, may of course accompany the act. The act which shocks and angers others may be the occasion of the sin of anger or cause a violation of charity.

Our English term *scandal* does not fully convey the hazard to spiritual good implied in the theological usage of the term. Quite frequently it rather indicates the shocking nature of a sin which is so reprehensible as to

affect the sensibilities of others. The very publicity accompanying the commission of certain sins may be the occasion of unjust or uncharitable
gossip. And the danger of scandal in the sense of occasion for disrespect
for religion is ever present.

2. The Biblical Use of the Term

The word *scandal* (*skándalon*) in the bible differs considerably from
the word as employed in moral theology. It is not restricted to actions
which manifest a lack of responsibility for the salvation of one's neighbor
and which place a culpable occasion of sin in his path. Often the inspired
writer uses the word *scandal* to characterize anything which can in any
way prove an occasion of another's sin. It includes the very thing which
summons him to decision and thereby either must lead to the ascent to the
good or to the descent into evil. Christ Himself, according to the prophecy
of Simeon, is the great scandal: "This child is destined for the fall and for
the rise of many in Israel, and for a sign that shall be contradicted." He is
the sign which occasions the contradiction through which the hearts of
many (not merely of the good, but also of the bad) shall be revealed (Lk
2:34f.). He is "a stumbling-stone and rock of scandal" (Rom 9:33; cf. Is
8:14; 28:16; 1 Pt 2:6f.; Mt 21:44).

By His very nature and mission, Christ would have to become a
"scandal" to the sinful world, the self-righteous Pharisees, and His own
people with their mundane messianic aspirations. His work with its
completion in the mission of the Holy Spirit would have to establish
clearly that sin in the world is rebellion against God and not merely
"disorder" or "misconception" (Jn 16:8f.). Obviously the Lord does not
attempt to avoid the clash. To the timorous objection of the disciples He
gives a very tart response: "Then his disciples came up and said to him,
'Dost thou know that the Pharisees have taken offense at hearing this
saying?' But he answered and said, 'Every plant that my heavenly Father
has not planted will be rooted up. Let them alone; blind guides they are
of blind men'" (Mt 15:12ff.). The Pharisees take umbrage at Christ
because they are blind. Christ must open their eyes whether the result will
be a still greater hardening in sin or their conversion. Their conversion, of
course, is the purpose of the "scandal" of Christ.

After His great Eucharistic promise Christ evidently prefers that even
His disciples should be scandalized rather than that He should compromise

His word of truth even slightly. He is just as unwilling to spare His own disciples the scandal of the Cross. Had He not prepared them for the test with all His loving patience? Though the prophecies of the passion are deferred to the later part of His public life, they are still in time to prepare the Apostles for Good Friday so that any defect of confidence could have been avoided. Peter even goes so far as to raise objection, spiritually hazardous, to the very mention of the coming passion. He makes himself a "scandal," a seducer of the Lord Himself (Mt 16:22f.).

Christ sets forth the scandal of His teaching, His person, and His Cross not that it be the occasion of another's fall, but that the sharp antithesis of His "scandal" might disturb man in his shameful perversion. The incipient shock should bring about a realization of the malice of certain thoughts and attitudes and make possible a total conversion to God. With this in mind we can explain the words of Christ, "Blessed are they who shall not be scandalized in me." The interpretation is: Blessed are they who permit themselves to be inwardly disturbed by the salutary shock of the scandal of My origin, My doctrine, and My passion so that their false ideals are destroyed and their eyes are opened to the saving truth.

Most strikingly did Christ place the great scandal of His claim to divinity before the high priest. He formulated His response with such clarity that it must have seemed to Caiphas as deliberately designed to invite condemnation. Christ fashioned this scandal in all sharpness so that it was impossible for the Great Council and all future generations to evade the decision, so that ultimately the faith of the ages could be based specifically on this "scandal" of His response.

As the Lord before them, so the Apostles in no way soft-pedaled the scandal of the Gospel, the scandal of the Cross—quite contrary to the attitude of the Gnosis.[137] Inexorably, Paul places in the very center of his preaching the doctrine of the Cross of Christ which was "to the Jews indeed a stumbling-block and to the Gentiles foolishness." He knows that Christ crucified is "the power of God and the wisdom of God" to those who are called (1 Cor 1:23f.; 2:2). Since the very heart of his preaching is the doctrine of the death of the true Son of God on the Cross, Paul must confront men with a decision on this very point without the slightest compromise or toning down of the "scandal."

Paul, too, proceeds with great caution and prudence in this weighty problem and unfolds his teaching progressively. He wishes to allow both Jew and Gentile converts ample time to mature so that they might more easily appreciate certain difficult insights. Thus he allows time for adjustment to the new. Accordingly, this great emancipator from Old Testament Law has his disciple Timothy circumcised to facilitate the acceptance of the Gospel by the Jews who might otherwise prejudicially close their hearts to his preaching. In his own inner manner of life he becomes all things to all men. "I have become to the Jews a Jew that I might gain the Jews: to those under the Law, as one under the law . . . that I might gain those under the Law. . . . To the weak I became weak, that I might gain the weak. I became all things to all men, that I might save all" (1 Cor 9:20ff.).

He admonishes the Roman Christians to avoid scandalizing those converts, still weak in the faith, who would be troubled by a flippant attitude toward the dietary prescriptions of the Old Testament (Rom 14 and 15). He reckons himself among the strong who consider no food unclean (Rom 14:14). Yet the determining point cannot be such knowledge and realization; it is rather the loving consideration for the salvation of the weak, of one's neighbor. No one may live to please himself, but he must take into consideration the frailty of others (Rom 15:1). One must be prepared to renounce the foods proscribed by the dietary and ritual laws of the Old Testament, even though it is no longer in force, rather than give a brother an occasion to sin. "Let us no longer judge one another, but rather judge this, that you should not put a stumbling-block or a hindrance in your brother's way" (Rom 14:13).

The Apostle, likewise, admonishes the Corinthians to avoid making their certain conviction that the idols are false and non-existent a source of confusion and distress to uninformed consciences, even to the extent of leading them to commit sin. Obviously the idols are nonentities. Therefore one could lawfully and with thanksgiving to the true God eat the meat first offered to the idols and then sold in the public market. But all these considerations must yield to the one supreme concern: one may not permit his conduct to become an occasion of sin to his neighbor. The following splendid passage clearly conveys the sentiments of Paul: "If food scandalizes my brother, I will eat flesh no more forever, lest I scandalize my brother" (1 Cor 8:13).

The Christian must be prepared, therefore, to restrict his freedom of action considerably should he discover that an act good in itself has become the occasion of spiritual ruin for others. In fact no action is altogether correct if one does not take into loving consideration the effect it might have on one's neighbor. "Let no one seek his own interests, but those of his neighbor" (1 Cor 10:24).

In the noted Antiochian incident St. Paul confronted St. Peter in an unequivocal defense of the new freedom from the ritual law of the Old Testament. It is clear that the saint no longer considered the law binding even though disregard for it might prove a serious scandal for the Judaizers (Gal. 2:11ff.). Peter had followed his course of action to avoid scandalizing the Jewish Christians. For this reason, not because of human respect and surely not because of any error in principle, he no longer ate at table with the Gentile Christians. This is not to deny that Peter had improperly appraised the effect of his own example which led the Judaizers to interpret an unbreakable rule out of his conduct. The result could only be that the purity of the Gospel was imperiled and the whole mission among the pagans placed in the gravest jeopardy. Thus was Paul constrained to demand of Peter that he should risk the scandal which the Jewish Christians might take because of the infractions of the obsolete Mosaic Law. This he did in order to preserve all the Christians from a far greater evil; namely, the grave danger of error in decisive questions of the Christian faith.[138]

3. Our Dispositions and the Various Species of Scandal

The sin of scandal has its roots in an inner attitude of unconcern for the salvation of others. The one who gives scandal in the worst sense of that term ignores the effect of his act on the salvation of his neighbor for the simple reason that he is not animated with supernatural love for his fellow man. Such a case is entirely different from that of the inculpable "giver of scandal." Despite all his love for his fellows it is still possible that he fails to note the circumstance of this effect of his act or appraises it falsely. In such an instance there is no sin of scandal. In the former case, however, each and every act takes on the malice of the evil disposition according to its culpability. Rarely is anyone so completely wrapped in himself that he does not even perceive the unwholesome effect of his conduct on others. The fact that one still gives scandal despite all this arises from motives of self-profit, from concern for unrestrained freedom of personal action, or from a self-indulgence which outweighs any concern for others.

The *foreseen effect* on the salvation of our neighbor is an essential element of the situation. The action can for various reasons produce a damaging or at least a dangerous effect on our neighbor. This may arise from the malice inherent in the act or from the fact that it is readily misconstrued as evil. On the other hand the evil may be due largely either to the frailty of others or, perchance, to their malicious disposition.

a. Scandal of Misconduct and Spiritual Mediocrity

The most hazardous and widespread scandal is the evil deed itself, the scandal of evil example, which is particularly enticing if found in one loved or one vested with authority or prestige. Its very presence and its identification with the milieu imparts to it a tremendous dynamic power of moral corruption. Even those who merely associate with the evil intensify this power and therefore in some way give scandal. The scandal is all the greater and more sinful, the more those who give bad example are in a position of social influence which contributes to the evil effect of their bad conduct. Though scandal arises only from external evil acts which are in some way within the view or knowledge of others, even purely internal sins imply a diminution of spiritual energies in the Mystical Body. Thus these, also, exercise a deleterious effect on others and pave the way for the actual scandal which flows from external sins.

Only the scandal which offers a particular and special danger must be confessed specifically in the sacrament of penance. The scandal involved in the danger inherent in all sin is implicitly confessed with the sin itself. A merely legalistic morality might readily fix its whole attention on the easily discernible scandal of the evil deed, while it slights or ignores that other scandal, no less perilous, given by countless Christians and entire Christian communities who have placed their light under a bushel and have falsified the witness of the Gospel through a self-satisfied spiritual mediocrity. The faithful who wish to examine their conscience in the mirror of the Gospel do not rest satisfied with mere inquiry into the scandal which they may give on the one hand, or take on the other.

This latter is the scandal of a specific legal minimalism with regard to the great commandment of love of God and love of neighbor. And concomitant with it is a disregard for the transparent piety of the Gospels because of a preference for saccharine devotional forms, for "edifying" literature and for the dripping "objects of devotion" which pass for religious art. To this is added an itching avidity for private revelation and prophecy, a nearly superstitious use of the sacramentals, and a meticulous observance of externals even in things most sacred.

This is the great scandal of a formalistic liturgy, inaccessible to humble folk, a leveling of the structure of piety and formation of the spiritual life. Every attempt to revitalize pastoral guidance is viewed with suspicion and made the object of complaint. And what shall we say of the salvation-egoism of so many "pious" persons who think only of their own souls and their own heaven, but not of the kingdom and dominion of God? Does not at times our excessive fear of giving scandal, if we oppose such things, choke the joy of faith in many converts, create in them the sense of musty narrowness, and finally make unbelievers and men of other faiths scorn the Church and turn against her "in good conscience?"

Pius XII stressed the point with very great emphasis in the following passage: "The worst obstacle to our efforts is probably not the express opposition of the enemies of God and immortal souls. It is rather the indifference, the unconcern, and the ironical sense of superiority on the part of those who consider themselves Christians and convinced practicing Catholics. To open their eyes, to make them realize the gravity of the evil and their own responsibility is not the least of our tasks."[139]

In all our forthrightness in facing up to this great and spiritually damaging scandal, we must never lose sight of the following significant point: we may never criticize the Church as though we were remote from her, absolutely aloof from any involvement in this scandal. Such an attitude would itself be the supreme scandal of Pharisaism. We must indeed be truthful; for God and His Church need no false apologetic. But the unimpeachable truth must begin with ourselves. Moreover, our stress of the subversive forms of scandal should not blind us to the hidden and visible holiness of the Church. To cite one example, we do not deny that the apostasy of vast masses of working people has a basis in the scandal of a "liturgy" and pastoral practice which is not virile and manly, but mediocre and commonplace, spiritless and dull. But this is a far cry from totally excusing all workers estranged from the Church—or ourselves—as being free from fault in this matter. There were always in the Church earnest protagonists of the social apostolate. There were always legitimate approaches and openings to the liturgy within reach of the workers and more acceptable to them. Nor was true and exemplary piety ever absent. We should not be carried to the extreme of considering ourselves as hopeless and helpless victims of this scandal-giving and scandal-taking. The

Church through her directives, through her teaching and her saints points the way by which we can effectively counteract this scandal.[140]

b. The Scandal of the Weak

Under certain circumstances serious scandal can also be given through actions which, apart from their effect on others, are good or indifferent. However, because of the appearance of evil which they are liable to create in special situations, they may readily disturb a weak conscience. Or they can give a spiritually less resolute individual an excuse for a specious justification of similar actions of his own, which, though not bad in themselves, may prove very dangerous. In this instance the external basis for taking scandal rests immediately on the moral weakness and labile character of one's neighbor. This is what we mean by the term *scandal of the weak* (*scandalum pusillorum*). But it is also to be ascribed to the lack of insight into the realities of the situation on the part of the "weak" individual, to a perceptibility that varies considerably in individuals. And as to the giving of scandal, the sinfulness is due to a lack of concern and consideration for the moral frailty of one's neighbor. St. Paul treats of such cases in chapters eight and nine of the First Letter to the Corinthians, and in the fourteenth and fifteenth chapters of the Letter to the Romans.

It is a serious duty to take into consideration the weakness of another insofar as this redounds to the good of his soul and is within the bounds of sound reason. However, we may not permit this concern for the frailty of others to divert us to a mode of action which in the long run would prove even more hazardous (cf. Gal 2). Nor may consideration for human frailty in others be carried to the extreme of jeopardizing our capacity for essential decision and joyful effort for the kingdom of God. Ordinarily concern for others does not oblige us to risk seriously a great personal loss, unless it is clearly established that one's neighbor is really in great peril.

Some hold that all obligation toward the spiritually weaker brother ceases once he has received a clearly presented correction and a realistic explanation of the matter. If he should still persist in taking scandal, he is himself at fault and the evil is his own responsibility. *Scandalum pusillorum* is converted into *scandalum pharisaicum*. He takes scandal hypocritically and no further consideration need be given him. Surely, by contrast to St. Paul's procedure, this solution of the problem of the scandal of the weak seems too simple and easy. It does not allow for the psychology of limited value appreciation. It also overestimates the power of the external word in relation to the force of the actual situation and especially individual or social prejudice. But surely in every instance this principle is always valid: when serious reasons forbid the omission of an act which can prove an occasion of sin to others because of their spiritual weakness, ordinarily at least a clear explanation of the act and its justification must be given to those who are spiritually imperiled.

In the light of the principle enunciated thus far, we must solve the following problems and particular cases. They offer the advantage of illustrating the general axiom but—we must caution the reader—do not furnish a facile and final solution. Every new situation must draw from the spirit of the Gospel its own proper solution based on openness to the concrete realities.[141]

Without a proportionately serious reason one may not request another to do an act which, though not in itself sinful, *would not* be performed without subjective guilt on his part. The act itself is not sinful; but the individual of whom we ask it is morally so weak, or his conscience is so erroneous, that it is evident beforehand that he will not be free from subjective guilt if he complies. Hence, one is not allowed under ordinary conditions to require an oath from one who, we fear, will perjure himself if he complies. Nor is one permitted to ask a priest to administer the sacraments to him if he prudently may assume that in all probability they will be administered sacrilegiously.

There is an essential distinction between being the occasion of an added sin flowing from an existing state of mortal sin and being the occasion of the loss of grace and the divine life by one who is in the state of grace, even though he may be weak. Merely to permit a sinful act, although one could prevent it by removing the occasion (for which one is not responsible in the first place), is not strictly and unqualifiedly on the level of positive scandal. One is permitted to allow the commission of the sin if the removal of the occasion is very difficult, or if non-interference regarding this single sin of another might result in emancipating the individual from the state of sin itself. Thus parents would be allowed to leave money lying openly in the home in the presence of a child who has repeatedly stolen money or is under grave suspicion of having done so. The motive would be to bring matters to a head with the purpose of thoroughly correcting the errant youngster. The same is permitted in regard to an unknown thief, if the primary intention is to expose him and thus safeguard one's own possessions. But no one is permitted to place an occasion or set up a test as a positive inducement to sin, for this is equivalent to direct temptation or seduction. Such a procedure might be an insidious trap for the innocent and—what is still worse—actually lead innocent individuals into entirely new sins.

One is never permitted to make use of positive means to lead others into any sin, not even into a lesser sin, with the purpose of deterring or dissuading them from committing a greater sin. However, merely to permit the commission of a lesser sin in order to prevent a greater sin is not the sin of scandal. In fact, we go so far as to hold that one would be allowed to reveal openly that he is prepared to permit the act externally. However, the sole motive must be the prevention of the greater sin. And tolerating this lesser evil must be the sole means of preventing the more heinous offence! This is the sense in which we understand those authors who hold that one is permitted to advise a lesser sin in some instances as means of preventing a greater sin. The actual object of such advice is, therefore, not the lesser sin itself—for one may never advise the commission of any sin—but the forceful admonition that one should at least shun the greater sin.

One can and in fact one must frequently omit purely positively-prescribed actions because of consideration for the moral frailty and religious sensibility of others. However, one is never permitted to carry the omission to such an extreme that it would appear to imply that we questioned the Church's authority or departed from the definite unequivocal confession of the faith; for this would indeed be one of the greatest of scandals. Works which are merely counseled we must under similar conditions at least postpone if we can hope to carry them out later without scandal to others. Even entry into religion or the priesthood might allowably be postponed in order to avoid a grave scandal to those who are spiritually weak. But still it could scarcely ever occur that one could stave off grave scandal to some individual only by means of renunciation of a spiritual vocation and at the same time lead him to salvation. Therefore it would be something exceedingly rare that this should be a valid reason for permitting, much less requiring, anyone to relinquish a vocation so important to the kingdom of God.

Representatives of the Church must rather forego a temporal advantage than expose others to danger of incurring a baneful prejudice against the faith and the Church. A cleric must be willing to yield one or other honorarium or stole fee rightly his due rather than repel the spiritually weak by an appearance of greed. The Church herself must be prepared rather to renounce temporal goods of vast extent (always within the realms of the possible and feasible) rather than permit large groups of men to be estranged from her. Naturally such renunciation must be based on the well-founded hope that the grave scandal will actually be averted.

A girl or a woman must be willing to give up many an enjoyment, many a dance, some unnecessary personal adornment, in fact even an occasional visit to church, if the renunciation should seem necessary or useful to preserve another from great temptation or to free him from such. If a girl should without good cause deliberately seek out the company of a man, even though she fully realizes that her presence is a source of grave temptation to him, she is guilty of a grave sin of scandal. This holds true even though she would be able to claim in her defense that she always dresses modestly, that she conducts herself properly, that she permits no sinful liberties; for even the interior sins which her very presence incites destroy the state of grace and involve another in spiritual ruin.

The final instances of scandal are here described to illustrate the point that it may be difficult, and perhaps well-nigh impossible, to determine with finality and in purely legal fashion what actually is and what is not scandal in concrete circumstances.

Two sisters are to wed in a double ceremony. It is, let us say, the custom in their parish for the bride to leave her corsage of white lilies at the feet of the statue of Our Lady. Because one of the sisters has had an illegitimate child the pastor forbids her to accompany her sister to the statue. She is to take her bouquet with her out of the church. What some people, but not the pastor, know is that the other sister had obtained an abortion. The pastor undoubtedly intends by his action to uphold premarital chastity. But does he succeed? Quite the contrary! Not only is the unhappy bride who is already a mother ridiculed by the worldly-wise as too stupid to prevent her exposure, but she is now publicly humiliated by her pastor for her sin. The difficulty is: does this humiliation appear as a sign of disapproval of sin or perhaps only as a reason to avoid getting caught in sin? In other words, was the sin of the girl, which was already public, truly scandal, and, if it was, does the form of reproof truly correct it or rather only beget worse scandal?

Possibly a hundred years ago the very same procedure would have had a truly wholesome effect. At that time no one so much as thought of abortion. The sanction placed on unwedded motherhood would have been accepted in the spirit of faith and contrition and might have proved a real deterrent for other girls, preventing them from yielding to any seduction or indulgence in sexual intercourse before marriage. But circumstances have changed, and with them the effects of certain actions otherwise good. One must constantly and carefully re-evaluate these things to determine well what is or what is not scandal.

Here is another example, but one concerned with the seeking of civil divorce. In some places there may be either no legal provision for separation or else the provisions are inadequate for the protection of rights. Sometimes also the legal separation of spouses is not the usual and best solution for the innocent party in an unfortunate marriage. Legal divorce may provide the only practicable or practiced solution.

Now the question is: should those who have obtained a civil divorce, no matter whether they are separated culpably or inculpably, be excluded from the sacraments until they have obtained the express permission of the diocesan ordinary to separate? To exclude such persons indiscriminately would likely create the impression in the public mind that the Church equates the civilly divorced who because of their faith in the indissolubility of marriage do not remarry with those who ignore the divine law and attempt remarriage during the lifetime of the previous legitimate spouse. The unintended consequence of such a practice would be to aid and abet remarriage by the civilly divorced and/or to embitter many against the Church. One might object that the "divorced" should humbly submit to the decision of the bishop and trustfully beg for re-admission to the sacraments. But this very type of objection ignores the essence of the giving of scandal: in view of the actual reaction of many of the faithful because of their difficulty in making "theological" distinctions, many do take scandal. Thus souls are placed in jeopardy, and many are brought to spiritual ruin. The sin of scandal in this instance lies in the fact that *under the given circumstances* the priest apparently has not sought that pastoral approach or method which is most effective in hindering the actual separation of persons who are validly married and, more especially, in hindering any subsequent attempts at remarriage.

A quite different practice, followed in many places, would seem to have gratifying results. Church authorities demand that Catholic parties who believe they have serious reasons to institute legal proceedings for "divorce" or who are the defendants in such suits first seek the counsel and direction of the episcopal authority. If this demand is made clear as to purpose and consequence and if petitions are handled expediently, the faithful can appreciate what is being done and why. They can also realize that, if one culpably fails to appeal to the episcopal authority before acting, he must later on humbly beg forgiveness for his culpable omission. This procedure would, as effectively as possible, erect a dam against any flood of hasty and unjustified separations and ward off the danger of remarriage. One should remember that it is especially the latter danger that should concern us today; it is so much the more serious and common.

In the same category with pastoral scandal is the practice of placing the occasional lapse into sin on a par with the deliberately habitual sin. Thus there are married people who actually live in accordance with the basic principles of responsible parentage in the sight of God, though they may occasionally fall into the sin of marital onanism due to human frailty. There are others who almost on principle misuse their marriage habitually. To place these two classes on an equal footing is a species of pastoral scandal. The consequence is that many become estranged from the sacrament of penance, and their will to wrestle earnestly (as they absolutely must) for responsible self-mastery is weakened. However, it should also be noted that possibly in certain regions where this misuse of marriage is relatively rare a procedure of this kind would hardly be a scandal.

In using the term *scandal* in these examples, it should be clearly understood that we do not imply any subjective guilt on the part of those responsible for the pastoral procedure. Obviously no one can render judgment in the matter of subjective guilt.

c. Scandal Due to Malice

Men who are concerned for the honor of God and the salvation of souls will seek to avoid, where it is easily possible, to give any occasion for sin. They will abstain even from good actions, which are not of obligation, rather than give evil men occasion to commit new sins. This attitude is particularly correct in that domain of human life where malice often conspires with frailty to lead men to sin. But the Christian must also realize that a truly Christian life itself is necessarily a stumbling block to a world which is hostile to God. The Holy in Person, Jesus Christ, by His very holiness most aroused and unmasked the malice of men. Their decision against Him opened an abyss of malice which men could never have conceived had He not come. "If I had not come and spoken to them, they would have no sin" (Jn 15:22). And the disciples of Jesus suffer the same fate. The hostility of Satan's world never fails to spew forth in wrath whenever aroused and challenged by the good deeds and holiness of Jesus' disciples. But one may never quail before this scandal. The Christian must face it resolutely (cf. Wis 2:10ff.).

The vigorous promulgation of the Gospel and the law of love included in the good tidings of salvation redounds to the deeper damnation of those who close their eyes to the light. But it is a great boon for all the undecided whose superficial mode of existence makes them waver: for them the Gospel preaching is a salutary scandal. It invites them with good tidings; it places them entirely under its judgment and forces them to decide for the good. As the biblical teaching on scandal shows, this challenge plays a tremendously decisive role in the divine plan of salvation. Christ Himself is in this sense the "great scandal"—and with Him the life of His disciples and the preaching of the Apostles. This jolt is effective in the crisis—the necessary crisis—to effect the healing of man in his illness.

From this we glean the basic pastoral principle for the preaching of the divine truths and for the whole pastoral activity. No one charged with the care of souls, and no lay apostle concerned with men's acceptance of the Gospel may ever overlook the essential alternative in decision; no apostle dare slight the great antithesis—the life-giving death of the beloved Son on the Cross—with which the plan of God confronts the "wisdom of this world." Gospel preaching and every apostolate must ultimately face man with a decision and force him to a clear *yes* or *no*. To remove the sting from the Gospel, to make it "acceptable" at all cost, is only to rob it of its force.

It is also important to bear in mind that in the preaching of the Gospel and the entire effort for the salvation of others we are cautioned against placing needless obstacles in their path. We must avoid confronting men with decisions at the inappropriate moment or in relation to accidentals. Such imprudent procedure might make us responsible if they should stumble and fall. The fault of our zeal would pervert the scandal of the Gospel into a scandal perilous to salvation. Above all, one is not permitted to grant individual demands a place of preference to the Gospel itself. Many requirements which the weak though willing hearers cannot now bear (cf. Jn 16:12) must await more mature knowledge. But at any cost not the slightest point of truth may be repudiated. Decision must be directed to the central and incommutable truth of the Gospel, to the very heart of the law of grace.

Perhaps the greatest scandal of all, the most hazardous for the world, is the inadequacy of the Christian testimony. We lack that full and complete clarity and decisiveness which is the salutary scandal of holiness and of total submission to the entire law of grace. As the holy people of God we must bear witness to the love of God and to the judgment of the world which is hostile to Him.

4. *Taking Scandal*

a. Sinful Taking of Scandal

Taking scandal in the strict sense of moral theology means the deliberate use of another's conduct, be it good or bad, as occasion for one's own sin. The action of another is only the occasion for sin. Even if it be sinful, it does not go beyond occasion or attraction. The efficient cause of taking scandal is always one's own free will. In consequence, the one who takes scandal is not excused on the plea that he is merely following his fellow man or even that everybody else is doing the very same thing.

A current example of scandal-taking of this kind is the "justified" attitude of some Catholics toward contraceptive birth control in married life, despite the clear moral instruction of the Church. Persuasive is the influence of public opinion (spread through conversation at work and at leisure, idealized by the idols of films and television, and expressly publicized and defended in the popular press and other popular literature, not excluding some religious journals). The "Joneses" create a very persuasive scandal that tends to paralyze man's sense of values. This influence is so effective that we hesitate to say, without qualification, that everyone who has received the clear and plain teaching of the Church is guilty of grave sin if he does not resist this public scandal.[142]

The most sinful form of scandal-taking, it might be added, is that of the world hostile to God; for its hatred flows quickly at the very thought and sight of good.

b. Hazardous but Not Sinful Scandal-taking

It often happens that men (particularly the young) look upon the perverted conduct of others as good and worthy of imitation because of the great confidence they have in the moral goodness of the one whom they admire. Their trust in the giver of scandal leads to inculpable imitation. But even should the scandal-taking in such instances be free from (formal) sin, it creates a very dangerous spiritual situation. It may seriously thwart the sound moral-religious development of the one who innocently takes such "scandal." But the fault is entirely on the part of the one responsible for the bad example.

At times it is most difficult to discern the true nature of the scandal. Often what is actually sinful taking of scandal is scarcely distinguishable from the merely hazardous. Where the greater fault lies is known only to God. But the warning of the Christ who shall judge rings in our ears: "Woe to the world because of scandal!" (Mt 18:7).

c. Salutary Scandal-Taking

The wholesome pain which mounts to incensed outrage is a morally proper response to the sin of others, provided of course that it be proportionate to the malice of the sin. If such scandal is morally correct— assuming that it is directed against the sin and not against the sinner—it will necessarily cry out for more resolute determination in the war against evil.

To the challenge of salutary scandal-giving and also to actual sinful scandal itself, there should be the response of a fruitfully corrective "taking of scandal." In this we must understand that there are two concepts of "scandal-taking." The goal of the divine permissive will permitting "scandals"—"It must needs be that scandals come" (Mt 18:7)— is the testing and confirming of the good man, challenging him with a summons to resolute and determined resistance to sin. But the complementary goal is also to stir the lax to decision and, of course, also to unmask the wicked and indolent.

5. Common Areas of Scandal

The few paragraphs we here add on certain areas in which scandal is common are specifically intended to conform to the traditional treatment in moral theology. Undoubtedly there is good reason for special stress in these areas, but it would be a fatal error to overlook the risk of scandal possible in other areas such as industry and social relations. Scandal may be as great and as perilous to man's salvation in these latter cases, as it is in those we are now to take up. The difference lies in this: scandal as we treat it in these paragraphs is in some measure intentional, the influence affecting others is in some way deliberate, even though not necessarily in the sense of direct seduction.

a. Fashions

1) *Moderation and Excess in Matters of Fashion.* Basically and in principle there is no objection to moderate beauty culture for women. God created in the two sexes the complementary desire to please. Women especially possess the wholesome desire of attractive cultivation of appearance. But there is a moral obligation to avoid all excess. A woman who neglects the care of her person, who is slovenly and untidy, can become a scandal to men. Women and girls are not forbidden to cultivate their beauty in rational accordance with their position and traditions, provided they avoid extravagance. Also in accord with reasonable custom they are even permitted to make use of the usual artificial aids (powder, lipstick, rouge, dyed or false hair, etc.). Of course one is tempted to ask: is not a natural, "unaffected" beauty far more refreshing?

In addition to the restraint and moderation which must be observed, the determining element in this matter is the motive animating the woman: does she want to please her husband or is she concerned with attracting other men? Does a girl adorn herself because of vanity? Is she bent upon a good and honorable marriage? Has she some frivolous flirtation in mind?

In judging the gravity of sins in this area we note that everything immoderate, surprising, or extravagant readily creates scandal and is usually an occasion of temptation for oneself and others. It is a grave or slight sin according to the motive and the scandal. One should note that the totally novel and unusual has a particularly luring effect. Nevertheless, if there is no indecency or impropriety but merely something immoderate and surprising, the doubtful cases are not to be judged as gravely sinful.

2) *Indecency in dress* is mortal sin as such (*ex genere suo*) because of the scandal which it creates. In our moral judgment on this point we should not overlook the danger incurred by the individual of undermining her own sense of shame and the resulting increase in the moral hazard of temptations. But it is also good to bear in mind that we cannot judge what is slightly or seriously improper in individuals with any mathemati-

cal standard assuring a universally valid norm for all times and places. The latest modes, by the very fact that they are unusual, readily have an improper and exciting effect, whereas those of long standing appear less enticing even though they may offend the tender sense of modesty no less. Low-cut, too-short, and diaphanous clothing, not to mention scant bathing attire on open beaches, in every case gives great scandal and leads to many interior and exterior sins. In judging the danger one is cautioned, on the one hand, against too great a leniency and, on the other, against any hasty accusation of mortal sin in individual instances as long as the scandal is not evident.

In instances in which the styles are not in themselves immoral or at least not seriously evil, the intention and attitude of mind constitutes perhaps the greatest danger. Therefore the confessor should not be quick to refuse absolution to a penitent merely because of the type of dress she wears. However, the commission of external sins in conjunction with indecent dress might justify a more severe verdict, condemning the styles as a source of the evil. Above all, we must insist that women at divine services, at the reception of the sacraments, or at Catholic gatherings appear in exemplary and becoming garb. But even at the reception of the sacraments the priest should not indulge in scolding those who appear in less-appropriate dress, much less deny them the sacraments, unless the scandal is patent and shocking. Only the most obviously scandalous dress could ever justify sending a woman from the church after she has come for Sunday Mass. The preacher surely cannot fail to say a word occasionally against indecent dress. But he too should be most cautious in his statements. It is no easy matter to state with exact precision where immodesty begins or where it becomes a mortal sin. Above all he should avoid crude and vivid forms of criticism which also are very likely to offend against modesty.

Even children can be taught to avoid violation of modesty in dress. Their clothing should be such that it in no way violates the sense of modesty but rather safeguards it. Parents can be guilty of grave scandal in this matter, for they can too easily cultivate vanity in their children, whose very innocence leaves them easy prey for the sensual and seductive.

b. Degenerate Art

Art in its degenerate forms can surround sin with the splendor of the beautiful and thus make it doubly seductive. And yet genuine art can also present the noble beauty of the nude human body in a way that the image does not become a temptation to sin for the normal man. It is the manner and mode of presentation of the nude or the draped body which is the source of scandal. Depicting the intimacy of love in vivid colors is calculated to incite passion and destroy reverence. It is no easy task even for a genuine artist to paint such themes without arousing temptations in many beholders. With all this in mind we must form the judgment regarding the sin, mortal or venial, involved in the production, exposition, and the sale of improper pictures and statues.

More concretely and specifically, we note that expositions or displays of art often offer a broad selection of works varying much in artistic merit and moral inoffensiveness. There may be noble and elevating examples of the finest art mingling with dubious nudes and actual pornography, not to speak of blasphemous conceptions of religious themes, all on the same display. To visit galleries or expositions of this kind is usually considered a proximate occasion of sin. Often one's presence may be a scandal to others. For this reason such places should be avoided. Should one, however, have a sound reason to visit them (as is the case for artists and art students) he is obliged to seek to make the proximate occasion a remote one by use of the usual necessary means to this end: prayer, renewal of good intention, caution in viewing the works themselves.

Degenerate art is particularly scandalous in our present-day movies. Since the scandal is public, the war against it must also be waged with concerted effort in the public forum. If these efforts are to be effective, they must stress the positive; especially should good films be encouraged and good movie houses patronized, at least to the extent that they make the better film offerings available. A substitute in wholesome entertainment must be found for the seductive and objectionable film. If we bear in mind that films may be objectionable in many other ways besides the incitement to lust, that some films simply are not intended for children or adolescents, we cannot fail to realize that the duty of parents and other guides of youth to supervise the movie fare of their children or charges is serious indeed. It would be a great boon if responsible Christian men should come to greater influence in the entire area of this influential medium of instruction and entertainment, from production to final screening. Meanwhile efforts should be made to increase Christian influence in the production, distribution, and showing of films to the end that baneful motion pictures be excluded. It has been suggested likewise that, as new theaters are built or as they change hands, men with a true social consciousness be urged to assume ownership or management with the same purpose in mind.[143]

c. Smut and Filth in Literature

Today's adults and adolescents are being inundated with a veritable flood of pornographic books, papers, magazines, and pictures. More than a scandal to the weak, the smut industry is a systematic commercial effort to seduce and pervert anyone who will pay the publisher's price. It is primarily a callous and vicious attack on human frailty which succumbs only too readily and willingly to the lure of sex. Offal in print is obviously lucrative. But the harm to souls, especially the souls of youth, is beyond all calculation. Every single individual must put forth every effort to counteract this evil as best he can. In its own evident interest the state has the obligation, as a protector of youth, to intervene through effective legislation. We concede that the problem is not an easy one. It is to reconcile the restriction of an evil press and vile literature with the essential and unrestricted freedom of the legitimate press. Above all, ways and means must be found to shut off the ceaseless flow of sewage from so many hidden fountains of defilement.

The individual and also the ecclesiastical hierarchy without an organized front of defense are rather helpless in the war against smut and filth. For this reason we find in this very area a highly important program for Catholic Action: a constant war against the publishers and peddlers through a clear perception of objectives, education of the masses (for example, in the art of effective protest lodged with editors, directors, publishers, sales and news agencies), introduction of legislative proposals, and above all, positive encouragement of a good press. The latter should not be restricted to the purely religious realm but made to attract even the religiously lukewarm. Encouragement must go far beyond the press in the sense of newspaper and magazine. We must promote the finest and noblest "illustrateds" (not excluding the "comic books"), news and bookstores and the establishment of good popular libraries; for we cannot hesitate in any way to explore and exploit all the modern possibilities for the dissemination of good and wholesome literature.

Bookstores are not permitted to offer immoral literature for public sale. In fact such action to a very large extent should be legally interdicted.

Moreover, one may sell only to those who, we may reasonably presume, have the right to purchase the literature which we offer. Objectively speaking, evil books which have been borrowed are not to be returned to an owner who is in bad faith in his possession or use, except for a serious and good reason. There can be no claim in this instance that the right of property is violated, for in the eyes of God no one has the right to possess such things.

6. Reparation for Scandal

First Principle: One who has given scandal culpably must endeavor to the best of his power to repair the evil he has done. He must attempt to nullify or destroy its evil effects and make good any spiritual damage wrought.

Second Principle: One who has offended not only against charity by giving scandal but has also failed in the fulfillment of the special duties of his state of life or even against justice is obliged by the same virtue to make reparation. Particularly parents, teachers, and directors of souls must as far as possible make good the damage wrought by their scandal. The obligation arises from their office or state. One who has led another into sin through threat or fear of violence or through insidious deception is bound in justice to restitution for the damage he has caused.

Third Principle: One who has given scandal publicly must make public restitution insofar as this is possible.

Fourth Principle: If complete restitution is outside the realm of possibility, the obligation to restitution by means of good example, prayer, and good works is all the more urgent and pressing to expiate the sins of those who have been misled through scandal.

The *seducer,* as far as in him lies, must attempt to exert direct influence for good upon the one whom he has misled, in order now to convert him. However, this is not always advisable because of the proximate danger that one may fall back into the old sins and lead one's neighbor more deeply astray. In such instances fervent prayer and special expiation is absolutely and unconditionally demanded. Often it is feasible to recommend the one who has been misled to the apostolic zeal of a third party.

Writers, politicians, artists, actors, theater owners, and others in similar positions who have given scandal should look to the very area where they have been active to make good the evil they have caused. Here they should find a rich and important area in which to work for good and thereby in some measure repair the evil they have done. It would be vain to hope for widespread results unless the individual himself first turned entirely to the good. To strive for his own conversion is his immediate duty arising from the obligation of reparation; a generous apostolate based on conversion is often the best form of reparation.

III. COMPLICITY IN THE SINS OF OTHERS

God has made us instruments and collaborators in the establishment of His kingdom of love. In brotherly fellowship we are to be witnesses to His love. And as such how can we permit ourselves to be misused as instruments of evil, as "accomplices" of the "world rulers of this darkness" (Eph 6:12)? And yet we all occasionally discover to our horror that our most exalted efforts sustained by the loftiest motives have served to lighten the task for others to carry out their nefarious designs!

What conclusions does Catholic moral theology draw from the exalted vocation of Christians and from the occasional tragic connection of their good actions with the machinations of the spirits of darkness? Must Christians withdraw from the world altogether, hold aloof from the industrial, social, cultural realms, remain as remote from the social order as possible, a small elect flock separated from the many, in order to be totally unblemished by the corruption of the great masses? If so, how could they bear witness in the midst of the world to the divine love and cooperate in the establishment of a fellowship of love reaching out to embrace all mankind? How is the word of the Lord to be applied in this context? "Let both grow together until the harvest; and at harvest time I will say to the reapers, Gather up first the weeds, and bind them in bundles to burn; but the wheat gather into my barn" (Mt 13:30). And what of the words of the Apostle who bade his followers "not to associate with the immoral—not meaning, of course, the immoral of this world, or the covetous, or the greedy, or idolators; otherwise you would have to leave the world" (1 Cor 5:9f.)? In the following pages we plan to treat first the concept and the moral quality of the various kinds of cooperation. Then we shall take up certain concrete problems to illustrate and apply these basic concepts.

1. *Principles Governing Cooperation*

Cooperation in the sin of another, in general, is any and every physical or moral assistance in the commission of a sinful action in union with others. In this sense the one who commands or directs, the one who seduces others to join, and the one who actually and immediately executes or carries out the work, all contribute significantly as cooperators. In this total context, even though the guilt of the various cooperators can be quite diverse in degree, the sin is still the same as to species. And the individual guilt is not lessened but rather increased by the very fact that many cooperate in the one same sinful project. The reason is evident. Cooperation in the sin also offends against love of neighbor insofar as cooperators encourage one another in the malice of their evil action or at least make the common sin possible. In the following pages we deal only with a specific kind of cooperation, namely, *cooperation in the execution* of a sinful deed: those who cooperate work with another who is *the principal,* who has already determined the course to be followed in the evil project.

This distinction is the basis of the essential differentiation between cooperation and scandal as such. Whereas scandal simply furnishes the occasion for another's sin, cooperation, as we treat it here, enters into the actual execution of a sinful action already determined. Naturally cooperation is not free from scandal insofar as one is readily confirmed in an evil design by the complicity of others and, through the very possibility of execution, is more determined to carry it out. There is of course the further possibility that a third party may take scandal in the strict sense of the term because of this very sin of cooperation. Where such scandal is not present, simple cooperation is *secundum naturam* less in conflict with the salvation of others than the scandal which is the occasion of an innocent's fall. We note also that the giver of scandal *in se* is not a cooperator in the full sense of the term because, unlike the cooperator, he is not involved in the actual commission of the deed and in its consequences. Thus it follows that guilty cooperation above all violates Christian love of self. As stressed above, this problem in all its complexity should not be viewed as purely individual or as confined to the narrow area of individual morality.

The highest aspect under which we study the avoidance of sinful cooperation is the duty of every Christian to assist in the external realization of the kingdom of God on earth. This obligation to spread the kingdom of God also embraces the duty of countermanding all jeopardy to God's honor and other's salvation.

a. Formal Cooperation

Basic to our entire appraisal of cooperation is the distinction between formal and merely material cooperation. Formal cooperation is every cooperation in the sin of another which by its inner purpose (*finis operis*) or deliberate intent (*finis operantis*) is characterized as complicity in the sin of another. The formal cooperator therefore places himself directly in the service of evil. Either through his own inner approval of the principal's sinful deed or through a cooperation which by its very nature is approval of the act he formally makes the act his own.

Formal cooperation is always sinful. We judge the degree of malice according to the malice of the sin in which one cooperates, according to the degree of one's actual cooperation, and according to the measure in which another's malice is confirmed. Especially great is the responsibility of the cooperator, if the execution of the evil deed would have been impossible without his cooperation.

Formal cooperation in the sins of others is always a violation of charity and likewise a specific offence against the virtue violated by the sinful deed which one has helped to commit. In sins of injustice formal cooperation bears with it the obligation of restitution *in solidum* with the principal agent (but secondarily and according to the degree of cooperation). This means that should the principal agent not make restitution, the cooperator would be obliged to furnish restitution in full; otherwise, he must merely provide his share according to the degree of his complicity.

b. Material Cooperation

Merely material cooperation is concerned with a good or at least with an indifferent act. The act, neither in itself (i.e., by its own inner purposiveness) nor by the intent of the agent, contributes to the sin of another, but is misused or misappropriated by the latter and is thus placed in the service of his sinful activity. It follows that ultimately there is in the act itself a perceptible possibility for misuse. The cooperator foresees with certainty or at least with probability that his act will be misused. If foresight is not the case, his action is not at all subject to any moral judgment regarding its misuse by another; for he cannot foresee this evil as arising from his own action which in itself was not directed to any evil end. (Had it been directed to an evil end, the cooperation would be formal.)

The presumption or the awareness that another will make evil use of one's action may arise from the special circumstances or from one's own unfortunate experience. Or others, perhaps even the evildoers themselves, may reveal the fact. The significance of the special circumstances creates a very knotty problem. At times they can be so shaped and fashioned that they pave the way to evil: an action indifferent in itself can be made to suit the very purpose of evil use. Hence circumstances can penetrate the structure of the action in such a way as to qualify it unequivocally for direct complicity in the sin of another. This is surely the case—no problem confronts us here—if the special circumstances are such that they make the action illicit, abstracting altogether from the evil intent of the other party.

A word of caution is in place. We must avoid any extreme position in this matter. If each and every circumstance, and even the mere foresight of the evil use, should make the action inwardly evil, then all distinction between material and formal cooperation would collapse.

Yet there is a great difference between one circumstance and another. Indeed the mere foreseeing of incidental evil effects is never so intimately bound up with the action, never so intimately enters into the action as does the sum total of circumstances which provoke or motivate the action and directly accompany it. A very controversial example taken from eighteenth-century moral theology should serve to illustrate this problem: a master charges his servant to help him climb in the boudoir window of his paramour or even to help him to break into a house for some evil purpose. The evil intent of the master is evident; it is obvious from all the circumstances. Now after a study of all the details of the case, some will argue: to break open a door or to help one through a window under special circumstances can be a work of love of neighbor (e.g., one could rescue sleeping children from a blazing home at night). In the case before us, however, this work which under other circumstances could be an heroic act of love is now totally perverted. But the actions themselves are not evil. What the servant does is therefore no more than material cooperation. In order to permit it there surely must be correspondingly serious reasons which in this instance must be very grave.

But it might be more to the point to reason as follows: the action in this case because of the circumstances of place and time, and above all because of the total absence of any morally good motivation, is so unequivocally determined as contributing to the sin of another that it can be conceived only as formal cooperation. It is not the abstract crashing of a door or the raising of a window. It is the concrete situation taken here and now. Breaking and entering the house *here and now* must be morally indifferent or morally good in order to be characterized as merely material cooperation in such an obvious instance of misuse for an evil purpose.

We hold that if an act is to be appraised as merely material cooperation, it must be such also in relation to the immediately determining circumstances, so that a clear-thinking man can, without wrestling with concepts or abstractions, simply say: "What I am doing is in itself good. I am doing it sincerely and with worthy motives. The perversion of my act is entirely due to human malice."

But he might have to arrive at the following conclusion: "I have no other reason to do this act. There is no other justification for it, except that it is demanded of me as a form of cooperation in another man's sin. In fact, under these circumstances I can think of no morally good purpose for which I should do it." In view of all this the man can no longer assume, "My good act is being perverted by the other man." Rather he must concede, "My act has no value at all except insofar as it contributes to the sin of another. And this is formal cooperation."

Let us stress one very significant point: the circumstance that one's act is in itself meaningful and justifiable is an important condition or presupposition for merely material cooperation. In taking this position, we abstract entirely from the question whether another perverts it or not: we hold that the act itself must be founded in right reason.

That an action materially contributes to an evil effect, which is to say that someone perverts our work to the service of sin, is a serious matter for our conscience. It is all the more serious if the act serves the evil purposes of another not merely remotely but also immediately and proximately. It is most serious if it should be the indispensable condition for the execution of that nefarious design.

First Principle: Love of self and love of neighbor (responsibility for the kingdom of God on earth) and the virtue which the principal agent purposes to violate oblige us, insofar as it is possible, to prevent our actions from being perverted to an evil end.

Second Principle: There are reasons which justify material cooperation, which may even suggest and advise it, if they do not go so far as to oblige it. These reasons must be the more valid and weighty *the greater the evil* to which our actions are perverted, *the more proximate our contribution or cooperation* in the sinful action of others, *the more certain our work will* really *be misused* or perverted, *the more probable that our refusal to* cooperate *could prevent the sin,* and, finally, *the greater the danger of scandal* to others. Let us note the following more specific norms which fall under this second principle:

1) Merely material cooperation is lawful if through such cooperation a higher good is assured and safeguarded or a greater evil is averted. However, according to the principle of the double effect,[144] no evil deed may be made the means to further the good, for the end does not justify the means.

2) In adducing what is the "greater good" or the "greater evil," we note that no private or personal gain or loss or fear of individual hurt or harm justifies proximate cooperation in an act which inflicts grave damage on a community (especially Church or state). The reason is evident: evil affecting a community is always greater than evil inflicted on one individual.

3) Remote cooperation on which the execution of the evil deed in no way depends is permitted for any proportionately good reason. Note again that formal cooperation is totally excluded.

4) Material cooperation in a deed which inflicts unjust damage on a third party is permitted only for the prevention of greater damage to others or to the cooperating agent himself. In this we assume of course that one has a right *per se* to do the deed which becomes a contributing factor or cooperates in inflicting the damage on others.

Third Principle: Material gain may not be our motive for material cooperation, nor should it be in the first instance a dread of material loss or damage. The motive should be primarily the prevention of spiritual hurt to oneself and others and the possibility of effective action "in the world."

It might be very easy for one who has withdrawn from the world and who is concerned only with the salvation of his own soul to condemn with smug horror every species of material cooperation. But one who "in the world" wills to be active for the kingdom of God and the salvation of those who are in spiritual jeopardy will view the matter in quite a different light. He is faced with a serious problem. Any hyper-rigorous stance respecting material cooperation—instance the moral rigorism represented by Tertullian in the early Church—simply renders the exercise of the lay apostolate totally impossible. Anyone who sets up in his moral code the rigid principle forbidding any action which might be perverted by others must, to cite but one example, renounce politics entirely. He will be obliged to remain aloof from many significant areas of apostolic activity.

As Christians we have a mission to sanctify all realms in the world which are not in themselves evil. Not only the Apostles but all Christians —specifically the laity—have received the word of Christ: "Even as thou hast sent me into the world, so I also have sent them into the world" (Jn 17:18). "I do not pray that thou take them out of the world, but that thou keep them from evil" (Jn 17:15). But we must be cautioned with all earnestness that there is one price we may never pay the world: we may never descend to its level nor be animated by its spirit; we may never do or further the evil works of the world in order to maintain ourselves "in the world." "Keep them from evil. They are not of the world, even as I am not of the world. Sanctify them in the truth" (Jn 17:15ff.).

The tremendous polarity of the Christian existence "in the world" and yet "not of the world" consists in this: we must avoid absolutely and unconditionally all formal cooperation in sin. This most precisely and exactly! But we must also prudently and wisely shun material cooperation, though we painfully permit that our good works now and again be perverted to evil ends. Perversion must not discourage us to the point of withdrawal from our mission in the world. To sustain the polarity in a truly Christian manner we must be both as "guiless as doves" and as "wise as serpents" (cf. Mt 10:16).

2. Examples of Licit and Illicit Cooperation

Each individual commandment presents countless problems of cooperation.[145] We can refer to only a few, selecting what seem to us the most typical examples. We urge the reader to recall what we have said above regarding the casuistic discussion of scandal. It is far from our mind to suggest final solutions. In fact, it is not at all possible to arrive at blanket solutions in every conceivable case if one takes into account every aspect of the problem. Our first task is to illustrate the universal principles which are always valid. The conclusions we arrive at in individual instances, however, may in their concrete application under different sets of circumstances involve new principles.[146]

a. Cooperation of Servants and Officials

A cook may prepare meat dishes on Friday or other days of abstinence if her Catholic employer demands it, although she knows or may reasonably surmise that as a Catholic he has no sufficient reason to consider himself exempt from the law of abstinence. If the employer is not a Catholic, she may assume that he is not bound by the Church law (e.g., if he is not baptized) or is in good faith in eating meat on these days. She has some obligation to admonish her Catholic employer if there is reason to hope he may listen. But in any case the cooperation is only material and remote. A butler or personal servant (e.g., chauffeur) may assume that his master is in good faith in instances of suspicious types of friendship. And even should it be certain that there exists an objectionable liaison, he would still be permitted to carry out the usual personal duties of a butler or personal servant. Such, for example, would be the following: to drive the car on various trips, to open the door for a questionable guest, to call the master of the house on the guest's arrival, to serve tea or meals, to prepare the guest rooms, and the like. But in each instance he must in some manner manifest his displeasure over any sinful relationship. However, if he does no more than the ordinary duties which any servant is to perform, he may rightly maintain that his services, good in themselves, are perverted to evil ends by his master. The situation would be different if direct furtherance of the sinful relationship were demanded: he might be asked to play the part of a spy or sentry, to convey secret messages and invitations in dead of night, to carry on seductive correspondence, to communicate sinful messages orally. All of this must be utterly excluded. The mere transmission of written messages, that is, the simple bearing of missives, even though the bearer may legitimately assume that they deal with illicit things, is not in itself formal cooperation in another's sin. The reason is that the action itself cannot necessarily be recognized by the servant as complicity in another's sin. And yet it is a very dubious service which he is not permitted to continue, except for very serious reasons, since this very conveyance of message can directly establish the conditions for sin. If he should continue to play the part of "postman," even after he has noticed the evil results, he could no longer innocently maintain that his actions are entirely licit, that they are merely perverted to evil ends by his employer; for his service rather creates the impression that the two are in full accord in an evil partnership.

In the light of these explanations we must conclude that no one may accept a position in which his ordinary duties are *frequently* perverted to evil ends unless he has very serious reasons for doing so. Similarly, those who render public service for hire (such as taxi drivers) are never permitted to direct inquirers to houses of sin, since such assistance makes the sin itself possible. But a driver would be allowed to drive a fare to a specific address given to him, even though he knew or could at least assume that the destination was sought for evil purposes. If, however, under the actual circumstances it appears that the driver is expected to contribute in some measure toward the evil itself, he would be obliged, as far as he could, to forego the fare, to give up the trip, or at very least to free himself of complicity by clearly indicating his disapproval with words similar to these: "I can take you to that address, but all I do is run a taxi; I don't provide any further 'service.'" One cannot merely shrug off such matters, but must shun even the appearance of contributing to the evil. If the driver can prevent the sin by refusal of his service, he is obliged to turn down the fare. In no instance is the mere loss of the price of the trip sufficient reason for permitting such a proximate material cooperation in sin.

The following points are applicable to men and women employees in stores: the sale of articles which in themselves can be put to good uses, but which here and now appear to be purchased for evil purposes is in itself material cooperation. This is understandable according to the circumstances and conditions already explained. However, the sale of objects which by their very nature serve no other purpose but sin (for example, various kinds of contraceptives, anti-pregnancy pills, etc.) is formal co-operation in the sin of the purchaser.

Pursuing the matter further, we point out an important distinction which should be made between the position of the *employed clerk* or *salesman* from whom the purchases are made and the *manager or owner* of the store. If an owner, manager, or self-employed salesman makes the sale, it is unquestionably illicit. No theologian questions this conclusion. But what shall we say of the simple salesclerk whose employer outlines his sales' duties? To my knowledge only Albert Schmitt[147] and Aertnys-

Damen[148] cast some doubt on the matter and permit the cooperation under certain circumstances. But they are very reserved in their view. They hold that, even though the cooperation may be considered material and not formal, the hazard of scandal is so great that it cannot readily be viewed as licit. Damen (and Schmitt appears to agree with him) presents the case as though the clerk is merely playing a very subsidiary and quasi-mechanical role. Material cooperation in this instance is merely relaying the article in question to the purchaser without any personal function or participation in the procedure (*simpliciter exhibet*). Perhaps one could reasonably interpret such a view so that it would be acceptable. L. Ruland argues in a similar vein: "Employees whose work is entirely under the direction and supervision of their managers or employers are not responsible for the content of letters, accounts, and entries which they must handle without any independent or personal decision at all. But to the degree and measure in which they are permitted to operate independently (for example, as heads of departments, purchasing agents, confidential clerks, and the like) their personal share in responsibility increases accordingly.[149] As to the specific point in question, Ruland makes his position quite clear: "Obviously, it is not lawful to provide or sell articles or to assist in their sale if they are of such a nature that they cannot at all be used for any morally good purpose.[150] And to add another name, Schilling also holds without any qualification that "to sell articles which are determined for an evil purpose is simply illicit."[151] He makes no distinction between the owner and the hired salesclerk.

Any pharmacist, druggist, or clerk in a drugstore who deals with the customers on the basis of businesslike understanding of the procedures in selling, and who is therefore quite aware of the immoral objects he is selling—and his knowledge is a basic professional requirement for his work—is, in my opinion, guilty of formal cooperation in every instance of sale. He cannot be excused from guilt merely on the score of having no choice. The excuse that he does merely what he is told is vapid. Excuses of this kind have been alleged in defense of the most unheard of crimes. A conscience attuned to the divine law steers clear of such an evasion and of the evil deed. This is not to deny that the manager or owner of the store in question obviously must be charged with far greater guilt than a mere clerk.

I should like to mitigate this severity of judgment in determining the morality of the cooperation provided by the *cashier* or *wrapping clerk* in the establishment. We should not condemn as formal cooperation the mere wrapping of the package or the registering of the sale after the article has been provided and sold. Any honest thinking man not absorbed in abstractions would still be able to say that the activity of the cashier and wrapping clerk is in itself indifferent, though it is misused in the worst way and perverted to evil purposes or at least readily open to perversion. But surely we cannot afford the same leniency regarding the role of the registered pharmacist, nurse, or saleslady who specifically searches for the article on the shelves or compounds and prepares the item. This latter activity essentially enters into the transaction. Conversely the business of wrapping the parcel and registering its sale is carried out just as effectively whether or not the clerk knows the nature of the article. He can be totally oblivious of its function and purpose. Accordingly he does not necessarily enter into the essential formality of the transaction. At any rate, as distasteful as the matter may be, we do not simply and unequivocally label it formal cooperation.

Formal cooperation of the professional pharmacist or informed salesclerk, we have already stated, is always unlawful. At most the confessor or pastor in some instances might be permitted to maintain a prudential silence regarding the objective sinfulness of the act. Of course the individual concerned must be acting in good faith because of invincible ignorance. And the silence of the director or pastor may not give the scandalous impression of implicit approval. To justify this silent toleration, there must be a weighty reason such as the prevention of a greater evil. The man in the position of which we are speaking may be keeping many people from sin. Or perhaps, if another should take his place, matters might become much worse. Nevertheless, if the confessor is asked directly about the licitness of the action, he must unreservedly declare that the cooperation is not allowed. It would be difficult to appraise the scandal which a person with a reputation for piety and virtue could give by the transactions just referred to—particularly if it were known that the confessor or director passed the matter over in silence. In such instances the spiritual guide must exercise the greatest prudence.

The cashier in our hypothetical drugstore might be permitted to continue her work with its considerable material cooperation only if there are the most serious reasons to do so, and again only under the assumption that scandal is avoided.

As to the sale of narcotics—distributed and peddled with greed and passion—our judgment is no less severe regarding all conscious cooperation. Even the pathetic pleas of the drug addict, though they might arouse false sympathy, do not justify cooperation in this vicious traffic.

b. Cooperation of Physicians, Nurses, and Hospital Personnel

For a physician to assist at an illicit operation is in most instances formal cooperation, for as a rule he must be ready to support every step of the principal physician or surgeon. In case of necessity he must be ready to take over. Merely passive assistance at the preliminary instruction and preparation for the work done at every operation is considered only material cooperation even for the physician, particularly if he can remain aloof from every appearance of approval of the illicit operation.

The interns, nurses, technicians, and hospital Sisters in the operating rooms have certain duties of a permanent nature, such as sterilization of instruments, preparation of drugs, administration of anaesthesia, handing of instruments during the operation, etc. All of this is merely material cooperation if the illicit operation (perhaps even an abortion) is something exceptional and accidental in relation to their routine work. Obviously, the hospital personnel in charge of the operating rooms, and even the nurses caring for the sick (who ordinarily cooperate only in a more remote way), and more particularly if they are members of a religious community of men or women, must make every effort to prevent their work being perverted to evil ends. As far as possible they must seek to prevent illicit activity; for surely the scandal could be very great if religious would as a regular practice place their cooperation at the service of physicians when they perform sinful operations. Obviously in a hospital under Catholic control the authorities have the serious obligation to forbid and prevent, if they humanly can, all such operations. Ordinarily hospital Sisters should come to an agreement with the administration of any hospital or clinic in order to free themselves from any obligation to assist at operations which the Church condemns because they are immoral. Such assurance and protection of a firm contract before taking over permanent service would remove any ground for fear and doubts in individual cases. They would not have to be harassed with scruples and obliged to confront the physician or surgeon with their misgivings over an occasional "borderline case."

However, even in these instances they cannot dispense with the prudent counsel of sound spiritual directors.

An earnest question: could it be that the spiritually fruitful activity of nuns in hospitals and clinics depends on an occasional more or less remote material cooperation in illicit operations and procedures? If such be the case, this cooperation can usually be considered justified, though formal cooperation in sin must always be excluded—and the material cooperation as well, if it be such that under the circumstances it is looked upon universally as tantamount to approval of immoral procedure.

If it is clear beyond all doubt that certain instruments serve only immoral purposes, it is formal cooperation to assist the physician by handing him these means of evil, particularly if he plainly indicates his purpose by such words as: "Hand me the instrument we use to interrupt pregnancy." However, if the instruments are also used for licit purposes and the other circumstances and arrangements are no different than usual— the instruments may ease parturition or facilitate premature birth—then one could not assume that merely assisting at an operation by handing the instruments to the physician would be formal cooperation. But even material cooperation is not allowed if the material cooperation itself gravely endangers the spiritual welfare of either the mother or the unborn infant and this could have been prevented by refusal to lend assistance.

Anyone engaged in *social or welfare work* of any kind (relief, unemployment, marriage counseling, care in public institutions, etc.) is morally forbidden to give misleading or persuasive instruction regarding contraceptive practices. In this connection the problem of counseling the "lesser evil" might arise. The suggestion that contraception is less evil than abortion might be advanced. However, to offer positive instruction regarding sinful methods about which the individual concerned is in complete ignorance is in our opinion not allowed. It can all too readily be considered real temptation or seduction.

It is immoral for *any* agency (the Armed Forces included) to distribute or disseminate means of contraception. This holds true even though employees are commanded to do so. The reason is apparent: such actions directly further sinful practices. But the furnishing of medication is not a formal cooperation in the sin. The purpose of the medication is the destruction of the bacillus after the sin has been committed. It is essentially the same as the treatment of a venereal disease already contracted. However, there is a point of caution: it is never allowed to present medication and means of cure as a deliberate inducement or invitation to sin—as may readily happen in some instances.

The practice of handling a contraceptive package to servicemen going on leave as "hygienic safeguards" in such a way as to make the leave dependent on this accession brings up the problem of cooperation on the part of those who distribute and those who accept contraceptives. Surely all who are responsible for the practice itself are formal cooperators in the sins which are or may be committed. Concerning the distribution, one might term *material cooperators* both those who merely pass out the articles and those who do no more than mechanically accept them. There is a serious reason for their conduct. The package is given and accepted as the material procedure bound up with leaving the camp and (as far as the material cooperator is concerned) is not at all used for sin.

To protest this practice may require courage—moral courage in this instance—but surely there are some who possess it in sufficient measure to risk rebuke and official displeasure to raise objections. The concern for bodily protection against disease, advanced under the hypocritical euphemism of "hygienic safeguard" while utterly disregarding the malice of the sin, is due to a totally false concept of culture and morals.

c. Various Forms of Cooperation: Taverns, Business, Service

If *tavern keepers* and *bartenders* encourage patrons "who have had enough" to take still another drink, they are guilty of actually inducing others to commit the sin of drunkenness. They formally cooperate in the sin. The same holds true of those who "treat" or serve such individual patrons drinks "on the house." If the bartender serves all customers indiscriminately, whether they drink to excess or not, he cooperates materially in a very questionable manner toward the sins of those who become intoxicated. His cooperation is a grave sin unless a correspondingly serious reason excuses him from guilt: such would be the creation of a very disturbing scene, violence, foul language, danger of hostility, etc. If parents squander in excessive drinking the money which should be used for food and clothing and other necessities in their homes, tavern keepers who continue to serve them are not only guilty of sinful cooperation in the sin of drunkenness; they are also guilty of grave injustice to the family of the drinkers and are obliged to make restitution to the impoverished family to the degree of the ill-gotten gain.

If the tavern keeper (the same is true of the proprietor or manager of a nightclub or dining place) offers the base attraction of lascivious entertainment or permits unseemly forms of dancing and deportment on the part of his patrons, etc., he is formally a cooperator in the sins which he knows will be committed. He is leading others into sin. However, if the evil is rather the exception and due to the excess of a few malicious individuals in an establishment which is decently conducted, the cooperation is no more than material and must be judged in accordance with the norms already laid down. Circumstances should determine whether it be sinful or not and the degree of sin. There is an especially serious obligation on the part of those who have charge of places of amusement (public parks, dance halls, etc.) where alcoholic beverages are sold to prevent abuses.

Merchants are not obliged, generally speaking, to investigate the possible misuse of their merchandise once it is in the purchasers' hands, provided the article itself belongs at least to the category of "indifferent things." If the seller foresees that the article will be put to evil use, the norms already laid down for material cooperation apply in his case also. The matter is quite different if the articles offered for sale are not in the category of "indifferent things." *Style shop operators, modistes,* and *merchants* who openly provide and sell indecent clothing are guilty of formal cooperation through seduction. Particularly objectionable is the lurid advertising of women's wear both in shop windows and in print. To attract customers or patrons to one's place of business or service (barbershops, etc.) by means of indecent or pornographic literature is strictly forbidden. Obviously to offer it for sale to all comers is likewise evil. Employees in such establishments must follow the norms we have explained above in the discussion of the moral obligations of the employees and others who work in drugstores.

Owners of motion picture theaters who bill evil films commit sin by seducing others to sin: they are guilty of grave scandal through the seduction of the moviegoers and also of formal cooperation in their sins. Even though the owner may not actually be the operator of the theater and may not have control of the films shown (e.g., he has leased it), he is still guilty of material cooperation in sin unless he has an adequately serious reason for permitting his contribution. Mere employees in the house who do only technical tasks are no more than material cooperators and are more readily excused from sin if the theatre does not consistently cater to morally objectionable films. They too are to follow the norms indicated above for material cooperation of employees in the sale of evil merchandise.

To rent rooms or apartments for sinful purposes (prostitution, rendezvouz for adultery, communistic cells, anti-Catholic propaganda, etc.) is indeed sinful in all instances. This holds even for what is often called legalized and supervised prostitution (authors in olden times were not as severe and categorical on this point). Objectively viewed, renting an apartment is surely "only" material cooperation; but it is a gravely scandalous one. However, it may happen that the room or apartment is rented or leased in perfectly good faith. In this instance the owner has the right *per se* to protest. In fact, if he is personally living in the house, he even has the duty to protest in order to eliminate any scandal. As to further obligation, much depends on the legal status of owner and renter. If the owner has no right to interfere unless the civil or criminal law is violated, it ordinarily would be sufficient for him to show his displeasure over the infringement of the moral law.

Owners and managers of *transportation or shipping services* (ships, railways, airlines, postoffice, etc.) and their employees who indiscriminately accept orders for shipping any kind of goods not expressly forbidden by law, or who offer transportation to all who purchase tickets, are not considered formal cooperators in the transportation of evil persons or things. The transportation of pernicious newspapers, pornographic literature, and other objects serving sinful purposes, as far as the actual handling of the materials is concerned, is ordinarily only material cooperation. The reason lies in the fact that the objects are merely conveyed and at that almost mechanically. The activity involved does not affect or promote the interior evil end of the object transported. The transportation worker often in fact is in no way aware of the contents of the packages he handles. Moreover, if we were to look upon the actions of workers in this field as formal cooperation, we would have to exclude practically all Christians from accepting or retaining jobs in public transportation service today.

Here we make the same essential distinction (as above) regarding the manager or self-employed worker. There is the transportation worker whose usual and undiversified tasks are perverted to evil uses in some instances. We have already dealt with his type of cooperation. But there is also the independent owner or employer who places his transportation facilities at the service of evil enterprises. In his case the personal attitude and spirit of free cooperation is tantamount to formal cooperation in sin.

d. Cooperation in Evil by Judges and Attorneys

A judge[152] may frequently be confronted by the predicament of pronouncing "justice" or "right" according to an *unjust law*. If by some legal provision he is permitted to withdraw from the case or is in some way able to avoid making a decision, he cannot be excused from the guilt of formal cooperation if he, nevertheless, decides the case. Should this withdrawal be impossible, then we must hold that his act goes no further than his pronunciation that the law applies in this particular instance, a decision which can be viewed as only material cooperation.

More difficult is the case in which the law is not only unjust but actually demands that something sinful in itself be done. We have a sad instance in the laws of those states requiring sterilization. Even worse would be a law demanding denial of the faith. No judge may cooperate in enforcing or applying these laws—particularly when the law requires the sterilization of individuals who have never committed the slightest crime, but who are considered "unfit" for marriage or parenthood because of heritage or mental deficiency! What shall we say of the decision of the court which must determine that a certain individual is to be classified as "unfit"? Some writers are inclined to doubt the guilt of a judge who must apply the law by making a decision according to the terms of the law, always provided that he does all in his power to avoid "passing the sentence." However, it seems to me that the official who is primarily responsible for the actual procedure, the physician or other official who makes the "certification" that this innocent individual is fit "only to be a descendant," is guilty of formal cooperation in sin. The law in this instance is no defense, for it requires something unjust, something no one is permitted to do. Obviously, those who actually carry out the law and perform the operation are principals in the crime.

In our age judges are often placed in a serious predicament because of the *divorce cases* brought before their courts. If a judge has in mind, when rendering his decision, complete agreement with the unchristian legislation which declares the matrimonial bond (assuming that there is a true marriage) dissolved and remarriage entirely lawful, then his cooperation is formal. But there is an alternative. The civil divorce laws may also be understood as going no further than regulating and restricting the civil effects of the marital union. The declaration that the civil effects of marriage (such as community of property and the use of the husband's name by the wife) are now no longer in force is morally permissible under certain circumstances. This holds even though one clearly foresees that this very declaration will be seized upon by many as an occasion and justification for attempting to enter a new and invalid "marriage."

What shall we say of the Catholic judge who is confronted by a couple whose marriage must be considered valid before God if neither party has a true right to seek an annulment of the civil effects of the marriage? In such instances the Catholic judge surely must make every effort to avoid a decision of divorce or separate maintenance.[153] Should he in no way be able to prevent the action, despite all his sincere efforts, we may look upon his granting of the divorce as material cooperation which is permitted for a grave reason; for loss of office would indeed be a grave consideration.

An *attorney* who is asked to represent a client whose case is unjust is in a far more delicate situation. He is never permitted to defend a case in which a third party, the state, or the Church is directly placed in jeopardy. Nor may he defend a case in direct violation of the divine law. Still he is permitted to shield a lawbreaker from punishment by means of his defense if he is sincerely convinced that the common good will not suffer. *A fortiori* he is allowed under similar conditions to work for a milder verdict than might be anticipated.

What we have said so far is concerned with principle. As indicated, we hold in principle that an attorney is not permitted to defend an action for divorce which is patently or in all probability not justifiable. However, we said nothing about the lawyer's approach in dealing with the clients themselves. Nothing about the ways and means of applying the principle! Some lawyers might reject the case indignantly and without any explanation. Thus the client would be more determined than ever to avoid all counseling and to go through with the divorce. Most probably he will seek an unscrupulous lawyer who will see to it that tempers are not permitted to cool for any hope of reconciliation.

Prudence suggests and experience proves that a capable Catholic lawyer should follow a totally different procedure which is psychologically far more amenable to reconciliation. Capable Catholic lawyers have saved countless marriages precisely because they were sympathetic and flexible.

Let us consider a hypothetical case: a client comes to a Catholic legal counselor in a very ugly mood. He and his wife have had a violent quarrel, replete with charges and countercharges. He wants a divorce. The counselor does not interrupt but hears him out. Then calmly he explains the legal points involved in all such cases. He then invites a somewhat subdued husband to return in about a week or ten days with all the evidence necessary to proceed legally in the courts. If this husband follows the more usual pattern he may simply drop the case. Experience shows that about four-fifths of the clients never return to pursue the divorce action further. The simple reason is that when tempers cool, the couples become reconciled and no longer think of divorce. But our prudent Catholic counselor is not without recourse even in dealing with those who do return with all the evidence and want the matter taken to court. Particularly when the couple has children and the difficulties are limited to the couple itself, can the marriage in most cases be saved. The lawyer also does well to have the couple seek the advice of a spiritual director whom both respect and admire.

Civil officials (justices of the peace, judges, mayors, etc.) may never voluntarily *officiate at a civil marriage* which as such is invalid or gravely illicit, provided they can refuse to assist at the ceremony without great loss to themselves. In order to prevent even the appearance of formal cooperation, they are obliged in every instance to manifest very clearly that their part in the procedure is not with a real matrimonial contract at all but only with certain civil effects which are assured by their presence.[154]

e. Cooperation in Scandalous Writing

Publishers, editors, managers, directive boards of publication firms, and their *advertisers* are guilty of formal cooperation in sin if they place their facilities at the service of the publication and dissemination of pernicious literature. Should the publication of this writing be no more than incidental to a much wider activity in spreading good and wholesome literature, then the individuals (e.g., members of the boards making the decisions) who were opposed to the work and had no voice in promoting it are not guilty of any cooperation. They are not obliged to give up their position if maintaining it does not cause grave scandal. If, however, the mere threat of resignation could prevent the grave departure from sound moral standards, one would be obliged to so act in certain serious cases.

Authors of morally correct (or indifferent) articles for immoral newspapers or magazines are at most guilty of material cooperation, which is morally permissible, as long as the evil publication is not sustained by one's contributing to it. Scandal, of course, must be avoided and there should be a corresponding weighty reason and good motive for the action, the latter being presumably to inject some element of good in an otherwise evil project. However, the hazard of scandal is never far removed from any cooperation, particularly if an author of note writes for a journal openly hostile to the Church or to morals.

To purchase advertising in disreputable newspapers or magazines is material cooperation in evil, for advertising of any kind contributes materially to financial support and is often the main source of profit. In fact, many newspapers could not exist without it. Serious also is cooperation even through *news and sports releases;* for regardless of the manner in which these are supplied, whether by agencies or individual writers or institutions, they constitute material cooperation in the evil wrought by an immoral press. Yet a good reason for the cooperation, as hinted above, is the well-founded hope that the contribution may be a balancing influence for good against evil. A prudent judgment, however, must be based on the actual circumstances in individual instances.

In a general way the work of *printers, typesetters, etc.* (not publishers) is material cooperation since their activity is usually not concerned as such with content, quality, and significance. But the owner of plant or press and its managers or directors are not to be considered free from mortal sin if they voluntarily place their facilities at the disposal of those who publish pornography and obscenity of whatever kind. However, it would be going too far to demand that they should be obliged to refuse to print the matter because of one or other incidental section or part when they could not prevent the publication as such anyway. The *employees,* concerned only with technical details of the whole work, cannot be aware of all the details of the various projects and of their moral correctness. But they would not be permitted to accept work or to continue at work in a plant which is devoted entirely to the printing of pornographic and immoral material, even though they should suffer considerable loss in refusing such employment.

f. Cooperation in Politics

No citizen is ever permitted to vote for a party or a candidate representing immoral or anti-Christian principles, for such a ballot is in itself approval and support of these principles and is therefore formal cooperation in evil. Because the principles of the Communist Party are utterly opposed to Christian doctrine and morality, the Holy Office[155] has declared that voting for the Party or support of it by keeping and disseminating Party literature is a grave sin. Before anyone guilty of this offense can be absolved and admitted to reception of the sacraments, he must renounce all allegiance to the Party and its principles and cease to support them. This holds also for those who protest that they reject the moral and philosophical errors of Communism; for not merely interior acceptance of heresy or error but even external support of it is gravely sinful as cooperation in a great sin which is a hazard to the common welfare.

Masonic and socialistic parties, which as a matter of principle are opposed to Catholic schools and deny every right of the unborn child, may not be supported. To cast a vote for such parties is support of an evil cause and is gravely sinful. Though conditions in English-speaking countries may differ radically from the political situation obtaining in other lands, the obligation of the voters to avoid support of principles and politicians opposing Christian moral ideals is everywhere present. Though there may be little open espousal of evil principles in our country, the very support of individuals and groups, or of parties as such, in preference to the common welfare is cooperation in a perversion of that right order which demands that the good of all take precedence over individual or party good.

Particularly distressing in political life is the absence of a real choice between one candidate and another or one party and the other. At times the voter can do no better than make the choice of the lesser of two or more evils. If he has no alternative in the choice of party or candidate because all advocate an immoral program or a program opposed to the principles of his faith, the Christian voter facing the actual situation either will have to abstain from voting altogether, unless this very refusal to vote will result in a greater evil, or he must turn to the party or candidate which is the lesser evil. He must choose that group or individual who, everything considered, is the most favorable to faith and morals or is the least hostile. Obviously, the very situation proclaims that the voters do not simply approve or support an immoral or evil program but merely shun the greater of two evils.

Anyone who runs for office under the banner of a party in which party discipline will force him to support legislation opposed to faith or morals cannot be excused from grave guilt of formal cooperation in sin. But should the party member be free within the party and in the assembly, (general assembly, house of representatives, senate, etc.) to oppose every and any program, seeking the office is not formal cooperation. Hence a Christian could permit his name to be placed on the ballot under the party symbol without committing sin, provided his action is not the source of scandal—when viewed in its total context—and does not promote but rather helps to retard the evil cause.

The member of a legislative body who *simply* votes in favor of legislation that is hostile to faith or morals is a formal cooperator in sin. However, if he has no alternative other than evil, he must then—again, depending on circumstances—choose the less pernicious in order to shun the greater evil. But the evidence of the circumstances themselves or an express declaration of the individual legislator must make very clear that his vote in favor of a bill is not an approval of the evil or injustice contained in it but only the choice of the lesser evil. In democratic legislative bodies, where floods of oratory usually accompany all legislative procedure, there should be no difficulty for any legislator to voice his honest convictions.

Policemen in executing an unjust law cannot be readily excused from sin when arresting an obviously innocent man. Nevertheless, one might conceivably view their act as only material cooperation if it is purely a mechanical execution of an order given them by their superiors, and if the circumstances are especially difficult for the ordinary police officer who has no power to make decisions in such matters. But should officials who do possess a degree of discretion in carrying out the law or the orders of their superior officers, or even subordinate officers, track down the innocent, ferret them out, or arrest them independently of express orders, they are by that very fact formally guilty in conscience as accessories of the unjust law and persecutors of the innocent.

A *soldier* (any serviceman) who follows orders in killing a patently innocent man or cooperates in the mass murder of innocents (we have examples in the mass murders of the Second World War, in the deliberate bombing of residential areas) is guilty of formal cooperation in the sin of murder. He is not to be excused from sin even though his crime is usually not so subjectively heinous as that of the superior officials who command the action.

We add the following by way of illustration to show how important in our Catholic casuistry is the doctrine that the circumstances of an action can give it a totally new meaning. There is a case in connection with the horrible persecution of the Church in Hungary which might be considered typical of many conflicts of conscience. A. Kelemen of Várna reports that the Communistic regime sought to prepare the way for the removal of the Primate of the country by means of petitions obtained under duress. "As the conflict of public conscience exceeded all bounds of human endurance, Cardinal Mindszenty resolved to make a bold new move which proved a great defeat for the state: the Cardinal informed his flock that they had his permission to sign the petitions demanding his removal. They might do so with a tranquil conscience since the signatures would be obtained through coercion and therefore would be invalid and worthless from the outset. He likewise very pointedly informed the ministerial presidium of his move."[156] Was such action on the great prelate's part lawful? Is not the signing of a petition demanding the arbitrary deposition of one's bishop formal cooperation in a sinful act? In an abstract casuistry it would be so. But in the concrete situation the signatures lose all meaning. The previous permission of the Cardinal makes this fully evident. Mindszenty would hardly be one to follow situation ethics in any matter of such importance, much less place his stamp of approval upon an evil action. He would not characterize as lawful or permissible anything which in itself—in the light of the total context—was evil.

g. Cooperation in False Rites

For a Catholic nurse to call the pastor of a sick Protestant at his request, or to arrange his sick room nicely and attractively for his visit is usually, under present day conditions and circumstances, not to be looked upon as formal cooperation in any false worship. This is particularly true *today* because we have every reason to assume that our separated brethren are in good faith. Moreover, as a rule, the assistance of the non-Catholic minister consists essentially of prayers and admonitions of a very general nature. He attempts to awaken in the patient a living faith and loving trust in God's providence and mercy and a sorrow for sin. Ordinarily the request of the sick man is no more than the expression of his desire for the consoling presence and advice which come with the visit of his pastor. Obviously, rather than a forbidden encouragement of heretical cult, the nurse's action is merely a kindly communication of charity. However, in this manifestation of love on the part of the Catholic, her attitude must always be such that she does not give the appearance of approving or supporting heretical doctrine or rites.

If Catholics at open gatherings of mixed groups make a *contribution* to the construction of a church for Protestant worship, in the conviction that it is better for them to pray together with a sincere desire to please God than to become a prey to indifferentism and unbelief, then there is no objection to be raised. However, we must always assume that there is no scandal. (Usually in English-speaking countries where many people of different faiths live together, there is little danger of scandal.) In some parts of the world Catholic bishops have—from the same motive and under the same conditions—made Catholic churches or church space available to Protestants for their services. This accommodation is made in a spirit of mutual regard and is an expression of love.

Under no condition may a Catholic be a *bridesmaid or best man* (i.e. an official or required witness) for a mixed marriage before a non-Catholic minister (or even before a civil official). Such an act is externally manifested support and approval of the grave sin committed by the Catholic party in this unfortunate attempt at marriage. In many dioceses the local ordinary lays down specific regulations about attendance at Protestant church services, funerals, marriages (also as to inclusion in the latter). From these prescriptions the faithful can readily learn, above all, to what extent such actions may cause scandal. They also clearly indicate the degree to which material cooperation may be permitted.

BIBLIOGRAPHY

Scandal

BRUCH, R. Die Bevorzugung des kleineren Uebels in moral theologischer Beurteilung, *ThG*, 1958, 241–257.

HUMBERT, H. Essai d'une théologie du scandale dans les synoptiques, *Biblica*, 35 (1954) 1–28.

JUNG, N. Scandale, *DTC* 14, 1246–1254.

SCHMITZ, O. *Vom Wesen des Aergernisses*. Berlin, 1925.

SCHOELLGEN, W. *Soziologie und Ethik des Aergernisses*. Duesseldorf, 1931.

———. Die Lehrpunkt von der Epikie und vom kleineren Uebel auf dem Hintergrund der Klugheit als einer sittlichen Tugend, *Anima* 15 (1960) 42–51.

The Fashions

BECK, H. *Schoenheit und Mode*. Stuttgart, 1956.

VON ROETHELI, E. Koerperkultur und Seelsorge. Eine Aussprache um Mode, Strandbad und Sauna, *Anima*, 2 (1947) 14–24.

Complicity in the Sins of Others

ABELLÁN, P. M. "De sententia fundata in lege injusta," *PRM*, 39 (1950), 5–33.

ABTS, D. *Some Religious and Ethical Problems in the Practice of Catholic Social Workers.* Washington, 1945.

CONNELL, F. J. *Morals in Politics and Professions. A Guide for Catholics in Public Life.* Westminster, Md.: Newman, 1946.

DELHAYE, PH. "Coopération médicale d'une religieuse," *L'Ami du clergé*, 68 (1958), 645–647.

Die Katholiken vor der Politik. ed. G. Kafka. Freiburg, 1958.

DIRKS, W. "Der Christ und die politische Demokratie," *Dokumente*, 14 (1957), 387–407.

GHOOS, J. "L'acte à double effet, étude de théologie positive," *EphThLov*, 27 (1951), 30–52.

LYNCH, J. J. "Notes on Moral Theology, Cooperation and Scandal," *ThSt*, 20 (1959), 235–238.

MILLER, J. *Gewissensfragen und Apostolatsaufgaben am Krankenbett.* 2 aufl. Innsbruck, 1958.

POSCHMANN, B. "Cooperatio in sacris," *ThPrQschr*, 104 (1956), 223ff.

ROSSI, J. "De cooperatione," *Perfice Munus*, 14 (1939), 657–666.

SCHOELLGEN, W. "Politische Wissenschaft und politische Ethik," *Aktuelle Moralprobleme* (1955), 211–219.

STEIGER, H. "Christliche Politik und Versuchung zur Gewalttaetigkeit," *Ho*, 52, (1959/60), 360–367.

SVOBODA, R. "Moraltheologische Probleme fuer die Seelsorge im Gastgewerbe," *Der Seelsorger*, 29 (1958/59), 394–401; HerderKorr 13 (1958/59), 459–463.

Additional Works in English

BANCROFT, JOHN R. *Communication in Religious Worship with Non-Catholics.* (Catholic University Studies in Sacred Theology, 75). Washington: Catholic Univ. Press, 1943.

CONNELL, FRANCIS J., C.SS.R. *Morals in Politics and Professions.* Westminster, Md.: Newman, 1946.

———. *Father Connell Answers Moral Questions.* ed. E. J. Weitzel. Washington: Catholic Univ. Press, 1959.

CONWAY, JOHN D. *Modern Moral Problems.* Chicago: Fides (Dome Books), 1961.

ELTZ, LOUIS A. *Cooperation in Crime* (Catholic University Studies in Canon Law, 156). Washington: Catholic Univ. Press, 1944.

McCARTHY, JOHN. *Problems in Theology* I. The Sacraments. Westminster, Md.: Newman, 1956. II. The Commandments. Westminster, Md: Newman, 1960.

MAHONEY, EDWARD J. *Questions and Answers.* I. Sacraments. London: Burns and Oates, 1946. II. Precepts. London: Burns and Oates, 1948.

PRAH, JOHN A. *Communication of Non-Catholics in Catholic Religious Rites.* (Catholic University Studies in Sacred Theology, 2nd Series, 98). Washington: Catholic Univ. Press, 1956.

Periodical Literature in English

BOUSCAREN, T. L. Cooperation with Non-Catholics: Canonical Legislation," *TheolS*, 3 (Dec., 1942), 475–512.

CONNELL, F. J. "Doctor's Cooperation in Contraceptive Devices," *AER*, 114 (Feb., 1946), 137–9.

——. "Sacraments for Dying Non-Catholics," *AER*, 127 (Sept., 1952), 225–6.

——. "Communication with Non-Catholics in Sacred Rites," *AER*, 111 (Sept., 1944), 176–88.

——. "Cooperation in Another's Sinful Act: Sale of Contraceptive Medicines, etc.," *AER*, 84 (May, 1931), 516–21.

Danagher, J. J. "Administration of Sacraments to Heretics and Schismatics," *Jur*, 13 (Oct., 1953), 357–81.

Kramer, J. G. "Administration of Sacramentals to Non-Catholics, *AER*, 85 (July, 1931), 39–47.

O'Malley, J. F. "Sale of Contraceptives" *HPR*, 40 (Dec., 1939), 282–90.

——. "Assistance of Nurses at Illicit Operations," *HPR*, 43 (Oct., 1942), 47–52.

Anon. "Reception of Sacraments from Non-Catholic Ministers," *ClerRev*, 37 (Nov., 1952).

NOTES AND REFERENCES

PRELUDE: THE BIBLICAL SOURCE

(pages xxi–xxxviii)

1. Cf. Vol. I, part one, chapter one.
2. Quoted in L. Bouyer, *The Meaning of Sacred Scripture,* trans. by M. P. Ryan (Notre Dame, Ind.: U. of Notre Dame Press, 1958), 21.
3. Spicq, *Agapè, Prolegomènes à une étude néo-testamentaire* (Paris, 1955), 94; cf. 205; "thus we have an ethic of love, a thing unknown in the whole history of religion: the moral life is conceived as the unfolding of love for God."
4. Spicq, 207.
5. Spicq, "Le morale de l'agapè selon le Nouveau Testament," in *LumVie,* 21 (May, 1955), 103–122.

BOOK ONE

NOTES AND REFERENCES

PART I
(pages 3–107)

1. Cf. II–II, q. 23, a. 7 and q. 4, a. 5; q. 17, a. 8.
2. T. Soiron, *Glaube, Hoffnung und Liebe* (Regensburg, 1934), 18.
3. We cannot refrain from expressing our surprise and shock over the attitude of such a noble spiritual thinker as Maritain. Undoubtedly misled by certain critics of the liturgical renewal and a few incidental excesses which everyone should deplore, he goes so far as to protest against too intense a cultivation of the liturgy. His concern is for the purity and vitality of the theological virtues. Not only does he go so far afield as to make of religion a second rate virtue constrained to accept its subordinate position in the Aristotelian scheme of virtues, he is also completely oblivious of the fact that the celebration of the divine mysteries is exercise of the theological virtues as well as of the virtue of religion. Only because Maritain places the divine virtues primarily in contemplation—wordless, motionless contemplation—and looks upon the external common form of the liturgy as an obstacle to purely spiritual contemplation, is he able to hold and defend the "primacy of contemplation" over the liturgy ("Liturgy and Contemplation," *Spiritual Life* 5 [June, 1959] 120). Participation in the liturgical life appears to Maritain as neither the only nor the necessary way to contemplation. For him the community celebration of the sacred mysteries is of less significance than solitary contemplation (*ibid.,* 131). L. Bouyer in *Liturgy and Contemplation,* by Jacques and Raissa Maritain, translated by J. W. Evans (New York: Kenedy, 1960), pertinently inquires why the writers look upon the contemplative life as though it were a thing apart, merely parallel to the genuine liturgical life which is really the true fountain of contemplation . . . There is a pressing need today, Bouyer continues, to show that mysticism, far from suppressing or constraining the liturgical life, normally flows from it. Ordinarily the mystical life is rooted in the deeper understanding and appreciation of the salvific mystery flowing to us in Christ. This is the very soul of the liturgy. And this understanding of the liturgy, progressively growing more real and effective in our minds and hearts, is animated and moved by faith which is fruitful in love (*VieSpir* 102 [April, 1960] 409).
4. III, q. 61, a. 4.
5. Cf. J. Gaillard, O.S.B., "Les sacrements de la foi," in *RevThom* 59 (1959) 5–31; 270–309 (with bibliography).
6. Originally the term *redonatio fidei* meant the baptismal profession of faith by the catechumen to whom the Church had granted a participation in her faith.
7. II–II, q. 11, a. 1.

8. R. Guardini, *The Life of Faith*, trans, J. Chapin (Westminster, Md.: Newman Press, 1962), 32. Translator's note: all the translations from German quoted throughout *The Law of Christ* are made by the present translator. They will, therefore, vary from the translated work cited in our text.

9. Cf. II–II, q. 4, a. 1.

10. First Council of the Vatican, D 1791; cf. D 1790, 1794, 1171, 1634ff., 1812. Note the words of the Council (D 1791): "Licet autem fidei assensus nequaquam sit motus animi caecus; nemo tamen 'evangelicae praedicationi consentire' potest, sicut oportet ad salutem consequendam, 'absque illuminatione et inspiratione Spiritus Sancti, qui dat omnibus suavitatem in consentiendo et credendo veritati' (Conc. Araus., n. 178 sqq.).

11. *III Sent.*, d. 24, a. 1, sol 2, ad 2; *De Veritate*, q. 14, a. 10, ad. 9.

12. Thomas says: "Mens creata reputatur informis, nisi ipsi Primae Veritati inhaereat (I, q. 106, a. 1, ad 3).

13. D 1796: "Ac ratio quidem, fide illustrata, cum sedulo, pie et sobrie quaerit, aliquam Deo dante mysteriorum intelligentiam eamque fructuosissimam assequitur tum ex eorum, quae naturaliter cognoscit, analogia, tum e mysteriorum ipsorum nexu inter se et cum fine hominis ultimo . . . Divina enim mysteria suapte natura intellectum creatum sic excedunt, ut etiam revelatione tradita et fide suscepta ipsius tamen fidei velamine contecta et quadam quasi caligine obvoluta maneant, quamdiu in hac mortali vita 'peregrinamur a Domino.' "

14. *In Joannis Evangelium*, 26, 3 (PL 35, 1608): "He who acts against his own will does not believe."

15. *De Veritate*, q. 14, a. 3, ad 10.

16. D 1814: "Si quis dixerit, assensum fidei christianae non esse liberum, sed argumentis humanae rationis necessario produci. . . . A. S."

17. Cf. D 1171, 1273, 1623ff., 1634ff., 1639, 1715, 1790, 1812, 2106f., 1154.

18. I, q. 43, a. 5, ad 2.

19. R. Guardini, *The Life of Faith*, 58.

20. *Ibid.*, 60.

21. *Ibid.*, 64f.

22. M. Scheler, *Vom Ewigen im Menschen* (3 aufl.; Berlin, 1933) 484, 491, 639, 685.

23. H. M. Christmann, "Geist und Glaube," *NO*, 4 (1950), 102f.

24. Soiron, *Glaube, Hoffnung, Liebe*, 76.

25. D 801: " 'Fides est humanae salutis initium,' fundamentum et radix omnis justificationis, sine qua impossibile est placere Deo (Heb 11:6) et ad filiorum eius consortium pervenire."

26. M. E. Boismard, "La foi selon saint Paul," *LumVie*, 22 (July, 1955), 65–89, particularly 85.

27. Guardini, *The Life of Faith*, 49.

28. *Ibid.*, 54.

29. Christmann, "Geist und Glaube," in *NO*, 4 (1950), 108. Cf. *Deutsche Thomasausgabe*, XV, 395. On p. 396 note these words: "It is clear that Thomas does not wish to deny that faith without charity (*fides informis*) is able to do good. Hence he does not place it entirely outside the category of virtue." But much depends on what is meant by *fides informis*. The faith of which St. James says, "The devils also believe and tremble" (Jas 2:19) has nothing in common with the virtue of faith. It is totally different from the faith of the Christian in the state of mortal sin, even though the same truths are its object. The sinner is still summoned and invited to conversion by the *dead faith* within him, something quite impossible to devils.

30. St. Augustine, *In Joannis Evangelium* 6. 47 (PL 35, 1610).

31. Cf. D 800: "Nam fides, nisi ad eam spes accedat et caritas, neque unit perfecte cum Christo, neque corporis eius vivum membrum efficit. Qua ratione verissime dicitur, 'fidem sine operibus mortuam' (Iac 2, 17 sqq.) et otiosam esse (can. 19), et 'in Christo Iesu neque circumcisionem aliquid valere, neque praeputium, sed fidem, quae per caritatem operatur' (Gal 5:6; 6:15)."

32. Cf. what we said above on the sacramental formation of the divine virtues.

33. Cf. D 1793: "Quoniam vero 'sine fide . . . impossible est placere Deo' (Heb 11:6) et ad filiorum eius consortium pervenire, ideo nemini unquam sine illa contigit justificatio, nec ullus, nisi in ea 'perseveraverit usque in finem' (Mt 10:22; 24:13), vitam aeternam assequetur."

34. Cf. Trent, D 801 (see note 25 above); cf. Vatican, D 1789: "Cum homo a Deo tanquam creatore et Domino suo totus dependeat et ratio creata increatae Veritati penitus subiecta sit, plenum revelanti Deo intellectus et voluntatis obsequium fide praestare tenemur (can. 1). Cf. also D 1793, cited above in note 33.

35. Cf. Trent, sess. VI, cap. 5, D 797: "Declarat praeterea, ipsius iustificationis exordium in adultis a Dei per Christum praeveniente gratia (can. 3) sumendum esse . . . ut qui per peccata a Deo aversi erant, per eius excitantem atque adiuvantem gratiam ad convertendum se ad suam ipsorum iustificationem, eidem gratiae libere (can. 4, 5) assentiendo et cooperando, disponantur."

36. *AAS* (1939), 406; (1940), 24 and 379. Cf. also P. Charles, S.J., "De participatione fidelium in honoribus Confucio exhibitis. Responsio S.C. P.F., May 28, 1935, Adnotationes," *PRM* 26 (1937), 87–108.

37. *AAS* 42 (1950), 142–147.

38. Cf. *CJC*, can. 1322ff. T. L. Bouscaren and A. C. Ellis, *Canon Law: a Text and Commentary* (3rd rev. ed.; Milwaukee: Bruce, 1957), 723–725. S. Woywod, *A Practical Commentary on the Code of Canon Law,* rev. by C. Smith (New York: Wagner, 1952), II, 107–110.

39. Cf. *CJC*, can. 1402. Bouscaren-Ellis, 771; Woywod, II, 153.

40. Cf. Ecclesiastical law on education in *CJC, can.* 1372–1383. Bouscaren-Ellis, 743–748; Woywod, II, 136–140.

41. Cf. *CJC*, Can. 1060ff. Bouscaren-Ellis, 505–510; Woywod, I, 699–706.

42. Cf. The sociological and pastoral aspects of mixed marriages are treated extensively in my work *Ehe in dieser Zeit* (Salzburg, 1960), 225–293. English translation in preparation.

43. F. Durrwell, C.SS.R., "Sainteté chrétienne, sainteté d'obéissance," *VieSpir* 95 (1956), 269.

44. Cf. II–II, q. 10, a. 5.

45. Significant is the attitude of Father Feeney who maintained that all those who do not belong to the Church will be damned. Cf. *AER,* 127 (Oct., 1952), 307–315. Cf. J. C. Fenton, "The Holy Office Letter on the Necessity of the Catholic Church," *AER,* 127 (Dec., 1952), 450–461.

46. Schism is external rupture of the unity of the Church by refusal to obey the lawful authority but without denial of any truths of faith. It is surely a grave sin against obedience and charity.

47. Cf. II–II, q. 10, a. 6.

48. Vatican, sess. III, cap. 3, D 1794: "Etenim benignissimus Dominus et errantes gratia sua excitat atque adjuvat, ut 'ad agnitionem veritatis venire' (1 Tm 2:4) possint, et

eos quos 'de tenebris transtulit in admirabile lumen suum' (1 Pt 2:9), in hoc eodem lumine ut perseverent, gratia sua confirmat, non deserens, nisi deseratur (cf. n. 804)."

49. D 1815: "Si quis dixerit, parem esse conditionem fidelium atque eorum, qui ad fidem unice veram nondum pervenerunt, ita ut catholici iustam causam habere possint fidem, quam sub Ecclesiae magisterio iam susceperunt, assensu suspenso in dubium vocandi, donec demonstrationem scientificam credibilitatis et veritatis fidei suae absolverint: A.S."

50. Cf. D 1794, note 48 above. Cf. D 804, 1170.

51. Adnotatio 20, Mansi 50, 95. Cf. H. Lange, "Alois Schmid und die vatikanische Lehre vom Glaubensabfall," *Schol,* 2 (1927), 342ff. See *Schol,* 6 (1931), 628f. (Lange's criticism of the article by Anselm Stolz: "Was definiert das vatikanische Konzil ueber den Glaubenszweifel?" *ThQschr,* 111 [1930], 519–560. See also G. Puentener, "Das vatikanische Konzil und die Verantwortlichkeit des Glaubensabfalls eines Katholiken," *DivThom* (F), 7 (1929), 414–445.

52. F. Mitzka, *Die Glaubenskrise im Seelenleben* (Innsbruck, 1928). A. Stoeckle, *Zur Psychologie des Glaubenszweifel* (2 aufl.; Mergentheim, 1922). G. Wunderle, *Glaube und Glaubenszweifel moderner Jugend* (Duesseldorf, 1932). D. Feuling, *Glaubensgewissheit und Glaubenszweifel* (Beuron, 1921).

53. Cf. P. Schmitt-Eglin, *Le mécanisme de la déchristianisation* (Paris, 1952).

54. The matter is treated somewhat briefly here. For an extensive work, cf. B. Haering, *Macht und Ohnmacht der Religion. Religionssoziologie als Anruf* (2 aufl.; Salzburg, 1957). Cf. also V. Schurr, *Seelsorge in einer neuen Welt* (3 aufl.; Salzburg, 1959).

55. Cf. St. Augustine, *In Joannis evangelium,* 43, 8 (PL 35, 1708); *Enarratio in Psalmum* 118, 163 (PL 37, 1592); *De civitate Dei,* lib. 14, 9 (PL 41, 416).

56. Cf. the author's studies in religious and pastoral sociology: *Macht und Ohnmacht der Religion* (2 aufl.; Salzburg, 1957), and *Ehe in dieser Zeit* (Salzburg, 1960), particularly pages 47–73.

57. Cf. J. Pieper, *Ueber die Hoffnung* (4 aufl.; Muenchen, 1949), 82f.

58. *Ibid.,* 49, 67.

59. M. Scheler, *Wesen und Formen der Sympathie,* 193; English translation: *The Nature of Sympathy* by P. Heath (New Haven: Yale U. Press, 1954).

60. St. Augustine, *Enchiridion sive de fide, spe et caritate* (PL 40, 286). For an English translation see St. Augustine, *Faith, Hope and Charity* (*Ancient Christian Writers,* 3; Westminster, Md.: Newman, 1947). Cf. Chapter 31. (For Augustine something of love is necessary for faith and hope.)

61. Cf. R. Egenter, *Gottesfreundschaft. Die Lehre von der Gottesfreundschaft in der Scholastik und Mystik des 12. und 13. Jahrhunderts* (Augsburg, 1928).

62. St. Augustine, *Enchiridion sive de fide, spe et caritate* (PL 40, 234). Cf. note 60.

63. E. Brunner, *The Divine Imperative,* trans. O. Wyon (London: Lutterworth, 1937), 192.

64. St. Bernard, *De diligendo Deo,* cap. 6 (Pl 182, 983f.).

65. *Ibid.,* cap. 4 (PL 182, 982).

66. F. Tillmann, *Die katholische Sittenlehre* (4 aufl.; Duesseldorf: Patmos, 1950), IV/1, 182.

67. St. Thomas, *Quaestio disp. de caritate,* a. 3; II–II, q. 23, a. 8.

68. Soiron, *Glaube, Hoffnung, Liebe,* 158.

69. St. Thomas, *In 1 Tm* 1:2.

70. Cf. II–II, q. 45, a. 3.

71. F. Tillmann, *Die katholische Sittenlehre,* IV/1, 182f.

PART II
(pages 111–346)

1. The words *holy, holiness* or *sanctity, sanctification,* as basic terms occur frequently in this work. The object and content of the virtue of religion are constantly referred to in these terms when we discuss the sacraments in the following pages.
2. The revealed name of God is treated as the object and the presupposition of the worship of God (in exercising the virtue of religion) in the following pages on the honor paid to God in His holy name.
3. Kittel in *ThW*, II, 247.
4. Cf. II–II, q. 81, a. 4.
5. Here we gain an insight into the biblical concept of *justice* which is one phase of the adorable and loving majesty of God. Under this aspect we can follow the Angelic Doctor and include the virtue of religion in the biblical concept of justice as its most noble ideal and profoundest summons. To place religion under the cardinal virtue of justice in the Aristotelian sense, to say the least, creates a problem.
6. II–II, q. 82. a. 2, ad 1.
7. *Ibid.,* q. 81, a. 5, ad 1.
8. *Ibid.,* q. 101, a. 3, ad 1.
9. The ethic of Marxism and, likewise, the ethic of Nicolai Hartmann, though their bases are different, are both obviously contrary to all religion.
10. R. Egenter, "Das Wesen der Religion und ihre Stellung im Tugendsystem nach dem hl. Thomas," *Der Mensch vor Gott;* Steinbuechel-Festschrift (Duesseldorf, 1948), 55–65.
11. *Ibid.,* 56; II–II, q. 81, a. 4, ad 1: "The virtue of religion commands all other virtues." Cf. q. 81, a. 1, ad 1.
12. II–II, q. 88, a. 5.
13. See pp. 92–97 on Man and Worship in chapter three of Vol. I of the *Law of Christ*.
14. In the psalms, canticles, and doxologies the inspired pages sing the praises of God.
15. II–II, q. 82, a. 2.
16. II–II, q. 82, a. 1.
17. The term *piety* as used in English is not to be equated strictly with the Latin *pietas*. As a natural virtue the Thomistic *pietas* is concerned only with one's relatives and one's country but not with God. Supernatural piety (*pietas*) for Thomas is not a virtue but essentially a gift of the Holy Spirit. Its essence can be grasped only in the light of the operation of the Holy Spirit in the supernatural area of the theological virtues.
18. II–II, q. 121, a. 1.
19. II–II, q. 83, a. 3.
20. II–II, q. 121, a. 1, ad 2 and 3.
21. II–II, q. 82, a. 3.
22. Note the pages in our third chapter of the first volume dealing with man as a body-soul totality in the imitation of Christ.
23. Dom P. Guéranger, *Institutions liturgiques* (Paris, 1841), II, 58.
24. D. 985: "Sanctorum quoque martyrum et aliorum cum Christo viventium sancta corpora, quae viva membra fuerunt Christi et templum Spiritus Sancti (cf. 1 Cor 3:16; 6:19; 2 Cor 6:16), ab ipso ad aeternam vitam suscitanda et glorificanda, a fidelibus veneranda esse, per quae multa beneficia a Deo hominibus praestantur: ita ut affirmantes, Sanctorum reliquiis venerationem atque honorem non deberi, vel eas aliaque sacra monumenta a fidelibus inutiliter honorari, atque eorum opis impetrandae causa

Sanctorum memorias frustra frequentari: omnino damnandi sint, prout iampridem eos damnavit et nunc etiam damnat Ecclesia."

D 986: "Imagines porro Christi, Deiparae Virginis et aliorum Sanctorum, in templis praesertim habendas et retinendas, eisque debitum honorem et venerationem impertiendam, non quod credatur inesse aliqua in iis divinitas vel virtus, propter quam sint colendae, vel quod ab eis sit aliquid petendum, vel quod fiducia in imaginibus sit figenda, veluti olim fiebat a gentibus, quae in idolis spem suam collocabant (cf. Ps 134:15ff.): sed quoniam honos, qui eis exhibetur, refertur ad prototypa, quae illae repraesentant: ita ut per imagines, quas osculamur et coram quibus caput aperimus et procumbimus, Christum adoremus, et Sanctos, quorum illae similitudinem gerunt, veneremur. Id quod Conciliorum, praesertim vero secundae Nicaenae Synodi, decretis contra imaginum oppugnatores est sancitum."

25. The significance of the holy sacraments in moral theology is not brought out most effectively and practically by means of an extensive tract with many individual propositions. Perhaps it would not be too extreme to say that the most sacramental form of moral theology should have no special tract on the sacramental duties. Rather all the parts should bear the impress of the cultal-sacramental forms of the Christian life. As to the positive norms of law, they should be treated in the study of canon law, the liturgy, and the rubrics.

26. Cf. III, q. 64, a. 2, ad 3.

27. Pius XII, *Mediator Dei, AAS* 39 (1947), 535.

28. Cf. D 852: "Si quis dixerit, in tribus sacramentis, baptismo scilicet, confirmatione et ordine, non imprimi characterem in anima, hoc est signum quoddam spirituale et indelebile, unde ea iterari non possunt: A.S." Cf. also D 411, 695.

29. Cf. G. Rauschen, *Patrologie* (Freiburg im B.: Herder, 1931), 18.

30. St. Cyril of Jerusalem, *Mystagogicae (Catecheses)*, 3, 3f. (PG 33, 429f.).

31. *Ibid.*, 21, 1 (PG 33, 1088f.).

32. St. Ambrose, *De Spiritu Sancto*, 1, 79 (PL 16, 725).

33. III, q. 63, a. 3.

34. B. Bartmann, *Lehrbuch der Dogmatik* (7 aufl.: Freiburg im B.: Herder, 1929), II, 222.

35. III, q. 63, a. 4, obj. 1, and ad 1.

36. Cf. St. Augustine, *De civitate Dei*, 20, 10 (PL 41, 676).

37. III, q. 62, a. 1, ad 1.

38. III, q. 63, a. 1; cf. q. 62, a. 5.

39. Bartmann, *op. cit.*, II, 214.

40. Paschasius Radbertus, *De corpore et sanguine Domini* 3, 1 (PL 120, 1275).

41. III, p. 63, a. 6.

42. F. Taymans, "Les sacrements et la vie du chrétien," *NRTh,* 69 (1947), 1027–1035; cf. part five of chapter eleven, no. 5 in our previous volume, on the sacramental dimension of conversion (pp. 404–419).

43. If health is restored through the sacrament of extreme unction a new cultal obligation arises. One who has received this favor must again say *yes* to God through a sacramentally consecrated acceptance of life and death with renewed zeal for the divine glory.

44. III, q. 65, a. 3. Matrimony as an unselfish bond of love is directed to this cultal meaning by the Creator.

45. Cf. Haering, "Eucharistie und Jungfraeulichkeit," *GeistLeben,* 25 (1952), 355–364.

46. R. Schnackenburg, *Das Heilsgeschehen bei der heiligen Taufe nach dem hl. Paulus* (Muenchen, 1950), 158.

47. J. Daniélou, S.J., *The Lord of History*, trans. Nigel Ambercrombie (Chicago: H. Regnery, 1958). H. Bouessé, *Le sauveur du monde: l'economie sacramentaire* (Doctrina sacra, 4; Chambery, 1951).

48. III, q. 61, a. 1, ad 3.

49. Cf. H. Preisker, *Das Ethos des Urchristentums* (Guetersloh, 1950).

50. O. Cullmann, *Christ and Time; The Primitive Christian Conception of Time and History*, trans. F. V. Filson (2nd ed.; Philadelphia: Westminster, 1950).

51. J. Daniélou, "Histoire marxiste et histoire sacramentaire," *Dieu Vivant*, 13 (1949), 105.

52. Schnakenburg, *op. cit.*, 193.

53. One fulfills the precept of the Church by worthy reception of Holy Communion in the paschal season, even though he made his confession before the season began.

54. *Mediator Dei, AAS* 39 (1947), 528.

55. Cf. Schnackenburg, *op cit.*, 163f.

56. *Mediator Dei, AAS* 39 (1947), 528.

57. J. Barbel, *Quellen des Heils* (Luxemburg, 1947), 20.

58. D 856: 'Si quis dixerit, receptos et approbatos Ecclesiae catholicae ritus in solemni sacramentorum administratione adhiberi consuetos aut contemni, aut sine peccato a ministris pro libito omitti, aut in novos alios per quemcunque ecclesiarum pastorem mutari posse: A.S." cf. D 1963ff. (Many theologians hold that the Church has the authority to determine and therefore to change the matter and form of some sacraments since Christ Himself did not specify in detail the sacramental sign. In such instances the minister of the sacrament would be obliged to follow the decisions of the Church *ad validitatem.*)

59. R. Bellarmine, *De sacramentis*, 1, 19.

60. D 946: "Etsi Missa magnam contineat populi fidelis eruditionem, non tamen expedire visum est Patribus, ut vulgari passim lingua celebraretur (can. 9). Quamobrem, retento ubique cuiusque ecclesiae antiquo et sancta Romana Ecclesia, omnium ecclesiarum matre et magistra, probato ritu, ne oves Christi esuriant, neve parvuli panem petant et non sit, qui frangat eis (Cf. Lam 4:4): mandat sancta Synodus pastoribus et singulis curam animarum gerentibus, ut frequenter inter Missarum celebrationem vel per se vel per alios, ex his, quae in Missa leguntur, aliquid exponant atque inter cetera sanctissimi huius sacrificii mysterium aliquod declarent, diebus praesertim Dominicis et festis."

61. Cf. J. Doelger, "Die Eingliederung des Taufsymbols in den Taufritus," *Antike und Christentum*, 4 (1934), 138–146.

62. III, q. 61, a. 4.

63. "Licet sacramentum baptismi non semper fuit necessarium ad salutem, fides tamen, cuius baptismus sacramentum est, semper necessaria fuit." (III, q. 68, a. 1, ad 1.)

64. "In quibus maxime operatur fides." (IV *Sent.*, d. 4, q. 1, a. 2.)

65. Cf. D 880: "Si non decet ad sacras ullas functiones quempiam accedere nisi sancte, certe, quo magis sanctitas et divinitas coelestis huius sacramenti viro christiano comperta est, eo diligentius cavere ille debet, ne absque magna reverentia et sanctitate ad id percipiendum accedat."

66. D 880; cf. also D 893: the Council of Trent condemns all those who teach the contrary doctrine. Cf. *CJC*, canon 856.

67. D 880, 893. Cf. *CJC*, canon 807.

68. Cf. K. Rahner, *Sendung und Gnade: Beitraege zur Pastoral-theologie* (Innsbruck: Tyrolia, 1959), 201–218. This noted theologian opposes the current conception that

Christ is sacramentally present in the communicant after he has consumed the Eucharistic Food.

69. III, q. 64, a. 2, ad 3.

70. Cf. D 938: ". . . Is igitur Deus et Dominus noster, etsi semel se ipsum in ara crucis, morte intercedente, Deo Patri oblaturus erat, ut aeternam illis [illic] redemptionem operaretur: quia tamen per mortem sacerdotium eius extinguendum non erat (Heb 7:24, 27), in coena novissima, qua nocte tradebatur, ut dilectae sponsae suae Ecclesiae visibile (sicut hominum natura exigit) relinqueret sacrificium (can. 1), quo cruentum illud semel in cruce peragendum repraesentaretur eiusque memoria in finem usque saeculi permaneret (1 Cor 11:23 sqq.), atque illius salutaris virtus in remissionem eorum, quae a nobis quotidie committuntur, peccatorum applicaretur: sacerdotem secundum ordinem Melchisedech se in aeternum (Ps 109:4) constitutum declarans, corpus et sanguinem suum sub speciebus panis et vini Deo Patri obtulit ac sub earundem rerum symbolis Apostolis (quos tunc Novi Testamenti sacerdotes constituebat), ut sumerent tradidit, et eisdem eorumque in sacerdotio successoribus, ut offerrent, praecepit per haec verba: 'Hoc facite in meam commemorationem, etc (Lc 22:19; 1 Cor 11:24), uti semper catholica Ecclesia intellexit et docuit (can. 2)."

71. III, q. 72, a. 5, ad 2.

72. D 882 . . . "in hoc 'unitatis signo,' in hoc 'vinculo caritatis,' in hoc concordiae symbolo. . . ."

73. *Mediator Dei, AAS* 39 (1947), 566.

74. *CJC*, can. 750, 751.

75. Cf. *Directoire pour la pastorale des sacrements à l'usage des diocèses de France* (Coutances: Editions Notre Dame, 1951), n. 15. Information on this Directory can be gleaned from *Worship* 29 (Sept., 1955), 469–474.

76. III, q. 68, a. 10; *CJC*, can. 745, 2, 2.

77. Vermeersch, *PRM,* 18 (1929), 143; *Theologiae moralis principia . . .* (3d ed.; Romae: P.U.G., 1945), II, n 37.

78. *CJC*, can. 731, 2.

79. Cf. Response of the Holy Office, dated November 15, 1941: *Il Monitore Ecclesiastico* 67 (1942), 114f. Cf. Responses of the Holy Office of July 25, 1630, Gasparri, *Fontes* IV, n. 721; July 20, 1898, Gasparri, *Fontes* IV, n. 2012; May 17, 1916 in Denzinger 2181a; on the problem in its entirety, cf. Vermeersch, *PRM,* 18 (1929), 123–148. J. Danagher, "Administration of the Sacraments to Heretics and Schismatics," *The Jurist* 13 (1953), 357–381. The decision of the Holy Office of May 17, 1916, as found in Denzinger 2181a is as follows: I. An schismaticis materialibus in mortis articulo constitutis, bona fide sive absolutionem sive extremam unctionem petentibus, ea sacramenta conferri possint sine abiuratione errorum? *Resp.:* Negative, sed requiri, ut meliori quo fieri possit modo errores reiciant et professionem fidei faciant.
II. An schismaticis in mortis articulo sensibus destitutis absolutio et extrema unctio conferri possit? *Resp.:* Sub conditione affirmative, praesertim si ex adiunctis conicere licet, eos implicite saltem errores suos reicere, remoto tamen efficaciter scandalo, manifestando scilicet adstantibus, Ecclesiam supponere, eos in ultimo momento ad unitatem rediisse.

80. *PRM,* 18 (1929), 127ff.

81. *Ibid.,* 147.

82. *loc. cit.*

83. *Ibid.,* 145.

84. *AAS* 44 (1952), 507–511.

85. Cf. *CJC*, canon 855.

86. Cf. *CJC*, canon 882.

87. In this connection a question arises regarding the final days of the great Russian convert Vladimir Soloviev who received the last sacraments from a Russian Orthodox priest. Was this act a renunciation of his conversion to the Catholic Church or simply a reception of the sacraments which must be judged as lawful for him in the hour of death. In this connection note Vladimir Szylkarski: "Soloviev und die katholische Kirche," in *Die Orientierung*, 18 (n. 4, 1954), 39ff. Surely many of the Orthodox groups separated from the Holy See for political or other reasons are not schismatic in mind and spirit. If the one Catholic Church is represented in vast areas only through such externally severed branches, the celebration of the liturgy and reception of the sacraments in these communities is not, in my opinion, an expression of opposition to the one true Church.

88. III, q. 64, a. 8, ad 2.

89. *Ibid.*, ad 3.

90. III, q. 64, a. 9, ad 1.

91. *Collectanea S.C.P.F.*, I, n. 593 and Gasparri, *Fontes I. C.*, VII, n. 4618 (January 21, 1788); *Collectanea S.C.P.F.*, I, n 939 and Gasparri, *Fontes I C.*, VII, n. 4795 (September 11, 1841).

92. Cf. *CJC*, can. 741 and can. 845, n. 2.

93. D 903: ". . . In eadem Ecclesia Dei custoditum semper fuit, ut nulla sit reservatio in articulo mortis, atque ideo omnes sacerdotes quoslibet poenitentes a quibusvis peccatis et censuris absolvere possunt."

94. *CJC*, canons 882, 884, 2252.

95. *CJC*, canons 207, 209.

96. D 873: "Si quis dixerit, sanctae confirmationis ordinarium ministrum non esse solum episcopum, sed quemvis simplicem sacerdotem: A.S."

97. *AAS* 38 (1946), 349; 40 (1948), 422. Cf. *CJC* canon 239, n. 23 (cardinals have the power to administer confirmation), canon 782. *AAS* 40 (1948), 41.

98. D 856; see above, note 58. *CJC*, canon 818.

99. *AAS* 52 (1960), 593–740.

100. *CJC*, canon 787.

101. Regarding the obligation to receive the sacrament of penance, see Vol. I, pp. 409–412, 447–467.

102. Cf. *CJC*, canons 853, 854, 860.

103. *CJC*, canon 854, § 4, and canon 860. Cf. Haering, "Erstkommunionvorbereitung durch die Familie," *Theologie der Gegenwart in Auswahl,* 3 (1960), 49–56.

104. *CJC*, canon 854, § 5.

105. Thomas Ohm, O.S.B., *Die Gebetsgebaerden der Voelker und das Christentum* (Leiden, 1948).

106. Elizabeth von Schmidt-Pauli, *Elemente und Naturalien in der Kirche* (Paderborn, 1937), 10.

107. There is no simply profane domain as such. All things are under the divine cult and dedicated to the divine worship or else through autonomous self-assertion under a Satanic countercult glorify the world.

108. Cf. *CJC*, canon 1151.

109. A. Veit, "Der Heimat- und Brauchtumgedanke in den Benediktionen der Kirche als befruchtendes Element des neuen kirchlichen Lebens," *Gestaltkraefte lebensnaher Seelsorge* (Freiburg, 1939), II, 266.

110. II–II, q. 13, a. 4.

111. Cf. principles on the application of the rules of prudence: more is at stake than the decision or right of the individual conscience. We must be concerned also with the honor and glory of God.

112. St. Alphonse Ligouri, *Homo Apostolicus,* tr. 8, n. 8.

113. "Lewd, obscene, insulting or blasphemous utterances when they are made solely for their own sakes and not to get across an idea can be punished by law." Edwin S. Newman: *The Law of Civil Rights and Civil Liberties,* Legal Almanac Series no. 13. Oceana Publications, N. Y., 1949, p. 18. This general proposition indicates that there are certain restrictions to free speech even in certain religious areas.

114. In addition to blasphemy and tempting God the sins against religion include sins against the oath, particularly perjury and violation of the promissory oath, and violation of the vow. Since they presuppose a special type of religious act, we shall treat them later as violations of these.

115. II–II, q. 122, a. 4, ad 3.

116. *CJC,* canon 1154.

117. *CJC,* canon 1179.

118. *CJC,* canon 1172.

119. *CIC,* canon 1173.

120. *CJC,* canon 2320.

121. Cf. Session IV of the Council of Trent. The decree on editing and using the sacred books says: "Post haec temeritatem illam reprimere volens, qua ad profana quaeque convertuntur et torquentur verba et sententiae Sacrae Scripturae, ad scurrilia scilicet, fabulosa, vana, adulationes, detractiones, superstitiones, impias et diabolicas incantationes, divinationes, sortes, libellos etiam famosos, mandat et praecipit, ad tollendam huiusmodi irreverentiam et contemptum et ne de cetero quisquam quomodolibet verba Scripturae Sacrae ad haec et similia audeat usurpare, ut omnes huius generis homines, temeratores et violatores verbi Dei, iuris et arbitrii poenis per Episcopos coerceantur." *Enchiridion Biblicum* (ed. 2), n. 64, p. 26.

122. *CJC,* canon 1150.

123. *CJC,* canons 2345, 2346.

124. Cf. T. McDonell, "Stipends and Simony," *IER,* 53 (June, 1939), 593–612; 54 (July/ August, 1939), 35–57, 159–175.

125. *CJC,* canons 727ff.

126. Cf. R. Egenter, *Kitsch und Christentum* (Ettal, 1950).

127. Trent, Session XXII. *Decretum de observandis et evitandis in celebratione Missae.* Cf. H. J. Schoeder, *Canons and Decrees of the Council of Trent* (St. Louis: B. Herder, 1941), 423f.

128. Cf. *DTC* VII, 603.

129. The case is different if an attempt is made to subdue or master the evil spirit by magical practices and hence not to pay honor to him.

130. Cf. the work of Thomas Ohm, O.S.B. with its immense wealth of information: *Die Liebe zu Gott in den nichtchristlichen Religionen* (Krailling vor Muenchen, 1950).

131. *CJC,* canon 2325.

132. Decree of April 1, 1898, *ASS* 30 (1897–98), 701; of April 27, 1917, *AAS* 9 (1917), 268.

133. II–II, q. 95, a. 5.

134. P. Schmidt, *Daemon Aberglaube* (Saarbruecken, 1938), 27ff.

135. II–II, q. 95, a. 5, ad 2.

136. Cf. D. Feuling, 'Das Kartenlesen psychologisch, philosophisch und theologisch gesehen," *Benediktine Monatsschrift* 17 (1935) 389–397.

137. Cf. Schmidt, *op. cit.,* 66ff.

138. *AAS* 34 (1942), 148; Cf. *PRM,* 31 (1942), 279–285.

139. St. John Chrysostom, *Contra Anomoeos* VII (PG 48, 766).

140. St. John Damascene, *De fide orthodoxa* 3, 24 (PG 94, 1089).

141. St. Augustine, *Enarratio in Psalmum* 85 (PL 37, 1086).

142. F. Heiler, *Das Gebet,* (4 aufl.; Muenchen, 1922), 489.

143. J. B. Hirscher, *Die christliche Moral* (Tuebingen, 1835), III, 85f.

144. St. Augustine, *Enchiridion sive de fide, spe et caritate* I, 7 (PL 40, 234).

145. *"Fac nos amare quod praecipis"* (Oration, 13th Sunday after Pentecost).

146. J. Zahn, *Einfuehrung in die christliche Mystik* (Paderborn, 1908), 188. Cf. II–II, q. 83, a. 12.

147. St. Augustine, *Epistola* 129, 9 (PL 33, 501).

148. J. P. Haas, "Gebetsformel und formelfreies Beten in der seelischen Entwicklung Jugendlicher," *ZAM* 9 (1934), 363–367.

149. D 1254: "Verbis et lingua gratias agere Deo, non est pro animabus internis, quae in silentio manere debent, nullum Deo impedimentum apponendo, quod operetur in illis; et quo magis Deo se resignant, experiuntur, se non posse orationem dominicam seu Pater noster recitare." (This proposition of Michael de Molinos was condemned by Innocent XI.) D 1564: "Doctrina, quae velut superstitiosam universe notat quamcunque efficaciam, quae ponatur in determinato numero precum et piarum salutationum; tanquam superstitiosa censenda esset efficacia, quae sumitur non ex numero in se spectato, sed ex praescripto Ecclesiae certum numerum precum vel externarum actionum praefinientis pro indulgentiis consequendis, pro adimplendis poenitentiis, et generatim pro sacro et religioso cultu rite et ex ordine peragendo:—falsa, temeraria, scandalosa, perniciosa, pietati fidelium iniuriosa, Ecclesiae auctoritati derogans, erronea." (Directed against the Synod of Pistoia.)

150. L. Ruland, *Foundations of Morality,* adapted into English by T. A. Rattler, ed. N. Thompson (*Pastoral Theology,* V. II; St. Louis: B. Herder, 1936), 192, 203.

151. Cf. D 956: "Si quis dixerit, Ecclesiae Romanae ritum, quo submissa voce pars canonis et verba consecrationis proferuntur, damnandum esse; aut lingua tantum vulgari Missam celebrari debere; aut aquam non miscendam esse vino in calice offerendo, eo quod sit contra Christi institutionem: A.S." (Council of Trent: canon 9 on the Sacrifice of the Mass.)

152. D 946, see above note 60.

153. Cf. K. Rahner, *Happiness Through Prayer,* trans. J. Henning and M. Carroll (Westminster, Md.: Newman, 1958).

154. II–II, q. 83, a. 17.

155. D 176: "Si quis invocatione humana gratiam Dei dicit posse conferri, non autem ipsam gratiam facere, ut invocetur a nobis, contradicit Isaiae Prophetae, vel Apostolo idem dicenti: 'Inventus sum a non quaerentibus me; palam apparui his, qui me non interrogabant' [Rom 10:20; cf. Is 65:1]" (2nd Council of Orange).

156. D 183: "Adiutorium Dei etiam renatis ac sanatis semper est implorandum, ut ad finem bonum pervenire, vel in bono possint opere perdurare" (2nd Council of Orange). D 472: "Quod ieiunare non oportet hominem nec orare, postquam gradum perfectionis huiusmodi fuerit assecutus; quia tunc sensualitas est ita perfecte spiritui et rationi subjecta, quod homo potest libere corpori concedere quidquid placet." (This proposition was condemned at the Council of Vienne.)

D 806: "Similiter de perseverantiae munere, . . . nemo sibi certi aliquid absoluta certitudine polliceatur, tametsi in Dei auxilio firmissimam spem collocare et reponere omnes debent . . . qui se existimant stare, videant, ne cadant et cum timore ac tremore salutem suam operentur, in laboribus, in vigiliis, in eleemosynis, in orationibus et oblationibus, in ieiuniis et castitate. . . ."

157. D 183, see note 156 above. Cf. also D 809, 826.

158. Cf. part one, chapter one, and the conclusion of this little book.

159. Hirscher, *Die christliche Moral* III, 94.

160. Cf. K. Rahner, "Das Gebet der Schuld," in *GeistLeben,* 22 (1949), 90–100.

161. Cf. what we said in chapter three on hope as a divine virtue.

162. D 923: "Si quis dixerit, pro peccatis, quoad poenem temporalem, minime Deo per Christi merita satisfieri poenis ab eo inflictis et patienter toleratis vel a sacerdote iniunctis, sed neque sponte susceptis, ut ieiuniis, orationibus, eleemosynis vel aliis etiam pietatis operibus, atque ideo optimam poenitentiam esse tantum novam vitam: A.S." (Council of Trent: canon 13 on the sacrament of Penance).

163. II–II, q. 82, a. 1.

164. Hirscher, *Die christliche Moral,* III, 88.

165. Cf. Deneffe, "Die dreifache Wirkung des Bittgebetes," in *StimmenZeit,* 102 (1921/22), 179ff.

166. II–II, q. 83, a. 14.

167. Cf. D 825: "Si quis dixerit, hominem renatum et iustificatum teneri ex fide ad credendum, se certo esse in numero praedestinatorum: A.S." (Council of Trent, canon 15 on justification.)

168. St. Augustine, *Epistola ad Probam* (PL 33, 501).

169. The prayer dialog with the saints, by comparison with our direct adoration of God, is prayer only in an analogical sense. It is communication corresponding to the communion of saints.

170. Cf. Haering, "Ehrfuerchtige Auslegung Roemischer Erlasse," *Klerusblatt,* (Munich) 38 (1958), 402–404; "Tugend der Epikie," *Klerusblatt,* 39 (1959), 406–408.

171. Alphonse Liguori, *Instit. catech.,* part. one, cap. one, § 4.

172. Cf. *CJC,* canons 125 and 126.

173. F. Tillmann, *Die katholische Sittenlehre* IV, 1, 215.

174. Hirscher, *Die christliche Moral,* III, 102.

175. *Didache* 8, 2f. as found in *Ancient Christian Writers* (Westminster, Md.: Newman, 1948), V. VI, 19.

176. Plato, *Kratilos,* 400 d.

177. Bietenhard, "oṅoma," in *ThW,* 5, 242–283.

178. *Ibid.,* 252f.

179. *Ibid.,* 248.

180. *Ibid.,* 271.

181. St. Alphonse Liguori, *Theologia Moralis,* lib. III, cap. 1, n. 128.

182. Cf. O. Schilling, *Lehrbuch der Moraltheologie* (Muenchen, 1927), II, 234.

183. A. Koch, *A Handbook of Moral Theology,* adapted and ed. by A. Preuss, V. IV (2nd rev. ed.; St. Louis: B. Herder, 1921), 187.

184. F. X. Linsemann, *Lehrbuch der Moraltheologie* (1878), 324.

185. Ruland, *Foundations of Morality,* 224f.

186. *Ibid.,* 150.

187. II–II, q. 88, a. 2.

188. *CJC,* canon 1307.

189. II–II, q. 88, a. 5.
190. II–II, q. 88, a. 11.
191. St. Augustine, *Epistula* 127 (PL 33, 489).
192. St. Augustine, *In Psalmum 75* (PL 36, 697).
193. St. Augustine, *In Psalmum 131* (PL 37, 1717).
194. II–II, q. 88, a. 6.
195. F. Vandenbroucke, *Le moine dans l'Eglise du Christ,* Louvain, 1947.
196. *CJC,* canon 1310.
197. Cf. J. Aertnys and C. Damen, *Theologia Moralis* (18th ed.; Romae: Marietti, 1951), I. n. 486.
198. II–II, q. 88, a. 3, ad 2.
199. Cf. *CJC,* canons 1307–1315.
200. *CJC,* canon 1312, § 1.
201. II–II, q. 88, a. 8.
202. *Ibid.,* ad 1.
203. *Ibid.,* ad 2.
204. *Ibid.,* corpus.
205. Cf. Aertnys-Damen, *Theologia moralis,* I, n. 492.
206. *CJC,* canon 1309.
207. We realize that some canonists today maintain that according to the present code of Church law parents are granted the right to release their children from vows. We do not wish to reject the validity of their view that the Church by positive law grants such a right to parents. There is some probability in the contention for the simple reason that parents can best judge whether their child has made a valid vow with full realization of the extent and nature of the obligation and his ability to carry it out or perhaps was lacking in proper understanding and insight. We assume of course that the parents have an understanding of the vow and a conscientious attitude toward the rights and duties of their children. Cf. A. Vermeersch and J. Creusen, *Epitome Iuris Canonici,* II 6th ed.; Mechliniae; Dessain, 1940), n. 643.
208. Aertnys-Damen, *Theologia moralis,* I, n. 493.
209. Usually one who has made the solemn profession (with solemn vows) in a religious order is not dispensed, but is re-admitted to the order when he has converted from his evil ways. By force of the vow he is obliged to strive for such betterment and re-acceptance.
210. Cf. II–II, q. 88, a. 3, ad 2.
211. According to the norm of canon 514, § 1.
212. *CJC,* canon 1313.
213. *CJC,* canon 1320.
214. *CJC,* canon 1309; note canon 81 regarding cases in which recourse to the Holy See is not possible.
215. *CJC,* canon 1314.
216. Tertullian, *De oratione* 23 (PL 1, 1191).
217. St. Jerome, *De die dominica paschae* (Analecta Maredsaus, III, 418).
218. St. Augustine, *Epistola ad Januarium* (PL 33, 215).
219. *Epistola Barnabae,* 15, 9 (PG 2, 771).
220. *Didascalia* 21.
221. Peter of Alexandria, *Epistola canonica* (PG 18, 508).
222. Maximus of Turin, *Homilia prima Pentecost.* (PL 57, 371).
223. St. Thomas, *III Sent.,* d. 37, q. 1, a. 5, sol. 3 and 3.

224. *Didache* 14, 1. R. de Journel, *Enchiridion Patristicum,* n. 8. *Ancient Christian Writers* (Westminster, Md.: Newman, 1948), V. VI, 23.

225. *Didascalia* 13.

226. St. Augustine, *De civitate Dei* 22, 30, 5 (PL 41, 804).

227. Cf. C. Feckes, *Christliches Vollkommenheitsstreben* (2 aufl.; Freiburg, 1953), 228.

228. Note that *Mediator Dei* rejects extremes and exaggerations and corrects misconceptions and false interpretations in explaining the sound and objective doctrine.

229. Cf. J. Eger, C.SS.R., *Messe als Mitte* (2 aufl.; Stuttgart, 1953).

230. Cf. J. Pascher, *Theologie des Kreuzes* (Muenster, 1948).

231. *Directoire pour la pastorale de la Messe à l'usage des diocèses de France* (2 me ed.; Coutances: Editions Notre Dame, 1960), n. 20.

232. St. Augustine, *Tractatus in Joannem* 26, 13 (PL 35, 612f.).

233. III. q. 73, a. 3; q. 79, a. 4. "Res huius sacramenti est unitas corporis mystici . . . est caritas."

234. Cf. B. Haering, "Die gemeinschaftsstiftende Kraft der Liturgie. Liturgiesoziologische Beobachtungen und Probleme," *Liturgisches Jahrbuch,* 7 (1957), 205–214, and "Religion als Gemeinschaft und als gemeinschaftsstiftende Macht," *Macht und Ohnmacht der Religion* (Salzburg, 1956), 31–50.

235. Pius XII, *Mystici Corporis, AAS* 35 (1943), 233.

236. Pius XII, *Mediator Dei, AAS* 39 (1947), 564. D 944: "Optaret quidem sancta Synodus, ut in singulis Missis fideles adstantes non solum spirituali affectu, sed sacramentali etiam Eucharistiae perceptione communicarent, quo ad eos sanctissimi huius sacrificii fructus uberior proveniret. . . ." (Trent: Doctrine . . . de sanctissimo Missae sacrificio, cap. 6.)

237. Pius XII, *loc. cit.*

238. Pius XII, *ibid.,* 566.

239. A. Troidl, *Mess- und Feiergestaltung* (Augsburg, 1958).

240. *CJC,* canons 1247, 1248; cf. also canon 12. Days of obligation in the universal Church are: all the Sundays of the year, the feasts of the Nativity, Octave of the Nativity, Epiphany, Ascension, Corpus Christi, Immaculate Conception and Assumption of the Blessed Virgin Mary, Saint Joseph, the Apostles Peter and Paul, All Saints. Of these the following are not feast days of obligation in the United States: the feasts of Epiphany, Corpus Christi, Saint Joseph, Saints Peter and Paul.

241. *CJC,* canons 1249, 866, § 1.

242. St. Ignatius of Antioch, *Ad Ephesios* 4 (PG 5, 735).

243. *CJC,* canon 2259.

244. For meaning of the terms, cf. *CJC,* canon 1188, § 2.

245. *CJC,* canon 1249.

246. E. Welty, *Vom Sinn und Wert der menschlichen Arbeit* (Heidelberg, 1946), 28.

247. Cf. J. Schildenberger, *Vom Geheimnis des Gotteswortes* (Heidelberg, 1950), 112ff. 138ff., 240f.

248. F. Tillmann, *Handbuch der katholischen Sittenlehre,* IV, 2, 153.

249. Pius XII, Constitutio *Sponsa Christi, AAS* 43 (1951), 13. Note that labor receives its sanctification from divine worship and is essential even for the soundness of the contemplative life.

250. Defect of such a spirit is evident in our social order in the lack of the spirit of willing sacrifice on the part of many women in respect to children. But it is also apparent in the endeavor of society itself to shirk the burden of responsibility toward the large family, so that the small family has become socially desirable. The bitter fruit will be

reaped in the next generation with the sharp divergences between the swelling ranks of the aged and retired unemployed and the struggling workers whose numbers show the population decline.

251. Cf. *Didache* 4, 6ff.; 12, 3ff.; *Letter of Barnabas* 10, 4 (PG 2, 753ff.).

252. Pius XI, *Quadragesimo Anno, AAS* 23 (1931), 221f.

253. J. Dreissen, "Die christliche Wertung der Arbeit," *Die Kirche in der Welt*, 2 (1949), 27.

254. F. Decurtins, "Medizinische Aspekte der Sonntagsheilung und -entheiligung," *Anima*, 4 (1949), 343ff.

255. Cf. II–II, q. 187, a. 3, ad 1 and ad 3; *De regimine principum*, I, 1.

256. Cf. M. Weber, *Die protestantische Ethik und der Geist des Kapitalismus* (Tuebingen, 1934). English translation: *Protestant Ethic and the Spirit of Capitalism* (London: Talcott Parsons, 1930).

257. Cf. P. Morant, "Der Tag des Herrn in der Heiligen Schrift," *Anima*, 4 (1949), 297.

258. Cf. J. Barbel, "Der christliche Sonntag in der Verkuendigung," *TrThZ*, 60 (1951) 17–30. (Extensive bibliography.)

259. *CJC*, canon 1248.

260. *CJC*, canon 1245, § 1.

261. *CJC*, canon 1245, § 3.

Book Two

NOTES AND REFERENCES

(pages 347–519)

1. Cf. F. Ebner, *Wort und Liebe* (Regensburg, 1935); *Das Wort und die geistigen Realitaeten* (Innsbruck, 1921).

2. St. Augustine, *Retractationes* 1, 83 (PL 32, 594).

3. II–II, q. 23, a. 5.

4. II–II, q. 44, a. 2.

5. Cf. Alszeghy, *Grundformen der Liebe: Die Theorie der Gottesliebe beim hl. Bonaventura*, (Rome, 1946).

6. St. Augustine, *De Trinitate* 8, 12 (PL 42, 959).

7. I–II, q. 77, a. 8.

8. St. Augustine, *De civitate Dei* 14, 28 (PL 41, 436).

9. Tillmann, *Die katholische Sittenlehre* IV, 2, 17.

10. Cf. Alszeghy, *op. cit.*, 178ff.

11. M. Scheler, *Ressentiment*, ed. L. A. Coser, trans. W. W. Holdheim (New York: Free Press of Glencoe, 1961), 109. Rather surprisingly, the same misconception is found in the Protestant theologian, H. Preisker, *Das Ethos des Urchristentums* (Guetersloh, 1949), 184: "This attitude which is found frequently in Judaism strikes at the very heart of the Christian position." On the face of it, we should judge the critic rather rash for finding in St. Paul—of all people—a Jewish perversion of the Gospel.

12. The Gospel of the Hebrews has preserved an even more striking *logion* of the Lord: "You should never rejoice if you do not look toward your brother in love" (St. Jerome, *Com. in Eph.* 5, 4 [PL 26, 520]).

13. Alphonse Liguori, *Theologia moralis*, lib II, n. 28; *Homo Apostolicus*, Tr. IV, cap. II, n. 17.

14. Aristotle, *Nichomachean Ethics*, 9. Cicero, *De amicitia*.

15. Aristotle, *Nichomachean Ethics,* 9, 7, 12.

16. Cf. Volume One, 230ff.: Spirit and Disposition.

17. Cf. Volume One, 550f.: The Hazard of False Perspectives.

18. Aertnys-Damen, *Theologia moralis,* I, n. 350. Cf. II–II, q. 26, a. 4.

19. Origen, *Homiliae in Canticum Canticorum* 3, 4 (PG 13, 156A).

20. *Didache* 2, 7. *Ancient Christian Writers:* (Maryland: Newman Press, 1948), V. VI, 16.

21. M. Scheler, *Vom Ewigen im Menschen,* 158.

22. Pius XII, address to the Fourteenth congress of the World Union of Catholic Women's Organizations, Sept. 29, 1957, *AAS* 49 (1957), 916; cf. *The Pope Speaks* 4 (Sept. 1958), 413–21 and 426.

23. "Certainly His mission as Redeemer was to liberate men from the slavery of sin, the extreme form of misery. Nevertheless, the greatness of His most sensitive heart could not allow Him to close His eyes to the suffering and the sufferers among whom He chose to live. Son of God and Herald of His heavenly kingdom, He was happy in bending compassionately over the wounds of humanity and the tattered rags of poverty. He was not satisfied with proclaiming the law of justice and charity; nor with condemning with withering anathemas the hardhearted, the inhuman, the selfish; nor with the warning that the final sentence of the Last Day will have as the norm of its judgment the exercise of charity, as the proof of the love of God. But He spent Himself personally in order to help, to heal, to feed. Certainly He did not ask whether and to what extent the misfortune before Him happened because the political and economic order of His time was defective or lacking. He was not indifferent to that. On the contrary, He is the Lord of the world and of its order. But just as His action as Savior was personal, so He wished to meet life's other misfortunes with a love that was personal. The example of Jesus is today, as every day, a strict duty for all" (Pius XII, Christian Message, Dec. 24, 1952, Paulist Press, p. 18f.).

24. St. Augustine, *Enarrationes in Psalmum 103,* n. 14 (PL 37, 1349).

25. Lactantius, *Divinae institutiones,* VI (PL 6, 676–684).

26. In his Lenten sermons over French television in 1956 (cf. *Man is Your Brother,* trans. R. Matthews, Westminster, Md.: Newman, 1958) one of the noblest apostles of fraternal love in our times, Abbe Pierre, listed the following as basic "preliminaries to freedom: bread, health, work, and instruction." May we not look upon them as a modern version of the corporal works of mercy, even though the theologian may raise an eyebrow at the inclusion of a modicum of knowledge and culture in the *corporal* works. However, since our world of technique places in science and know-how the key to possession and power and condemns the uneducated to menial labor and often to the distress of poverty or proletarization, something of education and culture should be included in our list. For this reason UNESCO follows the enlightened example of Catholic missionaries in foreign lands and goes to great length to raise the general cultural level of the economically undeveloped and depressed peoples. Nevertheless, if we view the whole matter from the Christian standpoint, it is evident that a one-sided consideration of knowledge as key to possession and power harbors a hazard for true human culture. Authentic communication of learning and genuine education must at all times embrace the spiritual works of mercy and thereby "instruct the ignorant." Nor is this by way of exception; for according to tradition the corporal and spiritual works of mercy form one harmonious whole. (Cf. Haering, *Ehe in dieser Zeit* [Salzburg, 1960], 489–560, for a study of the importance of the economic situation, the conditions of employment, and housing in the matter of family morals.)

27. St. Cyprian, *De habitu virg.* (PL 4, 449A).

28. St. Clement (PG 9, 617C, 640C).

29. St. Jerome, *Epistula 130*, 4 (PL 22, 1119).

30. St. Augustine, *Sermo* 61, 12 (PL 38, 413).

31. St. John Chrysostom, *In Matthaeum homilia* 50, 3 (PG 58, 508).

32. Cf. L. Lallement, *Histoire de la charité* (5 vols.; Paris, 1902–1912).

33. Linsenmann, *Moraltheologie*, 485.

34. Cf. the discussions on justice as a cardinal virtue and the study of earthly goods in relation to justice.

35. *Quadragesimo Anno; AAS* 23 (1931) 221f.

36. Cf. II–II, q. 32, a. 6.

37. St. Ambrose, *De Nabuthe* 12, 53 (PL 14, 747).

38. St. Augustine, *Sermo* 61 (PL 38, 413).

39. St. Augustine, *In Ps. 147*, 12 (PL 37, 1922).

40. II–II, q. 118, a. 4, ad 2, citing St. Basil. Cf. St. Giet, *Les idées et l'action sociales de saint Basile* (Paris, 1941).

41. St. Gregory the Great, *Homilia XL*, 3 (PL 76, 1305A).

42. D 1162.

43. Cf. St. Ambrose, *De officiis*, lib 1, 30, 144ff. (PL 16, 65ff.).

44. Cf. G. Gilleman, *The Primacy of Charity in Moral Theology*, trans. W. F. Ryan and W. Vachon (Westminster, Md.: Newman, 1959), 247.

45. Cf. F. Juergensmeier, *The Mystical Body of Christ as the Basic Principle of the Spiritual Life*, trans. H. G. Strauss (New York: Sheed & Ward, 1954), 319ff. E. Mersch, *The Theology of the Mystical Body*, trans. C. Vollert (St. Louis: B. Herder, 1951), 325–452. P. Glorieux, *Corps mystique et apostolate* (Paris, 1934), 71–80.

46. Pius XII, *Mystici Corporis, AAS* 35 (1943) 212. English trans. *Mystical Body of Christ*, No. 46 (Paulist Press).

47. Clement of Alexandria, *Stromata VII*, 2 (PG 9, 413); *Mystici Corporis, AAS* 35. (1943), 221. English translation, Paulist Press, No. 63.

48. Juergensmeier, *Mystical Body*, 273.

49. Clement of Alexandria, *Stromata VII*, 2 (PG 9, 413). Cf. K. Rahner, "Der Einzelne in der Kirche," *StimmenZeit*, 139 (1947) 260–276. A. Laepple, *Der Einzelne in der Kirche. Wesenszuege einer Theologie des Einzelnen nach J. H. Newman* (Munich, 1952).

50. Cf. what we have said regarding Person and Community in Volume One, pp. 79f.

51. *Mystici Corporis, AAS* 35 (1943) 229; English translation, no. 81 (Paulist Press).

52. Cf. J. Pascher, *Eucharisti. Gestalt und Vollzug* (2 aufl.; Freiburg and Muenster, 1935), 374–390.

53. *Mystici Corporis, AAS* 35 (1943) 232f; English translation, no. 89 (Paulist Press).

54. Cf. J. B. Umberg, S.J. *Zum Kampf geweiht. Vom Sinn der Firmung* (2 aufl.; Innsbruck, 1947). D. Koster, *Die Firmung im Glaubenssinn der Kirche* (Muenster, 1948). *La Maison-Dieu*, n. 38 (1952): *Le Baptême entrée dan le peuple de Dieu;* n. 54 (1958): *La Confirmation.*

55. III, q. 63, a. 3.

56. III, q. 72, a. 5, ad 2.

57. *Die Deutsche Thomasausgabe* Bd. 29, 534.

58. III, q. 72, a. 5.

59. M. Schmaus, *Katholische Dogmatik* (Munich, 1952), IV/1, no. 243, 177.

60. *Ibid.*, 178.

61. S. Lyonnet, "Un aspect de la 'prière apostolique' d'après saint Paul," *Christus*, 19

(1958), 22. Pius XII in the Encyclical *Fidei donum* (April 21, 1957) is very emphatic in stressing the obligation of prayer as the first duty of the apostolate to the pagan world for it arises from sincere gratitude for the gift of faith which we ourselves have received.

62. F. Wulf, "Das stellvertretende Leiden als Anruf unserer Zeit," *GeistLeben*, 21 (1948), 324.

63. Cf. R. Boehmer, "Victima Christi, Zur Begruendung des Suehnegedankens," *GeistLeben*, 22 (1949), 191–203.

64. Cf. the Gospel of the Mass for the Feast of the Sacred Heart of Mary.

65. Cf. Pius XI, *Miserentissimus Redemptor, AAS* 20 (1928), 165–187; *Caritate compulsi, AAS* 24 (1932), 177–194; Pius XII, *AAS* 34 (1942), 345f.; 37 (1945) 45–51.

66. St. Ignatius of Antioch, *Ad Ephesios* 21, 1 (PG 5, 756); *Ad Smyrnaeos* 10, 2 (PG 5, 856).

67. Cf. A. Heitmann, *Imitatio Dei. Die ethische Nachahmung Gottes nach der Vaeterlehre* (Rome, 1940).

68. Kant, bitterly hostile to the model ethic of Christianity, is a case in point. Note his *Grundlegung zur Metaphysik der Sitten* (ed. Cassirer), IV, 263f. English title: *The Moral Law or Kant's Groundwork of the Metaphysics of Morals,* trans. H. J. Paton (New York: Barnes & Noble, 1950). Cf. James Collins, *A History of Modern European Philosophy* (Milwaukee: Bruce, 1954), 515ff.

69. Tertullian, *Apologeticum* 39 (PL 1, 471). The actual words of Tertullian are: "The blood of Christians is a seed." Cf. Journel, *Enchiridion Patristicum* (St. Louis: Herder, 1953), n. 285.

70. Cf. Knowledge of Law and Experience of Value, in *The Law of Christ,* V. I, chapter four, II, 4 a., p. 124ff.

71. A. Rademacher, *Der Glaube als einheitliche Lebensform* (Bonn, 1937), 15.

72. E. Spranger, *Psychologie des Jugendalters,* 304.

73. *Ibid.,* 324.

74. M. Scheler, *Der Formalismus in der Ethik und die materielle Wertethik* (Halle, 1927), 599.

75. Cf. the tract on scandal in this volume.

76. Cf. CJC, canon 124.

77. Otto Schilling, *Lehrbuch der Moraltheologie* (2 aufl.; Stuttgart, 1952), II, 289.

78. This point is particularly stressed in the ethic of M. Scheler, which is both an ethic of love and of exemplary imitation. The concept of model and imitation in Scheler very correctly embraces the loving adherence to the person who is one's ideal and model.

79. The medieval theologians characterized the neglect of this duty *peccatum taciturnitatis.* Cf. *Summa fratris Alexandri* II B, n. 396–398, Quaracchi edition, V. III, 1930, 397–401. St. John of the Cross is exceedingly severe in his criticism of the craven and uncharitable silence maintained by subjects regarding the faults of their superiors which mar the peace and harmony of the religious life. A silence, he holds, which quite often is broken by harsh and unkindly criticism of the superior when his back is turned. *The Complete Works of Saint John of the Cross,* trans. and ed. by E. Allison Peers (Westminster, Md.: Newman, 1945), III, 314f.; ("Spiritual Sayings," nn. 12f.).

80. St. Augustine, *Contra litteras Petiliani* I, 29 (PL 43, 259); *Sermo* 49, 5 (PL 38, 323).

81. *Ibid.*

82. CJC, canon 1351.

83. Pius XII: Address to the Fifth National Convention of Italian Catholic Jurists, Dec. 6,

1953, *AAS* 45 (1953), 794. Cf. T. L. Bouscaren and J. I. O'Connor, *Canon Law Digest* (Milwaukee: Bruce, 1958), IV, 3–9.

84. Cf. particularly: V. Schurr, *Seelsorge in einer neuen Welt* (3 aufl.; Salzburg, 1959). Also Haering, *Ehe in dieser Zeit* (Salzburg, 1960).

85. Pius XII, in his address to the newly-created cardinals (Feb. 20, 1946), characterized the Church as the *life principle* of society with specific reference to the vocation of the laity in the world—*AAS* 38 (1946), 149. Any attempt to form a monopoly of exclusively Catholic societies would deprive the Church, and this means above all her laity, of the possibility to become truly the *life principle* of society. For this reason the Pope admonishes Catholics, particularly in countries where they constitute only a minority of the population, to cooperate with the neutral and non-Catholic movements and organizations, provided such cooperation furthers the common welfare and the glory of God. The Pope also urges an ever greater interest in the international organizations. —Address to the Second World Congress of the Lay Apostolate, October 5, 1957, *AAS* 49 (1957), 929.

86. Cf. CJC, canon 108. Priests who are not bishops also belong to the hierarchy of order.

87. The very core of priestly power in the Church is the Eucharistic celebration in the name of Christ and in His person. But the Eucharist does not mean merely sacrificial presence of Christ. It also means unity and harmony of all in the love of Christ, a still imperfect unity which looks forward eagerly to the perfect fulfillment when He shall come again.

88. In his coronation address (November 5, 1958), Pope John XXIII tenderly expressed the thought and ideal which was closest to his paternal heart: the commission of the Good Shepherd, given to the shepherd of the entire flock of Christ, to seek the sheep that were lost. To bring them back to the fold, though not the exclusive task, is still the first interest of the Roman pontiff. In the mind of Pope John this is the missionary problem in all its extent and beauty—*AAS* 50 (1958), 886.

89. Theodoret, "On 1 Cor 7:32" (PG 82, 283).

90. Cf. P. Winninger, *Vers un renouveau du diaconat* (Paris, 1958). J. Horneff, *Kommt der Diakon der fruehen Kirche wieder?* (Wien, 1959). W. Schamoni, *Married Men as Ordained Deacons,* trans. Otto Eisner (London: Burns and Oates, 1955).

91. Cf. A. M. Roguet, "La collégialité du sacerdoce," *Pastorale oeuvre commune;* Compt-rendu du Congrès de l'Union des oeuvres (1956), 129–145. B. Botte, "Charactère collégial du presbyterat et de l'épiscopat," *Etudes sur le sacrement de l'ordre* (Paris, 1957), 97–124; 442. R. Snoeks, "Concile oecoménique et collégialité épiscopale," *Évangéliser* 14 (1960), 609–621. J. Colson, "Évangélisation et collégialité apostolique," *NRTh,* 82 (1960), 349–372.

92. One still cannot fail to notice in some places that the capitulars at cathedrals and other priests who must "attend" the Mass of the bishop still make a practice of reciting their breviary during the Mass. "Finishing the office" in this manner is surely not calculated to raise the heart and mind to a spirit of priestly unity centering in the Eucharistic celebration. Even the purposive significance of the breviary prayers prescribed by the Church's law would be fulfilled more perfectly by active participation in the Eucharistic celebration, which is the Mass, than by the mere "execution" of the breviary text. This latter in great part does not directly harmonize with the texts prayed and sung by the celebrant and the people in holy Mass. (Cf. Instruction of the Sacred Congregation of Rites, September 3, 1958, in *Sacred Music and the Sacred Liturgy,* no. 36, page 14, NCWC publication.)

93. Pius XII, "Address to Religious Superiors," Feb. 11, 1958; *AAS* 50 (1958), 153ff.

94. Cf. J. Hamer, "Place des religieux dans l'apostolat de l'Eglise," *NRTh*, 81 (1959), 271–281. A Chavasse, *Eglise et Apostolat* (Tournai-Paris, 1953), 158–165. A. De Soras, "Les rôles respectifs du laïc, du prêtre et du religieux au sein de l'action ecclésiale," *Rev. Action populaire*, 88 (1955), 673–690.

95. Haering, "Froemmigkeit des Laien, Wege der Nachfolge Christi in der Welt," *WW*, 14 (1959), 179–189.

96. Note on this point the words of Pius XII spoken to the Congress of all religious on December 8, 1950, at Rome: "We frequently hear it said that love of neighbor is losing its religious character and gradually becoming laical. But in reality all acts of benevolence toward others which do not spring from faith but from some other motive or source are not truly love of neighbor in a Christian sense. . . . Those Catholic religious women who dedicate themselves to the service of the sick in the spirit of their institute and for the love of Christ create an atmosphere of singular effectiveness in their tasks which mere technical proficiency and medical progress cannot equal. We therefore ask the religious orders and congregations dedicated to the active life so to cherish their ideals that their work bears witness to its divine character and nourishes in their hearts the ardor of the Holy Spirit" (*AAS* 43 [1951], 33). In the same address the Pontiff stresses as particularly suitable to these institutes in this age: "breadth of view in ideals and judgment, unity and harmony in direction and organization, prompt and ready action" (*ibid.*, 35).

97. "This is the manner of preaching practiced by the Little Brothers and it is essential for a certain fulness of the apostolate even where pressing needs of the pastoral care exist. . . . This exclusiveness of ours is in some sort necessary so that we bear witness through our life itself to the presence of Jesus among men. Every compromise would becloud this testimony of our lives, for men would not be able to see clearly that ultimately the only important thing is to live the life of Jesus" (P. Voillaume, "Lettres aux petits Frères," *Information Catholique International* n. 79 [1958], 29). We should add that this simple and unpretentious life of the evangelical counsels in the midst of the world and officially approved as an authentic apostolate in the Church is not something modern or new. It has long existed in the Church. We recall the vocation of the virgins whose consecrated lives in the world in the very first centuries of the Christian era bore witness to the Christian faith and the exaltation of Christian morals. They gave testimony by their lives after the persecution as had the martyrs by their deaths in time of persecution. It is not generally known that in the middle of the past century a congregation of religious living in the world had already been formed. With surprisingly little delay it was approved by the Holy See. Most of the members of this congregation (Vierges de Jésus et Marie) live in the world not at all differing externally from the laity. In fact, ordinarily even their closest relatives are unaware that they are religious with vows of poverty, chastity, and obedience. Only the splendor of their lives bears witness to a love and utter detachment which flows from the most profound imitation of Christ.

98. G. Philips, *The Role of the Laity in the Church*, trans. J. Gilbert and J. Moudry (Cork: Mercier Press, 1955), 174.

99. The bibliography prepared in connection with the Second World Congress of the Lay Apostolate (*L'Apostolato dei laici. Bibliografia sistematica* [Milano, 1957]) lists no less than 2229 publications for the period of 1922 to 1957.

100. "The incorporation in the unity of the ecclesial mission, expressed in the very word *Church*, takes place in baptism and confirmation. These sacraments, however, are

participation in the mission of Christ to whom one is assimilated, participation in the missionary office of the Redeemer, participation in His unlimited authority and therewith in the dominion of God. The Christian is a man with tremendous authority." V. Schurr, *Seelsorge in einer neuen Welt* (2 aufl.; Salzburg, 1957), 64.

101. The First Roman Synod (art. 629) mentions the following as basis of this universally binding apostolate: 1) the love of God, 2) the love of neighbor, 3) the doctrine according to which all the members of the Mystical Body of Christ must be living and active members.

102. "It is a perversion of the true nature of the Church of God and her social character to distinguish in her a purely active element, the Church authorities, on the one hand, and a purely passive element, the laity, on the other. All the members of the Church are called to cooperate in the building up and perfecting of the Mystical Body of Christ." Pius XII, "Address to the Second World Congress of the Lay Apostolate," Oct. 5, 1957; *AAS* 49 (1957), 922. Cf. *Mystici Corporis, AAS* 35 (1943), 241.

Even more emphatic, if possible, is the utterance of Pope John XXIII: "Without the vigilant and zealous apostolate the profession of the Christian faith has no proper meaning. 'Every one is obliged to share his faith with others' (II–II, q. 3, a. ad 2). . . . Anyone who bears the name *Christian* clearly realizes that his first and fundamental obligation of conscience is to bear witness to the truth which he professes and to the grace by which he has been transformed spiritually" (*Princeps Pastorum, AAS* 51 (1959), 851f.

103. Pius XII, Address to the Second World Congress, *AAS* 49 (1957), 923.

104. *Ibid.,* 924.

105. That we have here only a question of terminology and not a final or ultimate evaluation is evident from the express words of this great teacher of the lay apostolate. According to Pius XII, the Catholic teacher, physician, engineer, and all others in similar professions who through professional training and dedicated purpose are at the highest level of their calling and at the same time also profoundly penetrated with the spirit of their Catholic faith, exercise an apostolate equal to that of the loftiest lay apostolate. *Ibid.*

106. *Directoire en matière sociale* of the French episcopate, n. 32. Cf. what we stated above on the *World Mission of the Laity.*

107. III, q. 72, a. 5, ad 2. Cf. Schurr, "Auch der Laie hat das Wort," *LebS,* 6 (1955), 1–11.

108. Y. Congar, "Esquisse d'une théologie de l'action catholique," *Cahiers du clergé rural,* 22 (1958), 391, with reference to the position of Karl Rahner, "L'apostolat des laïcs," *NRTh,* 78 (1956), 3–32.

109. V. Schurr, *Seelsorge in einer neuen Welt,* 65.

110. The Church has always shown the greatest concern for her music. Papal documents, from the *Motu Proprio* of St. Pius X to the recent decisions of Pius XII, make crystal clear how important is the competence of the well-trained layman in this area for the worthy celebration of the divine service. This competence is truly a splendid missionary force in our liturgy.

111. Pius XII, address on May 31, 1954, dealing with the teaching office of the bishops in the Church, *AAS* 46 (1954), 313.

112. Pius XII, Address to the Second World Congress of the Lay Apostolate, Oct. 5, 1957, *AAS* 49 (1957), 922.

113. *Ibid.,* 927.

114. *Ibid.,* 929.

115. The Roman synod treated this matter in the chapter on the directives for the lay

apostolate (art. 632–638). Special emphasis is placed on the need for the members of these organizations to be trained and equipped for an apostolate suited to modern needs and conditions.

116. *AAS* 14 (1922), 693. *AAS* 20 (1928), 385.

117. To the Second World Congress of the Lay Apostolate, Oct. 5, 1957; *AAS* 49 (1957), 922. Cf. K. Rahner, "Ueber das Laienapostolat," *Schriften zur Theologie* (Einsiedeln, 1955), II, 352f.

118. Roman Synod, 1960, art. 640.

119. John XXIII, *Princeps Pastorum, AAS* 51 (1959), 857; cf. address to Catholic Action group at Rome, *AAS* 52 (1960), 83–90; Roman Synod, art. 641.

120. Pius XII, *AAS* 49 (1957), 929.

121. Cf. address of Pius XII, May 31, 1954; cf. note 111.

122. Catholic publishers and their associates, as men of Christian learning and refinement, can make a tremendous contribution to this important apostolate. How highly the Church appreciates the apostolic labors in this sensitive area is evident from the honor she bestowed upon Frank Sheed, of Sheed and Ward Publishers, New York, by awarding him the degree of Doctor of Theology.

123. "It is necessary—and we consider it appropriate to refer to it constantly—that the methods and procedures of the apostolate be adapted to the conditions and needs of time and place. It is simply not possible to transfer to other places without any modification what has proved successful in one particular area." John XXIII, *Princeps Pastorum, AAS* 51 (1959), 856.

124. *AAS* 49 (1957), 882.

125. Attempts of this kind have been made through the "Zentralkomitee der deutschen Katholiken." (For the USA, cf. note 130.)

126. Cf. Schurr, *Seelsorge in einer neuen Welt,* 57ff.

127. Cf. J. Spielbauer, *Sorge um die andern* (5 aufl.; Freiburg, 1960).

128. Cf. B. Haering, *Macht und Ohnmacht der Religion,* 378–430.

129. Address of August 18, 1935; *AAS* 28 (1935), 66. Cf. also Mgr. Garrone, *L'Action catholique* (Paris, 1958), 13.

130. Cf. B. Haering, *Ehe in dieser Zeit* (Salzburg, 1960). Cf. also *National Catholic Almanac for 1961* (St. Anthony's Guild, Paterson, New Jersey) for summary information on the Family Life Bureau, Christian Family Movement, Cana Conference Movement, etc. (548f., 568f.).

Some notion of the network of organizational activity in the USA may be gained from the annual reports which are submitted at the Bishops' Meeting at Washington, D. C. The *National Catholic Welfare Conference* is a voluntary "association of the bishops of the United States, established in 1919, to serve as a central agency for organizing and coordinating the efforts of US Catholics in carrying out the social mission of the Church for the reconstruction of Christian society. It is a clearing house of information and a center for service on a national scale of Catholic works in fields of social significance—education, the press, immigration, social action, legislation, youth and lay organizations." *Ibid.,* 543.

The Department of Lay Organizations "serves as the channel for the interchange of information and service between the NCWC and the laity in their common work for the Church; promotes unity and cooperation between clergy and laity in matters that affect the general welfare; participates through Catholic lay representation in national and international movements involving moral questions; . . . promotes the 'participation of the laity in the apostolate of the hierarchy.'" *Ibid.,* 544.

Two national groups are particularly important: The National Council of Catholic Men and the National Council of Catholic Women, the former representing over 10,000 affiliated lay organizations, the latter over 12,000. Each has about nine million members. The Almanac lists fifteen entries under Catholic Action Groups; the Catholic associations, movements, and societies in the U. S. cover sixteen pages.

131. Address to the Second World Congress of the Lay Apostolate, Oct. 5, 1957; *AAS* 49, (1957), 822.

132. L. J. Suenens, *Theology of the Apostolate of the Legion of Mary* (Cork: Mercier, 1953).

133. The Roman Synod of 1960 has the following caution in article 661: "The members of Catholic Action should give evidence that they are outside and above political parties. But the correct formation of conscience for the right exercise of the rights and duties of citizens is one of their tasks. They must exercise an influence on politicians and statesmen whenever there is question of defense of the faith, good morals, and the right of the Church."

134. *Ibid.*, art. 662.

135. F. Tillman, *Die katholische Sittenlehre* IV/2, 277.

136. The previous references to seduction with the objective diversity of the sin were given special place largely because the term *seduction* conveys a somewhat different meaning in our vernacular than the word *scandal*.

137. Cf. J. Daniélou, *Théologie du judéo-christianisme* (Paris-Tournai, 1958), 291f.

138. Cf. H. M. Féret, *Pierre et Paul à Antioche et à Jerusalem. Le conflit des deux apôtres* (Paris, 1954). Cf. also, II–II, q. 43, a. 6, ad 2.

139. Pius XII, Address of September 28, 1948, to the delegates to the Congress of the International Association for the Protection of Young Girls: Moral Dangers For the Young Girl of Today. Cf. *Catholic Action* 30 (November, 1948), 3, 18–19.

140. The very same Bernanos who so sharply attacked the hypocritical members of the Church with the words, "You were for me in my infancy and youth an insufferable scandal which I could tolerate only insofar as I endeavored to comprehend you," also adds the words, "But this scandal must be. Christ wishes to disenchant us of our reason . . . you are a kind of sacramental sign of the great sacrament of the perpetual divine humiliation" (H. Urs von Balthasar, *Le chrétien Bernanos* [Paris, 1956], 310, citing Bernanos, *Lettre aux Anglais,* 152). Likewise E. Mounier who protests so vehemently against a dull and flabby Christianity and calls for a genuine saving scandal of a full Christian life, notes with Kierkegaard: "The protagonist of the faith presents to the man of our century not so much the scandal of the legendary as the scandal of the evasive middle-class existence. But it so seems that we must be tried in our very hearts by such matter of fact appearances" (*L'affrontement chrétien* [Paris, 1945–1948], 38).

141. Cf. Volume One, pp. 294–297 (on casuistry).

142. Cf. Haering, *Ehe in dieser Zeit*, 354–405.

143. We treat of the film and television problems in their relation to chastity in Volume Three.

144. See Volume One, pp. 106–108 (responsibility for effects), and pp. 289–294 (circumstances as determinants).

145. Cf. particularly the treatment of collective guilt in Volume One, pp. 84–87. Note also the problem of cooperation on the part of the spouses in marital relations in the pages on *usus matrimonii* in Volume Three.

146. There is a prudent observation of R. Brouillard which is worth citing: "The complex problem of cooperation is one of the knottiest in our theology. There are many solutions

which do not apply to all individual cases as they actually present themselves. It is frequently difficult to make a clean-cut and satisfactory decision. Of course we can lay down the general principles and broad lines which we must follow in deciding individual instances. But reality in its concrete forms and variations does not so readily fit into our conceptual categories." And the author imparts a final caution: "Our casuistry does not render superfluous any human and Christian prudence which comes to the rescue of our natural sense of reality and experience" "Cooperation," *Catholicisme,* ed. G. Jacquemet, V. III (Paris: Letouzey et Ané, 1952), col. 167.

147. A. Schmitt, "Mitwirkung zu fremden Suenden," *ThPrQschr* 87 (1934), 342–346.
148. Aertnys-Damen, *Theologia Moralis,* I, n. 403.
149. L. Ruland, *Morality and the Social Order,* adapted into English by T. A. Rattler, ed. N. Thompson (Pastoral Theology, V. III; St. Louis: B. Herder, 1942), 44.
150. *Ibid.*
151. O. Schilling, *Lehrbuch der Moraltheologie,* II, 311.
152. Cf. F. Connell, *Morals in Politics and Professions* (Westminster, Md.: Newman, 1955), 23–36.
153. Cf. address of Pius XII to Italian Catholic Jurists, November 6, 1949: "Not every application of an unjust law is equivalent to its recognition and approval. In such cases the judge can—and in fact he often must—permit the evil law to follow its course if this is the sole way to prevent an even greater evil. . . . As far as civil divorce is concerned, the Catholic judge may only for weighty reasons render a decision granting 'dissolution' in civil law of a marriage which is valid in the eyes of God and the Church. He may not ignore the fact that such a verdict not only has civil consequences but also contributes to the false image in the public mind: the erroneous impression will be created that the marital bond is actually dissolved." *AAS* 41 (1949), 597. Cf. *Canon Law Digest,* III, 10.
154. Cf. the reply of the Sacred Congregation of the Penitentiary, Feb. 13, 1900, quoted in Gasparri, *Tractatus Canonicus de Matrimonio* (ed. 9; Rome: Typis Polyglottis Vaticanis, 1932), II, 323.
155. Decree of the Holy Office, July 1, 1949; *AAS* 41 (1949), 334. The excommunication according to this decision affects only those who hold the communistic position philosophically, those who adhere to dialectical materialism.
156. A. Kelemen von Várna, *Die Stimme des Rufenden* (Saarlouis, 1950), 309.

INDEX

A

Aaron, xxiii
Abellán, 518
Abercius Inscription, 144
Abraham, xxvi
Abts, 518
Actio Catholica, 455
Adam, names animals, 270
Adam, A., 104
Adam, K., 62 f., 104
Adoration, 256f.; and love, 117
Adult, and act of faith, 29
Advertisers, in evil publications, 512 f.
Aertnys-Damon, 535, 538, 546; on cooperation in sale of contraceptives, 502 f.
Agapân, xxviii
Agápe, xxviii, 88, 302, 307, 313
Ahrens, 198
Alfano, 240
Algermissen, 200
Almsgiving, and Church Fathers, 392 ff.; Clement of Alexandria on, 393; comprehensive term for love of needy, 391; Cyprian on, 393; in early Church, 392; in Old Testament, 392; must be governed by prudence, 406; norms governing, 403 ff.; proper motivation for, 405; right manner and mode in, 405 f.; universal obligation, 391 ff.
Alphonse, St., 345, 532, 534, 537; and desire for revenge, 368; and prayer, 246; on misuse of Holy Name, 278; on prayer as means of grace, 257
Alszeghy, 104, 537
Alternative, supreme: accept or reject the Gospel, 486
Altruism, in love?, 351
Alvarez, 466
Ambercrombie, 529
Ambrose, St., 528, 539; on almsgiving by rich, 401
Amemptos, ámomos, katharós as biblical terms for moral excellence, 143

Amor benevolentiae, 87 f.
Amor complacentiae, 100
Amor concupiscentiae, 87, 100
Anastásimos, 299
Ancestors, veneration of, permitted?, 36 f.
Angermair, 104, 462
Anhofer, 241
Animals, not objects of love in strict sense, 361 f.; as objects of wonder, 361 f.
Anna, vow of, in Old Testament, 282
Antweiler, 62
Apostasy, collective, 60 ff.
Apostolate, and Eucharist, 445 ff.; and priesthood, 445 ff.; and tolerance, 430 ff.; and various states in the Church, 443; in marriage and family, 453; in sacraments, 410 f.; of contemplatives, 450 f.; official, and the various orders, 443 ff.; official hierarchical, 440 ff.; official, in relation to Christ, 442 f.; of laity and Catholic Action, 451 ff.; of prayer, 415 f.; priestly, and total giving, 448; universal, based on love of God and neighbor, and on active membership in Mystical Body, 543, n. 101; universal, of laity, 451 ff.; vocation to, 461 f.; zealous profession of faith demands, according to John XXIII, 543, n. 102
Apostolic fraternal love, Abbe Pierre on, 538, n. 26
Aristotle, 537 f.; and basis of friendship, 372
Arnold, 62, 464
Art, degenerate 490 ff.; galleries, 491; seductive, 490 ff.; unseemly presentation of sacred persons and themes in, 213 f.
Asmussen, 104, 198, 464
Astrology, 229 f.; propagandized, 224; scientifically preposterous, 230
Attention, in prayer, 260 ff.
Attitude, in prayer, 263
Attwater, 464, 466
Aubert, 465
Aubin, 241
Auer, A., 341, 464, 466

I

manded, 356 ff.; of neighbor, motive, 356 ff.; of neighbor, part of chief commandment, 360; of relatives and dear ones in distress, 362 f.; of self and neighbor: not equal in intensity of affection, 378; of self: priority of responsibility for self, 379 ff.; opposed to legalism, 95; order of preference in, 362 ff.; participation in life and love of Trinity involved, 88 f.; precept of, meaning, 98 ff.; redemptive, of Christ, xxxvi ff.; 416 f.; related to responsibility, 379 f.; related to value, 373 f.; rooted in person, 353; sentiment, disposition, explained, 373 ff.; signs of, manifested even to one's enemies, 369; supernatural, is entirely divine, 90; supernatural, penetrates areas of natural love, 355 f.; unity and diversity, 353 ff.; violation of, and sin, 363; virtue of, 83 ff.; virtue of, incorporation in divine life, 87 f.; virtue of, means share in love of Christ for Church, 86; wedded, in spirit of Christian friendship, 373; whom must we?, 360 ff.; works of, 100

Lowry, 345

Lucchini, 241

Lucien de Marie-Joseph, 81

Lumbreras, 81

Luther, and world alien to God, 191; denied vocation of superior perfection, 331; his work, *Daemonologie,* 237; objective discussion about, in the present age, 431

Lynch, J. J., 518

Lynch, Sister Miriam, 468

Lyonnet, 539

M

McAuliffe, 203

McCarthy, 14, 81, 518

McCormack, 199

McDonnell, 243, 532

McEvoy, 242

MacIvor, 345, 387

Mackenzie, 64

McLaughlin, 470

McManus, 203

McNabb, 64, 345

McNarney, 81

McReavy, 203, 344 f., 388

McSorley, 81

Mageean, 106

Mager, 240, 340

Magic, 235 ff.; pendulum, 232 f.; white, 237 f.

Magical practices, and origin of religion, 237; morality of, 238 f.

Magisterium, submission to, 48 ff.

Mahatma Gandhi, and prayer, 269

Mahoney, 470, 518

Mahr, 343

Malice against Christ, 485 f.

Malik, 65

Malone, 341

Man, in a world sanctified by the Incarnation, 191 f.; mystery of his Redemption, xxxv ff.

Mana cult, 237

Manders, 105

Manitou, 237

Marcel, 81

Marduk, 324

Maritain, J., 339, 345, 465; on liturgy and contemplation, 523

Maritain, R., 339, 345, 523

Marriage, apostolate, 453; cases involving possible scandal, 483 ff.; *church in miniature,* 308; civil and Catholic officials of, 512; compared to virginity, 149; mixed, hazards of, 46 f.; non-Catholic, at which Catholic assists, 47 f.; related to Christ and the Church, 413 f.

Marsot, 462

Martimort, 136, 200

Martin, 240

Martindale, 346, 388

Martyrdom, 30

Mary, and expiation, 416; and her prayer, 416; and hope, 80; *hyperdulia* paid to, 118

Masonic, political candidates, 514

Mass, and Christ's glory, 115; and state of grace, 317; center of Christian life, 307 ff.; community banquet, 309 ff.; *concelebration* discussed, 311; distractions during, 317; essentially *community* worship, 311; exterior attention at, 316 f.; fruitful participation at, 317 f.; going to confes-

A NOTE ON THE TYPE

IN WHICH THIS BOOK WAS SET

This book has been set in Granjon, a lovely Linotype face, designed by George W. Jones, one of England's great printers, to meet his own exacting requirements for fine book and publication work. Like most useful types, Granjon is neither wholly new nor wholly old. It is not a copy of a classic face nor an original creation, but rather something between the two—drawing its basic design from classic Garamond sources, but never hesitating to deviate from the model where four centuries of type-cutting experience indicate an improvement or where modern methods of punch-cutting make possible a refinement far beyond the skill of the originator. This book was composed by Progressive Typographers, Inc., York, Pa., printed by Wickersham Printing Company of Lancaster, Pa., and bound by Moore and Company of Baltimore. The design and typography of this book are by Howard N. King.